THE NEW BUSINESS

ENCYCLOPEDIA

THE NEW

BUSINESS

ENCYCLOPEDIA

Edited by

HENRY MARSHALL

Editor of THE BOOK OF BUSINESS ETIQUETTE
THE BUSINESS MAN'S DICTIONARY *and*
GUIDE TO ENGLISH

Revised, Up-to-date Edition

DOUBLEDAY & COMPANY, INC.
Garden City, N.Y.

Originally published under the title
THE BUSINESS ENCYCLOPEDIA

LIBRARY OF CONGRESS CATALOG CARD NUMBER 62–17419
COPYRIGHT © 1930, 1937, 1941, 1949, 1951, 1952, 1955, 1963
BY DOUBLEDAY & COMPANY, INC.

PRINTED IN THE UNITED STATES OF AMERICA

Anthony, Edward L., Chief, Management Methods Division, Small Business Administration, Washington, D. C.

Ball, Robert M., Commissioner, Social Security Administration, Washington, D. C.

Barrett, John Whitney, Business Writer, New London, Conn.

Bell & Howell Phillipsburg, Chicago, Ill.

Bendix Computer Division, Bendix Corporation, Los Angeles, Calif.

Brickman, William W., Chairman, Department of History of Education, New York University, New York, N. Y.

Brinkerhoff, Betty W., Writer and Editor, New York, N. Y.

Butler, Richard D., Agricultural Marketing Service, United States Department of Agriculture, Washington, D. C.

Corr, Arthur V., Instructor of Accounting, New York University, New York, N. Y.

Daro, E. Philip, Chairman, Data Processing Committee for Industry, Rutgers University, Metuchen, N. J.

Dickey, Norma H., Editor and Writer, Fort Lee, N. J.

Fluss, Felix F., Correspondent of European Business Publications, New York, N. Y.

Friden, Inc., San Leandro, Calif.

Gaffney, Wilbur G., Associate Professor, Department of English, University of Nebraska, Lincoln, Nebr.

General Binding Corporation, New York, N. Y.

Gode, Ralph E., Ex-Captain, Floral Park Rescue Squad, Floral Park, N. Y.

Heuer, Leone Ann, Director, Money Management Institute, Chicago, Ill.

Holden, Dr. John B., Director, Graduate School, United States Department of Agriculture, Washington, D. C.

Kellogg, Ted, Manager, Publicity and Information, Air-Conditioning and Refrigeration Institute, Washington, D. C.

Ladd, David L., Commissioner of Patents, United States Department of Commerce, Washington, D. C.

Langer, Howard J., Editor, *Scholastic Teacher;* former Editor, *Scholastic Magazines'* College and Careers Issue, New York, N. Y.

McKeon, William J., Associate Professor, School of Commerce, Accounts, and Finance, New York University, New York, N. Y.

National Cash Register Company, Dayton, Ohio

Parry, Natalie, Public Relations, New York, N. Y.

Peterson, Mrs. Esther, Director, Women's Bureau, and Assistant Secretary of Labor, Washington, D. C.

Picone, Alexander, Insurance Editor, *The Journal of Commerce,* New York, N. Y.

Remington Rand Division, Sperry Rand Corporation, New York, N. Y.

Rosett & Weinstein, Counselors at Law, New York, N. Y.

Roth, Julian, member Emery Roth and Sons, Architects, New York, N. Y.

Roth, Sidney G., Administrative Assistant in Charge of the Academic Department, Division of General Education, New York University, New York, N. Y.

Schiff, Michael, Associate Professor of Accounting, Graduate School of Business Administration, New York University, New York, N. Y.

Shaw, Grace G., former Associate Editor, C. L. Barnhart, Inc., Reference Books, Bronxville, N. Y.

Spafford, John L., Executive Vice President, Associated Credit Bureaus of America, Inc., St. Louis, Mo.

Tyng, Ed, Associate Editor, *The Journal of Commerce,* New York, N. Y.

von Struve, A. W., Public Information Officer, Bureau of the Census, Washington, D. C.

Warman, W. C., United States Savings and Loan League, Chicago, Ill.

Winter, Robert F., Teaching Fellow, Department of Economics, New York University, New York, N. Y.

Witaskin, Sidney, Certified Public Accountant, Brooklyn, N. Y.

Alphabetical Table of Contents

THE BUSINESSMAN AND THE CENSUS BUREAU

From a simple recording of population for the apportioning of seats in the House of Representatives, the census-taking activities of the United States government have become increasingly complex. Now the responsibility of the Bureau of the Census, an agency of the Dept. of Commerce, these activities are immensely helpful to the business community.

Reports made by the bureau may aid in economic or sales forecasting; analyzing market potentials, distribution, and sales performance; laying out sales territories; and in locating plants, warehouses, and stores. A manufacturer of dairy-farm equipment may use the Census of Agriculture to locate the counties in which the largest numbers of dairy farms are situated. He may use the Census of Business to find out what facilities exist in the same area to sell his product. And, once he has established his factory, he may check the work of his salesmen against figures indicating the comparative prosperity of the area. If a department store manager wants to examine a suburb as a possible site for a branch store, he can find out how many other stores are in the area and how much business they do. He can find out whether the number of people living in the area justifies the opening of another store. He can even find out whether the income level of the majority of the area's residents is high enough for the type of merchandise the store would expect to offer.

The variety of the censuses taken by the bureau is indicated in the following summaries.

The United States has been taking censuses regularly since 1790. The authority for censuses is embodied in the Constitution, in Section 2 of Article I, for the primary purpose of determining apportionment among states, on basis of population size, of seats in the House of Representatives of the Congress. Since 1902, the Bureau of the Census has been the permanent agency charged with responsibility for this work.

Censuses taken regularly are the censuses of population, housing, agriculture (including irrigation and drainage), manufactures, mineral industries, business (retail, wholesale, and service trades), and state and local government operation. Although legislation has been passed directing it, no census of transportation has yet been taken.

The Census of Population, or Decennial Census, first taken in 1790, counts the population of the nation and all of its subdivisions, such as states, counties, and cities, at ten-year intervals. It collects data on the characteristics of the population, such as age, sex, race, marital and family status, education, employment, income and occupation.

The Census of Housing, first taken in 1940 as a part of the Decennial Census, compiles detailed information on number and types of housing units, number of home owners and of renters, value, rents, condition and plumbing facilities, utilities, selected appliances, and related items.

The Census of Agriculture, first taken in 1840 and now taken every fifth year (in the years ending in "4" and "9"), provides data on number of farms, acreage in farms, value of land and buildings, uses of land, farm facilities and equipment, and specified crops harvested. Data also are presented on livestock and livestock products, fertilizer and lime used, and forest products cut and sold.

The Census of Business, first taken in 1930 and now taken every fifth year (to cover the years ending in "3" and "8"), covers the number of establishments, sales or receipts, and employees and payrolls for each kind of retail store and wholesale establishment and for selected service trades. These totals are shown for the nation and for many subdivisions such as states, counties, cities, and standard metropolitan statistical areas.

The Census of Manufactures, first taken in 1810 and now taken every fifth year (in the years ending in "3" and "8"), provides detailed data on manufacturing activity for geographic areas, individual industries, products shipped, and materials consumed. It shows how many plants there are, location, number of workers, wages paid to workers, expenditures for materials and for new plants and equipment, and how much the value of materials was increased by manufacturing. Some data also are given on inventories, manhours worked, and related items. Similar data are collected in the *Census of Mineral Industries,* which coincides with the canvass of factories.

The Census of Governments, first taken in 1850 and now taken every fifth year (in the years ending in "2" and "7"), provides statistics on the number and type of local governments, public employment, government finances—receipts, expenditures, indebtedness, and assets—and the value of taxable property.

The Congress has also provided for current surveys of social and economic subjects. These current reports cover population estimates, retail and wholesale trade, construction, housing vacancies, income, production of selected commodities, and other subjects.

Foreign-trade statistics also are collected by the Bureau of the Census from the reports of importers and exporters as filed with the Collector of Customs. The dollar value and net quantity of United States exports and imports by commodity, country of destination or origin and port of clearance are given, among other items.

The results of recent censuses are summarized below. Before going on, however, it might be well to note that the Census Bureau reports its data for four major regions of the United States. These are further divided into geographical divisions. The *Northeast* region consists of the *New England* division—the states of Maine, New Hampshire, Vermont, Massachusetts, Rhode Island, and Connecticut; and the *Middle Atlantic* division—the states of New York, New Jersey, and Pennsylvania. In the *North Central* region are grouped the *East North Central* division—the states of Ohio, Indiana, Illinois, Michigan, and Wisconsin; and the *West North Central* division—the states of Minnesota, Iowa, Missouri, North Dakota, South Dakota, Nebraska, and Kansas. The *South* includes the *South Atlantic* division—the states of Delaware, Maryland, Virginia, West Virginia, North Carolina, South Carolina, Georgia, and Florida, and the District of Columbia; the *East South Central* division —the states of Kentucky, Tennessee, Alabama, and Mississippi; and the *West South Central* division—the states of Arkansas, Louisiana, Oklahoma, and Texas. The *West* includes the *Mountain* division—the states of Montana, Idaho, Wyoming, Colorado, New Mexico, Arizona, Utah, and Nevada; and the *Pacific* division—the states of Washington, Oregon, California, Alaska, and Hawaii.

Population Characteristics

Since 1900, the population of the United States has increased by 103.1 million, or 135 per cent, from 76.2 million in 1900 to 179.3 million in 1960.[1] Of the nation's four major regions, only one—the West—has exceeded the national rate of gain. Since 1900, the West (including Alaska and Hawaii) has increased in population by 23.7 million, or 550 per cent, from 4.3 million in 1900 to 28.1 million in 1960. In total numbers, the South has shown the greatest gain since the turn of the century, with 30.5 million. In rate of increase, the South ranked second among regions, with a gain of 125 per cent. With a gain of 23.6 million, or 112 per cent, the Northeast had the smallest numerical increase, but it exceeded the North Central region's rate of 96 per cent. While the Northeast's population increased from

[1] Including residents of outlying areas under United States sovereignty or jurisdiction and members of the armed forces and civilians abroad, the total final population figure was 183,285,009.

21.0 million in 1900 to 44.7 million in 1960, the North Central region's count increased by 25.3 million, from 26.3 million in 1900 to 51.6 million in 1960.

The 1960 census—the 18th Decennial Census—recorded a total population for the United States of 179,323,175, an increase of 18.5 per cent over the 1950 total of 151,325,798. This increase of some 27,977,000 persons was the largest numerical increase in the nation's population in any ten-year period of its history.

Urban and Rural Population. About 70 per cent of the population in 1960 was urban, compared with 64 per cent in 1950. Of the total population in 1960, 125,-262,750, or 69.9 per cent, resided in urban areas; and 54,054,425, or 30.1 per cent, were residents of rural areas.

During the ten-year period, movement from rural areas and into metropolitan areas, particularly their suburbs, was substantial. While more people were concentrating in the metropolitan areas, many rural areas were losing population. Just under one-half, 1,537, or 49.4 per cent, of the total of 3,110 counties and county equivalents in the United States had fewer residents in 1960 than in 1950. A survey of the 1960 farm population showed that an average of 15,635,000 persons were living on rural farms in the 50 states in the 12-month period centered on April 1960. Of the total population, 8.7 per cent, or about 1 person in 12, was living on a farm.

The bulk of the country's population was concentrated in cities and towns. Of the total population, 42.4 per cent lived in the 676 cities of 25,000 or more. The total for these 676 top cities was 76 million.

Over 23 million persons lived in the top 12 cities. These most populous cities are:

RANK	CITY	POPULATION	RANK	CITY	POPULATION
1	New York	7,781,984	7	Houston	938,219
2	Chicago	3,550,404	8	Cleveland	876,050
3	Los Angeles	2,479,015	9	Washington	763,956
4	Philadelphia	2,002,512	10	St. Louis	750,026
5	Detroit	1,670,144	11	Milwaukee	741,324
6	Baltimore	939,024	12	San Francisco	740,316

Standard Metropolitan Statistical Areas. Approximately 84 per cent of the increase in the total population of the United States between 1950 and 1960 occurred in standard metropolitan statistical areas (S.M.S.A.'s),[1] that is, in cities of 50,000 or more and the outlying areas surrounding them. The 212 S.M.S.A.'s increased by 23.6 million persons, and of this increase 17.9 million occurred in the outlying parts of the S.M.S.A.'s and 5.6 million in the central cities. Thus the population increase in the outlying parts of the S.M.S.A.'s accounted for nearly two-thirds of the total population increase of the United States since 1950, as well as more than three-fourths of the total increase within S.M.S.A.'s. The growth of population in the central cities accounted for 20 per cent of the total population increase of the United States and 24 per cent of the increase within S.M.S.A.'s.

Within metropolitan areas, however, there were appreciable differences in population growth. In the decade 1950 to 1960, the population of central cities increased by only 11 per cent, whereas in the previous decade the corresponding increase was nearly 14 per cent. In the suburban ring, moreover, the 1950–60 increase was nearly 50 per cent, as compared with 35 per cent in the preceding decade. Considered as a proportion of the countrywide increase, the outlying parts, or suburban ring, accounted for about two-thirds of the total 1950–60 increase, but for slightly less than one-half of the 1940–50 increase.

Breakdown by Sex. America's women and girls outnumbered the men and boys

---

[1] The counties, cities, and towns constituting such areas, including their latest official census figures and other pertinent information, are available in "Standard Metropolitan Statistical Areas," a booklet sold by the Superintendent of Documents, United States Government Printing Office, Washington 25, D.C. (25¢).

in all sections of the United States except the Mountain and Pacific states and the Dakotas. Women and girls were more numerous in seven of the nation's nine geographic divisions. The ratio was 94.5 males to 100 females in the Middle Atlantic states. Conversely, the ratio was 101.2 males to 100 females in the Mountain states. For the other divisions, the ratios were between these two extremes. Among states, the proportions varied from 93.4 males per 100 females in Massachusetts to 132.3 males per 100 females in Alaska. The greatest difference in proportion of the sexes was in the District of Columbia, with 88.3 males to every 100 females.

Breakdown by Race. The Negro population of the United States was 18,871,831 in April 1960. This represented an increase of 3,829,545, or 25.5 per cent, between 1950 and 1960. The 1960 total represented 10.5 per cent of the 179,323,175 of all races enumerated in the 50 states. American Indians numbered 523,591, an increase of 166,092, or 46.5 per cent, over the 1950 census count of 357,499.

Figures for other minor races are:

Race	1960	1950	Per cent increase
Japanese	464,332	326,379	42.3
Chinese	237,292	150,005	58.2
Filipino	176,310	122,707	43.7

Breakdown by Age. The median age of the population of the United States was 29.5 years—down from 30.2 years in 1950. The 1960 census was the first to show a drop in the median age for any decennial period. The median age of the nation's population was 16 years in 1800 and 22.9 years in 1900.

About one in 11 persons in the United States was 65 years of age or over in 1960. There were 16,559,580 persons 65 years of age and over. This figure represented an increase of 4,264,882, or 34.7 per cent, over the 1950 count of 12,294,698 persons in the same age group.

At the other end of the age scale, there were 39,012,681 children under ten years of age, an increase of 9,507,416 over the 29,505,265 who were under ten years old in 1950.

Marital Status. There were 126,276,044 persons 14 years of age and over in 1960, of whom 27,792,782 were single and 85,166,281 were married—either for the first time or remarried after being widowed or divorced. Among the married persons were 2,214,418 who were separated from their spouses. Another 10,164,661 individuals were widowed; and 3,152,320 were divorced.

While the total number of persons 14 years old and over increased by 12.6 per cent from 1950 to 1960, the increase in the number of single persons was 7.0 per cent. Those married increased by 14.0 per cent; those divorced, however, increased by 28.3 per cent. The increase in the persons widowed in the ten-year period was 12.7 per cent. It was believed that some of these changes could be traced to the changes in age distribution already noted.

HOME OWNERSHIP

Three out of every five households in the United States, or approximately 33 million, owned their homes, according to results of the 1960 Census of Housing. This was the highest level of home ownership reported since 1890, the earliest year for which such census data are available.

In 1950 about 23.6 million, or 55 per cent of all households, owned their homes. At the turn of the century, only 47 per cent of the nation's households owned their homes, and the rate of home ownership remained relatively stable from then until 1940. At that time, some 44 per cent of the households owned the homes in which they were living. Dramatic increases in home ownership followed World War II, reaching 62 per cent of all households in 1960. Rates of home ownership in 1960 for white and nonwhite households were 64 per cent and 38 per cent, respectively. Whereas more than three out of five white households owned their homes, the rate for nonwhite households was less than two out of five.

PERSONAL INCOME

Each individual American—child, wage earner, retired person, etc.—shares in the income earned in the United States. The Census Bureau reports on personal income annually, helping to measure the progress of the economy. These estimates are for the nation as a whole, but the bureau's sister agency in the Dept. of Commerce, the Office of Business Economics, annually estimates the per capita income, by states. The 1960 personal income total was $401.6 billion; the per capita —or individual—share was $2,242. The state figures, however, ranged from a high of $3,094 for each person in Delaware to a low of $1,190 for a Mississippi resident. The accompanying table lists the states by income in four groups.

PERSONAL INCOME PER CAPITA BY STATE IN 1960

STATE	1960	STATE	1960
$1,000–1,500 per capita		*$2,001–2,500 per capita*	
Mississippi	$1,190	Kansas	$2,066
Arkansas	1,369	Minnesota	2,074
South Carolina	1,403	New Hampshire	2,108
Alabama	1,478	Nebraska	2,113
$1,501–2,000 per capita		Wisconsin	2,177
		Hawaii	2,192
Kentucky	1,555	Indiana	2,198
Tennessee	1,565	Missouri	2,214
North Carolina	1,584	Rhode Island	2,217
Georgia	1,622	Wyoming	2,262
Louisiana	1,630	Oregon	2,276
West Virginia	1,692	Pennsylvania	2,282
New Mexico	1,789	Colorado	2,301
Idaho	1,824	Washington	2,334
North Dakota	1,826	Michigan	2,355
Oklahoma	1,859	Ohio	2,367
Virginia	1,868	Maryland	2,415
Vermont	1,893	*$2,501 or more per capita*	
Maine	1,894	Massachusetts	2,548
South Dakota	1,919	Illinois	2,651
Utah	1,936	New Jersey	2,687
Texas	1,943	Alaska	2,724
Florida	1,949	California	2,753
Iowa	1,982	New York	2,853
Arizona	1,983	Nevada	2,854
Montana	1,996	Connecticut	2,871
		District of Columbia	3,000
		Delaware	3,094

CONTRACTS

A contract is an expression of an intention, by words or conduct, by two or more parties to affect their legal relationship. It is an agreement whereby each undertakes to do or not to do a particular thing. The word "agreement" implies a mutuality of rights and duties.

Contracts are said to be "express" when their terms are stated by the parties. Contracts are termed "implied in fact" when they are not expressly stated but their existence is determined from the acts and conduct of the parties. These are both true contracts. There is also another class of implied contracts, those which arise by implication of law. These occur without consent, a necessity of a true contract, and are known as quasi-contracts. A quasi-contract rests upon the equitable principle that a person shall not be allowed to enrich himself unjustly at the expense of another. It is an obligation which the law creates, in the absence of any agreement, when and because the acts of one party have placed in the possession of another money, or its equivalent, under such circumstances that in equity and good conscience he ought not to retain it. For example, if a doctor renders services to an unconscious person injured in an accident, the doctor is legally entitled to payment, even though the consent of the unconscious person was not obtained. The liability rests on a legal fiction created in the interest of justice. Other illustrations are found in the obligation to repay money received from another by mistake or through fraud, undue influence, or coercion.

Elements of a Contract. There are four elements to every contract. These are:

1. An *offer* by one party, duly accepted by the other. There is no contract until there is a definite meeting of the minds of the contracting parties upon all essential terms. This agreement occurs only when a definite and unconditional offer has been made by one party and unqualifiedly accepted by the other. A mere expression of intention is not an offer. An offer imports a willingness to incur a legal obligation. If one says to another, "I will sell my tennis racket for $10," it is an offer. If he says, "I intend to sell my tennis racket for $10," it is merely a declaration of intention. The acceptance of the former results in a binding and enforceable contract, whereas the latter is incapable of acceptance. An offer need not be in any particular form, but it must clearly import a willingness to be bound to the person to whom it is made. There is a vital distinction between an offer which, if accepted, creates a contract, and a *proposal* which is intended merely to open negotiations which may eventually result in a contract. Newspaper advertisements, letters, circulars, price lists, or catalogues distributed to prospective buyers, stating terms upon which goods are to be sold, are proposals, not offers.

To create a binding contract, there must be an unambiguous acceptance, showing a clear intention to accept the offer precisely as made. An intended acceptance which changes the terms of the offer is inoperative as an acceptance; it constitutes a new offer. A proposal to accept an offer if modified, or an acceptance subject to other terms and conditions than those stated in the offer, is equivalent to an absolute rejection. Such a proposal is a counteroffer, which, if it is to ripen into a contract, must be accepted by the party making the original offer.

An offer transmitted by mail is deemed accepted when the letter of acceptance is posted, even though it never reaches the party who made the offer, unless the latter party imposed the express condition that no contract should be made until the acceptance was received by him. If the language of the offer clearly indicates an intention to impose this condition, the contract is incomplete until the acceptance has been received. However, when an acceptance is transmitted by a different agency from that used or requested by the party who made the offer, the acceptance is not effective until it is received. To illustrate, when an offer which did not specify any particular mode of acceptance is sent by mail and accepted by telegraph, no contract results until the telegram is received by the party who made the offer.

The consent of the contracting parties must be free and voluntary. Consent may be affected by mistake of intention, misrepresentation, fraud, duress, or undue influence.

A party who signs a contract without reading it is bound by it. But, if his failure to read was induced by the other party's fraud, coercion, or undue influence, the signer's negligence will not bar relief and he can escape liability.

2. *Legal capacity* (as distinguished from physical or mental capacity) of all contracting parties is essential. By statute the age of legal capacity is 21. *Infants*

are those under 21; contracts of such persons are not void, merely voidable. This means that such contracts may be disaffirmed or ratified at the option of the infant. The other party to the contract, if adult, is bound by it. The defense of infancy is solely for the protection of the infant. When the infant ratifies the contract he assumes all liabilities and rights arising therefrom. When he disaffirms, he thereby avoids any liability. He can ratify the contract only after becoming 21. He can disaffirm all contracts, except deeds to real estate, either during infancy or within a reasonable time after becoming 21. Deeds to real estate can be disaffirmed only after he reaches 21. By statute in some states in certain instances contracts made by persons under 21 years of age are enforceable; for example: contracts by persons over 18 years of age engaged in business, which affect the business, and contracts affecting the relationship between depositor and savings banks.

Disaffirmance may be by express notice or by conduct which is manifestly inconsistent with the existence of the contract. Ratification requires affirmative action evidencing an intention to affirm the contract. The infant cannot ratify the beneficial parts and repudiate the detrimental parts. Once a contract is disaffirmed it cannot thereafter be ratified.

If a statute expressly permits an infant to enter into certain kinds of contracts, there is no right of disaffirmance. Marriage is such a contract.

Contracts made by a person after he has been adjudged *insane* are void; but contracts made by an insane person before such judicial declaration are voidable, not void. Insanity is a complete defense when performance of some contractual provision is still required, even though the other party made the contract without knowledge of the insanity, and before judicial declaration of insanity. But, if the contract is completely performed, the contract can be avoided by the incompetent, provided he returns all that he received under the contract. When such person is no longer insane he may affirm his contract.

A contract made by a person who was so *intoxicated* at the time that he did not know what he was doing is voidable by him but may be ratified when he becomes sober.

Formerly, *married women* had no right to enter into contracts. This restriction has been largely removed by statute; in most states married women may now make contracts as if they were single.

Aliens, although they are subjects of and owe sole allegiance to a foreign country, have the right to enter into contracts. Contracts between subjects of belligerent countries made after the commencement of war are void. If such contracts are made before war, they will be suspended during war, unless, from their nature, they are incapable of suspension, in which case they are not enforceable at the end of the war.

3. *Legality.* Contracts must have lawful purposes. Contracts contrary to statutory law or public policy are illegal. Illegality may affect only part of a contract. If the illegal part is severable from the legal part, the latter is enforceable by judicial action.

4. *Consideration.* No contract is valid without consideration. A valid consideration may consist of some right, profit, or benefit accruing to the party, or some forbearance, detriment, loss, responsibility, or some act or service given, suffered, or undertaken by the other party. However, by statute in some states certain kinds of contracts do not require consideration. Some of them are:

a. Agreements for purchase or sale of evidences of debt issued by government authorities or corporations and of stock of bank corporations or joint stock associations

b. Agreements to change, modify, or discharge contracts, leases, mortgages or other security interest, provided the agreement is in writing and signed

c. A written and signed assignment

d. A written offer to enter into a contract, stated therein to be irrevocable

e. A written and signed promise which is based on a past consideration expressed in the writing, if the consideration would have been valid but for the time when it was given or performed.

Formal and Informal Contracts. Contracts are either formal or informal. Most contracts are informal and may be oral; but, by statute, certain types of contracts must be in writing. They are:

1. Contracts which by their terms are not to be performed within one year from the time they are made

2. Contracts which provide for the payment of debts, defaults, or wrongs of another

3. Contracts by an executor or administrator of an estate to pay debts of the deceased out of his property

4. Contracts made in consideration of marriage, except promises to marry

5. Contracts for the sale of land, or a lease for more than one year

6. Contracts for the sale of goods above a certain value. This varies in the different states. In New York the amount is fixed at $500, except where goods are to be manufactured especially for the buyer and are not reusable for sale to others in the ordinary course of business. However, when the value exceeds $500, if: (a) the buyer accepts and receives a part of the goods; (b) pays part of the purchase price; or (c) the sale is by auction and the auctioneer makes a written memorandum of the sale, the contract is enforceable, even if it is not in writing

7. A promise to pay a debt when recovery has become barred by a statute of limitations

8. A promise to pay a debt discharged in bankruptcy

9. A promise to convey or assign a trust in personal property

10. A contract to bequeath property or make a will

11. A contract to establish a trust

12. An assignment of an interest in the estate of a deceased person

13. An authorization of an agent to sell land or create an interest therein or to lease land for more than one year

14. A contract to assign, or an assignment of, a life or health or accident insurance policy, or a promise to name a beneficiary of such policy

15. A contract to pay a fee for services rendered in negotiating the purchase, sale, exchange, or lease of land or of a business.

Oral contracts to pay compensation to an auctioneer, lawyer, or duly licensed real estate broker or salesman are valid.

Since contracts reflect the intention of the contracting parties, they should be in clear and unambiguous language. Pencil, chalk, ink, print, or typewriting may be used. The entire contract need not be on one piece of paper; an exchange of letters, telegrams, or other form of communication will suffice.

Usually, a contract is regarded as made at the place of acceptance and is interpreted according to the law of that place, unless it is to be performed elsewhere, in which case it is interpreted according to the law of the place where it is to be performed. Contracts affecting real property are generally interpreted in accordance with the laws of the place where the property is situated.

Many contracts specify the laws which shall govern their interpretation, and barring contrary public policy such provisions are controlling.

Generally, contracts are to be performed in the time specified in the contract. If no time is specified, the implication is that the contract is to be performed within a reasonable time.

A contract may provide that a certain amount as damages shall be paid for nonperformance. The enforcement of such a provision depends upon whether the amount is a penalty or liquidated damages. If it is a penalty, courts will not enforce it, and the aggrieved party can recover the actual damages only. It is not easy to determine when such an agreed amount will be considered to be a penalty. It is fairly safe to assume that if the amount is grossly in excess of the actual damages, the court will consider it a penalty. If the actual damages are uncertain and difficult to ascertain, the court will consider it to be liquidated damages.

Parties are bound to perform what they contracted to do. An Act of God will excuse nonperformance of a duty imposed by law, but it will not excuse a duty imposed by contract except where the parties so contemplated. Similarly, with some exceptions, supervening impossibility is not an excuse for nonperformance.

Liability. There are three kinds of liability: several; joint; and joint and several. When a "several obligation" is entered into by two or more persons in one instrument, it is the same as if each had signed separate instruments, although they may all relate to the same subject matter. Each is liable for his several promise, and cannot be held liable for the others. A joint contract is one in which two or more persons jointly bind themselves to fulfill its obligations; either of them may be held responsible for the whole debt. When one joint promisor pays more than his pro rata share, he is entitled to contributions from the others. Several persons may also bind themselves jointly as one party, and also severally as separate individuals; in such case all the promisors may be joined in one action, or may be sued separately. By statute, in many states joint liabilities are treated as joint and several liabilities.

Contract of Agency. An *agent* is a person authorized to act for another party called the principal. The relationship is based on consent, express or implied. It is implicit in the relationship that the agent may affect the legal relationship between the principal and third parties, and that the principal has the right to control the conduct of the agent. Lawyers, brokers, factors, and partners are all agents, but usually their authority is of a special character. A *general agent* is one who represents his principal in a particular line of business; for example, the manager of a store.

A *special agent* is one authorized to do some particular act, or to act upon some particular occasion. He acts usually in accordance with specific instructions, or under certain limitations necessarily implied by the nature of the act to be done.

A servant acts for the principal usually in accordance with instructions, while an agent represents the principal and acts in place and stead of the principal. Basically, however, the liability of the principal for torts of his agent is the same as that of a master for torts of his servant.

A *broker* is one who is engaged for others, on a commission basis, to negotiate contracts relative to property. A broker usually is not entrusted with the possession of the property and usually is not authorized to buy and sell it in his own name. Frequently a broker merely brings parties together to make a bargain, and does not complete a transaction.

Any person who has legal capacity to enter into a contract may appoint an agent and any person of legal age and sound mind can be an agent. Partnerships and corporations may be agents. An agent's authority is derived from consent of the principal; however, the principal's liability for his agent's contracts and acts is not limited to acts actually authorized but includes those implied from express authority and those which apparently have been delegated to the agent where the principal is responsible for the appearance of authority.

Generally, an agent upon whom is conferred authority involving trust and confidence has no power to appoint subagents, but the principal may confer such authority or it may be implied from the nature of the act to be performed or the nature of the agency. When an agent has determined upon the propriety of a certain course of action, he has implied authority to entrust the performance of any purely mechanical act to another. For example, an agent employed to sell land may employ a subagent to exhibit it, and an insurance agent may employ clerks to collect premiums and deliver policies. A subagent, appointed by express or implied authority of a principal, is, as far as third parties are concerned, the agent of the principal, and the acts of the subagent within the scope of his agency are binding upon the principal. If the agent has undertaken to transact certain business for the principal and appoints a subagent to assist him, even though the principal assents to this appointment the relation of principal and agent does not exist between the principal and subagent, although such relation does exist as far as third parties are concerned.

Appointment of Agents. Agents may be appointed orally, but an agency to buy and sell land or make leases for more than one year is required to be in writing. The usual way to appoint an agent is by means of a power of attorney.

Generally, agents are appointed by the principal, orally or in writing. However, if a person, by his affirmative conduct or silence, knowingly and without dissent permits another to act for him in a particular transaction, he will be estopped from repudiating the agency as against one who in good faith, and exercising reasonable prudence, has dealt with such apparent agent relying on such apparent authority. The acts of an unauthorized person on behalf of another may be subsequently adopted and affirmed. Such ratification is equivalent to prior authorization and binds the principal as effectively as though prior authority had been given.

Termination of Agency. A contract of agency may be terminated in three ways: (1) by the language of the agency agreement; (2) by acts of the parties; and (3) by operation of law.

If the agency is a general and continuing one, persons who deal in good faith with the agent are protected unless notice of revocation of the agent's authority is given. For example, a debtor is justified in paying an agent until notified by the creditor that the authority of the agent to receive payments has been revoked.

Some agencies are irrevocable by the principal. If an agent is authorized to collect a debt, and out of the proceeds reimburse himself for advances made to the principal, his authority may not be revoked by the principal; or if an agent is engaged to perform an act which entails personal liability and has actually incurred such liability, his authority to act may not be withdrawn by the principal; and if the agent has an interest in the subject matter of the agency, the principal may not revoke the power.

Death, insanity, or bankruptcy of either the principal or agent terminates the contract of agency. War or statutory law may also terminate the agency.

Obligation of Principal and Agent. A principal is liable for the torts of the agent committed in the performance of the agency. For example, when a manager affirms the act of a salesman who caused the arrest of a customer, the owner of the business will be held responsible. A principal is liable for the authorized frauds of his agent, and he may be liable in instances in which the agent was acting within the scope of his actual or apparent authority when the fraud was practiced.

An agent must exercise skill, care, and diligence in the performance of his duties. He must act in good faith and always be loyal to his principal. He may not acquire an interest adverse to that of his principal.

As a general rule, the agency agreement specifies how much and when the agent is to be paid for his services. If no amount is fixed the agent will be entitled to the reasonable value of the services rendered. He must have fully performed his duties before he is entitled to his compensation.

Patents for inventions made by an agent during an agency are considered the property of the agent, not of the principal, even though the invention is a direct outcome of information gained during the exercise of the agency. Generally, as a matter of business expediency, when it is known in advance that the agent is likely to make an invention (for example, if he is employed in a shop where mechanical appliances are designed or manufactured), it is customary for the company to provide by contract that all inventions made and discovered by their agents or employees shall belong to the company. Sometimes the employee is given additional compensation for such discoveries.

UNRESTRICTED POWER OF ATTORNEY[1]

Know all men, that I, John Doe, residing at ———, do hereby constitute and appoint Richard Roe, residing at ———, my true and lawful attorney for me, and in my name,

1. To enter upon and take possession of any lands, buildings, tenements, or other structures, or any part or parts thereof, that may belong to me, or to the possession whereof I may be entitled;

2. To ask, collect, and receive any rents, profits, issues, or income, of any and all of such lands, buildings, tenements, or other structures, or/of any part, or parts, thereof;

3. To make, execute, and deliver any deed, mortgage, or lease, whether with or without covenants and warranties, in respect of any such lands, buildings, tenements, or other structures, or of any part or parts thereof, and to manage any such lands, and to manage, repair, alter, rebuild, or reconstruct any buildings, houses, or other structures, or any part or parts thereof, that may now or hereafter be erected upon any such lands;

4. To demand, sue for, collect, recover, and receive all goods, claims, debts, moneys, interest, and demands whatsoever now due, or that may hereafter be due, or belong to me (including the right to institute any action, suit, or legal proceeding for the recovery of any land, buildings, tenements, or other structures, or any part or parts thereof, to the possession whereof I may be entitled), and to make, execute, and deliver receipts, releases, or other discharges therefor, under seal or otherwise;

5. To make, execute, endorse, accept, and deliver any and all bills of exchange, checks, drafts, notes, and trade acceptances;

6. To pay all sums of money, at any time or times, that may hereafter be owing by me upon any bill of exchange, check, draft, note, or trade acceptance made, executed, endorsed, accepted, and delivered by me, or for me, and in my name by my said attorney;

7. To sell any and all shares of stocks, bonds, or other securities now or hereafter belonging to me, that may be issued by any association, trust, or corporation, whether private or public, and to make, execute, and deliver an assignment or assignments of any such shares of stocks, bonds, or other securities;

8. To defend, settle, adjust, compound, submit to arbitration and compromise all actions, suits, accounts, reckonings, claims, and demands whatsoever that now are or hereafter shall be pending between me and any person, firm, or corporation, in such manner and in all respects as my said attorney shall think fit;

9. To hire accountants, attorneys at law, clerks, workmen, and others, and to remove them, and appoint others in their place, and to pay and allow to the persons to be so employed such salaries, wages, or other remuneration as my said attorney shall think fit;

10. To enter into, make, sign, execute, deliver, acknowledge, and perform any contract, agreement, writing, or thing that may, in the opinion of my said attorney, be necessary or proper to be entered into, made, or signed, sealed, executed, delivered, acknowledged, or performed;

11. To constitute and appoint, in his place and stead and as his substitute, one attorney or more for me, with full power of revocation; and

12. Without in any wise limiting the foregoing, generally to do, execute, and perform any other act, deed, matter, or thing whatsoever that ought to be done, executed, and performed or that, in the opinion of my said attorney, ought to be done, executed, or performed, in and about the premises, of every nature and kind whatsoever as fully and effectually as I could do if personally present.

And I, the said John Doe, do hereby ratify and confirm all whatsoever my said attorney, or his substitute, or substitutes, shall do or cause to be done in or about the premises, by virtue of this power of attorney.

[1] This is only a suggested form. The reader is advised to obtain a blank form, valid in his state, from a lawyer or legal stationer for use in specific transactions. Some states have enacted statutes which provide that certain short forms shall be deemed to include powers set forth at length in the statute.

In witness whereof, I have hereunto set my hand and seal, in (city), state of ————, on this ———— day of ————, 19–.

John Doe (L.S.)

In the presence of
John Doe, Jr.,
Richard Roe, Jr.

REVOCATION OF POWER OF ATTORNEY[1]

Know all men, that—

Whereas, I, John Doe, residing at ————, (city), (state), did, in writing, under date of ————, 19–, appoint Richard Roe, residing at (city), my true and lawful attorney, to demand, receive, sue for, and collect all claims, debts, moneys, and demands whatsoever due, or to become due, to me, all as in the said written power of attorney more particularly set forth; and

Whereas, I, the said John Doe, desire to terminate the said written power of attorney:

Now, therefore, I, the said John Doe, do hereby annul, cancel, revoke, and terminate the said written power of attorney, dated ————, 19–, and do hereby annul, cancel, revoke, and terminate all rights, powers, authorities, privileges, and immunities therein and thereby vested in, or given to, the said Richard Roe.

In witness whereof, in (city), state of ————, I have hereunto set my hand and seal, on the ———— day of ————, 19–.

John Doe (L.S.)

In the presence of
John Doe, Jr.,
Richard Roe, Jr.

Contracts of Sale. Most states have enacted statutes covering the entire subject of sales. A sale of goods is an agreement whereby the seller transfers the property in the goods to the buyer for a consideration called the price. The sale may be absolute or conditional. Mutual assent is necessary. The parties must have legal capacity to contract.

A contract to sell or a sale may be in writing (either with or without a seal), or by word of mouth, or partly in writing and partly by word of mouth, or may be inferred from the conduct of the parties.[2]

The sale may consist of goods which the seller owns or possesses at the time of the contract, or of goods to be manufactured or acquired by the seller after the making of the contract. The former are called "existing goods," the latter "future goods."

If the seller did not know that the goods were wholly perished at the time the agreement to sell was made, the agreement is void. If the goods have only partly perished or have wholly or partly deteriorated, the buyer may at his option treat the sale as avoided or take the remaining part, or as much as has not deteriorated, in which case he must pay the full agreed price if the sale is indivisible, or the agreed price for the goods in which the property passes if the sale is divisible. If the property is destroyed or damaged before the time agreed upon for title to pass, the buyer cannot be compelled to pay the price; if he has paid the price in advance it may be recovered.

The *price* for the goods is usually fixed in the contract. It may be left to be fixed in such manner as may be agreed, or it may be determined by the course of dealings between the parties. When not so determined, the buyer must pay a reasonable price, usually the market price at the time and place fixed by the contract for the delivery of the goods.

If the contract contains no specific contrary provision, the seller warrants by

---

[1] This is only a suggested form. The reader is advised to obtain a blank form, valid in his state, from a lawyer or legal stationer for use in specific transactions.

[2] Certain contracts of sale must be in writing. See *Formal and Informal Contracts,* earlier in this article.

implication that he has a right to sell and that the buyer shall enjoy *possession* of the goods as against the legal claim of others. This has no application to sales by sheriffs or auctioneers. If the sale is by description or sample, the goods must correspond to the description or sample. If they do not, the buyer may refuse to accept the goods; if he has taken them he may promptly return them. He may also bring an action against the seller for failing to deliver the goods agreed upon.

There is generally no implied warranty of *quality* nor of fitness for any particular purpose. The buyer makes the purchase at his risk. However, when the buyer expressly or by implication notifies the seller of the particular purpose for which the goods are required, and the buyer relies on the seller's skill or judgment, there is an implied warranty that the goods shall be reasonably fit for such purpose. When the goods are purchased by description from a seller who generally deals in such goods, there is an implied warranty that the goods are of merchantable quality. There is no implied warranty of fitness for any particular purpose if the goods are sold under a patent or trade name. If the buyer has examined the goods, there is no implied warranty as to obvious defects which the examination ought to have revealed. The warranty survives inspection when the defect is latent and not discoverable by reasonable care. An implied warranty of condition as to quality or fitness for a particular purpose may be annexed by the usage of trade.

Generally, and in the absence of contrary provisions, *payment* is due at the time of delivery. The unpaid seller has a lien for the purchase price on goods while he has possession of them. If the buyer becomes insolvent while the goods are in transit, the seller can stop shipment, resell the goods, and recover from the buyer the amount of his loss. But if the resale price is greater than the original contract price, the seller must refund the surplus to the buyer. The seller may also rescind the contract.

If the buyer has received the goods and wrongfully refuses to pay according to the terms of the contract, the seller may sue for the purchase price. The price may be recovered when it is payable on a certain day, irrespective of delivery, although title to the goods has not passed to the buyer. When the buyer wrongfully neglects or refuses to accept and pay for the goods, the seller may sue the buyer for non-acceptance. Generally, the measure of those damages will be a sum of money which puts the seller in as good a position as he would have been had the buyer accepted the goods. This loss can be ascertained if there is a market for the goods; then the loss to the seller would be the difference between the contract price and the market price at the time and place fixed in the contract. If there is no available market for the goods, the seller is entitled to receive the full amount of the damage which he sustained as a result of the breach of the contract.

The seller must *deliver* the goods in accordance with the terms of the contract. In the absence of contractual provisions or custom in the particular trade, it is generally presumed that the place of delivery is the seller's place of business. It is the buyer's duty to call for the goods, rather than the seller's duty to deliver. If the seller is required by the contract to deliver the goods, but no time is specified, the delivery must be made within a reasonable time. Since "a reasonable time" is somewhat indefinite, the buyer should give notice to the seller as to when he wishes delivery.

If the seller delivers a smaller quantity than is required by the contract, the buyer may reject the goods; but if he accepts the part delivered, knowing that the seller will not deliver the balance, the buyer must pay for what he accepts at the agreed contract price. If the buyer uses the goods before he knows that the seller is not going to deliver the balance required by the terms of the contract, the buyer will be liable only for the fair value of the goods to him and not for the contract price. If more is delivered the buyer may reject the whole or accept the goods included in the contract and reject the rest, but if the buyer accepts the goods, he must pay for them all at the contract price. Unless it is otherwise agreed, a buyer need not accept delivery in installments. If the contract provides for delivery in installments which are to be separately paid for, and the seller makes defective deliveries, or the buyer neglects or refuses to take delivery of, or to pay for, the installment, the remedies that the parties have against each other will in each case depend upon the terms of the contract; if no provision is made for such contingency, the circumstances of each case will determine whether the injured party may refuse to proceed further with the contract and sue for damages, or whether he can only sue for damages and not treat the whole contract as broken.

When the seller wrongfully neglects or refuses to deliver the goods, the buyer may sue for such nondelivery and recover his direct loss, which is the difference between the contract price and the market price at the time and place the contract is broken. If the seller repudiates the contract, the buyer may rescind the contract and recover the price paid.

BILL OF SALE[1]

Know all men by these presents,
that John Doe, residing at ————, (city), party of the first part, for and in consideration of the sum of ———— to him in hand, paid at or before the ensealing and delivery of these presents by Richard Roe, residing at ————, (city), party of the second part, the receipt whereof is hereby acknowledged, has bargained and sold, and by these presents does grant and convey unto the said party of the second part, his executors, administrators, successors and assigns the following:

The shoe store located at ————, (city), including stock and merchandise, fixtures, chattels, and equipment that are described in "Schedule A" hereto annexed and made part hereof, together with the good will and trade name of "The Bootery," heretofore used by the seller in the conduct of the said business.

To have and to hold the same unto the said party of the second part, his executors, administrators, successors, and assigns forever. And the party of the first part does for himself, and his heirs, executors, and administrators, covenant and agree, to and with said party of the second part, to warrant and defend the sale of the aforesaid shoe store business hereby sold to the party of the second part, his executors, administrators, successors, and assigns against all and every person and persons.

And the party of the first part does further covenant and agree, to and with the said party of the second part, that he will not re-establish, reopen, be engaged in, nor in any manner whatsoever become interested in, directly or indirectly, either as employee, as owner, as partner, as agent, or as stockholder, director, or officer of a corporation, or otherwise, in any business, trade, or occupation similar to the one hereby sold within a radius of five (5) square blocks from the address of the business hereby sold to the party of the second part, for a term of ten (10) years from the date of these presents.

In witness whereof, the party of the first part has set his hand and seal this ———— day of ————, 19–.

————————

Seller

(Annex a schedule of fixtures, chattels, etc.)

STATE OF ————
COUNTY OF ———— } ss:.

John Doe, being duly sworn, deposes and says; that he resides at ————, (city). That he is the same person who executed the within bill of sale. That he is the sole and absolute owner of the property described in said bill of sale and has full right to sell and transfer the same. That the said property and each and every part thereof is free and clear of any liens, mortgages, debts, or other encumbrances of whatsoever kind or nature.

That he is not indebted to anyone and has no creditors.

That there are no judgments existing against him, in any court, nor are there any

---

[1] This is only a suggested form. The reader is advised to obtain a blank form, valid in his state, from a lawyer or legal stationer for use in specific transactions.

replevins, attachments, or executions against him, now in force, nor has any petition in bankruptcy been filed by or against him.

That this affidavit is made for the express purpose and with the intent of inducing Richard Roe to purchase the property set forth and described in the foregoing bill of sale, knowing full well that he will rely upon this affidavit and pay a good and valuable consideration.

Sworn to before me this
————— day of —————, 19–.

Warranty. Warranties may be implied or expressed. An *express warranty* is an affirmative statement of fact made by the seller relating to the goods which induces the buyer to make the purchase. A statement of value or of opinion is not warranty.

The buyer has many remedies for a seller's breach of warranty. He may: (1) accept the goods and, when sued for the purchase price, apply the damages he suffered on either diminution or extinction of the price; (2) accept the goods and sue for damages; (3) refuse to accept the goods and sue for damages; or (4) rescind the contract and refuse to accept the goods; or (5) if the goods have been received, return them and recover the price paid.

In the absence of any express or implied agreement, the buyer's acceptance of the goods does not discharge the seller from liability for breach of warranty. But if, after accepting the goods, the buyer fails to give notice to the seller of the breach within a reasonable time after the buyer knows of such breach, the seller is not liable.

Option. An option is a privilege granted to a party to accept an offer within a stated time. If no consideration is given, the offer may be withdrawn at any time before acceptance,[1] but if the offer is accepted prior to such withdrawal it ripens into a binding contract. If any consideration is paid the offer is irrevocable for the stated period of time and may not be withdrawn before the expiration of such period.

Assignment. An assignment is a transfer of all right, title, or interest in the property or thing assigned from one person to another. It arises from contract or by operation of law, as when title to property passes to an executor or administrator of an estate, a trustee in bankruptcy, or a guardian.

TORTS

A tort is a violation of a legal right or duty. Moral wrongs are not torts. Torts do not arise from contract. Libel, slander, false arrest, malicious prosecution, deceit, fraud, assault, and conversion of personal property are torts.

SEALS

At common law, seals had great importance; without them certain contracts were not legal. By statute, it is now generally provided that the presence or absence of a seal upon a written instrument shall be without legal effect, except in specific cases that are governed by special statute.

BANKS AND BANKING

Banks are generally regarded as our most important financial institutions. It has been estimated that over 90 per cent of the business of the country is conducted by means of checks drawn by depositors against accounts they have in the banks. Banking functions are so important to the public interest that traditionally banks in the United States have been subject to broader regulation than any other type of

---

[1] In some states if the option is in writing and stated therein to be irrevocable the effect is the same as if consideration had been paid.

business. This regulation begins with the organization of the bank and is continued through regular supervision and examination by government authorities.

Organization of the Banking Structure. In this country there are two classes of banks, based on the authority from which they receive their charters. The Federal government charters *national banks,* while *state banks* are chartered under the authority of the legislatures and constitutions of each of the 50 states. The Comptroller of the Currency is the officer of the Federal government charged with the responsibility of granting charters for the establishment of national banks. The law establishes strict requirements covering the amount of capital to be supplied by the organizing stockholders, proof of need for the bank in the community, its prospects for success, and the general character of the proposed management. It is compulsory for national banks to be members of the Federal Reserve System, a system of "banks for the banks"; and of the Federal Deposit Insurance Corporation, another agency of the Federal government, which protects depositors against loss by insuring their accounts up to $10,000 per depositor.

The charters of state banks, granted under authority of the individual state legislatures, are obtained through the offices of the bank superintendents or commissioners, or banking boards, depending upon the method of incorporation adopted by the state. There is a reasonable degree of uniformity in the principles of incorporation among the various states. Differences lie in the specific application of the principles. For example, in some states the amount of capital required for organization is smaller than that prescribed in the Federal statute for national banks, while in other states the requirement is greater.

State banks may be classified in three different groups, according to the type of business they conduct: *commercial banks, trust companies,* and *mutual savings banks.* On the other hand, all national banks are classified as commercial banks, although they may do a combined commercial, trust, and savings business. Similarly, some state commercial banks and trust companies may perform all three functions.

Mutual savings banks are chartered only by states. They differ from commercial banks and trust companies in several important respects. Whereas the latter are organized by stockholders who buy stock and receive dividends from the profits earned, mutual savings banks do not have stock ownership; part of their earnings is distributed to their depositors as interest and part is retained as surplus to provide a protective cushion against losses, for the benefit of the depositors. Mutual savings banks do not offer a checking service, and the methods by which they may invest their money are usually more closely defined by law. Mutual savings banks exist only in Connecticut, Delaware, Indiana, Maine, Maryland, Massachusetts, Minnesota, New Hampshire, New Jersey, New York, Ohio, Oregon, Pennsylvania, Rhode Island, Vermont, Washington, and Wisconsin.

Banks chartered by the states have the option of membership in the Federal Reserve System. If they decide to join, they are also required to become members of the Federal Deposit Insurance Corporation. State banks which do not join the Federal Reserve System still may have their deposits insured by the F.D.I.C., provided they meet prescribed tests for admission similar to those required for the organization of national banks. In becoming members of either of these Federal instrumentalities, state banks subject themselves to Federal supervision in addition to that already exercised over them by the banking departments of the state in which they are chartered.

Banking Services. The following is a brief description of the principal banking services; not all banks necessarily provide all these services.

There are two types of deposits, commercial (or *demand*) and time (mostly *savings*). Commercial banks usually accept both types, while mutual savings banks confine their activities to savings deposits. Demand deposits are the basis for the check-payment system by which most business transactions are conducted. When you open a checking account, you fill out a card with your signature and other information which later will help the bank to identify you. The bank will provide you with a book of blank checks and a passbook. In making a deposit, you fill out a deposit slip which shows how much money, whether currency or checks from others, you wish to place in the bank. The teller enters the amount in your passbook and retains the deposit slip for the bank's records. (Some banks no longer issue passbooks for checking accounts, but use instead tellers machines. The depositor is given a receipt showing the amount deposited, the number on the receipt corresponding to the number on the bank's records.) After the account has been opened, you may draw checks on demand against the deposit. If you deposit checks, however, you may not draw against them until the bank has cashed them at the banks upon which they were drawn.

Checking accounts are adapted to the needs of the customer. If you draw only a few checks a month and wish to keep only a small amount of money on deposit, you may open a "special" checking account, on which you pay a nominal fee for each check drawn. Practices of banks differ. Some charge for deposit items as well. Some banks require that a balance be maintained, while others do not—although it is necessary, of course, for funds to be on deposit at the time a check is presented for collection against the account. Sometimes the bank will charge a small flat fee for the account, in addition to the charges for individual checks.

Other checking accounts are available for those who draw a relatively large number of checks each month and who are able to maintain a larger average balance. In determining whether to make a service charge on these accounts, the bank considers how many checks and deposits you have had during the month, as well as your average deposit balance. Your balance provides a source of income for the bank, against which the expenses for the checks and deposits are offset. If the credit earned on the balance is sufficient to cover the charges, you will not be required to pay anything for the services rendered. Otherwise a charge will be made in the following month.

The Checkbook. A check is an order upon a bank to pay from the depositor's account according to the instructions therein contained. It is payable on demand. A postdated check, one having a later date than that of delivery, is merely a promise to discharge a present obligation at a future date. The presumption is that the maker has an inadequate balance in the bank at the time of giving the check but will have enough at the date of presentation.

By statute a person who, with intent to defraud, shall make or draw or utter or deliver any check, draft, or order for the payment of money upon any bank or other depository, knowing at the time of such making that the maker or drawer has not sufficient funds with such bank for the payment of such check, although no express representation is made in reference thereto, shall be guilty of a misdemeanor. The making, drawing, uttering, or delivering of a check, payment of which is refused by the bank because of lack of funds, shall be prima-facie evidence of intent to defraud and of knowledge of insufficient funds. This statute has no application to a postdated check, since the implication of giving a postdated check is that the maker presently has not sufficient funds on deposit.

Checks are not only a convenient means of payment but also constitute permanent evidence and record of payment.

The following rules should be observed in making out checks and in the use of the stub which remains in the checkbook:

1. Know your balance. United States banks are not supposed to pay overdrafts, although this is done by banks in some other countries. Embarrassment, annoyance, and criminal prosecution will be avoided if you keep proper record of your bank balance and verify your bank statements.

2. Always write checks in ink; if possible, use a mechanical check writer to write the amount of the check.

3. Fill out the stub first; make complete entries.

4. Number the checks consecutively; be sure the numbers on the check and the stub correspond.

5. Be sure to date the check; write out or abbreviate the month. In many states a check made out on a Sunday or a legal holiday should be dated the following day.

6. Write distinctly; avoid flourishes. If you make a mistake do not cross out or rewrite; destroy the check and mark the check stub "Void."

7. Do not cross out the name of the bank on a check and write in the name of your own bank. Most banks, hotels, and department stores have blank checks for use by people who have forgotten their checkbooks. Use this form but make a note of the amount and the name of the payee and enter it in your checkbook as soon as possible by filling out the stub; destroy the check in your book for which this is the substitute.

8. Write out the full name of the payee. It is unwise to make checks payable to "Cash" or "Bearer." Such checks can be cashed by anyone who holds them and may be cashed by one not entitled to the money. Never sign completely or partially blank checks. If the payee's name does not fill the space then draw a line from the end of the name to the dollar sign. Begin writing the name as close as possible to the left of the line. This will prevent the insertion of additional names as payees. A check payable to more than one payee can be cashed by either payee unless the word "and" is used. Obviously, any person intending wrongfully to cash the check will insert the "or."

9. Be sure that the amount written in words corresponds to the amount in figures. If there is a difference, the amount in words will be considered the proper amount by the bank. Do not leave any blank space; begin as close as possible to the dollar sign and to the left on the line where you write out the amount. Fill the balance of the space by running a line to the word "Dollars."

Care and prudence must be exercised in drawing checks and in verifying accounts. The legal relationship between a bank and a depositor is that of debtor and creditor, and the bank can justify a payment on the customer's account only upon the actual direction of the depositor. The questions arising between the maker and the bank concerning checks, therefore, always relate to what the one has authorized the other to do. The question of the depositor's negligence, however, may arise in disputes between depositors and the bank. Such questions of negligence arise when the depositor, in drawing his check, has left blanks unfilled, or by some affirmative act of negligence has facilitated the commission of a fraud by those into whose hands the check may come. Now, while the drawer of a check may be liable when he draws the instrument so incompletely that it facilitates or invites fraudulent alterations, it is not the law that he is bound so to prepare the check that nobody else can successfully tamper with it. What affirmative acts of negligence will be legally attributable to the depositor cannot be categorically stated, but if the rules given above are followed in making out checks, the depositor will avoid the imputation of negligence.

The law places a duty upon the depositor to exercise diligence in examining his canceled vouchers and in notifying the bank within a reasonable time if forged checks have been paid by the bank. Failure to give such notice will absolve the bank from liability to the depositor. By statute it is provided that no bank shall be liable to a depositor for payment of a forged or raised check unless within one year after the return to the depositor of the voucher of such payment such depositor shall notify the bank that the check so paid was forged or raised.

A depositor may stop payment on a check he has drawn by telephoning instructions to the bank and then confirming by letter, or by filling out and delivering to the bank the form which most banks provide for this purpose.

Endorsements. Before a check can be cashed or deposited, it must be endorsed by the person to whom it is payable.

To endorse a check, turn it over and write your name near the top on the end farthest from the signature on the face of the check:

> *John Brown*

Spell your name as it is spelled on the face of the check. If this name is different from your regular signature, write your regular signature beneath it:

> *B. John Brown*
> *John Brown*

If you wish to pass a check on to someone else, the endorsement should be as follows:

> *Pay to the order of Henry Smith*
> *John Brown*

Then Henry Smith, upon presenting the check at the bank, must add his endorsement below yours:

> *Pay to the order of Henry Smith*
> *John Brown*
> *Henry Smith*

If the check is to be deposited, the endorsement may read:

> *For deposit*
> *John Brown*

or:

> *For deposit only*
> *John Brown*

A check endorsed:

> *Pay to the order of the First National Bank*
> *John Brown*

will be deposited unless John Brown owes the bank money, in which case it may be applied on the debt.

Persons who for one reason or another find it difficult to go to the bank often mail their checks to the bank with this form of endorsement.

If you are given a check on a bank where you are not known and are likely to have some difficulty in collecting, the best procedure is to have the maker of the check guarantee your signature. For instance, if Sam Jones made out such a check to Henry Smith, Henry Smith should endorse it in the regular way. Then Sam Jones should write just below this endorsement "Signature guaranteed, *Sam Jones,*" or "Signature O.K., *Sam Jones.*"

Certified Checks. For most purposes, a certified check is generally considered the equivalent of cash, since the bank on which it is drawn certifies that it will pay the check upon presentation. You fill out the check in the usual manner and take it to your bank, where the amount is immediately deducted from your balance, the check becoming a liability of the bank. As such, the check is acceptable, whereas your personal check might not be. Certification consists of stamping or marking the check "Certified" or "Accepted," together with the signature of the bank.

Cashier's Checks. A cashier's check is a check drawn by the bank upon itself and signed by an authorized officer. It is used to pay the bank's own bills and expenses or purchased by a depositor for remittances for which his own check might not be acceptable.

Bad and Postdated Checks. Nearly all the states have laws which provide that a person who issues a check or a person (whether he issued it in the beginning or not) who negotiates a check knowing that there are not funds enough to back it up, is guilty of a crime. The degree of crime varies in the several states; in some it is a misdemeanor, in others, a felony or larceny.

Postdated checks, that is, checks dated ahead of the day on which they are issued, are not considered bad checks unless there is behind them intent to defraud.

All checks should be presented promptly for payment.

No check is good when the maker is dead. The creditor can get his money only by filing a claim against the estate.

The Monthly Statement. At certain regular periods, usually on the first of every month, you receive from the bank an exact record of your transactions with and through the bank during the past month.

The statement should be carefully compared with your checkbook, item by item. The deposits are in one column. These should be added and checked against the deposits recorded in your checkbook and in your passbook.

The vouchers—canceled checks, drafts, promissory notes, etc., which the bank returns with the statement—should be arranged by date, then by numbers, and checked against the stubs in your checkbook.

If you find that a mistake has been made, go at once to the bank; however, don't assume a mistake has been made merely because all your checks are not there. The chances are that they have not yet been returned. You may find items that you did not expect, such as a small collection fee on out-of-town checks or a service charge because your average account has been below the minimum required by the bank. These should be noted in your checkbook in order to bring about the proper balance.

Joint Accounts. Joint bank accounts, which may be either checking or savings accounts, are payable to either of the two (or more) parties who enter into them. Another way in which a second person can be given access to an account is through a power of attorney. Sometimes persons who are going on long trips leave a power of attorney over their bank accounts with a trustworthy friend. Husbands and wives sometimes find this an easier way to handle their funds than the joint account. This makes it possible for both to have separate accounts and yet, in case of emergency, for each to draw upon the other.

Savings Accounts. A savings account is opened in about the same way as a checking account, but the passbook is much more important in the savings bank. In the checking account the passbook is simply a memorandum of deposits; in the savings account it contains a complete record of deposits and withdrawals and must be presented every time a transaction is made. If the deposit is made by mail the passbook should be mailed with it and the envelope registered. The book is balanced at the end of each transaction; there is no periodic statement of deposits and withdrawals as in the case of the checking account. On savings accounts, interest is paid to the depositor. There are many ways of computing this interest. The amount is entered the first time the depositor presents the passbook after the computation period is ended.

The depositor cannot issue a check against a savings account to be cashed by another person, but most savings banks furnish cashier's or treasurer's checks, often drawn on a commercial bank, to a payee designated by the depositor. Such cashier's checks are entered as withdrawals in the depositor's passbook.

Other Banking Services. A trust company or the trust department of a commercial bank may perform a variety of fiduciary services, such as acting as executor under a will, serving as trustee under trust agreements, managing property for others, investing funds, and acting as corporate trustee under bond issues. Some banks have foreign departments or specialists to facilitate transactions in international trade. They may secure and transfer foreign exchange, provide information concerning such trade, and afford a means for financing the import or export of goods and facilitating their actual movement through commerce.

Banks will rent, at a small annual fee, safe deposit facilities for the storage of valuables, such as jewels, securities, deeds, insurance policies, etc.

In meeting the financial needs of the community, a bank may perform a collection service on out-of-town items, bond coupons, public utility bills, matured bonds, and the like. It may provide business advisory service; some banks have established business or industrial development departments which afford information and advice regarding the community's property values, labor supply, plant locations, market data, and incorporation procedure. Banks act as agents for the United States Treasury in the sale and cashing of Savings Bonds. They sell travelers' checks, and some provide travel services. They may have an investment counsel service or may assist in the purchase or sale of securities. In agricultural communities, they may offer the farmer assistance in such matters as soil conservation, flood control, and scientific crop production. They help customers to secure technical advice in the financing and construction of homes. Banks are also an excellent source of credit information.

Bank Loans. The bank uses funds invested by stockholders and deposits made by its customers to lend to others for a wide variety of credit needs. In some banks, loan departments may be separated into commercial, industrial, mortgage, and personal divisions. The principal types of bank loans are as follows:

Personal loans, made to individuals to help them meet emergency financial needs. Loans may be repaid in installments or in a lump sum.

Installment purchase loans, made to individuals to finance the purchase of an automobile or other durable goods; such loans are secured by a chattel mortgage on the article.

Repair and modernization loans, made to individuals to finance home repairs and improvements.

Real estate loans, secured by real estate mortgages, and made to enable purchase of new or existing homes, farm land, or other property, under certain restrictions.

Commercial and industrial loans, which vary considerably, depending upon the type of business, the financial position of the borrower, the purpose of the loan, the security involved, etc. Such loans might include: (1) unsecured loans which are based on the bank's faith in the ability of the borrower to repay without specific security; (2) loans on warehouse receipts for goods in storage; (3) loans on other paper covering the movement of goods from seller to buyer; (4) loans on accounts or notes receivable by the borrower from his own customers; (5) agricultural loans to farmers for the production and storage of crops or the purchase of machinery; (6) term loans, repayable over a period of years, usually for capital purposes; (7) chattel mortgage loans, for example, on autos owned by a dealer pending sale to the public; (8) co-maker loans, in which a second party agrees to repay in the event that the borrower defaults; and (9) business loans on other assets, such as plant and equipment.

Security loans, made to investment dealers and others for the purpose of carrying or purchasing securities. For example, when a corporation decides to issue new securities, an investment house may agree to sell them for the corporation. The bank will lend money to the investment firm to carry the securities until they are sold.

Clearinghouses. In order to avoid the cumbersome process of actually interchanging money, banks send their checks to central places of exchange known as clearinghouses. Here the amounts the banks owe and the amounts due the banks are set against each other and the accounts balanced, the balance being either received or paid, as the case may be. Some clearinghouses are also collecting agencies. The Federal Reserve Banks act as clearinghouses for their customers.

An Outline of Banking History

"A million in the hands of a single banker is a great power; he can at once lend it where he will, and borrowers can come to him because they know or believe that he has it. But the same sum scattered in tens and fifties through a whole nation is no power at all: no one knows where to find it or whom to ask for it."

" 'The distinctive function of the banker,' says Ricardo, 'begins as soon as he uses the money of others'; as long as he uses his own money he is only a capitalist."

The first bank of any importance in the world was the Bank of Venice, which was established in 1171. The next most famous, historically speaking, was the Bank of Barcelona, established in 1401; it was the first to make use of the system of negotiating bills of exchange. In England banks grew out of the custom of merchants who, to protect themselves from theft, deposited their surplus funds with goldsmiths. The goldsmiths began to pay 6 per cent interest on the deposits, and banking as we know it today began. There are still in existence banks which owe their origin to these goldsmiths' establishments.

The first bank in the United States grew out of a patriotic desire to relieve the distress of Washington's troops. This was the Bank of Pennsylvania, organized in 1780 and destined to live only a very short time. The Bank of North America was established in 1781, the Bank of New York and the Bank of Boston in 1784.

The First Bank of the United States was established in 1791, the Second in 1816, Congress providing one-fifth of the capital of each. Until after the Civil War these two were the only banks in the United States which operated under

BOUNDARIES OF FEDERAL RESERVE DISTRICTS AND THEIR BRANCH TERRITORIES

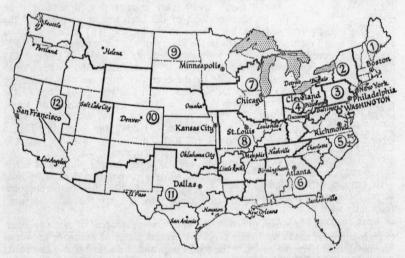

Hawaii and Alaska are considered part of District 12.

the national law. All others were organized according to the laws of the states in which they were established. It was in the period of depreciated currency and financial distress during and following the Civil War that the National Banking Act was passed. The act itself was passed in 1863. It was amended in 1864 and has been amended since.

It was the panic of 1907 that brought about a widespread desire to do something to improve United States banking methods. Following an investigation by the National Monetary Commission, the Federal Reserve Act was passed, which laid the foundation of the American banking system of today.

THE FEDERAL RESERVE SYSTEM

The Federal Reserve is the central banking system for the United States government and was set up under the Federal Reserve Act of 1913 to provide for a fluctuating demand for money and credit and for a greater degree of elasticity in the currency. Since enactment of the Employment Act of 1946, the Federal Reserve System has been guided also by the objectives of that act—"maximum employment, production, and purchasing power"—to the extent that the achievement of these goals can be assisted by monetary and credit policies.

The Federal Reserve System influences the supply and availability of money and credit by operations which affect the reserves that commercial banks are required to hold against their deposit liabilities. The amount of such reserves limits the amounts they can lend to clients or invest at any given time. By lowering the reserve requirements of the commercial banking system, the Federal Reserve can provide more funds, which tends to lower interest rates; when reserve requirements are raised the commercial banks' ability to lend and invest is restricted and interest rates tend to rise.

All national banks in the United States must be members of the Federal Reserve System; state banks which meet the requirements of the Federal Reserve Act may be members. Although some 7,000 of the nation's approximately 13,500 commercial banks are not members, the member banks hold more than 80 per cent of all commercial bank deposits. Member banks must keep their reserves (exclusive of vault cash, which counts as reserve) in Federal Reserve Banks.

The volume of reserves held by member banks is influenced by the Federal Reserve in three principal ways: (1) by changes in the percentage of reserves against deposits which member banks must keep in the Federal Reserve Bank of their district; (2) by increase or decrease of the "discount rate" on money which Reserve Banks advance to members; and (3) by purchase or sale of government securities in open markets.

The third method is the most frequently used instrument of Federal Reserve policy; purchases of Federal securities add to the national money supply, because the purchase price paid to the holders of the securities is added to their bank deposits and thereby swells the aggregate of bank deposits and reserves. Conversely, sales of Federal securities take money out of the public supply. Changes in discount rates—almost invariably made uniform at all Federal Reserve Banks within a few weeks—have a psychological influence by suggesting that money is being made easier or harder for commercial banks to borrow; such changes often supplement the open-market operations of the Federal Reserve. Increases or decreases in the percentage of reserve requirements are less frequently used as instruments of policy; when used, they permit a given volume of bank reserves to do more or less work, respectively. All three methods immediately affect the amount of money that commercial banks can make available to their clients, and therefore influence business planning and activity, demand and supply, and employment.

The Federal Reserve Banks provide by far the largest proportion of the currency in circulation in the United States. They perform important services for the United States Treasury Department in connection with new issues, exchanges, and redemptions of government securities. Most Treasury check payments move through the Reserve Banks. National check-collection and wire-transfer facilities are provided for member banks. "Involuntary" additions and subtractions in the national money supply result daily from vast "floats" of checks in process of collection. The Federal Reserve Bank of New York is also authorized to act as a depositary for international financial organizations and foreign monetary authorities.

At the apex of the Federal Reserve System is the Board of Governors of the Federal Reserve System, with headquarters in Washington, D.C. The board comprises seven members (governors) appointed to 14-year terms by the President (with Senate confirmation); two of these members are designated by the President as chairman and vice chairman for four-year terms, which are renewable. The board determines reserve requirements for member banks, reviews and determines the discount (sometimes called rediscount) rates, and exercises general supervision over the 12 Federal Reserve Banks.

The board appoints three of the nine directors of each Reserve Bank (the member banks choose the others) and approves the appointment of the president and first vice president of each regional Bank.

The Federal Open Market Committee directs the system's open-market operations and provides a periodic forum for monetary and economic discussions. Its 12 members comprise all seven Reserve Board governors and five representatives of the Reserve Banks, such representatives being elected annually by the boards of directors of certain specified Reserve Banks.

A 12-member Federal Advisory Council, traditionally composed of bankers, meets at least four times a year, confers with the board on business conditions, and makes recommendations to the board regarding the affairs of the Federal Reserve System. The directors of each Federal Reserve Bank designate one member to serve on this council.

The 12 individual Reserve Banks (with 24 branches) provide the nation's basic check-collection system, provide currency as needed by banks, lend money to member banks as required, examine state-chartered members, hold the member banks' reserves, and act as fiscal agents for the United States. The nine directors of each Reserve Bank administer their Bank, fix discount rates subject to Reserve Board review, and participate in the election of members of the Federal Open Market Committee and of the Advisory Council.

Member banks must subscribe 6 per cent of their capital and surplus (3 per cent paid in) for capital stock of the Reserve Bank of their district. Such stock is redeemable at face value, is refundable, and is limited to 6 per cent annual dividends, which are cumulative. All net earnings of Federal Reserve Banks after dividends and provision for maintaining surplus at the level of subscribed capital are paid to the United States Treasury as interest on outstanding Federal Reserve notes.

FEDERAL DEPOSIT INSURANCE CORPORATION

The corporation was created by the Banking Act of 1933, also known as the Glass-Steagall Act, which as well as the Banking Act of 1935 strongly affected the organization of banks.

The purpose of these acts and of the Emergency Acts of March and June 1933 was:[1] to meet emergency conditions in 1933, while the Act of 1935 incorporated

[1] Passages taken from the statement by M. S. Eccles, then of the Federal Reserve Board, before the Committee on Banking and Currency of the House of Representatives (March 4, 1935).

into permanent legislation the features of the emergency laws that had proved valuable; in addition, the legislation aimed to prevent the recurrence of speculative excesses which preceded the breakdown of the country's banking machine at that time.

The corporation was designed to insure depositors against loss in insured banks. With enactment of the Banking Act of 1935, insurance was established on a permanent basis and the individual coverage was determined at $5,000 per depositor; it was later extended to $10,000 per depositor.

All national and state banks which are members of the Federal Reserve System are insured by the corporation. Banks which are not members of the Federal Reserve System are admitted to insurance upon application and subsequent examination and approval by the corporation.

Applications for deposit insurance are granted by the board after giving consideration to the following factors, as prescribed by statute: the financial history and condition of the bank, the adequacy of its capital structure, its future earnings prospects, the general character of its management, the convenience and needs of the community to be served by the bank, and the consistency of the bank's corporate powers with the purposes of the Federal deposit insurance law.

The major functions of the corporation are to pay the depositors of insured banks which have closed without adequate provision having been made to pay claims of their depositors, and to act as receiver for all suspended national banks and for suspended state banks when appointed by state authorities. The corporation prevents the continuance or development of unsafe and unsound banking practices by periodical examinations of all insured banks which are not examined by other agencies of the Federal government, and by its supervisory powers over such banks.

Through its examination of banks, the corporation has exerted considerable influence upon the structure and character of banking. Of obvious concern to the corporation is the quality of bank assets. Even more important is the quality of bank management. Bank directors have been urged to take an active interest in their banks in order to carry out their heavy statutory responsibilities. Maintenance of adequate capital and regular provision for losses on assets are among banking practices consistently recommended by the F.D.I.C.

The three members of the board of directors of the corporation are appointed by the President, one of these being the Comptroller of the Currency.

The Federal Deposit Insurance Act was amended in 1960 to provide for a simpler method of determining deposit insurance assessments. The income of the corporation is obtained from semiannual assessments upon banks and interest upon its investments. Each bank is assessed 1/12 of 1 per cent of its average total deposits.

NEGOTIABLE INSTRUMENTS

Broadly defined, negotiable instruments are written promises or requests for the payment of money. A certain degree of uniformity in the law dealing with all forms of commercial paper was obtained by established custom and usage which, however, soon became inadequate to the needs of modern commerce. Consequently, uniformity was sought by statute. There is now a uniform Negotiable Instruments Law, which codifies the applicable legal principles; but one of the provisions of this uniform law expressly states that if a case is not covered thereby, the rules of the *law merchant*, *i.e.*, custom and usage, shall govern.

The term "negotiable" applies to any written instrument given as security for the payment of money, which may be transferred either by delivery or endorsement, vesting legal title in the party to whom it is so transferred. To be negotiable the instrument (1) must be in writing and signed by the maker, or drawer; no particular form of writing or signature is necessary; an authorized agent may sign his principal's name; (2) must contain an unconditional promise to pay a definite amount of money; (3) must be payable on demand, or at a fixed or ascertainable future time; (4) must be payable to order or to bearer; (5) if addressed to a drawee, must name or otherwise indicate that person with reasonable certainty.

If the instrument conforms to these requirements it is negotiable, even if it (1) is not dated; (2) does not specify the value given; (3) does not specify the place where it is made or payable; (4) designates a particular kind of current money in which payment is to be made.

Antedating or postdating an instrument does not invalidate it, provided neither is done for an illegal or fraudulent purpose. Title to an instrument so dated vests in the person to whom it is delivered on the date of delivery.

When the signature is forged or made without authorization it is wholly inoperative, unless the party against whom it is sought to enforce payment is precluded from setting up forgery or lack of authority. No hard-and-fast rule can be given as to when and under what circumstances a forged or unauthorizedly signed instrument can be enforced. This depends upon the particular facts of each case. Subsequent endorsers are not liable on a negotiable instrument if it is materially altered without their consent; those who do assent to the material alteration, however, remain liable. But when an instrument has been materially altered and is owned by a *holder in due course,* not a party to the alteration, he may enforce payment according to its original terms.

A holder in due course is a person who acquires the instrument, complete and regular on its face, in good faith and for value before it became overdue, and without prior notice that it had been previously dishonored (if such was the fact), and had no notice at the time it was endorsed or delivered to him that there was any infirmity in it, or that there was a defect in title of the person who negotiated it.

An alteration is material if it changes the date, the amount payable, the time or place of payment, or the currency in which payment is to be made, or if it in any other way alters the effect of the instrument.

The following are negotiable instruments: bills of exchange; trade acceptances; promissory notes; drafts; clearinghouse certificates; United States Treasury notes; bearer bonds and letters of credit. Any other form of instrument may be negotiable provided the previously mentioned minimum legal requirements are met.

Drafts. A draft is a written order by one person, called the *drawer,* upon another called the *drawee,* for the payment of a specified sum of money to a third person, the *payee.* The terms "draft" and "check" are sometimes used interchangeably. A draft, however, is distinguishable from a check by the fact that the drawee of a check is a bank, while the drawee of a draft may be any person or firm. There is also a difference between a cashier's check and a draft. A cashier's check is the primary obligation of the bank, which issues it, constituting a written promise to pay upon demand, whereas a draft is an order upon a third party drawn upon a deposit of funds. Drafts are payable at sight, on demand, or on a specified date.

The drawer by drawing the instrument admits the existence of the payee and agrees with the drawee and payee and the subsequent holders that on due presentment the draft will be accepted and paid according to its terms, and that if it be dishonored the drawer will pay the amount to the holder, or to any subsequent endorser who may be compelled to pay it.

The drawee's liability begins with his acceptance, which is an agreement on his part that he will pay. This is generally accomplished by writing the word

"Accepted" and the date across the face of the instrument and signing his name below it.

Nonpayment means that the instrument has been dishonored; all persons secondarily liable may be sued after notice of dishonor has been given to the drawer and each endorser, and any drawer or endorser to whom such notice is not given is discharged from liability. The notice may be given in writing or orally, either personally or by mail, within 24 hours. The form of notice should properly identify the instrument, and indicate that it has been dishonored by nonacceptance or nonpayment. Many negotiable instruments contain a provision waiving notice of dishonor. When same is embodied in the instrument it is bind-

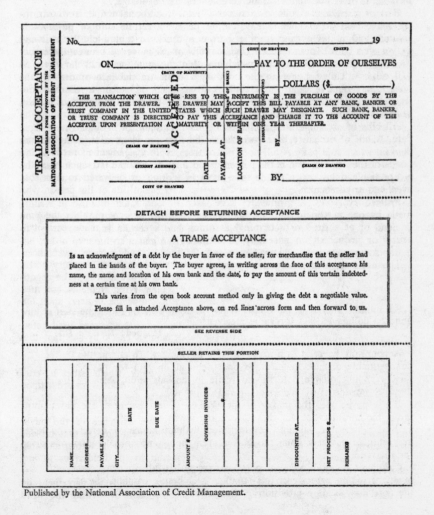

Published by the National Association of Credit Management.

ing on all parties, but where written above the signature of an endorser it is binding on him.

A *protest* is a declaration by a notary public certifying and specifying the necessary acts taken necessary to charge an endorser.

Trade Acceptance. A trade acceptance is a draft or bill of exchange drawn by the seller on the purchaser of goods sold, and accepted by such purchaser. Upon acceptance by the drawee it becomes in effect a promissory note. The acceptance makes the drawee primarily liable, and notice of presentment and demand for payment are not necessary.

The seller draws the draft and forwards it to the buyer with the invoice or mails it separately. The buyer signifies his acceptance by writing "Accepted" and filling in the date of acceptance, designating the bank at which it is to be paid, and signing it. He then returns it to the seller, who may hold it until it is payable, or may discount it. Trade acceptances are negotiable.

Bills of Exchange. A bill of exchange is an unconditional written order drawn by one person on another to pay a third person a certain sum of money, absolutely and in all events. It differs from a check in that a check is always drawn on a bank. There are two kinds of bills of exchange: (1) an *inland bill of exchange,* which is drawn and payable within the state; and (2) *foreign bills* (all others). Unless notice to the contrary appears on the face of the bill the holder may treat it as an inland bill. A foreign bill of exchange must be protested before the drawer can be held liable, but inland bills need no protest, notice of dishonor being sufficient.

All bills of exchange are payable on demand, at sight, or at some future fixed date. A bill of exchange bears two dates, the date on which it is made and the date on which it is paid. A bill does not operate as an assignment of funds in the hands of the drawee, who is the person called upon to pay the instrument, and he is not liable unless and until he accepts it in writing, although it is negotiable even before acceptance.

Promissory Notes. A promissory note is an unconditional promise in writing made by one person to another, and signed by the maker, engaging to pay on demand or at a fixed or determinable future date a certain sum of money "to order" or "to bearer." A note may be drawn by the maker to his own order, but it is not complete until endorsed by him.

The usual form of a note is:

New York, N.Y., ———, 19—

Six months after date I promise to pay to John Doe or order the sum of one hundred dollars ($100) for value received.

(Signed) *Richard Doe*

A note may be valid as a *nonnegotiable* instrument. To charge the maker of a nonnegotiable demand note, a personal demand on him for payment is necessary. A nonnegotiable note should recite its consideration. Such an instrument may be transferred by endorsement and delivery.

If the payee sues the maker of the note to collect payment, the payee must prove the consideration for the note. If the payee endorses a negotiable note to a third person for valuable consideration without notice of defects, the latter may enforce payment from the maker even though no consideration was given for the note.

Collateral Notes. Collateral notes are executed *only* in connection with, and pursuant to, an agreement; this stipulation is best exemplified by the fact that the note itself bears a provision to that effect.

COLLATERAL NOTE[1]

(city) ⸻

$⸻

On demand, for value received, John Doe promises to pay to Richard Roe or order, at his office, ⸻, (city), ⸻ dollars, with interest at the rate of six (6) per cent per annum, the said sum to be secured by the assignment to Richard Roe or order as collateral security for the payment of this and of all previous and subsequent obligations of John Doe, due or to become due, of certain accounts receivable, debts, claims, and demands created in favor of and belonging to John Doe, at the time of such assignment, and all moneys due, or to grow due thereon, together with all the right, title, and interest of John Doe in and to the merchandise, for the sale and delivery of which the said accounts arose; with the right on the part of the said Richard Roe and his assigns from time to time to demand such additional security as he or they may deem necessary; and, on failure to comply with any such demand, this obligation shall be deemed to be due and payable forthwith, without notice or demand; and with the further right to accept and substitute other assigned accounts subsequent to the date hereof, in lieu of accounts this day assigned, and to hold such other accounts as collateral on this loan, with the same rights and powers and under the same conditions as the accounts, and each of them, assigned and delivered herewith; with full power and authority to the said Richard Roe and his assigns to sell and deliver any and all of the said collateral security, at public or private sale, at the option of the said Richard Roe and his assigns, without demand, advertisement, or notice, and with the right on the part of the said Richard Roe and his assigns to be the purchaser thereof at such sale, free and discharged of any equity of redemption; and, after deducting all costs and expenses incident to the said sale and delivery, to apply the net proceeds to the payment of such just claims and obligations as may at the time of said sale be owing from John Doe to said Richard Roe or his assigns, whether due or to become due; and the undersigned agrees to remain and continue liable for any unpaid balance remaining.

This note is given in connection with a certain agreement between John Doe and Richard Roe, dated ⸻, 19–, and is to be interpreted in harmony with the said agreement.

RECEIPTS

A receipt is an acknowledgment in writing, signed by the person who gives it, that he has received certain personal property, which may be money or goods or both. If it is a receipt for property (see Warehouses), the property should be described sufficiently to be identified, and the terms under which it is to be stored or otherwise looked after should be stated. All receipts should be dated and signed. If an agent signs he should first write his principal's name, then his own beneath it, thus:

Robert Compton
By George Smith

If the receipt is for money, it should indicate whether the money is paid "on account" or "in full of account." If there is more than one account between the payer and the payee, the receipt should state to which account the money has been applied.

Many receipts are given simply by stamping "Paid in full" with initials or other identifying mark in ink on the face of a due bill. The returned voucher of a check is also considered a valid receipt, but most firms will give an additional receipt if it is requested.

[1] This is only a suggested form. The reader is advised to secure a form, valid in his state, from a lawyer or legal stationer for use in specific transactions.

A receipt is not necessary when a note is paid up, since the instrument itself then becomes a receipt.

If it can be proved that a receipt was given through mistake or fraud, it can be voided.

Receipts should be kept until after the time for action prescribed by the Statute of Limitation has passed. This varies in the different states and must be determined by consulting local statute books.

CARRYING MONEY

Letters of Credit. A letter of credit is a letter from a bank or business house addressed to one or more of its agents elsewhere requesting the payment of a certain sum of money to the person named in the letter. Letters of credit are used by persons traveling abroad, especially when large sums of money are needed.[1] Usually the person carrying a letter of credit has deposited with the

Letter of Credit

[1] Letters of credit are also used in export and import transactions. The purchaser obtains a letter of credit from a bank in favor of the seller. Upon presenta-

firm which issued it an amount equal to the sum mentioned in the letter. A small commission fee is charged by the concern issuing the letter.

The letter bears the signature of the holder. For further identification the bank or person issuing the letter, especially when the amount involved is a large one, often sends a letter through the mail to the agent or correspondent upon whom the letter of credit is drawn, giving a description of the holder and any other information which he may think helpful.

Letters of credit carry an expiration limit. This may consist of a notation, such

Letter of Credit issued by The American Express Company

tion of bills of lading and other necessary documents, the seller obtains payment or the bank on which it is drawn agrees to make payment in or at a stated time.

as "Available until ———", or "Drafts must be drawn before ———", or any one of a number of other forms.

Letter of Identification to Accompany Letter of Credit

Travelers' Checks. Travelers' checks are issued by banks, express companies, and some of the tourist agencies. They are either sight drafts or promissory notes. The person buying them signs when he buys and again when he presents them for payment, the signature establishing his identity. A small commission is charged. The usual rate is seventy-five cents for every $100 worth of checks, with a minimum fee of forty cents for $50 or less. The usual denominations of travelers' checks are $10, $20, $50, and $100.

Travelers' Check

SENDING MONEY AND VALUABLE MAIL

Money may safely be sent in the following ways:

Bank Check or Draft. This is the cheapest and nearly always (except for very small sums) the most convenient way to send money. An additional advantage is that there is no limit to the amount that can be sent.

Post Office Money Order. Domestic money orders are issued for any amount up to $100. A good way to send small sums. For fees, see Postal Information.

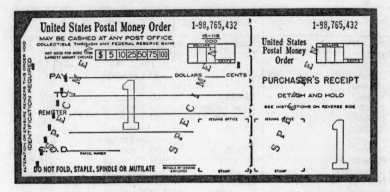

American Express Money Order. Such orders are as secure as a bank draft. They are sold by many thousands of druggists and others throughout the country and can be negotiated as freely as personal checks.

Bank Money Order. Most commercial and savings banks provide money-order service of varying types. In most cases, the money order is sold in blank, and the purchaser fills in the payee's name at the time of use.

Certified Letter. Certified mail service provides for a receipt to the sender and a record of delivery at the office of address. It is handled in the ordinary mails and no insurance coverage is provided. For fees, see Postal Information.

Registered Letter. Registered letters receive special handling and are therefore safer than ordinary letters. For fees, see Postal Information.

Stamps. Stamps should be sent to cover only very small amounts.

Coin. When it is not possible to send stamps, coins may be used. They should first be slipped inside a pasteboard card or otherwise protected so that they will not wear through the envelope or be recognized in transit.

Telegraph. Telegraph offices furnish blanks. See Telegraph Services.

VALUES OF THE PRINCIPAL FOREIGN MONETARY UNITS

Country	*Monetary Unit*	*Consisting Of*	*Recent Quotation*
Afghanistan[1]	Afghani	100 Puls	$ .05
Albania[1]	Lek	100 Qintar	.02
Argentina	Peso	100 Centavos	.0121
Australia	Pound	20 Shillings = 240 Pence	2.25
Austria	Schilling	100 Groschen	.0390
Belgium	Franc	100 Centimes	.0201
Bolivia	Boliviano	100 Centavos	.00009
Brazil[1]	Cruzeiro	100 Centavos	.0550
Bulgaria	Lev	100 Stotinki	.1470
Cambodia	Riel	100 Sen	.0287
Canada	Dollar	100 Cents	.9680
Chile	Escudo	100 Centesimos	.97
China	N.T. Dollar	100 Cents	.0255
Colombia	Peso	100 Centavos	.1160
Costa Rica[1]	Colon	100 Centimos	.1510
Cyprus	Pound	1,000 Mils	2.8225
Czechoslovakia	Crown	100 Hellers	.14
Denmark	Krone	100 Ore	.1453

[1] Official rate

VALUES OF THE PRINCIPAL FOREIGN MONETARY UNITS (*Cont.*)

Country	Monetary Unit	Consisting Of	Recent Quotation
Ecuador[1]	Sucre	100 Centavos	.0562
Egypt[1]	Pound	100 Piasters = 1,000 Mill.	2.8825
El Salvador	Colon	100 Centavos	.40
Ethiopia	Dollar	100 Cents	.41
Finland	Markka	100 Pennis	.0032
France	New Franc	100 Centimes	.2035
Germany (Western)	Deutsche Mark	100 Pfennig	.2502
Ghana	Pound	20 Shillings = 240 Pence	2.8276
Greece	Drachma	100 Lepta	.0335
Guatemala	Quetzal	100 Centavos	1.00
Guinea	Franc	100 Centimes	.0041
Haiti	Gourde	100 Centimes	.20
Honduras	Lempira	100 Centavos	.50
Hungary	Forint	100 Fillers	.0861
India	Rupee	Naye Paise	.2110
Indonesia[1]	Rupiah	100 Sen	.0224
Iran	Rial	100 Dinars	.0135
Iraq	Dinar	1,000 Fils	2.8136
Ireland (Republic)	Pound	20 Shillings = 240 Pence	2.8136
Israel[1]	Pound	100 Agorot	.56
Italy	Lira	100 Centesimi	.00161
Ivory Coast	Franc	100 Centimes	.0041
Japan	Yen	100 Sen	.0028
Korea (South)	Hwan	100 Chon	.00077
Laos	Kip	100 At	.0126
Libya	Pound	100 Piasters = 1,000 Mill.	2.8206
Mexico	Peso	100 Centavos	.0801
Morocco	Dirham	100 Moroccan Francs	.20
Netherlands	Guilder	100 Cents	.2780
New Zealand	Pound	20 Shillings = 240 Pence	2.8036
Nicaragua[1]	Cordoba	100 Centavos	.1430
Niger	Franc	100 Centimes	.0041
Nigeria	Pound	20 Shillings = 240 Pence	2.8286
Norway	Krone	100 Ore	.1405
Pakistan	Rupee	100 Paisas	.2113
Panama	Balboa	100 Centesimos	1.00
Paraguay	Guarani	100 Centimos	.0080
Peru	Sol	100 Centavos	.0375
Philippines[1]	Peso	100 Centavos	.4990
Poland	Zloty	100 Grosze	.25
Portugal	Escudo	100 Centavos	.0351
Rumania	Leu	100 Bani	.1666
Saudi Arabia	Riyal	20 Gurshes = 100 Halalah	.2235
Spain	Peseta	100 Centimos	.01675
Sudan	Pound	100 Piasters = 1,000 Mill.	2.88
Sweden	Krona	100 Ore	.1936
Switzerland	Franc	100 Centimes	.2315
Syria[2]	Pound	100 Piasters	.2805
Thailand[2]	Baht	100 Satang	.0480
Tunisia	Dinar	1,000 Mill.	2.40
Turkey[1]	Pound	100 Piasters	.1111

[1] Official rate   [2] Free rate

Union of South Africa	Rand	100 Cents	1.408
Union of Soviet Socialist Republics	Ruble	100 Kopecks	1.11
United Kingdom	Pound	20 Shillings = 240 Pence	2.8136
Uruguay[2]	Peso	100 Centesimos	.0925
Venezuela[1]	Bolivar	100 Centimos	.3000
Viet Nam	Piaster	100 Cents	.0288
Yugoslavia[1]	Dinar	100 Paras	.0013

[1] Official rate   [2] Free rate

HOUSEHOLD MONEY MANAGEMENT

In order to live safely within an income and to get the most value out of money spent, it is necessary to formulate a careful plan of spending and saving. This is known as *budgeting*. There are no set rules for the use of income, since the needs and requirements of people in various communities and income groups differ greatly. There are, however, certain general rules that should be followed if a budget is to be successful.

People who budget to improve their financial management design their own budgets, based on their goals and circumstances. They also stand ready to review their budgets from time to time, since what is good one year may be no good the next year.

Deciding your goals is a matter for family consultation. Children do not need to know all the details, but they need to have some understanding of the budget and the family situation, so that they, too, can work for the best use of the family money. It seems to give a child a feeling of security to know that his parents have a plan, even if the child cannot understand all of its details.

What should your income do? Are you young, faced with the many expenses of setting up a home? Do you have children who must be educated? Are you making as much money as you can expect to make in your present occupation? If you must set up a home, the major part of your income will probably go to satisfy that goal. If you have a home, but you must provide for college education for one or more children, your income may be heavily committed to tuition, board, and other school expenses. Perhaps you anticipate a raise, or you are just starting your career; then you may spend more to satisfy immediate needs, leaving less pressing ones to be met in the higher income period.

Before allotting your income, you must know what that income is. Under today's method of payment, take-home pay is the amount customarily left to the discretion of the individual. Federal income taxes, social security taxes, some state income taxes, insurance payments of one type or another, union dues, payments to professional associations, and pension-fund contributions may all have been withheld. Whenever such a deduction is made by the employer, the item may be dropped from consideration in setting up the budget, although a small amount should probably be set aside for additional tax payments, if necessary. In estimating income, add to take-home pay all bonuses, gifts, government or other allowances, and dividends or income from investments, as well as any rental income or commissions you receive.

Each family has various types of expenditures to make. It is usually possible to group these expenses, summarizing them as future expenses, day-to-day living costs, personal allowances, and savings for the future. They can be further classified as fixed or flexible expenses. The four groups would then be classified as *flexible*, or variable: day-to-day living costs, the expenses which are necessary for running a household; *fixed*: personal allowances, sums covering the individual family members' personal expenses, recreation, special lessons, and hobbies, etc., and savings; both *fixed and flexible*, depending on the nature of the expenditure: future expenses.

The following items are typical fixed expenses:
1. Taxes not already withheld by the employer
2. Rent or mortgage payments
3. Insurance premiums
4. Debt repayments
5. Fuel for home heating
6. School tuition, textbooks, and fees
7. Savings.

Typical flexible expenses are:
1. Food
2. Clothing
3. Medical and dental care
4. Home furnishings and household equipment
5. Contributions to charities, political groups, etc.
6. Annual subscriptions
7. Gifts and entertaining
8. Vacations.

The usual day-to-day living costs include: (1) utilities; (2) food; (3) laundry and dry cleaning, clothing, and shoe repairs; (4) household supplies and repairs; and (5) car upkeep or transportation.

Once the categories are more or less set in everyone's mind, estimating the amount of money to be set aside to meet each set of expenses is next. Where bills and canceled checks are involved, it is possible to obtain a reasonably accurate idea of the amount necessary. A careful check on expenses and a classification of them for a month or so will provide a guide to other amounts. Budgeting, it is easy to see, is not a matter for one night; it is necessary to spend some time and effort to make up a budget that will fit your needs and work for you.

After the family knows how much is spent on what, look at the records again. Think about the goals set up. Was the money set aside to meet school bills, or was there a wild flurry in August and September to raise the money? Was it possible to meet the insurance premiums, the tax bills, on time? If not, examine the other expenses. Perhaps the car has become uneconomical or too much entertaining has unbalanced household allotments. By reducing clothing expenditures, deferring the purchase of a desired home appliance, or by walking a few blocks and cutting down on gasoline consumption, it may be possible to meet the "must" expenses when they should be met. Minor changes in food costs— cheaper cuts of meat, for example—without cutting down on nutrition may also help. But if such measures do not help, take another look at the goals you have set up. Perhaps an out-of-town college is out of the question, and living at home will bring expenses to a manageable level. Perhaps one of the family could supply some extra income. But be sure that the expenses of working—there are always some—do not cancel out such extra money.

When there is enough money but it is not being allotted properly, violent ups and downs in the food budget, long stretches with no recreation, and too-long-deferred wardrobe buying make family life more difficult. The technique is to break down the over-all amounts necessary to meet large expenses into small weekly or monthly (or half-monthly, if you are paid that way) sums and deposit them in a bank account. For the longtime program—meeting the annual insurance premium, for instance—a savings account can be used. Deposit the required amount each payday, and when the premium is due the money will be there to pay it. For rent payments, utility bills, and other regularly recurring expenses, deposit the money in a checking account. Once the over-all level of expenses is smoothed out, you will need to do little bookkeeping, but for the first few months a simple set of books showing how much has been deposited for each item of expense to be met will be helpful. Many banks and other financial institutions will be glad to supply suitable booklets for this purpose.

WISE BUYING

Beyond adjusting your spending to your income, there are other aspects of wise money management. One of the techniques a housewife must perfect is wise buying, remembering that, as in budgeting, the key is deciding exactly what you want. It is helpful to write the desired qualities down, indicating to yourself which of them can be dispensed with, if necessary. Plan ahead and beware of shopping aimlessly. Make a list for each shopping expedition, particularly for frequently replenished supplies, from memorandums made when the need for a given item arises. It is best to plan your menus for a week or more, consulting advertisements and store announcements to find out what is readily—and inexpensively—available. One method of saving money in food buying is to shop as infrequently as you can manage, within the limits of your storage facilities.

For less frequently purchased items—clothing and home furnishings—you might keep a clipping file from newspapers, magazines, and consumer reports about possible purchases. Such a file is particularly helpful in keeping track of price fluctuations, so that you can take advantage of lower prices. It may also help you evaluate appliances and cut down on the time you spend "shopping around."

For staples—household linens, for instance—sales are useful. At such a time, the store buys in quantity and, by concentrating its sales in a short period, can pass on some of its savings to you. The merchandise is usually the same as that available during the regular season, but you should examine it closely. Buy a "second" or an "irregular" item only when you have decided that the flaw will not affect appearance or service. Seasonal sales for clearing stock may also help you save money if you buy early in the sale period and buy only items which require few or no major repairs or alterations.

Recognize your limits, and do not shop in stores which sell merchandise you know you cannot afford. There are many types of stores today. Some—such as the "discount" stores—offer lower prices because they provide few services; if you prefer to shop in such a store, it is doubly important that you know what you want and what it should cost. If you have little time and must do a great deal of shopping in one place, a department store with well-trained salespeople may be worth the slightly higher prices.

CONSUMER CREDIT

Traditionally, it has been slightly disreputable to use credit in any form, for the consumer at least. Upholders of such views point to the advisability of paying cash for all purchases. There are no credit or interest charges; and, if you have saved to make the purchase, you may well have accrued interest on the savings. But many pressures in the American economy have joined to make this point of view unattractive. Many persons prefer to use some forms of consumer credit, rather than do without conveniences.

Indeed, it is possible that you are using some forms of credit without realizing it. Repeated use of electricity, gas, and other "utilities," without payment for them until after use, is an example of *convenience credit*. Paying the paper boy or the milkman once a week are other examples of this type; another is the *charge account* in a department store.

Charge accounts can help you keep track of your expenditures and record your sales-tax payments, but they may encourage extravagance. Questions to ask yourself when considering such an account are: (1) what, if any, is the fee or service charge; (2) what items can be charged; (3) when must an item be paid for; and (4) does my personal management plan allow for the use of such an account? Ordinary charge accounts permit you to pay for your purchases once a month, by check; they do not involve credit charges. Special types of charge accounts include *revolving* accounts, into which you pay a specified sum each month; and *bank* charge accounts, in which the bank pays the merchant, who submits his bill to the bank for purchases made by you, and you pay the bank. Under some circumstances, a charge is rendered on any unpaid balance, after a certain period of time, by the bank.

Another form of consumer credit is time payment—*installment buying*. Such buying is arranged through a written contract between buyer and seller. Usually, a down payment is required in cash; and the balance is paid in regular installments, weekly or monthly. In addition, there is a carrying charge. You should not undertake installment buying unless you can afford it; the rule of thumb is to take on such installments only up to a total of 15 per cent of your take-home pay. Find out how much the credit service will cost, that is, add the down payment and the total installments and compare the sum with the cash price. In its simplest form, the difference is the cost of the credit. Shop around for the lowest credit cost as well as for the lowest price.

Before signing the contract, you should read the completely filled out document for the correctness of costs and agreements. Anything that is not written down and signed is not part of the contract. See that all charges are itemized, as well as any necessary descriptions and guarantees. And find out the answers to the following questions. If you become delinquent: (1) will there be additional charges; (2) will you have to pay the entire amount as soon as you miss one payment; and (3) will the item be repossessed? If you wish to prepay, can you do so, thus saving interest charges? Is there any penalty for prepayment?

A third form of consumer credit is the *cash loan*, which is available from banks, from consumer finance companies, from credit unions, and from industrial loan companies. The contract calls for payment of the loan plus a charge for the credit service, which varies with the source and is based on the varying costs of doing business.

To use any consumer credit wisely requires: (1) an understanding of the different forms of credit; (2) knowing the costs involved; (3) finding out the services offered; and (4) having confidence that your income will continue. It is important to remember that you should buy only those items which can comfortably be paid for out of current income. And it is necessary to make adjustments in your budget to allow for prompt payment of all such obligations.

SAVINGS AND INSURANCE

When your funds have been allotted to take care of your current expenses and those which can be anticipated, there remains another category to consider. To provide for the unexpected, for emergencies, and for the indeterminate future, a plan for savings and insurance should be set up, with, of course, the required allowances in the budget.

Savings. It is considered advisable for families to have a total of six months' earnings put away for emergencies. The only way in which such an amount can be amassed is through regular savings of small amounts, to which may be added the interest gained through putting these sums in a bank or into United States savings bonds.

There are many ways to save: (1) regular bank savings accounts; (2) club accounts—Christmas, vacation, etc., as arranged by your bank—requiring regular deposits weekly or semimonthly; (3) savings accounts in a savings and loan association; (4) United States savings bonds; and (5) life insurance.

The amount of money which you may accumulate through regular savings is indicated in the following table. If you save weekly, and the bank pays you 3½ per cent, compounded quarterly, a weekly deposit of $1 will total $52.90 in a year, etc.

Weekly Deposit	1 Year	3 Years	5 Years
$ 1	$ 52.90	$ 164.39	$ 283.93
5	264.50	821.95	1,419.65
10	529.00	1,643.90	2,839.30
20	1,058.00	3,287.80	5,678.60
25	1,322.50	4,109.75	7,098.25

The advantages of regularity of deposit cannot be stressed too much. Small deposits made systematically add up to sizable amounts in a relatively short time. Choosing a method of saving depends on the use to which you mean to put the money. If you want it for emergencies, put it in a regular savings account, where it will be readily available and will earn interest in the meantime. If you want to save for your children's education, United States savings bonds maturing in 10 years or 20 years may be useful. If you wish to save for retirement, insurance or other forms of saving, which are discussed elsewhere, will be of interest to you.

See Investing Money; Buying A Home. See also Savings Accounts under Banks and Banking; Interest.

Insurance. The need for insurance will be apparent if you stop to think how much a family spends annually to live and how unlikely it is that it can save enough money to go on living that way if its income stops. Even if the breadwinner does not die, he may be disabled or temporarily—by accident, perhaps—unable to work. Naturally, you cannot provide protection against every contingency. A basic insurance program, however, will provide life insurance on the family wage earner; health and accident, or, at least, hospitalization, insurance on the entire family; and a measure of protection for the family's investments in home, automobile, home furnishings, etc.

There are so many forms of insurance that it would be wise to consult a competent insurance agent. He should be licensed by your state or province and know his business thoroughly. When talking to him, be realistic in deciding what you can afford. Remember that you must continue to pay for insurance over a long period of time, and have a reasonably accurate estimate of your expected income in mind. You should know what the premium amounts to and when it must be paid; what the policy provides for; and what happens if you cannot continue to pay the premiums. If necessary, will you be able to borrow against the policy?

While insurance policies are discussed in detail elsewhere, briefly, the usual types of life insurance are: (1) *term insurance*—providing maximum protection for five or ten years and useful for the period when you are carrying a mortgage or another type of loan or while the children are in school—available at low premiums; (2) *straight* or *regular life*—for basic permanent protection—the cheapest form of insurance, which will build up a cash or loan value; (3) *limited-payment life*—for people with limited periods of high earnings—paid for within a stated period and remaining in force thereafter without further premiums, thus helpful for retired persons who are able to pay for it before retirement; (4) *endowment*—particularly suitable for savings, building up a sum of money within a stated term of years while protecting yourself with insurance at the same time—rather expensive.

For any type of insurance, it is advisable to pay premiums annually if you can. The single premium will be less than combined premiums paid in installments.

See also Insurance.

SALARY AND WAGES TABLE[1]

Per Year	Per Month	Per Semi-Month	Per Week	Per Day 5 day
2000.00	166.67	83.34	38.46	7.69
2025.00	168.75	84.38	38.94	7.79
2028.00	169.00	84.50	39.00	7.80
2040.00	170.00	85.00	39.23	7.85
2050.00	170.83	85.42	39.42	7.88
2075.00	172.92	86.46	39.90	7.98
2080.00	173.33	86.67	40.00	8.00
2100.00	175.00	87.50	40.38	8.08
2125.00	177.08	88.54	40.88	8.17
2132.00	177.67	88.84	41.00	8.20
2150.00	179.17	89.58	41.35	8.27
2160.00	180.00	90.00	41.53	8.31
2175.00	181.25	90.63	41.83	8.37
2184.00	182.00	91.00	42.00	8.40
2200.00	183.33	91.67	42.31	8.46
2220.00	185.00	92.50	42.69	8.54
2225.00	185.42	92.71	42.79	8.56
2236.00	186.33	93.17	43.00	8.60
2250.00	187.50	93.75	43.27	8.65
2275.00	189.58	94.79	43.75	8.75
2280.00	190.00	95.00	43.84	8.77
2288.00	190.67	95.33	44.00	8.80
2300.00	191.67	95.84	44.23	8.85
2325.00	193.75	96.88	44.71	8.94
2340.00	195.00	97.50	45.00	9.00
2350.00	195.83	97.92	45.19	9.04
2375.00	197.91	98.96	45.67	9.13
2392.00	199.33	99.67	46.00	9.20
2400.00	200.00	100.00	46.15	9.23
2425.00	202.08	101.04	46.63	9.33
2444.00	203.67	101.94	47.00	9.40
2450.00	204.19	102.09	47.12	9.42
2460.00	205.00	102.50	47.30	9.46
2475.00	206.25	103.13	47.50	9.52
2496.00	208.00	104.00	48.00	9.60
2500.00	208.33	104.17	48.08	9.62
2520.00	210.00	105.00	48.46	9.69
2525.00	210.42	105.21	48.56	9.71
2548.00	212.33	106.17	49.00	9.80
2550.00	212.50	106.25	49.04	9.81
2575.00	214.58	107.29	49.52	9.90
2580.00	215.00	107.50	49.61	9.92
2600.00	216.67	108.34	50.00	10.00
2625.00	218.75	109.38	50.48	10.10
2640.00	220.00	110.00	50.76	10.15
2650.00	220.83	110.42	50.96	10.19
2652.00	221.00	110.50	51.00	10.20
2675.00	222.92	111.46	51.44	10.29
2700.00	225.00	112.50	51.92	10.38
2704.00	225.33	112.67	52.00	10.40
2725.00	227.08	113.54	52.40	10.48
2750.00	229.17	114.59	52.88	10.58
2756.00	229.67	114.84	53.00	10.60
2760.00	230.00	115.00	53.07	10.61
2775.00	231.25	115.63	53.36	10.67
2800.00	233.33	116.67	53.85	10.77
2808.00	234.00	117.00	54.00	10.80
2820.00	235.00	117.50	54.23	10.85
2825.00	235.42	117.71	54.33	10.87
2850.00	237.50	118.75	54.81	10.96
2860.00	238.33	119.17	55.00	11.00
2875.00	239.58	119.79	55.29	11.06
2880.00	240.00	120.00	55.38	11.08
2900.00	241.67	120.84	55.77	11.15
2912.00	242.67	121.34	56.00	11.20
2925.00	243.75	121.88	56.25	11.25
2940.00	245.00	122.50	56.53	11.31
2950.00	245.83	122.92	56.73	11.35
2964.00	247.00	123.50	57.00	11.40
2975.00	247.92	123.96	57.21	11.44
3000.00	250.00	125.00	57.69	11.54
3016.00	251.33	125.67	58.00	11.60
3025.00	252.08	126.04	58.17	11.63
3050.00	254.17	127.09	58.65	11.73
3060.00	255.00	127.50	58.85	11.77
3068.00	255.67	127.84	59.00	11.80
3075.00	256.25	128.13	59.13	11.83
3100.00	258.33	129.17	59.62	11.92
3120.00	260.00	130.00	60.00	12.00
3125.00	260.42	130.21	60.10	12.02
3150.00	262.50	131.25	60.58	12.12
3172.00	264.33	132.17	61.00	12.20
3175.00	264.58	132.29	61.06	12.21
3180.00	265.00	132.50	61.15	12.23
3200.00	266.67	133.33	61.54	12.31
3224.00	268.67	134.33	62.00	12.40
3225.00	268.75	134.38	62.02	12.40
3240.00	270.00	135.00	62.31	12.46
3250.00	270.83	135.42	62.50	12.50
3275.00	272.92	136.46	62.98	12.60
3276.00	273.00	136.50	63.00	12.60
3300.00	275.00	137.50	63.46	12.69
3325.00	277.08	138.54	63.94	12.79
3328.00	277.33	138.67	64.00	12.80
3350.00	279.17	139.59	64.42	12.88
3360.00	280.00	140.00	64.62	12.92
3375.00	281.25	140.63	64.90	12.98
3380.00	281.67	140.84	65.00	13.00
3400.00	283.33	141.67	65.38	13.08
3420.00	285.00	142.50	65.77	13.15
3425.00	285.42	142.71	65.87	13.17
3432.00	286.00	143.00	66.00	13.20
3450.00	287.50	143.75	66.35	13.27
3475.00	289.58	144.79	66.83	13.37
3484.00	290.33	145.17	67.00	13.40
3500.00	291.67	145.84	67.31	13.46
3525.00	293.75	146.88	67.79	13.56
3536.00	294.67	147.34	68.00	13.60
3540.00	295.00	147.50	68.08	13.62
3550.00	295.83	147.92	68.27	13.65
3575.00	297.92	148.96	68.75	13.75
3588.00	299.00	149.50	69.00	13.80
3600.00	300.00	150.00	69.23	13.85
3625.00	302.08	151.04	69.71	13.94
3640.00	303.33	151.67	70.00	14.00
3650.00	304.17	152.09	70.19	14.04
3675.00	306.25	153.13	70.67	14.13
3692.00	307.67	153.84	71.00	14.20
3700.00	308.33	154.17	71.15	14.23
3720.00	310.00	155.00	71.54	14.31
3725.00	310.42	155.21	71.63	14.33
3744.00	312.00	156.00	72.00	14.40
3750.00	312.50	156.25	72.12	14.42
3775.00	314.58	157.29	72.60	14.52
3780.00	315.00	157.50	72.69	14.54
3796.00	316.33	158.17	73.00	14.60
3800.00	316.67	158.34	73.08	14.62

[1] By courteous permission of the Lefax Corporation, Philadelphia

Per Year	Per Month	Per Semi-Month	Per Week	Per Day 5 day
3825.00	318.75	159.38	73.56	14.71
3848.00	320.67	160.33	74.00	14.80
3850.00	320.83	160.42	74.03	14.81
3875.00	322.92	161.46	74.52	14.90
3900.00	325.00	162.50	75.00	15.00
3925.00	327.08	163.54	75.48	15.10
3950.00	329.17	164.59	75.96	15.19
3952.00	329.33	164.67	76.00	15.20
3960.00	330.00	165.00	76.15	15.23
3975.00	331.25	165.63	76.44	15.29
4000.00	333.33	166.67	76.92	15.38
4004.00	333.67	166.84	77.00	15.40
4020.00	335.00	167.50	77.31	15.46
4025.00	335.42	167.71	77.40	15.48
4050.00	337.50	168.75	77.88	15.58
4056.00	338.00	169.00	78.00	15.60
4075.00	339.58	169.79	78.37	15.67
4080.00	340.00	170.00	78.46	15.69
4100.00	341.67	170.84	78.85	15.77
4108.00	342.33	171.17	79.00	15.80
4125.00	343.75	171.88	79.33	15.87
4140.00	345.00	172.50	79.62	15.92
4150.00	345.83	172.92	79.81	15.96
4160.00	346.67	173.34	80.00	16.00
4175.00	347.92	173.96	80.29	16.06
4200.00	350.00	175.00	80.77	16.15
4212.00	351.00	175.50	81.00	16.20
4225.00	352.08	176.04	81.25	16.25
4250.00	354.17	177.09	81.73	16.35
4260.00	355.00	177.50	81.92	16.38
4264.00	355.33	177.67	82.00	16.40
4275.00	356.25	178.13	82.21	16.44
4300.00	358.33	179.17	82.69	16.54
4316.00	359.67	179.84	83.00	16.60
4320.00	360.00	180.00	83.08	16.62
4325.00	360.41	180.21	83.17	16.63
4350.00	362.50	181.25	83.65	16.73
4368.00	364.00	182.00	84.00	16.80
4375.00	364.58	182.29	84.13	16.83
4380.00	365.00	182.50	84.23	16.85
4400.00	366.67	183.34	84.62	16.92
4420.00	368.33	184.17	85.00	17.00
4425.00	368.75	184.38	85.10	17.02
4440.00	370.00	185.00	85.38	17.08
4450.00	370.83	185.42	85.58	17.12
4472.00	372.67	186.34	86.00	17.20
4475.00	372.92	186.46	86.06	17.21
4500.00	375.00	187.50	86.54	17.31
4524.00	377.00	188.50	87.00	17.40
4525.00	377.08	188.54	87.02	17.40
4550.00	379.17	189.59	87.50	17.50
4575.00	381.25	190.63	87.98	17.60
4576.00	381.33	190.67	88.00	17.60
4600.00	383.33	191.67	88.46	17.69
4620.00	385.00	192.50	88.85	17.77
4628.00	385.67	192.84	89.00	17.79
4650.00	387.50	193.75	89.42	17.88
4675.00	389.58	194.79	89.90	17.98
4680.00	390.00	195.00	90.00	18.00
4700.00	391.65	195.83	90.38	18.07
4725.00	393.75	196.88	90.87	18.17
4732.00	394.33	197.17	91.00	18.20
4740.00	395.00	197.50	91.15	18.23
4750.00	395.82	197.91	91.35	18.27
4775.00	397.91	198.96	91.83	18.37
4784.00	398.66	199.33	92.00	18.40
4800.00	400.00	200.00	92.31	18.46
4825.00	402.08	201.04	92.79	18.56
4836.00	403.00	201.50	93.00	18.60
4850.00	404.16	202.08	93.27	18.65
4860.00	405.00	202.50	93.46	18.69
4875.00	406.25	203.13	93.75	18.75
4888.00	407.33	203.67	94.00	18.80
4900.00	408.33	204.17	94.23	18.85
4920.00	410.00	205.00	94.62	18.92
4925.00	410.42	205.21	94.71	18.94
4940.00	411.67	205.84	95.00	19.00
4950.00	412.50	206.25	95.19	19.04
4975.00	414.58	207.29	95.67	19.13
4980.00	415.00	207.50	95.77	19.15
4992.00	416.00	208.00	96.00	19.20
5000.00	416.67	208.34	96.15	19.23
5025.00	418.75	209.38	96.63	19.33
5040.00	420.00	210.00	96.92	19.38
5044.00	420.33	210.17	97.00	19.40
5050.00	420.84	210.42	97.12	19.42
5075.00	422.92	211.46	97.60	19.52
5087.00	423.92	211.96	97.83	19.57
5096.00	424.67	212.34	98.00	19.60
5100.00	425.00	212.50	98.08	19.62
5125.00	427.08	213.54	98.56	19.71
5148.00	429.00	214.50	99.00	19.80
5150.00	429.17	214.59	99.04	19.81
5160.00	430.00	215.00	99.23	19.85
5175.00	431.25	215.63	99.52	19.90
5200.00	433.33	216.67	100.00	20.00
5220.00	435.00	217.50	100.38	20.08
5225.00	435.42	217.71	100.48	20.10
5250.00	437.50	218.75	100.96	20.19
5252.00	437.67	218.84	101.00	20.20
5275.00	439.58	219.79	101.44	20.29
5280.00	440.00	220.00	101.54	20.31
5300.00	441.67	220.84	101.92	20.38
5304.00	442.00	221.00	102.00	20.40
5325.00	443.75	221.88	102.40	20.48
5340.00	445.00	222.50	102.69	20.54
5350.00	445.83	222.92	102.88	20.58
5356.00	446.33	223.17	103.00	20.60
5375.00	447.92	223.96	103.37	20.67
5400.00	450.00	225.00	103.85	20.77
5408.00	450.67	225.34	104.00	20.80
5425.00	452.08	226.04	104.33	20.87
5450.00	454.17	227.09	104.81	20.96
5460.00	455.00	227.50	105.00	21.00
5475.00	456.25	228.13	105.29	21.06
5500.00	458.33	229.17	105.77	21.15
5512.00	459.33	229.67	106.00	21.20
5520.00	460.00	230.00	106.15	21.23
5525.00	460.42	230.21	106.25	21.25
5550.00	462.50	231.25	106.73	21.35
5564.00	463.67	231.84	107.00	21.40
5575.00	464.58	232.29	107.21	21.44
5580.00	465.00	232.50	107.31	21.46
5600.00	466.67	233.34	107.69	21.54
5616.00	468.00	234.00	108.00	21.60
5625.00	468.75	234.38	108.17	21.63
5640.00	470.00	235.00	108.46	21.69

Salary, Wages; Year, Month, Semi-Month, Weekly, Daily

Per Year	Per Month	Per Semi-Month	Per Week	Per Day 5 day
7020.00	585.00	292.50	135.50	27.00
7025.00	585.42	292.71	135.10	27.02
7050.00	587.50	293.75	135.58	27.12
7072.00	589.33	294.67	136.00	27.20
7075.00	589.58	294.79	136.06	27.21
7080.00	590.00	295.00	136.15	27.23
7100.00	591.67	295.84	136.54	27.31
7124.00	593.67	296.84	137.00	27.40
7125.00	593.75	296.88	137.02	27.40
7140.00	595.00	297.50	137.31	27.46
7150.00	595.83	297.92	137.50	27.50
7175.00	597.92	298.96	137.98	27.60
7176.00	598.00	299.00	138.00	27.60
7200.00	600.00	300.00	138.46	27.69
7225.00	602.08	301.04	138.94	27.79
7228.00	602.33	301.17	139.00	27.80
7250.00	604.17	302.09	139.42	27.88
7260.00	605.00	302.50	139.62	27.92
7275.00	606.25	303.13	139.90	27.98
7280.00	606.67	303.34	140.00	28.00
7300.00	608.33	304.17	140.38	28.08
7325.00	610.42	305.21	140.87	28.17
7332.00	611.00	305.50	141.00	28.20
7350.00	612.50	306.25	141.35	28.27
7375.00	614.58	307.29	141.83	28.37
7380.00	615.00	307.50	141.92	28.38
7384.00	615.33	307.67	142.00	28.40
7400.00	616.67	308.34	142.31	28.46
7425.00	618.75	309.38	142.79	28.56
7436.00	619.67	309.84	143.00	28.60
7440.00	620.00	310.00	143.08	28.62

Per Year	Per Month	Per Semi-Month	Per Week	Per Day 5 day
6550.00	545.83	272.92	125.96	25.19
6552.00	546.00	273.00	126.00	25.20
6575.00	547.92	273.96	126.44	25.29
6600.00	550.00	275.00	126.92	25.38
6604.00	550.33	275.17	127.00	25.40
6625.00	552.08	276.04	127.40	25.48
6650.00	554.17	277.09	127.88	25.58
6656.00	554.67	277.34	128.00	25.60
6660.00	555.00	277.50	128.08	25.62
6675.00	556.25	278.13	128.37	25.67
6700.00	558.33	279.17	128.85	25.77
6708.00	559.00	279.50	129.00	25.80
6720.00	560.00	280.00	129.23	25.85
6725.00	560.42	280.21	129.33	25.87
6750.00	562.50	281.25	129.81	25.96
6760.00	563.33	281.67	130.00	26.00
6775.00	564.58	282.29	130.29	26.06
6780.00	565.00	282.50	130.38	26.08
6800.00	566.67	283.34	130.77	26.15
6812.00	567.67	283.84	131.00	26.20
6825.00	568.75	284.38	131.25	26.25
6840.00	570.00	285.00	131.54	26.31
6850.00	570.83	285.42	131.73	26.35
6864.00	572.00	286.00	132.00	26.40
6875.00	572.92	286.46	132.21	26.44
6900.00	575.00	287.50	132.69	26.54
6916.00	576.33	288.17	133.00	26.60
6925.00	577.08	288.54	133.17	26.63
6950.00	579.17	289.59	133.65	26.73
6968.00	580.67	290.34	134.00	26.80
6975.00	581.25	290.63	134.13	26.83
7000.00	583.33	291.67	134.62	26.92

Per Year	Per Month	Per Semi-Month	Per Week	Per Day 5 day
6100.00	508.33	254.17	117.31	23.46
6120.00	510.00	255.00	117.69	23.54
6125.00	510.42	255.21	117.79	23.56
6136.00	511.33	255.67	118.00	23.60
6150.00	512.50	256.25	118.27	23.65
6175.00	514.58	257.29	118.75	23.75
6180.00	515.00	257.50	118.85	23.77
6188.00	515.67	257.84	119.00	23.80
6200.00	516.67	258.34	119.23	23.85
6225.00	518.75	259.38	119.71	23.94
6240.00	520.00	260.00	120.00	24.00
6250.00	520.83	260.42	120.19	24.04
6275.00	522.92	261.46	120.67	24.13
6292.00	524.33	262.17	121.00	24.20
6300.00	525.00	262.50	121.15	24.23
6325.00	527.08	263.54	121.63	24.33
6344.00	528.67	264.34	122.00	24.40
6350.00	529.17	264.59	122.12	24.42
6360.00	530.00	265.00	122.31	24.46
6375.00	531.25	265.63	122.60	24.52
6396.00	533.00	266.50	123.00	24.60
6400.00	533.33	266.67	123.08	24.62
6420.00	535.00	267.50	123.46	24.69
6425.00	535.42	267.71	123.56	24.71
6448.00	537.33	268.67	124.00	24.80
6450.00	537.50	268.75	124.04	24.81
6475.00	539.58	269.79	124.52	24.90
6480.00	540.00	270.00	124.62	24.92
6525.00	543.75	271.88	125.48	25.10
6540.00	545.00	272.50	125.77	25.15
6545.00	545.42	272.71	125.87	25.17

Per Year	Per Month	Per Semi-Month	Per Week	Per Day 5 day
5650.00	470.83	235.42	108.65	21.73
5668.00	472.33	236.17	109.00	21.80
5675.00	472.92	236.46	109.14	21.83
5700.00	475.00	237.50	109.62	21.92
5720.00	476.67	238.34	110.00	22.00
5725.00	477.08	238.54	110.10	22.02
5750.00	479.17	239.59	110.58	22.12
5760.00	480.00	240.00	110.77	22.15
5772.00	481.00	240.50	111.00	22.20
5775.00	481.25	240.63	111.06	22.21
5800.00	483.33	241.67	111.54	22.31
5820.00	485.00	242.50	111.92	22.38
5824.00	485.33	242.67	112.00	22.40
5825.00	485.42	242.71	112.02	22.40
5850.00	487.50	243.75	112.50	22.50
5875.00	489.58	244.79	112.98	22.60
5876.00	489.67	244.84	113.00	22.60
5880.00	490.00	245.00	113.08	22.62
5900.00	491.67	245.84	113.46	22.69
5925.00	493.75	246.88	113.94	22.79
5928.00	494.00	247.00	114.00	22.80
5940.00	495.00	247.50	114.23	22.85
5950.00	495.83	247.92	114.42	22.88
5975.00	497.92	248.96	114.90	22.98
5980.00	498.33	249.17	115.00	23.00
6000.00	500.00	250.00	115.38	23.08
6025.00	502.08	251.04	115.87	23.17
6032.00	502.67	251.34	116.00	23.20
6050.00	504.17	252.09	116.35	23.27
6060.00	505.00	252.50	116.54	23.31
6075.00	506.25	253.13	116.83	23.37
6084.00	507.00	253.50	117.00	23.40

[1] By courteous permission of the Lefax Corporation, Philadelphia

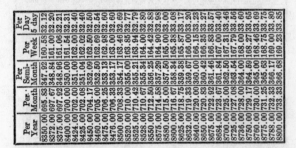

Per Year	Per Month	Per Semi-Month	Per Week	Per Day 5 day
7450.00	620.83	310.42	143.27	28.65
7475.00	622.92	311.46	143.75	28.75
7488.00	624.00	312.00	144.00	28.80
7500.00	625.00	312.50	144.23	28.85
7525.00	627.08	313.54	144.71	28.94
7540.00	628.33	314.17	145.00	29.00
7550.00	629.17	314.59	145.19	29.04
7560.00	630.00	315.00	145.38	29.08
7575.00	631.25	315.63	145.67	29.13
7592.00	632.67	316.34	146.00	29.20
7600.00	633.33	316.67	146.15	29.23
7620.00	635.00	317.50	146.54	29.31
7625.00	635.42	317.71	146.63	29.33
7644.00	637.00	318.50	147.00	29.40
7650.00	637.50	318.75	147.12	29.42
7675.00	639.58	319.79	147.60	29.52
7680.00	640.00	320.00	147.69	29.54
7696.00	641.33	320.67	148.00	29.60
7700.00	641.67	320.84	148.08	29.61
7725.00	643.75	321.88	148.56	29.71
7748.00	645.67	322.84	149.00	29.80
7750.00	645.83	322.92	149.04	29.81
7775.00	647.92	323.96	149.52	29.90
7800.00	650.00	325.00	150.00	30.00
7825.00	652.08	326.04	150.48	30.10
7850.00	654.17	327.08	150.96	30.19
7852.00	654.33	327.17	151.00	30.20
7860.00	655.00	327.50	151.15	30.23
7875.00	656.25	328.13	151.44	30.29
7900.00	658.33	329.17	151.92	30.38
7904.00	658.67	329.34	152.00	30.40

Per Year	Per Month	Per Semi-Month	Per Week	Per Day 5 day
7920.00	660.00	330.00	152.31	30.46
7925.00	660.42	330.21	152.40	30.48
7950.00	662.50	331.25	152.88	30.58
7956.00	663.00	331.50	153.00	30.60
7975.00	664.58	332.29	153.37	30.67
7980.00	665.00	332.50	153.46	30.69
8000.00	666.67	333.33	153.85	30.77
8008.00	667.33	333.67	154.00	30.80
8025.00	668.75	334.38	154.33	30.87
8040.00	670.00	335.00	154.62	30.92
8050.00	670.83	335.42	154.81	30.96
8060.00	671.67	335.84	155.00	31.00
8075.00	672.92	336.46	155.29	31.06
8100.00	675.00	337.50	155.77	31.15
8112.00	676.00	338.00	156.00	31.20
8125.00	677.08	338.54	156.25	31.25
8150.00	679.17	339.59	156.73	31.35
8160.00	680.00	340.00	156.92	31.38
8164.00	680.33	340.17	157.00	31.40
8175.00	681.25	340.63	157.21	31.44
8200.00	683.33	341.67	157.69	31.54
8216.00	684.67	342.34	158.00	31.60
8225.00	685.42	342.71	158.17	31.63
8250.00	687.50	343.75	158.65	31.73
8268.00	689.00	344.50	159.00	31.80
8275.00	689.58	344.79	159.13	31.83
8300.00	691.67	345.84	159.62	31.92
8320.00	693.33	346.67	160.00	32.00
8325.00	693.75	346.88	160.10	32.02
8340.00	695.00	347.50	160.38	32.08

Per Year	Per Month	Per Semi-Month	Per Week	Per Day 5 day
8350.00	695.83	347.92	160.58	32.12
8372.00	697.67	348.84	161.00	32.20
8375.00	697.92	348.96	161.06	32.21
8400.00	700.00	350.00	161.54	32.31
8424.00	702.00	351.00	162.00	32.40
8425.00	702.08	351.04	162.02	32.40
8450.00	704.17	352.09	162.50	32.50
8460.00	705.00	352.50	162.69	32.54
8475.00	706.25	353.13	162.98	32.60
8476.00	706.33	353.17	163.00	32.60
8500.00	708.33	354.17	163.46	32.69
8520.00	710.00	355.00	163.85	32.77
8525.00	710.42	355.21	163.94	32.79
8528.00	710.67	355.34	164.00	32.80
8550.00	712.50	356.25	164.42	32.88
8575.00	714.58	357.29	164.90	32.98
8580.00	715.00	357.50	165.00	33.00
8600.00	716.67	358.34	165.38	33.08
8625.00	718.75	359.38	165.87	33.17
8632.00	719.33	359.67	166.00	33.20
8640.00	720.00	360.00	166.15	33.23
8650.00	720.83	360.42	166.35	33.27
8675.00	722.92	361.46	166.83	33.37
8684.00	723.67	361.84	167.00	33.40
8700.00	725.00	362.50	167.31	33.46
8725.00	727.08	363.54	167.79	33.56
8736.00	728.00	364.00	168.00	33.60
8750.00	729.17	364.59	168.27	33.65
8760.00	730.00	365.00	168.46	33.69
8775.00	731.25	365.63	168.75	33.75
8788.00	732.33	366.17	169.00	33.80
8800.00	733.33	366.67	169.23	33.85

Per Year	Per Month	Per Semi-Month	Per Week	Per Day 5 day
8820.00	735.00	367.50	169.61	33.92
8825.00	735.42	367.71	169.71	33.94
8840.00	736.67	368.43	170.00	34.00
8850.00	737.50	368.75	170.19	34.04
8875.00	739.58	369.79	170.67	34.13
8880.00	740.00	370.00	170.77	34.15
8892.00	741.00	370.50	171.00	34.20
8900.00	741.66	370.83	171.15	34.23
8925.00	743.75	371.88	171.64	34.32
8940.00	745.00	372.50	171.92	34.38
8944.00	745.33	372.67	172.00	34.40
8950.00	745.83	372.92	172.12	34.42
8975.00	747.92	373.96	172.60	34.52
8996.00	749.67	374.84	173.00	34.60
9000.00	750.00	375.00	173.08	34.62
9025.00	752.08	376.04	173.56	34.71
9048.00	754.00	377.00	174.00	34.80
9050.00	754.16	377.08	174.04	34.81
9060.00	755.00	377.50	174.23	34.85
9075.00	756.25	378.13	174.52	34.90
9100.00	758.33	379.17	175.00	35.00
9120.00	760.00	380.00	175.38	35.08
9125.00	760.41	380.21	175.48	35.10
9150.00	762.50	381.25	175.96	35.19
9152.00	762.67	381.34	176.00	35.20
9175.00	764.58	382.29	176.44	35.29
9180.00	765.00	382.50	176.54	35.31
9200.00	766.66	383.33	176.92	35.38
9204.00	767.00	383.50	177.00	35.40
9225.00	768.75	384.38	177.40	35.48
9240.00	770.00	385.00	177.69	35.54
9250.00	770.83	385.42	177.88	35.58

Per Year	Per Month	Per Semi-Month	Per Week	Per Day 5 day
10,175.00	847.91	423.96	195.67	39.13
10,192.00	849.33	424.67	196.00	39.20
10,200.00	850.00	425.00	196.15	39.23
10,225.00	852.09	426.04	196.63	39.33
10,244.00	853.67	426.84	197.00	39.40
10,250.00	854.17	427.09	197.12	39.42
10,260.00	855.00	427.50	197.31	39.46
10,275.00	856.25	428.13	197.60	39.52
10,296.00	858.00	429.00	198.00	39.60
10,300.00	858.33	429.17	198.08	39.62
10,320.00	860.00	430.00	198.47	39.69
10,325.00	860.41	430.21	198.56	39.71
10,348.00	862.33	431.17	199.00	39.80
10,350.00	862.50	431.25	199.04	39.81
10,360.00	863.33	431.67	199.23	39.85
10,375.00	864.58	432.30	199.52	39.90
10,380.00	865.00	432.50	199.63	39.92
10,400.00	866.67	433.34	200.00	40.00
10,425.00	868.75	434.38	200.48	40.10
10,440.00	870.00	435.00	200.77	40.15
10,450.00	870.83	435.42	200.97	40.19
10,452.00	871.00	435.50	201.00	40.20
10,475.00	872.92	436.46	201.44	40.29
10,500.00	875.00	437.50	201.92	40.38
10,504.00	875.33	437.67	202.00	40.40
10,525.00	877.08	438.54	202.40	40.48
10,550.00	879.17	439.59	202.88	40.58
10,556.00	879.67	439.84	203.00	40.60
10,560.00	880.00	440.00	203.08	40.62
10,575.00	881.25	440.63	203.37	40.67
10,600.00	883.33	441.67	203.85	40.77
10,608.00	884.00	442.00	204.00	40.80
10,620.00	885.00	442.50	204.23	40.85

Per Year	Per Month	Per Semi-Month	Per Week	Per Day 5 day
9,724.00	810.33	405.17	187.00	37.40
9,725.00	810.42	405.21	187.02	37.40
9,750.00	812.50	406.25	187.50	37.50
9,775.00	814.58	407.29	187.98	37.60
9,776.00	814.67	407.34	188.00	37.60
9,780.00	815.00	407.50	188.08	37.62
9,800.00	816.67	408.33	188.46	37.69
9,825.00	818.75	409.38	188.94	37.79
9,828.00	819.00	409.50	189.00	37.80
9,850.00	820.83	410.42	189.42	37.88
9,875.00	822.92	411.46	189.90	37.98
9,880.00	823.33	411.67	190.00	38.00
9,900.00	825.00	412.50	190.38	38.08
9,925.00	827.08	413.54	190.87	38.17
9,932.00	827.67	413.84	191.00	38.20
9,950.00	829.16	414.58	191.35	38.27
9,960.00	830.00	415.00	191.54	38.31
9,975.00	831.25	415.63	191.83	38.37
9,984.00	832.00	416.00	192.00	38.40
10,000.00	833.33	416.67	192.31	38.46
10,020.00	835.00	417.50	192.69	38.54
10,025.00	835.41	417.71	192.79	38.56
10,036.00	836.33	418.17	193.00	38.60
10,050.00	837.50	418.75	193.27	38.65
10,075.00	839.58	419.79	193.75	38.75
10,080.00	840.00	420.00	193.85	38.77
10,088.00	840.67	420.34	194.00	38.80
10,100.00	841.67	420.84	194.23	38.85
10,125.00	843.75	421.88	194.71	38.94
10,140.00	845.00	422.50	195.00	39.00
10,150.00	845.83	422.92	195.19	39.04

Per Year	Per Month	Per Semi-Month	Per Week	Per Day 5 day
9,256.00	771.33	385.67	178.00	35.60
9,275.00	772.92	386.46	178.37	35.67
9,300.00	775.00	387.50	178.85	35.77
9,308.00	775.67	387.84	179.00	35.80
9,325.00	777.08	388.54	179.33	35.87
9,350.00	779.16	389.58	179.81	35.96
9,360.00	780.00	390.00	180.00	36.00
9,375.00	781.25	390.62	180.29	36.06
9,400.00	783.33	391.67	180.77	36.15
9,412.00	784.33	392.17	181.00	36.20
9,420.00	785.00	392.50	181.15	36.23
9,425.00	785.41	392.71	181.25	36.25
9,450.00	787.50	393.75	181.73	36.35
9,475.00	789.58	394.79	182.21	36.44
9,480.00	790.00	395.00	182.31	36.46
9,500.00	791.66	395.83	182.69	36.54
9,516.00	793.00	396.50	183.00	36.60
9,525.00	793.75	396.88	183.17	36.63
9,540.00	795.00	397.50	183.46	36.69
9,550.00	795.83	397.92	183.65	36.72
9,568.00	797.33	398.67	184.00	36.80
9,575.00	797.91	398.96	184.13	36.83
9,600.00	800.00	400.00	184.67	36.93
9,620.00	801.67	400.84	185.00	37.00
9,625.00	802.08	401.04	185.10	37.02
9,650.00	804.18	402.09	185.58	37.12
9,660.00	805.00	402.50	185.77	37.15
9,672.00	806.00	403.00	186.00	37.20
9,675.00	806.25	403.13	186.06	37.21
9,700.00	808.33	404.17	186.54	37.31
9,720.00	810.00	405.00	186.92	37.38

[1] By courteous permission of the Lefax Corporation, Philadelphia

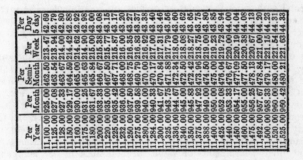

Per Year	Per Month	Per Semi-Month	Per Week	Per Day 5 day
11,544.00	962.00	481.00	222.00	44.40
11,550.00	962.50	481.25	222.12	44.42
11,575.00	964.58	482.29	222.60	44.52
11,580.00	965.00	482.50	222.69	44.54
11,596.00	966.33	483.17	223.00	44.60
11,600.00	966.67	483.33	223.08	44.62
11,625.00	968.75	484.38	223.56	44.71
11,640.00	970.00	485.00	223.85	44.77
11,648.00	970.67	485.34	224.00	44.80
11,650.00	970.83	485.42	224.04	44.81
11,675.00	972.92	486.46	224.52	44.91
11,700.00	975.00	487.50	225.00	45.00
11,725.00	977.08	488.54	225.48	45.10
11,750.00	979.17	489.59	225.97	45.19
11,752.00	979.33	489.67	226.00	45.20
11,760.00	980.00	490.00	226.15	45.23
11,775.00	981.25	490.63	226.44	45.29
11,800.00	983.33	491.67	226.92	45.38
11,804.00	983.67	491.84	227.00	45.40
11,820.00	985.00	492.50	227.31	45.46
11,825.00	985.42	492.71	227.40	45.48
11,850.00	987.50	493.75	227.88	45.58
11,856.00	988.00	494.00	228.00	45.60
11,875.00	989.58	494.79	228.37	45.67
11,880.00	990.00	495.00	228.46	45.69
11,900.00	991.67	495.84	228.85	45.77
11,908.00	992.33	496.17	229.00	45.80
11,925.00	993.75	496.88	229.32	45.86
11,940.00	995.00	497.50	229.62	45.92
11,950.00	995.83	497.92	229.80	45.96
11,975.00	997.92	498.96	230.29	46.06
12,000.00	1000.00	500.00	230.76	46.15

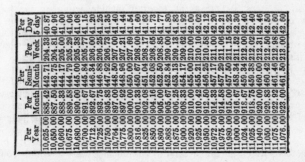

Per Year	Per Month	Per Semi-Month	Per Week	Per Day 5 day
11,100.00	925.00	462.50	213.47	42.69
11,125.00	927.08	463.54	213.94	42.79
11,128.00	927.33	463.67	214.00	42.80
11,150.00	929.17	464.59	214.42	42.88
11,160.00	930.00	465.00	214.62	42.92
11,175.00	931.25	465.63	214.90	42.98
11,180.00	931.67	465.84	215.00	43.00
11,200.00	933.33	466.67	215.38	43.08
11,220.00	935.00	467.50	215.77	43.15
11,225.00	935.42	467.71	215.87	43.17
11,232.00	936.00	468.00	216.00	43.20
11,250.00	937.50	468.75	216.35	43.27
11,275.00	939.58	469.79	216.83	43.37
11,280.00	940.00	470.00	216.92	43.38
11,284.00	940.33	470.17	217.00	43.40
11,300.00	941.67	470.84	217.31	43.46
11,325.00	943.75	471.88	217.79	43.56
11,336.00	944.67	472.34	218.00	43.60
11,340.00	945.00	472.50	218.08	43.62
11,350.00	945.83	472.92	218.27	43.65
11,375.00	947.92	473.96	218.75	43.75
11,388.00	949.00	474.50	219.00	43.80
11,400.00	950.00	475.00	219.23	43.85
11,425.00	952.08	476.04	219.72	43.94
11,440.00	953.33	476.67	220.00	44.00
11,450.00	954.17	477.09	220.19	44.04
11,460.00	955.00	477.50	220.38	44.08
11,475.00	956.25	478.13	220.67	44.13
11,492.00	957.67	478.84	221.00	44.20
11,500.00	958.33	479.17	221.15	44.23
11,520.00	960.00	480.00	221.54	44.31
11,525.00	960.42	480.21	221.63	44.33

Per Year	Per Month	Per Semi-Month	Per Week	Per Day 5 day
10,625.00	885.42	442.71	204.33	40.87
10,650.00	887.50	443.75	204.81	40.96
10,660.00	888.33	444.17	205.00	41.00
10,675.00	889.58	444.79	205.29	41.06
10,680.00	890.00	445.00	205.38	41.08
10,700.00	891.67	445.84	205.77	41.15
10,712.00	892.67	446.34	206.00	41.20
10,725.00	893.75	446.88	206.25	41.25
10,750.00	895.83	447.92	206.73	41.35
10,760.00	897.00	448.50	207.00	41.40
10,775.00	897.92	448.96	207.21	41.44
10,800.00	900.00	450.00	207.69	41.54
10,816.00	901.33	450.67	208.00	41.60
10,825.00	902.08	451.04	208.17	41.63
10,850.00	904.16	452.08	208.65	41.73
10,860.00	905.00	452.50	208.85	41.77
10,868.00	905.67	452.84	209.00	41.80
10,875.00	906.25	453.13	209.13	41.83
10,900.00	908.33	454.17	209.62	41.92
10,920.00	910.00	455.00	210.00	42.00
10,925.00	910.42	455.21	210.10	42.02
10,950.00	912.50	456.25	210.58	42.12
10,972.00	914.33	457.17	211.00	42.20
10,975.00	914.58	457.29	211.06	42.21
10,980.00	915.00	457.50	211.15	42.23
11,000.00	916.67	458.34	211.52	42.30
11,024.00	918.67	459.34	212.00	42.40
11,025.00	918.75	459.38	212.02	42.40
11,040.00	920.00	460.00	212.31	42.46
11,050.00	920.83	460.42	212.50	42.50
11,075.00	922.92	461.46	212.98	42.60
11,076.00	923.00	461.50	213.00	42.60

INVESTING MONEY

In selecting your investment objectives, serious consideration should be given to your earned income and annual savings; your age and health; your family responsibilities; the requirements in time and money, as well as the prospects, of your own business; maturing obligations such as mortgages; installment debt; educational expenses for children; and your own retirement objectives. These questions, of course, are tied into an insurance program and a liquid savings account for emergencies of illness, unemployment, disability, or general disaster, which in all well-run investment programs demand precedence.

Important guiding principles for an investor are: (1) secure adequate insurance and a savings account apart from any investable funds; (2) establish and maintain your investment objectives, whether for safety of principal, for income, for gradual growth of capital, or for speculative appreciation; (3) consult your bank or lawyer, and through them, a reputable investment or brokerage firm for advice on attaining your objectives; and (4) keep informed on your investments.

For the investor's protection, a great body of laws, both Federal and state, has been built up, particularly over the past 30 years. In part, such laws prohibit the fraudulent or deceptive schemes which lure the unwary on the promise of huge or "sure" profits; but most investors are concerned more with mistakes of judgment than with fraud in investments. The laws, especially the Federal securities acts (which are discussed under their own heading), emphasize in the main that full information be made available to investors, but no attempt is made by governmental authorities to render an opinion on investments. The investor, then, must be sure to get and use information intelligently and not rely solely on the laws. After all, there are traffic laws for our protection but one does not, therefore, blindly cross the street.

Among the pitfalls to avoid are: (1) "playing the market" for short-term gains, following "tips" or advice from dabblers, being impressed or swayed by mere masses of figures, or rushing to buy securities on impulse, or because they are popular; (2) retaining investments not on their basic merit but for sentimental reasons, or because they are still paying dividends, or because you have a loss; (3) entertaining or acting on vague ideas about the soundness of an industry or a company without bothering to learn the available facts; (4) being misled by the high or low price of a security, without relating it to earnings, dividends, assets, and other determinants of value (a $500 stock in one company, for example, may be a sounder and cheaper investment than a $5 stock in another company); and (5) forgetting that the past record and present data on an investment must be supplemented by an appraisal of its future.

The positive steps to take as an investor include acting on the four guiding principles outlined at the beginning of this section. Where investment is considered in a company's securities, obtain information on the company's assets, its products or services, its debts, the amount of stock outstanding, what it earns, and how it compares with other companies in the same line of business.

Generally speaking, the higher a yield or return promised on an investment, the greater the risk to the investor's capital. The expert investment adviser should be able to appraise the risks and possibilities in a speculative investment; but even the expert can give no guaranty of his appraisal. However, the amateur or occasional investor will serve his own ends well if he secures the help and counsel of a conscientious and reputable adviser.

There is no exact formula for solving the problems of investing money; but there is need to weigh all the factors, to consult an expert in whom you can have confidence, to settle on a choice of alternatives, and then to exercise that most elusive of qualities, patience. The total number of shareholders in public corporations in the United States was estimated in 1961 at 15,000,000.

For the new or small investor, there are two systems available under which an investing program can be begun without a large outlay of cash. These are the Monthly Investment Plan (MIP) offered by member firms of the New York Stock Exchange, and investment companies or mutual funds.

The MIP, developed by member firms of the New York Stock Exchange, enables the investor to buy shares or parts of shares in any one of more than 1,000 leading companies for as little as $40 per month or per quarter. Under this plan, the investor arranges with a member firm of the exchange to invest a certain regular amount in a stock of his own choice. If the stock sells for more than he wishes to invest at any one time, his account is credited with fractional shares. By investing regularly, it is also possible to take advantage of "dollar cost averaging," profiting by temporary downswings in price by getting more shares when the price is low and fewer when it is high; in this way the average cost of shares will be less than the average of the prices at the time of purchase.

Investment companies, popularly called mutual funds, are organizations in which investors pool their resources to buy stock in a variety of companies, thus by diversification reducing the risk inherent in all investing. There are investment companies to meet virtually all investing objectives: balanced funds, which invest for reasonable income, conservation of principal, and long-term growth of principal and income; stock funds, which seek long-term growth of principal and income; and income funds, which invest for the largest possible current income obtainable without assuming undue risks. In addition to diversification, mutual funds provide professional management and continuous supervision. Various funds offer various services, including automatic reinvestment of dividends and capital gains distributions; systematic investing plans, under which additional investments can be made at regular or convenient intervals; and systematic withdrawal plans, under which the shareholder may elect to receive a check for the same amount every month or at other convenient intervals.

A third method of investing for the beginner is the investment club. These clubs generally have two purposes: to provide investment experience and to build a nest egg for members. Typically, a club consists of ten or fifteen persons who meet at intervals to discuss and decide on investments. Each member pays a stipulated sum each month, which is invested in securities selected by the members; dividends and profits may be reinvested or divided proportionately among the members. Information and assistance in forming an investment club can be obtained from any member firm of the New York Stock Exchange.

See also Stock Exchanges.

BUYING A HOME[1]

Home ownership in the United States has risen to 62 per cent, based on the 1960 count of the United States Bureau of the Census. Ten years earlier, 55 per cent of the nation's families were in the home-owning category, and in 1940 only 44 per cent. In 1960 there were 32.8 million owner-occupied dwelling units in the United States, an increase of 39 per cent over 1950, and more than twice the figure of 20 years earlier. Two basic factors responsible for this trend have been the generally favorable economic climate and the general attitude that housing is an important indicator of a rising standard of living. The availability of mortgage credit through which home ownership is usually achieved has been an important contributing factor.

The home owner usually enjoys more space, more rooms, better design, and a better community than those who live in rented quarters. There are also in-

[1] For technical information concerning design and construction, see Home Design and Construction.

tangible advantages such as congeniality of neighbors and a sense of personal security.

Buying a home is a safe and sound investment. With each reduction of the mortgage on the property, a home owner adds to his original equity, until he eventually owns the home free and clear. An investment in a home also gives a preferred income-tax status, enabling a home owner to deduct interest payments and real estate taxes when filing his income-tax return.

The first decision that must be made is whether to own a home or to rent. Although a majority of the families in the United States now occupy their own homes, there will always be many persons who prefer to rent. Once a person has made the decision to buy, he should decide how much housing he can afford. There are several rules of thumb, of which the most important are: (1) that a home owner can afford roughly one week's pay out of a month's salary for housing expenses; and (2) that he can purchase a home costing roughly two and one-half times his annual income. Of course, these are only general rules. Obviously, families, like individuals, have different tastes, habits, and preferences. Some spend more on recreation than others. Some have more children and must budget more for food, clothing, and medical care and less for housing. By the same token, many families can allot more than a week's income for housing, because they have large incomes and prefer to use their homes for entertainment and for recreation.

Buying a home is the biggest single purchase made by most people in their lifetimes, and it is estimated that 90 per cent of the purchases of homes are accomplished through the use of mortgage credit. Home buyers today have a choice of three modern financing plans: the conventional loan; the V.A.[1]-guaranteed loan; and the F.H.A.[2]-guaranteed loan. The conventional loan is a transaction between the borrower and the lending institution. It does not involve any Federal government financial backing.

The sensible and safe approach is to buy or build a home properly located and of a design suitable to the family's way of life at a cost consistent with its income and under financing terms that are reasonable and considerate of the family's needs and ability to pay. Whether he is buying or building, the prospective home owner should consider the existence and placement of schools, churches, shopping facilities, and recreational facilities and whether the home will be convenient to his work with regard to distance and transportation costs. He should also consider the general appearance of the neighborhood and whether it is developing, static, or deteriorating; drainage of the lot and whether the area is subject to flooding; whether his prospective neighbors have incomes, types of work, and general living standards similar to his own; zoning ordinances pertaining to apartments, business, and industrial development; the condition of the streets; and public utility services.

The tax rate is a key point to check. It is possible to get an idea of a community's tax level from the city or village hall. The buyer should also check with some of the owners of homes in his price range in the community selected to get actual tax figures on specific homes and to find out what services are rendered by the local administration with tax money received. He should also inquire about the existence of special assessments for streets or sidewalks or the possibility of such assessments coming at a later time.

In purchasing an existing house, the prospective buyer should inquire into the age of the house, its structural qualities, heating and ventilation, insulation, plumbing, electric wiring, closets and storage space, room arrangements, and adaptability to his family. If a mortgage must be secured to complete the pur-

---

[1] Abbreviation for Veterans Administration.
[2] Abbreviation for Federal Housing Administration.

chase, it is possible to get some idea of the lending institution's valuation of the property by the amount it will lend. Independent appraisals can be secured in most communities at a reasonable cost.

Since most existing houses are acquired through the services of a realtor and most new houses are purchased directly from builders, it is important to select a realtor or builder who is reliable. In building a custom house, consideration should be given to the employment of an architect. Many new houses today are built as part of a project which has been planned by an architect. Changes during the process of construction, even though they seem to be minor, are quite expensive in relation to the results. Supervision of construction is also desirable. The local home-financing institution will be helpful on these matters.

When a home is found in the desired price range that meets the buyer's needs and he wishes to purchase it, he will be asked to sign a contract or agreement. Such an agreement will require a deposit or "earnest" money. It is suggested that the contract provide for the return of the "earnest" money in the event the required mortgage financing cannot be secured. It is also recommended that such documents be inspected by an attorney before they are signed.

Financing a Home

In financing the purchase of a home, it is important to make advance inquiries into the preliminary costs, the required down payment, and terms of the mortgage. Preliminary costs, generally paid by the borrower, include the appraisal fee, a mortgage tax (in some states), the cost of recording the mortgage, legal fees for obtaining a clear title covering the recording of the deed and mortgage and for the drawing of legal papers, a pro rata portion of prepaid taxes and insurance, survey costs, possible repair costs, and an initial service fee. When one is building a home on a custom basis, additional preliminary costs may include an architect's fee, inspection fees, insurance and interest during construction, and the cost of basic household equipment not included in the cost of the house.

In some types of government-guaranteed and -insured loans, the maximum interest rates are not always as high as current mortgage yields and, therefore, lenders may charge an additional item called a "discount" to compensate for this variation. In any event, it is well to secure in advance a statement from the lending institution of all costs and charges involved.

It is impossible to generalize on the cash down payment. Savings and loan associations and cooperative banks generally lend up to 80 per cent of the appraised value, and most of them are authorized to place a certain percentage of their assets in loans above an 80 per cent ratio but not exceeding 90 per cent. Savings banks, depending on state laws, can lend from 66⅔ per cent to 80 per cent of the appraised value, insurance companies 66⅔ per cent to 75 per cent, and commercial banks 60 per cent to 75 per cent of the appraised value. Exceptions are loans insured by the F.H.A. or guaranteed by the V.A., which are discussed later. As a practical matter, the down-payment requirement may often exceed the minimum provided by law and varies with economic conditions, the property itself, the borrower, and the judgment of the lender. Second-mortgage funds may be available to assist those who have insufficient cash funds to meet the down-payment requirements. The cost of such funds is often prohibitive, however, and usually such mortgages must be repaid within a few years. The borrower must take care not to commit himself for obligations he will be unable to meet. If second-mortgage financing is used, he should be sure that the second mortgage does not provide for a large payment, commonly called a "balloon payment," at the end of a specific term, usually before the maturity of the first mortgage.

With regard to manner of repayment, mortgage loans may be classified as straight mortgages and amortized or monthly payment loans. A straight mortgage loan requires that interest may be paid quarterly or semiannually, with the amount of the debt falling due generally in three, five, or ten years. Generally, *straight mortgages* are used only where the ratio of the loan to the value is rather small. The *amortized* or *monthly-payment mortgage* loan is repaid by monthly payments of interest and principal. The amount of the monthly payment depends primarily on the number of years to maturity and is usually a level monthly payment which will completely amortize the debt. From each month's payment there is first deducted an amount for interest; the remainder of the payment is applied toward the debt. Each month the amount of interest declines and the balance applied to debt reduction increases. This plan is most suitable for those receiving regular wages or salaries. Usually under this plan, too, the borrower is required to deposit each month one-twelfth of the estimated annual property taxes and insurance premiums; when these amounts fall due, they are paid by the lender out of the fund accumulated. These funds are known by different names, such as reserves, escrows, and impounds.

MONTHLY PAYMENTS REQUIRED TO REPAY AN AMORTIZED MORTGAGE OF $10,000

Maturity	5¼%	5½%	5¾%	6%	6¼%
15 years	$80.39	$81.71	$83.05	$84.39	$85.75
20 years	67.39	68.80	70.21	71.65	73.10
25 years	59.93	61.41	62.92	64.44	65.97
30 years	55.23	56.78	58.36	59.96	61.58
35 years	52.08	53.71	55.36	57.02	58.71

The F.H.A. does not grant loans. It is a government agency which insures the lender (not the borrower) against certain losses on mortgage loans. The borrower (not the lender) pays the insurance premium of ½ of 1 per cent per year, calculated on the balance of the loan, in addition to the interest charge. Loans insured by the F.H.A. carry an interest rate set by the Federal Housing Commissioner, subject to statutory limitations.

On Aug. 1, 1961, the F.H.A. would insure home loans up to a maximum maturity of 30 years on existing construction and 35 years on new construction, with F.H.A. inspection during the course of construction. It would insure up to 97 per cent of the first $15,000 of value, plus 90 per cent of value between $15,000 and $20,000, and 25 per cent of the appraised value in excess of $20,-000, with a maximum insurable loan on a single family home of $25,000. The actual effect of F.H.A. insurance is to set minimum down payments. Under the current law, minimum down payments would be $300 on a $10,000 house, $450 on a $15,000 house, $1,000 on a $20,000 house, $2,200 on a $25,000 house, and $5,000 on a $30,000 house.

The borrower must determine for himself how important the lower down payment and longer mortgage term are in relation to these factors. Certainly, there are advantages in dealing wholly with local lenders who know one's standing in the community and who are willing to grant special consideration in times of temporary financial difficulty. There is some question of the desirability of stretching the mortgage payments over too many years. Interest charges pile up rapidly when the loan is extended beyond 20 years. For example, interest on a $10,000, 20-year loan at 5½ per cent would total $6,512, compared with $10,440 for a 30-year loan. Thus, by paying $68.80 per month on a $10,000 loan instead of $56.78, an interest saving of $3,928 can be realized. As soon as the home is owned debt-free, the over-all housing costs decline substantially.

If possible, the borrower should secure a mortgage contract which permits prepayment in whole or in part (preferably without penalty); which permits making advance payments that can be applied to offset future delinquencies; and which provides that the borrower may secure additional loans at a later date, under the mortgage, for modernization or repairs. Since savings and loan associations typically finance homes only in their locality and do not sell them, the prospective home owner is more apt to find these and other favorable features in a mortgage contract with them.

The following table shows how payments are applied to both principal and interest on a $10,000 loan for 20 years at 5½ per cent.

MONTHLY AMORTIZED LOAN PAYMENTS ON A $10,000 LOAN FOR 20 YEARS AT 5½%

TIME		MONTHLY PAYMENT			BALANCE DUE AT END OF PERIOD
Years	Months	Total	Interest	Principal	
0	1	$68.80	$45.80	$23.00	$9,977.00
0	2	68.80	45.70	23.10	9,953.90
0	3	68.80	45.60	23.20	9,930.70
3	0	68.80	41.80	27.00	9,103.20
5	0	68.80	38.70	30.10	8,417.90
10	0	68.80	29.20	39.60	6,336.30
15	0	68.80	16.70	52.10	3,597.40
19	11	68.80	.60	68.20	62.00
20	0	62.30	.30	62.00	—

When home loans to veterans are made by local financial institutions, the V.A. guarantees up to 60 per cent of the loan, but not more than $7,500. This guarantee of the government to assume a substantial amount of the loss on a loan to a veteran was granted to encourage lenders to make 100 per cent or very low down-payment loans to veterans of World War II on homes at a preferred rate of interest. The loan guarantee is only available to veterans for loans on their own homes. Under an amendment effective in July 1961, eligible World War II veterans had until July 25, 1962, to avail themselves of this benefit, and this cut-off date might be extended to July 25, 1967, under a phase-out program based on the length of active service. For Korean war veterans, the cut-off date was Jan. 31, 1965, and under the phase-out program the final cut-off date was Jan. 31, 1975.

The special features of home loans to eligible veterans of World War II and the Korean conflict are the possibility of securing a loan with a very small, or no, down payment; up to 30 years to pay; some protection against paying an unreasonable price, since the V.A. will not guarantee the loan unless its designated appraisers find the interest rate to be reasonable in the current market; and a mortgage which permits prepayments without penalty.

DEEDS

A deed is a written instrument transferring title to real property. The person conveying the property is called the *grantor* and the person to whom title is transferred is called the *grantee*. Apart from statutory provisions, a deed requires: (1) competent parties, *i.e.*, the grantor and the grantee must have the legal capacity to transfer and acquire real property; (2) an adequate description of the real estate (in terms of monuments, metes and bounds, maps, lot and block numbers); (3) a valid or good consideration, *i.e.,* money, or love and affection, etc.; (4) proper and adequate language, indicating an intent to transfer legal title; and (5) a formal signing, execution, and delivery to the grantee.

Deeds are recorded in public offices designated by statute.

The most common forms of deed are *warranty deeds; bargain and sale deeds;* and *quit-claim deeds.*

Warranty Deed. A warranty deed contains five specific provisions for the benefit of the grantee:

1. Seizin, a covenant meaning that the grantor at the time of execution and delivery of the deed has legal title to the property and lawful authority to sell

2. Quiet enjoyment, a covenant meaning that the grantee and his heirs may at all times thereafter peaceably hold, use, and occupy the property free from claims of any other persons

3. Freedom from encumbrances, a covenant meaning that the property is free from all liens and encumbrances such as judgments, assessments, taxes, etc.

4. Further assurance, a covenant meaning that the grantor will thereafter, upon request and at his own expense, execute and obtain any and all other instruments to more effectively validate the title

5. Warranty of title, a covenant meaning that the grantor will forever warrant the title to the grantee and defend it against the claims of all other persons.

Bargain and Sale Deed. There are two kinds of bargain and sale deeds, one with covenant against grantor's acts, the other without such covenant. A bargain and sale deed grants to the purchaser all the interest of the seller. A covenant against grantor's acts is a covenant that the seller has not done anything whereby the property has been encumbered. Such deeds are usually used where the seller owns the property or may own less than a fee (full title). This deed requires pecuniary consideration.

Quit-Claim Deed. A quit-claim deed is one which purports to convey nothing more than the *interest* of the grantor, rather than the property itself; it stems from a release. The title to real property may be as effectually transferred by such a deed as by another form of conveyance. Such a deed conveys whatever title or interest the grantor may have, and only such title or interest. Except in so far as the grantee's rights may be enlarged by statute, he takes the property subject to existing encumbrances and the rights of others.

Deed in Escrow. A deed delivered in escrow is a deed *entrusted to a third person* until some stipulated condition has been fulfilled or some specified particular event has occurred. If the condition is not fulfilled or if the event does not occur, the grantor is entitled to a return of the deed.

Deed in Trust. A deed in trust is essentially a mortgage. It is a conveyance of the property intended to be pledged, to one or more trustees, who are to hold it for the benefit of a lawful holder of a note, bond, or other obligation of the grantor, permitting the latter to retain possession of the property and collect the rents thereof until default is made in the payment of the obligation, and with a power in the trustee or trustees, on such default, to sell the property and pay the obligation out of the net proceeds, returning the surplus, if any, to the grantor.

Trust Deed. A trust deed places property, real or personal or both, under the control of a person called a trustee for the benefit of another person or persons called beneficiary or beneficiaries. The trust deed differs from a deed in trust inasmuch as the latter refers to collateral for loans.

Acknowledgment. The acknowledgment of a deed is a *formal declaration* before a duly authorized public officer, generally a notary public, by the grantor that he is the person described in the instrument and the person who executed it.

DEED WITH FULL COVENANTS[1]

This indenture, made the ———— day of ———— between JOHN DOE, of No. ————
———— Street, (City), (State), and RICHARD ROE, of No. ———— ———— Street,
(City), (State)

————, party of the second part: *witnesseth,* that the party of the first part, in
consideration of ———— dollars lawful money of the United States, paid by the
party of the second part, does hereby grant and release unto the party of the second part, his heirs, executors, administrators, (if a corporation, "successors" instead of foregoing) and assigns forever, all that piece and parcel of land, known
and described as No. ———— ———— Street, (City), (State), and noted on the
land map of ———— County as being Section No. ————, Block No. ————,
more particularly described as follows: (Here insert description from prior deeds.
Also what mortgages the conveyance is subject to if any. Describe mortgage by
giving its amount, due date, interest, mortgagee, liber and page numbers in register's office where recorded.) together with the appurtenances and all the estate
and rights of the party of the first part in and to said premises.

To have and to hold the premises herein granted unto the party of the second
part ———— and assigns forever.

And the said JOHN DOE covenants as follows:

First: That said JOHN DOE is seized of the said premises in fee simple, and has
good right to convey the same.

Second: That the party of the second part shall quietly enjoy the said premises.

Third: That the said premises are free from encumbrances; except as hereinbefore set forth.

Fourth: That the party of the first part will execute or procure any further necessary assurance of the title to said premises.

Fifth: That said JOHN DOE will forever warrant the title to said premises.

In witness whereof, the party of the first part has hereunto set his hand and seal
the day and year first above written.
In presence of

(Signed) John Doe (seal)

(Acknowledgment)

QUIT-CLAIM DEED[1]

This indenture, made the ———— day of ————, nineteen hundred and ————
between JOHN DOE, of No. ———— ———— Street, (City), (State), and RICHARD
ROE, of No. ———— Street, (City), (State), party of the first part,

————, party of the second part, *witnesseth,* that the party of the first part, in
consideration of ———— dollars, lawful money of the United States, and other
good and valuable considerations to the party of the first part in hand paid by the
party of the second part, does hereby remise, release and quit-claim unto the
party of the second part, his heirs, executors, administrators (if a corporation,
"successors" instead of foregoing) and assigns forever, all that piece and parcel
of land known and described as No. ———— ———— Street, (City), (State), and
noted upon the land map of ———— County, as being Section No. ————, Block
No. ———— and more particularly described as follows: (Here insert description
from prior deed.)

Together with the appurtenances and all the estate and rights of the party of the
first part in and to said premises.

To have and to hold the premises herein granted unto the party of the second
part, his heirs, administrators, executors and assigns forever.

[1] This is only a suggested form. The reader is advised to obtain a blank form,
valid in his state, from a lawyer or a legal stationer for use in specific transactions.
Usually the form is prescribed by statute, but use of other forms is not prevented.
Bargain and sale deeds use the words "grant and release" in place of "remise, release, and quit-claim."

In witness whereof, the party of the first part has hereunto set his hand and seal the day and year first above written.

In the presence of

(Signed) *John Doe* (seal)

(Acknowledgment)

TRUST DEED[1]

This indenture, made this ———— day of ————, 19–, between JOHN DOE of No. ———— ———— Street, (City), (State), (hereinafter called the "grantor"), party of the first part, and ———— TRUST COMPANY, a corporation organized and existing under the laws of the state of ———— (hereinafter called the "trustee"), party of the second part, *witnesseth:* that the grantor in consideration of the sum of One Dollar ($1) to him in hand paid by the trustee, the receipt whereof is hereby acknowledged, and of the covenants hereinafter contained, hath sold, assigned, transferred and set over, and by these presents does sell, assign, transfer and set over unto the trustee the securities and property specified and described in a schedule hereto annexed and marked "Schedule A," the receipt of which securities and property is hereby acknowledged by the trustee.

To have and to hold the said securities and property to the said trustee, its successors or assigns upon the following express trust and conditions and with the powers and limitations hereinafter conferred and set forth, that is to say:

1. To collect and receive the rents, income, interest and dividends therefrom (hereinafter referred to as "income") and to pay the net income therefrom after deducting all proper charges and expenses to the grantor during his lifetime.

2. Upon the death of the grantor to pay over the principal of the said trust fund as he, the said grantor, may by his last will and testament appoint, and in default of such appointment, the same shall constitute and be disposed of as a part of his estate.

3. The trustee is expressly authorized and empowered (here insert whatever investment powers, with limitations or discretion, it is desired that the trustee shall have).

4. The grantor hereby expressly reserves the right at any time by a notice in writing, signed and acknowledged by him, and filed with the trustee, to revoke, cancel and annul this indenture and the trust hereby created, either in whole or in part, and he also reserves the right at any time, and from time to time, by a notice in writing, signed and acknowledged by him and filed with the trustee, to alter, amend and modify this agreement in any and every respect.

5. The trustee shall be entitled to the following compensation: (herein insert schedule for compensation).

6. The trustee shall have the right to resign at any time by giving written notice to the grantor.

7. The trustee by joining in this indenture signifies its acceptance of the trust.

In witness whereof the said parties have hereunto set their hands and seals the day and year first above written.

John Doe (seal)
———— TRUST COMPANY,
By Vice President.

Attest:
    Asst. Secretary (seal of company)
    (Acknowledgments)

REAL ESTATE MORTGAGES

A real estate loan is evidenced by a note or bond executed by the borrower. This note or bond is usually in negotiable form and secured by a security instru-

---

[1] This is only a suggested form. The reader is advised to obtain a blank form, valid in his state, from a lawyer or a legal stationer for use in specific transactions.

ment. Different forms of security instruments are used in different jurisdictions. The most common forms of security instrument are the *regular mortgage, trust deed,* and *deed in trust.* The security instrument is an instrument whereby a lien is created upon real estate or whereby title to real estate is reserved or conveyed as security for the payment of a debt or fulfillment of other obligation. The person who executes a mortgage is called a *mortgagor* and the person whose loan is secured, a *mortgagee.*

By statute, a binding and valid mortgage on real property must be *in writing.* Apart from express statutory requirements, no particular form is necessary, nor is any particular language required; it is only necessary that the instrument manifest a present purpose of the grantor or mortgagor to convey title of specified real estate to a designated person as the mortgagee. The instrument is held by the latter as security for the payment of a certain sum of money. The instrument must be executed or acknowledged before a public officer, generally a notary public, and recorded in a public office. The purpose of recording it is to give notice to others, who can then only acquire an interest in the mortgaged property subject to the mortgage. A mortgage, to be valid, must be delivered by the mortgagor.

Ordinarily the mortgagee has no right of possession prior to default. By statute, in some states, it is provided that after default in payment of the secured debt or other breach of the mortgage, the mortgagee is entitled to possession of the property, and may enter, peaceably or by appropriate legal proceeding.

In the absence of statute or agreement providing otherwise, the creditor may bring an action on the bond or note without first foreclosing the mortgage.

A valid judgment obtained in an action on a mortgage debt exists until the judgment is paid, and the mortgage remains a valid lien. The judgment does not discharge nor release the mortgage.

A mortgage can be assigned; the assignment must be in writing. Although the recording of an assignment of a mortgage is not prerequisite to its validity between the parties, under some statutes an assignee, *i.e.,* the person to whom it is assigned, must record his assignment to give constructive notice to third persons unless they are otherwise chargeable with notice.

In some states, by statute, a transfer of the debt secured by a mortgage carries with it the mortgage security and such an assignee succeeds to all the rights of the assignor.

The owner of mortgaged property may sell the property to a third party, without prejudice to the rights of the mortgagee. By selling the mortgaged property, the mortgagor does not relieve himself from his personal obligation on the secured debt.

If the purchaser does not agree to pay the mortgage, he is not personally liable to the mortgagor for its payment. He may, of course, expressly agree to pay the mortgage. When the land is sold subject to a mortgage, the mortgagee's lien continues, and the land is the primary fund for the satisfaction of the mortgage.

The lien of a mortgage continues until the debt is paid or the lien is extinguished by release or operation of law.

Foreclosure is a remedy by which the property may be subjected to sale for the payment of the debt for which the mortgage is security. This remedy is ordinarily necessary to cut off the mortgagor's equity of redemption, which is the right of the mortgagor to pay the full amount of the indebtedness with interest, in order to redeem the property. Once the mortgage is foreclosed, the mortgagor's title to the property vests in the mortgagee and amounts to a satisfaction of the mortgaged debt to the extent of the value of the mortgaged property, or, in the case of a sale thereof, to the extent of the amount realized therefrom.

FORM OF REAL ESTATE MORTGAGE[1]

This mortgage, made the ———— day of ———— nineteen hundred and ————, between ————, the mortgagor, and ————, the mortgagee,

Witnesseth, that to secure the payment of an indebtedness in the sum of ———— Dollars lawful money of the United States, to be paid ———— with interest thereon, to be computed from the date hereof at the rate of ———— per centum per annum, and to be paid on the ———— day of ———— next ensuing and ———— thereafter, ———— according to a certain bond or obligation bearing even date herewith, the mortgagor hereby mortgages to the mortgagee *all* that certain plot, piece or parcel of land, with the buildings and improvements thereon erected, situate, lying and being in the

(Here follows description of property.)

Together with all right, title and interest of the mortgagor in and to the land lying in the streets and roads in front of and adjoining said premises, and

Together with all fixtures, chattels and articles of personal property attached to or used in connection with said premises or which may hereafter be attached to or used in connection with said premises, including but not limited to furnaces, boilers, oil burners, radiators and piping, coal stokers, plumbing and bathroom fixtures, refrigeration, air conditioning and sprinkler systems, wash tubs, sinks, gas and electric fixtures, stoves, ranges, awnings, screens, window shades, elevators, motors, dynamos, refrigerators, kitchen cabinets, incinerators, and all other equipment and machinery, appliances, fittings, and fixtures of every kind in or used in the operation of the buildings standing on said premises, together with any and all replacements thereof and additions thereto, and the whole of said principal sum secured by said bond and this mortgage shall become due and payable, at the option of the mortgagee in the event of the removal, demolition or destruction in whole or in part of any of said fixtures, chattels or articles of personal property, unless the same are promptly replaced by similar fixtures, chattels and articles of personal property at least equal in quality and condition to those replaced, provided, however, that such substituted fixtures, chattels or articles of personal property be purchased free from any encumbrance and without reservation of title thereto in the seller.

Together also with any and all awards heretofore made and hereafter to be made to the present and all subsequent owners of said premises, including any award and awards for change of grade of any street affecting said premises, which said award and awards are hereby assigned to the mortgagee, who is hereby authorized and empowered to collect and receive such award and awards and to give proper receipts and acquittances therefor, and to apply the same toward the payment of the amount owing on this mortgage, notwithstanding the fact that the amount owing on this mortgage may not then be due and payable; and the mortgagor for himself, his heirs and all subsequent owners of said premises, hereby covenants and agrees with the mortgagee and the successors and assigns of the mortgagee, upon request by the holder of this mortgage to make, execute and deliver any and all assignments and other instruments sufficient for the purpose of assigning said award and awards to the holder of this mortgage, free, clear and discharged of any encumbrances of any kind or nature whatsoever.

and the mortgagor covenants with the mortgagee as follows:

1. That the mortgagor will pay the indebtedness as hereinbefore provided.

2. That no building on the premises shall be altered, removed or demolished without the consent of the mortgagee.

3. That the mortgagor will pay all taxes, assessments or water rates and in default thereof the mortgagee may pay the same.

4. That the mortgagor warrants the title to the premises.

[1] Because of differences in practice in the various states, it is suggested that forms in common use in the state where the property is located be procured from a lawyer or a legal stationer and used for specific transactions. This form is only a suggested one; it is in current use in New York.

5. That the mortgagor will keep the buildings on the premises insured against loss by fire for the benefit of the mortgagee; that he will assign and deliver the policies to the mortgagee; and that he will reimburse the mortgagee for any premiums paid for insurance made by the mortgagee on the mortgagor's default in so insuring the buildings or in so assigning and delivering the policies. The mortgagee is authorized, at its option, to collect, adjust and compromise any loss under any policies on said property and to apply the net proceeds, at its option, either as a credit on the mortgage debt or to restoring the improvements, or to deliver the same to the owner of said mortgaged premises.

6. That the mortgagor will, upon ten days' written demand by the mortgagee, deliver to the mortgagee receipted bills showing the payment of all taxes, assessments and water rates, and if such receipted bills are not delivered within said ten days, then all taxes, assessments and water rates appearing to be unpaid on the books of any officer for the collection of any such items shall be conclusively deemed to be unpaid, and all defenses of payment of any such items are hereby waived.

7. That the whole of said principal sum and interest shall become due, at the option of the mortgagee, after default in the payment of any instalment of principal for ten days, or after default in the payment of interest for fifteen days, or after default in the payment of any tax, assessment or water rate (including future instalments of assessments confirmed, whether said future instalments are liens or not) for thirty days after the same become payable, anything hereinbefore contained to the contrary notwithstanding, or immediately upon the actual or threatened alteration, removal or demolition of any building standing on the mortgaged premises, or after default after notice and demand either in assigning and delivering the policies insuring the buildings against loss by fire or in reimbursing the mortgagee for premiums paid on such insurance, as hereinbefore provided; or after default upon request in furnishing a statement of the amount due on the mortgage and whether any offsets or defenses exist against the mortgage debt, as hereinafter provided.

8. That in the event of a foreclosure of this mortgage said premises may be sold in one parcel, any provision of law to the contrary notwithstanding.

9. The rents, issues and profits of said mortgaged premises are hereby transferred and assigned to the mortgagee as further security for the payment of said indebtedness, and the mortgagor, for himself, his heirs and all subsequent owners of said premises, grants to the mortgagee license to enter upon said premises for the purpose of collecting the same and to let said premises or any part thereof, and to apply the rents, issues and profits, after payment of all necessary charges and expenses, on account of said indebtedness. This assignment and grant shall continue in effect until this mortgage is paid. The mortgagee hereby waives the right to enter upon said premises for the purpose of collecting said rents, issues and profits, and the mortgagor and any subsequent owner of said premises shall be entitled to collect and receive said rents, issues and profits until default under the covenants, conditions and agreements contained in this mortgage or the bond hereby secured, and the mortgagor for himself, his heirs, and all subsequent owners of said premises, covenants to use such rents, issues and profits in payment of principal and interest becoming due on this mortgage and in payment of taxes and carrying charges becoming due against said premises, but such right of the mortgagor and any subsequent owner to collect said rents, issues and profits may be revoked by the mortgagee upon any default, on five days' written notice. The mortgagor for himself, his heirs, and all subsequent owners of said premises, covenants that he will not, without the written consent of the mortgagee, receive or collect rent from any tenant of said premises or any part thereof for a period of more than one month in advance, and in the event of any default under this mortgage or the bond hereby secured, will pay monthly in advance to the mortgagee, or to any receiver appointed to collect said rents, issues and profits, the fair and reasonable rental value for the use and occupation of said premises or of such part thereof as may be in the possession of the mortgagor, his heirs, or any subsequent owner of said premises, and upon default in any such payment will vacate and surrender the possession of said premises to the mortgagee. The covenants con-

tained in this paragraph shall run with the land and bind the mortgagor, his heirs and all subsequent owners, tenants, sub-tenants and assigns of said premises or any part thereof.

10. That neither the value of the mortgaged premises nor the lien of this mortgage will be diminished or impaired in any way by any act or omission of the mortgagor, and that said mortgagor will not do or permit to be done to, in, upon or about said premises or any part thereof, anything that may in any wise substantially impair the value thereof, or substantially weaken, diminish or impair the security of this mortgage. This covenant shall run with the land and bind the mortgagor, his heirs and all subsequent owners of said premises.

11. That the whole of said principal sum shall become due at the option of the mortgagee if the buildings on said premises are not maintained in reasonably good repair, after notice of the condition of the building is given to the mortgagor, or upon the failure of any owner of said premises to comply with the requirements of any governmental department claiming jurisdiction within three months after an order making such requirements has been issued by any such department, or upon the failure of any owner of said premises or any person holding under said owner as tenant, lessee, or otherwise, to comply with all statutes, orders, requirements or decrees relating to said premises by any Federal, state or municipal authority.

12. That the mortgagee in any action to foreclose this mortgage shall be entitled, without regard to the adequacy of any security for the debt and without notice, to the appointment of a receiver.

13. That in the event of the passage of any law changing in any way the laws for the taxation of mortgages or debts secured by mortgage for state or local purposes, this mortgage shall, at the option of the mortgagee, become due and payable after thirty days' written notice to the mortgagor.

14. If any action or proceeding be commenced (except an action to foreclose this mortgage or to collect the debt secured thereby), to which action or proceeding the holder of this mortgage is made a party, or in which it becomes necessary to defend or uphold the lien of this mortgage, all sums paid by the holder of this mortgage for the expense of any litigation to prosecute or defend the rights and lien created by this mortgage (including reasonable counsel fees), shall be paid by the mortgagor, together with interest thereon at the rate of six per centum per annum, and any such sum and the interest thereon shall be a lien on said premises, prior to any right, or title to, interest in or claim upon said premises attaching or accruing subsequent to the lien of this mortgage, and shall be deemed to be secured by this mortgage and by the bond which it secures. In any action or proceeding to foreclose this mortgage, or to recover or collect the debt secured thereby, the provisions of law respecting the recovery of costs, disbursements and allowances shall prevail unaffected by this covenant.

15. That the mortgagor will receive the advances secured by this mortgage and will hold the right to receive such advances as a trust fund to be applied first for the purpose of paying the cost of improvement, and that he will apply the same first to the payment of the cost of improvement before using any part of the total of the same for any other purpose.

16. That the mortgagor within five days upon request in person or within ten days upon request by mail will furnish a written statement duly acknowledged of the amount due on this mortgage and whether any offsets or defenses exist against the mortgage debt.

17. That notice and demand or request may be in writing and may be served in person or by mail.

If more than one person joins in the execution of this mortgage, and if any be of the feminine sex, or if this mortgage is executed by a corporation, the relative words herein shall be read as if written in the plural, or in the feminine or neuter gender, as the case may be, and the words "mortgagor" and "mortagee" where used herein shall be construed to include their and each of their heirs, executors, administrators, successors and assigns.

In witness whereof, this mortgage has been duly executed by the mortgagor.

(Signed) John Doe (seal)

In presence of:

(2 witnesses)

> (Acknowledgment)

BOND SECURED BY MORTGAGE[1]

Know all men by these presents, that hereinafter designated as the obligor ——— do ——— hereby acknowledge ——— to be ——— justly indebted to ——— hereinafter designated as the obligee, in the sum of ——— Dollars, lawful money of the United States, which sum ——— said obligor ——— do ——— hereby ——— covenant to pay to said obligee, ——— or assigns, ——— with interest thereon to be computed from the date hereof, at the rate of ——— per centum per annum, and to be paid on the ——— day of ——— next ensuing, and

It is hereby expressly agreed that the whole of said principal sum and interest shall become due, at the option of said obligee, after default in the payment of any instalment of principal for ten days, or after default in the payment of interest for fifteen days, or after default in the payment of any tax, assessment or water rate (including future instalments of assessments confirmed, whether said future instalments are liens or not) for thirty days after same become payable, or immediately upon the actual or threatened alteration, demolition or removal of any building standing on the mortgaged premises or after default after notice and demand either in assigning and delivering policies insuring the buildings against loss by fire or in reimbursing the mortgagee for premiums paid on such insurance; or after default upon request in furnishing a statement of the amount due on the mortgage and whether any offsets or defenses exist against the mortgage debt.

And it is further expressly agreed that the obligation of this bond shall continue until said indebtedness shall be fully paid notwithstanding any waiver by the obligee of any breach of any condition or covenant of this bond or of the mortgage accompanying the same and notwithstanding any action to foreclose said mortgage and/or the settlement and/or discontinuance of such action and regardless of whether the due date of this bond shall have been extended or the terms modified by such settlement and/or discontinuance.

All the covenants and agreements contained in the mortgage covering the premises therein described and collateral hereto, are hereby made part of this instrument.

Signed and sealed this ——— day of ———.

In presence of

John Doe (seal)

> (Acknowledgment)

CHATTEL MORTGAGES

A chattel mortgage is a *conveyance of a legal or equitable right in personal property,* as security for the payment of money. In some states it operates to pass legal title of the property to the mortgagee, but in other states it merely creates a lien.

Any kind of personal property can be the subject of a chattel mortgage. There must be consideration for a chattel mortgage.

Unless required by statute, no particular form of words is necessary to create a chattel mortgage, and any language is sufficient if it indicates an intention to create a lien on personal property to secure payment of a debt.

The chattel mortgage must (1) describe the property and its location; and (2)

---

[1] Because of differences of practice in the various states, it is suggested that forms in common use in the state where the property is located be procured from a lawyer or a legal stationer and used for specific transactions. This form is only a suggested one; it is in current use in New York.

state the amount of indebtedness, and when and how it is payable. The instrument must be executed and filed in accordance with statutory provisions to be valid and effective against third persons, but not between the mortgagor and mortgagee.

The generally accepted rule is that legal title to the mortgaged property is vested in the mortgagee on default by the mortgagor.

Prior to default, in the absence of statute or agreement between the parties, the general rule is that the mortgagee has the right to possession, but in some states the courts have decided that the right of possession is vested in the mortgagor. A mortgagor in possession must not impair the rights of the mortgagee.

When the mortgagor complies with the terms of the chattel mortgage, it is discharged and, generally, a satisfaction is signed by the mortgagee and filed in the same office in which the chattel mortgage was filed. If the debt is not paid, the mortgagee may foreclose the chattel mortgage and out of the net proceeds of the sale of the mortgaged goods satisfy the debt; he must remit the surplus, if any, to the mortgagor. Generally, the procedure to foreclose is regulated by statute, which also provides in what manner the sale is to be conducted.

MORTGAGE ON GOODS OR CHATTELS[1]

To all to whom these presents shall come, know ye that, I, JOHN DOE, of No. ———— ———— Street, (City), (State), party of the first part, for securing the payment of the money hereinafter mentioned, and in consideration of the sum of one dollar to me duly paid by RICHARD ROE, of No. ———— ———— Street, (City), (State), party of the second part, at or before the ensealing and delivery of these presents, the receipt whereof is hereby acknowledged, have bargained and sold, and by these presents do grant, bargain and sell unto the said party of the second part, (here insert goods sold) and all other goods and chattels mentioned in the schedule hereunto annexed, and now in the (here insert location of goods) to have and to hold, all and singular the goods and chattels above bargained and sold, or intended so to be, unto the said party of the second part, his executors, administrators and assigns forever. And JOHN DOE the said party of the first part, for his heirs, executors and administrators, all and singular the said goods and chattels above bargained and sold unto the said party of the second part, his heirs, executors, administrators and assigns, against JOHN DOE the said party of the first part and against all and every person or persons whomsoever, shall and will warrant, and forever defend. Upon condition, that if JOHN DOE the said party of the first part, shall and do well and truly pay unto the said party of the second part, his executors, administrators or assigns, (here insert the sum of money owing, the time of payment, rate of interest, interest dates, etc.), then these presents shall be void. And JOHN DOE the said party of the first part, for his executors, administrators and assigns, does covenant and agree to and with the said party of the second part, his executors, administrators and assigns, that in case default shall be made in the payment of the said sum above mentioned, or any part thereof then it shall and may be lawful for, and JOHN DOE the said party of the first part, does hereby authorize and empower the said party of the second part, his executors, administrators and assigns, with the aid and assistance of any person or persons, to enter his dwelling-house, store, and other premises, and such other place or places as the said goods or chattels are or may be placed, and take and carry away the said goods or chattels, and to sell and dispose of the same for the best price they can obtain; and out of the money arising therefrom, to retain and pay the said sum above mentioned, including interest, cost of sale, etc., and all charges touching the same; rendering the overplus (if any) unto JOHN DOE or to his executors, administrators or assigns. And until default be made in the payment of the said sum of money it is understood and agreed that JOHN DOE is to remain and continue in the quiet and peaceable possession of the said goods and chattels, and the full and free enjoyment of the same. If from any cause said

[1]This is only a suggested form. The reader is advised to obtain a blank form, valid in his state, from a lawyer or a legal stationer for use in specific transactions.

property shall fail to satisfy said debt, interest, costs and charges, the said JOHN DOE, party of the first part, covenants and agrees to pay the deficiency.

In witness whereof, JOHN DOE, the said party of the first part, has hereunto set his hand and seal the ———— day of ———— one thousand nine hundred ————. Sealed and delivered in the presence of

(Signed) John Doe (seal)

(Acknowledgment)

(Here follows the schedule referred to in the contract.)

LEASES

A lease is a *contract for the use and possession of real estate* for a specified period of time; it requires the *lessee,* or tenant, to pay the *lessor,* or landlord, an agreed rental. A lease for more than one year is void unless the contract, or some note or memorandum thereof, expressing the consideration, is in writing subscribed and not merely signed by the party to be charged, or by his lawful agent, whose authority must be in writing. In some states leases for more than a specified number of years must be recorded.

Generally the rights, duties, and obligations of the parties are fixed by the terms of the lease after preliminary negotiations.

In the absence of agreement, the landlord does not warrant that the leased premises are fit for use and occupancy.[1] This is a matter to be determined by the tenant after inspection.

If there is no express prohibition against assignment or subleasing, the tenant may do so without the landlord's consent. Most leases, however, prohibit that this be done; when it is permitted, the lease generally provides that the original tenant shall remain liable for the payment of rent and the other terms of the lease, notwithstanding the assignment or subletting.

The shortage of space for housing and business purposes prevalent since World War II has led Congress and most states to pass statutes regulating and controlling the rights of owners and occupants of such space. The state statutes are not uniform. The primary purposes of all these statutes are (1) to prevent landlords from evicting tenants after the expiration of their leases; (2) to fix maximum rentals; and (3) to establish procedures for procuring increases or decreases in rent.

These statutes, as originally passed or later amended, have been held constitutional.

LEASE OF AN OFFICE OR LOFT BUILDING[2]

Agreement, made this ———— day of ———— nineteen hundred and ———— *between* ———— hereinafter designated as the Landlord, and ———— hereinafter designated as the Tenant, *Witnesseth,* that the said Landlord does hereby let unto the said Tenant, and the said Tenant does hereby hire from the said Landlord ———— Borough of ———— New York City, to be used and occupied for the business of ———— for the term of ———— to commence on the ———— day of ———— and to end at nine o'clock in the forenoon on the ———— day of ———— at the yearly rent of ———— lawful money of the United States, payable as follows: ————.

The above letting is upon the following conditions, all and every one of which said Tenant covenants and agrees to and with said Landlord to keep and perform.

First: Neither the Tenant nor his heirs, executors or administrators shall assign or encumber this lease, and the said premises, or any part thereof, shall not be let or underlet, nor used or <u>permitted to be used</u>, for any purpose other than

---

[1] Some states have enacted statutes to the contrary.

[2] This is only a suggested form. The reader is advised to obtain a blank form, valid in his state, from a lawyer or legal stationer for use in specific transactions.

above mentioned, nor by any other person without the written consent of said Landlord.

Second: The Tenant shall take good care of the premises and fixtures, make good any injury or breakage done by such Tenant or any agents, clerks, servants, or visitors, and shall quit and surrender said premises, at the end of said term, in as good condition as the reasonable use thereof will permit; and shall not make any additions, alterations, or improvements in said premises, nor permit any additional lock or fastening on any door, without the written consent of the Landlord; and all alterations, partitions, additions, or improvements which may be made by either of the parties hereto upon the premises, except movable office furniture other than partitions, put in at the expense of the Tenant, shall be the property of the Landlord, and shall remain upon and be surrendered with the premises, as a part thereof, at the termination of this lease, without disturbance, molestation, or injury, but injury caused by moving said movable furniture in or out shall be repaired at the expense of the Tenant.

Third: In case of damage, by fire, or other action of the elements, to the demised premises, the Landlord shall repair the same with all reasonable dispatch, after notice of the damage. But in case the building generally throughout (though the herein demised premises may not be affected) be so injured or destroyed that the Landlord shall decide, within a reasonable time, to rebuild or reconstruct the said building, then this agreement shall cease and come to an end, and the rent be apportioned and paid up to the time of such injury or destruction, provided, however, that such damage or destruction as hereinbefore mentioned be not caused by the carelessness, negligence, or improper conduct of the Tenant, agents, or servants. No claim for compensation shall be made by the Tenant by reason of inconvenience, damage, or annoyance arising from the necessity of repairing any portion of the building, however the necessity may occur.

Fourth: The Landlord agrees to use due diligence in operating the elevators in said building, and in furnishing steam for heating the premises between October 15 and April 15 in each year, during the hours between 8 o'clock A.M. and 6 o'clock P.M., Sundays and Holidays excepted; but it is expressly agreed that if the operation of the elevators, or the furnishing of steam heat ———— shall cease by reason of accident, strike, repairs, cleaning out boilers, alterations or improvements to be made or done to any part of the apparatus or appurtenances belonging thereto, or any cause beyond the control of the Landlord, the obligations of the Tenant under the terms of this lease shall not be affected thereby, nor shall any claim accrue to the Tenant by reason thereof.

Fifth: The Landlord shall not be liable for any damage or injury to the demised premises, for goods, wares, merchandise, or property of the Tenant contained therein, by reason of any damage done or occasioned by or from electric wiring, plumbing, water, gas, steam or other pipes, or sewage or the breaking of any electric wire, the bursting, leaking or running of water from any cistern, tank, washstand, water closet or waste pipe, radiator or any other pipe, in, above, upon, or about said building or premises; nor for any damage occasioned by electricity, or water, snow, or ice being upon or coming through the roof, skylight, trap door, or otherwise, or for any damages or injuries arising from acts or neglect of the cotenants, or occupants of the same building, or of any owners or occupants of adjacent or contiguous property, or any other cause.

Sixth: The following RULES AND REGULATIONS shall be faithfully observed and performed by the Tenant and the clerks, servants, and agents of such Tenant, to wit:

(a) The sidewalks, entry, halls, passages, staircases, and elevators shall not be obstructed, nor used for any other purpose than for ingress and egress, nor shall any property of any kind be moved in or out of the building between 9 o'clock A.M., and 5 o'clock P.M.

(b) The toilet rooms, water closets, urinals, and other water apparatus shall not be used for any purposes other than those for which they were constructed, and no improper substance or articles shall be thrown therein, nor shall any faucet be left open nor any water wasted.

(c) The sashes, sash doors, windows, glass doors, and any skylights that reflect or admit light in to the halls or other places of said building shall not be covered or obstructed.

(d) No one shall mark, paint, or drill into, or in any way deface the walls, ceilings, partitions, floors, wood, stone or iron work; and no nails, hooks, or screws shall be driven or inserted in any part of the walls or woodwork of said building.

(e) If Tenants desire telegraphic or telephone connections, the Landlord will direct the electricians as to where and how the wires are to be introduced; and without such direction no boring or cutting for wires will be permitted.

(f) No sign, advertisement, notice, or device shall be inscribed, painted or affixed on any part of the outside or inside of said building, except of such color, size, and style or in such places upon or in said building, as shall be first designated by said Landlord.

(g) All lettering on doors or windows shall be ordered and done by the Landlord's painter at the expense of the lessee.

(h) No machinery of any kind will be allowed to be operated on the premises without the written consent of the Landlord.

(i) No Tenant shall do or permit anything to be done in said premises, or bring or keep anything therein, or permit anything to be brought or kept therein, which shall in any way increase the rate of fire insurance on said building, or on the property kept therein; nor use the demised premises, or any part thereof, nor suffer or permit their use in any business of such a character as to increase the rate of fire insurance on said building or on the property kept therein.

(j) The Tenant covenants and agrees not to do or permit anything to be done in or about said premises, or bring or keep anything therein, or permit anything to be brought or kept therein, which shall in any way conflict with the orders, ordinances, regulations, or rules of the state or any department thereof, the municipality of the City of New York, or any department thereof, or of any public or municipal authority, or of the New York Board of Fire Underwriters, or the requirements of any policy of fire insurance upon said building, or upon any property contained therein.

(k) The Landlord shall have the power to prescribe the weight and position of iron safes; and they shall, in all cases, stand on two-inch-thick strips to distribute the weight; and all damage done to the building by taking in or putting out a safe, or during the time it is in or on the premises, shall be repaired at the expense of the Tenant. Safes shall be moved only after 5 o'clock P.M.; and no safe will be allowed to be moved upon the elevators; and safes shall only be moved by competent persons acceptable to the Landlord.

(l) The Landlord shall not be responsible to any Tenant or other person for any loss of property from said leased premises, or damage done to furniture or effects, however occurring, whether said loss or damage occur or be done through or by any employees, or by any other person whatsoever.

(m) The Landlord shall have the right to enter any of the leased rooms, at reasonable hours in the day, to exhibit the same to applicants to hire, and to put up upon them the usual notice "To Let," which said notice shall not be removed by any Tenant during the six months next preceding the time of expiration of the lease of the premises.

(n) Nothing shall be thrown by the Tenants, their clerks or servants, out of the windows or doors, or down the passages of the building, and Tenants shall not make or permit any improper noises in the building, or interfere in any way with other Tenants, or those having business with them. Nor shall any animals or birds be brought or kept in or about the building.

(o) The lessee shall not use the premises, or any part thereof, nor permit the same to be used for the business of stenography, typewriting, or other copying or similar occupation, nor permit any employee to carry on such business in or from the premises.

(p) The use of the elevator for moving purposes is subject to the consent of the Landlord and first to be obtained therefor.

(q) No illuminating oil or fluid shall be used or kept on the premises, and no stove or other heating apparatus employed in the rooms; nor shall any shades be used other than those supplied by the lessor, or awning permitted, unless first approved by the lessor.

(r) The Landlord reserves the right to make such further rules and regulations as, in the judgment of the Landlord, may from time to time be needful for the safety and protection of the premises and its care and cleanliness, and for the preservation of good order therein, which rules and regulations when so made shall have the same force and effect as if originally made a part of this lease.

Seventh: The Tenant agrees that the Landlord and representatives shall have the right, during the term, to enter into and upon said premises, or any part thereof, or any part of said building, at all reasonable hours, for the purpose of inspecting the same, to see that the covenants on the part of the Tenant are being kept and performed; and of examining the same, or making such repairs, alterations, additions, or improvements therein as may be necessary for the safety, preservation, or improvement thereof, or which the Landlord may for any reason deem desirable. But the Tenant shall not be entitled to any damages or rebate on account of the making of any repairs, alterations, improvements or enlargements of said building, nor shall the Tenant be relieved from liability under this lease in consequence thereof.

Eighth: The Tenant having deposited with the Landlord the sum of ———— dollars, as security for the payment of the rent and performance of the covenants herein contained on the part of the Tenant, and as an inducement to the Landlord to enter this lease upon the terms and covenants herein contained, it is expressly understood and agreed that for special and peculiar reasons applicable to this lease, the Landlord shall be entitled to hold and retain the said deposit in the event of any breach on the part of the Tenant in respect to any of the covenants herein contained, without regard to the amount of damage suffered by the Landlord in consequence of such breach; but that if the Tenant shall carry out and perform all the covenants and agreements required to be carried out and performed by the Tenant, then at the expiration of the time herein limited for the term of this lease the said deposit shall be returned to the said Tenant.

Ninth: It is further agreed that, in case the said demised premises shall be deserted or vacated, or in the event of the insolvency of the Tenant, either before or after the commencement of the term, or if default shall be made in the payment of rent, or any part thereof, at the time specified herein, or if default shall be made in the performance of any of the covenants and agreements, conditions, rules, and regulations herein contained or hereafter established, as herein provided, on the part of the Tenant, this lease shall (if the Landlord so elect) become null and void thereupon, and the Landlord shall have the right to re-enter or repossess the said premises, either by force, summary proceedings, surrender, or otherwise, and dispossess and remove therefrom the Tenant, or other occupants thereof, and their effects, without being liable to any prosecution therefor, and to hold the same as if this lease had not been made; and, in such case, the Landlord may, at his option, relet the premises, or any part thereof, as the agent of the Tenant; and the Tenant agrees to pay the Landlord the difference, as ascertained, from time to time, between the rents and sums hereby reserved and agreed to be paid by the Tenant and those otherwise received, on account of rents of the demised premises, during the residue of the term remaining at the time of re-entry or repossession. The Tenant hereby expressly waives the service of notice of intention to re-enter, or of instituting legal proceedings to that end. The Tenant waives and will waive all right to trial by jury in any summary proceeding hereafter instituted by the Landlord against the Tenant in respect to the demised premises. The Tenant waives all rights to redeem under §1437 of the Civil Practice Act.

Tenth: In addition to any other legal remedies, for violation, or attempted or threatened violation, by or on the part of the Tenant or any one holding or claiming under him, of any of the covenants herein contained, the same shall, in addition to all other legal remedies, be restrainable by injunction.

Eleventh: The said Landlord covenants that the said Tenant, on paying the said yearly rent, and performing the covenants aforesaid, shall and may peaceably and quietly have, hold, and enjoy the said demised premises for the term aforesaid.

Twelfth: The consent of the Landlord, in any instance, to any variation of the terms of this lease, or the receipt of rent with knowledge of any breach, shall not be deemed to be a waiver as to any breach of any covenant or condition herein contained, nor shall any waiver be claimed as to any provision of this lease unless the same be in writing, signed by the Landlord or his authorized agent. This instrument may not be changed orally.

Thirteenth: This lease shall be subordinate to any mortgage or mortgages which shall, at any time, or from time to time, be placed upon said premises, or any part thereof.

Fourteenth: The covenants herein contained shall bind and inure to the benefit of the parties hereto, and their respective successors, heirs, executors, and administrators.

In witness whereof, the parties have interchangeably set their hands and seals or caused these presents to be signed by their proper corporate officers and caused their proper corporate seals to be hereto affixed the day and year first above written.
Signed, sealed, and delivered in
    the presence of
    (Acknowledgments)

LEASE OF AN UNFURNISHED HOUSE[1]

This indenture, made the ———— day of ———— in the year one thousand nine hundred and ———— *between* ———— hereinafter known as Landlord and ———— residing at ———— hereinafter known as Tenant, *Witnesseth,* that the said Landlord has letten, and by these presents does grant, demise and to farm let, unto the said Tenant and the said Tenant has agreed to take and hereby does take from the said Landlord ———— with the appurtenances for the term of ———— to commence at noon on the ———— day of ————, 19— and to end at noon on the ———— day of ————, 19—.

And the said Tenant hereby covenants and agrees that he will pay unto the said Landlord, the ———— rent of ———— dollars payable as follows, viz.: ———— dollars on signing of lease, receipt of which is hereby acknowledged.

And that at the expiration of the said term the said Tenant will quit and surrender the premises hereby demised in as good state and condition as they were in at the commencement of the term, reasonable use and wear thereof and damages by the elements excepted.

And the Landlord does covenant that the said Tenant on paying the said rent, and performing the covenants herein contained shall and may peaceably and quietly have, hold, and enjoy the said demised premises for the term aforesaid.

And the said Tenant covenants that if the said premises, or any part thereof, shall become vacant during the said term, the said Landlord or agents may re-enter the same, either by force or otherwise, without being liable for any prosecution therefor; and relet said premises as the agent of the said Tenant, and receive the rent thereof, applying the same first to the payment of such expenses as the Landlord will be put to in re-entering, and then to the payment of the rent due by these presents; the balance (if any) to be paid over to said Tenant, who shall remain liable for any deficiency.

And the said Tenant hereby further covenants that if any default be made in the payment of said rent, or any part thereof, at the time above specified, or if any default be made in the performance of any other covenants or agreements herein contained, the said hiring, and the relation of Landlord and Tenant, at the option of said Landlord shall wholly cease and determine; and the said Landlord shall and may re-enter said premises, and remove all persons therefrom; and the said Tenant hereby expressly waives the service of any notice in writing of intention to re-enter, as provided for in the third section of an act entitled "An Act to Abolish Distress for Rent, and for Other Purposes," passed May 31, 1846.

It is understood and agreed, between the parties hereto:

[1] This is only a suggested form. The reader is advised to obtain blank forms, valid in his state, from a lawyer or legal stationer for use in specific transactions.

First: That the Tenant will pay all charges for water, electricity, telephone, and gas used during the term of this lease or any renewal thereof.

Second: That during the last three months of this lease or any renewal thereof, the Landlord or his agent, shall have the privilege of displaying the usual "For Sale" and "To Let" signs on the premises and to show the property to prospective purchasers or tenants.

Third: That in case the Tenant has the privilege of renewing this lease, the Tenant shall give notice in writing to the broker or Landlord of his intention at least three months prior to the expiration hereof.

Fourth: That the Tenant shall use the premises hereby leased exclusively for a private residence, and that the Tenant will not, without the consent of the Landlord, assign this lease, nor let or underlet the whole or any part of the said premises, nor make any alterations therein or thereupon under the penalty of forfeiture and damage.

Fifth: That if the said premises or any part thereof shall, during said term or previous thereto, be slightly damaged by fire, the premises shall be promptly repaired by the Landlord and an abatement will be made for the rent corresponding with the time during which and the extent to which said premises may have been untenantable; but if the building or buildings should be so damaged that the Landlord shall decide to rebuild, the term of this lease shall cease and the aggregate rent be paid up to the time of the fire.

Sixth: The Tenant agrees that the Landlord or broker shall have the right to enter into and upon said premises, or any part thereof, at all reasonable hours for the purpose of examining the same, or making such repairs or alterations as may be necessary for the safety and preservation thereof.

Seventh: That the Tenant shall keep the fixtures in said house or on said premises in good order and repair; shall keep the faucets in repair; the furnace, smoke pipe, and flues clean and the electric bells in order, and shall at the Tenant's expense make all required repairs to the plumbing work, range, heating apparatus, and electric light or gas fixtures whenever damage shall have resulted from misuse, waste, or neglect, it being understood that the Landlord is to have same in good order when giving possession.

Eighth: That the Tenant is to comply with all the sanitary laws, ordinances and rules and all orders of the Board of Health or other authorities affecting the cleanliness, occupancy, and preservation thereof for the demised premises and the sidewalks connected to the said premises, during said term of this lease.

Ninth: That the Landlord agrees that the Tenant shall have the free use of all fruit, vegetables, and other products of the premises during the term of this lease, and the Tenant agrees that the Tenant will permit no waste or injury to the trees, shrubbery, or vines or remove same from the premises and that the grounds shall be kept at all times in neat order and condition.

Tenth: That the Landlord agrees that the oil burner shall be clean and in good working condition on giving possession to the Tenant and said Tenant agrees to pay for the annual servicing of the oil burner by a servicing company acceptable to the Landlord.

Eleventh: The Tenant agrees that this lease shall be subject and subordinate to any mortgage or mortgages now on said premises or which any owner of said premises may hereafter at any time elect to place on said premises, and to all advances already made or which may be hereafter made on account of said mortgages, to the full extent of the principal sums secured thereby and interest thereon; and the Tenant agrees upon request to hereafter execute any paper or papers which the counsel for the said Landlord may deem necessary to accomplish that end; and that in default of the Tenant so doing the Landlord is hereby empowered to execute such paper or papers in the name of the Tenant and as the act and deed of the Tenant; and this authority is hereby declared to be coupled with an interest and not revocable.

Twelfth: That the Landlord agrees to deliver the premises to the Tenant in a broom-clean condition, with all rubbish removed, and the Tenant agrees to leave the premises in the same condition upon the termination of this lease.

The covenants and conditions herein contained shall apply to and bind the heirs, executors, and legal representatives of the parties hereto. This instrument may not be changed orally.

In witness whereof, the parties to these presents have hereunto set their hands and seals, the day and year first above written.

In the presence of

. . . .

. . . .

. . . .

LEASE OF AN APARTMENT[1]

This indenture, made the ——— day of ——— in the year one thousand nine hundred and ——— between ——— as Landlord, and ——— as Tenant.

Witnesseth, that the said Landlord has let unto the said Tenant, and the said Tenant has hired from the said Landlord, apartment No. ——— on the ——— floor of the premises known as No. ———, City of ———, County of ———, for the term of ———, commencing on the ——— day of ———, nineteen hundred and ———, and ending on the ——— day of ———, nineteen hundred and ———, at noon, to be used and occupied as a strictly private dwelling apartment for the said Tenant and members of his family only and for no other purpose, at the yearly rental or sum of ——— dollars, payable in equal monthly payments of ——— dollars, in advance on the first day of each and every month during the said term.

First: This lease is granted upon the express condition, however, that in case said Landlord, his agents or assigns, shall deem objectionable or improper any conduct on the part of said Tenant or occupant of said apartment, said Landlord, his agents or assigns may give the Tenant five (5) days notice of said Landlord's intention to terminate this lease and tender return of the rent paid on account of the unexpired term; and upon the expiration of said notice this lease shall terminate as effectually as if such date of expiration were the date fixed herein for its termination; and thereupon said Landlord, his agents or assigns shall have full license and authority to re-enter and have full possession of said premises, either with or without legal process, by means of summary proceedings or any other method prescribed by law; and in consideration of the above letting said Tenant consents that said Landlord, his agents and assigns, shall not be liable to prosecution for damages for so resuming possession of said premises.

Second: The said premises are also leased upon the further covenants and conditions between the parties hereto.

Third: Said Tenant shall take good care of the premises and fixtures, make good any injury or breakage done by the Tenant, servants, or visitors of the Tenant, and any damage caused by the overflow or escape of water, steam, or gas resulting from the negligence of the Tenant, or visitors or servants of the Tenant. The Tenant shall quit and surrender said premises at the end of said term in as good condition as the reasonable use thereof will permit; and shall not make any alterations, additions, or improvements in said premises without the written consent of the said Landlord; and all alterations, additions, or improvements which may be made by either of the parties hereto upon the premises, except movable furniture put in at the expense of the Tenant, shall be the property of the Landlord, and shall remain upon and be surrendered with the premises, as a part thereof, at the termination of this lease, without disturbance, molestation, or injury; but injury caused by moving said movable furniture in and out shall be repaired by the Tenant. That any and all shelves, locks, plumbing fixtures, or any other improvements that the Tenant may place or cause to be placed in the said apartment shall immediately become a part of the house and the property of the Landlord.

Fourth: That the Tenant shall not expose any sign, advertisement, illumination, or projection in or out of the windows or exteriors, or from the said building, or upon or in any place, except such as shall be approved and permitted in writing by the Landlord or his duly authorized agent. Tenant shall only use such shades

---

[1] This is only a suggested form. The reader is advised to obtain a blank form, valid in his state, from a lawyer or a legal stationer for use in specific transactions.

in the front windows as may be approved by the Landlord; and the Tenant shall not keep or maintain any dogs in or about said premises nor permit any other party to keep or maintain therein any dog or domestic animals without the written consent of the Landlord.

Fifth: The Tenant hereby agrees not to assign this agreement, or underlet the premises or any part thereof, or make any alterations in the apartment or premises without the Landlord's or agent's consent in writing, and will not use the said premises, or any part thereof, or permit the same to be used for any other purpose than that of private dwelling apartment for the Tenant and the Tenant's immediate family, or for any purposes deemed extra hazardous on account of fire, under penalty of damages and forfeiture of this lease.

Sixth: That the Tenant shall, in case of fire, give immediate notice thereof to the Landlord, who shall thereupon cause the damage to be repaired as soon as reasonably convenient, and no claim for compensation shall be made by reason of inconvenience, annoyance from loss arising from necessity of repairing any portion of the building; but if the premises be so damaged that the Landlord shall decide to rebuild, the accrued rent shall be paid by the Tenant up to the time of the fire, and the term shall then cease and the Tenant shall immediately surrender said premises and all interest therein to the Landlord.

Seventh: The Tenant agrees to conform to the rules and regulations governing said house, which are printed on this lease and which are made part of this lease, and to any reasonable alterations thereto or new rule or regulation that may be deemed necessary for the protection of the building and the general comfort and welfare of the occupants of the same; and also shall comply with all rules, orders, ordinances, and regulations of the city government, and of any and all its departments and Bureaus applicable to the said premises, and with the requirements of the Board of Fire Underwriters and the Fire Insurance Exchange, which may in anywise relate to or affect the premises hereby leased; and upon default in any of the covenants contained in this paragraph this lease may at the option of the Landlord terminate and the Tenant after five days' written notice shall vacate the premises; and in default thereof the Landlord shall have the right to proceed against the Tenant as a holdover after expiration of the term of the Tenant.

Eighth: That the Landlord is exempt from any and all liability for any damage or injury to person or property caused by or resulting from steam, electricity, gas, water, rain, ice, or snow, or any leak or flow from or into any part of said building, or from any damage or injury resulting or arising from any other cause or happening whatsoever, unless said damage or injury be caused by or be due to the negligence of the Landlord. Said Tenant shall give to said Landlord or agents, prompt written notice of any accident to or defects in the water pipes, gas pipes, or warming apparatus, to be remedied by the Landlord with due diligence.

Ninth: That in case of default in any of the covenants or if the premises become vacant, the Landlord may re-enter by means of summary proceedings or any other method prescribed by law, with or without notice of an intention so to do, and resume possession and relet the premises in his own name, without terminating this lease or in any manner affecting the obligation of the Tenant to pay the rent herein covenanted to be paid; in which event, however, there shall be credited to the account of the Tenant the amount received from reletting after deducting the expenses of such summary or other proceedings as may be necessary in order to regain possession under this provision, as well as the cost of reletting the premises, and repairing and redecorating if any; and the execution of a new lease for the same premises shall not terminate the Tenant's liability or obligations hereunder, which shall in any event remain in full force and effect for the full term of this lease; and a Tenant, who has once vacated may not re-enter without the consent of the Landlord or his agents, and no act or thing done by the Landlord or his agents during the term hereby granted, shall be deemed an acceptance or a surrender of said premises, and no agreement to accept a surrender of said premises shall be valid, unless the same be made in writing and personally subscribed by the Landlord. And the Landlord further reserves the right to rent the premises for a longer period of time than fixed in the original lease without releasing the original Tenant from any liability. The Tenant hereby expressly waives any and all right of redemption in the event the Tenant shall be dispossessed by judgment or warrant, of any court or judge, and the Tenant waives and will waive all right to trial by jury in any summary proceeding hereafter instituted by the Landlord against the Tenant in respect of the demised premises or in any action brought to recover rent or damages hereunder.

Tenth: That the Tenant shall exhibit the premises to prospective tenants daily at reasonable hours during four months prior to the expiration of the lease, and in the event of the Tenant's absence hereby agrees to arrange for such exhibiting of the premises. The Tenant agrees not to interfere with the Landlord's renting to a new Tenant. That the Landlord or his agent shall also be permitted at any time during the term to visit and examine the premises at any reasonable hour of the day, and workmen may enter at any time, when authorized by the Landlord or his agents to make or facilitate repairs in any part of the building; and if the Tenant shall not be personally present to open and permit an entry into said premises, at any time, when for any reason an entry therein shall be in the judgment of the Landlord or his agents necessary or permissible hereunder, for the protection of the building or property therein, or to make such repairs, or to show such apartment to prospective tenants, the Landlord or his agents may forcibly enter the same without rendering himself or them liable to any claim or cause for action for damages by reason thereof without in any manner affecting the obligations and covenants of this lease; it is, however, expressly understood that the right and privilege hereby reserved does not impose, nor does the Landlord assume by reason thereof, any responsibility or liability whatsoever for the care and supervision of said premises, or any of the pipes, fixtures, appliances, or appurtenances therein contained or therewith in any manner connected.

Eleventh: No claim shall be made by, or compensation paid to, the Tenant, family, or servants by reason of inconvenience, annoyance, loss, or damage arising from the necessity of repairing any portion whatsoever of the building, its machinery or appliances, however the necessity may occur.

Twelfth: The Landlord is in no event, liable for any loss of, or damage to, the property of the Tenant, family, servants, or guests, howsoever such damage or loss may arise, and whether such property be contained in the demised premises, in the storage room, or in any other portion of said building or any place appurtenant thereto.

Thirteenth: The Tenant hereby agrees to pay to the Landlord as often as is demanded all charges for telephone service and telephone tolls used by the Tenant; and all such charges shall be added to and considered a part of the rent. If such charges are not immediately paid by the Tenant when the same shall fall due as herein set forth, the Landlord may, at his option, without any notice to said Tenant discontinue such telephone service, and such discontinuance by said Landlord shall in no way affect the obligation of the Tenant under this lease, and the Landlord shall be under no obligation to install telephone service.

Fourteenth: The Landlord will furnish to the Tenant without additional charge, steam heat during the winter months, and hot and cold water; and it is further mutually understood and agreed upon by and between the parties hereto, that in case it shall become necessary or proper at any time, from accident, or for improving the condition or operation of the heating apparatus, plumbing, boilers, machinery, electric plant, or anything appertaining thereto, to omit the operating of said light or heating apparatus or other service, until all necessary repairs or improvements shall have been made and completed, the Landlord shall be at liberty to do the same without in any manner or respect affecting or modifying the obligations or covenants of the said Tenant herein contained, or rendering the Landlord liable for any damage or offset by reason thereof.

Fifteenth: The Tenant agrees that this lease shall be subject and subordinate to any renewal of any mortgage or mortgages now on said premises or any new mortgage or mortgages which any owner of said premises may hereafter at any time elect to place on said premises; and the Tenant agrees, upon request, to hereafter execute any paper or papers which the Landlord may deem necessary to accomplish that end, and in default of the Tenant so doing, that said Landlord be and is hereby empowered to execute such paper or papers in the name of the Tenant, and as the act and deed of said Tenant, and this authority is hereby declared to be coupled with an interest and not revocable.

Sixteenth: That this agreement shall be binding on the heirs, executors, administrators, and assigns of both parties.

Seventeenth: The Landlord acknowledges the receipt of the sum of ———— dollars from the Tenant to be retained by the Landlord as security for the performance by the Tenant of each term, covenant, and condition of this lease on the part of the Tenant to be performed, which said sum of money the Landlord agrees to return to the Tenant at the termination of this lease provided the Tenant has fully complied with all the terms, covenants, and conditions herein contained.

Eighteenth: The Tenant hires said premises after examination, and without any representation on the part of the Landlord, and no representative or agent of said Landlord is authorized to make any representations in reference thereto or to vary or modify this agreement in any way. This instrument contains all the agreements and conditions made between the parties hereto. Any additions thereto, or alterations or changes in this contract, or other agreements hereafter made or conditions created, to be binding, must be in writing signed by both parties; and it is agreed that this provision cannot be waived except by writing, duly signed by the parties hereto.

Nineteenth: It is understood and agreed that the space on the roof is provided by the Landlord of this building to accommodate the Tenants in the airing and drying of clothing, with the express understanding that the space is furnished gratuitously by the Landlord, and the Tenants using the same for any purpose do so at their risk, and with the express stipulation and agreement that the Landlord shall not be liable for any loss of property thereon, nor for any damage or injury whatever.

Twentieth: The obligation of the Tenant to pay the full rent herein reserved shall not be affected by, and the Tenant agrees and hereby does waive the legal effect of any future act or omission on the part of the Landlord with respect to, the tenantability of the premises hereby let, or the building of which they are a part, unless the Tenant shall give to the Landlord or Landlord's agents at his principal place of business immediate written notice of said act or omission and a reasonable time to perform his legal duty with respect to the condition complained of.

Twenty-first: The failure of the Landlord to insist upon strict performance of any of the covenants or conditions of this lease, or to exercise any option herein conferred in any one or more instances, shall not be construed as a waiver or relinquishment for the future of any such covenants, conditions, or options; the same shall be and remain in full force and effect.

Twenty-second: That in the event of a bona fide sale, subject to this lease, the Landlord, or Landlord's assigns, shall have the right to transfer the aforementioned security to the vendee for the benefit of the Tenant, and the Landlord, or Landlord's assigns, shall be considered released by the Tenant from all liability for the return of such security.

Twenty-third: It is further mutually understood and agreed upon by and between the parties hereto, that if the operation of the elevators shall cease by reason of accident, strikes, repairs, alterations, or improvements to be made or done to any part of same or appurtenances thereto, or any cause beyond the control of the Landlord, the obligation of the Tenant under the terms of this lease shall not be affected thereby, nor shall any claim accrue to the Tenant by reason thereof.

Twenty-fourth: That this letting and hiring shall be extended and renewed by and against the parties hereto for the further term of ———— years from the expiration of the term granted hereby, at the same rental without any deduction or concession, and upon all the above terms, conditions, and covenants, unless either party on or before the first day of ———— next preceding the termination of any term granted hereby shall give notice to the other of an intention to surrender or have possession of the premises, as the case may be. Notice by the Landlord to the Tenant must be given by sending the same by United States Registered Mail. Notice by the Tenant to the Landlord must be given by sending the same by United States Registered Mail. This clause shall be and continue operative likewise with respect to any renewals or extensions hereof.

Twenty-fifth: This lease and the obligations of the Tenant to pay rent hereunder and perform all of the other covenants and agreements hereunder on part of the Tenant to be performed shall in nowise be affected, impaired, or excused because the Landlord is unable to supply or is delayed in supplying any service expressly or impliedly to be supplied or is unable to make, or is delayed in making any repairs, additions, alterations, or decorations or is unable to supply or is delayed in supplying any equipment or fixtures if the Landlord is prevented or delayed from so doing by reason of governmental pre-emption in connection with a national emergency declared by the President of the United States, or in connection with any rule, order, or regulation of any department or subdivision thereof of any governmental agency, or by reason of the conditions of supply and demand which have been or are affected by war.

In witness whereof, the parties have interchangeably set their hands and seals or caused these presents to be signed by their proper corporate officers and caused their proper corporate seal to be hereto affixed the day and year first above written. Signed, sealed, and delivered
in the presence of

RULES AND REGULATIONS

1. The front stoop entries, passages, halls, corridors, or stairways shall not be obstructed by any of the tenants, nor be used by them for any purposes except ingress or egress to their respective apartments, and the sidewalks shall not be in any manner obstructed.

2. Tenants shall not incumber the fire escapes or dumb-waiters or place flowerpots or any other articles on the window sills or doorcaps of the building, nor shall they waste nor unreasonably use water supply.

3. All garbage and refuse shall be sent down to the basement from apartments and kitchens at the time called for by the janitor.

4. The water closet and other water apparatus shall not be used for any other purposes than those for which they are constructed, and no sweepings, rubbish, rags, ashes, or other substances shall be thrown therein. Any damage resulting to them from misuse shall be borne by the tenant causing the same.

5. No tenant shall do anything, nor permit anything to be done in the premises, nor bring or keep anything therein, which will in any way increase the rate of fire insurance on the building or on the property kept therein, or conflict with the laws relating to fire.

6. Tenants, or their servants shall not make or permit any unseemly or disturbing noises, nor interfere in any way with other tenants, or those having business with them; nor throw anything out of the windows or doors, or down the dumb-waiter, passages, or skylights of the building; nor mark or defile the water closets, or the walls, windows, and doors of the building.

7. It is understood and agreed that the owner shall be in nowise responsible to any tenant for any loss of property, however occurring, or for any damage done to furniture or other effects by the janitor or any of his employees.

8. No animal shall be kept in or about the premises without the written consent of the landlord or agent.

9. The window shades and awnings for the building are to be kept in good order by the tenants.

10. Servants, except nurses accompanying children, shall have ingress and egress through the basement only, and are not to make entrance or exit by main entrance.

11. Tenant shall give immediate notice to the superintendent of any accident or injury to the water pipes, gas pipes, gas fixtures, or dumb-waiters in the building.

12. Bicycles and baby carriages shall not be taken in or out of the building through main entrance.

13. Hall boys shall not be sent on private messages during hours they are on duty.

14. Hours for closing entrances at night will be fixed and noticed in agent's office, and are to be complied with.

15. No peddlers shall be allowed on the premises.

16. Each tenant must, upon the termination of the within lease, return all keys of the apartments and appurtenances or pay for same.

17. No tenant shall make or permit any disturbing noises in the building by himself, his family, friends, or servants; nor do or permit anything by such person that will interfere with the rights, comforts, or conveniences of other tenants. No tenants shall play upon, or suffer to be played upon, any musical instrument, or operate a radio in the demised premises between the hours of ten o'clock P.M. and the following eight o'clock A.M. if the same shall disturb or annoy other occupants of the building. No tenant shall operate a phonograph or a radio loud-speaker between the hours of ten o'clock P.M. and the following nine o'clock A.M.

LIENS

Liens, or charges upon real or personal property, are of different types. A *common law lien* is the right that a party has to retain possession of personal property of another until a debt secured by such property is paid. A *statutory lien* is created by statute. *Mechanic's liens, garagekeeper's liens, factor's liens, hospital liens*, etc., are statutory. An equitable lien is a right recognized in equity, although not at law, to have property applied in payment of a particular debt. For example, a purchaser of real property who has paid either the whole or part of the purchase price and sues to rescind the contract because of fraud may have a lien declared upon the property in the action brought to recover the money paid, in order that if the judgment is not paid he can enforce the equitable lien against the property.

Liens are also classified as *general* and *special*. A general lien is the right to retain the property of another to secure a balance due from the owner. A special lien is a charge on a particular piece of property, which is held for the payment of a particular debt, in priority to the general debts of the owner.

Lienholders may enforce their liens by sale of the property only after fully complying with the applicable statutes; until then they only have the right to possession.

A lien may be lost by *operation of law,* such as by destruction of the property on which it exists, or if the lien is created by law, by the *death or bankruptcy* of the owner of the property. In some states the lien is discharged if a legal proceeding to enforce it is not instituted within the statutory time. A lien is discharged by payment of the secured debt.

LICENSES

A license is a permission granted by a governmental agency to carry on a business or occupation which, without such license, would be illegal. It is not a contract between the authority (be it Federal, state, or municipal) and the person to whom it is granted; it creates no vested right. Generally, a license fee must be paid to the granting authority. Such licenses are granted for two primary reasons: (1) to protect the public interest through governmental supervision and regulation; (2) to collect taxes.

Some typical businesses and practitioners that must be licensed are: automobile driving schools; banks; businesses of salvage; businesses charging storage fees; liquor businesses; collection agencies; drug stores; bail-bonding companies; insurance companies; theater ticket agencies; engineers; certified accountants; lawyers; dentists; doctors, etc.

A *real estate license* is an authorization by the owner permitting another to do something to the property or to use land for a particular purpose without, however, giving such person an interest in the property. It is merely a personal privilege, and is always revocable. A typical license is the privilege granted by a landlord to a tenant to install a television aerial on the roof of the building or to erect a sign. If such privilege is granted for a consideration, it is not a license. These informal licenses may be written or oral. Such licenses are not assignable.

A licensing agreement with respect to copyrights and patents is a right to make, use, or sell the patented or copyrighted article.

ASSIGNMENT

An assignment is a transfer of property or of any interest from one party to another. Assignments of copyrights or patents are governed by Acts of Congress.

ASSIGNMENT OF PATENT[1]

Whereas, JOHN DOE, of (City), County of —— and State of ——, did obtain Letters Patent of the United States, for an improvement in —— which Letters Patent are numbered —— and bear date the —— day of —— 19—; and *whereas* JOHN DOE is —— now the sole owner of said patent and of all rights under the same; and *whereas* RICHARD ROE, of (City), County of —— and State of ——, is desirous of acquiring

an

   interest in the same;

the entire

Now, therefore, to all whom it may concern, be it known that, for and in consideration of the sum of —— dollars to me the said JOHN DOE in hand paid, the receipt whereof is hereby acknowledged, I, the said JOHN DOE, have sold, assigned, transferred and by these presents do sell, assign and transfer unto the said RICHARD ROE, his executors, administrators and assigns the —— whole right, title, and interest in and to the said invention, described as an improvement in —— and in and to the Letters Patent therefor aforesaid; the same —— to be held and enjoyed by the said RICHARD ROE for his own use and behoof and for the use and behoof of his legal representatives, to the full end of the term for which the said Letters Patent are or may be granted, as fully and entirely as the same would have been held and enjoyed by me had this assignment and sale not been made.

In testimony whereof, I have hereunto set my hand and affixed my seal at (City) in the County of —— and State of —— this —— day of —— 19—.
In presence of: *John Doe* (seal)

ATTACHMENTS

Writ of Attachment. Attachment is a proceeding for the seizure of property before judgment. It is not a common-law right, but is a *statutory* remedy and can be used only as part of a pending action. It does not initiate a law suit, although in proper circumstances it may be obtained before the summons is served. The purpose of this remedy is to enable the creditor to obtain possession of and hold the debtor's property until the recovery of judgment, and thereby prevent him from disposing of it to frustrate the purpose of the action.

Since it is a statutory remedy, it is within the legislative power to determine the actions in which, and the conditions under which, it may be resorted to. It is generally limited to actions brought to recover sums of money arising out of contract. It is ordinarily given to creditors and is available against all debtors, whether corporate or individual.

Statutes generally permit an attachment to issue on the property of a debtor on the ground that he has absconded, or absents himself, or keeps himself concealed for the purpose of defrauding his creditors or of avoiding service of process.

The procedure to obtain a writ of attachment is regulated by statute; and all statutory requirements must be strictly followed. Generally the statutes require

[1] This is only a suggested form. The reader is advised to secure a form from a legal stationer for use in specific transactions.

the creditor-plaintiff to submit an affidavit setting forth the facts to justify the issuance of the writ; and he must furnish a bond to indemnify the debtor for any loss or injury the latter may suffer as a result of the attachment if it proves wrongful.

Generally, all property of the debtor except such property as is exempted by statute is subject to attachment for his debts. Bank deposits, shares of stock, money, fixtures, goods, merchandise, and other personal property may be attached, as well as real property.

Property Exemptions. Most states have specifically exempted certain property from attachment by creditors. The underlying reason for such exemptions is to protect debtors from destitution, which would make them and their families public charges. These exemption statutes are founded on public policy.

In most states certain amounts of wearing apparel, food, household goods and furniture, a mechanic's tools, burial grounds, and a limited amount of life insurance and of wages are exempt.

Garnishment. Garnishment is a statutory proceeding whereby the creditor seeks to obtain payment of his claim from money or property of the debtor which is in the possession of a third person.

A valid and final judgment against the debtor is the basis for the remedy.

In some states the proceeding may not be instituted until an execution on the judgment against the debtor's nonexempt property has been returned unsatisfied.

Wages and salary due the judgment debtor over a certain amount may be garnished, as well as any other property in the hands of third persons which belongs to the judgment debtor.

Body Attachment. A body attachment is an execution against the person of the judgment debtor. This remedy permits the sheriff to arrest the debtor and imprison him until he pays the judgment or it is discharged by law. The proceeding is strictly regulated by statute. It can only issue in certain types of actions, such as those involving embezzlement, misappropriation, fraud, and the like. It is a very drastic remedy and is permissible only as a last resort, when all other remedies have failed to obtain payment.

In some states various classes of persons such as idiots, lunatics, infants, members of the legislature while performing their legislative duties, persons in military service, and females are exempt from arrest on execution.

BAIL

An arrested person prior to trial and a convicted person prior to sentence may, in the court's discretion, obtain his liberty from jail until his trial or until sentence is imposed, by posting bail in an amount fixed by the court.

The object of requiring bail is to compel the defendant to appear in court for trial or sentence. If cash is not available, a bail bond may be furnished. If he fails to appear at the required time the bail is forfeited. The United States Constitution provides that excessive bail shall not be demanded.

BAILMENT

A bailment is the delivery of personal property for a special purpose, the property to be returned to the owner after the purpose has been fulfilled. The person who delivers the property is called a *bailor* and the person to whom it is delivered is called the *bailee*.

There are several kinds of bailment: (1) bailments for the benefit of both parties, as when jewelry is left with another to be exhibited and sold for a commission; (2) bailments for the sole benefit of the bailor, as when goods are temporarily left by the purchaser with the seller and no storage fee is to be paid; and (3) bailments for the sole benefit of the bailee, as when a neighbor borrows a lawn mower for a short period of time and pays nothing for the privilege of using it.

The essence of a bailment is the delivery and acceptance of the subject matter of the bailment. To be valid it must be for a legal purpose. The title to the property always remains with the bailor; the bailee merely has a temporary possessory right.

The *rights, duties,* and *liabilities* of the parties are determined from the express or implied terms of the bailment contract.

When a bailment is for mutual benefit, the bailee, in the absence of special contract, must exercise ordinary care and is responsible for ordinary negligence. Ordinary care is that care and attention which, under the circumstances, a man of ordinary prudence would use if he were dealing with his own property; the want of such care is ordinary negligence. Such a bailee is not an insurer. He is not responsible for losses necessarily incident to the property's use, nor for losses caused by infirmities in the thing itself nor by natural causes, such as fire, storm, or other acts of God.

When a bailment is for the sole benefit of the bailor, the bailee is liable only for gross negligence or bad faith, which is the failure to exercise slight care and caution.

All bailees are responsible for affirmative acts of negligence and fraud. The subject matter of the bailment must be returned to the bailor, and if the bailee refuses to do so after demand, or otherwise misappropriates or converts the property, he is liable to the bailor.

The bailee is not entitled to compensation if the bailment is for the sole benefit of either the bailor or the bailee; he is entitled to reasonable payment in the absence of express or implied agreement in all other cases. All bailees are entitled to repayment of any disbursements necessarily incurred by them in preserving or protecting the subject matter of the bailment.

Bailees who by their skill or labor confer some benefit on the bailed property have a lien thereon for the reasonable value of their services.

The duration of the bailment depends upon the intention of the parties; or, if the bailment is for a limited time, the lapse of such time terminates the bailment.

The liability of certain bailees is regulated and limited by statute. An example is that of hotelkeepers. Generally, they are absolutely responsible for property delivered to their care; but by providing a safe and posting a certain form of notice they may limit their liability to a certain amount of money for a loss if it is not due to their own affirmative negligence.

NEGLIGENCE

Negligence is the failure to exercise the degree of care required by the circumstances of a particular situation. It is measured by the conduct of a reasonable and prudent person. *Actionable negligence, i.e.,* negligence for which legal redress can be obtained, arises only from a violation of duty. It is doing something which duty to another requires not to be done, or failing to do something which duty requires to be done.

There are three *degrees* of negligence: ordinary; slight; and gross. They have been previously defined in the subject matter of bailments.

DEMURRAGE

It is usual to insert a clause in an agreement between the owner of a vessel and a charterer or shipper of merchandise to the effect that a specified number of days shall be allowed for loading or unloading cargo.

Demurrage is the money paid to the owner of a vessel by the charterer or shipper of merchandise by boat for an improper and unreasonable delay in unloading cargo after the expiration of such specified time.

GUARANTY AND SURETY

Guaranty and surety are closely related, guaranty being a form of surety. There are, however, one or two essential differences. A surety is part of a principal contract. It is a direct assumption of responsibility and the surety is liable from the moment the contract is made. If the principal fails, the surety must pay and is not entitled to demand or notice. A guaranty is a collateral contract, separate and distinct from the main contract. The guarantor agrees to pay if the principal cannot, and the creditor cannot approach the guarantor until he has made all reasonable effort to collect from the principal. The guarantor is entitled to demand and notice.

A surety or a guarantor is relieved of his obligations if he was persuaded to assume them through misrepresentation or through concealment of material facts. For warranty, see Contracts.

INSURANCE

Insurance has been defined as "a provision, or contract, by which the risk of pecuniary loss arising from death or personal injury, or from destruction of, or damage to, property owing to perils of any kind to which an individual, the insured, may be exposed, is undertaken by a group of persons or a corporation, called the insurers. As consideration an appropriate premium is paid to the insurers, either in a single sum or by periodical payments."

The contract is called the policy.

The events insured against are called risks or perils.

The thing insured is called the insurable interest.

Marine Insurance. The oldest known form of insurance is marine insurance, which, as its name implies, was originally insurance against perils at sea.

There are two forms of marine insurance: that by which the *owner's interests*, including the body of the ship, are protected, and that by which the *cargo* is protected. Limits are imposed upon the kind of trading that can be done; when these limits are overstepped additional premiums are required.

The ordinary cargo insurance policy protects against perils of the sea, pirates, thieves, jettison, and barratry (breach of trust on the part of the master of the ship resulting in injury to the owner or the cargo of the ship). Further protection must be had through special clauses. In some policies the cargo is protected only after it is actually on the ship; in others it is protected from shipper's to consignee's warehouse. This is partly regulated by custom, the custom varying in different kinds of shipments, and partly by special arrangements of the one holding the insurance policy. Policies may be valued. The value includes freight and insurance charges plus a reasonable profit. For unvalued policies the value must be determined at the time of the loss. A number of policies contain an average clause by which the person taking out the insurance agrees to pay a certain percentage of loss, usually, in American policies, 5 per cent. Other policies are f.p.a. (free from particular average).

Inland marine risks are divided into three groups: (1) domestic shipments; (2) bridges, tunnels, and other instrumentalities of transportation and communication; and (3) personal property floater risks.

The Personal Property Floater covers in one policy loss from fire, windstorm, tornado, smoke, smudge, falling aircraft, vehicular damage, burglary, robbery, larceny, and theft. It covers not only the domicile of the assured, but also his personal property and that of members of his family anywhere in the world.

Other personal floaters featuring the all-risks protection of inland marine insurance cover broadly the kind of items indicated by their titles: camera floater, stamp- and coin-collection floater, fur and jewelry floater, personal effects and articles floater, and musical instruments floater.

Radioactive-contamination insurance is available for risks eligible for inland marine coverage. It is written under a separate form and only in conjunction with an inland marine policy covering the property against loss by other perils.

Fire Insurance. An owner of property, real or personal, or anyone with an insurable interest in property may insure to the extent of his interest. Insurable interest requires that the insured stand in such relation to the property as to be pecuniarily interested in its preservation and directly injured by its destruction. Generally, the standard fire insurance policy in use in the several states insures against direct loss by fire and lightning. It does not cover the risk of fire caused by war, invasion, insurrection, rebellion, revolution, civil war, or usurped power.

By endorsement, known as Extended Coverage Endorsement, the policy may be extended to include direct loss or damage from the perils of windstorm, hail, explosion, riot, riot attending a strike, civil commotion, aircraft, vehicles, and smoke—that is, smoke due to a sudden, unusual, and faulty operation of any heating unit when such unit is connected to a chimney by a smokepipe and is on the premises of the insured. Smoke from fireplaces or industrial apparatus is excluded.

By still another endorsement, the Additional Extended Coverage Endorsement, which is available only for dwellings, the policy may be extended to include direct loss or damage from the perils of water damage, explosion of steam boiler, vandalism and malicious mischief, vehicle damaged by owned vehicles, fall of trees, objects falling from weight of snow, freezing of plumbing, collapse, landslide, and breakage of glass.

The fire policy is the basic coverage contract used in most multiple-line package policies. The package policies are designed for business and dwelling risks alike. The more recent contracts are the home owner's policies, the apartment house owner's policy, the tenant's policy, commercial property coverage, public and institutional property coverage, and the farm owner's property policy. In general, they cover—in addition to the risks related to the fire insurance policy— loss or damage caused by burglars and thieves, and, at the same time cover the insured against his liability hazards arising out of the use of his home or deriving from the operation of his business.

Life Insurance. Life insurance is a means whereby a person may have a portion of his income continued to his dependents after his death, or to himself in his old age. Life insurance premiums are based upon three factors: (1) the expected mortality experience among the individuals insured; (2) the rate of interest which the life insurance company expects to earn on its invested funds; and (3) the costs of operating the insurance company. Premiums are payable in advance, and are paid on an annual, semi-annual, quarterly, or sometimes monthly basis in ordinary insurance. Industrial life insurance premiums are generally collected weekly, or sometimes monthly, at the home of the insured. Industrial life insurance is insurance for amounts usually not over $1,000.

Three types of ordinary insurance are available: (1) Whole Life, with protection being provided throughout life. This may be accomplished by either a *straight life policy,* for which premiums are paid throughout life, or by a *limited-payment policy,* for which the premium payment period is limited to a certain number of years, such as 20 or 30 years; (2) Term Insurance, which provides *temporary protection* for a designated period; the term policy may be *convertible* without medical examination within a specified number of years to either whole life or endowment insurance, or it may be *renewable* without a medical examination at the end of the term, the premium for the renewed policy being higher than that for the original one, since the policyholder is older and his chance of death greater; (3) Endowment Insurance, which provides life insurance protection for a stated period in combination with an increasing savings element; the face amount of the policy is paid to the policyholder at the end of the endowment period.

Life insurance contracts may be terminated: (1) by death, at which time the proceeds are paid to the person the insured designated to receive them (the beneficiary); (2) by maturity as an endowment, when the proceeds are paid to the insured person; (3) by lapse for nonpayment of premium; or (4) within the contestable period, by company proof that the insured committed fraud in procuring the contract. If the insured is unable to continue paying premiums, he may surrender his policy and receive a stipulated cash surrender value.

Instead of surrendering his policy for cash, the insured may apply his cash value to purchase a paid-up policy for a reduced amount of protection, or he may choose an extended term insurance policy which provides protection for the same amount as the original contract, but for a limited period. The policyholder who wishes to keep his insurance in force but who needs funds, may borrow from the accumulated cash value of his policy, the policy itself being the security for the loan.

Upon termination of a policy by death or maturity, the proceeds may be paid in a lump sum or under an optional mode of settlement. The settlement options generally available are those which pay the face value of the contract: (1) periodically for a designated number of years; (2) as a specific amount periodically until the proceeds are exhausted; (3) as a life annuity to the beneficiary. A fourth option specifies that the proceeds are to be held by the company for later disposition, the interest earnings being paid to the beneficiary or added to the fund. Where it is intended to provide for the beneficiary's continued support after the insured dies, it is generally wise to avoid payment of the proceeds in a lump sum, choosing instead an option which will assure the beneficiary an adequate, well-administered, and certain income.

The primary purpose of life insurance is to provide a family with income after the breadwinner's death. Life insurance also provides an excellent medium for saving toward particular goals, such as the accumulation of funds for education of children, for retirement, etc., and is also much used to provide for payment of a debt in case of death.

Business life insurance is life insurance used to protect a business or the family of a businessman from the financial loss which results from the death of someone associated with the business. This gives assurance of business continuity to the firm and full value of business equity to the family of the deceased. There is no basic difference between business life insurance and the life insurance used for personal and family needs—both are insurance on the lives of individuals. The protection set up by business firms, however, involves many more complex details to meet legal, financial, tax, and technical problems. It is, in fact, life insurance custom tailored to the individual business.

Business life insurance is written for a number of specific purposes, chief among which are: (1) key-man protection, to reimburse for loss or provide replacement in the event of the death of a key employee; (2) partnership insurance, to retire a partner's interest at death; (3) corporation insurance, to retire a shareholder's interest at death; and (4) proprietorship insurance, to provide for maintenance of business upon the death of a sole proprietor. Group insurance, usually provided by the employer or business management, is another form of life insurance to protect the family in the event of the death of the breadwinner.

Accident, Health, and Compensation Insurance. Accident and health insurance provides a weekly income to the insured in the event of disability by accident or sickness and a fund to the beneficiary in case of death by accident. Such insurance is closely related to compensation insurance, which covers accidents which occur to employees while at work. The various types of policies include:

1. Ticket policies, which are sold at the ticket offices of airports and railroad stations, and provide for the payment of certain sums if injury by accident occurs within a specified time—a day, a week, a month, 90 days, etc.

2. Limited policies, which cover particular kinds of accidents.

3. General policies, which more or less cover all types of accidents.

4. The newest form of health insurance, which provides for hospitalization and medical expenses, as well as weekly payments during disability.

The most recent form of health insurance is the major medical insurance. It is usually sold on a group basis and provides up to $10,000—even higher in some policies—for nearly any illness or accident to employees or members of their families, usually starting slightly above the level at which a regular health or hospitalization policy stops. The maximum benefit may apply on a per-illness or per-injury basis or to the total amount of expenses for several illnesses. Since major medical benefits apply on an individual basis, the members of one family may receive several times the stated maximum benefit limit of the policy if several family members are stricken at any one time.

Under the group insurance approach, major medical expense protection is offered on either a supplementary or comprehensive basis. On a supplementary basis, catastrophe protection is provided as a complement to basic hospital, surgical, and regular medical expense protection already in existence. There frequently is an uninsured margin of medical expense, say $100, between the basic and supplementary plans.

Comprehensive plans are designed to provide both basic and catastrophe protection to the insured group. These plans are commonly offered with an initial "deductible" amount. The supplementary plans are the most popular. Under both plans, the insurance company pays 75 to 80 per cent of all covered hospital and medical expenses above the deductible amount.

Casualty Insurance and Suretyship. Casualty insurance is written to protect the insured from loss due to injury to his person or property (except losses covered exclusively by life, fire, or marine companies) and from liability for damages for death or injury to the person or property of others. Casualty insurance covers public liability, property damage liability, workmen's compensation, employers' liability, accident and health liability; automobile and aircraft collision; water damage, plate-glass damage; burglary, robbery, and theft; damage to boilers and machinery, and to elevators; animals; check alteration and forgery, and credit insurance.

The surety branch of the business provides fidelity and surety bonds indemnifying against dishonesty of employees, breach of contract, certain bank losses, the failure of public officials to faithfully perform their duties; license bonds; court and fiduciary bonds; and many other types of bonds required by law or used in business transactions.

Automobile Insurance. The most common types of policies covering automobiles are: Liability, Property Damage, and Fire and Theft. Complete protection is assured when Collision insurance is added to these basic coverages.

The Liability policy insures against legal liability "for damages on account of bodily injuries sustained by any person or persons other than the owner or his employees engaged in operating or caring for the automobile, as a result of the ownership, maintenance, use of the automobile covered." The rates for this policy and for the property damage policy depend upon the type of car (private, taxicab, truck, etc.), the territory in which it is to be used (the hazards and therefore the rates being much higher in large cities where there are more people and more cars), the motive power and price of the automobile, and the driver (the cost being less where the owner is the driver).

The usual policy provides a payment of $5,000 for injuries to one person in one accident and $10,000 for injuries to more than one person in one accident, but there are many arguments in favor of larger policies. The company generally agrees to make investigations and settle claims, to pay for immediate surgical care for the injured, to defend the insured in suits, and to pay legal costs, the total liability of the company being limited to the amount on the face of the policy. The policy generally runs for the period of a year. Accidents occurring when the car is subjected to extraordinary use—as in speed contests or, in the case of private automobiles, when they are being operated for hire—are not covered by the ordinary policy and must be made the subject of special arrangements.

The most recent form of automobile insurance is the safe-driver insurance plan, under which motorists pay insurance rates based on their driving records. Under this merit-rating plan, motorists with clear driving records during the immediate past three years receive a discount of 10 to 20 per cent off their liability and collision insurance premiums. Drivers with a record of accidents and serious traffic-violation convictions pay higher rates, ranging from 10 to 150 per cent above the basic rates.

The Property Damage policy provides payment for damage to the property of others not carried in the car covered by the insurance policy. The company's liability is limited to the amount on the face of the policy. The usual policy is for $5,000.

Collision insurance covers damages to the owner's car through collision with a moving or stationary object. Damages are based on either the value of the car or the cost of repair.

There are two kinds of fire insurance policies, valued and unvalued; in the first, the value of the automobile is agreed upon in advance and in the second, the value is determined at the time of the loss.

Under the Comprehensive Fire and Theft policy, the company makes full payment in the case of theft or damage not caused by collision or upset, such as scratching and marring by hail, windstorm, flying objects, etc.

Theft insurance covers only the automobile itself, not its contents.

Aviation Insurance. During recent years aviation risks of every description have been insured under standard forms of policies and at published rates.

Planes are classified in accordance with the use to which they are put, as (1) private business and pleasure; (2) commercial, including or excluding instruction; and (3) scheduled air lines.

Miscellaneous Insurance. There are many other kinds of insurance. Public events may be insured against rain; certain broadcasts are insured against S O S calls. Protection may be had against hail, windstorms, tornadoes, earthquakes, theft, forgery, riots, explosions, and so on through a long list. See also the articles on Workmen's Compensation and Social Security Act.

ANNUITIES

The ends served by annuities and by life insurance are directly opposite. Whereas life insurance is bought in order to create an estate, protecting the insured against the hazard of not living long enough to accumulate an estate through his earnings, annuities are purchased in order to liquidate an already accumulated estate, providing the purchaser with protection against the hazard of outliving his income.

An annuity is, strictly speaking, an annual payment of a definite sum of money. Many annuities, however, are payable semiannually, quarterly, monthly, or even weekly, notwithstanding the definition of annuity.

The person receiving an annuity is called the *annuitant,* and the period during which payments are made is called the *term of the annuity*. In purchasing an annuity, one must pay the present value of all future annuity payments, the present value being the amount which, placed at interest now, will be sufficient to provide the periodic payments when they fall due.

Two general kinds of annuities are most common. One, the *life annuity*, pays a guaranteed income to the annuitant throughout his life, no matter how long he lives. If he dies before the annuity payments have equaled the cost of the annuity, the sum which has not been returned to him is used to provide continued life payments to the annuitants who live to collect much more than the cost of the annuity.

The other most common kind of annuity is an *annuity certain*. An annuity certain provides payments for a specified period. At the end of that period, all payments cease.

One of the most popular forms of annuities sold by life insurance companies is a combination of a life annuity and an annuity certain. This type of annuity provides payments for the life of the annuitant. If the annuitant dies within a specified period, payments continue to a beneficiary until the end of that period.

Deferred annuities are also available. The purpose of these is to permit a person to make deposits with the life insurance company while he is young and still working, the deposits being returned to him as an annuity after he has retired. Either life annuities or annuities certain may be purchased on a deferred basis.

Annuities are frequently purchased by retired persons. They provide an excellent investment for old people because an annuity is much safer than most stocks and bonds and involves no managerial expense, worry, or care to the investor, because the rate of return is the highest commensurate with safety, and because an annuity provides an income which cannot be outlived.

Joint and survivor annuities may be purchased by two persons wishing to provide themselves with an income that neither can outlive. The advantage of this type of contract is that the income payments do not cease at the death of the first person, but continue until the death of the second joint annuitant.

Since each annuity payment to the annuitant consists of a portion of the annuity principal, as well as interest earned on the remaining fund—whereas other investments can provide a life income safely only by restricting payments to interest—the monthly income from annuities is generally much greater than that from other investments. Because of this, a person may invest a portion of his savings in an annuity, devote the balance of the savings to some other use, and still realize as great a return from the annuity portion as he would receive from investing his total savings elsewhere. Thus, people frequently purchase annuities from which they receive a large, regular income, and use the balance of their savings to provide advanced education for their children, to help them get started in business, or to present a sizable gift to a philanthropic, charitable, or educational institution.

Premiums for life annuities are computed on the basis of mortality tables. There are many kinds of annuity tables. The table accompanying this article is one of the most useful. It shows the amount of an annuity certain of $1.00 at the end of each period. To find the amount of an annuity of $15,000, simply multiply the amount of $1.00 for a given period at a given rate. For instance, find the amount of an annuity of $15,000 at 5 per cent for 10 years. Looking at the table, you see that the amount of $1.00 at 5 per cent for 10 years is 12.577893. For practical purposes, let us call it $12.58. Multiplying this by 15,000 we have $188,700, which is the answer. There is no way to calculate the amount of an annuity in perpetuity, since there is no end point from which to work.

In large organizations annuity calculations are done by machines.

TABLE SHOWING AMOUNT OF ANNUITY OF $1.00 AT END OF EACH PERIOD

No. of years	Annual Rates of Interest				
	3 per cent	4 per cent	4-1/2 per cent	5 per cent	6 per cent
1	1.	1.	1.	1.	1.
2	2.03	2.04	2.045	2.05	2.06
3	3.0909	3.1216	3.137025	3.1525	3.1836
4	4.183627	4.246464	4.278191	4.310125	4.374616
5	5.309136	5.416323	5.470710	5.525631	5.637093
6	6.468410	6.632975	6.716892	6.801913	6.975319
7	7.662462	7.898294	8.019152	8.142008	8.393838
8	8.892336	9.214226	9.380014	9.549109	9.897468
9	10.159106	10.582795	10.802114	11.026564	11.491316
10	11.463879	12.006107	12.288209	12.577893	13.180795
11	12.807796	13.486351	13.841179	14.206787	14.971643
12	14.192030	15.025805	15.464032	15.917127	16.869941
13	15.617790	16.626838	17.159913	17.712983	18.882138
14	17.086324	18.291911	18.932109	19.598632	21.015066
15	18.598914	20.023588	20.784054	21.578564	23.275970
16	20.156881	21.824531	22.719337	23.657492	25.672528
17	21.761588	23.697512	24.741707	25.840366	28.212880
18	23.414435	25.645413	26.855084	28.132385	30.905653
19	25.116868	27.671229	29.063562	30.539004	33.759992
20	26.870374	29.778079	31.371423	33.065954	36.785591

EXPECTATION OF LIFE IN THE UNITED STATES[1]

AGE	Total Population	White		Non-White	
		Males	Females	Males	Females
0	69.4	67.2	73.7	60.6	65.5
1	70.4	68.1	74.2	62.8	67.3
5	66.7	64.3	70.5	59.3	63.8
10	61.8	59.5	65.6	54.5	59.0
15	57.0	54.7	60.7	49.7	54.1
20	52.2	50.0	55.9	45.0	49.3
25	47.5	45.4	51.0	40.6	44.6
30	42.8	40.7	46.2	36.3	40.1
35	38.1	36.0	41.4	32.0	35.7
40	33.6	31.5	36.7	28.0	31.5
45	29.1	27.1	32.1	24.1	27.5
50	24.9	22.9	27.6	20.5	23.7
55	21.0	19.2	23.3	17.3	20.3
60	17.3	15.7	19.2	14.5	17.4
65	14.0	12.7	15.4	12.1	14.0
70	11.1	10.1	12.0	10.9	13.1

"BEST" WEIGHT OF MEN AND WOMEN

Many adult Americans are overweight. This represents a serious health condition in view of the known relationship of body weight to health and longevity. Recent actuarial studies have shown that average weights of American men, particularly at the younger ages, are higher than of men a generation ago. The greatest gain in weight with age now occurs when men are between 25 and 40 years. Among women, however, the average weights, particularly at the younger ages, are less than they were, and today's pattern shows little gain in weight for women with increasing age until after 45.

[1] Based on 1958 statistics. Figures denote years.

These findings underscore the need for the younger businessman to be acutely conscious of the importance of weight control. Life insurance studies have consistently shown that overweight men experience a significantly higher mortality rate than those of average or less than average weight. A first step toward weight control is to know one's own best weight. The chart below shows the latest tables of desirable weights (that is, those associated with the lowest mortality).

DESIRABLE WEIGHTS FOR MEN AND WOMEN[1]
According to Height and Frame. Ages 25 and Over

Height (In Shoes)[2]	Weight in Pounds (In Indoor Clothing)		
	Small Frame	Medium Frame	Large Frame
Men			
5' 2"	112–120	118–129	126–141
3"	115–123	121–133	129–144
4"	118–126	124–136	132–148
5"	121–129	127–139	135–152
6"	124–133	130–143	138–156
7"	128–137	134–147	142–161
8"	132–141	138–152	147–166
9"	136–145	142–156	151–170
10"	140–150	146–160	155–174
11"	144–154	150–165	159–179
6' 0"	148–158	154–170	164–184
1"	152–162	158–175	168–189
2"	156–167	162–180	173–194
3"	160–171	167–185	178–199
4"	164–175	172–190	182–204
Women			
4' 10"	92– 98	96–107	104–119
11"	94–101	98–110	106–122
5' 0"	96–104	101–113	109–125
1"	99–107	104–116	112–128
2"	102–110	107–119	115–131
3"	105–113	110–122	118–134
4"	108–116	113–126	121–138
5"	111–119	116–130	125–142
6"	114–123	120–135	129–146
7"	118–127	124–139	133–150
8"	122–131	128–143	137–154
9"	126–135	132–147	141–158
10"	130–140	136–151	145–163
11"	134–144	140–155	149–168
6' 0"	138–148	144–159	153–173

[1] Prepared by the Metropolitan Life Insurance Co. and derived primarily from data of the Build and Blood Pressure Study, 1959, Society of Actuaries.
[2] One-in. heels for men and 2-in. heels for women.

Proper Diet Plus Exercise—The Keys to Weight Control

Physicians hold that the chief cause of overweight is the combination of too much food and too little exercise. When more food is eaten than the body requires, the excess is retained as extra fat. Glandular disturbances are only occasional factors in overweight. Heredity plays some role, but even here changes in family eating customs and the adoption of new eating habits can help individuals from traditionally overweight families to reduce. In pregnancy and middle age, too, attention to calories—the measure in which food values are expressed—plus proper exercise, can prevent the storing up of excess fat. Temperament is sometimes at the root of a weight problem, but frequently many people consume an undue amount of high-calorie foods simply because they are ignorant of what foods provide the best nutrition. The accompanying food plan shows a healthful selection of foods for various age groups and available at moderate cost.

CANNING, QUICK-FREEZING, AND STORING FOOD AT HOME

In the home, as in business, long-range planning frequently results in added efficiency and economy. Many homemakers find it thrifty and labor-saving to can or quick-freeze certain foods when they are in season or low in price, and to serve them later, in season or out.

The housewife who decides to preserve foods by these methods must always remember three important rules: (1) in order to stop the action of enzymes in foods and prevent spoilage by organisms (bacteria, molds, and yeasts) present at all times in air, water, and soil, follow all directions with utmost care; (2) insure success by purchasing only top-quality material and equipment; (3) use sanitary precautions. Hands, food, containers, equipment, and work surfaces should be scrupulously clean.

The general directions given below should be supplemented by booklets available from the United States Department of Agriculture and state agricultural colleges or extension services; these booklets contain scientifically tested, step-by-step directions, and timetables adaptable to all home food-preservation.

Canning Equipment. You will need a steam-pressure canner for poultry, meats, and low-acid vegetables, such as beans and corn; a water-bath canner (any deep vessel of tin, aluminum, enamelware, or galvanized iron, at least 12 in. deep) with a tight-fitting cover for processing tomatoes, fruits, and pickled vegetables; a rack on which to place jars in canner so that they do not touch bottom; glass jars (tins may be used but require a special sealer) and lids; new rubber rings (unless self-sealing type of closure is used); large pan or kettle for hot water; tongs for lifting hot jars; long-handled spoons (wooden, if possible) for stirring; colander; jar funnel; spatula or knife; measuring cups; measuring spoons.

Preliminary Steps. Figure yield of canned food from fresh, in order that you may prepare sufficient number of jars. Examine jars and lids. Discard any with chips, dents, or cracks which would cause breakage. Wash glass jars and lids (except those with sealing compound) in hot, soapy water. Rinse well in hot water. Then keep the jars hot until time to fill them.

Methods. Two canning methods are used today, each suited to specific groups of food. They are (1) boiling-water bath, for processing tomatoes, fruits, and pickled vegetables; (2) steam-pressure canner, absolutely essential for processing poultry and meats, corn, beans, and other common vegetables. For safety's sake these foods require processing at a temperature above that of boiling water, to insure killing heat-resistant bacterial spores which may spoil or produce toxins in low-acid canned foods.

FOOD PLAN AT MODERATE COST[1]

Suggested Weekly Quantities of Food (as Purchased, Assuming Average Choices Within Groups) for 19 Sex-Age Groups

Family members	Milk, cheese, ice cream (Qt.)	Meat, poultry, fish (Lb.)	(Oz.)	Eggs (No.)	Dry beans, peas, nuts (Lb.)	(Oz.)	Flour, cereal, baked goods (Lb.)	(Oz.)	Citrus fruit, tomatoes (Lb.)	(Oz.)	Dark-green and deep-yellow vegetables (Lb.)	(Oz.)	Potatoes (Lb.)	(Oz.)	Other vegetables and fruit (Lb.)	(Oz.)	Fats, oils (Lb.)	(Oz.)	Sugar, sweets (Lb.)	(Oz.)
Children:																				
Under 1 year	6	1	4	6	0	0	0	12	1	8	0	2	0	8	1	8	0	1	0	2
1–3 years	6	1	12	6	0	1	1	0	1	8	0	4	1	12	2	12	0	4	0	4
4–6 years	6	2	4	6	0	1	1	12	2	0	0	4	1	0	4	0	0	6	0	10
7–9 years	6	3	0	7	0	2	2	0	2	4	0	8	1	12	4	12	0	10	0	14
10–12 years	6½	4	0	7	0	4	2	12	2	8	0	12	2	4	5	8	0	10	0	14
Girls:																				
13–15 years	7	4	8	7	0	2	2	12	2	8	0	12	2	4	5	12	0	12	0	14
16–19 years	7	4	4	7	0	2	2	8	2	8	0	12	2	0	5	8	0	10	0	12
Boys:																				
13–15 years	7	4	12	7	0	4	4	0	2	12	0	12	3	0	6	0	0	14	1	0
16–19 years	7	5	8	7	0	6	5	0	3	0	0	12	4	4	6	4	1	2	1	2
Women:																				
20–34 years	3½	4	4	6	0	2	2	4	2	8	0	12	1	8	5	12	0	8	0	14
35–54 years	3½	4	4	6	0	2	2	0	2	8	0	12	1	4	5	4	0	8	0	12
55–74 years	3½	4	4	6	0	2	1	12	2	4	0	12	1	4	4	4	0	6	0	8
75 years and over	3½	3	12	6	0	2	1	12	2	4	0	12	1	0	3	12	0	6	0	8
Pregnant	7	4	0	7	0	2	2	4	3	8	1	8	1	8	5	12	0	8	0	12
Lactating	10	5	0	7	0	2	2	12	5	0	1	8	2	12	6	4	0	12	0	12
Men:																				
20–34 years	3½	5	8	7	0	4	4	0	2	12	0	12	3	0	6	8	1	0	1	4
35–54 years	3½	5	4	7	0	4	3	8	2	12	0	12	2	8	5	12	0	14	1	0
55–74 years	3½	5	0	7	0	2	3	4	2	12	0	12	2	4	5	8	0	12	0	14
75 years and over	3½	5	0	7	0	2	2	12	2	8	0	12	2	0	5	4	0	10	0	12

[1] From "Yearbook of Agriculture," 1959.

Do not try to process foods in the oven. This method not only is inefficient in destroying bacteria but may cause jars to explode.

Do not use open-kettle cooking for canning. The United States Department of Agriculture warns that cooking food in an ordinary kettle, removing it to hot jars, and sealing without processing may permit entry of spoilage organisms. This method is reserved for processing jellies and jams, in which the cooking-down process and concentration of sugar help in preventing spoilage.

Boiling-Water Bath—Steps to Take. Prepare ¾ to 1 cup syrup for each quart jar of fruit. In general, the three types of syrup used are: thin syrup—1 cup sugar to 3 cups water or fruit juice; medium syrup—1 cup sugar to 2 cups water or juice; heavy syrup—1 cup sugar to 1 cup water or juice. Syrup is prepared by boiling for 5 minutes over low flame until sugar dissolves. If fruits are juicy merely add sugar directly to fruit and heat without adding liquid—in this case use about ½ cup sugar to 1 quart fruit. When sugar is scarce replace with mild honey or corn syrup for up to half the sugar required. Sweetening helps preserve color, shape, and flavor but is not needed to prevent spoilage; food may be processed in boiling water and sweetened just before serving.

Sort fruit for size and ripeness; use only firm, fresh fruits, neither too ripe nor too green. Handle only as much as can be processed at one time. Wash carefully, in small quantities, in wire basket or colander. Lift fruit from water; avoid bruising. Repeat, washing several times, rinsing container each time. Dip peaches or tomatoes briefly in boiling water to loosen skins, then dip for a moment in cold water, using wire basket. Peel and prepare fruits or tomatoes as required (coring, pitting, slicing). At this point drop apples, peaches, and apricots into water containing 2 tbs. each of salt and vinegar to the gallon—they should be drained just before heating—to prevent discoloration.

Peaches and tomatoes may be heated or not, as you prefer, before packing and processing. Soft berries, such as red raspberries, are best packed without preheating. Firm berries are best preheated.

For a *hot pack,* place fruit in boiling sugar syrup or boiling water and heat so that fruit is cooked through but not soft. Quarter tomatoes, and bring to boil, stirring often. While food is heating lift clean jars from water; set in shallow, cloth-lined pan; put hot, wet rubber ring on jars requiring ring. Now fill jars. Pack food in loosely, leaving ½ in. space at top of jar. Cover fruit with boiling liquid, filling within ½ in. of jar top. Tomatoes should be packed to ½ in. of top, with ½ tsp. salt for pints, 1 tsp. for quarts. Remove air bubbles by running spatula down sides of jar. As each jar is filled wipe rim and rubber ring with clean, damp cloth and adjust closure.

When all jars are filled place on rack in canner. Fill canner with enough boiling water to reach 1 in. to 2 in. above jars, adding boiling water, if necessary, to maintain this level. Jars should not touch each other. When required processing time is up, remove jars and complete sealing when required. Never open a jar to replace any liquid which may have been lost in processing. To do so would permit entry of bacteria.

Strawberries require a slightly different procedure. To these berries add ½ cup sugar to each quart fruit and bring slowly to a boil; remove from stove and allow to stand overnight. Next day bring quickly to boil, then pack in jars for canning in a boiling-water bath.

For a *cold pack* of peaches, tomatoes, or red raspberries pack the raw food into jars as for hot pack. Add salt but no water to tomatoes. Add boiling syrup to cover fruits.

Steam-Pressure Canner—Steps to Take. Poultry, meats, and all garden vegetables (*except* tomatoes) should be canned this way. The time required for processing varies with each food. Follow manufacturer's directions for care of canner, use, and timing, and make use of supplementary bulletins.

Beef, veal, mutton, lamb, pork, poultry, and game can be canned successfully at home. Do not can mixtures such as hashes and stews, chile con carne, pork and beans, scrapple, cereal, or vegetable soups, etc., unless tested home-canning procedures are available.

Follow these general steps:

Fill canner with 2 to 3 in. of water. Place hot, filled jars on rack, permitting steam to flow freely about each jar. Always fasten canner cover securely so that steam escapes only at open petcock or weighted gauge opening.

When steam begins to escape steadily from opening, permit it to escape for 7 to 10 minutes so that air is forced from canner. Then close petcock and watch pressure gauge until desired number of pounds is reached. Begin specific timing the instant desired pressure is reached. Maintain constant pressure level by regulating stove heat—do not try to regulate pressure by opening petcock.

When processing required for individual food is completed remove canner from heat. Permit canner to stand 1 minute to 2 minutes after pressure has reached zero point. Never hasten cooling by applying cold water or cloths. Open petcock gradually or remove weighted gauge. Unfasten canner cover with extreme care, tilting it far side up, so that steam escapes away from face and hands.

Remove jars. Complete sealing immediately if jars are not self-sealing. As with boiling-water bath, never reopen jars to add liquid which may have been lost during processing.

Canning at High Altitudes. Because the boiling point of water decreases with increasing altitude, those living in elevated regions must allow longer processing time in the water bath, or increased pressures, to reach the temperature (240° F.) which insures the destruction of spoilage organisms in low-acid foods. *Boiling-water bath:* If you live at an altitude of 1,000 ft. or more, for each 1,000 ft. above sea level add 1 minute to processing time for fruits and tomatoes, if time needed is 20 minutes or less. If time needed is 20 minutes or more, add 2 minutes for each 1,000 ft. *Steam-pressure canner:* For meats and low-acid vegetables, increase pressure by 1 lb. for each 2,000 ft. of altitude. You may need to have a weighted gauge regulated for altitude by the manufacturer.

To Close Jars. Several types of glass jars are used for canning, each having a different type of closure. Sealing of the various types is carried out as follows: (1) *Porcelain-lined screw cap with rubber ring,* suitable for standard Mason jar. When rubber-ringed jar is ready for closing, screw cap on tightly, then turn back ¼ in. After jar is taken from canner turn cap back and screw tightly. (2) *Wire bail with glass lid and rubber ring.* When rubber-ringed jar is ready for closing, cover with glass lid. Leaving short wire up, snap long wire over into groove on top of lid. After jar is taken from canner push short wire down. (3) *Flat metal lid edged with sealing compound,* held in place by metal screw band; fits standard Mason jar. When jar is ready for closing, place lid on it with sealing compound resting on jar. Fasten metal band down tightly with hand—never use implement for this. After canning do not tighten further or you may break seal. (4) *Glass lid and rubber ring,* held in place by metal screw band; suitable for standard Mason jar. When jar is ready for closing, fit wet rubber ring on glass lid. Place lid on jar with rubber side down. Screw metal band on tightly, then turn back about ¼ turn, making certain that band and jar mesh. Do not make too tight. After canning screw tightly.

Cooling and Testing Jars. Cool jars overnight, top side up, on thick cloth or paper surface. Keep out of draft. Next day turn jars partly over to test for leaks. To test self-sealing jars tap with spoon, listening for clear, ringing sound denoting complete seal.

Wipe jars. Label with name of contents, date, and, if more than one lot is canned in a day, lot number. Store in cool, dry place where food can neither freeze nor become too warm.

Examine carefully for spoilage before using. Do not use any canned food showing such spoilage signs as bulging can ends, rings, or jar lids; gas bubbles or leakage; spurting liquid, bad odor, or mold when opened. For safety, before tasting *boil* vegetables and meat for 10 minutes. *Warming is not enough.* Destroy any spoiled food by burning or burying deep in the ground to insure that neither man nor animal will eat it.

FREEZING AND STORAGE

Home Freezing Units. Freezing is a highly modern technique of preserving foods which has won many advocates among homemakers. The numerous types of zero storage cabinets available include individual units as small as 3 or 4 cu. ft. in size. Thus, even the small city or town family without access to home-grown produce can save time as well as money by purchasing a supply of commercially frozen food (all-food, with no waste in bone, hulls, etc.) and storing it in the freezer (thereby reducing marketing trips to a minimum), or by purchasing items when plentiful and freezing them at one time. The infinite variety of foods adaptable to home freezing includes cakes, rolls, breads, cooked dishes, and desserts. Ice cream storage is one of the most popular features.

Among the types of freezers on the market are: (1) *Walk-in freezer,* usually a built-in room, although sometimes prefabricated—a large home freezer suited to small farms or estates where quantity storage is called for; (2) *Two-temperature units*—contain ordinary refrigerator space plus a separate freezing compartment of from 1 cu. ft. to 4 cu. ft. The frozen-food compartment here is not to be confused with the ice-cube compartment of the regular automatic refrigerator. The latter is suitable for storing small amounts of frozen food for little more than a week or two; (3) *Top-opening chest*—square, oblong, or cylindrical in shape; and (4) *Upright freezer*—has either front- or side-opening doors.

If your unit is not equipped with a warning device indicating power failure, it is wise to purchase such an alarm and adapt it to your freezer.

Best results with freezers are gained by following manufacturers' directions and using supplementary literature. General directions are given below.

Foods Suitable for Freezing. Most fruits, vegetables, poultry, meats, and fish can be successfully frozen. As in canning, use best-quality food. Cucumbers, endive, lettuce, uncooked celery, radishes, whole tomatoes, and a few others are unsuited to freezing. Work with chilled food—even vegetables which require heating should be chilled before packaging and freezing.

How to Preheat Vegetables. Preheating vegetables for freezing is accomplished by scalding with boiling water or by steaming. This step is necessary to destroy enzymes which would cause food deterioration. Time needed for preheating varies with individual foods.

Wash vegetables thoroughly and peel or cut as if readying for ordinary cooking.

To preheat with boiling water, place vegetables in colander or wire basket with handle, and immerse in large kettle of boiling water. Use 1 gal. of water for each pound of vegetables. Preheat no more than 1 lb. at a time. Start counting time when vegetable is immersed in boiling water. Agitate (to insure even heating) by moving colander or basket to and fro. The boiling-water method is practicable for most vegetables. Broccoli has better flavor when preheated with steam.

To preheat with steam, use a 6- to 12-qt. kettle with a rack placed on bottom. Again, work with no more than 1 lb. of produce at a time. Pour slightly more than 1 in. of water on bottom of kettle. When water reaches rolling boil place colander or basket with vegetables on rack and cover steamer tightly. Begin timing immediately. This method of blanching is especially suited to cut-up vegetables and cut sweet corn.

At 5,000 ft. or more above sea level 1 minute should be added to scalding time.

How to Cool Vegetables After Preheating. Remove container immediately after scalding and plunge it under cold running water or into pan of ice water. Cool vegetables thoroughly before proceeding with packaging.

How to Prepare Fruits. Wash fruits thoroughly. Remove stems or skins and slice if necessary. Peaches and apricots may be peeled as described for canning. Fruits do not require blanching, except in the case of apples, which must be heated by either of the methods described or may be treated with an antidarkening agent.

For protection during storage and thawing most fruits need the addition of dry sugar or cold syrup. In general it is recommended that sugar alone be used on juicy fruits, such as strawberries, which will form their own syrup. The specified proportion of sugar should be sprinkled over fruit and stirred in, preferably with a fork, until berries are covered with juice. Sugar syrup is prepared by mixing sugar and water, or white corn syrup and water, in proportions specified for each fruit. In order to prevent discoloration of peaches, apricots, cherries, plums, and pears, add ½ tsp. ascorbic acid (vitamin C) to syrup for every quart of syrup just before adding to fruit.

Packaging Materials. Numerous packaging materials are available in department and hardware stores. Among the types offered are heavily waxed paperboard cartons; re-usable rigid containers of tin, glass, or plastic; tin cans (some foods require special lacquer linings in tin cans); special round or square glass containers; lightweight aluminum boxes with aluminum lids that can be sealed to the box with a small tool supplied with the box; and moistureproof, vaporproof wrappings. Make your choice on the basis of price, size, convenience, etc.; most freezer containers and packaging materials available today give satisfactory results when used correctly.

Meat and Fish. Any good fresh meat or fish can be frozen satisfactorily. Duration of top quality and flavor under storage varies with individual meats. Some meat shops are equipped to cut up, package, wrap, and label meats for your home freezer at no extra cost.

Meats for freezing should be prepared in fairly small packages, since these freeze more rapidly than large packages. All meats should be chilled before freezing. In general they should be cleaned as for service at the table. They require no precooking—are frozen raw.

Meat requires extremely careful packaging to protect it from drying out and becoming rancid. Smoked meats demand extra-careful wrapping to prevent escape of their odors to other items.

Fish and shellfish should be frozen on the same day they are caught, if possible; otherwise they must be under constant refrigeration until freezing time. Fish should be scaled, beheaded, eviscerated, and otherwise cleaned, just as for table service. Large fish should be cut into fillets and steaks. Some home economists recommend immersing fillets and steaks of cod and haddock (never fatty fish such as mackerel and salmon) for 20 seconds to 1 minute in brine of 1 lb. salt to 4½ qts. water before packing.

Clams, scallops, and oysters must be shucked before freezing. The raw meats may be washed under a spray of clean cold water, or in a 2½-per-cent brine, and drained. Fruit and vegetable containers may be used here with inner liner of moistureproof, vaporproof cellophane and with space allowed for expansion.

Crab and lobster must be cooked as for table service. Cooked, picked crab meat and lobster meat should be packed in jars with 2½-per-cent brine, allowing space for expansion during freezing.

Shrimps should have heads and appendages removed and discarded. Some authorities advise freezing uncooked (cooked shrimp toughens during storage) in shells; others advise shelling before packing.

Whole meats and fish are wrapped tightly in moistureproof, waterproof material especially prepared for freezer storage. Among these materials are cellophane, aluminum foil, and coated paper. Always protect your foods with good quality material. Special sealing tape is used. Large irregular-shaped pieces, such as roasts, are usually further protected by overwrapping in stockinette or heavy paper. Small cuts of meat and fish may be wrapped in lined cartons. To give whole fish extra protection, some people freeze it in the regular manner, then dip it in thoroughly chilled ice water, drain, and repeat the process until an ice glaze forms. Fish is then rewrapped in moistureproof, vaporproof material, sealed, and returned to freezer.

Sandwiches for Lunch Box or Parties. The home freezer enables you to make and store a two-weeks' supply of sandwiches at one time, avoiding morning hustle, and economizing by using left-overs. Use day-old bread. Spread softened (not melted) butter or margarine on entire surface of each slice—it will prevent fillings from soaking bread. Fillings suitable for freezing include cheese, sliced or ground poultry or meat, peanut butter, and hard-cooked egg yolk (hard-cooked egg white is not suitable). In fact, almost any filling except salad greens, tomatoes, jellies, mayonnaise, and salad dressing may be used. Wrap sandwiches individually in moistureproof, vaporproof material, and pack several in a carton, taking care not to mash them. Sandwiches can go directly from freezer to lunch box, will be thawed by noon. *Canapés* and party sandwiches are usually wrapped and placed in cartons in layers. Each layer is separated from the others by a double thickness of wrapping material. Fancy loaves for ribbon sandwiches should be frozen whole and cut after thawing.

Thawing. Most frozen vegetables may be cooked without thawing. Meats and fish may be cooked while frozen, but even cooking and a saving in cooking time result from two-thirds thawing.

Labeling. Because different foods have different lasting capacities, it is important to label each package with the date of packing and freezing and a description of contents. A china-marking pencil may be used. Take inventory of stored foods at regular intervals.

TAXES

A tax is a compulsory sum of money payable to a governmental unit. Practically every such unit, Federal (United States), state, city, county, town, village, water district, school district, etc., imposes taxes of one form or another. Almost every time a legislature convenes, either a new type of tax is voted or tax rates or other provisions of some tax law are changed. With few exceptions, taxes imposed temporarily become part of the permanent tax structure. By reason of continued amendments, additions, and exceptions, most tax laws now require expert interpretation, and the courts have added to the complexities.

Taxes are often classified as *direct* or *indirect*. This distinction is important because of provisions of the United States Constitution requiring direct taxes to be laid in proportion to population. Accordingly, an amendment to the Constitution became necessary to validate the United States income tax, which is a direct tax. Direct taxes are those imposed on a person, *e.g.,* a poll tax; or on a business, *e.g.,* a license fee. Indirect taxes are those levied on articles, *e.g.,* customs duties on imported goods, or excise taxes on certain manufactured articles.

Politically and economically, there is usually greater opposition to direct taxes than to indirect, because the taxpayer realizes a direct tax is being paid whereas indirect taxes are often hidden in the price of the merchandise.

The United States government levies and collects many different taxes, among them the income tax and the estate tax.

United States Income Tax. The current provisions of the United States Income Tax may be learned through application to the local Collector of Internal Revenue. Each year before this tax becomes due, the Treasury Department sends to each taxpayer who filed a tax return for the preceding year a booklet containing forms and information to assist in completing the tax return. Additional forms and many pamphlets covering specific types of returns and problems are also available on request. The personal income tax is a graduated tax, starting at 20 per cent and increasing to 91 per cent as income increases. Partnerships are not taxed as such, but each partner reports his share of the partnership income. The corporate income tax presently taxes the first $25,000 of income at 30 per cent and the balance at 52 per cent.

Taxpayers should keep detailed records to help in preparing returns and to prove the entries in the return. If the taxpayer keeps his books on a fiscal basis his return must be made on that basis; if he keeps them on a calendar basis he must make the return on that basis. If the taxpayer's accounting period is other than a fiscal year (a period of 12 months ending on the last day of a month other than December) or if he has no annual accounting period or does not keep books, income must be computed on a calendar year basis. A new taxpayer (other than a partnership, which is governed by a number of rules depending on the partners' tax years) can begin on any basis he likes, subject to the foregoing; if he wishes to change his tax year, permission must be obtained from the Tax Commissioner, except with respect to (1) certain corporate situations; (2) partnerships, where all principal partners have the same taxable year to which the partnership changes; and (3) newly married couples, so that both will have the same tax year in order to file a joint return. (There are some exceptions.) Wherever a change of taxable year is made, a return for the short intervening period is required. Application for permission to make a change should be made on a special form (now #1121) to the Commission of Internal Revenue, Washington 25, D.C., on or before the last day of the month following the close of the short taxable year required to effect the change.

Federal personal income taxes are payable under the "pay-as-you-go" plan in two ways: (1) by *withholding* the amount due from wages or salaries; and (2) by quarterly *declaration and payment of estimated tax* for incomes not subject to the withholding tax. The balance of the tax is payable on April 15, after the close of the calendar year upon which the tax is reckoned; or if it is reckoned on a fiscal year, on the 15th day of the third month following the end of the year. If the taxpayer has overpaid his taxes, a refund will be made on the basis of the taxpayer's return filed at the end of the year.

Certain credits are allowed against the tax, such as for income taxes paid to foreign governments, retirement income, and a credit of a percentage of certain dividends.

Methods of filing returns include (1) separate returns; (2) a joint return with a spouse, on both of which either detailed deductions or standard deductions may be claimed; and (3) a short form limited to certain income levels on which only standard deductions may be claimed. When using the last named, the taxpayer may pay the tax or complete the return except for tax calculations and the District Director will compute the tax and bill the taxpayer for any amount due.

Joint returns may include the benefit of "splitting" income between the parties so that each part is taxed in a lower bracket before being added together for the total tax liability.

Exemptions are those portions of gross income specifically excluded by law from tax. These include personal exemption and additional specific exemptions for the taxpayer's old age or infirmity, and for dependents, definitions of which are given in the prevailing tax law.

In addition, the principal items of income normally exempt from tax are: (1) proceeds of a life insurance policy which has been paid on the decease of the insured; (2) the value of gifts, bequests, or inheritances (this value is not taxable to the recipient, unless the items involve receipt of income at intervals—for example, if items of a gift of real estate specify that the recipient will get the income from the gift at intervals, such income is taxable); (3) certain interest income, including interest on any obligation of a political subdivision of the United States, interest on United States government obligations issued before March 1, 1941, to the extent provided in the particular obligations; (4) sickness and injury benefits, as a general rule; (5) war veteran pensions, mustering-out pay, and other armed forces benefits, except retirement pay; (6) social security benefits; (7) railroad retirement pensions; (8) annuities and pensions to the extent of the "cost" of the annuity, the cost representing the total of the actual payments made for the annuity or pension; and (9) military service pay within prescribed limits.

Income that must be reported for tax purposes always includes: (1) salaries and wages; (2) competitive prizes and awards; (3) bonuses and tips; (4) alimony and separate maintenance payments; (5) rents and royalties; (6) interest on certain United States savings bonds; (7) regular dividends[1] and interest on investments and tax refunds; (8) gambling winnings; (9) real estate profits; (10) rewards; and (11) income in forms other than money (meals, lodging, capital stock, etc.).

Capital gains and losses refer to results of the sale or exchange of stocks, bonds, and personal residence or other real or personal property if not a dealer therein; they must be reported in accordance with a special set of income tax rules. The period of time the capital asset is held is important in determining whether a profit or loss is long-term or short-term. If the asset is held for six months or less, the gain or loss on the disposal of the asset is short-term; an asset held longer than six months may only incur a long-term gain or loss. Treatment of gains or losses in each category depends on the latest tax law.

With respect to the sale of a personal residence which is the taxpayer's principal home, there is a special provision which permits postponement of payment of capital gains tax if a new residence is purchased. The new residence must be purchased and used within one year before or after sale of the old residence. In such event, the capital gains tax is not payable until the new residence is sold. There is also a special rule which permits postponement of the count of the time if the taxpayer goes on active duty (over 90 days) with the armed forces until his service ends or four years after sale, whichever comes first. Also the investment in the new house must be as much as, or more than, was realized from the sale of the old.

There are other items of expense or loss which are properly deductible from gross income before the income tax is figured. The basic principle governing deductions is that the taxpayer must be able to point to some specific provision of law or regulation which authorizes that deduction, and that he must be able to prove he is entitled to such deduction.

In the broad category of deductions, not necessarily applicable to everybody, are business and professional expenses; bad debts which become worthless in the

---

[1] At present the first $50 of such dividends is excluded from income and 4 per cent of the dividends, subject to certain limitations, are allowed as a credit. The law permitting this exclusion and deduction was passed to alleviate the double tax caused by the tax on corporate earnings and another tax when such earnings were distributed as dividends. In the early 1960's, however, there was agitation to abolish this exclusion and credit.

tax year and will remain worthless; depreciation; charitable and other similar contributions (up to a limited percentage of the adjusted gross income); casualty and burglary losses and medical expenses of over a specified percentage of adjusted gross income, not reimbursed by insurance; interest expense; state income and other state taxes, except estate and gift taxes; union initiation fees and dues.

Penalties for neglect or fraud in connection with income tax returns vary. Understatement of the amount of the tax through negligence or disregard of rules is penalized by fine, as is delay without reasonable cause. The penalty for understatement with fraudulent intent to evade tax, or willful failure to pay a tax or file a return, is a greater fine plus costs; in addition a prison sentence may be imposed. For aiding in a false return a similar penalty is imposed. An interest penalty is charged when a tax is due and not paid.

Tax returns may be inspected by the government only under orders issued by the President of the United States. The returns of an individual may be inspected by that individual, his attorney, or, if he is deceased, his executor, heirs, or next of kin. The joint return of a husband and wife may be inspected by either. Corporate returns may be inspected by the president, vice president, secretary, or treasurer of the company, or by bona fide stockholders who own one per cent or more of the outstanding stock. Certain congressional committees may inspect income tax returns, and copies of returns may be furnished in court cases in which the United States is an interested party, or to a United States grand jury. The unofficial disclosure of information is severely penalized.

Excess profits taxation applied to business has become a feature of Federal legislation during emergency periods. Such taxation is based on a classification of earnings into two categories—one considered "normal" or peacetime income, and the other considered attributable to the incidence of wartime or emergency conditions rather than to the efforts of the taxpayer. The first excess profits tax in 1917 laid the groundwork for similar temporary taxes in subsequent periods. Two methods have been used for determination of "normal" profits; i.e., the "average income" of a specified earlier base period, and the "invested capital" method, which employs an arbitrary percentage of the taxpayer's invested capital during the taxable year. These methods have been used either separately or in combination in excess profits tax laws.

United States Estate Tax. Under United States law, citizens and resident aliens (nonresident aliens are also subject to tax on property in the United States; this is a specialized subject and no attempt is made to discuss it here) are subject to a tax on their net estate, computed on value on the date of death or, at the option of the personal representatives, on value one year later. The gross estate includes all property owned by the decedent regardless of kind or location, except real estate situated outside of the United States. It includes life insurance payable to the estate or named beneficiaries, except where the beneficiary was the owner of the policy and decedent had no rights therein. Jointly held property is presumed to be the sole property of the decedent, subject to proof that the other joint tenant contributed thereto. Gifts made within three years of death are presumed to have been made in contemplation of death and, subject to contrary proof, are included in the gross estate; gifts made prior to the three years are not included in the estate. Other included types of property are transfers in which deceased retained an interest, certain annuities, and certain rights or powers over property.

Deductions for debts; funeral and administration expenses, including counsel fees and commission of executors or administrators; charitable gifts; an exemption of $60,000; and a "marital deduction" are allowed to be taken from the gross estate to compute the taxable estate. The estate remaining is taxed at graduated rates from 3 per cent to 77 per cent. There are allowed certain credits against the tax for state estate taxes, Federal gift taxes, foreign death taxes, and prior transfers—*i.e.,* part of Federal estate tax paid with respect to property inherited by decedent ten years before or two years after decedent's death.

The "marital deduction" is allowed in any amount up to 50 per cent of the "adjusted gross estate" as to property which passes to the surviving spouse (including property includable in the gross estate which passed during decedent's lifetime); as to a legal life estate or trust for benefit of the spouse, as to which the spouse has full rights of disposition of the remainder on her death or sooner; and as to life insurance payable in certain ways.

United States Gift Tax. This tax is payable by any citizen and by aliens under certain circumstances. To compute the tax all gifts made after June 6, 1932, are added together. The tax is payable yearly. Gifts for public and charitable purposes are excluded. An exclusion, currently $3,000, of gifts made to any number of individuals during the calendar year, is allowed. To qualify for the exclusion, the gift must be of a present interest except gifts to minors under specified conditions. A spouse is permitted to consent to a gift made by the other spouse, and it is assumed that in such event one-half the gift is made by the consenting spouse, thus permitting a $6,000 exclusion. A marital deduction similar to that allowed with respect to estate taxes is also allowed.[1] There is also a lifetime exemption of $30,000. The current rates range from 2¼ per cent to 57¾ per cent.

In addition to the foregoing, the United States imposes excise taxes, unemployment insurance taxes, Federal Old Age Benefit (Social Security) taxes, gasoline taxes, and many others.

The various states also levy many different taxes, among the principal of which are:

Gasoline Tax. All states.

Income Tax. All states except Florida, Illinois, Maine, Michigan, Nebraska, Nevada, New Jersey, Ohio, Pennsylvania, Rhode Island, South Dakota, Texas, Washington, West Virginia, and Wyoming. The New Hampshire income tax is based on interest and dividends only, excluding savings-bank interest.

Sales and Use Taxes. All states except Alaska, Delaware, Idaho, Massachusetts, Minnesota, Montana, Nebraska, New Hampshire, New Jersey, Vermont, Virginia, and Wisconsin. Texas limits tax to automobiles, television sets, and playing cards. Massachusetts taxes meals.

Property Taxes. All states except Hawaii, Maryland, New Mexico, New York, and North Dakota.

Automobile Licenses. All states.

Inheritance Taxes or Estate Taxes. All states levy one or the other or both. In some states, however, the tax is only the amount the Federal estate tax law allows as a credit (if paid) against Federal estate taxes. In such states the net effect is the same as though no state estate tax were payable. Among such states are Alabama, Arkansas, Florida, and Georgia. All states have provision to assure the Federal credit except South Dakota and West Virginia.

Some of the other taxes levied by various states are poll taxes, deed and mortgage filing, employer and employee unemployment insurance, disability, cigarette, wine and liquor, privilege, mortgage, admission, motor excise, motor vehicle oil, tobacco products, mineral, documentary stamps, beer, etc.

Sales taxes are imposed by New York City, Denver, Baton Rouge, and New Orleans. Admission taxes are imposed by Chicago, New York City, Cincinnati, Cleveland, and Columbia. Philadelphia imposes an amusement tax. Income taxes are imposed by Louisville, Ky.; St. Louis, Mo.; Dayton, Cincinnati, Columbus, Toledo, Springfield, and Youngstown, Ohio; and Erie, Pittsburgh, Philadelphia, and Scranton, Pa. Cigarette taxes are imposed by New York City and

---

[1] In order to be sure to take advantage of the deductions counsel should be consulted.

by Memphis, Tenn., which latter also imposes a liquor tax. New York City imposes a tax on hotel occupancy.

Cities, counties, villages, and townships generally impose taxes on real estate. Tax assessors are persons appointed to value each property and apportion the tax according to value. The assessment roll is a list of property owners, a brief description of the property, the assessed value, and the tax levied. The assessed valuation is the base upon which the tax is calculated. Payments assessed for local benefits such as street paving, sidewalk, sewers, etc., are not taxes and are called assessments. Such assessments must be levied legally; that is, they must be announced to the taxpayer far enough ahead of their due dates for him to be heard if he thinks the assessment is unjust. Real estate taxes become liens on the property the day they are due; if they are unpaid, the property may eventually be sold to satisfy the tax claim. A tax lien is prior to a mortgage lien. All mortgagees and all purchasers of real estate should have tax searches made. Inheritance taxes also must be paid before a real estate title is clear.

CORPORATIONS

A corporation is created pursuant to law and has a legal entity entirely separate and distinct from the individuals who compose it, with the capacity of continuous existence, notwithstanding changes in its membership. It has the right to buy, hold, and convey property, make contracts, sue and be sued, and to exercise such other powers and privileges as are conferred on it by law. The stockholders are not liable for corporate debts, except under certain circumstances and only by reason of specific statutory provision.

A corporation should be organized by a lawyer familiar with the law of the state in which the corporation is to function.

A corporation can be organized only for legal purposes, which must be set forth in the certificate of incorporation. This corporate charter is in essence a contract between the state and the corporation. Unless there is statutory right or unless such power is specified in the certificate, the state has no power to withdraw or change the certificate after acceptance. The certificate is filed in a state office upon payment of a statutory fee.

Every corporation must have a name; this name is set forth in the certificate of incorporation. The name must not conflict with that of another corporation, nor be so similar to it that the new name will deceive the public and result in confusion or unfair competition; and no corporation can appropriate to its exclusive use geographical or generic terms.

The business policies of the corporation are controlled by the directors, who are elected by the stockholders.

The internal affairs of a corporation are regulated and defined in its bylaws. These bylaws are binding upon the directors, officers, and stockholders. They are adopted by the stockholders or board of directors. No bylaw can conflict with or be contrary to what is set forth in the certificate nor be in violation of any statute.

The *capital stock* of a corporation is the sum fixed by the certificate as the amount with which the corporation is to do business. Capital is the fund contributed by the stockholders to the corporation.

The power of a corporation to issue stock depends on its certificate and the state laws under which it is organized. A *share* of capital stock is the interest that a stockholder has in the corporation. The shares of stock are represented by a certificate, which he may transfer by sale or otherwise to another person. At times, such right is restricted by an agreement between stockholders, called stockholders' agreement.

Kinds of Stock. The owner of *common stock* is entitled to pro rata dividends without any priority or preference over any other shareholder but equally with all other stockholders, except preferred stockholders. A common stockholder is an owner of the corporate business in the proportion that his stock bears to the entire stock; he is ordinarily entitled to participate in the management, profits, and assets of the corporation. In some corporations the common stock is divided into classes, with each class having different rights, sometimes with respect to voting power or dividends or other rights or combinations thereof.

Preferred stock generally entitles the holders to dividends in priority to the holders of the common stock. Sometimes the owners of such stock are also, or only, preferred as to assets upon dissolution of the corporation; that is, they receive their share of assets before the holders of common stock. However, the preferences accorded such stockholders are many and varied; some are mentioned below. The law requires that the rights and preferences of each kind of stock be set forth on the certificate of stock.

Dividends are payable only out of profits, never out of capital. No corporation may guarantee that it will pay dividends, but a corporation may guarantee that the stockholders of another corporation will receive dividends.

Dividends on preferred stock may be *cumulative* or *noncumulative*. A cumulative dividend carries over from year to year; if the corporation has no profits and declares no dividend in any one year the deficit is paid as soon thereafter as dividends are earned and declared. Holders of common stock receive no dividends until all cumulative dividends are paid. Noncumulative dividends do not carry over from year to year; sometimes if not paid in any year they are never payable; sometimes if earned but not paid they remain payable. Payment of dividends on preferred stock may be assured by means of a sinking fund, provided earnings are available to be added to such fund.

Preferred stockholders usually have no right to vote except on certain questions; for instance, as to whether more preferred stock shall be issued. Nonvoting stock may be issued; but a stockholder with the right to vote his stock may not thereafter be deprived of such right.

There are several types of preferred stock: (1) nonparticipating preferred stock, which entitles the owner to receive a certain dividend and nothing more; (2) simple participating preferred stock, which entitles the owner to receive the specified dividend, after which payment the balance of earnings is shared equally by the holders of the common and preferred stock; and (3) special participating stock, which may be arranged according to any scheme which the directors of the corporation may devise, with the stipulation that the arrangement must be provided for in the certificate of incorporation.

Redeemable stock is stock which a corporation has the right to buy back from its holders upon the terms fixed in the certificate of incorporation. The right to do so is optional with the corporation.

Convertible stock is stock of one class which may be exchanged for stock of another class, usually preferred stock which may be exchanged for common stock. The right to do so is optional with the stockholder.

Holding Companies. A holding company is a company formed to own and control the stock of other corporations. The holding company's income is derived from the interest or dividends upon the stock and securities which it holds of the other corporations. Such companies are legal as long as they do not operate in restraint of trade or in violation of the antitrust laws. Such corporations engaged in interstate commerce are regulated by Federal statutes.

Subsidiary Companies. A subsidiary company is a company whose entire or whose controlling stock is owned by another corporation, called the parent corporation.

PARTNERSHIP

The statutory law of partnerships varies in the different states. In essence, a partnership is a legal relation arising from contract between two or more persons who agree to pool their money and labor to engage in a lawful business or trade and share profits and losses equally or in specified proportions.

All property brought into the partnership or acquired by partnership funds becomes partnership property. Land may be acquired in the partnership name, and can be sold only in the partnership name.

A *secret partner* actually shares the profits and losses of the business, but the fact that he does is not generally known by outsiders. A *dormant partner* is one who takes no active part in the business and whose association with it is also unknown. Such a partner is liable for contracts made by the active and known partners in the partnership name, as well as for implied contracts of the firm. A *nominal partner* is one who is designated a partner, but who in fact is not a partner. He is, however, liable for partnership debts.

Every partner is an agent of the partnership for all business purposes. The acts of each partner bind the partnership as well as all the other partners, unless the partner so acting has no authority to act for the partnership in the particular matter, and the person with whom he is dealing knows that he has no such authority. An act by the partner which is not apparently for the partnership business will not bind the partnership unless it is authorized by the other partners. All partners are required to act in (1) assigning the partnership property for the benefit of creditors; (2) disposing of the good will of the business, or doing anything which would make it impossible to carry on the ordinary business of the partnership; and (3) confessing a judgment or submitting a partnership claim to arbitration. No act of any partner in contravention of a restriction on his authority will bind the partnership to persons who have knowledge of the restriction.

Whereas the liability of a stockholder in a corporation is limited to the extent of his interest in the corporation as represented by the amount of his stock, the *liability of a partner* is not limited to the extent of his investment, except in those states which provide for the formation of limited partnerships or joint stock companies.

Generally, partners are *fiduciaries* to each other and must act equitably; no partner may obtain any personal interest adverse to his partners' interest or that of the partnership. A partner may be entitled to an accounting whenever he is wrongfully excluded from the partnership or whenever circumstances render it just and reasonable.

A partnership is *dissolved* by the expiration of the time fixed in the agreement for its duration, or by the completion of the purpose for which it was formed, or by the will of all partners, either before or after the time fixed for its duration; and any partner can bring about a dissolution if no term has been fixed nor particular purpose has been specified in their agreement. It may also be dissolved by operation of law; for instance, if any event occurs which makes the enterprise unlawful or if one or more partners are inducted into military service. The court can also decree dissolution if any partner becomes incapable of performing his partnership duties or has been judicially declared an incompetent. There are many other statutory causes for dissolution by the court; these vary in the different states.

Death dissolves a partnership; and the heirs do not succeed to membership in the firm unless it was expressly so provided in the agreement.

Regardless of the cause of the dissolution, the partnership continues to function until all partnership affairs are completely wound up. Dissolution does not put an end to partnership contracts nor change the liability of partners to third persons.

In the absence of an express agreement between the partners and a partnership creditor, a retiring partner continues to remain liable for partnership contracts made before dissolution. The person to whom the retiring partner transfers his interest in the partnership does not thereby become a member of the firm unless the other partners consent thereto. A retiring partner should give public notice of his retirement, and personal notice to all those with whom he personally dealt on behalf of the firm.

The liability of a partner in a limited partnership is limited to his capital investment. Such partnerships must be drawn up in strict accord with the statutory law of the state in which they are formed. Some limited partnerships are so similar to corporations that they are taxed as such. Rules setting forth the characteristics which would have such result have been promulgated by the U.S. Treasury Department. A limited partnership must be composed of one or more general partners whose liability is unlimited. Today limited partnerships are most commonly used for the ownership and operation of real estate and the financing of theatrical and entertainment enterprises in order to avoid the double taxation inherent in corporate operation.

A *joint stock association* has some of the attributes of a corporation as well as of a partnership; but it is based on a written agreement between the parties and not on a state charter. Joint stock associations are now quite rare; the contents of the agreement and other matters affecting their rights and liabilities are regulated by statutes which differ from state to state.

ARTICLES OF CO-PARTNERSHIP[1]

Article of agreement, made the ———— day of ———— nineteen hundred and ———— between JOHN DOE, of No. ———— ———— Street, (city), (state), and RICHARD ROE of No. ———— ———— Street, (city), (state), as follows: The said parties above named have agreed to become co-partners in business, to sell furniture and by these presents do agree to be co-partners together under and by the name or firm of DOE AND ROE in the buying, selling and vending all sorts of goods, wares and merchandise to the said business belonging, and to occupy the suite of offices (here describe the firm property), their co-partnership to commence on the ———— day of ————, 19—, and to continue for the term of ———— years, that is to say until the ———— day of ————, 19—, and to that end and purpose the said JOHN DOE agrees to deposit in the ———— bank ———— dollars in the firm name by the ———— day of ————, 19—, and the said RICHARD ROE agrees to deposit in the ———— bank ———— dollars in the firm name by the ———— day of ———— 19— (or any property that each is to contribute), to be used and employed in common between them for the support and management of the said business, to their mutual benefit and advantage.

And it is agreed by and between the parties to these presents, that at all times during the continuance of their co-partnership, they and each of them will give their attendance, and do their and each of their best endeavors, and to the utmost of their skill and power, exert themselves for their joint interest, profit, benefit and advantage, and truly employ, buy, sell, and merchandise with their joint stock, and the increase thereof, in the business aforesaid.

And also, that they shall and will at all times during the said co-partnership, bear, pay, and discharge equally between them, all rents, and other expenses that may be required for the support and management of the said business; and that all gains, profit and increase that shall come, grow or arise from or by means of their said business, shall be divided between them, in the following proportions:— to the said JOHN DOE—50%; to the said RICHARD ROE—50%, and all loss that shall happen to their joint business by ill commodities, bad debts or otherwise, shall be borne and paid between them.

And it is agreed by and between the said parties, that there shall be had and kept

---

[1] This is only a suggested form. The reader is advised to obtain a form, valid in his state, from a lawyer or legal stationer for use in specific transactions.

at all times during the continuance of their co-partnership, perfect, just, and true books of account, wherein each of the said co-partners shall enter and set down, as well all money by them or either of them received, paid, laid out and expended in and about the said business, as also all goods, wares, commodities and merchandise, by them or either of them bought or sold, by reason or on account of the said business, and all other matters and things whatsoever, to the said business and the management thereof in anywise belonging; which said books shall be used in common between the said co-partners, so that either of them may have access thereto, without any interruption or hindrance of the other.

And also, the said co-partners, once in (here insert stated periods when accounts shall be made) or oftener if necessary, shall make, yield and render, each to the other, a true, just and perfect inventory and account of all profits and increase by them, or either of them made, and all losses by them, or either of them, sustained; and also all payments, receipts, disbursements and all other things by them made, received, disbursed, acted, done, or suffered in this said co-partnership and business; and the same account so made shall and will clear, adjust, pay and deliver, each to the other, at the time their just share of the profits so made as aforesaid.

And the said parties hereby mutually covenant and agree, to and with each other, that during the continuance of the said co-partnership, neither of them shall nor will endorse any note, or otherwise become surety for any person or persons whomsoever, without the consent of the other of the said co-partners. And at the end or other sooner termination of their co-partnership the said co-partners, each to the other, shall and will make a true, just and final account of all things relating to their said business, and in all things truly adjust the same; and all and every the stock and the stocks, as well as the gains and increase thereof, which shall appear to be remaining, either in money, goods, wares, fixtures, debts or otherwise, shall be divided between them.

In witness whereof the parties have on the day first above written, affixed their hands and seals.

Sealed and delivered in the presence of:

John Doe (seal)
Richard Roe (seal)

(Acknowledgment)

DISSOLUTION OF PARTNERSHIP[1]

This agreement made the ——— day of ——— one thousand nine hundred ——— between JOHN DOE, of No. ——— ——— Street, (city), (state), party of the first part and RICHARD ROE, of No. ——— ——— Street, (city), (state), party of the second part,

Witnesseth: whereas the parties hereto have formed a co-partnership for the purpose of selling furniture under the firm name of DOE AND ROE and have maintained and continued said partnership up to the present time, and

Whereas the parties hereto have agreed that the partnership existing between them should be dissolved and at an end, and

Whereas an accounting of the assets and liabilities of the said firm has been duly had by the parties hereto, for the purpose of ascertaining the condition of said co-partnership business, and on said accounting it was found that a true statement of the conditions and of the affairs of such co-partnership are as set forth in the schedule of assets and liabilities hereto annexed, and made part hereof, and

Whereas the parties hereto have agreed to distribute said assets in the following manner: To JOHN DOE—50% of all the assets, to RICHARD ROE—50% of all the assets.

Now in consideration of the sum of One Dollar each to the other in hand paid, the receipt whereof is hereby acknowledged, and in consideration of the foregoing premises the parties hereto agree to terminate and dissolve said co-partnership and each of the parties hereto hereby severally releases the other of and from any and all manner of obligations growing out of the said partnership, and it is further Agreed that the party of the first part, in consideration of the sum of ——— dol-

[1] This is only a suggested form. The reader is advised to obtain a form, valid in his state, from a lawyer or legal stationer for use in specific transactions.

lars paid to him by the party of the second part the receipt whereof is hereby acknowledged, has transferred, assigned and set over and by these presents does assign, transfer and set over unto said party of the second part, his executors, administrators and assigns, all right, title, interest and share of, in and into the assets and property of every kind, nature and description of said partnership, together with the good will of the business thereof, and it is further

Agreed that none of said partners has signed or endorsed the firm name to any commercial paper, nor other evidence of debt, nor incurred any obligation nor liability, contingent or actual, in behalf of said co-partnership, except as mentioned or included in the accounting herein set forth, and it is further

Agreed by the parties hereto that the party of the first part shall and will pay and discharge all the firm obligations and liabilities referred to and mentioned in the accounting hereinbefore set forth, without contribution by the party of the second part thereto; and that the said party of the first part does hereby agree to save, indemnify and keep harmless the said party of the second part of and from any and all such firm obligations and liabilities and of and from all damage, cost, charge and expense occurring through the default or failure of the party of the first part to promptly and fully pay and discharge the same.

In witness thereof, the parties hereto have hereunto set their hands and seals, the day and year first above written.
Witness:

(Signed) John Doe (seal)
Richard Roe (seal)

(Acknowledgment)

SCHEDULE

ASSETS

Cash on hand and in bank .... $............
Outstanding accounts as per schedule hereunto annexed ....
Stock on hand ....
Fixtures, machinery and fittings ....
Miscellaneous property as per schedule annexed ....
                                         Total assets $............

LIABILITIES

For merchandise as per annexed schedule .... $............
Money loaned as per annexed schedule ....
Notes or other obligations as per annexed schedule ....
Miscellaneous liabilities as per schedule annexed ....
                                         Total liabilities $............

STOCK EXCHANGES

A stock exchange is a place where securities are bought and sold. The three leading stock exchanges in the world are the London Stock Exchange, the Paris Bourse, and the New York Stock Exchange. The largest in the United States is the New York Stock Exchange, though there are others of considerable importance, among which the American Stock Exchange (formerly the New York Curb Exchange) may especially be mentioned.[1] New issues and other issues which, for one reason or another, are either not willing or not able to meet the requirements of the New York Stock Exchange may still be listed on the American or some other exchange.

The investing public is now protected by the Securities and Exchange Commission (S.E.C.), which was established in 1934 to administer the Securities

---

[1] Other stock exchanges in the United States include those in Boston, Mass.; Cincinnati, Ohio; Colorado Springs, Colo.; Detroit, Mich.; Honolulu, Hawaii; New Orleans, La.; Philadelphia-Baltimore; Pittsburgh, Pa.; Richmond, Va.; Salt Lake City, Utah; San Francisco, Calif.; Spokane, Wash.; and Wheeling, W. Va.; the Midwest Exchange in Chicago, Ill.; and the Pacific Coast Exchange, in San Francisco and Los Angeles, Calif.

Act of 1933 and the Securities Exchange Act of 1934. Under the provisions of these two acts, issuers of securities to be sold in interstate commerce or through the mails are required to file with the Commission and furnish to prospective buyers all basic information concerning the securities offered. Neither the Commission nor the Exchange passes on the soundness of the securities; its aim is to give the public the truth. Penalties are imposed for fraudulent or misleading statements. On the flotation of foreign securities the domestic fiscal agent of the issuer is held responsible. The Commission is empowered in various ways to prevent the manipulation of stocks and unreasonable speculation on the exchanges.

The more than 1,350 members of the New York Stock Exchange may be roughly divided into five groups: commission house brokers; floor brokers; specialists; odd-lot dealers; and traders. Commission brokers represent, on the trading floor, firms which primarily do business with the public. Floor brokers execute orders for other brokers. Specialists, as the name implies, undertake to make markets in securities, acting as dealers, besides executing orders entrusted to them for execution in such securities. Odd-lot dealers accommodate buy-and-sell orders for less than the customary 100-share round lot. Traders deal primarily for their own account. The brokers' minimum commissions are fixed by the rules of the exchange.

All orders given to brokers are considered canceled at the end of the day upon which they were entered, unless express provisions are made to the contrary. Orders may be given to buy or sell at the market price or at a specified price. In buying stock the broker is required to buy, if possible, at a lower price than the one specified. In selling stock he must sell either at the specified price or a higher one. One of the most common specified-price orders is the stop-loss order. This is used when a customer buys on margin. He names a certain price below the market price at which he wishes his broker to sell, should the market value of the security decline, so as to "stop" his losses. Many orders are given to brokers with instructions that they are "good till canceled." These are commonly known as G. T. C. orders. Before placing an order, the prospective buyer or seller can ascertain the approximate price of a stock by asking his broker for quotations. This is the current highest bid to buy, and lowest offer to sell, the stock in question.

Prices of stocks are designated in various ways according to the kinds of transactions that are taking place.

The *bid price* is the price offered by a prospective purchaser of stock.

The *asked price* is the price asked by the seller of a stock.

The *actual price* is the price at which the transaction is finally concluded.

The *market price* is the price at which a security is selling at a specified time. If no transactions are taking place at the time, the bid and asked prices are given.

The *nominal price* is an estimated price when there are no bid and asked prices.

A *firm price* is one which is quoted and held to for a certain period. It is generally used between brokers when stocks are not active.

The *exhaust price* is the price at which the holder's margin will be exhausted.

Buying on margin is buying partly on credit. The buyer advances a percentage of the money required for the entire number of stocks bought, the percentage varying with different stocks and with different brokers. The following estimate has been made, but the variations between the amounts listed here and actual conditions may be very wide indeed:

The initial maximum credit value of a registered security for margin purposes, as prescribed by the Federal Reserve System pursuant to the Securities Exchange Act (1947), is 70 per cent of its current market value. The general

ANNUAL RATE OF RETURN ON DIVIDEND-PAYING STOCKS AT VARIOUS PRICES[1]

Based on Par Value of $100

Price	1%	2%	2½%	3%	3¼%	3½%	3¾%	4%	4¼%	4½%	4¾%
20	5.00	10.00	12.50	15.00	16.25	17.50	18.75	20.00	21.25	22.50	23.75
21	4.76	9.52	11.90	14.28	15.47	16.66	17.85	19.04	20.23	21.42	22.61
22	4.54	9.08	11.35	13.62	14.75	15.89	17.02	18.16	19.29	20.43	21.56
23	4.34	8.68	10.85	13.02	14.10	15.19	16.27	17.36	18.44	19.53	20.61
24	4.16	8.32	10.40	12.48	13.52	14.56	15.60	16.64	17.70	18.72	19.76
25	4.00	8.00	10.00	12.00	13.00	14.00	15.00	16.00	17.00	18.00	19.00
27½	3.64	7.27	9.09	10.91	11.82	12.73	13.64	14.55	15.46	16.37	17.28
30	3.33	6.67	8.33	10.00	10.83	11.66	12.49	13.33	14.16	14.99	15.82
32½	3.08	6.15	7.69	9.23	10.00	10.77	11.54	12.31	13.08	13.85	14.62
35	2.86	5.71	7.14	8.57	9.28	10.00	10.71	11.43	12.14	12.86	13.57
37½	2.67	5.33	6.66	8.00	8.67	9.33	10.00	10.67	11.34	12.00	12.67
40	2.50	5.00	6.25	7.50	8.12	8.75	9.37	10.00	10.62	11.25	11.87
42½	2.35	4.71	5.88	7.06	7.65	8.23	8.82	9.41	10.00	10.58	11.17
45	2.22	4.44	5.55	6.67	7.22	7.78	8.33	8.89	9.44	10.00	10.55
47½	2.11	4.21	5.26	6.32	6.85	7.37	7.90	8.42	8.95	9.47	10.00
50	2.00	4.00	5.00	6.00	6.50	7.00	7.50	8.00	8.50	9.00	9.50
52½	1.90	3.81	4.76	5.71	6.18	6.66	7.13	7.62	8.09	8.57	9.04
55	1.82	3.64	4.55	5.45	5.90	6.36	6.81	7.27	7.72	8.18	8.63
57½	1.74	3.48	4.35	5.22	5.65	6.09	6.52	6.96	7.39	7.83	8.26
60	1.67	3.33	4.16	5.00	5.42	5.83	6.25	6.67	7.09	7.50	7.92
62½	1.60	3.20	4.00	4.80	5.20	5.60	6.00	6.40	6.80	7.20	7.60
65	1.54	3.08	3.85	4.62	5.00	5.39	5.77	6.15	6.53	6.92	7.30
67½	1.48	2.96	3.70	4.44	4.81	5.18	5.55	5.93	6.30	6.67	7.04
70	1.43	2.86	3.57	4.29	4.65	5.00	5.36	5.71	6.07	6.42	6.78
72½	1.38	2.76	3.45	4.14	4.48	4.83	5.17	5.52	5.85	6.21	6.55
75	1.33	2.67	3.33	4.00	4.33	4.66	4.99	5.33	5.66	5.99	6.32
77½	1.29	2.58	3.22	3.87	4.19	4.51	4.83	5.16	5.48	5.80	6.12
80	1.25	2.50	3.12	3.75	4.06	4.37	4.68	5.00	5.31	5.62	5.93
82½	1.21	2.42	3.02	3.64	3.94	4.24	4.54	4.85	5.15	5.45	5.75
85	1.18	2.35	2.94	3.53	3.82	4.12	4.41	4.71	5.00	5.30	5.59
87½	1.14	2.29	2.86	3.43	3.71	4.00	4.28	4.57	4.85	5.14	5.42
90	1.11	2.22	2.77	3.33	3.61	3.88	4.16	4.44	4.72	4.99	5.27
92½	1.08	2.16	2.70	3.24	3.51	3.78	4.05	4.32	4.59	4.86	5.13
95	1.05	2.11	2.63	3.16	3.42	3.68	3.94	4.21	4.47	4.73	4.99
97½	1.03	2.05	2.56	3.08	3.34	3.59	3.85	4.10	4.36	4.61	4.87
100	1.00	2.00	2.50	3.00	3.25	3.50	3.75	4.00	4.25	4.50	4.75
105	.95	1.90	2.37	2.86	3.10	3.33	3.57	3.81	4.05	4.28	4.52
110	.91	1.82	2.27	2.73	2.96	3.18	3.41	3.64	3.87	4.09	4.32
115	.87	1.74	2.17	2.61	2.83	3.04	3.26	3.48	3.70	3.91	4.13
120	.83	1.67	2.08	2.50	2.71	2.91	3.12	3.33	3.54	3.74	3.95
125	.80	1.60	2.00	2.40	2.60	2.80	3.00	3.20	3.40	3.60	3.80
130	.77	1.54	1.92	2.31	2.50	2.69	2.88	3.08	3.27	3.46	3.65
135	.74	1.48	1.85	2.22	2.40	2.59	2.77	2.96	3.14	3.33	3.51
140	.71	1.43	1.78	2.14	2.32	2.49	2.67	2.86	3.04	3.21	3.39
145	.69	1.38	1.72	2.07	2.24	2.41	2.58	2.76	2.93	3.10	3.27
150	.67	1.33	1.66	2.00	2.17	2.33	2.50	2.67	2.84	3.00	3.17
155	.65	1.29	1.61	1.94	2.10	2.26	2.42	2.58	2.74	2.90	3.06
160	.63	1.25	1.56	1.87	2.03	2.18	2.34	2.50	2.66	2.81	2.97
165	.61	1.21	1.51	1.82	1.97	2.12	2.27	2.42	2.57	2.72	2.87
170	.59	1.18	1.47	1.76	1.91	2.05	2.20	2.35	2.50	2.64	2.79
175	.57	1.14	1.42	1.71	1.85	1.99	2.13	2.29	2.43	2.57	2.71
180	.56	1.11	1.39	1.67	1.81	1.95	2.09	2.22	2.36	2.50	2.64
185	.54	1.08	1.35	1.62	1.75	1.89	2.02	2.16	2.29	2.43	2.56
190	.53	1.05	1.31	1.58	1.71	1.84	1.97	2.11	2.24	2.37	2.50
195	.51	1.03	1.28	1.54	1.67	1.79	1.92	2.05	2.18	2.30	2.43
200	.50	1.00	1.25	1.50	1.62	1.75	1.87	2.00	2.12	2.25	2.37
210	.48	.95	1.19	1.43	1.55	1.67	1.79	1.90	2.02	2.14	2.26
220	.45	.91	1.13	1.36	1.47	1.58	1.69	1.82	1.93	2.04	2.15
230	.43	.87	1.08	1.30	1.41	1.51	1.63	1.74	1.85	1.95	2.07
240	.41	.83	1.03	1.25	1.35	1.45	1.55	1.67	1.77	1.87	1.97
250	.40	.80	1.00	1.20	1.30	1.40	1.50	1.60	1.70	1.80	1.90
260	.38	.77	.96	1.15	1.24	1.34	1.43	1.54	1.63	1.73	1.82
270	.37	.74	.92	1.11	1.20	1.29	1.38	1.48	1.57	1.66	1.75
280	.36	.71	.89	1.07	1.16	1.25	1.34	1.43	1.52	1.61	1.70
290	.34	.69	.86	1.03	1.11	1.20	1.28	1.38	1.46	1.55	1.63
300	.33	.67	.83	1.00	1.08	1.16	1.24	1.33	1.41	1.49	1.53

[1] By courteous permission of the Lefax Corporation, Philadelphia.

ANNUAL RATE OF RETURN ON DIVIDEND-PAYING STOCKS AT VARIOUS PRICES (*Cont.*)

Based on Par Value of $100

Price	5%	5¼%	5½%	5¾%	6%	6½%	7%	8%	9%	10%	12%
20	25.00	26.25	27.50	28.75	30.00	32.50	35.00	40.00	45.00	50.00	60.00
21	23.80	24.99	26.18	27.37	28.56	31.94	33.32	38.08	42.84	47.60	57.12
22	22.70	23.83	24.97	26.10	27.24	29.51	31.78	36.32	40.86	45.40	54.48
23	21.70	22.78	23.87	24.95	26.04	28.21	30.38	34.72	39.06	43.40	52.08
24	20.80	21.84	22.88	23.92	24.96	27.04	29.12	33.28	37.44	41.60	49.92
25	20.00	21.00	22.00	23.00	24.00	26.00	28.00	32.00	36.00	40.00	48.04
27½	18.18	19.09	20.00	20.91	21.82	23.64	25.45	29.00	32.73	36.36	43.60
30	16.67	17.50	18.33	19.16	20.00	21.66	23.33	26.67	30.00	33.33	40.00
32½	15.38	16.15	16.92	17.69	18.46	20.00	21.54	24.62	27.69	30.77	36.92
35	14.29	15.00	15.72	16.43	17.14	18.57	20.00	22.86	25.71	28.57	34.29
37½	13.33	14.00	14.66	15.33	16.00	17.33	18.67	21.33	24.00	26.67	32.00
40	12.50	13.12	13.75	14.37	15.00	16.25	17.50	20.00	22.50	25.00	30.00
42½	11.76	12.35	12.93	13.52	14.12	15.29	16.47	18.82	21.18	23.53	28.23
45	11.11	11.66	12.22	12.77	13.33	14.44	15.56	17.78	20.00	22.22	26.67
47½	10.53	11.06	11.58	12.11	12.63	13.68	14.74	16.84	18.95	21.05	25.26
50	10.00	10.50	11.00	11.50	12.00	13.00	14.00	16.00	18.00	20.00	24.00
52½	9.52	9.99	10.47	10.97	11.43	12.38	13.33	15.24	17.14	19.05	22.86
55	9.09	9.54	10.00	10.45	10.91	11.82	12.73	14.55	16.36	18.18	21.82
57½	8.70	9.13	9.57	10.00	10.43	11.30	12.17	13.91	15.65	17.39	20.87
60	8.33	8.75	9.16	9.58	10.00	10.83	11.67	13.33	15.00	16.67	20.00
62½	8.00	8.40	8.80	9.20	9.60	10.40	11.20	12.80	14.40	16.00	19.20
65	7.69	8.07	8.46	8.84	9.23	10.00	10.77	12.31	13.85	15.38	18.46
67½	7.41	7.78	8.15	8.52	8.89	9.63	10.37	11.85	13.33	14.81	17.78
70	7.14	7.50	7.85	8.21	8.57	9.28	10.00	11.43	12.86	14.29	17.14
72½	6.90	7.24	7.59	7.93	8.28	8.97	9.66	11.03	12.41	13.79	16.55
75	6.67	7.00	7.33	7.66	8.00	8.66	9.33	10.67	12.00	13.33	16.00
77½	6.45	6.77	7.09	7.41	7.74	8.38	9.03	10.32	11.61	12.90	15.48
80	6.25	6.56	6.87	7.18	7.50	8.12	8.75	10.00	11.25	12.50	15.00
82½	6.06	6.36	6.66	6.96	7.27	7.87	8.48	9.70	10.91	12.12	14.55
85	5.88	6.17	6.47	6.76	7.06	7.65	8.24	9.41	10.59	11.76	14.12
87½	5.76	6.04	6.33	6.61	6.86	7.43	8.00	9.14	10.29	11.43	13.71
90	5.51	5.79	6.06	6.34	6.67	7.12	7.78	8.89	10.00	11.11	13.33
92½	5.41	5.68	5.95	6.25	6.49	7.03	7.57	8.65	9.73	10.81	12.97
95	5.26	5.52	5.78	6.04	6.32	6.84	7.37	8.42	9.47	10.53	12.63
97½	5.13	5.39	5.64	5.90	6.15	6.66	7.18	8.21	9.23	10.26	12.31
100	5.00	5.25	5.50	5.75	6.00	6.50	7.00	8.00	9.00	10.00	12.00
105	4.76	5.00	5.23	5.47	5.71	6.18	6.67	7.62	8.57	9.52	11.43
110	4.55	4.78	5.00	5.23	5.45	5.90	6.36	7.27	8.18	9.09	10.91
115	4.35	4.57	4.78	5.00	5.22	5.65	6.09	6.96	7.83	8.70	10.43
120	4.17	4.38	4.58	4.79	5.00	5.41	5.83	6.67	7.50	8.33	10.00
125	4.00	4.20	4.40	4.60	4.80	5.20	5.60	6.40	7.20	8.00	9.60
130	3.85	4.04	4.23	4.42	4.62	5.00	5.38	6.15	6.92	7.69	9.23
135	3.70	3.88	4.07	4.25	4.44	4.81	5.19	5.93	6.67	7.41	8.89
140	3.57	3.75	3.92	4.10	4.29	4.64	5.00	5.71	6.43	7.14	8.57
145	3.45	3.62	3.79	3.96	4.14	4.48	4.83	5.52	6.21	6.90	8.28
150	3.33	3.50	3.66	3.83	4.00	4.33	4.67	5.33	6.00	6.67	8.00
155	3.23	3.39	3.55	3.71	3.87	4.19	4.52	5.16	5.81	6.45	7.74
160	3.12	3.28	3.43	3.59	3.75	4.06	4.38	5.00	5.63	6.25	7.50
165	3.03	3.18	3.33	3.48	3.64	3.94	4.24	4.85	5.45	6.06	7.27
170	2.94	3.09	3.23	3.38	3.53	3.82	4.12	4.71	5.29	5.88	7.06
175	2.86	3.00	3.14	3.28	3.34	3.71	4.00	4.57	5.14	5.71	6.86
180	2.78	2.92	3.06	3.20	3.33	3.61	3.89	4.44	5.00	5.56	6.67
185	2.70	2.83	2.97	3.10	3.24	3.51	3.78	4.32	4.86	5.41	6.49
190	2.63	2.76	2.89	3.02	3.16	3.42	3.68	4.21	4.74	5.26	6.32
195	2.56	2.69	2.81	2.94	3.08	3.33	3.59	4.10	4.62	5.13	6.15
200	2.50	2.62	2.75	2.87	3.00	3.25	3.50	4.00	4.50	5.00	6.00
210	2.38	2.50	2.62	2.74	2.86	3.10	3.33	3.81	4.29	4.76	5.71
220	2.27	2.38	2.49	2.60	2.73	2.95	3.18	3.64	4.09	4.55	5.45
230	2.17	2.28	2.38	2.50	2.61	2.82	3.04	3.48	3.91	4.35	5.22
240	2.08	2.18	2.28	2.38	2.50	2.70	2.92	3.33	3.75	4.17	5.00
250	2.00	2.10	2.20	2.30	2.40	2.60	2.80	3.20	3.60	4.00	4.80
260	1.92	2.01	2.11	2.20	2.31	2.50	2.69	3.08	3.46	3.85	4.62
270	1.85	1.94	2.03	2.12	2.22	2.40	2.59	2.96	3.33	3.70	4.44
280	1.79	1.88	1.97	2.06	2.14	2.32	2.50	2.86	3.21	3.57	4.29
290	1.72	1.80	1.89	1.97	2.07	2.24	2.41	2.76	3.10	3.45	4.14
300	1.67	1.75	1.83	1.91	2.00	2.16	2.33	2.67	3.00	3.33	4.00

Example.—A $100 par value stock paying 1 per cent and purchased at $20 gives a return of 5 per cent. Similarly, a $100 par value stock paying 3½ per cent purchased at $70 gives a return of 5 per cent. For par values less or greater than $100, multiply the "rate of return" figures by P , where P is the par value.

maintenance margin, prescribed by the New York Stock Exchange, is 25 per cent of the security's market value.

The holder may be called upon to put up more margin and more and more and more, if the value of the stock decreases. It is through marginal trading that big sums of money are made in the market, but big sums are lost in the same way. Margin buying is no game for a man who has not money enough to cover his account if there is a sudden drop in market prices.

Selling short is a term used to describe the operation of selling securities one does not own. The seller is betting that the price will go down. He asks his broker to sell short at, say, 90 and cover at 85. The broker sells the stock and then, since the exchange rules demand delivery the fourth business day following the date of the transaction, borrows the stock to make the delivery. The stock is lent in return for payment of the market price. This is returned, with interest, if there is interest, or premium, when the broker buys the stock, for delivery to the lender, at 85. The seller has made the difference between 90 and 85 minus broker's commission, transfer taxes, and interest fees. Selling short is confined as a rule to professional operators in the market.

Much of the trading in the stock exchange is done on borrowed money. There are two kinds of loans, *time loans* and *call loans.* The first is for a definite period, say for 60 days or a year. The rate of interest is agreed upon and does not change, although if the value of the securities placed for collateral falls below the required margin, more securities or money may be demanded. The second, or call, loan, is not for a stated time but is renewed every day. The interest is subject to change from day to day, and the day's activities depend largely upon whether call money is high or low.

All stock exchange transactions are given immediate publicity through the *ticker tape.* As soon as a sale is made it is recorded on the stock ticker. Each stock has a certain symbol, and the symbols and the prices are recorded on the tape. A strip of tape is reproduced below with a translation of the symbols.

TICKER TAPE

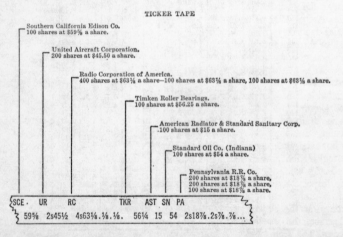

When the tumult and shouting have died, the buyer of a share or a group of shares of stock has a small piece of paper known as a *stock certificate* to show for it, which represents, in effect, a partnership in the business of that company. He should not put it away and forget it. Stocks fluctuate too much to make this wise. If he loses it he should at once notify the corporation and the broker through whom he bought it.

As time goes on the company which issued the stock may float another issue. In this case the original stockholders will have the privilege of buying a certain number of the new shares (allotted according to the number of old shares they held). This privilege is called a *right*. Rights may be extremely valuable or they may be almost worthless, depending upon the subscription price and the market price of the issue. Rights are negotiable and may be bought and sold.

The same general principles set forth above with regard to stocks apply to transactions in bonds.

Stockholders are part owners in a corporation; *bondholders* have lent it money at interest and are its creditors. The usual principal amount on the face of a bond is $1,000 but the delivery of two $500 bonds instead of one $1,000 bond is considered a good delivery. There are also a number of $100 bonds ("baby bonds") on the market.

On coupon bonds the contracts for the payment of interest are on the coupons, which, as they mature, are detached from the bond and may be presented at the bank for payment like a check or draft.

Those who hold registered bonds have their names registered with the agent or maker of the bond. Fully registered bonds are registered as to both principal and interest, and the interest payments are made by check or draft mailed to the owner of the bond. Bonds which are registered as to principal only carry coupons, which are like the ones on regular coupon bonds.

Most bonds are secured by actual property and constitute in effect a mortgage on property. Government bonds, however, are not secured, and there is a certain type of unsecured bond, called debenture, which is sometimes issued by firms of long standing and excellent reputation. A debenture is a promise to pay, and the validity of the promise depends upon the amount of profit the firm makes.

SECURITIES ACTS

Under the jurisdiction of the Securities and Exchange Commission,[1] the Securities Act of 1933 is designed to compel full and fair disclosure to investors of material facts regarding securities[2] publicly offered and sold in interstate commerce, or through the mails, and to prevent fraud in the sale of securities.

Dealers who participate in the sale of new securities must provide their customers with a prospectus. This prospectus is a condensation of the data contained in the registration statement which the issuer must place on file with the Commission before an issue of securities may be offered for public sale.

The Commission has prescribed special forms for filing this information. Each form is designed to record for investors the pertinent information about the securities, the company, the management, and the purpose of issue, together with financial statements, options, salaries, contracts, etc.

A registration statement must become effective before the securities may be offered for sale. A registration statement and prospectuses are available for public inspection and must undergo an examination by the Registration Division, which is composed of a staff of accountants, security analysts, examiners, and attorneys. If the statement appears to be misleading, inaccurate, or incomplete on its face, the issuer is advised and may file amendments to meet these deficiencies. The Commission is empowered to refuse registration in cases in which the issuer fails to supply required data, or to suspend registration if it develops

[1] The Commission also administers the Public Utility Holding Company Act of 1935, the Investment Company Act of 1940, and the Investment Advisers Act of 1940.

[2] There are certain exceptions, including domestic government securities and limited intrastate offerings (under certain conditions).

after registration has become effective that information is lacking or misleading. Registration may be refused or suspended only after public hearing.

The examination of a registration statement is concerned only with the completeness and accuracy of the information. It is not to be considered as a finding by the Commission that the registration statement is true, accurate, or complete, or that the security has investment merit.

The act provides for civil and criminal liability on the part of issuers and others for the fraudulent sale of securities and protects investors against such outright frauds as bucket shops and "sell-and-switch" devices. Prior to the enactment of this law, stock swindlers could escape justice merely by stepping across a state line.

The aims of the Securities Exchange Act of 1934 are threefold: to prevent unfair practices in the securities markets; to regulate the use of credit to finance trading in securities; and to provide the investor with information through the filing of periodic reports with the Commission and the exchanges on which the securities are listed.

Under this act stock exchanges must be registered with the Commission, as must brokers and dealers who transact business in the over-the-counter market; and provisions are made for civil remedies for injured investors and criminal penalties for violations.

The Trust Indenture Act of 1939 is applicable to certain bonds, debentures, notes, and similar debt securities. It requires that any debentures under which such securities are issued conform to prescribed standards designed to safeguard the rights and interests of the purchasers of such securities. Among other things, the indenture trustee must be "independent" and free of any conflicting interests which might interfere with the full performance of duties in behalf of the investor.

BLUE SKY LAWS

"Blue sky" laws are the securities acts by which the states exercise control over the sale of stocks, bonds, and other securities within their borders. The first of these laws was passed in Kansas in 1911. Its purpose was to stop the sale of securities based upon worthless or nonexistent oil wells in Oklahoma. The name is said by some authorities to have come about because the corporations were capitalized out of the blue sky; by others equally competent it is said to have been because the blue sky was the limit to what the corporations offered.

The provisions of the present-day laws vary, but most of them require a sworn statement listing the securities, together with definite and accurate information as to the basis upon which they were issued.

Many securities which may be lawfully issued in one state are not within the law in another state. Anyone contemplating an issue should consult a competent attorney.

BANKRUPTCY[1]

A person in bankruptcy is one who has been declared a bankrupt by a Federal (United States) court. The purposes of the bankruptcy law are (1) to bring

[1] The subject of bankruptcy is a highly technical field. This article is designed as a brief summary of the fundamentals. Any specific situation must be considered individually with careful attention to the provision of the Bankruptcy Act (available through the Superintendent of Documents, Washington, D.C.), the General Orders and Forms in Bankruptcy prescribed by the United States Supreme Court, the rules of the local District Court, the exemptions provided for under state laws, and the pertinent court decisions.

about an equitable distribution of the bankrupt's property among his creditors; (2) to discharge the honest bankrupt from his obligations and enable him to start anew unencumbered; and (3) to reorganize and rehabilitate debtors who are not necessarily insolvent, but who are temporarily hard pressed.

The Federal Constitution gives Congress the power to pass a bankruptcy law which shall have authority throughout the country. The several states may enact statutes to cover points which have not been covered by Federal legislation but they may not pass laws to complement or to provide additional or auxiliary regulations to a Federal Bankruptcy Act when in force.

The Bankruptcy Act now in force is the Act of 1898 as amended by the Act of 1938. This latter amendatory act is known popularly as the Chandler Act.

In addition there are several specific acts affecting the situation: the Corporate Reorganization Act of 1934; the Frazier-Lemke Farm Mortgage Act of 1935; the Debtors' Relief Act of 1933, supplemented 1935; the Railroad Reorganization Act of 1933, amended 1935; the Municipal Debt Adjustment Act of 1937; and the Chandler Railroad Adjustment Act of 1939.

Municipalities, farmers, railroads, and wage earners especially have profited by the new laws. Banks and insurance companies are still excluded from the benefits of the acts. The bankruptcy of a corporation does not release its officers, directors, or stockholders, as such, from any liability under the laws of a state or territory in the United States.

Candidates for Bankruptcy. Any person owing debts, no matter how small in amount or number, may file a petition in voluntary bankruptcy. A debtor with but one small debt and no assets may therefore file such a petition. Generally, provable debts are dischargeable.

Minors, aliens, and, in all states where they can contract debts, married women, may be entitled to the benefits of the act.

The estate of a deceased debtor cannot be declared bankrupt, but if a debtor dies after bankruptcy proceedings have been instituted, they shall proceed just as if he were alive, in so far as this is possible.

Involuntary bankruptcy proceedings are instituted by a creditor or group of creditors filing a petition to have the debtor adjudicated a bankrupt and his assets taken into custody for distribution to his creditors. The alleged bankrupt has the opportunity of contesting the claim asserted against him.

An involuntary petition may be filed against any natural person, excepting a wage earner or a farmer, and may be filed against any corporation except municipal, railroad, insurance, or banking corporations or a building and loan association.

When the debtor's creditors are 12 or more in number, at least three of the creditors are required to join in filing the petition for involuntary bankruptcy. If there are fewer than 12 creditors, one creditor may file. A petition may be filed by such creditors only if:

1. The debtor owes $1,000 or more

2. The creditors who file the petition have provable claims against the debtor totaling $500 or more in excess of any securities which they may hold

3. The debtor has committed an act of bankruptcy within four months of the filing of the involuntary petition. The act defines six acts of bankruptcy, namely (a) conveyances in fraud of creditors; (b) voluntary transfers of property to give preferences to certain creditors while insolvent; (c) permitting any creditor to obtain a lien upon the debtor's property through legal proceedings while the debtor is insolvent which has not been vacated or discharged; (d) making a general assignment for the benefit of creditors; (e) permitting while insolvent the appointment of a receiver or trustee to take charge of the debtor's property; (f) admitting in writing inability to pay debts and willingness to be adjudged a bankrupt.

In either a voluntary or an involuntary petition, application may be made for the appointment of a receiver if it is deemed that the interest of the creditors requires protection against loss of assets.

Property Exemptions. Property exemptions are prescribed by the laws of the state in which the proceedings are held and vary from one state to another. In most states the tools and implements of the bankrupt's trade, his household furniture and wearing apparel (within limits), and his homestead are exempt. Pension money is exempt.

Duties of a Bankrupt. The bankrupt shall:

1. Attend the first meeting of his creditors, if directed by the court or a judge thereof to do so, and the hearing upon his application for a discharge, if filed

2. Comply with all lawful orders of the court

3. Examine the correctness of all proofs of claims filed against his estate

4. Execute and deliver such papers as shall be ordered by the court

5. Execute to his trustee transfers of all his property in foreign countries

6. Immediately inform his trustee of any attempt, by his creditors or other persons, to evade the provisions of this act, coming to his knowledge

7. In case of any person having to his knowledge proved a false claim against his estate, disclose that fact immediately to his trustee

8. Prepare, make oath to, and file in court within ten days after adjudication if an involuntary bankrupt, and within ten days after the filing of a petition if a voluntary bankrupt, unless in either case further time is granted, a schedule of his property, showing the amount and kind of property, the location thereof, its money value, in detail, and a list of his creditors, showing their residences, if known (if unknown that fact to be stated), the amount due each of them, the consideration thereof, the security held by them, if any, and a claim for such exemptions as he may be entitled to, all in triplicate—one copy of each for the clerk, one for the referee, and one for the trustee

9. File in triplicate a statement of his affairs within five days prior to the first meeting of creditors

10. When present at the first meeting of his creditors, and at such other times as the court shall order, submit to an examination concerning the conduct of his business, the cause of his bankruptcy, his dealings with his creditors and other persons, the amount, kind, and whereabouts of his property, and, in addition, all matters which may affect the administration and settlement of his estate; but no testimony given by him shall be offered in evidence against him in any criminal proceedings

11. When required by the court, prepare, verify, and file with the court in duplicate a detailed inventory.

Provable Claims. All claims against the estate of a bankrupt must be filed within six months of the date first set for the first meeting of creditors or they will not be allowed, and must be under oath signed by the creditor containing a statement of the claim, consideration therefor, the securities held, if any, and the payments made on the claim, if any, and that the claim is justly owing. The court may shorten the time to file claims to less than six months, but cannot extend the time. An unliquidated claim is not allowed until liquidated. Unliquidated claims against the bankrupt may, pursuant to applications to the court, be liquidated in such manner as it shall direct, and may thereafter be proved and allowed against his estate. Claims of secured creditors are allowed to the extent of the difference between the value of their security and the amount owed.

Debts which may be proved and allowed against the estate of a bankrupt are the following:

1. A fixed liability as evidenced by a judgment or an instrument in writing, absolutely owing at the time of the filing of the petition against him, whether then payable or not, with any interest thereon which would have been recoverable at

that date, or with a rebate of interest upon such as were not then payable and did not bear interest

2. Due as costs taxable against an involuntary bankrupt who was at the time of the filing of the petition against him plaintiff in a cause of action which would pass to the trustee and which the trustee declines to prosecute after notice

3. Founded upon a claim for taxable costs incurred in good faith by a creditor before the filing of the petition in an action to recover a provable debt

4. Founded upon an open account, or upon a contract express or implied

5. Founded upon provable debts reduced to judgments after the filing of the petition and before the consideration of the bankrupt's application for a discharge, less costs incurred and interest accrued after the filing of the petition and up to the time of the entry of such judgments

6. Founded upon an award of industrial accident commissions having jurisdiction of workmen's compensation cases when the injuries occurred prior to adjudication

7. Founded upon claims for damages in a negligence action instituted prior to and pending at the time of the filing of a petition in bankruptcy

8. Founded upon contingent debts and contingent contractual liabilities

9. Founded upon claims for anticipatory breach of contract, including unexpired leases of real or personal property, with the exception that landlords' claims are limited to one year's rent for the year following the date of surrender of the premises or the re-entry plus unpaid accrued rent.

Bankruptcy Courts and Referees. The United States district courts are the "courts of bankruptcy" or bankruptcy courts. As all questions of both law and fact in relation to the rights of various parties must be decided in the bankruptcy proceedings, it is provided that the judges in each district may appoint *referees* who are charged with the duty of hearing the testimony of all parties and deciding all such questions as may arise. Referees are appointed for terms of two years and take the same oath of office as that prescribed for judges of the United States courts. The Bankruptcy Act is in effect administered by the referees, subject to review by the judges. Each case as it comes up is assigned to a referee, whose duty it is to adjudicate and pass upon all such questions arising therein in the first instance.

Trustees. The *trustee* is an officer of the court. Trustees are appointed by the creditors, at their first meeting after the adjudication, or if they fail to do so, by the court. It is the duty of the trustee to collect assets, reduce them to money, and close up the estate as soon as it can be done, with due regard for the interests of those concerned. Except in matters which are more or less routine, the trustee should consult the wishes of the creditors. The power of removing a trustee rests solely with the judge, though creditors may institute proceedings for his removal. A trustee may resign, but the resignation is ineffectual unless the judge or the referee consents. If a trustee dies or is removed, his place may be filled in the same way that he was appointed, or the decision may be to have his joint trustees carry on without the addition of another person. A trustee designates the attorney to handle the estate. Creditors must therefore be particularly concerned as to the competence of both the trustee and the attorney designated by him, since great care is often necessary to uncover bankruptcy fraud, to trace concealments, or to recover preferences or transfers which have been made.

Compositions. The National Bankruptcy Act provides that debtors may settle with their creditors by means of a compromise. If the bankrupt and a majority of his creditors can come to an agreement about the settlement basis and can get the agreement approved by the court, the agreement becomes binding on all the creditors. This agreement is known as a *composition.* If it is not approved, bankruptcy proceedings continue in the regular way.

Assignments. It is also possible for debtors to make *assignments* in trust, whereby they turn all their assets over to a trustee to sell and distribute the profits among the creditors. There is much less publicity attached to this procedure than to regular bankruptcy proceedings, since it is a private matter between the debtor and his creditors, but in most states the assignment must be recorded. If the creditors are not satisfied, they can have the assignments set aside by filing petition of bankruptcy. Individual debtors usually do not make assignments for the benefit of creditors, since such a proceeding does not result in a discharge of indebtedness to creditors.

Debts Not Affected by a Discharge in Bankruptcy. A *discharge in bankruptcy* releases a bankrupt from all of his provable debts, except such as:

1. Are due as a tax levied by the United States, the state, county, district, or municipality in which he resides, except real estate taxes where the liability for the tax is on the land rather than on the owner

2. Are liabilities for obtaining property by false pretenses or false representation, or for wilful and malicious injuries to the person or property of another, or for alimony due or to become due, or for maintenance or support of wife or child, or for seduction of an unmarried female, or for breach of promise of marriage accompanied by seduction, or for criminal conversation

3. Have not been duly scheduled in time for proof and allowance, with the name of the creditor, if known to the bankrupt, unless such creditor had notice or actual knowledge of the proceedings in bankruptcy

4. Were created by his fraud, embezzlement, misappropriation, or defalcation while acting as an officer or in any fiduciary capacity

5. Are for wages due to workmen, clerks, traveling or city salesmen, or servants, which have been earned within three months before the date of commencement of the proceedings in bankruptcy

6. Are due for moneys of an employee received or retained by his employer to secure the faithful performance by such employee of the terms of a contract of employment

Debts Which Have Priority. The following claims are entitled to priority in the order listed:

1. Administration costs which are the actual and necessary costs of preserving the estate subsequent to filing the petition

2. Creditors' expenses in successfully opposing a bankrupt's discharge or confirmation of an arrangement or wage earner's plan or in discovering evidence resulting in the conviction of any person under the act

3. Wage claims not exceeding $600 to each claimant which have been earned within three months before the date of the beginning of the bankruptcy proceeding. Wage earners' claims exceeding $600 or wages earned outside the three months' period participate as general claims

4. Taxes due to the United States or any state or subdivision thereof

5. Debts owing to any person who by the laws of the United States is entitled to priority, and rent owing to a landlord who by state law is entitled to priority.

Conduct of Bankrupt Preventing Discharge. A bankrupt may be denied a discharge not only from undischargeable debts but from all his debts if any of the following circumstances or situations has occurred. The circumstances prior to the proceeding which will result in the denial of a discharge to the bankrupt are:

1. The destruction of his books by the bankrupt or his failure to keep books of account or records unless the court considers such acts or failure to have been justified

2. The making or publishing of a materially false written financial statement by means of which credit or an extension of credit was obtained

3. The transfer or concealment of any of the bankrupt's property within one year of the filing of the petition with intent to hinder, delay, or defraud his creditors

4. The obtaining of a previous discharge in bankruptcy or the confirmation of a composition, arrangement, or wage earners' plan under the act within six months prior to the present bankruptcy proceeding.

The circumstances occurring subsequent to the filing of the petition which may result in the denial of a discharge are:

An offense punishable by imprisonment under the act, such as the concealment of any property of a bankrupt estate or transfer of property in contemplation of the bankruptcy proceeding or the concealment or falsification of a document relating to the affairs of the bankrupt; and during the course of a proceeding under the act, by the bankrupt's refusal to obey a lawful order or answer a material question asked by the court, or by making a false oath or account in or relating to the bankruptcy.

Dividends. Dividends of an equal per cent shall be declared and paid on all allowed claims, except such as have priority or are secured.

The first dividend shall be declared within 30 days after the adjudication, if the money of the estate in excess of the amount necessary to pay the debts which have priority and such claims as have not been, but probably will be, allowed equals five per cent or more of such allowed claims. Dividends subsequent to the first shall be declared upon like terms as the first and as often as the amount shall equal ten per cent or more and upon closing the estate. Dividends may be declared oftener and in smaller proportions if the judge shall so order: *Provided,* That the first dividend shall not include more than 50 per cent of the money of the estate in excess of the amount necessary to pay the debts which have priority and such claims as probably will be allowed: and provided further, That the final dividend shall not be declared within three months after the first dividend shall be declared.

The rights of creditors who have received dividends, or in whose favor final dividends have been declared, shall not be affected by the proof and allowance of claims subsequent to the date of such payment or declarations of dividends; but the creditors proving and securing the allowance of such claims shall be paid dividends equal in amount to those already received by the other creditors if the estate equals so much before such other creditors are paid any further dividends.

Whenever a person shall have been adjudged a bankrupt by a court without the United States and also by a court of bankruptcy, creditors residing within the United States shall first be paid a dividend equal to that received in the court without the United States by other creditors before creditors who have received a dividend in such court shall be paid any amounts.

A claimant shall not be entitled to collect from a bankrupt estate any greater amount than shall accrue pursuant to the provisions of this act.

If dividends remain unclaimed for six months after the final dividend has been declared the trustee must pay them into the court. If they remain unclaimed for a year the court shall distribute them among the creditors whose claims have been allowed but not fully paid. What is left is paid to the bankrupt. Minors have a year after coming of age to claim such dividends.

STATUTES OF LIMITATION

Statutes of limitation fix an arbitrary time within which every form of action shall be brought. The statutes vary in the different states. Different periods of limitation are provided for different types of actions. The term of the limitation is computed from the time the cause of action arises, unless the statute provides otherwise. For example, when a person borrows money and agrees to repay the loan one year later, and the statute of limitations is six years, the action can be commenced within six years from the time provided for repayment.

The primary purpose of such statutes is to prevent the enforcement of stale or fraudulent claims after proper vouchers and evidence may have been lost, or when it may be impossible to establish the facts because of faulty memory, death, or unavailability of witnesses.

Such statutes will not ordinarily have a retroactive effect. However, within constitutional limitations, a statute of limitation may apply to causes of action which accrued before the enactment of the statute, as well as to causes of action which accrued thereafter.

The statute of limitation may be waived under certain circumstances; for example, by written acknowledgment of the indebtedness before expiration of the statutory period. Likewise, payment of interest or part of the principal will in almost all cases have the effect of causing the term within which action may be brought to begin anew from the date of the payment of interest or the part of the principal. Similarly, in many states, time absent from the state during which a summons cannot be served within the state is added to the statutory term. In some states a claim outlawed by the statute of limitation may be revived through the execution of a formal acknowledgment of the indebtedness by the debtor.

In the absence of statute, criminal prosecutions are not barred by the lapse of time. However, some states have statutes specifying the time within which criminal prosecutions must be commenced. Such statutes are regarded as acts of grace or amnesty. The period of limitation applicable to particular crimes is determined by the statutory provision in the jurisdiction in which the offender is prosecuted.

Under the Federal statutes, an indictment or information for an offense punishable by death may be found at any time without regard to any statute of limitation. As to crimes arising under the internal revenue laws the limitation is three years, except as to offenses involving the defrauding or attempting to defraud the United States, or the offense of willfully attempting in any manner to evade or defeat any tax or the payment thereof; or offenses with respect to the preparation or presentation of false or fraudulent returns, affidavits, claims, or documents, and conspiracies to evade any tax or payment thereof. In these cases the limitation is six years. Under the Bankruptcy Act, an indictment or information must be filed within three years after the commission of any offense arising under the act. However, the offense of concealment of assets is deemed continuing until the final discharge, and the period of limitations does not begin to run until the final discharge.

THE GOVERNMENT OF THE UNITED STATES

Men must either govern or be governed; they must take part in the control of their own lives, or they must lead subject lives, helplessly dependent in the little things and great things of life upon the will and power of others.
—ELIHU ROOT.

THE PRESIDENT

The President of the United States is chosen by the electoral college, the membership of which is selected by the various states according to whatever method they choose. Each state has as many members in the electoral college as it has members in both houses of Congress. In case of a tie, the House decides by a majority of states, each state having one vote.

The candidate for the Presidency must be a natural born citizen of the United States, at least 35 years old, and must have lived within the United States for 14 years.

The President receives a salary of $100,000 a year, plus a taxable expense allowance of $50,000 and a nontaxable sum not to exceed $40,000 a year for travel and official entertainment expenses.

The Constitution of the United States directs that the President, before he enters on the execution of his office, shall take the following oath or affirmation:

"I do solemnly swear (or affirm) that I will faithfully execute the office of President of the United States, and will, to the best of my ability, preserve, protect, and defend the Constitution of the United States."

It is the duty of the President as the head of the government to see that the provisions of the Constitution are carried out, that laws are enforced, treaties respected, and decisions of the Federal courts strictly observed.

In the administration of his duty he is aided by a cabinet of ten members. These ten members, each the head of an important department, are appointed by the President subject to the approval of the Senate. They meet regularly, and the President may summon them at any time for a special meeting. The meetings are informal; no formal record of the proceedings is kept, and the discussions are, as a rule, kept secret. In case of the removal, death, resignation, or inability of both the President and the Vice President, the Speaker of the House of Representatives, upon his resignation as Speaker and Representative, shall act as President. Should there be no Speaker, or should he fail to qualify, the president pro tempore of the Senate becomes the President. In the absence of both a Speaker and president pro tempore of the Senate, the cabinet officers succeed to the Presidency in the following order:

Secretary of State	Secretary of the Interior
Secretary of the Treasury	Secretary of Agriculture
Secretary of Defense	Secretary of Commerce
Attorney General	Secretary of Labor
Postmaster General	

Members of the cabinet are not allowed to sit in either the Senate or the House of Representatives.

They receive salaries of $25,000 a year, and have under secretaries and assistants with salaries ranging from $22,500 down.

The President has great influence throughout the judicial department of the government through his power of appointing Federal judges, even though these appointments must have the approval of the Senate. Federal judges are appointed for life or during good behavior and can be removed only by impeachment.

The President is by virtue of his office Commander in Chief of the armed forces, and in time of war has almost absolute control of the economic resources and man power of the country.

The President theoretically determines foreign policy but is constantly held in check by the Senate. He may negotiate treaties, but the Senate must confirm them. He appoints diplomats and consuls, but these, too, are subject to the approval of the Senate.

The President receives the ambassadors and other ministers of foreign countries and may dismiss them, no matter how serious the consequences which may follow.

The President has unlimited power to grant pardons or reprieves for offenses against the United States.

The President is required by the Constitution to send or deliver from time to time a message to Congress on the state of the country, with recommendations for such legislation as he may think desirable. The Presidential message may have great influence, especially when his party is in control, but the President has no power to enforce his desires; he can merely state them. See The Constitution of the United States.

The only direct control he has over legislation is through the fact that he can veto any Act of Congress that does not win his approval, and even this is not unlimited. Every act or resolution must be presented to the President after it has been passed by Congress. If he signs it or fails to return it within ten days, it becomes a law. If he returns it with a statement of his reasons for disapproving it, this constitutes a veto, and the measure is killed unless it goes again before both houses and wins a two-thirds vote, in which case it becomes a law in spite of the veto.

If the President retains a bill without signing it for more than ten days (Sunday excepted) it automatically becomes a law unless it was passed within ten days of the adjournment of Congress, in which case the President may retain or "pocket" the bill, which does not then become a law but is killed without a direct veto and without the risk of being passed over a veto. This veto is provided for in the Constitution, Article I, Section 7, Clause 2.

THE CABINET

The duties of the ten departments headed by cabinet members are indicated by the titles of the departments.

The *Department of State* has charge of foreign affairs. It issues passports and in general supervises relations with other countries. The Secretary of State is custodian of the national archives and keeper of the Great Seal of the United States. The Department of State is older than the Constitution. Before the Declaration of Independence was issued, the Continental Congress had found it necessary to establish a Department of Foreign Affairs, a Treasury Department, a War Department, and a Post Office Department. All these departments were immediately re-established by the first Congress which met under the Constitution, and, although their duties have been modified and enlarged in various ways, all four have continued active until the present day.

The *Department of the Treasury* acts as the financial agent of the government. Its duties include the collection of Federal taxes, customs duties, and internal revenue; the minting of coin and printing of paper money, stamps, etc.; the supervision of the national banks; the detection of counterfeiters and smugglers; the maintenance of the coast guard, and the construction and maintenance of United States government buildings throughout the country.

This department also prepares an annual budget, which, however, is mainly suggestive, since the authority to determine expenditures and appropriations lies with Congress.

The *Departments of War, Navy,* and *Air Force* were reorganized in 1947 as the *Department of Defense*. The secretaries of these departments do not have cabinet status, but are represented in the cabinet by the *Secretary of Defense,* who coordinates the functions of all three departments. The *Secretary of the Army* is in charge of organizing, training, and maintaining the Army. His responsibilities include control of Army appropriations and expenditures; development of improved weapons and matériel; and defense of coastal cities and harbors of the United States and of the Panama Canal. The *Department of the Navy* has charge of the construction and maintenance of vessels, the maintenance of Navy yards, and the administration of the personnel and equipment of the Navy. The *Department of the Air Force* was created from the Army Air Forces in 1947 and includes all military aviation forces, combat and service, and otherwise assigned. It is organized and trained for prompt and sustained air offensive and defensive operations.

The *Attorney General,* who is head of the Department of Justice, is the chief law counselor of the United States. Upon request he is required by statute to render advice to the President or to any one of the executive departments. The Department of Justice passes upon the validity of titles to public lands bought by the United States for the erection of public buildings and acts in all litigation where the United States is concerned. The Attorney General appears sometimes in the Supreme Court but seldom in the lower courts.

The *Post Office Department* has a much greater number of employees than any other department. Besides carrying the mails, the department operates the postal savings banks and handles a great deal of currency through money orders.

The *Department of the Interior* has charge of pensions, public lands, Indian affairs, national parks, reclamation service, and a variety of other matters which do not fit directly into any other department.

Few of the departments render so direct and personal a service as the *Department of Agriculture*. For its duties, see The Department of Agriculture.

The *Department of Commerce* has charge of the development of foreign and domestic trade. The National Bureau of Standards functions under this department which also has charge of the licensing and inspection of steamboats, the regulation of fisheries, the regulation and maintenance of the lighthouse service, the making of coastal and geodetic surveys, the taking of the census, issuing of patents, and the publication of commercial statistics.

The *Department of Labor* has charge of the administration and enforcement of statutes designed to advance the welfare of wage earners in the United States, to improve their working conditions, and to advance their opportunities for profitable employment. The department is directed by the Secretary of Labor and is composed of several major units, including the Bureau of Labor Standards, the Bureau of Labor Statistics, the Wage and Hour and Public Contracts Divisions, and the Women's Bureau.

The *Department of Health, Education, and Welfare* has assumed the functions of the former Federal Security Agency, administering the health, education, and welfare legislation of the United States.

CONGRESS

The legislative department of the United States government is known as Congress and consists of two houses, the Senate and the House of Representatives. Each state has two Senators who are elected by popular vote for a period of six years. Senators may serve as many terms as their followers will allow. A Senator must be 30 years old and, if he is an alien, he must have been a citizen of the United States for nine years and must be a resident of the state in which he is elected. His salary is $22,500 a year. In addition to its lawmaking power, the Senate confirms the appointments made by the President, ratifies treaties, and tries impeachments.

Members of the House of Representatives are elected by the people for a period of two years and may be re-elected. The number of Representatives from each state is based upon the population figures from that state at the last official census. (It was to determine the number of Representatives, as a matter of fact, that the census was instituted.) The census is taken every ten years. A Representative must be 25 years old, and, if he is an alien, he must have been a citizen of the United States for seven years and must be a resident of the state which elects him. His salary is $22,500 a year. The House of Representatives has the sole power of presenting impeachments, just as the Senate has the sole power of trying them.

THE FEDERAL COURTS

At the head of the Federal courts stands the Supreme Court. The Supreme Court has nine members, a Chief Justice who receives a salary of $35,500 a year, and eight associate justices with salaries of $35,000 each. This court is the highest judicial authority in the United States. From its decisions there is no appeal.

The Supreme Court has jurisdiction over cases involving foreign ambassadors, public ministers, consuls, etc.; cases governed by admiralty and maritime laws;

cases in which the United States is a party; and cases between a citizen of the United States and of a foreign state, between citizens of different states or citizens of the same state claiming land granted by another state, between a state and its citizens, etc. Its greatest power is the right to declare any Federal or state statute null and void if a majority of the justices find it unconstitutional.

There are ten circuits in the United States, in each of which there are circuit judges, the number depending upon the amount of judicial work to be done. The circuit judges sit with the district judges, thus forming the Circuit Courts of Appeal.

Below the Circuit Court is the District Court, which is the lowest Federal court. If a district is large it may be subdivided, and each subdivision may be presided over by one or more judges.

Circuit judges receive $25,500 and district judges $22,500 a year.

The Court of Claims hears all citizen claims against the Federal government. It consists of a chief and four associate judges, who receive $25,500 a year.

The Court of Customs and Patent Appeals consists of a presiding judge and four associate judges, who receive $25,500 a year. Formerly this court was called the Court of Customs Appeals and acted as the final court of appeal in matters connected with the administration of the tariff laws. In 1929 the title was changed to the United States Court of Customs and Patent Appeals. In addition to tariff questions, it now handles all matters connected with appeals from the Patent Office in patent and trademark cases which were formerly under the jurisdiction of the Court of Appeals in the District of Columbia.

THE CONSTITUTION OF THE UNITED STATES

PREAMBLE

We, the people of the United States, in order to form a more perfect Union, establish justice, insure domestic tranquillity, provide for the common defense, promote the general welfare, and secure the blessings of liberty to ourselves and our posterity, do ordain and establish this Constitution for the United States of America.

ARTICLE I

Section 1. (Legislative powers; in whom vested)

All legislative powers herein granted shall be vested in a Congress of the United States, which shall consist of a Senate and House of Representatives.

Section 2. (House of Representatives, how and by whom chosen. Qualifications of a Representative. Representatives and direct taxes, how apportioned. Enumeration. Vacancies to be filled. Power of choosing officers, and of impeachment.)

1. The House of Representatives shall be composed of members chosen every second year by the people of the several States, and the electors in each State shall have the qualifications requisite for electors of the most numerous branch of the State Legislature.

2. No person shall be a Representative who shall not have attained to the age of twenty-five years, and been seven years a citizen of the United States, and who shall not, when elected, be an inhabitant of that State in which he shall be chosen.

3. Representatives and direct taxes shall be apportioned among the several States which may be included within this Union, according to their respective numbers, which shall be determined by adding to the whole number of free per-

sons, including those bound to service for a term of years, and excluding Indians not taxed, three fifths of all other persons. The actual enumeration shall be made within three years after the first meeting of the Congress of the United States, and within every subsequent term of ten years, in such manner as they shall by law direct. The number of Representatives shall not exceed one for every thirty thousand, but each State shall have at least one Representative; and until such enumeration shall be made, the State of New Hampshire shall be entitled to choose 3; Massachusetts, 8; Rhode Island and Providence Plantations, 1; Connecticut, 5; New York, 6; New Jersey, 4; Pennsylvania, 8; Delaware, 1; Maryland, 6; Virginia, 10; North Carolina, 5; South Carolina, 5; and Georgia, 3.[1]

4. When vacancies happen in the representation from any State, the Executive Authority thereof shall issue writs of election to fill such vacancies.

5. The House of Representatives shall choose their Speaker and other officers; and shall have the sole power of impeachment.

Section 3. (Senators, how and by whom chosen. How classified. State Executive, when to make temporary appointments, in case, etc. Qualifications of a Senator. President of the Senate, his right to vote. President pro tem., and other officers of the Senate, how chosen. Power to try impeachments. When President is tried, Chief Justice to preside. Sentence.)

1. The Senate of the United States shall be composed of two Senators from each State, chosen by the Legislature thereof, for six years; and each Senator shall have one vote.

2. Immediately after they shall be assembled in consequence of the first election, they shall be divided as equally as may be into three classes. The seats of the Senators of the first class shall be vacated at the expiration of the second year, of the second class at the expiration of the fourth year, and of the third class at the expiration of the sixth year, so that one third may be chosen every second year; and if vacancies happen by resignation, or otherwise, during the recess of the Legislature of any State, the Executive thereof may make temporary appointment until the next meeting of the Legislature, which shall then fill such vacancies.

3. No person shall be a Senator who shall not have attained to the age of thirty years, and been nine years a citizen of the United States, and who shall not, when elected, be an inhabitant of that State for which he shall be chosen.

4. The Vice President of the United States shall be President of the Senate, but shall have no vote, unless they be equally divided.

5. The Senate shall choose their other officers, and also a President pro tempore, in the absence of the Vice President, or when he shall exercise the office of President of the United States.

6. The Senate shall have the sole power to try all impeachments. When sitting for that purpose, they shall be on oath or affirmation. When the President of the United States is tried, the Chief Justice shall preside: and no person shall be convicted without the concurrence of two thirds of the members present.

7. Judgment of cases of impeachment shall not extend further than to removal from office, and disqualification to hold and enjoy any office of honor, trust or profit under the United States; but the party convicted shall nevertheless

---

[1] See Article XIV, Amendments.

be liable and subject to indictment, trial, judgment and punishment, according to law.

Section 4. (Times, etc., of holding elections, how prescribed. One session in each year.)

1. The times, places and manner of holding elections for Senators and Representatives, shall be prescribed in each State by the Legislature thereof; but the Congress may at any time by law make or alter such regulations, except as to places of choosing Senators.

2. The Congress shall assemble at least once in every year, and such meeting shall be on the first Monday in December, unless they shall by law appoint a different day.

Section 5. (Membership, quorum, adjournments. Rules. Power to punish or expel. Journal. Time of adjournments, how limited, etc.)

1. Each House shall be the judge of the elections, returns and qualifications of its own members, and a majority of each shall constitute a quorum to do business; but a smaller number may adjourn from day to day, and may be authorized to compel the attendance of absent members, in such manner, and under such penalties as each House may provide.

2. Each House may determine the rules of its proceedings, punish its members for disorderly behavior, and, with the concurrence of two thirds, expel a member.

3. Each House shall keep a journal of its proceedings, and from time to time publish the same, excepting such parts as may in their judgment require secrecy; and the yeas and nays of the members of either House on any question shall, at the desire of one fifth of those present, be entered on the journal.

4. Neither House, during the session of Congress, shall, without the consent of the other, adjourn for more than three days, nor to any other place than that in which the two Houses shall be sitting.

Section 6. (Compensation. Privileges. Disqualification in certain cases.)

1. The Senators and Representatives shall receive a compensation for their services, to be ascertained by law, and paid out of the Treasury of the United States. They shall in all cases, except treason, felony and breach of the peace, be privileged from arrest during their attendance at the session of their respective Houses, and in going to and returning from the same; and for any speech or debate in either House, they shall not be questioned in any other place.

2. No Senator or Representative shall, during the time for which he was elected, be appointed to any civil office under the authority of the United States, which shall have been created, or the emoluments whereof shall have been increased during such time; and no person holding any office under the United States, shall be a member of either House during his continuance in office.

Section 7. (House to originate all revenue bills. Veto. Bill may be passed by two thirds of each House, notwithstanding, etc. Bill not returned in ten days to become a law. Provisions as to orders, concurrent resolutions, etc.)

1. All bills for raising revenue shall originate in the House of Representatives; but the Senate may propose or concur with amendments as on other bills.

2. Every bill which shall have passed the House of Representatives and the Senate, shall, before it become a law, be presented to the President of the United States; if he approve he shall sign it, but if not he shall return it, with his objections, to that House in which it shall have originated, who shall enter

the objections at large on their journal, and proceed to reconsider it. If after such reconsideration two thirds of that House shall agree to pass the bill, it shall be sent, together with the objections, to the other House, by which it shall likewise be reconsidered, and if approved by two thirds of that House it shall become a law. But in all such cases the votes of both Houses shall be determined by yeas and nays, and the names of the persons voting for and against the bill shall be entered on the journal of each House respectively. If any bill shall not be returned by the President within ten days (Sundays excepted) after it shall have been presented to him, the same shall be a law, in like manner as if he had signed it, unless the Congress by their adjournment prevent its return, in which case it shall not be a law.

3. Every order, resolution, or vote to which the concurrence of the Senate and House of Representatives may be necessary (except on a question of adjournment) shall be presented to the President of the United States; and before the same shall take effect, shall be approved by him, or being disapproved by him, shall be repassed by two thirds of the Senate and the House of Representatives, according to the rules and limitations prescribed in the case of a bill.

Section 8. (Powers of Congress.)

The Congress shall have power:

1. To lay and collect taxes, duties, imposts and excises, to pay the debts and provide for the common defense and general welfare of the United States; but all duties, imposts and excises shall be uniform throughout the United States;

2. To borrow money on the credit of the United States;

3. To regulate commerce with foreign nations, and among the several States, and with the Indian tribes;

4. To establish an uniform rule of naturalization and uniform laws on the subject of bankruptcies throughout the United States;

5. To coin money, regulate the value thereof, and of foreign coin, and fix the standard of weights and measures;

6. To provide for the punishment of counterfeiting the securities and current coin of the United States;

7. To establish post offices and post roads;

8. To promote the progress of science and useful arts, by securing for limited times to authors and inventors the exclusive rights to their respective writings and discoveries;

9. To constitute tribunals inferior to the Supreme Court;

10. To define and punish piracies and felonies committed on the high seas, and offenses against the law of nations;

11. To declare war, grant letters of marque and reprisal, and make rules concerning captures on land and water;

12. To raise and support armies, but no appropriation of money to that use shall be for a longer term than two years;

13. To provide and maintain a navy;

14. To make rules for the government and regulation of the land and naval forces;

15. To provide for calling forth the militia to execute the laws of the Union, suppress insurrections, and repel invasions;

16. To provide for organizing, arming, and disciplining, the militia, and for governing such part of them as may be employed in the service of the United

States, reserving to the States respectively, the appointment of the officers, and the authority of training the militia according to the discipline prescribed by Congress;

17. To exercise exclusive legislation in all cases whatsoever, over such district (not exceeding ten miles square) as may, by cession of particular States, and the acceptance of Congress, become the seat of the Government of the United States, and to exercise like authority over all places purchased by the consent of the Legislature of the State in which the same shall be, for the erection of forts, magazines, arsenals, dockyards, and other needful buildings; and

18. To make all laws which shall be necessary and proper for carrying into execution the foregoing powers, and all other powers vested by this Constitution in the Government of the United States, or in any department or officer thereof.

Section 9. (Provision as to migration or importation of certain persons. Habeas Corpus. Bills of attainder, etc. Taxes, how apportioned. No export duty. No commercial preference. Money, how drawn from Treasury, etc. No titular nobility. Officers not to receive presents, etc.)

1. The migration or importation of such persons as any of the States now existing shall think proper to admit, shall not be prohibited by the Congress prior to the year one thousand eight hundred and eight, but a tax or duty may be imposed on such importation, not exceeding ten dollars for each person.

2. The privilege of the writ of habeas corpus shall not be suspended, unless when in cases of rebellion or invasion the public safety may require it.

3. No bill of attainder or ex post facto law shall be passed.

4. No capitation, or other direct, tax shall be laid, unless in proportion to the census or enumeration hereinbefore directed to be taken.

5. No tax or duty shall be laid on articles exported from any State.

6. No preference shall be given by any regulation of commerce or revenue to the ports of one State over those of another: nor shall vessels bound to, or from, one State, be obliged to enter, clear, or pay duties in another.

7. No money shall be drawn from the Treasury, but in consequence of appropriations made by law; and a regular statement and account of the receipts and expenditures of all public money shall be published from time to time.

8. No title of nobility shall be granted by the United States: and no person holding any office of profit or trust under them, shall, without the consent of the Congress, accept of any present, emolument, office, or title, of any kind whatever, from any king, prince, or foreign state.

Section 10. (States prohibited from the exercise of certain powers.)

1. No State shall enter into any treaty, alliance, or confederation, grant letters of marque and reprisal, coin money, emit bills of credit, make anything but gold and silver coin a tender in payment of debts, pass any bill of attainder, ex post facto law, or law impairing the obligation of contracts, or grant any title of nobility.

2. No State shall, without the consent of the Congress, lay any impost or duties on imports or exports, except what may be absolutely necessary for executing its inspection laws: and the net produce of all duties and imposts, laid by any State on imports or exports, shall be for the use of the Treasury of

the United States; and all such laws shall be subject to the revision and control of the Congress.

3. No State shall, without the consent of Congress, lay any duty of tonnage, keep troops, or ships of war in time of peace, enter into agreement or compact with another State, or with a foreign power, or engage in war, unless actually invaded, or in such imminent danger as will not admit of delay.

ARTICLE II

Section 1. (President; his term of office. Electors of President; number and how appointed. Electors to vote on same day. Qualification of President. On whom his duties devolve in case of his removal, death, etc. President's compensation. His oath of office.)

1. The Executive power shall be vested in a President of the United States of America. He shall hold his office during the term of four years, and, together with the Vice President, chosen for the same term, be elected, as follows:

2. Each State shall appoint, in such manner as the Legislature thereof may direct, a number of electors, equal to the whole number of Senators and Representatives to which the State may be entitled in the Congress: but no Senator or Representative, or person holding an office of trust or profit under the United States, shall be appointed an elector.

3. The electors shall meet in their respective States, and vote by ballot for two persons, of whom one at least shall not be an inhabitant of the same State with themselves. And they shall make a list of all the persons voted for, and of the number of votes for each; which list they shall sign and certify, and transmit sealed to the seat of the Government of the United States, directed to the President of the Senate. The President of the Senate shall, in the presence of the Senate and House of Representatives, open all the certificates, and the votes shall then be counted. The person having the greatest number of votes shall be the President, if such number be a majority of the whole number of electors appointed; and if there be more than one who have such a majority, and have an equal number of votes, then the House of Representatives shall immediately choose by ballot one of them for President: and if no person have a majority, then from the five highest on the list the said House shall in like manner choose the President. But in choosing the President, the vote shall be taken by States, the representation from each State having one vote; a quorum for this purpose shall consist of a member or members from two thirds of the States, and a majority of all the States shall be necessary to a choice. In every case, after the choice of the President, the person having the greatest number of votes of the electors shall be the Vice President. But if there should remain two or more who have equal votes, the Senate shall choose from them by ballot the Vice President.[1]

4. The Congress may determine the time of choosing the electors, and the day on which they shall give their votes; which day shall be the same throughout the United States.

5. No person except a natural born citizen, or a citizen of the United States, at the time of the adoption of this Constitution, shall be eligible to the office of President; neither shall any person be eligible to that office who shall not

---

[1] This clause is superseded by Article XII, Amendments.

have attained to the age of thirty-five years, and been fourteen years a resident within the United States.

6. In case of the removal of the President from office, or of his death, resignation, or inability to discharge the powers and duties of the said office, the same shall devolve on the Vice President, and the Congress may by law provide for the case of removal, death, resignation, or inability, both of the President and Vice President, declaring what officer shall then act as President, and such officer shall act accordingly, until the disability be removed, or a President shall be elected.

7. The President shall, at stated times, receive for his services, a compensation, which shall neither be increased nor diminished during the period for which he shall have been elected, and he shall not receive within that period any other emolument from the United States, or any of them.

8. Before he enter on the execution of his office he shall take the following oath or affirmation:

"I do solemnly swear (or affirm) that I will faithfully execute the office of President of the United States, and will, to the best of my ability, preserve, protect, and defend the Constitution of the United States."

Section 2. (President to be Commander in Chief. He may require opinions of Cabinet officers, etc., may pardon. Treaty-making power. Nomination of certain officers. When President may fill vacancies.)

1. The President shall be Commander in Chief of the Army and Navy of the United States, and of the militia of the several States, when called into the actual service of the United States; he may require the opinion, in writing, of the principal officer in each of the executive departments, upon any subject relating to the duties of their respective offices, and he shall have power to grant reprieves and pardons for offenses against the United States, except in cases of impeachment.

2. He shall have power, by and with the advice and consent of the Senate, to make treaties, provided two thirds of the Senators present concur; and he shall nominate, and by and with the advice and consent of the Senate, shall appoint ambassadors, other public ministers and consuls, judges of the Supreme Court, and all other officers of the United States, whose appointments are not herein otherwise provided for, and which shall be established by law: but the Congress may by law vest the appointment of such inferior officers, as they think proper, in the President alone, in the courts of law, or in the heads of departments.

3. The President shall have power to fill up all vacancies that may happen during the recess of the Senate, by granting commissions which shall expire at the end of their next session.

Section 3. (President shall communicate with Congress. He may convene and adjourn Congress, in case of disagreement, etc. Shall receive ambassadors, execute laws, and commission officers.)

He shall from time to time give to the Congress information of the state of the Union, and recommend to their consideration such measures as he shall judge necessary and expedient; he may, on extraordinary occasions, convene both Houses, or either of them, and in case of disagreement between them, with respect to the time of adjournment, he may adjourn them to such time as he shall think proper; he shall receive ambassadors and other public ministers;

he shall take care that the laws be faithfully executed, and shall commission all the officers of the United States.

Section 4. (All civil offices forfeited for certain crimes.)

The President, Vice President and all civil officers of the United States, shall be removed from office on impeachment for, and conviction of, treason, bribery, or other high crimes and misdemeanors.

ARTICLE III

Section 1. (Judicial powers. Tenure. Compensation.)

The judicial power of the United States, shall be vested in one Supreme Court, and in such inferior courts as the Congress may from time to time ordain and establish. The judges, both of the Supreme and inferior courts, shall hold their offices during good behavior, and shall, at stated times, receive for their services, a compensation, which shall not be diminished during their continuance in office.

Section 2. (Judicial power; to what cases it extends. Original jurisdiction of Supreme Court. Appellate. Trial by jury, etc. Trial, where.)

1. The judicial power shall extend to all cases, in law and equity, arising under this Constitution, the laws of the United States, and treaties made, or which shall be made, under their authority; to all cases affecting ambassadors, other public ministers and consuls; to all cases of admiralty and maritime jurisdiction; to controversies to which the United States shall be a party; to controversies between two or more States; between a State and citizens of another State; between citizens of different States; between citizens of the same State claiming lands under grants of different States, and between a State, or the citizens thereof, and foreign states, citizens or subjects.

2. In all cases affecting ambassadors, other public ministers and consuls, and those in which a State shall be party, the Supreme Court shall have original jurisdiction. In all the other cases before mentioned, the Supreme Court shall have appellate jurisdiction, both as to law and fact, with such exceptions, and under such regulations as the Congress shall make.

3. The trial of all crimes, except in cases of impeachment, shall be by jury; and such trial shall be held in the State where the said crimes shall have been committed; but when not committed within any State, the trial shall be at such place or places as the Congress may by law have directed.

Section 3. (Treason defined. Proof of. Punishment of.)

1. Treason against the United States, shall consist only in levying war against them, or in adhering to their enemies, giving them aid and comfort. No person shall be convicted of treason unless on the testimony of two witnesses to the same overt act, or on confession in open court.

2. The Congress shall have power to declare the punishment of treason, but no attainder of treason shall work corruption of blood, or forfeiture except during the life of the person attainted.

ARTICLE IV

Section 1. (Each State to give credit to the public acts, etc., of every other State.)

Full faith and credit shall be given in each State to the public acts, records, and judicial proceedings of every other State. And the Congress may by general laws prescribe the manner in which such acts, records, and proceedings shall be proved, and the effect thereof.

Section 2. (Privileges of citizens of each State. Fugitives from justice to be delivered up. Persons held to service having escaped, to be delivered up.)

1. The citizens of each State shall be entitled to all privileges and immunities of citizens in the several States.

2. A person charged in any State with treason, felony, or other crime, who shall flee from justice, and be found in another State, shall on demand of the Executive authority of the State from which he fled, be delivered up, to be removed to the State having jurisdiction of the crime.

3. No person held to service or labor in one State, under the laws thereof, escaping into another, shall, in consequence of any law or regulation therein, be discharged from such service or labor, but shall be delivered up on claim of the party to whom such service or labor may be due.

Section 3. (Admission of new States. Power of Congress over territory and other property.)

1. New States may be admitted by the Congress into this Union; but no new State shall be formed or erected within the jurisdiction of any other State; nor any State be formed by the junction of two or more States, or parts of States, without the consent of the Legislatures of the States concerned as well as of the Congress.

2. The Congress shall have power to dispose of and make all needful rules and regulations respecting the territory or other property belonging to the United States; and nothing in this Constitution shall be so construed as to prejudice any claims of the United States, or of any particular State.

Section 4. (Republican form of government guaranteed. Each State to be protected.)

The United States shall guarantee to every State in this Union a Republican form of government, and shall protect each of them against invasion; and on application of the Legislature, or of the Executive (when the Legislature cannot be convened) against domestic violence.

ARTICLE V

(Constitution; how amended. Proviso.)

The Congress, whenever two thirds of both Houses shall deem it necessary, shall propose amendments to this Constitution, or, on the application of the Legislatures of two thirds of the several States, shall call a convention for proposing amendments, which, in either case, shall be valid to all intents and purposes, as part of this Constitution, when ratified by the Legislatures of three fourths of the several States, or by conventions in three fourths thereof, as the one or the other mode of ratification may be proposed by the Congress; provided that no amendment which may be made prior to the year one thousand eight hundred and eight shall in any manner affect the first and fourth clauses in the Ninth Section of the First Article; and that no State, without its consent, shall be deprived of its equal suffrage in the Senate.

ARTICLE VI

(Certain debts, etc., declared valid. Supremacy of Constitution, treaties, and laws of the United States. Oath to support Constitution, by whom taken. No religious test.)

1. All debts contracted and engagements entered into, before the adoption of this Constitution, shall be as valid against the United States under this Constitution, as under the Confederation.

2. This Constitution and the laws of the United States which shall be made in pursuance thereof; and all treaties made, or which shall be made, under the authority of the United States, shall be the supreme law of the land; and the judges in every State shall be bound thereby, any thing in the Constitution or laws of any State to the contrary notwithstanding.

3. The Senators and Representatives before mentioned, and the members of the several State Legislatures, and all executive and judicial officers, both of the United States and of the several States, shall be bound by oath or affirmation, to support this Constitution; but no religious test shall ever be required as a qualification to any office or public trust under the United States.

ARTICLE VII

(What ratification shall establish Constitution.)

The ratification of the Conventions of nine States, shall be sufficient for the establishment of this Constitution between the States so ratifying the same.

AMENDMENTS TO THE CONSTITUTION OF THE UNITED STATES[1]

AMENDMENT . I

(Religious establishment prohibited. Freedom of speech, press, and petition.)

Congress shall make no law respecting an establishment of religion, or prohibiting the free exercise thereof; or abridging the freedom of speech, or of the press; or the right of the people peaceably to assemble, and to petition the Government for a redress of grievances.

AMENDMENT II

(Right to keep and bear arms.)

A well-regulated militia being necessary to the security of a free State, the right of the people to keep and bear arms, shall not be infringed.

AMENDMENT III

(Conditions for quartering of soldiers.)

No soldier shall, in time of peace be quartered in any house, without the consent of the owner, nor in time of war, but in a manner to be prescribed by law.

AMENDMENT IV

(Regulation of right of search and seizure.)

The right of the people to be secure in their persons, houses, papers, and effects, against unreasonable searches and seizures, shall not be violated, and no warrants shall issue, but upon probable cause, supported by oath or affirmation, and particularly describing the place to be searched, and the persons or things to be seized.

---

[1] The Amendments I to X are commonly known as The Bill of Rights.

AMENDMENT V

(Provisions concerning prosecution, trial, and punishment. Private property not to be taken for public use without compensation.)

No person shall be held to answer for a capital, or otherwise infamous, crime unless on a presentment or indictment of a Grand Jury, except in cases arising in the land or naval forces, or in the militia, when in actual service in time of war or public danger; nor shall any person be subject for the same offense to be twice put in jeopardy of life or limb; nor shall be compelled in any criminal case to be a witness against himself, nor be deprived of life, liberty, or property, without due process of law; nor shall private property be taken for public use, without just compensation.

AMENDMENT VI

(Right to speedy trial, witnesses, etc.)

In all criminal prosecutions, the accused shall enjoy the right to a speedy and public trial, by an impartial jury of the State and district wherein the crime shall have been committed, which districts shall have been previously ascertained by law, and to be informed of the nature and cause of the accusation; to be confronted with the witnesses against him; to have compulsory process for obtaining witnesses in his favor, and to have the assistance of counsel for his defense.

AMENDMENT VII

(Right to trial by jury.)

In suits at common law, where the value in controversy shall exceed twenty dollars, the right of trial by jury shall be preserved, and no fact tried by a jury, shall be otherwise re-examined in any court of the United States, than according to the rules of the common law.

AMENDMENT VIII

(Excessive bail or fines and cruel punishment prohibited.)

Excessive bail shall not be required, nor excessive fines imposed, nor cruel and unusual punishments inflicted.

AMENDMENT IX

(Rule of construction of Constitution.)

The enumeration in the Constitution, of certain rights, shall not be construed to deny or disparage others retained by the people.

AMENDMENT X

(Rights of States under Constitution.)

The powers not delegated to the United States by the Constitution, nor prohibited by it to the States, are reserved to the States respectively, or to the people.

AMENDMENT XI

(Judicial powers construed.)

The following amendment was proposed to the Legislatures of the several states by the Third Congress on March 5, 1794, and was declared to have been ratified in a message from the President to Congress, dated January 8, 1798.

The judicial power of the United States shall not be construed to extend to any suit in law or equity, commenced or prosecuted against one of the United States by citizens of another State, or by citizens or subjects of any foreign state.

AMENDMENT XII

(Manner of choosing President and Vice President.)

The following amendment was proposed to the Legislatures of the several states by the Eighth Congress on December 12, 1803, and was declared to have been ratified in a proclamation by the Secretary of State, dated September 25, 1804. It was ratified by all the states except Connecticut, Delaware, Massachusetts, and New Hampshire.

The electors shall meet in their respective States, and vote by ballot for President and Vice President, one of whom, at least, shall not be an inhabitant of the same State with themselves; they shall name in their ballots the person voted for as President, and in distinct ballots the person voted for as Vice President, and they shall make distinct list of all persons voted for as President, and of all persons voted for as Vice President, and of the number of votes for each, which list they shall sign and certify, and transmit sealed to the seat of the Government of the United States, directed to the President of the Senate; the President of the Senate shall, in the presence of the Senate and House of Representatives, open all the certificates and the votes shall then be counted; the person having the greatest number of votes for President, shall be the President, if such number be a majority of the whole number of electors appointed; and if no person have such majority, then from the persons having the highest number not exceeding three on the list of those voted for as President, the House of Representatives shall choose immediately, by ballot, the President. But in choosing the President, the votes shall be taken by States, the representation from each State having one vote; a quorum for this purpose shall consist of a member or members from two thirds of the States, and a majority of all the States shall be necessary to a choice. And if the House of Representatives shall not choose a President whenever the right of choice shall devolve upon them, before the fourth day of March next following, then the Vice President shall act as President, as in the case of the death or other constitutional disability of the President. The person having the greatest number of votes as Vice President shall be the Vice President, if such number be a majority of the whole number of electors appointed, and if no person have a majority, then from the two highest numbers on the list, the Senate shall choose the Vice President; a quorum for the purpose shall consist of two thirds of the whole number of Senators, and a majority of the whole number shall be necessary to a choice. But no person constitutionally ineligible to the office of President shall be eligible to that of Vice President of the United States.

AMENDMENT XIII

(Slavery abolished.)

The following amendment was proposed to the Legislatures of the several states by the Thirty-eighth Congress on February 1, 1865, and was declared to have been ratified in a proclamation by the Secretary of State, dated December 18, 1865. It was rejected by Delaware and Kentucky; was conditionally ratified by Alabama and Mississippi; and Texas took no action.

1. Neither slavery nor involuntary servitude, except as a punishment for crime

whereof the party shall have been duly convicted, shall exist within the United States, or any place subject to their jurisdiction.

2. Congress shall have power to enforce this article by appropriate legislation.

AMENDMENT XIV

(Citizenship rights not to be abridged.)

The following, popularly known as the Reconstruction Amendment, was proposed to the Legislatures of the several states by the Thirty-ninth Congress on June 16, 1866, and was declared to have been ratified in a proclamation by the Secretary of State, dated July 23, 1868. The amendment got the support of 23 Northern states; it was rejected by Delaware, Kentucky, Maryland, and ten Southern states; California took no action. Subsequently it was ratified by the ten Southern states.

1. All persons born or naturalized in the United States, and subject to the jurisdiction thereof, are citizens of the United States and of the State wherein they reside. No State shall make or enforce any law which shall abridge the privileges or immunities of citizens of the United States; nor shall any State deprive any person of life, liberty, or property, without due process of law; nor deny to any person within its jurisdiction the equal protection of the laws.

(Apportionment of representatives in Congress.)

2. Representatives shall be apportioned among the several States according to their respective numbers, counting the whole number of persons in each State, excluding Indians not taxed. But when the right to vote at any election for the choice of electors for President and Vice President of the United States, Representatives in Congress, the executive and judicial officers of a State, or the members of the Legislature thereof, is denied to any of the male inhabitants of such State, being twenty-one years of age, and citizens of the United States, or in any way abridged, except for participation in rebellion, or other crime, the basis of representation therein shall be reduced in the proportion which the number of such male citizens shall bear to the whole number of male citizens twenty-one years of age in such State.

(Power of Congress to remove disabilities of United States officials for rebellion.)

3. No person shall be a Senator or Representative in Congress, or elector of President and Vice President, or hold any office, civil or military, under the United States, or under any State, who, having previously taken an oath, as a member of Congress, or as an officer of the United States, or as a member of any State Legislature, or as an executive or judicial officer of any State, to support the Constitution of the United States, shall have engaged in insurrection or rebellion against the same, or given aid and comfort to the enemies thereof. But Congress may by a vote of two thirds of each House, remove such disability.

(Validity of public debts.)

4. The validity of the public debt of the United States, authorized by law, including debts incurred for payment of pensions and bounties for services in

suppressing insurrection and rebellion, shall not be questioned. But neither the United States nor any State shall assume or pay any debt or obligation incurred in aid of insurrection or rebellion against the United States, or any claim for the loss or emancipation of any slave; but all such debts, obligations and claims shall be held illegal and void.

5. The Congress shall have power to enforce, by appropriate legislation, the provisions of this article.

AMENDMENT XV

(Equal rights for white and colored citizens.)

The following amendment was proposed to the Legislatures of the several states by the Fortieth Congress on February 27, 1869, and was declared to have been ratified in a proclamation by the Secretary of State, dated March 30, 1870. It was not acted on by Tennessee; it was rejected by California, Delaware, Kentucky, Maryland, and Oregon and was ratified by the remaining 30 states; New York rescinded its ratification, January 5, 1870. New Jersey rejected it in 1870, but ratified it in 1871.

1. The right of the citizens of the United States to vote shall not be denied or abridged by the United States or by any State on account of race, color, or previous condition of servitude.

2. The Congress shall have power to enforce the provisions of this article by appropriate legislation.

AMENDMENT XVI

(Income Taxes Authorized.)

The following amendment was proposed to the Legislatures of the several states by the Sixty-first Congress on July 12, 1909, and was declared to have been ratified in a proclamation by the Secretary of State, dated February 25, 1913. The income tax amendment was ratified by all the states except Connecticut, Florida, Pennsylvania, Rhode Island, Utah, and Virginia.

The Congress shall have power to lay and collect taxes on incomes, from whatever sources derived, without apportionment among the several States, and without regard to any census or enumeration.

AMENDMENT XVII

(United States Senators to be elected by direct popular vote.)

The following amendment was proposed to the Legislatures of the several states by the Sixty-second Congress on May 16, 1912, and was declared to have been ratified in a proclamation by the Secretary of State, dated May 31, 1913. It got the vote of all the states except Alabama, Delaware, Florida, Georgia, Kentucky, Louisiana, Maryland, Mississippi, Rhode Island, South Carolina, Utah, and Virginia.

1. The Senate of the United States shall be composed of two Senators from each State, elected by the people thereof for six years; and each Senator shall

have one vote. The electors in each State shall have the qualifications requisite for electors of the most numerous branch of the State Legislatures.

(Vacancies, when governor may fill by appointment.)

2. When vacancies happen in the representation of any State in the Senate, the executive authority of such State shall issue writs of election to fill such vacancies: Provided, That the Legislature of any State may empower the Executive thereof to make temporary appointment until the people fill the vacancies by election as the Legislature may direct.

3. This amendment shall not be so construed as to affect the election or term of any Senator chosen before it becomes valid as part of the Constitution.

AMENDMENT XVIII

(Prohibition of liquor.)

The following amendment was proposed to the Legislatures of the several states by the Sixty-fifth Congress on December 18, 1917; on January 29, 1919, the United States Secretary of State proclaimed its adoption by 36 states and declared it in effect as of January 16, 1920.

1. After one year from the ratification of this article the manufacture, sale, or transportation of intoxicating liquors within, the importation thereof into, or the exportation thereof from the United States and all territory subject to the jurisdiction thereof for beverage purposes is hereby prohibited.

2. The Congress and the several States shall have concurrent power to enforce this article by appropriate legislation.

3. This article shall be inoperative unless it shall have been ratified as an amendment to the Constitution by the Legislatures of the several States, as provided in the Constitution, within seven years from the date of the submission hereof to the States by the Congress.

AMENDMENT XIX

(Nationwide woman suffrage.)

The following amendment was proposed to the Legislatures of the several states by the Sixty-fifth Congress, having been adopted by the House of Representatives, May 21, 1919, and by the Senate, June 4, 1919. On August 26, 1920, the United States Secretary of State proclaimed it in effect, it having been adopted (June 10, 1919–August 18, 1920) by three quarters of the states.

1. The right of citizens of the United States to vote shall not be denied or abridged by the United States or by any State on account of sex.

2. Congress shall have power to enforce the provisions of this article by appropriate legislation.

AMENDMENT XX

(Beginning of terms of President, Vice President, Senators, and Representatives.)

The following amendment was proposed to the Legislatures of the several states by the Seventy-second Congress in March 1932, a joint resolution to that effect having been adopted, first by the House, and then, on March 2, by the Senate. On February 6, 1933, the Secretary of State proclaimed it in effect, 39 of the 48 states having ratified.

Section 1. The terms of the President and Vice President shall end at noon on the 20th day of January, and the terms of Senators and Representatives at noon on the 3rd day of January, of the years in which such terms would have ended if this article had not been ratified; and the terms of their successors shall then begin.

Section 2. The Congress shall assemble at least once in every year, and such meeting shall begin at noon on the 3rd day of January, unless they shall by law appoint a different day.

Section 3. If, at the time fixed for the beginning of the term of the President, the President-elect shall have died, the Vice President-elect shall become President. If a President shall not have been chosen before the time fixed for the beginning of his term, or if the President-elect shall have failed to qualify, then the Vice President-elect shall act as President until a President shall have qualified; and the Congress may by law provide for the case wherein neither a President-elect nor a Vice President-elect shall have qualified, declaring who shall then act as President, or the manner in which one who is to act shall be selected, and such person shall act accordingly until a President or Vice President shall have qualified.

Section 4. The Congress may by law provide for the case of the death of any of the persons from whom the House of Representatives may choose a President whenever the right of choice shall have devolved upon them, and for the case of the death of any of the persons from whom the Senate may choose a Vice President whenever the right of choice shall have devolved upon them.

Section 5. Sections 1 and 2 shall take effect on the 15th day of October following the ratification of this article (1933).

Section 6. This article shall be inoperative unless it shall have been ratified as an amendment to the Constitution by the Legislatures of three fourths of the several States within seven years from the date of its submission.

AMENDMENT XXI

(Repeal of the Eighteenth [Prohibition] Amendment.)

The following amendment, embodied in a joint resolution of the Seventy-second Congress (Senate, February 16, 1933, by 63 to 23; House, February 20, 1933, by 289 to 121), was transmitted to the Secretary of State on February 21 and he at once sent copies to the governors of the states. The amendment went into effect December 5, 1933, having been adopted by 36 of the 48 states.

Section 1. The eighteenth article of amendment to the Constitution of the United States is hereby repealed.

Section 2. The transportation or importation into any State, Territory, or Possession of the United States for delivery or use therein of intoxicating liquors, in violation of the laws thereof, is hereby prohibited.

Section 3. This article shall be inoperative unless it shall have been ratified as an amendment to the Constitution by conventions in the several States, as provided in the Constitution, within seven years from the date of the submission hereof to the States by the Congress.

AMENDMENT XXII

(Limiting Presidential Tenure.)

The following amendment was proposed to the Legislatures of the several states by the Eightieth Congress in March 1947; it was ratified by three fourths of the states and went into effect in February 1951.

Section 1. No person shall be elected to the office of the President more than twice, and no person who has held the office of President, or acted as President, for more than two years of a term to which some other person was elected President shall be elected to the office of President more than once. But this article shall not apply to any person holding the office of President when this article was proposed by the Congress, and shall not prevent any person who may be holding the office of President, or acting as President, during the term within which this article becomes operative from holding the office of President or acting as President during the remainder of such term.

Section 2. This article shall be inoperative unless it shall have been ratified as an amendment to the Constitution by the Legislatures of three fourths of the several States within seven years from the date of its submission to the States by the Congress.

AMENDMENT XXIII

(Voting rights for the District of Columbia.)

The following amendment was proposed to the Legislatures of the several states by the Eighty-sixth Congress in 1960, a resolution to that effect having been adopted by the House of Representatives on June 14 and by the Senate on June 16. Ratification by 38 states within seven years was necessary for the amendment to become effective.

Section 1. The District constituting the seat of Government of the United States shall appoint in such manner as the Congress may direct:

A number of electors of President and Vice President equal to the whole number of Senators and Representatives in Congress to which the District would be entitled if it were a State, but in no event more than the least populous State; they shall be in addition to those appointed by the States, but they shall be considered, for the purposes of the election of President and Vice President, to be electors appointed by a State; and they shall meet in the District and perform such duties as provided by the twelfth article of amendment.

Section 2. The Congress shall have power to enforce this article by appropriate legislation.

THE CIVIL SERVICE

All branches of the public service that are not military, legislative, or judicial belong to the civil service. Civil service positions exist in the Federal government and in state, county, and municipal governments.

The Federal civil service consists of about 2,300,000 positions and represents practically every kind of job. Most positions are in the competitive service; when vacancies occur, they are filled through open competitive examinations or by other procedures provided for under the system, such as promotion, transfer, and reinstatement.

The government provides a true career service, with pay based on actual responsibilities, and with low-cost life insurance and health benefits partially financed by the government, promotion on merit, paid vacation and sick leave, and a liberal retirement system.

Opportunities for employment are good in many fields, particularly physical science and engineering. College-caliber recruits are sought for jobs in more than 60 occupational fields, and they are encouraged to make careers in government with the goal of becoming the top managers and experts of future years. Examinations are publicized through such means as notices posted on bulletin boards in post offices and other Federal buildings, and notices sent to schools, public libraries, organizations, periodicals, and newspapers.

Examinations vary in nature according to the types of position for which they are held. Each is designed to test the ability of the applicant to perform the duties of the position applied for, or to test his ability to learn how to perform them. Some examinations consist of, or include, a written test; others consist of an appraisal of the applicant's experience or training, as described in his application form.

For complete information about an examination, the examination announcement (a printed or processed bulletin) should be consulted. These bulletins are furnished, upon request, by whatever office is announcing a particular examination: (1) examinations for positions in Washington, D.C., and, in some cases, throughout the country, are announced by the commission's central office in Washington, D.C.; (2) examinations for positions in a civil service region (a state or group of states) and certain local examinations (for example, those held for positions in post offices) are announced by the commission's 11 regional offices; and (3) examinations for many types of positions in Federal establishments such as navy yards, arsenals, and veterans' hospitals are announced by boards of U.S. civil service examiners located at those establishments.

Further information may be obtained from the United States Civil Service Commission, Washington 25, D.C.

RANK OF GOVERNMENT OFFICIALS OF THE UNITED STATES

Even in a democratic country like ours, a strict order of precedence is followed by government officials. Protocol in ranking government officials varies, but the following is the most generally accepted order:

The President
The Vice President
President pro tempore of the Senate
Foreign Ambassadors
Chief Justice of the Supreme Court
United States Senators
Speaker of the House
Representatives
Associate Justices of the Supreme Court
Secretary of State
Diplomatic Corps (other than ambassadors)
Secretary of the Treasury
Secretary of Defense
The Attorney General
The Postmaster General
Secretary of the Interior
Secretary of Agriculture
Secretary of Commerce
Secretary of Labor
Secretary of Health, Education, and Welfare
Secretaries of the Army, Navy, and Air Force
Governors of the States

STATE NICKNAMES, FLOWERS, MOTTOES, AND OTHER DATA

State	Nickname	Capital	Date admitted to Union
ALABAMA	Cotton State	Montgomery	Dec. 14, 1819
ALASKA	(None)	Juneau	Jan. 3, 1959
ARIZONA	Grand Canyon State	Phoenix	Feb. 14, 1912
ARKANSAS	Land of Opportunity	Little Rock	June 15, 1836
CALIFORNIA	Golden State	Sacramento	Sept. 9, 1850
COLORADO	Centennial State	Denver	Aug. 1, 1876
CONNECTICUT	Constitution State	Hartford	Jan. 9, 1788
DELAWARE	Diamond State, First State	Dover	Dec. 7, 1787
FLORIDA	Sunshine State	Tallahassee	March 3, 1845
GEORGIA	Cracker State, Peach State, Empire State of the South	Atlanta	Jan. 2, 1788
HAWAII	Aloha State	Honolulu	Aug. 21, 1959
IDAHO	Gem State	Boise	July 3, 1890
ILLINOIS	Prairie State	Springfield	Dec. 3, 1818
INDIANA	Hoosier State	Indianapolis	Dec. 11, 1816
IOWA	Hawkeye State	Des Moines	Dec. 28, 1846
KANSAS	Sunflower State, Jayhawk State	Topeka	Jan. 29, 1861
KENTUCKY	Blue Grass State	Frankfort	June 1, 1792
LOUISIANA	Pelican State	Baton Rouge	April 30, 1812
MAINE	Pine Tree State	Augusta	March 15, 1820

Flower	Motto	Origin of state name
Camelia	*Audemus Jura Nostra Defendere* (We Dare Defend Our Rights)	Perhaps from Indian tribe name, Alabama
Forget-me-not	(None)	From Aleutian word meaning "great land"
Saguaro Cactus	*Ditat Deus* (God Enriches)	From Indian word "Arizonac," meaning "small spring"
Apple Blossom	*Regnat Populus* (The People Rule)	Algonquin name of the Quapaw Indians
Golden Poppy	*Eureka* (I Have Found It)	An imaginary island named in a 16th-century Spanish romance
Rocky Mountain Columbine	*Nil Sine Numine* (Nothing Without the Deity)	Spanish word for "red"
Mountain Laurel	*Qui Transtulit Sustinet* (He Who Transplanted Continues to Sustain)	Indian, "Quonecktacut," meaning "long river" or "river of pines"
Peach Blossom	Liberty and Independence	From Lord De La Warr, of England, Governor of Virginia
Orange Blossom	In God We Trust	Spanish words, "Pascua Florida," or Feast of Flowers
Cherokee Rose	Wisdom, Justice, and Moderation	From King George II, of England
Hibiscus	*Ua Mau Ke Ea O Ka Aina I Ka Pono* (The Life of the Land Is Preserved in Righteousness)	Not certain; perhaps from the native name of the original home of the Polynesians
Syringa	*Esto Perpetua* (Mayest Thou Exist Forever)	Indian, meaning "light on the mountains"
Native Violet	State Sovereignty, National Union	Indian word meaning "warriors or men"
Peony	The Crossroads of America	State of Indians
Wild Rose	Our Liberties We Prize and Our Rights We Will Maintain	A Sioux tribe, the Ioways or Aiouez, meaning "sleepy ones"
Sunflower	*Ad Astra per Aspera* (To the Stars Through Difficulties)	Name of a Sioux tribe, meaning "people of the south wind"
Goldenrod	United We Stand, Divided We Fall	From Wyandot name, "Kentah-teh," meaning "land of tomorrow"
Magnolia	Union, Justice and Confidence	From King Louis XIV, of France
White Pine Cone and Tassel	*Dirigo* (I Guide)	From ancient province in France

STATE NICKNAMES, FLOWERS, MOTTOES, AND OTHER DATA

State	Nickname	Capital	Date admitted to Union
MARYLAND	Free State, Old Line State	Annapolis	April 28, 1788
MASSACHUSETTS	Bay State, Old Colony State	Boston	Feb. 6, 1788
MICHIGAN	Wolverine State	Lansing	Jan. 26, 1837
MINNESOTA	North Star State, Gopher State	St. Paul	May 11, 1858
MISSISSIPPI	Magnolia State	Jackson	Dec. 10, 1817
MISSOURI	Show-me State	Jefferson City	Aug. 10, 1821
MONTANA	Treasure State	Helena	Nov. 8, 1889
NEBRASKA	Cornhusker State	Lincoln	March 1, 1867
NEVADA	Sagebrush State, Silver State	Carson City	Oct. 31, 1864
NEW HAMPSHIRE	Granite State	Concord	June 21, 1788
NEW JERSEY	Garden State	Trenton	Dec. 18, 1787
NEW MEXICO	Land of Enchantment	Santa Fe	Jan. 6, 1912
NEW YORK	Empire State	Albany	July 26, 1788
NORTH CAROLINA	Tar Heel State	Raleigh	Nov. 21, 1789
NORTH DAKOTA	Sioux State, Flickertail State	Bismarck	Nov. 2, 1889
OHIO	Buckeye State	Columbus	March 1, 1803
OKLAHOMA	Sooner State	Oklahoma City	Nov. 16, 1907
OREGON	Beaver State	Salem	Feb. 14, 1859
PENNSYLVANIA	Keystone State	Harrisburg	Dec. 12, 1787

Flower	Motto	Origin of state name
Black-eyed Susan	*Scuto Bonae Voluntatis Tuae Coronasti Nos* (With the Shield of Thy Good-will Thou Hast Covered Us)	From Queen Henrietta Maria, of England, wife of Charles I
Mayflower	*Ense Petit Placidam Sub Libertate Quietem* (By the Sword We Seek Peace, but Peace Only Under Liberty)	Algonquin name, "Massadchu-es-et," meaning "great-hill-small-place"
Apple Blossom	*Si Quaeris Peninsulam Amoenam Circumspice* (If You Seek a Pleasant Peninsula, Look Around You)	From the Mishigamaw or Mishawiguma Indians, whose name meant "great water"
Moccasin Flower	*L'Étoile du Nord* (The Star of the North)	From Sioux words meaning "sky-colored water"
Magnolia	*Virtute et Armis* (By Valor and Arms)	Indian words, "Maesi"— "large," "Sipu"—"river"
Hawthorn	*Salus Populi Suprema Lex Esto* (The Welfare of the People Shall Be the Supreme Law)	Name of a Sioux tribe
Bitterroot	*Oro y Plata* (Gold and Silver)	Mexican-Spanish for "mountainous"
Goldenrod	Equality Before the Law	An Omaha Indian name for the "wide river" Platte
Sagebrush	All for Our Country	A Spanish word, meaning "snow-clad"
Purple Lilac	Live Free or Die	From the County of Hampshire, in England
Purple Violet	Liberty and Prosperity	From the Island of Jersey
Yucca	*Crescit Eundo* (It Grows As It Goes)	From "mexitli," Aztec war god
Rose	*Excelsior* (Ever Upward)	From the Duke of York (1664)
Dogwood	*Esse Quam Videri* (To Be Rather Than To Seem)	From Charles I, of England
Wild Prairie Rose	Liberty and Union, Now and Forever, One and Inseparable	From Sioux word meaning, "alliance with friends"
Scarlet Carnation	With God, All Things Are Possible	Iroquois name, meaning "great"
Mistletoe	*Labor Omnia Vincit* (Labor Conquers All Things)	Choctaw, meaning "red people"
Oregon Grape	The Union	Probably from Spanish word "Orejon," meaning "big-eared men"
Mountain Laurel	Virtue, Liberty and Independence	Named in honor of William Penn, father of the founder

STATE NICKNAMES, FLOWERS, MOTTOES, AND OTHER DATA

State	Nickname	Capital	Date admitted to Union
RHODE ISLAND	Little Rhody	Providence	May 29, 1790
SOUTH CAROLINA	Palmetto State	Columbia	May 23, 1788
SOUTH DAKOTA	Coyote State, Sunshine State	Pierre	Nov. 2, 1889
TENNESSEE	Volunteer State	Nashville	June 1, 1796
TEXAS	Lone Star State	Austin	Dec. 29, 1845
UTAH	Beehive State	Salt Lake City	Jan. 4, 1896
VERMONT	Green Mountain State	Montpelier	March 4, 1791
VIRGINIA	The Old Dominion	Richmond	June 25, 1788
WASHINGTON	Evergreen State	Olympia	Nov. 11, 1889
WEST VIRGINIA	Panhandle State, Mountain State	Charleston	June 20, 1863
WISCONSIN	Badger State	Madison	May 29, 1848
WYOMING	Equality State	Cheyenne	July 10, 1890

Flower	Motto	Origin of state name
Violet	Hope	"Isle of Rhodes," name chosen by colony General Court in 1644
Yellow Jessamine	*Animus Opibusque Parati* (Prepared in Soul and Resources) and *Dum Spiro, Spero* (While I Breathe, I Hope)	(See North Carolina)
Pasque Flower	Under God the People Rule	(See North Dakota)
Iris	Agriculture, Commerce	From "Tennese," name of chief Cherokee town
Bluebonnet	Friendship	From an Indian word meaning "friends" or "allies"
Sego Lily	Industry	From an Indian tribe, named the Utes
Red Clover	Freedom and Unity	From the French words "vert" and "mont," meaning "green mountain"
Dogwood	*Sic Semper Tyrannis* (Thus Always to Tyrants)	In honor of Elizabeth, the "Virgin Queen" of England
Rhododendron	*Al-Ki* (Bye and Bye)	In honor of George Washington
Rhododendron	*Montani Semper Liberi* (Mountaineers Always Freemen)	(See Virginia)
Violet	Forward	From an Indian name
Indian Paintbrush	*Cedant Arma Togae* (Let Arms Yield to the Gown)	From Wyoming Valley, Pa. Word means "alternating mountains and valleys"

RANK IN THE ARMED FORCES OF THE UNITED STATES

In the United States the Army outranks the Navy because it was established first. In England the opposite is true, the Navy there being the older service. The President of the United States is Commander in Chief of both the Army and the Navy. Below him, in order, are the following:

Army and Air Force	*Navy*
General of the Army	Fleet Admiral
General of the Air Force	Admiral
General	Vice Admiral
Lieutenant General	Rear Admiral
Major General	Commodore
Brigadier General	Captain
Colonel	Commander
Lieutenant Colonel	Lieutenant Commander
Major	Lieutenant
Captain	Lieutenant (Junior Grade)
First Lieutenant	Ensign
Second Lieutenant	
(in the Air Force, Lieutenant)	

Enlisted men's ratings are, in the *Army:* private (recruit), private first class, corporal, sergeant, staff sergeant, sergeant first class, 1st sergeant, master sergeant, warrant officer, chief warrant officer (W-2, W-3, W-4); in the *Navy:* seaman recruit, seaman apprentice, seaman, petty officer (3rd, 2nd, and 1st class), chief petty officer, senior chief petty officer, master chief petty officer, warrant officer, chief warrant officer (W-2, W-3, W-4); in the *Air Force:* airman, airman (3rd, 2nd, and 1st class), staff sergeant, technical sergeant, master sergeant, senior master sergeant, chief master sergeant, warrant officer, chief warrant officer (W-2, W-3, W-4).

In the Army, all holding the rank of second lieutenant or higher are addressed in writing and speech by their titles. Below the rank of second lieutenant they are introduced by their titles and addressed by them in writing, but in speech they are addressed or referred to as "Mr."

In the Navy all holding the rank of commander or higher are addressed by their titles in writing and speech. Those below the grade of commander are introduced by their titles, and so addressed in letters, but in ordinary speech they are addressed and referred to as "Mr."

The President, in this capacity, and indeed in all others, is addressed as "Mr. President" and "Sir." His wife (as are all other wives of American officials) is addressed simply as "Mrs."

VOTING QUALIFICATIONS IN THE VARIOUS STATES[1]

Alabama: Previous residence required, two years in the state, one year in the county, three months in the district. The voter must pay all poll taxes owed for the two years next preceding the election at which voting is intended. Persons who have served honorably in the armed forces during hostilities, even if there has been no declaration of war, are exempt from poll taxes. Registration is permanent unless removed for cause. Absentee voting is permitted; absentee registration occurs as part of the absentee voting procedure.

Alaska: Previous residence required, one year in the state, 30 days in the dis-

---

[1] All states having permanent registration, with the exception of Alabama, Delaware, Florida, Maine, Mississippi, Nebraska, New Hampshire, and South Dakota, make it subject to cancellation for failure to vote at certain specified intervals.

trict. Voters must be able to read or speak English. Registration is permanent in some areas. Absentee voting is permitted.

Arizona: Previous residence required, one year in the state, 30 days in the district. Voters must read or speak English. Registration is permanent for all but irrigation-district elections. Absentee registration and voting are permitted.

Arkansas: Previous residence required, one year in the state, six months in the county, one month in the district. Poll tax is required. There is no registration law. Absentee voting is permitted.

California: Previous residence required, one year in the state, 90 days in the county, 54 days in the district. Voter must have been a citizen for 90 days. Registration is permanent. Absentee registration and voting are permitted.

Colorado: Previous residence required, one year in state, 90 days in county, 30 days in town or city, 15 days in district. Registration permanent for all except certain minor elections. Absentee registration and voting permitted.

Connecticut: Previous residence required, one year in the state, six months in the district. Voters must pass a literacy test. Registration is permanent. Absentee voting is permitted, but absentee registration is permitted only to members of the armed forces and the merchant marine.

Delaware: Previous residence required, one year in state, three months in county, 30 days in district. A literacy test is required. Registration is permanent. Absentee voting is permitted, but absentee registration is restricted to members of armed forces and merchant marine and certain other special groups.

Florida: Previous residence required, one year in the state, six months in the county. Registration is permanent. Absentee voting is permitted.

Georgia: Previous residence required, one year in state, six months in county. Under 1949 law, all voters must pass a literacy test or qualify by answering ten to 30 prescribed oral questions. Registration is permanent unless removed for cause. Absentee voting is permitted, but absentee registration is permitted only to members of the armed forces, their spouses and dependents.

Hawaii: Previous residence required, one year in the state, three months in the district. Literacy in English or Hawaiian is required. Registration is permanent for all elections. Absentee registration and voting are permitted.

Idaho: Previous residence required, one year in the state, 90 days in the county, and 30 days in the district. Voters must be registered for state and Federal elections, and registration is permanent for all state and Federal elections. Absentee balloting is permitted. Voting without registration in a Federal, state, or county election is permitted only to members of the armed forces and the merchant marine and certain other special groups.

Illinois: Previous residence required, one year in the state, 90 days in the county, 30 days in the precinct. Voters must be registered for state and Federal elections; registration is permanent for all state and Federal elections; however, it may be cancelled if a voter fails to vote in a four-year period. Absentee balloting is permitted. Registration must be in person.

Indiana: Previous residence required, six months in the state, 60 days in the township, and 30 days in the district. Registration is permanent for all except minor elections. Absentee registration and balloting are permitted.

Iowa: Previous residence required, six months in the state, 60 days in the county, ten days in the district. Registration is permanent in some areas and in others is required every four years for all except certain minor elections. No literacy test is required. Absentee registration and balloting are permitted.

Kansas: Previous residence required, six months in the state, 30 days in the township. Registration is permanent in some areas and periodic in others. No literacy test is required. Absentee registration and balloting are permitted.

Kentucky: Previous residence required, one year in the state, six months in the county, 60 days in the district. Registration is permanent for all elections. No literacy test is required. Absentee balloting is permitted. Absentee registration is permitted only for members of the armed forces and the merchant marine and certain other special groups.

Louisiana: Previous residence required, one year in the parish, four months in the municipality, three months in the district. A literacy test is required but may be waived if the person can pass certain specifications. Registration is permanent in some areas but is required every four years in others. Absentee balloting is permitted. There is no absentee registration.

Maine: Previous residence required, six months in the state, three months in the county, three months in the district. Registration is permanent. Absentee registration is permitted under specific conditions. Absentee balloting is permitted.

Maryland: Previous residence required, one year in the state, six months in the county, and six months in the district. Registration is permanent in some areas and periodic in others. Absentee registration is permitted for members of the armed forces and merchant marine and certain other special groups. Absentee balloting is permitted.

Massachusetts: Previous residence required, one year in the state, six months in the town or city. A literacy test is required. Registration is permanent for all elections. Absentee registration is permitted for members of the armed forces and the merchant marine and several other specific groups. Absentee balloting is permitted in general elections only.

Michigan: Previous residence required, six months in the state, 30 days in the district. Registration is permanent for all elections. Absentee registration and balloting are permitted.

Minnesota: Previous residence required, six months in state, 30 days in district. Voter must have been a citizen 90 days. Registration is permanent in some areas and periodic in others. Absentee registration and balloting permitted.

Mississippi: Previous residence required, two years in the state, one year in the district (ministers of the Gospel and their wives may vote after six months' residence in the district). Voters from 21 to 60, except those specifically exempted, must pay poll tax. A literacy test is required. Registration is permanent unless removed for cause, but a separate registration is required for municipal elections. Absentee registration and balloting are permitted for members of the armed forces and the merchant marine and certain other special groups.

Missouri: Previous residence required, one year in the state (but only 60 days when voting for Presidential or Vice Presidential electors), 60 days in the county or district. Registration is permanent in some areas and required every four years in others. Absentee registration is permitted for members of the armed forces and the merchant marine and certain other special groups. Absentee balloting is permitted.

Montana: Previous residence required, one year in the state, 30 days in the county or district. Registration is permanent for all except certain minor elections. Absentee registration is permitted for members of the armed forces and the merchant marine and certain other special groups and to others absent from their county but within the U.S. continental limits. Absentee balloting is permitted.

Nebraska: Previous residence required, six months in the state, 40 days in the county, ten days in the district. Registration is permanent in some areas but required every four years in others. Absentee registration and balloting (the latter only for primary and general elections) are permitted.

Nevada: Previous residence required, six months in the state, 30 days in the county, ten days in the district. Registration is permanent for all elections. Absentee registration and balloting are permitted.

New Hampshire: Previous residence required, six months in the state and district. Voters must pass a literacy test. Registration is permanent for all elections. Absentee registration is permitted for members of the armed forces and the merchant marine and certain other special groups. Absentee balloting is permitted in biennial (general) elections only.

New Jersey: Previous residence required, six months in the state, 60 days in the county. Registration is permanent for all elections. Absentee registration is permitted in cases of physical incapacity. Military service voters are not required to register. Absentee balloting is permitted.

New Mexico: Previous residence required, 12 months in the state, 90 days in the county, 30 days in the district. Registration is permanent. Absentee registration is permitted. Absentee balloting is permitted but not in elections for state, county, or local officials.

New York: Previous residence required, one year in the state, four months in the county, 30 days in the district. One who became eligible to vote after Jan. 1, 1922, must, except for physical disability, be able to read and write English. The voter must have been a citizen for 90 days. Registration is permanent in some areas and annual in others. Absentee registration is permitted. Absentee balloting is permitted for armed forces personnel and their absentee relatives in general and local elections only and for others in general elections only.

North Carolina: Previous residence required, one year in the state, 30 days in the district. There is a literacy test. Registration is permanent. Absentee balloting is permitted. Absentee registration is permitted for members of the armed forces and certain other special groups; it is permitted for others in general elections only.

North Dakota: Previous residence required, one year in the state, 90 days in the county, 30 days in the district. There is no registration requirement for Federal or state elections, but persons who are not members of the armed forces or the merchant marine or certain other special groups may be required to register for a municipal election. Absentee balloting is permitted.

Ohio: Previous residence required, one year in the state (none when voting for Presidential and Vice Presidential electors), 40 days in the county, and 40 days in the district. Registration is permanent in some areas and periodic in others. Absentee balloting is permitted. Registration is not required for members of the armed forces who vote by a special absentee ballot; others must register in person where required. Absentee balloting is permitted.

Oklahoma: Previous residence required, one year in the state, six months in the county, 30 days in the district. Registration is permanent in all except school-district elections. Registration is not required for absentee voters who are members of the armed forces or merchant marine or other special groups; others must register in person.

Oregon: Previous residence required, six months in the state, 30 days in the district. There is a literacy test. Registration is permanent. Absentee registration and balloting are permitted.

Pennsylvania: Previous residence required, one year (six months, if the voter was previously an elector or native of the U.S.) in the state, two months in the district. Registration is permanent. Absentee registration and balloting are permitted.

Rhode Island: Previous residence required, one year in the state, six months in the district. Registration is permanent. Absentee registration is permitted for members of the armed forces and merchant marine and certain special groups. Absentee balloting is permitted in certain special state elections.

South Carolina: Previous residence required, two years in the state (except for ministers of the Gospel, teachers in public schools, and their spouses, who may vote after residence of six months), one year in the county, four months in the district. Property ownership may be claimed as an alternative to literacy. Registration is on a decennial basis. Absentee registration and balloting are permitted for members of the armed forces and certain other special groups.

South Dakota: Previous residence required, one year in the state, 90 days in the county, 30 days in the district. Registration is permanent for some elections only. Absentee registration and balloting are permitted.

Tennessee: Previous residence required, 12 months in the state, three months in the county. Registration is permanent for all elections. Absentee registration and balloting are permitted.

Texas: Previous residence required, one year in the state, six months in the county, six months in the district. A poll tax is assessed on citizens 21 to 60 years of age, with certain specific exemptions. The state constitution contains registration provisions, but no registration system exists. Absentee balloting is permitted.

Utah: Previous residence required, one year in the state, four months in the county, 60 days in the district. The voter must have been a citizen for 90 days. Registration is permanent except for certain minor elections. Absentee registration is permitted for members of the armed forces and the merchant marine and certain other special groups. Absentee balloting is permitted.

Vermont: Previous residence required, one year in the state, three months in the township. Registration is periodic; it is not required for absentee members of the armed forces and merchant marine and certain other special groups. Absentee balloting is permitted.

Virginia: Previous residence required, one year in the state, six months in the county, 30 days in the district. A literacy test is required. A voter must owe no past-due taxes. Registration is permanent except in some cities. Registration is not required for members of the armed forces; others must register in person. Absentee balloting is permitted.

Washington: Previous residence required, one year in the state, 90 days in the county, 30 days in the district. A literacy test is required. Registration is permanent except for irrigation-district elections. Temporary absentee registration for "service" voters is permitted; all others must register in person. Absentee balloting is permitted.

West Virginia: Previous residence required, one year in the state, 60 days in the county. Registration is permanent for all except special elections. Absentee registration and balloting are permitted.

Wisconsin: Previous residence required, one year in the state (but no residence requirement when voting for Presidential and Vice Presidential electors), ten days in the district. Registration is permanent in some areas. Absentee registration and balloting are permitted.

Wyoming: Previous residence required, one year in the state, 60 days in the county, ten days in the district. A literacy test is required. Registration is periodic. Absentee registration and balloting are permitted.

LEGAL AND PUBLIC HOLIDAYS IN THE UNITED STATES[1]

January	1.	New Year's Day: In all the states, D.C., Canal Zone, Guam, Puerto Rico, Virgin Islands.
January	8.	Anniversary of the Battle of New Orleans: In Louisiana.
January	19.	Robert E. Lee's Birthday: In Ala., Ark., Fla., Ga., Ky., La., Miss., N.C., S.C., Tenn., and Texas. In Va., known as Lee-Jackson Day.
January	20.	Inauguration Day: Observed every fourth year since 1937, in the District of Columbia.
January	30.	Franklin D. Roosevelt's Birthday: In Kentucky and the Virgin Islands.
February	12.	Lincoln's Birthday: Alaska, Ariz., Calif., Colo., Conn., Del., Ill., Ind., Iowa, Kans., Ky., Md., Mich., Minn., Mo., Mont., Nebr., N.J., N.Y., N.D., Ohio, Ore., Pa., S.D., Tenn., Utah, Vt., Wash., W. Va., Wyo., and the Virgin Islands.
February	14.	Admission Day: In Arizona.
February	22.	Washington's Birthday: In all the states except Hawaii (where it is Presidents' Day), Nev., Okla., and Wis.; also in D.C., Canal Zone, Guam, Puerto Rico, and Virgin Islands.
March	2.	Texas Independence Day: In Texas.
March	15.	Andrew Jackson's Birthday: In Tennessee.
March	17.	Evacuation Day: In Boston and the remainder of Suffolk County, Mass.
March	22.	Emancipation Day: In Puerto Rico.
March	25.	Maryland Day: In Maryland.
March	26.	Kuhio Day: In Hawaii.
March	30.	Seward's Day: In Alaska.
April		Fast Day (fourth Monday): In New Hampshire.
April	12.	Halifax Independence Day (date of passage of Halifax Independence Resolutions): In North Carolina.
April	13.	Thomas Jefferson's Birthday: In Alabama and Missouri.
April	16.	De Diego's Birthday: In Puerto Rico.
April	19.	Patriots' Day: In Maine and Massachusetts.
April	21.	San Jacinto Day: In Texas.
April	22.	Arbor Day: In Nebraska.
April	26.	Confederate Memorial Day: In Ala., Fla., Ga., and Miss.
April	28.	Arbor Day: In Utah.
May	4.	Rhode Island Independence Day: In Rhode Island.
May	10.	Confederate Memorial Day: In S.C. and N.C.

[1] Based on "Bank and Public Holidays Throughout the World," 1961 ed., Copyright 1960 by Morgan Guaranty Trust Company of New York.

May	20.	Anniversary of the signing of the Mecklenburg Declaration of Independence: In North Carolina.
May	30.	Decoration Day or Memorial Day: In all states except Ala., Fla., Ga., Ky. (where it is also Confederate Memorial Day), Miss., S.C., and Texas. In La. and Tenn., known as Confederate Memorial Day.
June	11.	Kamehameha Day: In Hawaii.
June	14.	Flag Day: In Pennsylvania.
June	20.	West Virginia Day: In West Virginia.
June	22.	Organic Act Day: In the Virgin Islands.
July	4.	Independence Day: In all states, D.C., Canal Zone, Guam, Puerto Rico, and Virgin Islands.
July	13.	Nathan Bedford Forrest's Birthday: In Tennessee.
July	17.	Birthday of Muñoz Rivera: In Puerto Rico.
July	24.	Pioneer Day: In Utah.
July	25.	Constitution Day: In Puerto Rico. Supplication Day: In the Virgin Islands, marking start of hurricane season.
July	27.	Barbosa's Birthday: In Puerto Rico.
August	1.	Colorado Day: In Colorado.
August	14.	World War II Memorial Day: In Arkansas. Victory Day: In Rhode Island.
August	16.	Bennington Battle Day: In Vermont.
August	30.	Huey P. Long's Birthday: In Louisiana.
September		Labor Day (first Monday): In all states, D.C., Canal Zone, Guam, Puerto Rico, and Virgin Islands.
September	9.	Admission Day: In California.
September	12.	Defenders' Day: In Maryland.
October	12.	Columbus Day: In Ala. (where it is also Fraternal Day), Ariz., Calif., Colo., Conn., Del., Fla. (where it is also Farmers' Day), Ga., Ill., Ky., La., Md., Mass., Minn., Mo., Mont., Nebr., N.H., N.J., N.M., N.Y., Ohio, Pa., R.I., Texas, Utah, Vt., Wash., W. Va., and Puerto Rico. Discovery Day: In Ind. and N.D.
October	25.	Thanksgiving Day (local): In Virgin Islands, to celebrate close of hurricane season.
October	31.	Nevada Day: In Nevada.
November		General Election Day (first Tuesday after the first Monday in November): In every state except Ala., Alaska, Conn., Ga., Idaho, Kans., Ky., Mass., Minn., Miss., Nebr., Nev., N.M., Utah, and Vt.; also in D.C. In some of the states it is a half holiday or a bank holiday.
November	11.	Veterans Day or Armistice Day: In all states, D.C., and Puerto Rico.
November	19.	Discovery Day: In Puerto Rico.
November		Thanksgiving Day (by proclamation of the President, traditionally, the last Thursday in November): In all states, D.C., Canal Zone, Guam, Puerto Rico, and Virgin Islands.
December	25.	Christmas Day: In all states, D.C., Canal Zone, Guam, Puerto Rico, and Virgin Islands.

Other frequently observed holidays are: Mother's Day, the second Sunday in May; Armed Forces Day, the third Saturday in May; Father's Day, the third Sunday in June.

Shrove Tuesday is celebrated in Ala., in some Fla. cities, and some La. parishes. Good Friday is a public holiday in Calif. (noon to 3 P.M.), Conn., Del., Fla., Hawaii, Ill., Ind., La., Md., Minn., N.J., N.D., Pa., Tenn., Canal Zone, Guam, Puerto Rico, and the Virgin Islands.

COUNTY GOVERNMENT IN THE UNITED STATES

Every state in the United States is divided into counties except Louisiana, where the divisions are known as parishes. In all there are about 3,100 counties. There is no uniformity as to the number in each state. Texas, for instance, has 254 while Delaware has only three.

County administration is a local matter for each state to decide; consequently, there is a great variety of systems throughout the country. The county has in all cases comparatively little legislative authority; it is for the most part an agent of administration under the state government. In most states the county is the district of record for deeds, administration of estates, probate of wills, etc. Roads, bridges, education, etc., are usually county concerns. Relief is sometimes a county job, and in many states the county is the school district. City and county government sometimes merge to a certain extent, as in the case of New York City, which includes five counties. In most states the principal county offices are elective. The county seat is the town or village selected for the headquarters of the county administration. It is often the most important settlement in the county.

MUNICIPAL GOVERNMENT IN THE UNITED STATES

Essentially, municipal government provides those public services which people living together in urban places need for their community existence. Most commonly these services are police protection, fire prevention and fire fighting, sanitation, construction of city streets and recreation facilities, and maintenance of public service enterprises, such as water supply and electric power. The municipality is recognized as the government "closest to the people" because of the fundamental character of these services, as well as because of the local nature of municipal government. The suspension of vital municipal services would present an immediate threat to the life and property of the community. The larger the city, the more profound is this dependence on municipal functions.

In colonial times, municipal governments were characterized by colonial governors. Of course, cities as they now exist were unimaginable and local government was rudimentary. One of the first municipal officials was the "town crier." He often served as a kind of constable for the city fathers. Early municipal functions were keeping a curfew, making and enforcing simple sanitary regulations, and maintaining law and order in the community. Since then, the United States has evolved from an agricultural into an industrial nation, and the majority of the population has moved from farms to cities and towns. Now about two thirds of the population lives in urban places. This has heightened tremendously the need for new and expanded municipal services.

The burgeoning of cities and towns has brought into existence municipal services unheard of in the 19th century—planning and zoning, municipally owned rapid transit lines, air-pollution control, a variety of health services, and many others. Traffic engineering and regulation have become prime concerns of city governments throughout the nation, and hundreds of municipalities now provide offstreet parking facilities.

Municipal and industrial growth have been parallel and interdependent in the

United States. The services of a modern municipality now enable people to live together comfortably in large urban communities; this situation provides the necessary working force for industrial mass production.

Yet during this tremendous urban growth and flux, the legal relationship of municipalities to their state governments has not changed greatly. In some states new municipal charters must still be approved by the state legislature. In many states rural-minded legislatures tend to dominate municipal affairs. Gradually, however, states are adjusting to the increasing importance of municipal governments by granting them "home rule"—broad powers of local self-government. Basically, home rule authorizes municipal voters to adopt the kind of city or town charter they desire, within broad limits, or to amend the charter in existence. At present more than 20 states have some kind of constitutional or statutory provisions for home rule, although not all of them are in effect.

As municipal voters acquired greater freedom to choose and manage their local governments, municipal fiscal structures were strengthened. At one time the property tax on real estate was almost the sole source of municipal income. Today, to enable them to meet increased demands for services, many municipalities are permitted to tax local sales, tobacco, theater admissions, wages, etc. In some states cities have broad powers to levy such nonproperty taxes; in other states these powers are virtually nonexistent. Cities and towns are also adding to their revenues by fees and service charges, such as for sewer rental. Municipal income is augmented further by shares of state-collected taxes and other forms of state aid.

There are four major forms of municipal government in the United States: the *weak mayor* form, the *strong mayor* form, the *commission* form, and the *council-manager* form. The growth of cities and the complexity of municipal services has caused a healthy ferment of controversy about the relative strengths and weaknesses of these forms. The weak mayor form is gradually becoming extinct except in small towns. The commission form, first adopted as an emergency plan in Galveston, Texas, after the flood of 1900, enjoyed a vogue for several decades but is being gradually abandoned. The strong mayor form predominates in big cities. The council-manager form is a 20th-century development designed to cope with modern problems of municipal management. It has become increasingly popular, and though not a panacea, will unquestionably continue to grow. The basic characteristics of each form are as follows:

Commission Form. Commissioners (usually five) elected at large by a majority vote. They serve both as municipal legislators and as administrative heads of municipal departments. The plan fails to focus responsibility and authority in a single executive and can easily lead to "buck-passing" unless an unusual degree of cooperation prevails among commissioners. Especially in big cities, the plan tends toward administrative ambiguity. Since the commissioners both vote municipal funds and spend them, there is no adequate control of spending.

Weak Mayor Form. Councilmen elected by wards. Most administrative heads elected also—at least the treasurer, the city attorney, and usually some others. The mayor is elected, usually by direct popular vote, sometimes by the council. Administrative boards are elected to enact council policies. A basic disadvantage of this type of administration is that too many officials are elected, thus causing a high turnover of top administrators and failing to attract competent career men. This pattern scatters responsibility and action so widely that it is virtually unworkable in a city of any size.

Strong Mayor Form. The mayor elected at large. Councilmen elected by wards. The mayor may veto acts of the council, and has authority to hire and fire department heads. He is the chief executive of the municipality, and is responsible also for preparing the budget and submitting it to the council. The strong mayor form fixes responsibility adequately but does not separate the policy-making and administrative functions. This form can be very effective, but only if the mayor combines exceptional political acumen with keen executive abilities.

Council-Manager Plan. A small council elected at large. The council hires a city manager as chief administrator. The council decides all policy matters; the manager is responsible for all municipal administration. He has the power to hire and fire department heads and others. The manager is also responsible for drafting the budget and presenting it to the council. The plan adequately separates the policy-making and administrative functions, and focuses responsibility for each. This form of municipal government was first adopted by Sumter, S.C., in 1912. Today the number of United States municipalities with this kind of charter is nearly 1,000.

JUSTICE OF THE PEACE

A justice of the peace holds a judicial office of ancient origin. His election or appointment, term of office, and jurisdiction are governed by constitutional or statutory provisions. To be eligible for such office the candidate must have certain qualifications: he must be over 21 years old, a citizen of the United States, and of the state in which he seeks office. In some states the candidate must be a male, in others females are eligible; in some states only lawyers can qualify.

The Justice's Court is an inferior tribunal having civil jurisdiction in particular cases generally limited to $200. The proceedings in civil matters are less formal and technical here than in other courts, but a justice of the peace is bound by the general rules of evidence applicable to other courts; he is not merely an arbitrator, but must decide cases according to the weight of evidence and established principles of law. Generally, either plaintiff or defendant may have a trial by jury. This jury may consist of either six or twelve persons.

The justice of the peace also has some criminal jurisdiction. Under most statutes it does not cover felonies, but is limited to the trial of specified misdemeanors and minor offenses for which the punishment on conviction is fixed by statute. In some states justices of the peace have inquisitorial power; like grand juries, they may inquire into crimes committed or believed to have been committed within their territorial jurisdiction. They may also act as committing magistrates, with the power to conduct preliminary hearings, to remand the accused to jail, to discharge the accused, or to admit him to bail on all charges except murder, pending the outcome of the action of the grand jury; or to hold him for trial in a higher court having jurisdiction over the particular crime. However, such committing magistrate has no power to try the case.

JURIES

A jury is a group of selected persons sworn to render a fair and just verdict on the evidence presented to them and in accordance with the presiding judge's charge citing the applicable principles of law.

Trial by jury is constitutionally guaranteed to litigants, but there is not a mandatory right to a jury trial in all classes of cases. The right exists only in cases for which it existed at common law or as it was granted by statute at the time of the adoption of the Constitution. In some states the right may be waived in all cases, both civil and criminal; in others it cannot be waived in criminal cases of a specified character, such as felonies, nor in a capital case, *i.e.,* murder. The right to waive depends upon constitutional or statutory provision.

A *special jury* is a jury ordered by the court on due application in cases for which a fair and impartial trial cannot otherwise be had, or in cases of unusual importance or intricacy. Such juries are sometimes called "blue ribbon" juries.

The United States Supreme Court has held trial by these juries to be constitutional.

A *grand jury* is a body of men selected and summoned according to statutory provision. After being impaneled and sworn, a grand jury is charged by the court to inquire into a crime alleged to have been committed within its jurisdiction. Its duty is to ascertain whether prima facie grounds for a criminal prosecution have been made out, sufficient to warrant bringing the accused to trial. If sufficient evidence is presented, an indictment is returned charging the accused with the commission of a particular crime. No presumption of guilt arises from such indictment; it is merely an accusation. The guilt or innocence of the accused is determined after a trial, which is based on the indictment. Ordinarily, the accused and his witnesses are not entitled to appear before the grand jury, unless such right is granted by statute. The proceedings are secret.

The qualifications, composition, sex, number, and selection of all juries in civil and criminal proceedings is governed by constitutional or statutory provisions. At common law a grand jury must be composed of not less than 12 nor more than 23 people, but the number is now generally fixed by constitutional or statutory provision. A unanimous opinion of the grand jury is not necessary before an indictment may be returned; nor is a unanimous opinion of the jury necessary for a verdict in civil or criminal cases. The statutes specify how many grand jurors must agree to return an indictment, and how many jurors must be in accord as to what the verdict shall be in civil or criminal cases.

A *coroner's jury,* composed of a specified number of people, fixed by statute, conducts an inquest to determine the cause of death when there is reason to believe that it was not due to natural causes, and in cases of death by clearly non-natural causes, to obtain evidence of possible criminality.

The coroner is a public officer who summons the jurors. The office is ancient; it has been abolished by statute in some states.

AFFIDAVITS

An affidavit is a written statement under oath taken before an officer authorized by statute to administer an oath, for instance, a judge, a notary public, or a commissioner of deeds. It must specify the venue, *i.e.,* the state and county in which the affidavit is made, and must state facts within the personal knowledge of the person making the affidavit; or, if it contains statements not within the personal knowledge of such person, the source of such facts must be stated. The affidavit must be signed. An illiterate person can sign by making a cross or other symbol. The person making the affidavit is called the *affiant* or *deponent.* At the end of the affidavit is the statement, "Sworn to before me this   day of 19—," under which the person before whom the affidavit is made signs his name and writes his title. This statement is called a *jurat.* Under proper circumstances an affirmation may replace the oath.

An affidavit differs from a *deposition* in that the former is voluntary and made without notice to the adverse party in the litigation; the latter, however, is generally made in answer to specific questions propounded under a court order or other legal notice.

LAW

Constitutional law is that branch of jurisprudence which deals with the formation, adoption, construction, and interpretation of state constitutions and the Federal constitution. In its respective domain, each is the supreme law; but no state constitution or statute is constitutional if it is in conflict with the constitution of the United States, and no state statute is constitutional if it is in conflict with the constitution of its state.

Statutory law is law found in the various statutes enacted by the legislative bodies of the states or by Congress.

Common law originated and developed in England, where it was administered by secular as distinguished from ecclesiastical tribunals. It is a flexible body of jurisprudence based upon decisional law designed to serve the interests of society, and is susceptible of adaptation to new conditions. It does not depend on positive legislative enactment, although many statutes are a codification of common-law principles, and in the absence of statutory law common-law principles prevail.[1]

Maritime law has reference to the legal principles that apply to ship owners, seamen, shipping, and other maritime matters.

Commercial law has reference to the legal principles that apply to commercial paper, such as notes, bills of exchange, drafts, etc.

International law has reference to the legal principles which govern the interrelations of sovereign states.

THE COPYRIGHT LAW OF THE UNITED STATES[2]

Copyright is the exclusive property right of an author (including designer, composer, engraver, printer, draftsman, photographer, sculptor, or artist) of an intellectual production to reproduce and sell copies of his work and grant other rights respecting the use of the product of his intellect.

The purpose of the copyright law is "to promote the progress of science and useful arts by securing for a limited time to authors and inventors the exclusive right to their respective writings and discoveries."

Those who are entitled to copyright protection in the United States are:

1. The *author* of a work, if he is a citizen of the United States, if he is an alien living here at the time of the first publication of his work, or if he is a citizen of a country which grants to citizens of the United States the benefit of copyright on substantially the same basis as to its own citizens.

2. The *proprietor* of a work; that is, the person who derives his title to the work from the author. If the author is not entitled to copyright protection the proprietor cannot claim it.

3. The *executors, administrators,* or *assigns* of the author or the proprietor of a work.

Generally speaking, the copyright of material in magazines, newspapers, dictionaries, encyclopedias, and other compilations, is held in the name of the proprietor, but the author may, if he wishes, retain the right to his contribution if it is published separately also, or if he applies for a separate registration for it. Because of income tax regulations, an increasing number of authors are having copyrights taken out in their own names, but where authors wish to retain their copyright and yet have their publishers named as copyright claimants it is pro-

[1] This is true in all states of the United States except Louisiana, where common law is not effective.

[2] Subject to amendment or change. The material in this chapter refers to copyrights under United States Statute Law. In addition, an author of an unpublished work has a right to prevent publication, copying, or use of his unpublished work without his consent, called a common-law copyright. Currently studies are in progress with a view to enactment of a new copyright law. Copies of these studies, which contain history of the copyright law and discussion of copyright law and problems, may be obtained from the Superintendent of Documents, Washington 25, D.C. Copyright problems are extremely complex; in all instances the advice of a skilled practitioner should be obtained.

vided that "the legal title to a copyright vests in the person in whose name it is taken out, but it may be held in trust for the true owners."

Title 17 of the United States Code provides that the application for registration of any work "shall specify to which of the following classes the work in which copyright is claimed belongs."

Class A. Books published in the United States (Application Form A)

Books or periodicals first published in a foreign language outside the United States (Application Form AB Foreign)

Books or periodicals in the English language first published outside the United States (Application Form AB Ad Interim)

Class B. Periodicals (Application Form B)

Contributions to periodicals (Application Form BB)

Class C. Lectures, sermons, addresses, prepared for oral delivery (Application Form C)

Class D. Dramatic or dramatico-musical compositions (Application Form D)

Class E. Musical composition, author a citizen or domiciled in the United States, or published in the United States (Application Form E)

Musical composition, author not a citizen or not domiciled in the United States, or not published in the United States (Application Form E Foreign)

Class F. Maps (Application Form F)

Class G. Works of art; models or designs for works of art (Application Form G)

Class H. Reproductions of a work of art (Application Form H)

Class I. Drawings or plastic works of a scientific or technical character (Application Form I)

Class J. Photographs (Application Form J)

Class K. Prints and pictorial illustrations (Application Form K)

Prints or labels used for articles of merchandise (Application Form KK)

Class L. Motion-picture photoplays (Application Form LM)

Class M. Motion pictures other than photoplays (Application Form LM)

The first term of copyright is 28 years, which is computed, in the case of a work published in the first instance, from the date of publication; and, in the case of an unpublished work, from the date of registration. In the 28th year a renewal application (Form R) may be made to secure a second term of 28 years. Form RR is to be used for renewal of copyright of a print or label used for articles of merchandise. Not all the complexities of problems of copyright renewal have been resolved, despite numerous decisions including those of the United States Supreme Court.

Copyright may be secured for:

Unpublished Works. These include lectures, sermons, addresses, or similar productions for oral delivery; dramatic, musical, and dramatico-musical compositions; photographs; works of art (drawings, paintings, and sculptures); plastic works; motion-picture photoplays; and motion pictures other than photoplays.

The copyright procedure for such works is to file a claim of copyright with registration fee, to be accompanied as follows:

In the case of lectures, sermons, addresses, and dramatic, musical, and dramatico-musical compositions, one *complete* copy of the work, which may be written by hand or typewritten but must be clean and legible, with the sheets fastened securely together, should be deposited.

In the case of unpublished photographs, one copy of the work should be deposited.

In the case of works of art, models, designs, etc., a photograph or other identifying reproduction should be deposited.

In the case of motion-picture plays, the title and a description and one print from each scene or act should be deposited.

In the case of motion pictures other than photoplays, the title and a description, with not less than two prints taken from different sections of the motion picture, should be deposited.

Any work in this group, if published—that is, if reproduced in copies for sale—must be deposited a second time and registered as a published work.

Published Works. Published works are those which are printed or otherwise produced and "placed on sale, sold, or publicly distributed."

The fee for copyright registration is $4 except that in the case of a commercial print or label it is $6. The fee for renewal registration is $2, except for renewal of a print or label, which fee is $6.

New versions of a work must be copyrighted on their own account. This does not mean that mere corrections or additions need an extra copyright. The dramatization of a story, the photoplay version of a drama, etc., must have independent copyrights.

Foreign books and periodicals first published abroad can be copyrighted in the United States for ad interim copyright by registering and depositing the book or periodical in the United States Copyright Office within six months from the date of foreign publication. The copyright thus secured lasts for five years from the date of publication. The Copyright Office issues import statements for 1,500 copies of books or periodicals of foreign origin which have been registered for ad interim copyright. These imported copies must bear copyright notices. Whenever during the existence of the five-year ad interim copyright the book or periodical is manufactured, published, and registered in the United States, the copyright is extended for the usual copyright term with the regular opportunity available for renewal.

Effective Sept. 16, 1955, the United States became a charter member of The Universal Copyright Convention. Accordingly, on and after the effective date, works by nationals of, or first published in, member countries and which contain the prescribed notice (see below) receive automatic copyright protection in this country without compliance with other United States formalities. Likewise, United States authors receive protection in all contracting countries merely by the fact of publication with the prescribed notice in the United States.

The usual form of copyright notice for books, periodicals, dramatic and musical compositions is "Copyright, 19— (fill out with the year of publication), by ——— (fill out with the name of the claimant)." However, if Universal Copyright as well as United States protection is desired, the notice should be: "©, 19— (fill out with year of publication), by ——————————— (fill out with the name of the claimant)."

In the case of books and dramatic compositions, the notice should be on the title page or the page immediately following; in the case of a periodical, on the title page or first page of the text. The notice in the case of a musical composition should be on the title page or the first page of music.

On maps, works of art, drawings, photographs, and prints the notice may consist of the letter C, inclosed within a circle, thus, ©, accompanied by the initials, monogram, mark, or symbol of the holder of the copyright, but somewhere on the work should appear the name of the copyright holder himself. The prescribed notice must be affixed to each copy of the work published or offered for sale in the United States.

Promptly upon publication two complete copies of the best edition of the work should be sent to the copyright office, with a proper application for registration (such application may be had free upon request from the Copyright Office at Washington, D.C.) and a money order for the amount of the legal registration fee ($4). "Promptly" means "without unnecessary delay." Nevertheless, court decisions have held that deposit many years later is effective.

In the United States copyrights are good for 28 years. Application for renewal should be filed by the author (or some person legally entitled to do so) one year before the expiration of the existing term. The copyright is then good for another 28 years. The registration fee for renewal of copyright is $2. Failure to renew within the specified time terminates the copyright.

Nearly all the civilized nations of the world were represented at the Berne Copyright Convention, held in 1885–86. Through this and later conventions, arrangements were made by which a copyright issued in one country was to be respected in all countries which were parties to the Berne Convention. In general, the term of copyright was to last for 50 years after the death of the author. The United States was not a party to these deliberations, but a number of foreign countries have agreed to give protection to American authors under reciprocal copyright agreements with the United States government. United States authors can obtain protection in foreign countries under the Berne Convention by securing copyright in Great Britain or Canada simultaneously with the United States copyright.

Copyright relations have been established by proclamation of the President with Argentina, Australia, Austria, Belgium, Canada, Chile, Costa Rica, Cuba, Czechoslovakia, Denmark, Finland, France, Germany, Great Britain and the British possessions, Greece, India, the Irish Free State, Israel, Italy, Luxemburg, Mexico, Monaco, The Netherlands and possessions, New Zealand, Norway, Poland, Portugal, Rumania, Spain, Sweden, Switzerland, Tunis, and the Union of South Africa.

Copyright proclamations have been issued securing copyright control of mechanical musical reproduction in the United States to citizens or subjects of Argentina, Australia, Austria, Belgium, Brazil, Canada, Chile, Cuba, Czechoslovakia, Denmark, Finland, France, Germany, Great Britain, Greece, India, the Irish Free State, Israel, Italy, Luxemburg, Monaco, The Netherlands, New Zealand, Norway, Poland, Rumania, Spain, Sweden, Switzerland and the Union of South Africa.

Copyright treaties have also been entered into with China, Japan, Hungary, Italy, Rumania, and Thailand. The Copyright Convention of Mexico of 1902 was ratified by the United States and became effective from June 30, 1908, and is now in force between the United States and Salvador; the other parties became parties to the Buenos Aires Convention, which practically replaced the 1902 Convention. The Pan-American Copyright Convention signed at Buenos Aires in 1910 was proclaimed July 16, 1914, and is effective between the United States and Argentina Bolivia, Brazil, Chile, Colombia, Costa Rica, Dominican Republic, Ecuador, Guatemala, Haiti, Honduras, Nicaragua, Panama, Paraguay, Peru, and Uruguay. The following are signatories to the Universal Copyright Convention: Andorra, Argentina, Austria, Belgium, Brazil, Cambodia, Canada, Chile, Costa Rica, Cuba, Czechoslovakia, Denmark, Ecuador, France, German Federal Republic, Ghana, Haiti, Holy See, Iceland, India, Ireland, Israel, Italy, Japan, Laos, Lebanon, Liberia, Lichtenstein, Luxemburg, Mexico, Monaco, Nicaragua, Nigeria, Pakistan, Panama, Paraguay, Philippines,[1] Portugal, Spain, Sweden, Switzerland, United Kingdom, and the United States.

Upon application to the Register of Copyrights a search will be made of the records, indexes, or deposits for such information as they may contain relative to specific copyright claims. The applicant for a search should state clearly the nature of the work under consideration, its title, the name of the claimant of

[1] Philippines has withdrawn accession. No determination of legal effect has been made.

copyright, and the probable date of its entry. The fee for such searches is $3 an hour for each hour of time consumed in making the search.

A copyright owner may bring suit for infringement and receive damages covering his loss and whatever profit the infringer may have made. Suits for infringement cannot be maintained in court until copies of the work have been deposited in the Copyright Office and registration made. The owner of a copyright has a certificate of registration which is prima facie evidence.

The Copyright Office, Library of Congress, Washington 25, D.C., will give further information.

PATENT LAW OF THE UNITED STATES

The Patent Office was established to administer the patent laws enacted by Congress in accordance with Article I, section 8, of the United States Constitution. The first of these laws was enacted April 10, 1790, but the Patent Office as a distinct bureau in the Department of State dates from 1802. The office was transferred from the Department of the Interior, where it had been since 1849, to the Department of Commerce in 1925. The present basic patent law is the Act of July 19, 1952, as embraced in Title 35, United States Code.

Under the United States patent laws only the inventor may apply for a patent, with certain exceptions. If a person who is not the inventor should apply, the patent—if it were obtained—would be void. If the inventor is dead, the application may be made by his legal representatives. If the inventor is insane, the application may be made by his guardian. If two or more persons make an invention jointly, they apply for a patent as joint inventors. A person who makes a financial contribution is not a joint inventor and cannot be joined in the application as an inventor, but an interest may be assigned to him. A patent is personal property and may be sold or mortgaged; it may be bequeathed by a will, and it may pass to the heirs of a deceased patentee. The patent law provides for the transfer or sale of a patent, or of an application for patent, by an instrument in writing, referred to as an assignment, which may transfer the entire interest or a part interest. The assignment, grant, or conveyance of any patent or application for patent should be acknowledged before a notary public or officer authorized to administer oaths or perform notarial acts.

A patent, which is issued in the name of the United States under the seal of the Patent Office, contains a grant to the patentee and a printed copy of the specification and drawing. The grant is of "the right to exclude others from making, using, or selling the invention throughout the United States" for the term of 17 years. The term of a patent can be extended only by an Act of Congress.

The application for patent is made to the Commissioner of Patents and includes: (1) a written document, which comprises a petition, a specification (description and claims), and an oath; (2) a drawing in those cases which admit of a drawing; and (3) the filing fee of $30 (plus an additional $1 for each claim in excess of 20). The application must be in English and must be legibly written in permanent black ink on one side of the paper. It should contain a clear, exact description of the invention, or if it is an improvement on a former invention, an exact description of its relation to that invention. The specification should contain the name and address of the inventor, the name of the invention, its general object, a detailed description, the claim or claims of the inventor as to just what part he considers his invention. It must be signed by the applicant. The applicant must swear (and there is a special form the oath must take) that he believes he is the original inventor. Blank forms are not supplied by the Patent Office, but specimen forms are shown in the pamphlet "General Information Concerning Patents."

A drawing must show every feature of the invention specified in the claim. Standards are specified in detail so that the drawings will be uniform in style and can be readily understood. A model will not be admitted unless specifically called for.

If the patent application is found to be allowable, a notice of allowance is sent the applicant, and a fee for issuing the patent is due within six months from the date of the notice.

The preparation of an application for patent and the conducting of proceedings in the Patent Office requires knowledge of patent law and Patent Office practice, as well as knowledge of the scientific or technical matters involved in the particular invention. While the inventor may prepare and file his own application and conduct the proceedings in the Patent Office himself, most inventors employ the services of patent attorneys or patent agents. The Patent Office publishes a list of such persons who are available to new clients; the list is arranged by states, cities, and foreign countries.

Inventors should prepare a record in the form of a sketch or drawing or written description promptly after the first conception of the invention, asking a trustworthy friend to sign his name as a witness; thereafter a carefully dated record of other steps taken in working on the invention should also be kept. Dated and witnessed records may be very important in case it becomes necessary to offer proof as to activities in connection with the invention.

The question whether or not patent applications should be filed in foreign countries depends largely upon the nature of the invention and its probable use abroad. Application in foreign countries should be made within a year after the date of application in the United States.

The United States courts only can handle questions of patent infringement, but the government, as well as the private individual, may be sued.

TRADEMARK LAW OF THE UNITED STATES

A trademark includes any word, name, symbol, device, or combination thereof adopted and used by a manufacturer or merchant to identify his goods and distinguish them from those manufactured or sold by others. The primary function of a trademark is to indicate origin, but trademarks also serve to guarantee the quality of goods and, through advertising, to create and maintain a demand for the product. Rights in a trademark are acquired only by use and the use must ordinarily continue if the rights so acquired are to be preserved. Most often words are chosen for their popular appeal and advertising value. An application for registration of a trademark must be filed in the name of the owner in the Patent Office in Washington, D.C. The registration fee is $25.

Trademarks may be protected in the United States in the following ways. Common-law rights, acquired by priority of adoption, ensure protection against infringement and unfair competition in the use of the trademark, even in the absence of registration. Registration on the so-called Principal Register of the Federal Trade Mark Act or Lanham Act (effective July 5, 1947) affords benefits not otherwise available. Registration of a trademark in the Patent Office does not in itself create or establish any exclusive rights but is recognition by the government of the right of the owner to use the mark in commerce to distinguish his goods from those of others. Registration on the Principal Register is constructive notice of the registrant's claim of ownership and prima facie evidence of the validity of the registration, the registrant's ownership of the mark, and the registrant's exclusive right to use the mark in commerce. After the registration has remained on the register for five years, it is subject to cancellation only on the grounds that the mark was obtained fraudulently, has been abandoned, or has become the common descriptive name of the goods to which it is applied.

After five years of continued use, upon the filing of an appropriate affidavit, the mark may acquire incontestability status and prima facie evidential value of the certificate becomes conclusive.

Requirements for registration on the Principal Register of the Lanham Act are as follows. The trademark must be used "in commerce"; that is, commerce within the control of Congress. Trademarks used on a local basis only may be protected by state laws, but they do not come under Federal control. The trademark must be actually in use at the time of application, either on merchandise or on displays associated with merchandise; use in advertising alone is not enough. The trademark must not violate certain statutory prohibitions: it must not contain immoral or scandalous matter; it must not be descriptive or misdescriptive of the goods of the applicant. The name or portrait of a living individual may be registered only if the written consent of such person is given. Registration of national insignia or emblems, such as the Red Cross emblem, is not permitted.

The Lanham Act permits the registration of geographical or descriptive words or surnames on the Principal Register, if they have acquired distinctiveness or a so-called "secondary meaning." The act also provides for registration of so-called service marks; *i.e.,* trademarks used by dry cleaners, railroads, insurance companies, etc., to indicate their services rather than merchandise made by them. Under the act, so-called certification marks and collective marks also may be registered.

Registration not available on the Principal Register of the Lanham Act may be secured on that act's Supplemental Register, which is a continuation of a register first created in 1920. Such registration does not constitute constructive notice and has no prima facie evidential value, but does give the right to sue in the United States courts. The Lanham Act provides for the registration of labels, packages, and configurations of goods on the Supplemental Register. Commercial labels and advertisements may also be copyrighted as such at the Library of Congress.[1] Supplementing Federal laws are trademark registration statutes in all of the 50 states. These laws cover a wide variety of business devices and usually provide for criminal remedies for willful infringement. Many of the states permit registration of trademarks before they are actually in use. State registration is limited to business activities carried on exclusively within the state.

The United States is a party to two international conventions: the Paris Convention for the Protection of Industrial Property as last revised in London in 1934 and the Washington Pan-American Convention of 1929. Both afford protection against unfair competition and trademark infringement for citizens and residents of the contracting countries.

CUSTOMS REGULATIONS OF THE UNITED STATES

The laws of the United States require, generally speaking, that the baggage of returning residents be examined by customs officers. As a returning resident you must declare all articles acquired abroad at the first customs port you reach when you come back to the United States. At a seaboard port, a written declaration will probably be required to speed you through customs. Members of a family residing in one household and traveling together may file a single declaration. You will be required to list articles which (1) you are bringing home for someone else at that person's request; (2) you intend to sell or use in your business; (3) do not accompany you on your return; and (4) consist of liquor and cigars when they exceed the limitation described under *Exemptions.* If the total value of acquired articles exceeds $200 for each member of your family, you will be required to list all articles acquired abroad. Declaration forms should

---

[1] See Copyright Law of the United States.

be prepared and handed to the purser or steward well in advance of arrival.

In making either an oral or written declaration, tell the customs officer what you actually paid. Do not guess; he knows more about values than you realize. If you acquired any article by gift, tell the customs officer as best you can the fair retail value. Although values for customs purposes are determined in most instances on wholesale value, you must state the price paid.

Exemptions. The term exemption simply means that if on your trip abroad, and as an incident of the trip, you acquire articles for your personal or household use and properly declare them at the port of your arrival in the United States, you are entitled to free entry of the articles, subject to the limitations on liquors and cigars mentioned below, up to the value of $200, $300, or even $500 depending upon the circumstances. If, however, you ordered the articles before you left the United States, the exemptions do not apply. The wearing of any article purchased abroad does not exempt it from duty. Remember that the exemptions are lost on any article which you fail to declare on your return from the trip on which you acquired it. Members of a family residing in one household and traveling together may combine their exemptions and apply the total exemptions to the value of all articles which they acquired on the trip.

The $200 exemption usually doesn't apply unless you have been outside the country for at least 48 hours on the trip from which you are returning. However, if you return through a port along the California-Mexico border, a 24-hour absence is sufficient for articles acquired in Mexico. Likewise, if you return through a port in Texas, Arizona, or New Mexico, there is no time restriction at all for articles acquired in Mexico. In no case is this exemption allowable more often than once in any 31-day period. A U.S. resident returning from the Virgin Islands is permitted an exemption of $200 for articles for personal or household use, no matter how short his period of absence. However, not more than $100 of the $200 may be applied to articles acquired elsewhere than in the Virgin Islands; furthermore, articles not acquired in the Virgin Islands may be included in the exemption only if the resident has been absent for at least 48 hours. The $300 exemption is in addition to the $200 exemption. You can get the $300 exemption only if you have been abroad not less than 12 full days and have not claimed it within six months prior to your return from this trip. If you sell within three years any article passed free under this exemption, the article will become subject to forfeiture, unless the duty from which the article was exempted is paid at the port of importation before such article is sold.

The $200 exemption will always be applied before the $300 exemption, but you may obtain both exemptions if you meet the conditions on which each depends.[1]

If you have crossed the border at one point and you swing back into the United States in order to travel to another point in the foreign country, you run the risk of losing your exemptions if you fail to meet certain requirements. If you make a "swing back" be sure to ask the nearest customs officer about these requirements.

Not more than one gallon of alcoholic beverage nor more than 100 cigars may be included in the exemption. These amounts may be included under either exemption, but not both. Additional quantities will be subject to duties and internal-revenue taxes. Customs officers will not release liquors destined to any state for use in violation of its laws.

Personal or household effects, professional books, or tools of trade or occupation which you prove you took out of the United States are duty-free on—or

---

[1] Under a law that went into effect on Sept. 9, 1961, the $200 exemption was reduced to $100 (except for residents returning from the Virgin Islands), and the $300 exemption was suspended. Unless further legislation should change the situation, the $200 and $300 exemptions will be restored automatically on July 1, 1963.

after—your return if properly declared or entered. If you take abroad an automobile or other vehicle, airplane, or boat for noncommercial use, you may bring it back duty-free by proving to the customs officer that it was taken out of the United States. This proof may be a customs certificate of registration obtained before departure. See Motoring Outside the United States.

Prohibited and Restricted Articles. If under the law an article is not allowed to be brought into this country, the customs officer cannot permit you to have it. Examples of prohibited articles are narcotics, drugs containing narcotics, obscene publications and articles, lottery tickets, etc. You cannot bring in certain specified fruits, vegetables, plants, cuttings, and seeds. Other kinds of plants and unprocessed plant products must be inspected or treated before you can bring them in.

The entry of fresh, chilled, or frozen meats from cloven-footed animals (cattle, sheep, goats, swine, deer, antelope, etc.) from any country in which rinderpest or foot-and-mouth disease is known to exist is prohibited. For all practical purposes, you may consider cured and cooked meats prohibited.

The entry of pets (cats, dogs, monkeys, and psittacine birds such as parakeets and parrots) is subject to the regulations of the Public Health Service, Department of Health, Education, and Welfare. If you wish information regarding such importations, contact the nearest Public Health Service quarantine officer.

The importation (as well as the purchase abroad) of all merchandise originating in some countries, such as Communist China or North Korea, is prohibited without a Treasury license, which may be considered unavailable to tourists. If in doubt, check with the U.S. Consulate offices before making purchases, particularly if traveling in Far Eastern countries.

BALANCE OF INTERNATIONAL PAYMENTS
(in millions of dollars)

ITEM	1925	1935	1945	1950	1955	1956	1957	1958	1959	1960 (prel.)
Exports of goods and services	6,348	3,265	16,273	14,427	22,328	26,284	29,168	25,606	25,683	29,065
Military transfers under grants			(1)	526	2,325	2,579	2,435	2,281	1,974	1,765
Other goods and services	6,348	3,265	16,273	13,901	20,003	23,705	26,733	23,325	23,709	27,300
Merchandise, adjusted	5,011	2,404	12,473	10,117	14,280	17,379	19,390	16,263	16,282	19,409
Transportation	318	189	1,308	1,033	1,420	1,642	1,999	1,672	1,646	1,816
Travel	83	101	162	419	654	705	785	825	902	968
Misc. services: Private[5]	8	82	453	607	879	1,087	1,168	1,205	1,390	1,413
Government	16	18	1,288	132	122	123	133	142	144	164
Military transactions				(1)	204	158	372	296	302	335
Income on investments	912	621	589	1,593	2,444	2,611	2,881	2,922	3,043	3,205
Imports of goods and services	5,261	3,137	10,232	12,098	17,937	19,829	20,923	21,053	23,537	23,327
Merchandise, adjusted	4,291	2,462	5,245	9,108	11,527	12,804	13,291	12,951	15,294	14,722
Transportation	391	206	420	818	1,204	1,408	1,569	1,636	1,759	1,942
Travel	347	245	309	754	1,153	1,275	1,372	1,460	1,610	1,744
Misc. services: Private[5]			153	247	486	543	563	613	683	634
Government	23	28	1,440	250	242	264	810	805	802	808
Military expenditures	39	41	2,434	576	2,323	2,955	3,105	3,412	3,109	3,048
Income on investments	170	155	231	345	502	580	653	676	880	929
Balance on goods and services	1,087	128	6,041	2,329	4,391	6,455	8,245	4,553	2,146	5,738
Unilateral transfers, net [to foreign countries (−)]	−403	−182	−7,113	−4,533	−4,811	−4,977	−4,753	−4,619	−4,398	−4,254
Private remittances	−373	−162	−473	−444	−444	−580	−543	−540	−575	−633
Government	−30	−20	−6,640	−4,089	−4,367	−4,447	−4,210	−4,079	−3,823	−3,621
Military supplies and services				−526	−2,579	−2,435	−2,435	−2,325	−1,974	−1,765
Other	−30	−20	−6,640	−3,563	−2,042	−1,868	−1,775	−1,798	−1,849	−1,856
U.S. capital, net [outflow of funds (−)]	−899	544	−1,569	−1,421	−1,521	−3,619	−4,133	−3,815	−2,728	−4,965
Private	−917	543	−550	−1,265	−1,211	−2,990	−3,175	−2,844	−2,375	−3,856
Government	27	1	−1,019	−156	−310	−629	−958	−971	−353	−1,109
Foreign capital, net [outflow of funds (−)]	241	968	2,085	1,913	1,454	1,304	691	1,226	3,721	2,427
Long-term investments in U.S.[3]	301	320	−104	53	846	530	361	24	555	297
Short-term and other liquid liabilities	−60	648	2,189	1,859	1,108	1,274	330	1,202	3,166	2,130
Gold sales [purchases (−)]	100	−1,822	548	1,743	41	−306	−798	2,275	731	1,702
Foreign capital and gold, total	341	−854	2,633	3,655	1,495	1,498	−107	3,501	4,452	4,129
Errors and omissions	−135	364	8	−30	446	643	748	380	528	−648

FOREIGN TRADE

Goods shipped into a country are called imports; those sent out of a country are called exports. Both imports and exports are valued at the customs house or in some other authorized place. In this way it is possible for all countries to issue periodical returns showing the relationship between exports and imports. The difference between imports and exports is known as "the balance of trade." The basis of the official statistics of the United States are export declarations and customs entry declarations filed with the United States customs officials at the time of exportation or at the time of importation of the merchandise or preceding its arrival. Charges incidental to the transportation of goods from country to country are taken into account in calculation of the balance of payments between the United States and foreign countries. Practices among countries vary greatly and the subject of valuation is extremely complex.

Balance of Payments. The term balance of payments represents the income of a country from payments by other countries—including payments for all "exports" (commodities, merchandise), services, interest on loans, dividends and profits from investments in foreign countries—compared with similar outgoing payments to other countries. The balance of payments of any given country will be plus (active) or minus (passive) depending on whether the income or the outgo is the greater. In 1894 the United States began to maintain an active balance of payments; however, because of rising expenditures (as, for instance, for foreign aid and military establishments in foreign countries), the United States balance of payments has recently become passive.

A country's balance of payments, in turn, affects its gold reserves, and for settlement of its international obligations gold bullion must be released. Between 1952 and 1960, United States reserves declined from about $23,000,000,000 to $18,000,000,000, although the country still held some 45 per cent of the world's monetary gold supply. The dwindling of United States gold stocks also affected the ratio of coverage of the dollar; in 1945 Treasury-held gold stocks covered 42.1 cents of every dollar; by June 30, 1960, the support had sunk to 36.48 cents.

The export of gold at the fixed price of $35 an ounce—often aggravated by heavy speculation against the dollar in expectation of a possible devaluation of the American currency—has maintained the parity between the dollar and other currencies.

Export and Import Trade. The dwindling of American gold stocks has served to emphasize the importance to the American economy of the export trade. Realizing that out of 300,000 American companies with exportable products, only about 12,000 do an active export business, the United States Department of Commerce takes a strong interest in promoting export efforts. A very important phase is participation in international trade fairs and special exhibitions, which give even small industries an opportunity to show their merchandise in many parts of the world. American products tend to have a certain appeal and can be sold abroad even when the domestic product might be a little less expensive. Consumer goods of all kinds, ranging from kitchen utensils, fabrics, and portable tools to gasoline engines, are eagerly bought in many parts of the world.

In each of the 33 strategically located field offices of the Department of Commerce in the United States, there are experts who will advise firms interested in exporting concerning the problems involved. Trade lists of principal importers, processors, wholesalers, distributors, sales agents, and service organizations are available, grouped by country and by individual commodity; information also is given about size, type of operation, sales territory covered, and other details. In addition, the World Trade Directory Reports give background details concerning particular foreign companies. Manufacturers wishing to visit potential customers overseas also may be introduced to the appropriate persons in foreign service posts who can give on-the-spot briefing concerning the possibilities of an export program.

Exports can no longer be regarded as a pleasant bonus to America's domestic profit. Americans are skillful in meeting competition at home and must be at least equally skillful in meeting foreign competition. The responsibility for developing American international trade cannot be left solely to the large firms; more medium-sized and small businesses must enter the competition if the United States economy is to remain healthy and prosperous.

Foreign trade is a two-way street, however; a nation that wants to sell its goods to other nations must buy from them as well. Imports basically provide either goods not produced domestically or goods that can compete favorably in price with domestic merchandise. In the 1940's American industry scoffed at stainless-steel cutlery; undaunted, Japanese manufacturers developed—with American help —inexpensive steel tableware which is retailed at low prices in American variety stores. American factories later followed suit, producing a better-styled product which sold at higher prices.

Generally speaking, American industry aims at mass production for the mass market. Consequently a certain proportion of the consuming public looks for better-made and better-styled goods even at higher prices. Here too, imports fill the gap by offering such items as food specialties, chinaware, watches, cameras, lighting fixtures, and a wide variety of goods.

Firms wishing to import may make contact with foreign factories or stores abroad by consulting the trade specialist in the field offices of the Department of Commerce. Trade lists, trade directories, and the "Foreign Commerce Weekly," all published by the department, will provide ample leads. In special cases additional information and names of exporting companies may be obtained from the commercial attaché at the United States Embassy in the country in question. Inquiries at foreign consulates in the United States and the chambers of commerce linking America with foreign countries, as well as advertising in foreign tradepapers may produce valuable information on new sources.

Foreign Currency Futures. This aspect of international trade may be of importance to the American exporter or importer in avoiding loss through currency fluctuations. If an importer buys a certain commodity priced in foreign currency (for instance, pound sterling, or German marks) payable in 30, 60, or 90 days, he can insure himself against fluctuation in the interval by buying the pounds or marks at the current rate for specified future delivery. Conversely, an American manufacturer having received an order from West Germany to be paid in marks can immediately sell the marks to be delivered in 60, 90, or 120 days when he makes delivery of the goods.

NATURALIZATION[1]

A foreigner born outside the jurisdiction of the United States is considered an alien[2] until he is naturalized. An alien is entitled to all the privileges of citizenship except political rights. He can buy and sell, make contracts, and sue and be sued; he is entitled to the full protection of the government in his person and his property.

An applicant's first step toward naturalization is the filing of a petition for naturalization. He may, if he wishes, make a declaration of intention at any time before filing the petition. Children of naturalized persons, if under 16 years of age at the time of their parents' naturalization and residing in the United States, may derive citizenship through their parents. Foreign-born children of United States citizens are generally considered citizens of the United States.

The citizenship of a married woman[3] is not the same as that of her husband. Any person who meets all other requirements and whose spouse is a citizen of the United States is eligible for naturalization if the person has been lawfully admitted for permanent residence and has resided in the United States for three

---

[1] The Immigration and Naturalization Service is a part of the United States Department of Justice, Washington, D.C. There are 32 district offices, located in the larger cities. Specific questions should be addressed to these district offices.

[2] Current legislation requires that each alien notify the Attorney General, in writing, of his current address, in January of each year.

[3] See also Rights and Duties of Husband and Wife.

years immediately preceding the filing of the petition. The person must have lived in marital union with his citizen spouse during the entire three-year period and the spouse must have been a citizen for the entire period.

Generally, an alien may be admitted to citizenship only if (1) immediately preceding the date of his petition he has resided continuously in the United States for at least five years and in the state for at least six months, and has been physically present in the United States for at least half of the required period of residence; (2) he has resided continuously in the United States from the date of his petition to the time of his admission to citizenship; and (3) he is a person of good moral character, attached to the principles of the Constitution of the United States, and well disposed to the good order and happiness of the United States.

At the hearing of the petition, residence in the state and other qualifications shall be proved by the oral testimony of at least two credible witnesses, citizens of the United States. These witnesses should know the applicant for at least six months. If the witnesses have not known the applicant for the entire five-year period of United States residence, the applicant will be required to name additional witnesses who knew him for the remainder of the required time. These witnesses may make a sworn statement in the place where they live.

Absence from the United States for a continuous period of more than six months and less than one year during the period immediately preceding the date of filing the petition for citizenship shall cause presumption of a break in the continuity of residence, but such presumption may be overcome by presentation of satisfactory evidence that the applicant had a reasonable cause for not returning to the United States sooner.

Absence from the United States for a continuous period of one year or more during the period immediately preceding the date of filing the petition shall break the continuity of such residence. However, under certain conditions permission may be obtained from the Immigration and Naturalization Service to be absent for a year or more without breaking the required residence. Such permission may be granted to persons employed by the United States government, an American research institution, an American firm engaged in development of foreign trade and commerce of the United States, or a public international organization of which the United States is a member. Such permission also is granted to members of the clergy of a religious denomination having a bona fide organization within the United States, or persons engaged solely by a religious denomination or an interdenominational mission organization having a bona fide organization within the United States, as missionaries, brothers, nuns, or sisters.

A petition generally may not be heard until at least 30 days after it is filed. The Commissioner of Immigration and Naturalization has authority to designate examiners to conduct preliminary examinations on petitions for naturalization and to make recommendations to the court empowered to naturalize aliens.

NATIONAL FLAG CODE[1]

1. The flag should be displayed only from sunrise to sunset, or between such hours as may be designated by proper authority. It should be displayed on national and state holidays and on historic and special occasions.

2. When carried in a procession with another flag or flags, the flag of the United States should be either on the marching right, *i.e.*, the flag's own right, or in front of the center in a line of other flags.

3. When displayed with another flag against a wall from crossed staffs, the flag of the United States should be on the right—the flag's own right—and its staff should be in front of the other flag.

---

[1] Rules, as adopted by the National Flag Conference.

4. When a number of flags are grouped and displayed from staffs, the flag of the United States should be in the center or at the highest point.

5. When flags of states or cities or pennants of societies are flown on the same halyard with the flag of the United States, the national flag should always be at the peak. When they are flown from adjacent staffs the flag of the United States should be hoisted first. No flag or pennant should be placed above or to the right.

6. When flags of two or more nations are displayed they should be flown from separate staffs of the same height and the flags should be of approximately equal size.

7. When the flag is displayed from a staff projecting horizontally or at an angle from the window sill, balcony, or front of a building, the union of the flag should go to the head of the staff unless the flag is at half-staff.

8. When the flag of the United States is displayed in a manner other than by being flown from a staff it should be displayed flat, whether indoors or out. When displayed either horizontally or vertically against a wall or in a window, the union should be uppermost and to the flag's own right, *i.e.,* to the observer's left.

9. When displayed over the middle of the street, as between buildings, the flag should be suspended vertically with the union to the north in an east-and-west street or to the east in a north-and-south street.

10. When used on a speaker's platform, the flag should be displayed above and behind the speaker. It should never be used to cover the speaker's desk nor to drape over the front of the platform. If flown from a staff it should be on the speaker's right.

11. When used in unveiling a statue or monument, the flag should not be allowed to fall to the ground but should be carried aloft to wave out, forming a distinctive feature.

12. When flown at half-staff, the flag is hoisted to the peak for an instant and then lowered to the half-staff position; before lowering the flag for the day it is raised again to the peak. By "half-staff" is meant lowering the flag to one-half the distance between the top and bottom of the staff. If local conditions require, divergence from this position is permissible. On Memorial Day, May 30, the flag is displayed at half-staff from sunrise until noon and at full staff from noon until sunset.

13. Flags flown from fixed staffs are placed at half-staff to indicate mourning. When the flag is displayed on a small staff, as when carried in parade, mourning is indicated by attaching two streamers of black crepe to the spearhead, allowing the streamers to fall naturally; this may be done only by order of the President of the United States.

14. When used to cover a casket, the flag should be placed so that the union is at the head and over the left shoulder. The flag should not be lowered into the grave nor allowed to touch the ground.

15. When the flag is displayed in the body of a church it should be from a staff placed on the congregation's right as the members face the clergyman. The service flag, the state flag, or other flag should be at the left of the congregation. If it is in the chancel, or on the platform, the flag of the United States should be placed on the clergyman's right as he faces the congregation, and other flags on his left.

THE PLEDGE TO THE FLAG

I pledge allegiance to the flag of the United States of America and to the republic for which it stands, one nation under God, indivisible, with liberty and justice for all.

MONETARY SYSTEM OF THE UNITED STATES

GOLD COIN

Weight: 15 5/21 grains to the dollar
Fineness: 900–1000, or 1/35 ounce of pure gold
Denominations: $2.50, $5, $10, $20

The United States government does not issue any gold coin, nor permit hoarding of gold. Section 5 of the Gold Reserve Act of 1934 provided that no gold should thereafter be coined for domestic use and that all gold coins should be withdrawn from circulation.

SILVER COIN

Standard Dollar: Unlimited as to use for legal tender. Receivable for all public dues; exchangeable for silver certificates and other forms of money.
Weight: 412.5 grains
Fineness: 900–1000
Ratio to gold: 15.988 to 1

Other Silver Coins: Legal tender. Receivable for all public dues; exchangeable for minor coin; *i.e.,* five-cent pieces or one-cent pieces.
Weight: 50¢, 192.9 grains; 25¢, 96.45 grains; 10¢, 38.58 grains
Fineness: 900–1000
Ratio to gold: 14.953 to 1

MINOR COIN

Weight: five-cent piece, 77.16 grains (75 per cent copper, 25 per cent nickel)
Weight: one-cent piece, 48 grains (95 per cent copper, 5 per cent tin and zinc)

PAPER CURRENCY

On July 10, 1929, the Treasury began to issue a small-size paper currency to replace the old larger-size currency. In less than a year this was practically accomplished. The new currency is 6⅛ in. × 2⅝ in. The back designs are uniform for each denomination; the face designs, too, are essentially the same, but with small characteristic variations.

The portraits assigned to the faces and the embellishments for the backs of the several denominations are as follows:

Denomination	Portrait on face	Embellishment on back
$1	Washington	Ornate One
$2	Jefferson	Monticello
$5	Lincoln	Lincoln Memorial
$10	Hamilton	U. S. Treasury
$20	Jackson	White House
$50	Grant	U. S. Capitol
$100	Franklin	Independence Hall
$500	McKinley	Ornate Five Hundred
$1,000	Cleveland	Ornate One Thousand
$5,000	Madison	Ornate Five Thousand
$10,000	Chase	Ornate Ten Thousand

The United States issues the following kinds of paper currency:

Gold Certificates.—These were issued against gold coin and against gold bullion for greater convenience in handling. Denominations, $10, $20, $50, $100, $500, $1,000, $5,000, $10,000. The United States government issues gold certificates only to Federal Reserve Banks.

Silver Certificates.—These are issued against deposits of silver or against silver coins. They are legal tender and are receivable for all public dues and are redeemable in silver dollars at the Treasury. Denominations, $1, $2, $5, $10, $20, $50, $100.

United States Notes.—These are notes guaranteed by the United States government. They are legal tender for all debts, customs, and interest on the public debt.

Federal Reserve Notes.—These are a first lien upon all the assets of the Federal Reserve Bank by which they are issued. They are full legal tender. They constitute the principal part of the circulating medium.

National Bank Notes.—These notes were issued by the national banks and guaranteed by the national government, the bank in question depositing whatever security was required; said security not exceeding the capital of the bank. In 1935 the Treasury called for redemption the only government securities on which national banks might issue notes and their issue thereupon ceased.

United States Mints are in Philadelphia, San Francisco, and Denver. Assay offices are in New York and Seattle.

United States Bullion Depositories are at Fort Knox, Ky. (*gold*) and West Point, N.Y. (*silver*).

THE SECRETARY AND HER WORK

The secretary occupies a pivotal spot in any office. Because she handles her employer's correspondence, telephone calls, and appointments, she interprets him on many occasions to others in the company, to persons in other firms, and sometimes—as in a medical or legal practice—to members of the public.

Because of her unique position on the business team, the secretary must be dependable, accurate, and poised without being arrogant or aggressive. Above all, because she is entrusted with many confidential details of her employer's business, and often of his personal life, she must be a person of unquestionable discretion and integrity.

Important Secretarial Duties

Incoming Correspondence. Each piece of mail should be opened, stamped with a date stamp, and collected in a folder for the employer's perusal. Retain an envelope only if it bears an address or some other detail not in the letter. Mail may be sorted in terms of significance, with important letters in one pile and routine items in another.

If the employer is out of town, the secretary frequently acknowledges letters of importance during his absence. She writes that her employer is away and—as the case may be—she has forwarded the letter to him, has called the matter to his attention by telephone, or is holding the letter for his attention. Before a letter is forwarded, a copy should be made so that the message is not lost.

Outgoing Mail. The secretary is responsible for the appearance and accuracy of all letters sent out. Neat letters, clearly phrased, facilitate understanding between her employer and the outside world and create an image of efficiency.

The following practices are useful in maintaining high standards in correspondence:

1. Always keep the current shorthand pad and pencil in the same place, ready for dictation at a moment's notice. Date the pad each day; if the unused pages seem inadequate for the probable dictation for the day, have a fresh pad ready.

2. For the most favorable hearing position, face the person dictating, whenever possible. If dictation is too rapid, interrupt by repeating the last word you have written down. Check an unfamiliar name or word by repeating it. If you have doubt about a spelling, try to find out from the person dictating where it can be checked. Proper names and unfamiliar words are best spelled out in longhand. A name that is used frequently can be designated by a special symbol.

3. Sentence endings and question marks are often evident from voice alone, although some persons specify punctuation as well as paragraphs when dictating. If not specified, the secretary must insert these herself. Where grammar is incorrect, she must make corrections, being careful not to change the meaning intended.

4. If extra copies of a letter are needed, make a notation immediately preceding the letter. If immediate attention must be given any item dictated, indicate by marks in colored pencil, attaching a paper clip, or turning down the page corner. Draw a line after each letter in the pad and two lines to denote the close of a dictation period.

5. Names and addresses should be checked against letters being answered. As each letter is transcribed, a vertical pencil line is drawn through the notes for it. The carbon copy of the new letter is attached to the original correspondence.

6. Analyze placement of each letter on the page before typing it. If carrying material over to a new page, save at least a paragraph to be carried over. Before removing a page from the typewriter, check it for errors and make corrections. When one line contains several errors or if errors on the page are numerous, it is quicker and cleaner to retype the page.

7. Finished letters should be placed in a folder for the employer's signature.

Other Secretarial Duties. The secretary creates good will for her employer and company through the friendliness and interest she projects in her telephone voice. An ability to recognize regular callers from their voices alone is a great asset. When calls are taken after going through a switchboard, the secretary may say, "Mr. Jones' office, Miss Brown speaking." If there is no switchboard, she says, "Smith Brothers, Miss Brown speaking." If a caller does not identify himself, she asks, "May I tell him who's calling?" If the employer does not wish to accept certain calls, she says, "He's not available just now. May I give him your message?"

In placing outgoing calls, the secretary is uniformly pleasant with employees to whom she speaks in other firms. When she greets visitors to the office, her manner is friendly even when she must tell a visitor that her employer cannot see him. If she has any doubt as to whether an unexpected caller is welcome, she asks him to wait: "I'll see if Mr. Jones is free just now." In many offices, the secretary ushers expected visitors into the office of her employer and makes the introductions.

Many other tasks are performed by secretaries; they vary from office to office. Among such jobs are making travel arrangements, taking minutes of business conferences or board meetings, and preparing an employer's manuscript for publication. In cases where she feels the need of specialized information, as in manuscript preparation, she will work more efficiently if she consults specialized reference books.

See also charts on How to Correct Proof and Proofreaders' Marks; A Guide to Abbreviations; and related information in this encyclopedia.

FILING

Filing, the classification and storage of records, is a vital procedure in virtually every business. Accuracy is the primary factor in successful filing, since protracted hunting for a needed document is costly in time and therefore in money. Four systems of filing are in general use:

Alphabetic. The foundation of all filing and the most widely used system, it consists of filing all names and subjects in alphabetical order.

Geographic. A system which features grouping first by location and then by name and subject, it is useful for sales organizations and for firms with sizable mailing lists.

Subject. This system is helpful in separating and grouping documents pertaining to various phases of a business. In this method it is advisable to file under names of actual objects, such as "Maps," "Pamphlets," "Photographs," rather than under abstract headings.

Numeric. Widely employed in work of a scientific nature, this system allots a number to each subject or name; an alphabetic card file provides the index for the numbers. Probably the best-known numeric system is the Dewey Decimal Classification used in libraries.

Other Methods of Data Recording. In many offices a diary is kept which notes the important activities of each day, *e.g.*, major business transactions, travel arrivals and departures of staff members, important telephone calls, and similar items. A scrapbook is useful for recording printed matter, such as newspaper clippings and advertisements; the use of rubber cement produces an efficient paste-up job. A daily record or daily file is helpful where correspondence is heavy and frequent reference to it is made. Here, an extra carbon copy of each outgoing letter is made; these copies can then be bound in alphabetical order by day, week, or month, depending on the volume.

Where a follow-up, or tickler, system is needed, a box of index cards bearing reminders can be effective if it is consulted each day. In another reminder system, papers and letters needing further attention may be filed chronologically in a folder, which is checked daily for current and pending items.

Some organizations which must preserve extensive documentary records use microfilm recording to conserve space. Using the microfilm process, material is photographed on 35-millimeter film, which can then be viewed through a special projector. Preserving data on cards or rolls of this film can greatly reduce storage needs.

STEPS IN FILING

Unless filing is of a fixed, everyday nature, material must be marked to indicate where it should be filed. The person in authority marks the filing indication on the item to be filed, usually with a colored pencil. The name or subject under which it should be filed is underlined or circled; if neither is mentioned, the classification is written in the upper right-hand corner.

Material can be sorted before filing; for example, in alphabetic filing, all items can be separated under major alphabetic headings—"A," "B," and so on—then arranged alphabetically within each letter classification. Within the file itself, colored labels and tiny metal file signals in various colors simplify identification of material, especially when various sets of files are in use; replacement of material in the files is also facilitated. A number of efficient filing arrangements bearing prepared guides and labels are available for purchase.

Cross References. Many items can be filed under more than one classification. In such cases, cross-reference slips may be placed under alternate classifications referring back to the main heading under which the item has been filed.

Alphabetization. Two systems of alphabetizing are used, one following dictionary style, the other following telephone-directory style. The dictionary method adheres to strict alphabetical order; the telephone-directory method alphabetizes by first unit; or, if first units are the same, by second unit; or, if second units are the same, by third unit, and so on.

Dictionary Style	Telephone Directory Style
Mason Housebuilders Co.	Mason House Wares
Mason House Wares	Mason Housebuilders Co.
Mason, James	Mason, J. C.
Mason, J. C.	Mason, James
Mason, John	Mason, John

Mc and Mac are filed as they occur alphabetically:

Mabon Company
MacArdle, John
MacFeeley, Kent
Mack, William
Mackintosh, Henry W.
MacLennan, George L.
McGinnis, Herbert
McMinnies, Mary J.
Mearns, William

In firm names, abbreviations are treated as they are written:

NYC Plumbing Co.
OK Garage

Numerals are filed as though they were spelled out:

Nightingale, Everett S.
9 Park Place, Inc.

Common abbreviations, such as Ft., Mt., and St., are alphabetized as if they were spelled out. Titles, such as Dr., Mrs., Rev., should be ignored, except in book indexing, where this form is used:

Jones, Dr. James J.
Jones, Rev. James J.

POSTAL INFORMATION

HANDLING MAIL

Saving Money on Postage. There are many ways in which an alert businessman can save money on postage. Letters with advertising matter enclosed often weigh more than 2 oz., thereby requiring more postage, when the message they carry might just as effectively be presented on material weighing less than 2 oz. The savings may be small on a few circulars, but if there are 10,000 to be sent out there will be a considerable saving on the lot if the less-than-two-ounce rule is observed. In the same way business reply cards now make it possible for commercial organizations to pay only for the return postage that will mean something to them, instead of broadcasting actual stamps. There are special mailing permits, which are well worth investigation when a large volume of mail is handled.

Business Reply Cards and Envelopes. It is possible, instead of sending a post card or a stamped envelope with a circular for the return order, to send a card or an envelope on which postage need not be paid until it has returned to the office where it originated. Persons wishing this privilege must make application to the postmaster and must conform with the established rules and regulations.

Business reply envelopes and cards may be distributed by mail or otherwise, in any quantity, for return through the domestic mails to the permit holder. They may not be sent to foreign countries, for they cannot be returned therefrom. The permit holder pays the regular rate of postage plus a prescribed amount for each card or envelope returned to him. Collection of postage is made in the regular manner by the letter carrier or other postal employee at time of delivery.

Keeping Mailing Lists Up to Date. The best way to keep a mailing list up to date is to keep a careful check on the responses which it brings in, but sometimes other methods also are necessary. One of the most valuable of these is to ask the post office to check the list. The post office will eliminate dead names and correct all addresses.

Another valuable method for use in keeping up-to-date lists is the "Form 3547" procedure, whereby the mailer of advertising matter may request notice to be sent to him on a card in the event the mail is undeliverable as addressed. This particular service is restricted to matter sent as third- or fourth-class mail and for a purpose other than to obtain the address of an individual. Your local post office will furnish details.

Recalling Mail. It is possible to recall mail after it has been deposited in the mail box or post office up to the time of its delivery. A form may be obtained at any post office. The expense of the recall, which may include telegraphing if the mail has already been dispatched, is borne by the recaller and must be deposited with the postmaster at the time the application is filled out. There is no expense if the mail has not left the office at which it was first deposited.

DOMESTIC POSTAGE RATES

First Class. Letters and written and sealed matter, 5¢ for each ounce or fraction thereof. Post cards and private mailing cards, 4¢ each.

Second Class. Newspapers and periodical publications with second-class mail privileges (copies mailed by private individuals), 4¢ for the first 2 oz.; 1¢ for each additional ounce or fraction thereof, or the fourth-class rate, whichever is lower.

Third Class. (limit 15 oz.) Circulars and other miscellaneous printed matter, and merchandise, 4¢ for the first 2 oz.; 2¢ for each additional ounce or fraction thereof.

Books (including catalogs) of 24 pages or more (at least 22 of which are printed), seeds, cuttings, bulbs, roots, cions, and plants, 4¢ for the first 2 oz.; 2¢ for each additional ounce or fraction thereof.

Bulk lots of identical pieces may be mailed under permit in quantities of not less than either 20 lb. or 200 pieces, at the rate of 18¢ a lb. or fraction thereof, in the case of circulars, miscellaneous printed matter, and merchandise; and 12¢ a lb. or fraction thereof, in the case of books or catalogs having 24 pages or more, seeds, plants, etc., with a minimum charge of 2⅝¢ a piece. The bulk mailing fee must be paid at or before the first mailing in each calendar year.

Special Rates for Books. Books containing no advertising matter other than incidental announcements of books may be mailed at the rate of 9.5¢ (in 1963 and 10¢ thereafter) for the first lb. and 5¢ for each additional pound or fraction thereof.

Fourth Class or Parcel Post. (1 lb. and over) Merchandise, books, printed matter, and all other mailable matter not in first or second class. The limit of size is 100 in. in combined girth and length, and the limit of weight is 70 lb., except for parcel post mailed at any first-class post office for delivery at any other first-class post office, in which case the size of the parcel is limited to 72 in. in combined girth and length and the weight is limited to 40 lb. in Zones 1 and 2, and 20 lb. in Zones 3 to 8. The higher size and weight limits also apply to parcels mailed at or to any second-, third-, or fourth-class post office; to or from any rural or star route; to or from any Army-Air Force or Fleet post office; and to, from, or between any territory or possession of the United States.

Zones. There are eight numbered parcel post zones, determined as follows: The United States and its territories and possessions are divided into units identical with a quarter of the area formed by the intersecting parallels of latitude and meridians of longitude. The zones are based on the straight-line distance between the unit of area in which the mailing post office is located and the unit of area in which the post office of address is located, measured from the center of one unit to the nearest point in the other. The zone equivalents of straight-line distances are shown in the column headings of the accompanying rate chart.

FOURTH CLASS (PARCEL POST) ZONE RATES

Weight, 1 pound and not exceeding—	Local	Zones						
		1 and 2	3	4	5	6	7	8
		Up to 150 miles	150 to 300 miles	300 to 600 miles	600 to 1,000 miles	1,000 to 1,400 miles	1,400 to 1,800 miles	Over 1,800 miles
2 pounds	$0.24	$0.33	$0.35	$0.39	$0.45	$0.51	$0.53	$0.64
3 pounds	.26	.38	.41	.47	.55	.64	.74	.83
4 pounds	.28	.43	.47	.55	.65	.77	.90	1.02
5 pounds	.30	.48	.53	.63	.75	.90	1.06	1.21
6 pounds	.32	.53	.59	.70	.85	1.03	1.22	1.40
7 pounds	.34	.58	.65	.77	.95	1.16	1.38	1.59
8 pounds	.36	.63	.71	.84	1.05	1.29	1.54	1.78
9 pounds	.38	.68	.77	.91	1.15	1.42	1.70	1.97
10 pounds	.40	.73	.83	.98	1.25	1.55	1.86	2.16
11 pounds	.42	.77	.89	1.05	1.35	1.67	2.02	2.34
12 pounds	.44	.81	.95	1.12	1.45	1.79	2.18	2.52
13 pounds	.46	.85	1.01	1.19	1.55	1.91	2.34	2.70
14 pounds	.48	.89	1.07	1.26	1.65	2.03	2.50	2.88
15 pounds	.50	.93	1.13	1.33	1.75	2.15	2.66	3.06
16 pounds	.52	.97	1.18	1.40	1.85	2.27	2.81	3.24
17 pounds	.54	1.01	1.23	1.47	1.95	2.39	2.96	3.42
18 pounds	.56	1.05	1.28	1.54	2.05	2.51	3.11	3.60
19 pounds	.58	1.09	1.33	1.61	2.15	2.63	3.26	3.78
20 pounds	.60	1.13	1.38	1.68	2.25	2.75	3.41	3.96
21 pounds	.62	1.17	1.43	1.75	2.34	2.87	3.56	4.14
22 pounds	.64	1.21	1.48	1.82	2.43	2.99	3.71	4.32
23 pounds	.66	1.25	1.53	1.89	2.52	3.11	3.86	4.50
24 pounds	.68	1.29	1.58	1.96	2.61	3.23	4.01	4.68
25 pounds	.70	1.33	1.63	2.03	2.70	3.35	4.16	4.86
26 pounds	.72	1.37	1.68	2.10	2.79	3.47	4.31	5.04
27 pounds	.74	1.41	1.73	2.17	2.88	3.59	4.46	5.22
28 pounds	.76	1.45	1.78	2.24	2.97	3.71	4.61	5.40
29 pounds	.78	1.49	1.83	2.31	3.06	3.83	4.76	5.58
30 pounds	.80	1.53	1.88	2.38	3.15	3.95	4.91	5.76

| Weight, 1 pound and not exceeding— | Zones | | | | | | | |
	Local	1 and 2 Up to 150 miles	3 150 to 300 miles	4 300 to 600 miles	5 600 to 1,000 miles	6 1,000 to 1,400 miles	7 1,400 to 1,800 miles	8 Over 1,800 miles
31 pounds	$0.82	$1.57	$1.93	$2.45	$3.24	$4.06	$5.05	$5.93
32 pounds	.84	1.61	1.98	2.52	3.33	4.17	5.19	6.10
33 pounds	.86	1.65	2.03	2.59	3.42	4.28	5.33	6.27
34 pounds	.88	1.69	2.08	2.66	3.51	4.39	5.47	6.44
35 pounds	.90	1.73	2.13	2.73	3.60	4.50	5.61	6.61
36 pounds	.92	1.77	2.18	2.80	3.69	4.61	5.75	6.78
37 pounds	.94	1.81	2.23	2.87	3.78	4.72	5.89	6.95
38 pounds	.96	1.85	2.28	2.94	3.87	4.83	6.03	7.12
39 pounds	.98	1.89	2.33	3.01	3.96	4.94	6.17	7.29
40 pounds	1.00	1.93	2.38	3.08	4.05	5.05	6.31	7.46
41 pounds	1.02	1.97	2.43	3.15	4.14	5.16	6.45	7.62
42 pounds	1.04	2.01	2.48	3.22	4.23	5.27	6.59	7.78
43 pounds	1.06	2.05	2.53	3.29	4.32	5.38	6.73	7.94
44 pounds	1.08	2.09	2.58	3.36	4.41	5.49	6.87	8.10
45 pounds	1.10	2.13	2.63	3.43	4.50	5.60	7.01	8.26
46 pounds	1.12	2.17	2.68	3.50	4.59	5.71	7.15	8.42
47 pounds	1.14	2.21	2.73	3.57	4.68	5.82	7.29	8.58
48 pounds	1.16	2.25	2.78	3.64	4.77	5.93	7.43	8.74
49 pounds	1.18	2.29	2.83	3.71	4.86	6.04	7.57	8.90
50 pounds	1.20	2.33	2.88	3.78	4.95	6.15	7.71	9.06
51 pounds	1.22	2.37	2.93	3.84	5.03	6.26	7.84	9.22
52 pounds	1.24	2.41	2.98	3.90	5.11	6.37	7.97	9.38
53 pounds	1.26	2.45	3.03	3.96	5.19	6.48	8.10	9.54
54 pounds	1.28	2.49	3.08	4.02	5.27	6.59	8.23	9.70
55 pounds	1.30	2.53	3.13	4.08	5.35	6.70	8.36	9.86
56 pounds	1.32	2.57	3.18	4.14	5.43	6.81	8.49	10.02
57 pounds	1.34	2.61	3.23	4.20	5.51	6.92	8.62	10.18
58 pounds	1.36	2.65	3.28	4.26	5.59	7.03	8.75	10.34
59 pounds	1.38	2.69	3.33	4.32	5.67	7.14	8.88	10.50
60 pounds	1.40	2.73	3.38	4.38	5.75	7.25	9.01	10.66
61 pounds	1.42	2.77	3.43	4.44	5.83	7.36	9.14	10.82
62 pounds	1.44	2.81	3.48	4.50	5.91	7.47	9.27	10.98
63 pounds	1.46	2.85	3.53	4.56	5.99	7.58	9.40	11.14
64 pounds	1.48	2.89	3.58	4.62	6.07	7.69	9.53	11.30
65 pounds	1.50	2.93	3.63	4.68	6.15	7.80	9.66	11.46
66 pounds	1.52	2.97	3.68	4.74	6.23	7.91	9.79	11.62
67 pounds	1.54	3.01	3.73	4.80	6.31	8.02	9.92	11.78
68 pounds	1.56	3.05	3.78	4.86	6.39	8.13	10.05	11.94
69 pounds	1.58	3.09	3.83	4.92	6.47	8.24	10.18	12.10
70 pounds	1.60	3.13	3.88	4.98	6.55	8.35	10.31	12.26

Air Mail. Mail of all classes, except that which may be damaged by low temperatures or high altitudes. Air mail is carried by air and by the fastest connecting surface carriers and is given the most expeditious handling in dispatch and delivery. Weight is limited to 70 lb. and size to 100 in. in combined length and girth. Postage is charged according to weight at the rates in the accompanying table (for weights over 20 lb., consult the post office), except that when first-class mail is enclosed the rate may not in any instance be less than 5¢ an oz.

AIR MAIL

Weight	Kind of Mail	Rate
8 ounces or less	Air postal or post cards	6¢ each.
	Letters and packages	8¢ an ounce.
	Business reply:	
	Air cards	7¢ each.
	Air mail other than cards:	
	Weight not over 2 ounces	7¢ an ounce, plus 2¢ per piece.
	Weight over 2 ounces	7¢ an ounce, plus 5¢ per piece.

Weight over 8 ounces, and not exceeding:	Rate					
	NOTE: Where amount is shown in boldface type, see note below regarding first-class mail.					
	Zones 1, 2, and 3	Zone 4	Zone 5	Zone 6	Zone 7	Zone 8
1 pound	**$0.68**	*$0.73*	*$0.78*	*$0.83*	*$0.83*	*$0.88*
2 pounds	**1.16**	**1.23**	**1.34**	*1.47*	*1.55*	*1.68*
3 pounds	**1.64**	**1.73**	**1.90**	*2.11*	*2.27*	*2.48*
4 pounds	**2.12**	**2.23**	**2.46**	*2.75*	*2.99*	*3.28*
5 pounds	**2.60**	**2.73**	**3.02**	*3.39*	*3.71*	*4.08*
6 pounds	**3.08**	**3.23**	**3.58**	*4.03*	*4.43*	*4.88*
7 pounds	**3.56**	**3.73**	**4.14**	*4.67*	*5.15*	*5.68*
8 pounds	**4.04**	**4.23**	**4.70**	*5.31*	*5.87*	*6.48*
9 pounds	**4.52**	**4.73**	**5.26**	*5.95*	*6.59*	*7.28*
10 pounds	**5.00**	**5.23**	**5.82**	*6.59*	*7.31*	*8.08*
11 pounds	**5.48**	**5.73**	**6.38**	*7.23*	*8.03*	*8.88*
12 pounds	**5.96**	**6.23**	**6.94**	*7.87*	*8.75*	*9.68*
13 pounds	**6.44**	**6.73**	**7.50**	*8.51*	*9.47*	*10.48*
14 pounds	**6.92**	**7.23**	**8.06**	*9.15*	*10.19*	*11.28*
15 pounds	**7.40**	**7.73**	**8.62**	*9.79*	*10.91*	*12.08*
16 pounds	**7.88**	**8.23**	**9.18**	*10.43*	*11.63*	*12.88*
17 pounds	**8.36**	**8.73**	**9.74**	*11.07*	*12.35*	*13.68*
18 pounds	**8.84**	**9.23**	**10.30**	*11.71*	*13.07*	*14.48*
19 pounds	**9.32**	**9.73**	**10.86**	*12.35*	*13.79*	*15.28*
20 pounds	**9.80**	**10.23**	**11.42**	*12.99*	*14.51*	*16.08*

Note: Parcels containing first-class matter and destined for Zones 1 through 5 must bear postage at the rate of 5¢ for each ounce or fraction thereof.

Special Handling. This service provides the most expeditious handling, dispatch, and transportation, but does not include special delivery at the office of address. The special handling postage charge on fourth-class matter is 25¢ for parcels weighing not more than 2 lb.; 35¢ for parcels weighing more than 2 lb. but not more than 10 lb.; and 50¢ for parcels weighing more than 10 lb.

Special Delivery. This service provides handling and transportation in the same manner and with the same expedition as first-class mail, plus immediate delivery at the office of address during prescribed hours to (1) points within a radius of 1 m. of any post office, station, or branch; (2) points within the delivery limits of any post office having letter carrier service; and (3) points within ½ m. of a rural route if there is a passable road. The fees, in addition to regular postage, are: (first class and air mail, including air parcel post) 30¢ up to 2 lb.; 45¢ over 2 lb. up to 10 lb.; 60¢ over 10 lb.; (all other classes) 55¢ up to 2 lb.; 65¢ over 2 lb. up to 10 lb.; and 80¢ over 10 lb.

Registered Mail. Added protection for valuable mail and evidence of mailing and delivery may be obtained by having it registered. All classes of mail may be registered, except that fourth-class mail must be prepaid with postage at the first-class rate. Registry fees for domestic mail are: when declared value is $0.00 to $10, 50¢; $10.01 to $100, 75¢; $100.01 to $200, $1.00; $200.01 to $400, $1.25; $400.01 to $600, $1.50; $600.01 to $800, $1.75; $800.01 to $1,000, $2.00. For declared valuation in excess of $1,000, consult the post office. Fees for return receipts (requested at time of mailing), showing to whom and when delivered, 10¢; showing to whom, when, and address where delivered, 35¢; (requested after mailing) showing to whom and when delivered, 25¢; delivery restricted to addressee only, 50¢.

Insurance. Third- and fourth-class mail or air mail may be insured against loss, rifling, or damage by having it insured. Insured air mail may contain incidental first-class enclosures. Liability is limited to $200. The fees in addition to postage are: when liability is $0.01 to $10, 10¢; $10.01 to $50, 20¢; $50.01 to $100, 30¢; $100.01 to $200, 40¢. Return receipts and restricted delivery may be obtained (for mail insured for more than $10) at the following fees: receipts (requested at time of mailing) showing to whom and when delivered, 10¢; showing to whom, when, and address where delivered, 35¢; (requested after mailing) showing to whom and when delivered, 25¢; delivery restricted to addressee only, 50¢.

Certified Mail. Any mail of no intrinsic value on which first-class postage has been paid will be accepted as certified mail, providing for a receipt to the sender and a record of delivery at the office of address, at a fee of 20¢. Return receipts and restricted delivery are available at the fees for these services on insured mail (see above).

C.O.D. (Collect-on-Delivery) Service. Under this service patrons may mail an article for which they have not received payment and have the price and the cost of the postage collected from the addressee when the article is delivered. The fees include insurance against loss, rifling, or damage and failure to receive the amount collected from the addressee. Rates according to liability are shown in the accompanying table.

Money Orders. Domestic money orders may be purchased at all post offices, branches, and stations in the United States and its possessions. The maximum amount for a single money order is $100; however, there is no limitation on the number of orders that may be purchased at one time. Domestic money orders are payable at any United States post office or may be collected through any bank in the same manner as depositing or cashing a check. The fees are: $0.01 to $10, 20¢; $10.01 to $50, 30¢; $50.01 to $100, 35¢.

Liability (and C.O.D. collection to $200)	C.O.D. Fees	
	Registered	Unregistered
$0.01 to $5	$0.80	$0.30
$5.01 to $10	.80	.40
$10.01 to $25	1.10	.60
$25.01 to $50	1.10	.70
$50.01 to $100	1.20	.80
$100.01 to $150	1.40	.90
$150.01 to $200	1.40	1.00
$200.01 to $300	1.50	⎫ Liability for unregistered C.O.D.
$300.01 to $400	1.60	⎪ mail is limited to $200; for
$400.01 to $500	1.70	⎪ registered C.O.D. $1,000,
$500.01 to $600	1.80	⎬ same as for other registered
$600.01 to $700	1.90	⎪ mail. Collection for C.O.D.
$700.01 to $800	2.00	⎪ mail, unregistered or regis-
$800.01 to $1,000	2.10	⎭ tered, is limited to $200.
Restricted delivery	50¢	50¢
Notice of nondelivery	5¢	5¢
Alteration of charges or delivery	10¢	10¢

FOREIGN SURFACE POSTAGE RATES

Letters and Letter Packages. To Canada and Mexico, 5¢ per oz. or fraction; to all other countries, 11¢ for the first ounce and 7¢ for each additional ounce or fraction. The weight limit is 4 lb., 6 oz., except that to Canada it is 60 lb. The maximum dimensions are 36 in. in length, breadth, and thickness combined, with the greatest length 24 in. In the form of a roll, the length (the maximum of which is 32 in.) plus twice the diameter is limited to 40 in. The minimum dimensions are 4 in. in length and 2¾ in. in width on the address side. A roll may not be less than 4 in. in length, nor may the length plus twice the diameter be less than 6¾ in.

Post Cards. To Canada and Mexico, 4¢ each; 8¢ with reply paid. Maximum dimensions, 6 × 4¼ in.; minimum dimensions, 4 × 2¾ in.

Printed Matter. For circulars and miscellaneous prints: to Canada and Mexico, 3¢ for the first 2 oz. and 1½¢ for each additional ounce; to other countries, 5¢ for the first 2 oz. and 3¢ for each additional 2 oz. or fraction.

For permanently bound books having at least 22 printed pages and containing no advertising other than incidental announcements of books, and printed sheet music, 3¢ for the first 2 oz. and 1½¢ for each additional 2 oz. or fraction, except to the following countries, for which the rate is 2¢ for the first 2 oz. and 1¢ for each additional 2 oz.: Argentina, Bolivia, Brazil, Canada, Chile, Colombia, Costa Rica, Cuba, Dominican Republic, Ecuador, Guatemala, Haiti, Republic of Honduras, Mexico, Nicaragua, Panama, Paraguay, Peru, El Salvador, Uruguay, and Venezuela. Weight limits for printed matter in general are 6 lb. 9 oz.; for books, catalogs, and directories, 11 lb., with the following exceptions: (1) to Paraguay and Peru the weight limit is 11 lb.; (2) to Argentina, Bolivia, Brazil, Fernando Po, Rio Muni, Spain (including Balearic Islands, Canary Islands, and Spanish offices in Northern Africa), and Spanish West Africa, the weight limit is 22 lb.; (3) to Chile, Colombia, Costa Rica, Cuba, Dominican Republic, Ecuador, Guatemala, Haiti, Republic of Honduras, Mexico, Nicaragua, Panama, El Salvador, Uruguay, and Venezuela, the weight limit is 33 lb. The limits on dimensions are the same as for letters (see above).

Samples of Merchandise. To Canada and Mexico, 3¢ for the first 2 oz., 1½¢ for each additional ounce; other countries 5¢ for the first 2 oz., 3¢ for each additional 2 oz. or fraction. Minimum charge, Canada and Mexico, 10¢; other countries, 12¢. Weight limit, Canada and Mexico, 16 oz.; other countries, 18 oz. Dimensions, the same as for letters (see above).

Commercial Papers. To all countries, 5¢ for the first 2 oz., 3¢ each additional 2 oz. or fraction. Minimum charge, 12¢. Weight limit, 4 lb. 6 oz. Dimensions, same as for letters (see above).

Small Packets. To all countries that accept such classifications (consult post office), 5¢ for each 2 oz. or fraction, with a minimum charge of 25¢. Weight limit, 2 lb. 3 oz. Dimensions, same as for letters (see above).

Eight-Ounce Merchandise Packages. Such packages are accepted only to Canada, Chile, Cuba, Guatemala, Haiti, Paraguay, and Peru. The rate to Canada is 3¢ for the first 2 oz. or fraction and 1½¢ for each additional ounce, with a minimum charge of 10¢; to the other countries a flat rate of 25¢ per package applies. Weight limit is 8 oz. Dimensions are the same as for letters (see above).

Registration. The service is available to practically all countries. Consult the postmaster for fees.

INTERNATIONAL RATES FOR ALL AIR MAIL AND FOR SURFACE PARCEL POST

Country	Letters and letter packages (per ½ oz.) Cents	Other Articles (prints, samples, small packets, etc.) First 2 oz.	Each addl. 2 oz. or fraction	Parcel Post First 4 oz.	Each addl. 4 oz. or fraction	Frequency (dispatches per week)	Transit time (days, except where shown in hours)	Surface Parcel Post First 2 lbs.	Each additional pound or fraction	Max. wt. for parcel post (surface or air) Lbs.
Argentina	15[4]	$0.40	$0.20	$1.56	$0.67	7	1–2	$0.90	$0.35	44
Australia	25	.50	.30	1.66	.76	7	2	.90	.35	22
Austria	15	.40	.20	1.71	.46	7	2	.90	.35	44
Bahamas	13	.30	.10	1.53	.16	7	1 hr.	.80	.30	22
Belgium	15	.40	.20	1.39	.42	7	1–2	.90	.35	44
Bermuda	13	.30	.10	1.12	.22	7	3 hr.	.80	.30	33
Bolivia	15[3]	.40	.20	1.57	.43	7	1–2	.90	.35	44
Brazil	15	.40[4]	.20	1.87	.49	7	1–2	.90	.35	44[4]
Bulgaria	15	.40[2]	.20	1.36	.47	7	3	.90	.35	22
Burma	25	.50[2]	.30	2.10	.91	7	3–4	.90	.35	22
Canada	8[1]	[1] [2]	----	----	----	7	1	.80	.30	25
Chile	15	.40[2]	.20	1.85	.55	7	2	.90	.35	22
China (Formosa)	25[3]	.50[2]	.30	1.56	.66	7	3	.90	.35	44[4]
China (Mainland)	25[3]	.50[2]	.30	----	----	7	3	----	----	----
Colombia	15[3]	.40[2]	.20	1.82	.31	7	1	.90	.35	44
Costa Rica	13	.30	.10	1.31	.26	7	1	.80	.30	44
Cuba	13	.30[2]	.10	1.36	.17	7	1 hr.	.80	.30	22
Czechoslovakia	15	.40	.20	1.38	.48	7	2	.90	.35	44
Denmark	15	.40	.20	1.35	.45	7	1	.90	.35	44
Dominican Rep.	13	.30	.10	1.42	.23	7	1	.80	.30	44
Ecuador	15[4]	.40	.20	1.76	.30	7	1	.90	.35	44
Ethiopia	25	.50	.30	1.80	.69	7	3	.90	.35	44
Finland	15	.40	.20	1.38	.49	7	2	.90	.35	44
France	15	.40	.20	1.89	.42	7	1	.90	.35	44

Air Service
Aerogrammes—11 cents each to all countries.
Air Mail Post Cards (single)—11 cents each to all countries except Canada and Mexico (5¢).

[1] The "per ounce" air mail letter rate applies.
[2] Small packets not accepted.
[3] Merchandise prohibited in letters or letter packages.
[4] Restrictions apply. Consult post office.

INTERNATIONAL RATES FOR ALL AIR MAIL AND FOR SURFACE PARCEL POST

Country	Letters and letter packages (per ½ oz.) Cents	Other Articles (prints, samples, small packets, etc.) First 2 oz.	Each addl. 2 oz. or fraction	Parcel Post First 4 oz.	Each addl. 4 oz. or fraction	Frequency (dispatches per week)	Transit time (days, except where shown in hours)	Surface Parcel Post First 2 lbs.	Each additional pound or fraction	Max. wt. for parcel post (surface or air) Lbs.
Germany	15	.40	.20	1.34	.44	7	1–2	.90	.35	44⁴
Ghana	25	.50	.30	1.85	.58	5	2	.90	.35	22
Great Britain	15	.40	.20	1.32	.42	7	1	.90	.35	22
Greece	15	.40	.20	1.66	.53	7	2	.90	.35	22
Guatemala	13⁴	.30²	.10	1.59	.29	7	1	.80	.30	44
Hungary	15	.40	.20	1.37	.48	7	2–3	.90	.35	44
India	25	.50²	.30	1.70	.80	7	2–3	.90	.35	22
Iran	25	.50	.30	1.70	.61	7	3	.90	.35	44
Iraq	25	.50	.30	1.89	.60	7	2–3	.90	.35	44
Ireland	15	.40	.20	1.31	.42	7	1	.90	.35	22
Israel	25	.50	.30	1.86	.57	7	2	.90	.35	22
Italy	15³	.40²	.20	1.67	.49	7	1–2	.90	.35	44
Japan	25³	.50	.30	1.39	.50	7	2	.90	.35	22
Liberia	25	.50	.30	1.42	.53	4	2	.90	.35	22
Mexico	8¹	1	2	----	----	7	1	.80	.30	44
Morocco	15	.40	.20	1.67	.49	7	1–2	.90	.35	44
Netherlands	15	.40	.20	1.50	.42	7	1	.90	.35	44
New Zealand	25	.50	.30	1.89	.67	7	2–3	.90	.35	22
Nicaragua	13	.30	.10	1.32	.26	7	1	.80	.30	44
Norway	15	.40	.20	1.35	.45	7	1	.90	.35	44
Pakistan	25	.50²	.30	2.20	.77	7	2–3	.90	.35	22
Panama	13⁴	.30	.10	1.58	.28	7	1	.80	.30	70⁴
Paraguay	15	.40²	.20	1.57	.43	7	2	.90	.35	44
Peru	15⁴	.40²	.20	1.83	.37	7	1	.90	.35	44
Philippines	25	.50	.30	1.93	.74	7	2–3	.90	.35	44⁴
Poland	15	.40	.20	1.65	.47	7	2	.90	.35	44
Portugal	15	.40²	.20	1.30	.40	7	1	.90	.35	22
Rumania	15³	.40²	.20	----	----	7	3	.90	.35	22
Salvador, El	13	.30⁴	.10	1.40	.27	7	1	.80	.30	44
Saudi Arabia	25³	.50	.30	1.97	.63	6	2	.90	.35	22
South Africa	25	.50²	.30	1.69	.80	5	2–3	.90	.35	11
Spain	15	.40	.20	1.77	.44	7	1–3	.90	.35	44⁴
Sweden	15	.40	.20	1.35	.45	7	1	.90	.35	44
Switzerland	15	.40	.20	1.52	.43	7	1	.90	.35	44
Syria	25	.50	.30	1.57	.58	5	2	.90	.35	44⁴
Thailand	25	.50	.30	2.08	.74	5	3	.90	.35	22
Turkey	15	.40	.20	1.44	.54	7	2	.90	.35	44
U.S.S.R.	25⁴	.50⁴	.30	1.81	.60	7	2	.90	.35	44
United Arab Republic	15	.40²	.20	1.47	.58	5	2	.90	.35	44
Uruguay	15⁴	.40	.20	1.86	.56	7	1–2	.90	.35	44
Venezuela	15³	.40	.20	1.72	.26	7	1	.90	.35	44
Yugoslavia	15	.40	.20	1.38	.49	7	2	.90	.35	44

Air Service
Aerogrammes—11 cents each to all countries.
Air Mail Post Cards (single)—11 cents each to all countries except Canada and Mexico (5¢).

[1] The "per ounce" air mail letter rate applies.
[2] Small packets not accepted.
[3] Merchandise prohibited in letters or letter packages.
[4] Restrictions apply. Consult post office.

Special Delivery. The service is not available to all countries. Consult the postmaster.

Air Mail and Surface Parcel Post. These mail services are available to virtually all parts of the world. The accompanying table lists representative rates, frequency of dispatch, transit time, and maximum weights.

DEAD-LETTER OFFICE

The dead-letter office is anything but dead; it is one of the most active of all the post office departments, receiving millions of undeliverable letters a year, a large proportion of which are Christmas cards. All of these are without return address on the outside. They are opened and those with addresses inside are returned to the senders. The fee for this service is 5¢.

Parcels are treated in the same way, except that instead of returning them and collecting the fee at the other end, the department notifies the sender (when his address can be found) that the parcel is being held for a specified amount of postage. Insured parcels are held for six months, ordinary parcels for 60 days. Parcel sales are held periodically at each dead-letter branch post office.

ABBREVIATIONS ACCEPTED BY THE POST OFFICE

Abbreviations should never be used in formal writing, nor in any place where they would create doubt as to the meaning.

The following abbreviations are officially recognized by the Post Office Department.

Ala., Alabama	N. C., North Carolina
Ariz., Arizona	N. Dak., North Dakota
Ark., Arkansas	Nebr., Nebraska
Calif., California	Nev., Nevada
Colo., Colorado	N. H., New Hampshire
Conn., Connecticut	N. J., New Jersey
C. Z., Canal Zone	N. Mex., New Mexico
D. C., District of Columbia	N. Y., New York
Del., Delaware	Okla., Oklahoma
Fla., Florida	Pa., Pennsylvania
Ga., Georgia	P. I., Philippine Islands
Ill., Illinois	P. R., Puerto Rico
Ind., Indiana	R. I., Rhode Island
Kans., Kansas	S. C., South Carolina
Ky., Kentucky	S. Dak., South Dakota
La., Louisiana	Tenn., Tennessee
Mass., Massachusetts	Tex., Texas
Md., Maryland	Va., Virginia
Mich., Michigan	Vt., Vermont
Minn., Minnesota	Wash., Washington
Miss., Mississippi	W. Va., West Virginia
Mo., Missouri	Wis., Wisconsin
Mont., Montana	Wyo., Wyoming

No provision has been made by United States postal authorities for abbreviations of Alaska and Hawaii.

TELEGRAPH SERVICES

Modern systems of communication are so intertwined and interlaced that it is possible for almost anyone at any time to be in almost instantaneous touch with any part of the world. Cables have been sent from New York to London and answers received in less than a minute, and telephone conversations between New York and Paris are commonplace.

The services which the various communication systems have to offer have been classified and the businessman needs to be familiar with the classifications and the advantages they offer.

Domestic Service

The regular *telegram* is accepted at any hour of the day or night for immediate delivery. It has the right of way over all other traffic. The minimum charge is for 15 words, low extra-word charges being reckoned on words in excess of 15. It should be used when quick service is needed. The *day letter* is subordinate to full-rate messages. The delay in transmission is usually slight, and the cost is reckoned on a minimum basis of 50 words. Fifty words can be sent for about 45 per cent more than the cost of a 15-word telegram. Code language may be used. The *night letter* is accepted any time during the day and at night until 2 A.M. for delivery the following morning. The cost of a 50-word night letter is less than the full-rate message and varies according to the distance it is to be sent. The cost of additional words is small. This is the least expensive service for long messages and is much used by businessmen in place of letters when speed is essential. Code language may be used.

How to Write a Telegram. All telegrams should be as brief as they can be and yet state their messages clearly. Punctuation marks, including the period (or decimal point), comma, colon, semicolon, dash or hyphen, parentheses, quotation marks, and apostrophe are free, but words such as "stop," "quote," "comma," and "semicolon," when written out, are charged as one word each. Abbreviations, figures, letters, and other signs such as $, &, /, ' (for feet), and " (for inches), are counted at the rate of one word for each five characters in messages between points within the United States and between the United States and Mexico or Alaska.[1] For example, each of the following is counted as one word: AM or A.M., PM or P.M., NY or N.Y., B.&O., COD or C.O.D., 1st, 2nd, $25.05, 12345, and AB175. A group of letters, figures, or signs containing more than five characters is counted as two or more words; for example, #78694 (two words). If abbreviations are separated by spaces (A. M., N. Y., B. & O.), they are counted as one word for each character. Proper and personal names in the message are charged for according to the way they are normally written: for example, New York City (three words), Du Pont (two words), Vandewater (one word). Initials, if not spaced, count as one word (R.L.S.). If spaced, they count as one word for each letter; for example, R. L. S. (three words).

Any dictionary word from any one of the following languages may be used and counted as one word: English, German, French, Italian, Dutch, Portuguese, Spanish, and Latin. All groups of letters which do not form dictionary words from one of the languages mentioned above are counted at the rate of five letters to a word.

On a domestic telegram the address and signature are free. The address should be as full as possible to facilitate prompt delivery. Code addresses cannot be used in domestic messages. Messages addressed to two people are charged for as two telegrams, and a separate copy is delivered to each person. If a telegram is addressed to John Brown *or James Smith,* the italicized words are charged for.

---

[1] In telegrams between points in the United States and Canada, and St. Pierre and Miquelon Islands, these signs are counted as one word each.

If the message is not to be signed, the word "Unsigned" should be written in place of the signature. When there is more than one signature, all except the last are counted and charged for. In *"John Brown and* James Smith", the italicized words are charged for, but in a family signature like "John and Mary," no extra charge is made.

The sender can have a report made as to whether his message is delivered by writing "Report delivery" immediately following the addressee's name. These words are charged for and the reply, wired collect to the sender, will state when and to whom the message was delivered.

If the sender desires to have his message repeated back (and this is a good way to insure accuracy in important messages) he should write "Repeat back" at the top of the message. The repetition will cost one half as much as the regular rate, and, in addition, the sender has to pay for the words, "Repeat back."

Messages to be sent collect will be accepted from holders of Western Union collect cards, which may be obtained through application from members of reputable social or commercial organizations, and from any responsible person or business firm.

Direct Customer-to-Customer Services. Instant two-way telegraphic communication at special time-distance rates is available through *Telex.* Users can dial other Telex subscribers in the United States, Canada, and Mexico City in seconds. International Telex is available to overseas points. *Private wire systems* are communications systems leased to telegraph users for fast, economical volume transmission of messages and data. A system may extend hundreds or even thousands of miles and interconnect a company's offices and plants in as few as two and as many as hundreds of cities. *Intrafax* is a leased facsimile system which speeds intracompany communications automatically in facsimile "picture" form. *Desk-Fax* and *teleprinter* facilities offer direct connections between the customer and the telegraph office. There are now 38,000 compact facsimile machines called Desk-Fax, which serve as electronic messengers, sending and receiving messages in "picture" form automatically at the push of a button. The teleprinter is operated from a typewriter-like keyboard and sends and receives messages over a direct circuit to a similar printer at the telegraph office.

Other Telegraph Services. Money may be sent and received quickly and safely by *telegraphic money order,* either by fast wire or overnight by low-rate night letter. Supplemental messages may be sent with the money. *Messenger errand service* covers a wide variety of individual errands performed by telegraph messengers. They deliver parcels, circulars, samples, and sales promotional material. Messengers will also set up window and counter displays, pick up canceled credit cards and handle other special assignments. *Market Research and Public Opinion Survey Service* provides regional and nationwide market and opinion surveys and TV-radio listener surveys, which are made by telephone interview or by messenger pick-up and delivery of questionnaires. *Hotel-Motel Reservation Service* will quickly obtain reservations in hotels and motels nationwide and confirm them telegraphically by the Western Union reservation bureau. *Special-occasion greetings* are sent on such occasions as birthdays, weddings, anniversaries, and holidays. Special blanks and colorful envelopes are used. *CandyGram* is a novel candy-with-telegram service through which a box of candy is delivered, with a personal telegram, throughout the United States.

International Service

International cable and radio messages are constructed similarly to domestic telegrams, except that registered (abbreviated) code addresses may be used to save tolls, and code words (secret language) are permitted in the full-rate classification. Each word in the address, text, and signature is counted and charged for.

The *full-rate* classification of international service, which is the standard fast service for messages in plain language, in secret (code or cipher) language, or in a combination of plain and secret languages, is subject to a minimum charge for seven words.

The *letter telegram* classification of international service, which is for messages in plain language *only*, is charged for at one half the per-word rates applicable to full-rate messages, with a minimum charge for 22 words. This is an overnight service with delivery generally being made the day after the filing date; but in certain countries delivery may be made in the morning of the second day after the filing date. Letter Telegram messages are designated by the indicator "LT," which is placed before the address, and counted and charged for as one word. Secret language is *not* admitted but registered (abbreviated) code addresses may be used in the address or signature of such LT messages.

In the address of an international cable or radio message, the name of the country of destination is seldom necessary. Unregistered addresses should not be unduly shortened, since senders are responsible for incorrect or insufficient addresses and corrections or amplifications can be made only by sending a paid-service message at the full rate.

Each plain language (dictionary) word appearing in messages in the full-rate and letter telegram (LT) classifications is counted at the rate of 15, or fraction of 15, letters to the word and any figures or figure-groups appearing in such messages are counted at the rate of five, or fraction of five, figures to the word. Punctuation marks (period, comma, colon, question mark, apostrophe, hyphen or dash, and fraction bar or stroke) are counted and charged for as one word each when used in their normal sense. The two signs forming parentheses () or quotation marks (" " or ' ') are together counted as one word when they enclose one or more words or groups. However, when the preceding punctuation marks appear in a group of figures or in a group of letters, they are each counted as one figure or one letter in the group and not as a separate word. The apostrophe ('), hyphen or dash (−), and quotation mark (") may alternately be used to designate minutes or feet, the subtraction sign, and seconds or inches, respectively, and when so used with a group of figures are each counted as a figure in the group in which they appear. The dollar sign ($) and the pound sterling sign (£) cannot be transmitted overseas and to facilitate the handling of his message, the sender should substitute acceptable equivalents for such signs. Secret language, consisting of nondictionary words, which is admitted only in messages in the full-rate classification, is counted at the rate of five, or fraction of five, characters to the word.

Cable money orders provide a quick way to send funds to many foreign countries. The money is deposited at the telegraph office and a cable money order is sent abroad. Payment is made through a foreign representative. A message can be sent at a slight additional cost.

Ship radiogram communication with ships at sea in all parts of the world is provided by radiomarine-telegraph companies. Only the full-rate message classification is available, which classification is subject to a minimum charge for seven words.

TELEPHONE SERVICES

The telephone wires leading from home or office make it possible for each subscriber to reach more than 130,000,000 other telephones around the world. The calls may travel along open wire, by underground and undersea cables, or be beamed through the air as radio signals. In the future, the calls may be transmitted by satellites orbiting the earth.

Telephone service is continuous. The telephones in homes and offices are linked by wire and cable to a central office, where calls are connected to other telephones by wire or radio. The instruments are available in various colors and models.

Basic Service. Charges for basic service vary. In some cases the basic monthly charge is for unlimited calls in a local area. In others, a certain number of messages are included in the basic monthly charge, with added charges for each additional message or "message unit." Rates for some calls to distant points are lower between 6 P.M. and 4:30 A.M. (local time), on some holidays, and all day Sunday.

Most telephones in the United States are dial-operated. More than half of the country's telephone users can dial their own long-distance calls by using a three-digit area code and the number of the distant telephone. This service is called Direct Distance Dialing. Operators are always available to accept regular calls, emergency calls, information requests, and calls requiring special assistance.

Types of Out-of-Town Calls. The calls most easily made are *station-to-station* calls, in which the caller will talk with anyone who answers. Charging begins as soon as the called telephone is answered. *Person-to-person* calls are those in which the caller specifies the particular person, department, or extension telephone to be reached. Rates are higher than for station-to-station calls, but charging does not begin until the called person, department, or extension answers. *Collect calls* are those that are charged to the called telephone; however, the charges must first be accepted at the called telephone. In addition, a service known as "bill to third telephone" permits the transfer of long-distance charges to a telephone in the United States and Canada other than one of the two between which conversation is held. *Credit card calls* are those in which the charges on a long-distance call are billed to a specified telephone. Credit cards may be obtained by applying at the local telephone business office. The card is issued on a yearly basis and contains a number which is recorded by the operator for billing purposes. *Mobile and marine service,* both local and long-distance, enables callers to reach automobiles, trucks, aircraft, and boats equipped for the service. *Public coin telephone service* is available at many locations, including thousands of outdoor telephone booths on highways and streets. *Conference service* permits a caller to have his telephone connected simultaneously with several others at different locations. There is an extra charge for this service.

Special Services. Many businesses subscribe to *private-line service,* which permits them to make unlimited calls between two points at a flat rate. A system called *Wide Area Telephone Service* (WATS) provides unlimited calls from the subscriber's telephones to all telephones within an area he selects. This service is available at fulltime rates with unlimited use of the service 24 hours a day, or at measured-time rates, permitting use for a given number of hours a month. There are six WATS areas, the largest of which encompasses the entire United States (except Hawaii and Alaska). A businessman may arrange for a special "collect call" number, whereby he is automatically billed for telephone calls from his customers in a specific area. The collect number is usually identified by an *Enterprise* prefix. Telephone directories listing these numbers carry the notation, "No charge for Enterprise call." Regional or national advertising in the *Yellow Pages* is possible in any or all of the 4,000 Yellow Pages directories on a one-contract, one-monthly-bill basis.

Special Equipment. All telephone services and equipment are available to the businessman. Each business, however, has particular communications problems. To help solve these problems and increase efficiency, Bell System and other telephone companies have communications consultants specially trained to survey a customer's needs and recommend the appropriate service and equipment. In addition, service advisers are available to assist customers in obtaining maximum use of telephone equipment. *Data-Phone service* enables customers to transmit information such as sales reports, inventory information, orders, and other records over regular telephone lines at various speeds. A Data-Phone set, associated with the telephone, accepts and converts information from business machines for transmittal over telephone lines. At the receiving end, the information is reconverted by another data set and fed to an appropriate business machine. *Teletypewriter service* in some respects does for the written word what the telephone does for the spoken word. It can reproduce copies of messages at distant points. Messages may be transmitted manually or fed to the teletypewriter via prepunched tape. *Private Line Teletypewriter Service* can be tailored to provide written communication between two points on the premises or to many points in distant cities. In addition, *Teletypewriter Exchange Service* (TWX) is provided through a vast network of teletypewriter central offices and circuits spanning the nation. Over this network, more than 54,000 stations communicate with one another in written form, or send messages to a number of points simultaneously. *Speakerphones* are regular telephone instruments which have microphones and loudspeakers associated with them to permit talking without holding the phone. *Call Directors* are desk-top instruments with up to 30 pushbuttons that permit call answering and holding, signaling, interoffice communication, conference arrangements, and addition of another person to a call already in progress. *Switchboards* are available for every size of business. Arrangements can be made for complete internal dial systems, direct inward and outward dialing, and calling to and from extensions. *Centrex,* for example, is available for large users, making possible the saving of space by installing the equipment, in some instances, on telephone company property. *Bellboy Signaling Service* enables a customer to keep in touch with his home or office by means of a miniature radio receiver which may be carried on the person. The receipt of a signal indicates that he is to call a pre-arranged number.

TRANSPORTATION

*"If our industrial progress is to continue, there is nothing more important to industry, whether on the farm or in the city, than the proper organization and operation of an adequate system for the distribution of our products. Everyone who lives in the United States should be interested in distribution. It is the necessary link between production and selling, and neither can function properly unless this third partner is efficient."—*IRVING T. BUSH, Founder of the Bush Terminal Company.

COMMON CARRIERS

A person or organization which transports goods or people or both from one place to another for a price is called a *common carrier.* The fact that the common carrier announces himself in business becomes a standing offer to the public which turns into a contract as soon as it is accepted. The carrier cannot refuse anyone or anybody without good reason. He is not required to transport dangerous commodities such as dynamite or nitroglycerin, and he is not required to carry goods when his means of transport are already fully occupied. The rules by which the carrier regulates his business are usually announced. (See post office regulations or the terms on the back of a receipt from the express company.) While the goods are in his hands the carrier must exercise due care as to their safety, for which, as a matter of fact, he is responsible unless the loss or damage is caused by an act of God or of the public enemy. The bill of lading is evidence of the contract between the sender and the carrier. The carrier is not legally responsible for the safety of human passengers if it can be proved that he has taken due care toward insuring it.

Common carriers are of many kinds—trains, motor buses, automobiles, airplanes, steamships, etc. Telephone and telegraph companies are also common carriers, though not in quite the same sense as carriers of actual property. They do not, for instance, insure the correctness of the messages that they transmit.

An operator must send the message exactly as it is given to him. It may not make sense to him but it is possible that it will mean something to the person for whom it is intended. An operator can refuse to accept a message if it is illegible, but once he has accepted it he must send it as best he can. The message is not considered delivered until it is received by the person to whom it is addressed. Mere delivery to a messenger boy is not real delivery. The employees of telephone and telegraph companies are strictly bound to secrecy, and even if they are summoned into court they are protected against having to repeat dispatches or make testimony with regard to their contents.

DELIVERY SERVICES

The conduct of modern business frequently requires the sending of various articles—other than by United States mail—from one point to another by economical and expeditious means. Such articles may range from letters for delivery by hand within a particular city or town, to packages—or even pets—for delivery across the country. Various services have been developed to meet these needs. Among them are:

Messenger Service. In addition to the errand service offered by Western Union, messenger service is available for the delivery or pickup of articles within easy reach by public transportation. Most such services bond their employees for the security of customers who wish to transmit money, negotiable papers, or other valuables. See also Telegraph Services.

Railway Express Service. Large and small packages can be shipped expeditiously by railroad between cities by means of the Railway Express Agency, which has offices throughout the country. Pickup and delivery service is available within city limits. Packages may be shipped prepaid or collect. Railway Express also provides an air express service for more rapid transportation.

Air Express Service. Most major airlines maintain air express service, providing pickup and delivery to points on their regularly scheduled routes.

Truck Express Service. Trucking companies throughout the United States are linked in a loose chain via which packages can be shipped across the country. Slower than air express or Railway Express, this service is correspondingly less expensive for shipments in which time is not a prime factor. Generally there is an extra charge for inside delivery; *i.e.,* delivery to a particular office or apartment within a building.

WAREHOUSES

Warehouses are of several different types, but broadly speaking may be divided into those used for general merchandise storage and those used for the storage of perishable commodities requiring refrigeration. Merchandise warehouses serve manufacturers and distributors of nonperishable commodities while refrigerated warehouses provide scientific refrigeration and controlled humidity for the storage of perishable foods, certain drugs, florists' stocks, etc. In addition to storage, these warehouses usually provide such other services as pool car distribution, repacking and coopering, distribution, and in the case of refrigerated warehouses, quick freezing, refrigerator-car icing, pipeline refrigeration, etc.

Warehouses may be distinguished as public (which store goods for others) or private (which store only their own goods). All public warehouses issue warehouse receipts which may be used as collateral for loans against the commodities represented by the receipt.

Some warehouses specialize in the handling and storage of one commodity such as household goods, tobacco, cotton, grain, etc.

Bonded Warehouses. The term bonded warehouse implies various types of protection to the storer. State-bonded or state-licensed warehouses cover fidelity or personal security aspects of the storage problem. Federal-bonded warehouses are those in which the government has permitted the approved warehouse to set aside for storage imported merchandise not yet released from the government's custody. There are also *Internal Revenue Bonded Warehouses,* which set aside space for storage of alcohol, liquor, cigarettes, etc.; *United States Warehouse Act Bonded Warehouses,* wherein certain agricultural commodities are stored at government expense; and warehouses bonded under the Quarantine Acts, which are permitted to store plant and animal products prior to inspection. There are in addition several government departments which require performance bonds from warehousemen contracting government-owned, or government-controlled, goods.

ANTITRUST DIVISION OF THE DEPARTMENT OF JUSTICE[1]

The Antitrust Division of the Department of Justice is assigned the responsibility of enforcing the Federal antitrust statutes. The basic antitrust law is the Sherman Act of 1890, which prohibits all contracts, combinations, and conspiracies which unreasonably restrain or monopolize interstate or foreign commerce. This statute contains both criminal and civil provisions. Violations under the criminal provisions may be punished by a maximum fine of $50,000 or imprisonment for one year, or both. Violations of a civil nature may be enjoined by civil decrees which may, as appropriate, order positive action to prevent continuation of the violation and to restore competitive conditions. The Sherman Act has since been supplemented by other enactments, such as the Clayton Act and the Robinson-Patman Act.

Under our economic system, resources are allocated, goods produced, and prices set in response to consumer pressures exerted via free markets. The general objective of the Antitrust Division is to insure that this system of competitive enterprise is maintained unhampered by artificial restraints interposed by private business. The division places particular emphasis upon its efforts to prevent such anticompetitive activities as price-fixing, boycotts, and unreasonable refusals to deal with any party so requesting, as well as the prevention of mergers and acquisitions the effect of which may be substantially to lessen competition or tend to create a monopoly. The division also maintains a program for reviewing instances of identical bids submitted to Federal agencies to determine if there has been a violation of the antitrust laws. Finally, the division acts as counsel for various other Federal agencies defending their orders and other actions in the Federal courts.

INTERSTATE COMMERCE COMMISSION

The Interstate Commerce Commission is an independent agency of the United States government, created in 1887 to supplement the provision established in the Constitution for complete freedom of trade among the states. The commission is headed by 11 commissioners, appointed by the President and confirmed by the Senate, for terms of seven years. The Interstate Commerce Act, which created the agency, declared that common carriers between the states were subject to regulation, that their charges should be reasonable, and that there should be no special rates, rebates, or preferences.

The authority of the commission as established extended only to regulation of railroads. The first major addition to the law, in 1906, provided for enforcement of commission orders and extended its jurisdiction to include express companies, pipelines (except water and gas), and sleeping-car companies. The Motor Carrier Act of 1935 (now Part II of the Interstate Commerce Act) brought interstate motor carriers under the commission's jurisdiction, and the Transportation Act of 1940 (now Part III of the act) extended its jurisdiction to water carriers

---

[1] Information supplied by the Antitrust Division, Department of Justice.

operating in interstate commerce coastwise, intercoastally, and upon inland waterways.

Among other measures widening the commission's scope are the Transportation Act of 1920, which extended its authority over rates, and a 1942 amendment which provided for regulation of freight forwarders; and the Transportation Act of 1958, which reduced the number of agricultural commodities exempt from I.C.C. regulation when transported by motor carrier, and authorized the commission to permit discontinuance of railroad service under certain conditions and to guarantee repayment of certain loans to railroads.

COOPERATIVES

A cooperative is a business organization in which members pool their buying and selling in order to obtain the greatest advantage in prices and costs. The cooperative operates on a nonprofit basis, returning its profits to the members in proportion to their use of the organization.

Cooperatives exist in many fields, notably those of farm marketing and supplies, rural electric supply, and housing. In recent years urban consumer groups have begun to utilize the cooperative system. Group health plans and mutual insurance companies also are forms of cooperative.

The Central Bank for Cooperatives in Washington, D.C., and its twelve district banks were established under authority of the Farm Credit Act of 1933 to provide a permanent source of credit to farmers cooperatives. The district bank makes loans to farm cooperatives, which in turn own part of the capital stock of the bank, increasing their investment by purchasing stock in proportion to their current interest payments and through the payment of patronage refunds by the banks in the form of stock.

An important form of cooperative association is the credit union, which makes loans to members at low interest rates out of the pooled savings of all the members. Credit unions are formed among persons having a common bond of association, occupation, or residence.

Credit unions may be chartered under the Federal Credit Union Act of 1934, created "to establish a Federal Credit Union System, to establish a further market for securities of the United States and to make more available to people of small means credit for provident purposes through a national system of cooperative credit." The act is administered by the Bureau of Federal Credit Unions, a division of the Social Security Administration.

CHAMBERS OF COMMERCE

A chamber of commerce[1] is a voluntary association which unites the businessmen of the community for the promotion and protection of commercial interests, the improvement of business opportunities, and the general betterment of the city, county, or state which it serves.

The first in the United States was the New York Chamber of Commerce, founded in 1768 by 20 merchants. It received a royal charter from London in 1770; it was reincorporated by act of the state legislature in 1784 as the Chamber of Commerce of the State of New York. Meanwhile, Charleston, S.C., and Boston, Mass., each founded a chamber of commerce in 1773. Today there is a chamber of commerce or comparable organization in every city of commercial importance in the United States, and a similar organization on a broader area level in most of the states.

The Chamber of Commerce of the United States, in cooperation with six uni-

---

[1] A board of trade is a similar organization, which concentrates principally, however, on advancement and protection of the interests of the business community.

versities in various sections of the country, sponsors summer Institutes for Organization Management for training chamber-of-commerce and trade-association executives.

Established in 1912, the Chamber of Commerce of the United States is a federation of more than 3,700 voluntary organizations of businessmen—local and state chambers of commerce, and trade and professional associations—and 27,500 firms and individuals. It has an underlying membership of 3,000,000.

Through voluntary organized action, the national chamber, with 26 specialized departments, has as its goals: (1) to promote the concepts of limited government, a free-market economy, and the self-reliance of the individual; (2) to strengthen and improve competitive enterprise, and to safeguard and preserve our representative form of government; (3) to create new job opportunities and to keep the economy expanding.

The official organs of the national chamber are *Nation's Business,* published monthly in Washington, and *Washington Report,* published weekly. In addition to the regular publications, each of the 26 departments issues special reports, studies, and research papers throughout the year. It has headquarters in Washington, D.C., and divisional offices in principal cities.

NATIONAL ASSOCIATION OF MANUFACTURERS

The National Association of Manufacturers of the United States of America (frequently abbreviated N.A.M.) is a voluntary organization of nearly 20,000 proprietorships, partnerships, firms, or corporations, 83 per cent of which employ fewer than 500 employees. Founded in 1895 in Cincinnati, Ohio, the association set as its objectives ". . . the promotion of the industrial interests of the United States, the fostering of the domestic and foreign commerce of the United States, the betterment of the relations between employer and employee, the protection of the individual liberty and rights of the employer and employee, the dissemination of information among the public with respect to the principles of individual liberty and ownership of property, the support of legislation in furtherance of those principles, and opposition to legislation in derogation thereof."

Member companies are represented by a 175-man board of directors elected annually by the membership. Additionally, some 3,200 representatives of member companies serve on 13 policy committees responsible for the preparation of policy recommendations for consideration by the board of directors.

The programs of the N.A.M. include the annual Industrial Relations Institute and Congress of American Industry; workshops and clinics on industrial relations; visual economic programs; the TV series "Industry on Parade"; and the Public Affairs Program. Its many publications include the *N.A.M. News* (weekly), economic research studies, and various news services for newspapers, company house organs, churches, and women's clubs.

In addition to its New York City headquarters, there are offices in Washington, D.C., and 13 division and regional offices throughout the country.

NATIONAL INDUSTRIAL CONFERENCE BOARD

The National Industrial Conference Board, an independent and nonprofit institution for business and industrial fact-finding through scientific research, was founded in 1916. The board conducts objective research in the fields of economics, business management, and human relations. It publishes *Business Record* and *Management Record* (monthlies), *Economic Almanac* (biennial), and periodic studies in business economics, business practices, and personnel policies. Information also is distributed through press releases and conferences. The work of the board is supported by more than 3,700 subscribing associates, including business organizations, trade associations, government bureaus, labor unions, libraries, individuals, and colleges and universities.

FEDERAL TRADE COMMISSION

The purpose of the Federal Trade Commission is to protect the public from, and to move against, unfair trade practices occurring in commerce.

Most of the commission's activities are directed against deception of the public by false and "bait" advertising; fictitious pricing; exaggerated claims for the efficacy of drugs and cosmetics; and misrepresentations of the quality of products. In addition, the commission polices the labeling of furs and textiles.

The commission attacks monopoly-breeding favoritism, such as price discrimination by means of reduced brokerage fees and the practice of giving larger advertising allowances or costly services to favored customers. The commission also works to limit mergers, acquisitions, and consolidations of companies which tend to lessen competition or create a monopoly in a particular line of commerce. See also Advertising.

The legislation under which the commission functions includes: the Federal Trade Commission Act of 1914; the Clayton Act, sections 2, 3, 7, 8, and 11 (1914); the Webb-Pomerene Export Trade Act (1918); the Wheeler-Lea Act (1938); the Robinson-Patman Act (1936); the Wool Products Labeling Act of 1939; Public Law 15, 79th Congress (1945); the Lanham Trade Mark Act (1946); the Oleomargarine Act (1950); Public Law 899, 81st Congress (1950); the Fur Products Labeling Act (1951); the Flammable Fabrics Act (1953); Public Law 85-909, 85th Congress (1958); and the Textile Fiber Products Identification Act (1958).

BETTER BUSINESS BUREAUS

A Better Business Bureau is an agency maintained by business to protect both the consumer and the businessman from fraud, misrepresentation, and sharp practices in commercial transactions. It strives to give this protection through the promotion of advertising and selling practices which are fair to consumer and businessman alike.

The first Better Business Bureaus were organized on a local level in 1912. There are now some 117 bureaus in the United States, Canada, and Mexico.

Better Business Bureaus publish a 138-page consolidation of the various standards and recommendations which they have adopted, the "Guide for Retail Advertising and Selling." Some of these recommendations are based on law, others on legal decisions and rulings by government agencies. In addition, a loose-leaf publication service, "Do's and Don'ts in Advertising Copy," covering similar ground but in greater detail, is maintained.

Business usually cooperates voluntarily with the bureaus. Moreover, public exposure of violation of bureau standards is often highly effective in stopping unfair practices. Such exposure usually comes about when a consumer reports to his local bureau any practice he believes to be questionable.

DISHONEST SALESMANSHIP[1]

Although the world of business is in the main fair in its dealings with the public, a few unscrupulous companies prey on the public and the good name of business by promoting unfair schemes. More than 800 such schemes are known, all of them relying on universal human desires such as the wish to gain wealth, or health, or something for little or nothing. To defeat such schemes, the consumer and merchant should deal only with legitimate, responsible concerns; should investigate a business concern, its past record, and the representations made before investing in any proposition; and should read all business agreements and understand them fully before signing.

[1] Sources: National Better Business Bureaus, Inc., and the Federal Trade Commission.

Among the most common among fraudulent sales schemes are the following: *Misuse of Comparative Prices.* In this scheme, all types of articles, but chiefly appliances, are advertised at a fictitious "regular price," which is given as the basis of comparison with the sale price. The difference is represented as a saving.

"Bait" Advertising. This practice appears in two common forms. In the first, brand-name merchandise is advertised at greatly reduced prices. In the second, inferior merchandise is advertised as quality merchandise and at startlingly low prices. The aim in both instances is merely to attract the customer to the store. When the customer attempts to purchase the advertised merchandise, the sales person speaks of it in a derogatory way, states it has been "sold out," or in some other high-pressure way seeks to switch the customer's interest to more expensive goods. Another form of "bait" is the offer of credit terms which are not actually available as represented.

Advance Listing Fees. The salesman requests an advance fee to list for sale such items as a home, a business, or rooms for rent. Unscrupulous promoters frequently charge listing fees (sometimes as high as thousands of dollars) and then render no service beyond the publication of an advertisement in a brochure having valueless circulation.

Door-to-Door Selling. Door-to-door salesmen may use a variety of "scare" tactics, hoping to frighten home owners into buying their products to remedy alleged health or safety hazards. A common misrepresentation involves savings in fuel bills that will result from installation of storm doors and windows. In another method, the salesman represents that the home owner's house has been selected as a model for a particular improvement, which will be done at a reduced rate in order to interest others in the area in having the same type of service performed. Commissions are promised on resulting sales but are not forthcoming. In all home improvement projects, the customer is advised to know his contractor. In any door-to-door sales, the customer should realize that even the signing of a simple order blank commits him to a legally binding contract. Having signed, the customer has no redress, no matter how shoddy the article or false the claims.

Vending Machines. Advertisements, often printed in "Help Wanted" columns, claim that a comfortable living can be made with little effort from part-time servicing of vending machines for nuts, confections, and other merchandise. Advertisers represent that they will set the prospect up in business with an established route, choice locations for the machines, and merchandise supplied at cost if he will buy one or two machines. The purchaser eventually realizes that he has been sold out-of-date machinery and that his earnings, if any, have been vastly exaggerated.

Collection Agencies. Some collection agencies charge fees which turn out to be greater than the sums they have been retained to collect. The merchant should always read with care the collection-agency contract.

Vanity, or Subsidy, Publishing. Publishers of this type offer glowing promises for publication of books to authors who have not been able to achieve publication by established publishing houses. The author is required to pay a substantial sum for the printing but is assured of 30 per cent or 40 per cent royalties on retail sales of the book. The investment may run from several hundred dollars to several thousand, in return for which the author receives numerous copies of his book.

Correspondence Schools. Some such schools falsely represent their ability to secure employment for persons taking their courses. One of the most frequent deceptions is the claim that a school is associated with the Civil Service or can guarantee Federal employment. The standing of correspondence schools can be checked with state educational accreditation authorities.

Cosmetic and Health Schemes. Frequent misrepresentations in this area relate to bust developers, cancer "cures," hair coloring and hair growing, and obesity.

Medical authorities state that no device, substance, or service can permanently develop the bust. Skin creams sold as "tissue builders" or as "skin foods" are useless for those purposes. When treated in its early stages by a reputable physician, cancer may be cured; however, quacks and "institutes" of doubtful standing which advertise cancer "cures" should be avoided. Weight reduction cannot be effected by any external application. Reducing preparations should never be taken internally without consultation with one's physician.

PASSPORT REGULATIONS OF THE UNITED STATES

A passport is a travel document of identity and nationality, internationally recognized, issued to a person who is a national of the country by which it is issued. A passport indicates that it is the right of the bearer to receive the protection and assistance of the diplomatic and consular offices of his government, and it requests the officials of foreign governments to permit the bearer to travel in their territories and, in case of need, to give him all lawful aid and protection. United States passports are issued by the Passport Office of the Department of State, which provided the information included in this chapter.

United States passports are not required for travel to any territory or waters, continental or insular, subject to the jurisdiction of the United States, including the (Panama) Canal Zone. In addition, they are not required by some countries in the Western Hemisphere, including Canada and Mexico, for brief tourist travel. Further information regarding such countries may be obtained from travel agents or the consular officials of the countries to be visited. Most foreign countries have consular representatives in the principal cities of the United States. The Passport Office issues on request a circular entitled "Passports Not Required of United States Citizens," which lists the countries in the Western Hemisphere not requiring passports.

An application for a passport may be made before a clerk of a Federal or state court authorized by law to naturalize aliens; at one of the Passport Agencies located in Boston, Chicago, Los Angeles, Miami, New Orleans, New York, San Francisco, Seattle, and Washington, D.C.; or before the Special Passport Representative at Honolulu, Hawaii.

An applicant for a passport must present proof of United States citizenship. A native-born citizen should present his birth or baptismal certificate, or an affidavit of his birth executed by a parent, a close blood relative, or some other person having personal knowledge of the date and place of his birth. A naturalized citizen should present his naturalization certificate. Persons claiming citizenship through a native or naturalized citizen must submit evidence of citizenship of the person through whom they claim citizenship. A previously issued passport will be accepted as evidence of United States citizenship.

An applicant is required to establish his identity to the satisfaction of the clerk of court or passport agent either through personal knowledge, by the presentation of an acceptable document of identification, or by an identifying witness. The following documents are acceptable provided they contain the signature and either a photograph or physical description of the applicant: a previous passport; a naturalization certificate; a driver's license; or a government (Federal, state, municipal), industrial, or business identification card or pass. An identifying witness who has known the applicant for at least two years is required only when the applicant cannot satisfactorily establish his identity otherwise.

Two duplicate photographs, both signed by the applicant and taken within the previous two years, must accompany the passport application. A group photograph is preferred when a wife and/or children are to be included in the passport. Photographs may be in color or in black and white; they must be full-faced, on thin unglazed paper, with a light background, and not over 3 × 3 in. nor less than 2½ × 2½ in. in size.

The senior member of a family may include members of his immediate family in his passport. This means that a husband may include his wife and minor children in his passport, or that a woman may include her minor children in her passport. It is not necessary for a wife or children to appear when they are included in a husband's application.

The fee for a new passport is $9. The execution fee is an additional $1 unless the application is executed by clerks of state courts authorized to collect $2.

A passport issued on or after Sept. 14, 1959, is valid for three years and may be renewed for an additional two-year period, but the final date of expiration shall not be more than five years from the original date of issue. Passports may be renewed by forwarding a completed renewal application or letter requesting renewal, the passport, and renewal fee ($5) to the Passport Office, Department of State, Washington 25, D.C.; or to one of the Passport Agencies; or to the Special Passport Representative at Honolulu, Hawaii. Persons abroad may have passports renewed by United States consular or diplomatic officials.

It is the responsibility of the bearer of the passport to obtain any necessary visas. Most countries require an American citizen to obtain a visa from one of their consular officials in the United States if he wishes to enter their territory. A visa is generally a stamped notation in a passport indicating that the bearer is to be permitted to enter the country involved for a certain purpose and length of time. A number of foreign countries waive the visa requirement for certain kinds of travel, such as the brief visits of tourists. Most Western European countries do not require visas for temporary visits, the specific time depending on the individual country; travelers should check the length of time for which the visa will be waived. Certain foreign visas are valid for one trip only or bear time restrictions. When you apply to a foreign consular officer for a visa, make it a point to tell him how many trips you plan to make into his country and the length of time you intend to stay. Travelers by air must comply with the same visa regulations that apply to travelers by land or water.

Further information regarding visas may be obtained from travel agents or the consular officials of the countries to be visited. The Passport Office issues on request a circular entitled "Fees Charged by Foreign Countries for the Visa of United States Passports." In addition to a list of visa fees, the circular includes current information concerning the waiving of the visa requirement by various foreign countries.

Further information may be obtained by writing to the Passport Office, Department of State, Washington 25, D.C.

AUTOMOBILE DRIVING COSTS AND TAX ALLOWANCES[1]

Owning and operating an automobile constitutes a major expense for America's nearly 60,000,000 car owners. Car costs fall into two broad categories, variable and fixed. The first relates to the number of miles driven, how hard the car is used, and the costs of repairs and service. The second includes insurance, taxes (license and registration fees, use and property taxes), and depreciation.

Variable Costs. The best way to determine the average cost of gas is as follows: Fill the tank until the gas is visible in the filler neck and record the mileage on the odometer. Drive normally until the tank is almost empty, have it refilled to the same point as when the test was started, then divide the number of miles driven by the number of gallons required to refill the tank. This will indicate the number of miles per gallon. As for depreciation, the figures may vary widely. For instance, money saved by neglecting needed repairs will ultimately show up in the form of increased depreciation. The best practice is to keep an accurate record of all expenditures for repairs and replacement of parts. Tire

---

[1] Source: American Automobile Association.

costs also vary greatly from car to car. According to one study, the average cost per mile is slightly more than half a cent.

Fixed Costs. Among these is insurance, included because premiums do not vary with the number of miles driven. To determine total cost, add all premiums directly related to car operation (public liability, property damage, collision, fire and theft, medical payment). Property and use taxes are fixed annual costs. Federal and state excise taxes and sales taxes should be considered part of the original cost of the car and should not be prorated in determining annual costs. License and registration fees should be treated the same as taxes. There is no set formula for determining depreciation. It merely represents the difference between the purchase price of a car and its ultimate selling price. Most business firms arbitrarily fix car depreciation at 25 per cent per year, but this would not prove realistic for the private-car owner.

Income Tax Deductions. First the car owner must determine whether or not his car qualifies as being used for business purposes. If so, certain deductions are allowed, such as the operating costs listed above, parking, etc. The Internal Revenue Service has prepared a special worksheet, Form 2106, for use in reporting certain business expenses; the reverse side of this is useful for computing automobile business expenses, and it may be attached to the individual income-tax return. This form may be obtained from the District Director of Internal Revenue.

The various methods used for computing depreciation in connection with income taxes are quite complex. In general, however, an annual prorated deduction is allowed, depending on the length of time the owner expects to use the car and the loss he expects to take in replacing it.

ABOUT TRAFFIC LAWS[1]

Throughout most of the United States there is heavy emphasis on enforcement of traffic laws. With the support of the Federal government, traffic laws—both state and municipal—are fairly uniform throughout the country.

A major exception is the regulation of speed. Speed laws vary so much from state to state, within communities, on various types of highways, and from day to night that any chart would be hopelessly complex.

More and more states have accepted speed zoning—adjusting the top allowable speeds to the realities of the road, which makes it imperative that drivers observe the speed-limit signs. In every state there is strong emphasis on enforcement of speed regulations, and so-called radar or other speed-determining devices are in operation by state highway patrolmen, city police, county sheriffs, or others. Unmarked cars may be used and in a few states there is surveillance from the air.

Speed limits are subject to change, sometimes without apparent reason. In some small towns, the low speed limit of the built-up area may extend far beyond it. The driver is advised to keep a sharp watch for speed signs, or he may deputize a member of his party to do so.

Improper passing, a major cause of arrest, is not only illegal in all states but is one of the most dangerous of all driving maneuvers. However impatient a driver may be, he should never try to pass another car until he is absolutely certain that there is plenty of room to get back into the proper lane in time.

In Event of Arrest. Despite all safety precautions, the most well-meaning driver may inadvertently break a traffic rule and be arrested. When this happens, American Automobile Association experts, who have handled thousands of arrest complaints, offer this advice. No matter how unjustified the arrest may seem, remain calm. Even if the judicial authority before whom the case is heard is an

---

[1] Source: American Automobile Association.

apparently ignorant justice of the peace, it is almost certain to be futile to engage in an altercation with him. Determine the amounts involved in a fine or a bond. In some places these are identical; in others the bond may be substantially higher. When they are the same, a motor-club membership card may be left in lieu of cash. These cards are generally accepted, and in at least nine states acceptance is mandatory.

POINT SYSTEMS[1]

As part of a continuing program to bring about driver improvement, a number of states have adopted what is known as the "point system." Motor vehicle administrators long have had the power to suspend or revoke licenses for extremely serious violations, but the problem remained as to how to cope with the driver guilty of numerous but less serious violations which nevertheless were potential accident-breeders. A method was needed to identify such drivers and, through warning or barring them temporarily from driving, to prevent a more serious violation or a bad accident.

As a result, point systems have been adopted by almost half the states and by several Canadian provinces. There are wide variations in the number of points assigned for a given violation, the number of points requisite for suspension, the legislative authority for the program, and policies for publicizing the point system. In general, however, the systems work as follows:

A schedule is set up assigning a certain number of points to various types of violation. Convictions for violations (and in some states, forfeiture of bond) as well as accident involvement are reported to the state motor vehicle administrator. When the points have reached a certain level, a letter is sent to the individual warning him that he faces loss of the right to drive if he continues to violate regulations. At a higher level of points, the driver may be called for a personal interview. Finally, if the offender fails to correct faulty driving practices and the points go above a predetermined level, the driving license is suspended.

A question on which the states are divided is whether to ascribe points for alleged violations taking place outside the driver's home state. So-called "speed traps," justices of the peace and constables operating under the fee system, and the general inability of a motorist away from home to get an impartial trial have complicated this problem. The American Automobile Association maintains that out-of-state convictions or forfeitures of bond should not be mandatory in assigning points, but should depend on the circumstances in each case.

Among the states and provinces which by 1961 had adopted the point system as part of driver improvement programs are: Alabama, Arizona, California, Connecticut, District of Columbia, Indiana, Iowa, Kentucky, Louisiana, Maine, Manitoba, Michigan, Minnesota, Nebraska, New Brunswick, New Jersey, New York, Nova Scotia, Ohio, Oklahoma, Ontario, Oregon, Rhode Island, South Carolina, Utah, Washington, and Wisconsin.

DRIVER'S SAFETY INFORMATION

Questions and Answers[2]

QUESTIONS

	True	False
1. It is safer to keep your vehicle in the center of the road when driving in a fog to avoid driving off the highway	....	....

---

[1] Source: American Automobile Association and American Association of Motor Vehicle Administrators.

[2] Compiled by the Automobile Club of New York. The questions cover the type of information required by New York State of applicants for a driver's license, but they are applicable for drivers throughout the United States.

2. The warning for steep hills, narrow bridges, or similar hazards is a diamond-shaped sign   ....
3. When carrying passengers, all buses must stop before crossing railroad tracks   ....
4. On streets and highways, vehicles always have the right of way over pedestrians   ....
5. Square traffic signs usually indicate a sharp curve in the road ahead   ....
6. The purpose of traffic signals is to permit fast-moving vehicles to save time   ....
7. At an uncontrolled intersection, the vehicle coming from your left always has the right of way   ....
8. When driving in a fog, it is best to have headlights on high beam   ....
9. On a three-lane highway the center lane is for passing only   ....
10. Stop and then proceed with caution when you see a square traffic sign   ....
11. An eight-sided sign means a full stop   ....
12. It is permissible to allow someone else to use your driver's license only in case of emergency   ....
13. The left hand and arm of the driver is extended outward horizontally before making a left turn   ....
14. It is not necessary to watch for pedestrians as long as you have the green light in your favor   ....
15. A section of the road set aside for parking of vehicles is called a safety zone   ....
16. In addition to the written information on highway signs, the color and shape of these signs give very definite information   ....
17. Four-wheel brakes in good condition should stop a car traveling at 30 m.p.h. within 67 ft.   ....
18. Extending the left hand and arm upward is the proper hand signal for a right turn   ....
19. Under normal conditions, right turns may be made at a faster speed than left turns   ....
20. You can stop your vehicle quicker on a dirt road than you can on a concrete highway   ....
21. Before backing a vehicle, it is always necessary to turn around and observe to the rear   ....
22. Most accidents happen at night, particularly during the winter months   ....
23. In the event of a tire blowout, you should apply brakes immediately   ....
24. Railroad crossing ahead is indicated by a square traffic sign   ....
25. When parking on an incline, set the hand brake and cramp the front wheels into the curb   ....
26. At 40 m.p.h., a vehicle equipped with four-wheel brakes should stop within 120 ft.   ....

27. When traffic permits, it is not necessary to stop when emerging from a driveway   ....
28. Place your car in the lane nearest to the right curb when preparing for a right turn   ....
29. Vehicles are not permitted in a safety zone   ....
30. If your vehicle is difficult to steer, wheel alignment may need checking   ....
31. A diamond-shaped traffic sign means "stop"   ....
32. Do not pass vehicles at intersections   ....
33. A vehicle equipped with four-wheel brakes must stop within 190 ft. when traveling at 50 m.p.h.   ....
34. Use caution when you see a square traffic sign   ....
35. Never pass a school bus while flashing red lights are on and children are being received or discharged   ....
36. At an intersection, pedestrians have the right of way only when there is a traffic light at the intersection which is green in their favor   ....
37. A round traffic sign indicates a railroad crossing ahead   ....
38. The hand signal for slowing down is given with the left hand and arm extended downward   ....

ANSWERS

All of the test statements should have been answered "True," with the exception of those whose numbers appear below. The statements appearing here provide the correct information after each number listed.

1. Under foggy conditions, drive very slowly on the extreme right of the road with bright lights deflected.
4. When there are no traffic signals or they are not operating, drivers must yield the right of way to pedestrians.
5. Square signs mean caution; be prepared to meet a possible operating hazard.
6. We have traffic signals to prevent accidents and facilitate traffic.
7. At an uncontrolled intersection, the vehicle coming from your right has the right of way.
8. Headlights should be deflected in fog.
10. A square traffic sign means caution.
12. A driver's license may never be used by anyone other than the person to whom it is issued.
14. As an operator, you must realize that pedestrians may be unreasonable, but since they have so little chance to survive a collision with your destructive vehicle, you must protect them.
15. A safety zone is a section of roadway for the use of pedestrians. Motorists are not permitted to drive in a safety zone.
19. A right turn must ordinarily be made at a slower speed than a left turn.
20. A car will not stop as quickly on a loose gravel or dirt road as it will on a hard-surface road.
23. If you have a tire blowout, do not disengage clutch or apply brakes until speed is reduced materially.
24. Railroad crossing ahead is indicated by a round sign.

27. In a business or residence district, when you drive from an alley, driveway, or building, you must stop just before driving on to a sidewalk and yield the right of way to all vehicles on the road.

31. A diamond-shaped sign means reduce speed for permanent physical hazards such as curves, steep hills, and narrow bridges.

36. When there are no traffic signals or they are not operating, drivers must yield the right of way to pedestrians.

GASOLINE TAX RATES BY STATES[1]

(Cents per gallon)

State	Rate	State	Rate	State	Rate
Alabama	7	Louisiana	7	Ohio	7
Alaska	7	Maine	7	Oklahoma	6½
Arizona	5	Maryland	6	Oregon	6
Arkansas	6½	Massachusetts	5½	Pennsylvania	7
California	6	Michigan	6	Rhode Island	7
Colorado	6	Minnesota	5	South Carolina	7
Connecticut	6	Mississippi	7	South Dakota	6
Delaware	5	Missouri	3	Tennessee	7
Florida	7	Montana	6	Texas	5
Georgia	6½	Nebraska	7	Utah	6
Hawaii[2]	8½–11	Nevada	6	Vermont	6½
Idaho	6	New Hampshire	7	Virginia	7
Illinois	5	New Jersey	5	Washington	7½
Indiana	6	New Mexico	6	West Virginia	7
Iowa	6	New York	6	Wisconsin	6
Kansas	5	North Carolina	7	Wyoming	5
Kentucky	7	North Dakota	6	District of Columbia	6

Compiled by the American Automobile Association

[1] 1961 rates; Federal, county, and municipal taxes not included.
[2] Rate varies by counties.

AUTOMOBILE TOURING MILEAGE IN THE UNITED STATES[1]

Cities in the South	Asheville, N. C.	Atlanta, Ga.	Birmingham, Ala.	Charleston, S. C.	Columbia, S. C.	Jacksonville, Fla.	Knoxville, Tenn.	Memphis, Tenn.	Miami, Fla.	Nashville, Tenn.	New Orleans, La.	Richmond, Va.	Savannah, Ga.	Tampa, Fla.	Washington, D. C.	W. Palm Beach, Fla.
Asheville, N. C.		209	348	281	166	436	112	531	791	306	736	389	300	621	487	724
Atlanta, Ga.	209		161	306	225	327	194	408	678	258	512	564	273	482	633	611
Birmingham, Ala.	348	161		467	386	423	269	251	796	214	357	719	434	566	769	792
Charleston, S. C.	281	306	467		122	267	407	730	618	601	776	425	109	466	533	551
Columbia, S. C.	166	225	386	122		309	285	649	757	479	749	371	151	508	479	593
Jacksonville, Fla.	436	327	423	267	309		528	728	351	585	664	158	199	683	763	284
Knoxville, Tenn.	112	194	269	407	285	528		419	879	194	617	406	418	829	928	812
Memphis, Tenn.	531	408	251	730	649	728	419		1059	225	929	406	869	928	67	
Miami, Fla.	791	678	796	618	757	351	879	1059		929	1015	869	730	829	1123	992
Nashville, Tenn.	306	258	214	601	479	585	194	225	929		538	644	531	780	703	869
New Orleans, La.	736	512	357	776	749	664	617	406	899	538		1100	667	672	1203	855
Richmond, Va.	389	564	719	425	371	664	450	869	1015	644	1100		506	863	108	948
Savannah, Ga.	300	273	484	109	151	158	418	730	509	531	667	506		357	606	442
Tampa, Fla.	621	482	566	466	508	199	683	829	272	780	672	863	357		971	232
Washington, D. C.	487	633	769	533	479	763	928	1123	703	1203	108	606	971			1056
W. Palm Beach, Fla.	724	611	792	551	593	284	812	992	67	869	855	948	442	232	1056	

[1] Source: American Automobile Association.

AUTOMOBILE TOURING MILEAGE

Cities in the East	Albany, N. Y.	Atlantic City, N. J.	Baltimore, Md.	Boston, Mass.	Buffalo, N. Y.	Burlington, Vt.	Charleston, W. Va.	Chicago, Ill.	Cincinnati, Ohio	Cleveland, Ohio	Columbus, Ohio	Detroit, Mich.	Evansville, Ind.	Gettysburg, Pa.	Hagerstown, Md.	Harrisburg, Pa.
Albany, N. Y.		262	336	175	282	154	729	806	716	467	607	534	947	314	351	278
Atlantic City, N. J.	262		135	345	437	426	555	809	640	489	532	658	874	176	210	160
Baltimore, Md.	336	135		412	375	493	420	697	505	363	397	532	739	54	75	74
Boston, Mass.	175	345	412		464	259	788	990	880	651	772	735	1097	416	452	394
Buffalo, N. Y.	282	437	375	464		386	458	526	435	190	327	254	667	321	306	301
Burlington, Vt.	154	426	493	259	386		844	912	821	573	713	640	1053	468	504	432
Charleston, W. Va.	729	555	420	788	458	844		494	200	271	179	367	393	382	346	418
Chicago, Ill.	806	809	697	990	526	912	494		294	354	315	272	297	639	700	689
Cincinnati, Ohio	716	640	505	880	435	821	200	294		248	108	254	234	459	429	487
Cleveland, Ohio	467	489	363	651	190	573	271	354	248		140	165	480	309	301	335
Columbus, Ohio	607	532	397	772	327	713	179	315	108	140		188	342	347	320	382
Detroit, Mich.	534	658	532	735	254	640	367	272	254	165	188		452	478	470	504
Evansville, Ind.	947	874	739	1097	667	1053	393	297	234	480	342	452		705	662	724
Gettysburg, Pa.	314	176	54	416	321	468	382	639	459	309	347	478	705		36	36
Hagerstown, Md.	351	210	75	452	306	504	346	700	429	301	320	470	662	36		72
Harrisburg, Pa.	278	160	74	394	301	432	418	689	487	335	382	504	724	36	72	
Indianapolis, Ind.	775	707	566	947	495	881	308	186	108	308	175	280	172	522	495	557
Lake George, N. Y.	60	334	401	219	328	94	765	869	778	529	669	596	1009	376	413	340
Louisville, Ky.	822	749	614	989	544	930	268	300	109	357	217	363	125	568	538	596
Montreal, Que.	234	506	573	353	387	93	845	865	822	574	714	593	1045	545	585	509
New York, N. Y.	143	124	191	221	377	301	597	831	660	508	555	631	897	211	236	173
Norfolk, Va.	465	357	235	618	606	721	405	889	605	559	584	767	798	269	261	305
Philadelphia, Pa.	241	62	98	314	369	394	518	757	586	427	481	596	823	118	144	103
Pittsburgh, Pa.	476	357	235	576	222	628	228	462	291	132	186	301	528	177	162	196
Portland, Me.	242	452	501	107	522	203	939	1047	957	708	848	775	1188	523	559	501
Quebec, Que.	399	671	738	387	552	258	1089	1030	887	739	879	758	1210	710	750	674
Richmond, Va.	480	280	145	557	523	638	318	802	518	474	497	643	711	186	178	222
St. Louis, Mo.	1018	953	818	1193	729	1127	583	294	343	554	421	526	172	768	501	802
Toledo, Ohio	579	601	475	763	299	685	310	242	197	112	131	57	395	421	413	438
Toronto, Ont.	382	570	484	573	109	479	567	511	493	296	436	239	691	430	415	410
Washington, D. C.	373	172	37	449	376	530	367	698	497	368	395	522	737	78	70	114
White Mts., N. H.	220	451	518	167	493	107	921	1019	928	680	820	747	1160	532	569	496

Cities in the West	Bismarck, N. D.	Boise, Idaho	Calgary, Alta.	Cheyenne, Wyo.	Chicago, Ill.	Dallas, Texas	Denver, Colo.	Duluth, Minn.	El Paso, Texas	Grand Canyon, Ariz.	Helena, Mont.	Houston, Texas	Kansas City, Mo.	Los Angeles, Calif.	Memphis, Tenn.	Mexico City, Mexico
Bismarck, N. D.		1145	834	723	884	1333	783	454	1418	1576	668	1579	863	1849	1387	2534
Boise, Idaho	1145		914	797	1784	1686	860	1507	1407	771	582	1932	1505	1086	2080	2764
Calgary, Alta.	834	914		1066	1800	2001	1134	1270	1927	1312	422	2247	1750	1657	2274	3106
Cheyenne, Wyo.	723	797	1066		994	921	104	1028	847	866	681	1167	692	1211	1190	2026
Chicago, Ill.	884	1784	1800	994		1006	1022	495	1522	1813	1596	1107	517	2175	542	2168
Dallas, Texas	1333	1686	2001	921	1006		817	1182	632	1067	1619	246	540	1446	478	1200
Denver, Colo.	783	860	1134	104	1052	817		1104	743	872	785	1613	645	1268	1104	1789
Duluth, Minn.	454	1507	1270	1028	495	1182	1086		1814	1814	1831	1122	1428	2176	999	2382
El Paso, Texas	1418	1407	1927	847	1522	632	743	1814		636	1526	757	1094	814	1110	1977
Grand Canyon, Ariz.	1576	771	1312	866	1813	1067	872	1814	636		890	1350	1336	526	1459	2013
Helena, Mont.	668	582	422	681	1596	1619	785	1831	1526	890		1865	1331	1235	1542	2707
Houston, Texas	1579	1932	2247	1167	1107	246	1613	1122	757	1350	1865		786	1571	588	1130
Kansas City, Mo.	863	1505	1750	692	517	540	645	1428	1094	1336	1331	786		1742	451	1740
Los Angeles, Calif.	1849	1086	1657	1211	2175	1446	1268	2176	814	526	1571	1742	57		1865	2191
Memphis, Tenn.	1387	2080	2274	1190	542	478	1164	999	1110	1459	1935	588	478	1865		1657
Mexico City, Mexico	2534	2764	3106	2026	2168	1200	1789	2382	1977	2013	2707	1130	1740	2191	1657	
Milwaukee, Wis.	795	1793	1685	1003	91	1057	1061	467	1611	1869	1505	1196	563	2187	631	2257
Minneapolis, Minn.	449	1532	1309	874	435	1200	932	154	1569	1677	1159	1274	488	2210	886	2228
New Orleans, La.	1733	2237	2505	1425	998	504	1280	1405	1124	1557	2123	367	892	1938	406	1497
Omaha, Neb.	658	1297	1545	507	487	705	556	521	1202	1373	1146	951	205	1718	683	1905
Portland, Ore.	1382	478	859	1275	2262	2090	1338	1836	1885	1249	714	2410	1983	1026	2558	3262
Reno, Nev.	1603	606	1390	1007	2001	1885	1042	1972	1201	659	912	2009	1709	480	2228	2671
Salt Lake City, Utah	970	380	921	475	1469	1353	514	1440	1027	391	499	1595	1177	736	1696	2321
St. Louis, Mo.	1120	1758	2016	945	294	674	898	692	1228	1589	1677	813	253	1925	307	1882
San Antonio, Texas	1608	1884	2181	1101	1243	275	864	1457	566	1292	2052	205	815	1380	732	925
San Francisco, Calif.	1736	840	1571	1241	2199	1850	1298	2206	1252	897	1146	2009	1943	404	2132	2629
Santa Fe, N. M.	1237	1322	1594	514	1369	661	410	1494	333	484	1195	907	856	890	1043	1710
Seattle, Wash.	1302	547	779	1307	2076	2280	1407	1756	1954	1318	634	2479	1957	1217	2627	3331
Spokane, Wash.	993	444	470	998	1923	1939	1102	1447	1851	1215	325	2190	1648	1415	2260	3032
Vancouver, B. C.	1418	690	791	1423	2348	2364	1527	1872	2097	1461	750	2615	2073	1360	2685	3457
Winnipeg, Man.	448	1751	917	1128	934	1410	1252	430	1907	1809	1116	1656	910	2154	1385	2610
Yellowstone Nat'l Pk.	558	440	558	498	1346	1327	602	1067	1252	748	183	1665	1070	1093	1708	2524

[1] Source: American Automobile Association

IN THE UNITED STATES (Cont.)[1]

Indianapolis, Ind.	Lake George, N. Y.	Louisville, Ky.	Montreal, Que.	New York, N. Y.	Norfolk, Va.	Philadelphia, Pa.	Pittsburgh, Pa.	Portland, Me.	Quebec, Que.	Richmond, Va.	St. Louis, Mo.	Toledo, Ohio	Toronto, Ont.	Washington, D. C.	White Mts., N. H.	Cities in the East
775	60	822	234	143	465	241	476	242	399	480	1018	579	382	873	220	Albany, N. Y.
707	334	749	506	124	273	62	357	452	671	280	953	601	570	172	451	Atlantic City, N. J.
566	401	614	573	191	228	98	235	501	738	145	818	475	484	87	518	Baltimore, Md.
947	219	989	353	221	618	314	576	107	387	557	1193	763	573	449	167	Boston, Mass.
495	328	544	387	377	606	369	222	522	552	528	729	299	109	576	493	Buffalo, N. Y.
881	94	930	93	301	721	394	628	203	258	638	1127	685	479	530	107	Burlington, Vt.
308	765	268	845	597	405	518	228	939	1089	818	533	810	567	867	921	Charleston, W. Va.
186	869	800	865	831	889	707	462	1047	1080	802	294	242	511	698	1019	Chicago, Ill.
108	778	109	522	660	605	586	291	957	987	518	343	197	493	497	928	Cincinnati, Ohio
308	529	357	574	508	659	427	132	708	739	474	554	112	296	368	680	Cleveland, Ohio
175	669	217	714	555	584	481	186	848	879	497	421	131	436	395	820	Columbus, Ohio
280	596	363	593	631	767	596	301	775	758	643	526	57	239	522	747	Detroit, Mich.
172	1009	125	1045	897	798	823	528	1188	1210	711	172	395	691	737	1160	Evansville, Ind.
522	376	563	545	211	269	118	177	523	710	186	768	421	480	78	532	Gettysburg, Pa.
495	413	538	585	236	261	144	162	559	750	178	501	413	415	70	569	Hagerstown, Md.
557	340	596	509		305	103	196	501	674	222	803	438	410	114	496	Harrisburg, Pa.
	837	114	873	730	713	656	361	1016	1038	626	246	223	519	570	993	Indianapolis, Ind.
837		887	174	209	540	303	538	265	339	546	1083	641	440	438	201	Lake George, N. Y.
114	887		956	769	673	695	403	1096	1121	586	265	306	602	606	1043	Louisville, Ky.
873	174	956		381	699	475	609	282	165	718	1119	650	354	610	186	Montreal, Que.
730	209	769	381		329	93	369	228	546	336	976	620	486	228	327	New York, N. Y.
713	540	673	699	329		237	427	725	864	87	938	671	715	191	656	Norfolk, Va.
656	303	695	475	93	237		295	421	640	243	902	539	478	135	430	Philadelphia, Pa.
361	538	403	609	369	427	295		697	774	344	607	244	331	236	694	Pittsburgh, Pa.
1016	265	1096	282	228	725	421	697		280	664	1262	820	624	556	96	Portland, Me.
1038	339	1121	165	546	864	640	774	280		883	1248	815	519	775	242	Quebec, Que.
626	546	586	718	336	87	243	344	664	883		851	586	632	108	663	Richmond, Va.
246	1083	265	1119	976	938	902	607	1262	1248	851		469	765	816	1239	St. Louis, Mo.
223	641	306	650	620	671	539	244	820	815	586	469		296	480	792	Toledo, Ohio
519	440	602	354	486	715	478	331	624	519	632	765	296		488		Toronto, Ont.
570	438	606	610	228	191	135	236	556	775	108	816	480	488		560	Washington, D. C.
993	201	1043	186	327	656	430	694	96	242	663	1239	792		560		White Mts., N. H.

Milwaukee, Wis.	Minneapolis, Minn.	New Orleans, La.	Omaha, Neb.	Portland, Ore.	Reno, Nev.	Salt Lake City, Utah	St. Louis, Mo.	San Antonio, Texas	San Francisco, Calif.	Santa Fe, N. M.	Seattle, Wash.	Spokane, Wash.	Vancouver, B. C.	Winnipeg, Man.	Yellowstone Nat'l Pk.	Cities in the West
795	449	1733	658	1382	1603	970	1129	1608	1736	1237	1302	993	1418	448	558	Bismarck, N. D.
1793	1532	2237	1297	478	606	380	1758	1884	840	1322	547	444	690	1751	440	Boise, Idaho
1685	1339	2505	1545	859	1390	921	2016	2181	1571	1594	779	470	791	917	575	Calgary, Alta.
1003	874	1425	507	1275	1007	475	946	1101	1241	514	1307	998	1423	1128	498	Cheyenne, Wyo.
91	435	998	487	2262	2001	1469	294	1248	2199	1369	2139	1923	2348	934	1346	Chicago, Ill.
1057	1028	504	705	2090	1883	1358	474	275	1850	661	2280	1939	2364	1410	1327	Dallas, Texas
1061	932	1280	556	1388	1064	514	898	864	1298	410	1407	1102	1527	1252	602	Denver, Colo.
467	154	1405	521	1836	1912	1440	692	1457	2206	1494	1756	1447	1872	430	1067	Duluth, Minn.
1611	1569	1124	1202	1885	1201	1027	1228	566	1252	333	1954	1551	2097	1907	1252	El Paso, Texas
1869	1677	1557	1373	1249	659	391	1589	1202	897	484	1818	1215	1461	1809	748	Grand Canyon, Ariz.
1505	1159	2123	1146	714	912	499	1677	1782	1146	1195	684	325	750	1116	183	Helena, Mont.
1196	1274	367	951	2410	2009	1595	813	205	2009	907	2479	2190	2615	1656	1665	Houston, Texas
563	488	892	205	1983	1709	1177	253	815	1943	856	1957	1648	2073	910	1070	Kansas City, Mo.
2187	2210	1938	1718	1026	480	736	1925	1380	404	890	1217	1415	1360	2154	1093	Los Angeles, Calif.
631	886	406	683	2553	2228	1696	307	732	2182	1043	2627	2260	2685	1385	1708	Memphis, Tenn.
2257	2228	1497	1905	3262	2671	2321	1882	925	2629	1710	3331	3032	3457	2610	2524	Mexico City, Mexico
																Milwaukee, Wis.
346																Minneapolis, Minn.
938	1340															New Orleans, La.
496	367	1097														Omaha, Neb.
2219	1873	2668	1910													Portland, Ore.
2010	1818	2389	1514	779												Reno, Nev.
1478	1286	1857	982	858	532											Salt Lake City, Utah
383	579	713	458	2238	1962	1430										St. Louis, Mo.
1332	1303	572	980	2362	1928	1396	949									San Antonio, Texas
2244	2050	2297	1748	712	284	766	2196	1784								San Francisco, Calif.
1419	1842	1165	966	1800	1104	875	1109	841	1207							Santa Fe, N. M.
2139	1793	2784	1390	191	970	927	2311	2427	903	1829						Seattle, Wash.
1830	1484	2443	1471	889	1050	824	2002	2328	1101	1520	309					Spokane, Wash.
2255	1909	2868	1896	334	1113	1070	2427	2945	143	425	143	425				Vancouver, B. C.
845	499	1802	705	1820	1966	1418	1078	1685	2200	1671	1740	1431	1747			Winnipeg, Man.
1338	1092	1807	963	839	810	357	1401	1466	1004	1012	775	443	892	993		Yellowstone Nat'l Pk.

MOTORING OUTSIDE THE UNITED STATES

Many American tourists visiting foreign countries prefer to take their own automobile with them for ease in sightseeing. This is a relatively simple procedure, and one with which motoring associations, such as the American Automobile Association, can be of great assistance in supplying the necessary customs documents for taking the car into foreign countries and bringing it back to the United States.

In Europe there are two types of customs documents that make traveling easy: the Triptyque, if only one country is to be visited; and the Carnet de Passage en Douanes, for more than one country. These make it unnecessary to deposit a duty when entering a foreign country or crossing the border between countries. Many European countries waive even these formalities; some require a temporary import card, valid usually for a few weeks; others have abolished all requirements if the tourist is strictly on visitor status. Turkey, and all East European countries require one or the other.

Carnets are required (and valid for varying lengths of time) in the following countries: Aden, Aegean Islands, Algeria, Angola, Argentina, Australia, Basutoland and Swaziland, Bechuanaland, British East Africa, Burma, Cambodia, Cameroon, Ceylon, Chile, Comoro Islands, Costa Rica, Cyprus, Czechoslovakia, Egypt (United Arab Republic), Fiji, French Oceania, French West Africa, Gibraltar, Hong Kong, Hungary, India, Indonesia, Iran, Iraq, Israel, Jordan, Laos, Lebanon, Libya, Malagasy, Malta, Mauritius, Morocco, Mozambique, New Caledonia (French territory), New Zealand, Nyasaland, Pakistan, Paraguay, Peru, Philippines, Poland, Reunion Island, Rhodesia (Northern and Southern), St. Pierre and Miquelon Islands, Seychelles Islands, Somalia, Southwest Africa, Sudan, Surinam, Syria (United Arab Republic), Tangier, Thailand, Togo, Trinidad, Tunisia, Turkey, Union of South Africa, Uruguay, and Viet Nam.

To facilitate travel abroad, a World Convention on International Road Traffic was signed in Geneva, Switzerland, in 1949. Americans motoring abroad may take out an international driving permit (I.D.P.) in the United States, which eases motor travel in the ratifying countries. These are: Afghanistan, Argentina, Australia, Austria, Belgium, Cambodia, Ceylon, Chile, China (National Republic), Cuba, Czechoslovakia, Denmark, Dominican Republic, Egypt (United Arab Republic), Finland, France, Gambia, Ghana, Greece, Haiti, Ireland, Israel, Italy, Jamaica (British West Indies), Jordan, Laos, Luxemburg, Malaya (Federated States), Mauritius, Monaco, Morocco, Netherlands, New Zealand, Norway, Peru, Philippines, Poland (with translation), Portugal (Macao excepted), Singapore, Spain, Surinam, Sweden, Switzerland, Syria (United Arab Republic), United Kingdom, U.S.S.R., Vatican City, Viet Nam, and Yugoslavia. Germany requires a German translation of a valid U.S. license.

Cars need not be registered with customs when taken into Canada. On return, the tourist merely establishes ownership by showing his state registration card.

To take a car into Mexico, a permit must be obtained from the Mexican customs office at the port of entry, but applications may be had at the American Automobile Association offices in Laredo, Brownsville, El Paso, or Nogales. No official government charge is made for these, which are valid for 90 days and renewable for an additional 90 days. The permit must be returned for cancellation on leaving the country, and at that time proof of ownership is required, in the form of title, license registration, or notarized bill of sale.

Travel in Central America involves burdensome red tape. Although all six republics—Guatemala, El Salvador, Honduras, Nicaragua, Costa Rica, and Panama—share a common language, each has its own particular set of requirements for visiting tourists. Passports with visas, or tourist cards, are needed for all, and in some cases exit visas are also necessary. Special documents are obligatory for taking in an automobile; these are available from motoring associations. A single insurance policy valid in all six countries is unavailable. Some of the countries require smallpox vaccinations and certificates of health and good conduct. The prudent tourist will check carefully with his local motoring association on conditions in the country he intends to visit.

AUTOMOBILE MANUFACTURERS ASSOCIATION

The Automobile Manufacturers Association, founded in 1913, is an organization through which motor vehicle manufacturers voluntarily cooperate in carrying out programs that promote efficient, safe, and economical manufacture and use of motor vehicles.

The purpose of the association is to assist in the solution of problems affecting the industry and to promote free competition in the manufacture, distribution, sale, and servicing of the industry's products.

This purpose is implemented through the following three basic types of activity: (1) the maintenance of services that can be more efficiently or effectively rendered on an industry-wide basis than on a separate-company basis; (2) the collection of factual information concerning the manufacture, distribution, and use of motor vehicles and the distribution of such information to interested private and public groups; and (3) cooperative activity with other industrial, social, or governmental groups to solve problems arising from the manufacture and use of passenger and commercial vehicles.

Publications of the Automobile Manufacturers Association include *Automobile Facts* (monthly); *Automobile Facts and Figures* (annual); and *Motor Truck Facts* (biennial). The association also distributes news releases, booklets, films, and educational materials on automotive subjects. It maintains, at its headquarters office in the New Center Building, Detroit, Mich., an extensive automotive library and a large collection of historical automotive photographs. It is the sponsor of the National Automobile Shows, usually held in Detroit. Offices also are maintained in New York City and Washington, D.C.

THE AMERICAN AUTOMOBILE ASSOCIATION

The American Automobile Association (abbreviated A.A.A.), founded in 1902, is the world's largest motor federation, comprising some 750 state associations, motor clubs, and branches located throughout the United States, Canada, Panama, and Puerto Rico. More than 7,000,000 motorists belong to the organization through membership in their local affiliated motor clubs.

The A.A.A. is a civic, nonprofit organization; its affairs, policies, and activities are guided by a board of directors recruited from among its membership; they serve without compensation. Since it has no stockholders, its revenues are devoted to providing specialized services for members and for the promotion of improved motoring conditions for all motorists.

Among the association's objectives are: fair and equitable taxation of the motor vehicle; dedication of motor-vehicle revenues exclusively to highway purposes; elimination of discriminatory motor-vehicle levies; uniformity of motor-vehicle laws; Federal aid for highway construction; a 40,000-mile interstate system of high-type highways geared to the needs of modern traffic; elimination of parking problems; roadside zoning; building greater safety into the highways; extension of driver training in the high schools of the nation; promotion of travel, both at home and abroad; and elimination of travel barriers among nations.

HORSEPOWER

One horsepower is equal to 33,000 foot-pounds per minute, or 550 foot-pounds per second.

Note that power involves both the work done and the time involved. The unit of work is the foot-pound, which is equal to lifting one pound one foot. The 33,000 foot-pounds can be performed in any way, such as lifting 33,000 pounds one foot, a thousand pounds 33 feet, or one pound 33,000 feet. For example, it might take a man several days to shovel 33,000 pounds of dirt one foot into the air in a wheelbarrow, but a steam shovel could lift 2,000 pounds 16.5 feet in one minute to produce one horsepower. Work is not only lifting a weight, but moving anything against a resistance, such as turning a grindstone. If the stone had a circumference of two feet and rotated at 3,300 revolutions per minute, the stone surface would be moving at a rate of 6,600 feet per minute. If the grinding friction was five pounds, the power required to rotate the stone would be one horsepower.

TO ESTIMATE THE HORSEPOWER OF A GASOLINE ENGINE

The results obtained by using the formula given below are not exact but are close enough for all practical purposes.

Let

x=Horsepower

a=Area of one piston in square inches

b=Number of cylinders

c=Stroke of engine in feet

d=Revolutions per minute

e=Constant 1000 for four-cycle, 900 for two-cycle

then

$$x = \frac{a \times b \times c \times d}{e}$$

A boiler requires for each nominal horsepower 30 to 35 pounds of water an hour.

ELECTRICAL POWER

The kilowatt hour is the unit of electrical power. It is equal to 1.341 horsepower. Ordinarily we speak of so many kilowatts of power, but, strictly speaking, this is incorrect. We really mean a certain amount of electrical energy flowing for one hour.

CAREERS IN THE 1960'S

Two hundred years ago, Richard Arkwright revolutionized the cotton-textile industry with the invention of cotton-spinning machinery. There were riots in many areas of Great Britain as hand spinners and hand weavers protested this threat to their livelihood. Troops were used to put down the disturbances.

What happened?

In little more than a quarter of a century, textile employment in Britain rose from fewer than 8,000 jobs to 320,000 jobs!

The 1960's will see a repetition of the 1760's—barring a major war. Automation will revolutionize industry—but many more jobs will be created in the process.

The big problem for American industry will be finding workers who can be trained for the technical jobs that will open up in the process. This means a better-educated working force than ever before in American history. In 1960 the United States had a population of 180,000,000; by 1970 it will have 208,000,000. In 1960 the American work force was nearly 70,000,000; by 1970 it will be nearly 87,000,000.

But the jobs will be very different—skilled jobs, technical jobs, jobs requiring thoughtful men and women who have the background for training. Many of today's job areas, such as teaching and medicine, will continue to expand. Other job areas, such as coal mining and rail transportation, will shrink.

Following is a summary of the major job areas, and what may be expected in salary. (Salaries, of course, will vary in different parts of the country—smaller in the South and higher in the Far West. Inflation may raise these salaries somewhat, while recession may tend to lower them.)

Accountancy. As local, state, and national taxes continue to expand, there will be an increasing demand for accountants—by individuals as well as by business firms. A college degree is a *must*. Starting salary is between $3,000 and $5,000. Established accountants earn $10,000 to $15,000.

Agriculture. Most of the large farms throughout the United States have introduced automation. There will be fewer jobs on farms in 1970 than there were in 1960. In 1950, 12 per cent of the labor force was engaged in farm work; by 1960 the figure had dropped to 9 per cent, and by 1970 it will be down to 6 per cent. (However, there will be more jobs in fields related to agriculture—such as food packaging.)

Aircraft and Spacecraft. As the 1960's began, about 1,000,000 workers were engaged in aircraft, spacecraft, and missile work. By the 1970's—with man reaching for the planets—the number of workers will be even higher. Jobs cover all kinds of engineers, scientists, and technicians, as well as metallurgists, mathematicians, assemblers, mechanics, etc. A topnotch science background is required. The salary range is wide, although generally high.

Air Transportation. This area of the economy is expected to boom through the 1960's—particularly in overseas flights. Trips abroad on long week ends will become fashionable with the new fast jets. Experienced pilots earn as much as $20,000; mechanics, $6,000; airline agents, $5,000; stewardesses as much as $4,000. High-school graduation is necessary, with some college preferred.

Atomic Energy. Technical workers and craftsmen will be needed in the manufacture of reactors and radiation recording devices, and in research. College degrees are required. The starting salaries are high.

Clerical Occupations. Most job opportunities for women will remain clerical —largely because of huge turnover. Salaries vary widely, in some areas starting as low as $2,500. Many firms use "fringe benefits" to attract workers: long vacations, discounts on company products, health insurance plans, etc.

Construction. Building is expected to boom throughout the 1960's. The building of roads, schools, hospitals, and homes will create need for more carpenters, bricklayers, masons, etc. Jobs might increase by 30 per cent over the decade.

Engineering. There are many fields of engineering, ranging from aeronautical and agricultural to electrical and mining engineering. Best opportunities will lie in aeronautical and chemical engineering, poorest opportunities in mining. A college degree is a must; in many instances, graduate work is extremely helpful. Starting salaries range from $4,000 to $5,000; advanced salaries may go up to $15,000.

Government Service. As the demand for expanded government services increases, jobs will become available in such areas as public health, sanitation, welfare, and education. By 1970, such jobs will rise at least 25 per cent.

Insurance. At least 30 per cent more job openings are likely in this field by 1970. Agents handle life insurance, auto insurance, health insurance, retirement plans, fire and theft insurance, liability insurance, etc. Salaries start at around $4,000.

Manufacturing. Emphasis will be on new consumer goods. This area will probably create at least 15 per cent more jobs during the decade, ranging from factory workers to foremen, supervisors, executives, etc.

Medicine. The big demand for physicians, dentists, and nurses will undoubtedly see no letdown. Training for medicine or dentistry, however, requires huge outlays for education. Once established, doctors and dentists earn top five-figure salaries. Practical nurses average up to $3,500, while registered nurses earn up to $5,000. The practical nurse needs a high-school education, plus about a year of specialized training. The registered nurse needs up to four years of special schooling beyond high school.

Mining. Automation will continue to be felt—particularly in coal mining. A major problem of the 1960's will be the retraining of miners—who have become technologically unemployed—for other jobs. Jobs will increase, however, in the areas of crude petroleum and gas.

Office Work. Jobs will increase over the decade, but automation will demand skilled workers: operators of tabulating machines, programmers, etc.

Rail Transportation. Airlines will continue to make inroads into rail travel. Rail freight, however, will thrive. In general, opportunities in railroading will diminish. Brakemen and conductors average from $3,000 to $9,000, depending on the type of work (yard work, freight trains, passenger trains, etc.).

Real Estate. With the flight to suburbia proceeding rapidly—and the growth of major highways—real estate opportunities will continue to expand. Real estate salesmen start at an average salary of $3,000 to $4,000. Most, however, work on commission.

Retail Stores. Job opportunities will open up in the suburban shopping centers. As the supermarkets expand, the small store owner will face stiff competition. Jobs will rise by about 25 per cent.

Sales. The biggest increase in sales jobs will be part-time workers in retail stores. This field will be particularly important for both married women and students seeking part-time work. In addition to such jobs, there will continue to be opportunities for door-to-door selling. College students may be able to finance school expenses by summer sales jobs.

Science. Scientists may include astronomers, chemists, physicists, biologists, geologists, etc. Generally, the demand will be heavy. Best prospects are in physics (especially nuclear physics) and chemistry. Biology and geophysics provide good opportunities, geology and astronomy fair opportunities. College degrees are required in *all* science fields. Starting salaries vary according to academic degree: with B.S., $5,000; with M.S., $6,000 to $7,000; with Ph.D., as high as $10,000. The exception is in astronomy, where starting salaries are not much above $6,000.

Services. Besides the services listed here, there are hundreds of others that may be performed at home. Many skilled people set up workshops in their basements to turn out products ranging from jewelry to cabinets. Women type envelopes for addressing companies, or telephone prospective buyers for door-to-door salesmen to follow up. Free-lance artists and writers work at home. Some women set up day nurseries; others give music lessons or special tutoring. Home services are particularly well adapted for handicapped people who may find it difficult to travel to an office daily. Information on jobs for the handicapped and rehabilitated may be obtained from J.O.B. (Just One Break), 717 First Ave., New York City; American Federation of the Physically Handicapped, P.O. Box 827, Brooksville, Fla.; the Institute for the Crippled and Disabled, 400 First Avenue, New York City; the local Veterans' Administration office; or the local Division of Vocational Rehabilitation of the United States Employment Service.

Skilled Trades. There will be a big demand for electricians, machinists, workers in building trades, and tool and die makers. Because many of these trades are controlled by unions, it is prudent to assess union requirements before deciding to enter a particular trade.

Teaching. The shortage of teachers will continue through the 1960's. Teachers of mathematics, science, and foreign languages will continue to be in great demand. Salaries vary widely through the United States. In 1961, for example, the average classroom teacher in Mississippi earned $3,415 a year; in California, $6,700. Teaching jobs require a college degree. In some areas, a master's degree is needed for high-school teaching.

EDUCATION—THE KEY TO GOOD JOBS

Young people still in school should seek assistance from the school guidance officer in deciding what field most interests and suits them, and what courses should be taken in high school to prepare for future training. During the 1950's, 60 per cent of those entering the work force were *at least* high-school graduates, with 22 per cent having had some college education. But in the 1960's it is estimated that 70 per cent of the job-seekers will be at least high-school graduates, and 26 per cent will have had some college.

The value of education was the basis of a United States Department of Labor survey of 22,000 boys and girls who entered the labor market during the 1950's. At least 85 per cent of the boys who graduated from high school earned $50 or more weekly, but only 56 per cent of those who dropped out of school earned as much. Among girls, half of the graduates earned $50 or more weekly, as opposed to 18 per cent of the dropouts. However, 15 per cent of the boy dropouts and 39 per cent of the girl dropouts earned less than $40 a week. Only three per cent of the boy graduates and 14 per cent of the girl graduates earned as little.

The United States Census Bureau[1] estimates that an elementary-school graduate can expect to earn $110,000 during his lifetime; a high-school graduate, $155,000; a college graduate, $260,000. (As salaries go up during the 1960's, these figures can be expected to rise proportionately.)

Most teenagers are ambitious for college training. At the beginning of the decade, the Institute of Student Opinion, sponsored by *Scholastic Magazines,* polled a sampling of 7,200 junior and senior high school students about college plans. Of those interviewed, 63 per cent said they expected to go to college upon graduation from high school; 20 per cent were undecided. Of those who expected to go to college, only 35 per cent said they would have enough money to pay college expenses. Most students indicated that they intended to work their way through school. As high as 24 per cent expected to win scholarships. Less than eight per cent expected to take loans for tuition.

Although more scholarships have become available than ever before, there are not nearly enough to satisfy the huge percentage who seek them. For information on scholarships, students may read the "Lovejoy-Jones College Scholarship Guide," or "College Ahead!" by Eugene S. Wilson and Charles A. Bucher. Many books and pamphlets on the subject are available. The Superintendent of Documents, U.S. Government Printing Office, Washington 25, D.C., offers inexpensive pamphlets such as "Financial Aid for College Students" and "Costs of Attending College."

Students seeking aid should check the college of their choice to see if it is part of the Federal Student Loan Program. They may be able to borrow up to $1,000 a year and repay it over a ten-year period after graduation. Such loans are particularly valuable if a teaching career is decided upon; up to 50 per cent

[1] See also The Businessman and the Census Bureau.

of the loan may be forgiven for those becoming fulltime public-school teachers in elementary or secondary schools.

VOCATIONAL INFORMATION

Government agencies, both state and Federal, publish up-to-date reports giving vocational information in various fields. These reports, often in pamphlet or booklet form, are available to the public at cost.

Outstanding are the "Occupational Outlook" series published by the Bureau of Labor Statistics of the United States Department of Labor. The "Occupational Outlook Handbook," which is revised frequently, may be purchased from the Superintendent of Documents, United States Government Printing Office, Washington 25, D.C.

"Occupations in the Federal Civil Service" lists opportunities in the various occupations and tells how these civil-service jobs are filled. Another pamphlet is "Opportunities for Women in the Federal Civil Service." Free copies can be obtained from the United States Civil Service Commission, Washington, D.C.

Jobs for Women

Many young women who plan to marry right after high school feel there is no point in preparing themselves for jobs—not even typing or stenography. But the fact is that 60 per cent of all women gainfully employed are married. Aside from the "insurance" aspect of the possibility of widowhood, many women prefer to return to work when their children are grown. Other women like to work part-time so that their families may enjoy some of the "extras" that cannot be afforded from the husband's income alone.

The best job opportunities for women lie in clerical, secretarial, and sales jobs. About a third of American working women hold such jobs. The other two thirds are scattered among 500 job categories listed by the United States Census, among which are nurses, teachers, dietitians, social workers, lawyers, scientists, and doctors.

As for part-time jobs, many women work as retail sales clerks, waitresses, practical nurses, beauty operators, household helpers, substitute teachers, nurses, government clerks, etc.

Inexpensive pamphlets on employment for women, prepared by the Women's Bureau of the Department of Labor, may be obtained from the Superintendent of Documents. One particularly useful booklet is "Part Time Employment for Women." Another is "Trade and Industrial Education for Girls and Women," prepared by the United States Office of Education.

Jobs in the Armed Forces

Career opportunities in the armed forces should not be overlooked. Job training is available in literally hundreds of civilian-related occupations. The armed forces need aviators and engineers, cooks and bakers, photographers and doctors, clerks and typists.

The Army, Navy, Air Force, Marine Corps, and Coast Guard maintain 250 specialized training schools. The four service academies offer commissions and college degrees to qualified young men.

There are also opportunities for women in the services, as secretaries, X-ray technicians, cryptographers, laboratory technicians, etc. Local recruiting offices will provide information; the United States Department of Defense, The Pentagon, Washington 25, D.C., has prepared a number of pamphlets on how its training programs help young men and women in their civilian career fields.

Jobs Abroad

With so many American installations overseas, there are a number of job opportunities available. Most numerous are teaching jobs—especially at armed forces dependents' schools. There are also mission schools established by religious organizations, and schools set up by certain American corporations (*e.g.,* United Fruit in Central America, Aramco in the Middle East).

American construction firms conducting building operations overseas hire both skilled workers (*e.g.,* carpenters, painters) and professionals (*e.g.,* doctors and lawyers).

Most public libraries have reference sources which list some of these firms, and several books have been published on possibilities of finding jobs in foreign countries.

The United States government has a wide range of jobs abroad. Most of these are in the armed forces, but there are also civilian jobs in the Peace Corps, the United States Information Agency, the International Cooperation Administration, and the Department of State. These agencies should be contacted in Washington.

Summer Jobs

Summer jobs are highly important for young people, not only because of the money they bring in, but because they give a taste of what the job world is like. Youngsters learn what employers expect of their workers, how to conduct themselves in business, and how to assume responsibility.

Most summer jobs are seasonal: camp counselors, waiters and busboys at summer resorts; soda dispensers in candy stores and luncheonettes; pickers and packers on farms; car washers, etc.

The Federal government has some summer jobs available. Descriptive booklets include "Summer Employment with the U.S. Department of the Interior," available from the department, Washington 25, D.C.; and "Summer Employment in Federal Agencies" (pamphlet 45), available from the United States Civil Service Commission, Washington 25, D.C.

The Department of Labor has published an inexpensive pamphlet, "Summer Jobs for Students," listing several dozen jobs for boys and girls in the 14–15 and 16–17 age brackets. It is available from the Superintendent of Documents, U.S. Government Printing Office, Washington 25, D.C.

HOW TO LOOK FOR A JOB

During the great depression of the 1930's, when competition for the few jobs available was so keen, job-hunting became something of a science. In job clinics, career conferences, and round-table discussions on job-hunting techniques, authorities in employment work established specific formulas for planning, organizing, and carrying through a job hunt. As a result, the old haphazard methods have practically ceased to exist. Today, most job-hunters—at least those who have benefited from vocational counseling services in school or college—know that employers expect applicants to have prepared themselves sufficiently to know what they are offering and to be reasonably sure that they are offering it in the right place. Such preparation is an essential preliminary to the actual job hunt.

Preparation. The job-seeker should maintain the mental attitude that he is not so much asking for a job as he is offering for sale a commodity that has a market value. After the psychological preparation come the concrete steps in preparation.

The prospective job-hunter will need to determine (1) the nature of the service he proposes to offer; (2) the market value of this service, *i.e.*, what employers are generally paying for such service; (3) the qualifications he possesses in the way of (a) general education and specialized training; (b) work experience; (c) special aptitudes or talents (whether he is qualified, for instance, to work in the theater or the movies, radio or television, writing, or some other field of artistic expression); and (4) which business, profession, or organization may need the service he has to offer.

Looking for a Job. After preparation the next step is to locate a likely "prospect." The *"Help-Wanted" columns* of the local newspapers are an obvious source; less obvious but equally important are the advertisements in trade publications. Certain employers (notably those employing workers with technical training and skills) who do not ordinarily advertise in the newspapers often advertise in their trade publications.

The job-seeker should read the advertisement carefully for the *key words* to determine exactly what the employer is looking for. He should answer[1] the ad by giving specific examples of the kind of experience or talent called for in the advertisement. Instead of saying "I have had considerable experience in teaching," he should say "For ten years I was an instructor in the Department of History at Clinton High School."

One should never write that he can "do anything" unless the ad calls for a home handyman—and even that requires special skills which should be listed: carpentry, painting, gardening, etc.

Another obvious source is the *employment agency.* A recent graduate of a college or a business or technical school will, of course, make full use of whatever placement facilities it has to offer. State employment offices and such organizations as the "Y" should also be utilized. Commercial employment agencies charge a fee for their services, often a week's salary, which is usually paid by the employee placed but sometimes by the employer.

Friends and acquaintances can often help. They sometimes know of an opening, or will be on the lookout; or they may give letters of introduction to persons who might be in a position to help with advice, information, or further introductions.

Sometimes a strategically placed *advertisement* is useful, but as a rule only if the job-seeker is experienced in a specialized field—for example, if he is an advertising copywriter, an executive, an engineer, or a chemist. Advertisements usually are best placed in a trade, professional, or technical publication.

If efforts in these directions fail to produce an opening, it may be advisable to try *independent prospecting.* A list should be made of organizations which have a fairly constant need for the type of service to be offered, and a letter of application sent to each, with a carefully prepared summary of the writer's education, training, and experience.[1]

This letter and summary deserve the utmost effort; they will be the basis for an estimate of the applicant and his qualifications.

The letter should reflect some quality of the writer—a measure of originality and individuality that will cause it to stand out from the general run. Trick devices, however, should never be used. The letter should be brief, and mention only matters which bear directly on the writer's qualifications for the job in question. Each copy should be individually typed, on suitable stationery, and be correct in every detail of spacing, placing, and typing. The English, punctuation, and spelling should be flawless. The summary—or résumé, as it is usually called —should be typed on a separate sheet. It should give in skeleton form the facts, with dates, of the applicant's general education; specialized training, work

[1] See also Letters of Application.

experience, if any, and other pertinent assets, such as extracurricular activities, foreign travel, and knowledge of foreign languages.

Many "career" books give advice on job-hunting, with sample letters of application and sample résumés. These examples are well worth studying; but the fact remains that a letter of application and résumé will prove effective only in so far as they truly represent the writer, and show sound thinking on his individual problem.

The Interview. One day, as a result of the job hunt, will come an appointment for an interview. This is a crucial occasion. In no longer than it takes for the job-seeker to walk from the door to the chair by the interviewer's desk, he can win or lose a job. His dress, posture, manner of carrying himself, his walk, the expression on his face—all these things will tell the interviewer a great deal that will enter into his decision.

The task before the applicant is to convince the shrewd, experienced person behind the desk not only that the applicant has what it takes to make a success of the job in question, but that he is an individual the interviewer will be proud to have in his organization. He knows that skills are not too difficult to find, but that outstanding quality is a rare commodity.

Individual quality, therefore, is what the job-hunter should seek to register the moment he enters the interviewer's office. Appearance and bearing are the important criteria. It is essential to be neatly and conservatively dressed; quiet, reserved, and dignified in manner, and yet, as far as the natural nervousness inevitable to the occasion permits, at ease.

The interviewer should be permitted to take the lead and set the tone of the interview; but if the applicant is encouraged to talk he should not be afraid to speak up. He should remain physically quiet, without fidgeting, swinging his feet, drumming with his fingers, or fussing with his hair or clothing. He should not smoke unless invited to do so. He should answer questions fully and pleasantly. The interviewer should be permitted to introduce such matters as salary, paydays, hours of work, vacations, and holidays. The applicant should confine himself to presenting his qualifications for the work and his interest in securing it.

He should watch carefully for indications that the interviewer is ready to terminate the interview. Many an eager job-seeker lingers on and on, hoping to add one more point in his favor, and as a result talks himself out of a job. When the interviewer says, "We'll let you know," or "You'll be hearing from us," it is the cue for departure. It is enough then to thank the interviewer for his courtesy and to express the hope of being considered for the position.

APTITUDE TESTING

America is test-happy, and the job applicant may find himself required to take a whole battery of tests before he is accepted for a job. There are literally hundreds of aptitude tests, but they measure only nine or ten different abilities. The odds are that no applicant can do well in *all* of them. He will do very well in some, poorly in others, and probably score in between on most. But his score will show the kind of job for which he is best qualified.

What kinds of abilities do the tests measure?

1. Solving arithmetic and number problems
2. Understanding written material
3. Visualizing two-dimensional objects in three dimensions, called "spatial perception" by the experts
4. Working with the hands
5. Working with the fingers
6. Clerical ability
7. Memory

8. Figuring out how things work
9. Solving problems through reasoning.

If a job applicant is given some of these tests, he should take them in stride and do the best he can. He should not be discouraged if he misses out on a job because he failed a test; it probably means that he is not really qualified for the particular job, and perhaps should look elsewhere.

For an opportunity to take some aptitude tests, students should contact the school guidance counselor. Colleges, United States and state employment services, and the Veterans' Administration can provide information on how and where such tests may be taken. Many libraries have reference materials on self-measurement.

PERSONNEL SELECTION

The employees of a business are a vital factor in its efficient operation. Hiring the right person for a job involves not only finding a worker who can perform certain duties, but finding someone who will fit in well with the organization and who will enhance the local reputation of the business. A store clerk, for example, can either build up a faithful following or drive customers away to a competitor.

A small businessman must usually hire local workers, and often finds himself in direct competition with big business firms who scout local talent for the most promising workers. The small businessman, however, can reduce this handicap in several ways. He can (1) meet the wages offered by larger concerns; (2) offer experience in a wider variety of related jobs; and (3) stress the opportunity for more rapid advancement and greater responsibility.

WHERE TO FIND WORKERS

Employment Agencies. Federal, state, and privately operated employment agencies maintain lists of qualified workers in every field, and will recommend workers at no cost to the employer. Some private agencies specialize in certain types of work and can readily recommend good workers in their fields.

Advertising. Newspaper want ads can be a quick way to find workers interested in a certain type of job. Such ads should be carefully prepared to make sure that they specify exactly the qualifications desired. Careful wording will avoid interviews with unqualified persons who might answer a vaguely worded ad. The "Help-Wanted" sections in local newspapers offer numerous examples of such advertising.

Nearby Schools. Most high schools, technical schools, and colleges maintain placement services for graduates. These services are always a good source of young workers anxious to learn a particular type of work, or to obtain experience in certain fields.

Local Contacts. In a small town, business associates, business clubs, and other organizations often know who is seeking a job and who is qualified for certain work.

WHAT TO LOOK FOR IN AN EMPLOYEE

The employer should be a good judge of personalities and be able to assess the qualifications of the person he is considering for a job. Necessary personal qualifications, of course, vary with different types of work, but certain traits, such as cooperativeness, eagerness to work, and neatness, are desirable in all fields.

An interview affords the best means for the employer to get acquainted with an applicant and to study him carefully. The employer should try to put the applicant at ease during the interview, and should speak in a friendly manner.

The gruff or stern approach often defeats the purpose of finding a good worker and frequently results in making the applicant nervous and ill at ease.

During the interview the employer should inquire into the past experience or training of the applicant in relation to the particular type of job open, and into his general educational background. The exact duties of the job should be thoroughly explained, and the employer should question the applicant on his ability to perform the work.

Employment application forms can also be used to good advantage. Often an applicant not qualified for the present opening is able to fill other jobs that might be open in the future. With the applications on file, the employer always has a list of possible workers on hand. Such forms should provide adequate space for the following information: (1) name, address, and telephone number of applicant; (2) age, marital status, and social security number; (3) record of schools attended, the length of attendance, and the student's major subjects; (4) previous jobs held, type of work done, length of employment, and salary received; and (5) the names of at least three local residents, other than relatives, who can give character references. Space should also be provided for any additional remarks the applicant might wish to make, such as why he desires a particular job, or why he feels qualified for it.

If time permits, the following procedure is recommended in hiring a worker: (1) have the applicant fill out the company application form; (2) make a mutually convenient appointment for an interview; (3) study the application form and refer to it during the interview; (4) allow time for consideration of the relative merits of various applicants; (5) notify the chosen applicant, and send notes to the rejected applicants to the effect that the position has been filled and that their interest has been appreciated.

WHAT IS PERSONNEL WORK?[1]

What does a personnel man do? Primarily, he sees to it that manpower is used in the most effective way possible. For example, he tries to fit the right employee into the most suitable job. The personnel man in business and industry fills another important need by finding out what causes friction and helping to prevent or correct it.

In general, the functions of a personnel department in business and industry may include: (1) hiring, which involves judging and testing prospective employees; (2) training employees in their jobs; (3) wage administration, which includes setting salaries and wage rates, as well as cutting down waste time and motion; (4) settling labor-relations problems, involving negotiation and administration of union contracts, handling of grievances, and maintenance of good rapport with union officials; (5) developing the attitude of management and individual employees toward each other, which involves determining personnel policies and explaining them; and (6) encouraging safety and health, through the prevention of accidents and through safety education, inspection, physical examinations, and sanitation.

There are also special services, which may include housing assistance, restaurant management, social clubs, counseling, and publishing employee news organs.

ORGANIZATION OF A SMALL BUSINESS

The economy of the United States—from the standpoint of the size and number of business concerns—is largely an economy of small businesses. Of more

[1] Excerpts from "Should You Go into Personnel Work?" by Cyrus S. Ching, as told to Harold Baron, pamphlet, © 1956, New York Life Insurance Company.

than 4,000,000 business establishments in the country, over 90 per cent are usually classified as small business.[1]

Small firms are in almost all fields of business. They are concentrated in the retail and service fields, but they also help to maintain a sound and prosperous economy through construction, manufacturing, wholesaling, and mining.

The establishment of a successful small business, whether from scratch or by purchasing a going concern, is not an easy task. The owner can expect hard work and long hours as well as intensive competition from both small and large concerns. Problems constantly arise demanding immediate decisions, decisions which in the long run determine success or failure.

Inadequate sales, competitive weakness, unwise credit practices, and excessive fixed assets are reported as the causes of business failures. A recent study estimated that during 1960 poor management because of inexperience and incompetence was the basic cause of most failures.[2]

In 1953 Congress established the Small Business Administration (abbreviated S.B.A.) to advise and assist the nation's small business concerns. The S.B.A. assists small business by: (1) helping it obtain private financing; (2) lending money when private financing is not available; (3) licensing privately owned small business investment companies which extend equity-type capital; (4) lending money to state and local development companies; (5) lending for replacement of businesses that have been destroyed by disaster; (6) helping small business to get a fair share of government orders and contracts; (7) assisting small firms in solving production problems; (8) assisting small firms with management problems; and (9) financing research into the problems of small business.

Selecting the Right Business. The fact that inexperience is a primary cause of failure indicates that a prospective businessman should observe one basic rule in selecting a business: He should select a field with which he is familiar.

Thus, many persons have no problem about what business they should enter: they go into the one in which they have been employed, the one they know best. The selection of a business, however, is more complicated for individuals with little or no experience.

In such instances, the individual should determine the business he believes he would like most. Then he should obtain from government and nongovernment sources all available information concerning that line of business. If his evaluation indicates there is a future for that type of business, his next step is to determine the qualifications required for its operation. Then he should match these qualifications against his own background, ability, and experience. If he meets all the qualifications except experience, he should work for someone in the field and thus acquire sufficient experience and knowledge.

Establishing a New Business. After selecting the kind of business to operate, the prospective businessman is ready to consider the problems connected with starting a new business. The primary considerations are: (1) capital requirements and sources of funds; (2) form of business organization to be used; and (3) location of the business.

Capital Requirement. The amount of capital required to start a business varies widely, depending on the kind of business, type of establishment, location, and many other factors. This makes it impossible to set an average minimum that will apply to all small businesses. The new businessman needs cash or credit

[1] According to the Small Business Administration, "small business" includes the following: manufacturing plants with 250 employees or less; wholesale firms with $5,000,000 or less annual sales; retail stores, service establishments, with annual sales of $1,000,000 or less; and construction establishments with average of $5,000,000 or less for the preceding three years.

[2] "Why Businesses Fail: Year Ended December 31, 1960" *Dun's Review,* March 1961.

to cover opening expenses and a reserve of cash or credit to carry the business until it becomes self-supporting. This varies from a few months for some businesses to three years or more for others. Capital requirements should not be underestimated, because insufficient capital often causes failure.

Sources of Funds. The three principal sources of securing funds are:

1. Initial Capital. The risks of starting a small business are so great that the owner must be willing to invest his own savings. Traditionally, the initial capital for establishing a business is furnished by the owner. Occasionally it is supplemented by relatives or friends.

2. Short-Term Credit. Even though earnings are plowed back, short-term credit is usually needed to handle current operating expenses until payment has been received from sales. Sources of short-term credit are: (a) bank loans—usually from two to six months; (b) trade credit from suppliers—30 to 90 days; and (c) loans from commercial credit firms or from banks against inventory, accounts receivable, and other collateral—six to 12 months.

3. Term Loans. The small businessman seeking to expand or modernize his business needs credit for one year to five years or longer. Three important sources of term-loan assistance are commercial banks, venture capital organizations, and the Small Business Administration.

Form of Business Organization. The *proprietorship* is an organization that is owned by one person. It provides the greatest freedom of action to the owner, who usually manages the business, receives all profits, and bears all losses. However, creditors have a legal claim not only on the investment in the business but also on the personal assets of the owner.

The *partnership* is an association of two or more persons by mutual agreement to operate a business for profit. It usually provides greater financial resources than the individual proprietorship and enables the business to offer a more comprehensive and efficient service. Outstanding characteristics are (1) unlimited liability of each partner; (2) termination by death or withdrawal of partner or by acceptance of a new partner; and (3) the fact that the acts of one partner, within the scope of the business, are binding upon the other partners.

The *corporation* is an artificial legal entity—separate and apart from its stockholders, officers, and directors. It may sue or be sued without in any way affecting the individuals. It can make contracts and other business transactions as though it were an individual. The corporate form of organization is more expensive to establish and requires more records than the other two types of organization. However, it offers the advantage of limited liability. Its stockholders are liable only to the extent of their investment in the corporation.

Location. In many instances the small businessman opens in his home town, where he has friends, relatives, and business contacts. Personal feelings are important, but the most important factor should be whether the location will support the business profitably.

In evaluating a town or city the emphasis should be on population, employment, income, and competitive trends. An analysis of what has happened in the past and of the present situation provides important bases for estimating future trends.

Buying a Going Business. The possibility of buying a going business should also be considered. The classified sections of all major newspapers and of many trade papers give detailed listings of businesses offered for sale.

The same problems of capital, form of organization, and location encountered in establishing a new business must be considered in the purchase of a going business. The advantages and disadvantages should be carefully weighed. Sometimes owners of small establishments, for personal reasons, are forced to sell their businesses at bargain prices. By purchasing a going business it may be possible to obtain a well-equipped plant in a good location, or a well-furnished store with adequate stock. Less working capital may be needed, since income will be forthcoming from the start, and smaller outlays will be required for new equipment, fixtures, and stock.

The advantages can be determined, however, only by a careful study of all phases of the business. The owner may be trying to unload an unprofitable business—unprofitable because of mismanagement, or poor location, or for other reasons. The equipment, fixtures, and stock on hand may have been poorly selected for the requirements of the business.

An analysis of the financial statements and business records of the concern, together with a review of the income tax returns, will help not only to determine whether to purchase the business, but also to establish a fair price.

Advice should be sought from local banks, suppliers, and other sources familiar with the type of business. Such advice may help to prevent the investment of time, effort, and money in a business that is doomed to failure from the start.

Merchandising Problems. Sound buying policies are essential. Sound buying results in having on hand the goods the customers want at the prices they are willing to pay. It is based on a careful analysis of the problems of *what, when, where,* and *how much* to buy. Buying policies should never be controlled solely by a desire for quantity discounts or special prices, or by attempts to anticipate a rising price trend. It is important not to over-buy, for serious financial trouble may result.

A sound and effective pricing policy is also essential. It should cover all the operating expenses of a business and also return to the owner a fair and reasonable profit. Adequate accounting records, containing current information on all operations of the business, are the basis of a sound pricing policy.

The general price level the business expects to maintain should be determined at the time of reviewing and evaluating all the factors bearing on the establishment of the business. Competitors' prices should be observed; the general price level should be kept in line with competing stores selling similar goods. The prices of individual items must conform to the general price policy of the business. In determining the principles of individual items it is essential that the markup[1] needed to cover both operating expenses and a fair net profit be accurately determined. Most public libraries have numerous publications covering the basic principles of determining prices—how to determine costs, markup, selling prices, and profit margins.

After the individual prices are computed, they should again be compared with competitors' prices. If the average price is much below that of competitors a review should be made, to insure that no operating expenses were overlooked; if the average price greatly exceeds that of competitors, a study of sources of supply, rent, and salaries is indicated.

Selling and Advertising. In many small businesses, selling is primarily a matter of personal salesmanship, with the owner and one or two salesmen doing the selling. In such instances the sales program should especially consider the personalities of the people selling, and their knowledge of the needs and desires of customers. The sales program should also consider the number of potential customers who cannot be reached through personal salesmanship alone. Advertising should be employed to inform potential customers concerning the goods carried and the services offered by the business. Advertising[2] draws customers into the place of business; effective personal salesmanship consummates the sales.

Many forms of advertising are available for small business concerns—display signs, newspapers, magazines, direct mail, shopping news, handbills, outdoor billboards, classified section of the telephone directory, radio, television, and newsletters. In selecting the media to be employed consideration should be given

---

[1] See also the section on Markup.
[2] See also sections on Advertising and Salesmanship.

to the size of the trading area served by the business, the type of business, and customers' buying habits. A neighborhood store may find handbills and direct mail, together with a hanging display sign, most effective. If the trading area covers a large part of the city, local newspapers, "spot" radio announcements, television, and outdoor billboards may be most productive.

Record Keeping. Small businesses should keep a record of all business assets, current and fixed, and of claims against the business; *i.e.,* liabilities. All expenses of the business should be recorded; daily sales records should be totaled, to permit recording of income. If the business offers credit, a record must be kept of the amount owed by customers. The common terms for these records are General Ledger, Journal, Cash Book, Sales Book, and Accounts Receivable Ledger.[1]

These records will permit the owners to prepare a balance sheet showing the financial condition of the business, and a profit-and-loss statement showing whether the business is operating at a profit or a loss.

Government Regulations and Restrictions. Businesses are subject to numerous laws and regulations. Small firms are no exception. Therefore, it is wise to obtain legal advice on those that may affect a particular business.

Nearly all small concerns are subject to some form of governmental licensing control, the degree of regulation depending upon the type and location of the establishment. Certain businesses, such as restaurants, hotels, barbershops, and beauty shops, usually have quite detailed licensing requirements. Others, such as dry goods stores, encounter relatively few controls.

Some states impose legal restrictions on the employment of women and minors. Certain states have laws limiting the working hours of men. Another important consideration is the matter of minimum wages paid in business establishments. In addition, almost all states have workmen's compensation laws.

Taxes. The following are some of the principal types of taxes[2] the small business owner-manager must consider in planning and operating a business:

1. Income Taxes. The Federal income tax laws apply somewhat differently to corporations than to partnerships and individual proprietorships. For corporations there may be several taxes (*e.g.,* normal tax, surtax, and excess profits tax) on income before it is distributed to stockholders, and another tax on this income when it has been received by stockholders as dividends. There may also be a penalty tax on undistributed corporation income.

For a partnership or an individual proprietorship, there is no income tax levied on the business as such, but earnings are taxed at individual income tax rates, whether distributed or not, and usually at a somewhat higher rate.

Public Law 85-866, "The Technical Amendments Act of 1958," makes it possible under certain conditions for small corporations to be taxed as partnerships. This and other small-business tax benefits should be investigated by the owner-manager with the help of his tax adviser.

Employers must comply with the withholding tax law; *i.e.,* hold back a portion of the wages of each employee as an advance payment on his personal income tax.

2. Social Security Taxes. Under the Federal Social Security Act, the small businessman is required to deduct taxes from employee wages for old-age and survivors insurance and for unemployment compensation.

3. Other Federal Taxes. Manufacturers and retailers excise taxes, license fees, and occupational taxes are other principal Federal taxes. The Internal Revenue Service has complete information concerning all Federal taxes.

The principal state taxes are property, license, sales, and use taxes, unemployment compensation, and income taxes. The most important local taxes are

---

[1] See also section on Keeping Accounts.
[2] See also section on Taxes.

property, license, sales, and income. The state tax commissions and county and city officials have complete information concerning state and local taxes.

Keeping Up to Date. The small business owner-manager, if he is to operate at a profit and maintain his competitive position in his industry or trade, must keep informed of new techniques of production, merchandising, and management in his particular field. He must understand trends and developments affecting business conditions in general and his firm in particular. The successful owner is always endeavoring to improve his marketing methods and continually checking his product, pricing, and service policies to insure that they are giving as much customer satisfaction as possible.

Sources of Information. The S.B.A. issues nine classes of management and technical publications: (1) Management Aids for Small Manufacturers; (2) Technical Aids for Small Manufacturers; (3) Small Marketers Aids; (4) Aids Annuals, available from the Superintendent of Documents, Washington 25, D.C.; (5) Small Business Bulletins, which include bibliographies devoted to individual types of business; (6) Management Research Summaries; (7) Small Business Management Series, available from the Superintendent of Documents; (8) Starting and Managing Series, describing the problem of starting and operating a specific type of enterprise, available from the Superintendent of Documents; and (9) Small Business Research Series, consisting of selected, higher-level academic studies of small business management problems.

SHOULD YOU START A SMALL BUSINESS OF YOUR OWN?[1]

The information presented in the previous section makes it clear that the person who seeks to be his own boss will face many problems. He may also gain many satisfactions not found in working for others. Before risking the loss of savings and borrowed funds, however, the individual who plans to start his own business should carefully evaluate the problems he will face and his own qualifications for meeting them.

Following is a check list based on questions compiled by the Small Business Administration. Each item is designed to stimulate thoughtful consideration of important questions directly related to starting and maintaining a business.

CHECK LIST FOR STARTING YOUR OWN BUSINESS

Are You the Type? Have you rated your personal qualifications regarding initiative, attitude toward others, leadership, responsibility, organizing ability, industriousness, ability to make decisions, sincerity, perseverance, and physical energy?

Have you had some acquaintances rate you on such qualifications?

Have you carefully considered those qualities in which you are weak? Have you taken steps to improve in these areas or to find an associate whose strong points will compensate for your weaknesses?

What Business Should You Choose? In what business have you had previous experience?

In what business do you know the characteristics of the goods or services you will sell?

Do you have special technical skills, such as those needed by a pharmacist, plumber, electrician, or radio repair man, which may be used in business?

Have you studied current trends to be certain the new business you are planning is needed?

---

[1] Based on material in "Starting and Managing a Small Business of Your Own" (SBA 1.15:1) Small Business Administration (1958). Available from the Superintendent of Documents, Washington 25, D.C.

Should You Buy a Going Business? Have you considered the advantages and disadvantages of buying a going business?

Have you compared what it would take to equip and stock a new business with the price asked for the business you are considering buying?

How Much Should You Pay for It? Have you checked the owner's claims about the business with his copies of his income-tax returns?

Are the sales increased by conditions which are not likely to continue?

Is the stock a good buy? How much would have to be disposed of at a loss? How much is out of date, unsalable, or not usable?

Are the fixtures and equipment and/or the machinery modern? Or would they be unsuitable? Overvalued? In poor condition?

Are you going to buy the accounts receivable? Are you sure they are worth the asking price?

Does the present company have good will to offer? Have you been careful in your appraisal of its worth?

Would you assume the liabilities? Are the creditors willing to have you assume the debts?

Have you consulted a lawyer to be sure that the title is good?

Has your lawyer checked to see if there is any lien on record against the assets you are buying?

Are there any accumulated back taxes to be paid?

Is this a bulk sale? Has the bulk-sales law been complied with?

Why does the owner wish to sell?

What do the suppliers think of the proposition?

What Are Your Chances for Success? Are business conditions good or bad in the city and neighborhood where you are planning to locate?

Are current conditions good or bad in the line of business you are planning?

What Will Be Your Return on Investment? How much will you have to invest in your business?

What will be your net profit?

Will the net profit divided by the investment result in a rate of return which compares favorably with the rate you can obtain from other investment opportunities?

How Much Capital Will You Need? What income from sales or services can you reasonably expect in the first six months? The first year? The second year?

What is the gross profit you can expect on these volumes of business?

What expenses, including your own salary, can you forecast as being necessary?

Are the net profit and salary adequate?

Have you compared this income with what you could make as an employee?

Are you willing to risk uncertain or irregular income for the next year? Two years?

Have you made an estimate of the capital you will need to open and operate this business until income equals expenses?

Where Can You Get the Money? How much have you saved which you can put into the business immediately?

How much do you have in the form of other assets which you could, if necessary, sell or on which you could borrow to get additional funds?

Have you some place where you could borrow money to put into the business?

Have you talked to a banker? Does he think enough of your venture to lend you money?

Do you have a financial reserve available for unexpected needs?

How does the total capital, available from all sources, compare with the estimated capital requirements?

Should You Share Ownership with Others? Do you lack needed technical or management skills which can be most satisfactorily supplied by one or more partners?

Do you need the financial assistance of one or more associates?

If you do (or do not) share the ownership with associates, have you checked the features of each form of organization (individual proprietorship, partnership, corporation) to determine which will best fit your operation?

Where Should You Locate? Have you considered population, labor supply, possible income, and competitive trends in relation to selection of the city or town where you wish to locate?

In selecting the area within the city or town, have you considered where your type of business is most likely to flourish?

Are you familiar with buying power in the area, zoning ordinances, parking and transportation facilities, and natural barriers (such as hills and bridges)?

For a manufacturing plant, have you considered the condition and suitability of the building, transportation, parking facilities, and type of lease?

For a store or service establishment, have you checked on the competition, traffic flow, parking facilities, street location, physical aspects of the building, type of lease, history of the site (has the building remained vacant for any length of time and if so, why?), and the amount, speed, cost, and quality of transportation?

Are You Familiar with the Problems of Buying? In estimating your total stock, have you considered in what quantities and how often the user buys your product?

What share of the market do you think you can get?

Have you broken this total estimate down into the major lines to be carried?

What characteristics, specifications, or properties will you require in your materials or parts?

Has your stock selection been guided by an analysis of customer preference?

Have you set up a model stock assortment to follow in your buying?

Will it be cheaper to buy large quantities infrequently or small quantities frequently, weighing price differentials for large orders against capital and space tied up?

Have you decided what merchandise to buy from manufacturers? From wholesalers?

Have you planned to make your account more valuable by concentrating your buying?

Have you considered affiliating with a voluntary or cooperative group?

Have you worked out any stock-control plans to avoid overstocks, understocks, out-of-stocks?

How Will You Price Your Products and Services? Have you decided upon your price range?

What prices will you have to charge to cover your costs and obtain a profit?

How do these prices compare with prices of competitors?

Have you investigated possible legal restrictions on your establishment of prices?

What Are the Best Methods of Selling? Have you studied both direct and indirect sales promotion methods used by competitors?

Have you outlined your promotional policy?

Why do you expect customers to buy your product or service—price, quality, distinctive styling, or other factor?

Are you going to do outside selling?

Are you going to advertise in newspapers? Magazines?

Are you going to do direct-mail advertising?

Are you going to use handbills?

Are you going to use radio advertising?

Are you going to use television?

Are you going to use displays?

How Will You Select and Train Personnel? Will employees supply skills you lack?

What skills are necessary?

Have you written job descriptions for prospective employees?

Are satisfactory employees available locally?

What is the prevailing wage scale?

What do you plan to pay?

Would it be advantageous or disadvantageous to hire someone now employed by a competitor?

What labor legislation will affect you?

Have you planned your training and follow-up procedures?

What Other Management Problems Will You Face? Are you going to sell for credit?

Do you have the additional capital necessary to carry accounts receivable?

What will be your returned-goods policy?

Have you considered other policies which must be established in your business?

Have you planned how you will organize the work, including the distribution of your own time and effort?

What Records Should You Be Prepared to Keep? Have you planned a book-keeping system?

Have you planned a merchandise control system?

Have you obtained any standard operating ratios for your type of business which you plan to use as guides?

What additional records are necessary?

What system are you going to use to keep a check on costs?

Do you need any special forms or records? Can they be bought from stock? Must they be printed?

Are you going to keep records yourself? Hire a bookkeeper? Have an outsider come in periodically?

What Laws and Regulations Will Affect You? Is a license to do business necessary? State? County? City?

Have you checked the police and health regulations as they apply to your business?

Are your operations subject to interstate commerce regulations?

What Tax and Insurance Problems Will You Have? Have you worked out a system for paying the withholding tax for your employees?

Have you worked out a system for handling sales taxes? Excise taxes?

Has fire insurance been purchased? Windstorm? Use and occupancy?

Has insurance protecting against damage suits and public liability claims been purchased?

Has workmen's compensation insurance been provided?

Has burglary and hold-up insurance been considered?

What other hazards should be insured against?

Will You Keep Up to Date? How do you plan to keep up with improvements in your trade or industry?

TECHNIQUES OF MANAGEMENT

Business management consists of (1) administration, the formulation of policy; and (2) organization, putting into effect the determined policies. Normally, businesses are organized functionally; *i.e.,* into divisions each of which is concerned with a particular activity, such as marketing, production, and personnel, with a manager heading each division. The activities of the various divisions are coordinated toward common long-range objectives; they must be sufficiently flexible to obtain efficient contribution from all divisions of the organization and to permit successful adaptation to changing conditions.

This chapter examines the principles followed by successful managers.

LEADERSHIP QUALITIES

An effective leader must possess or develop certain character traits if he is to make his maximum contribution to the organization. Among these are:

Determination. Real leaders have faith in their own strength and the drive vital for success. They give subordinates the "lift" necessary to get the job done. Ability to overcome handicaps, both human and mechanical, constitutes a major part of leadership responsibilities.

Foresight. Employees see in their jobs mainly what the leader wants them to see. A true leader, therefore, gives to his staff a sense of purpose which binds them into an integrated work force.

Fidelity. Workers admire a leader who fights for their rights. Leaders must defend subordinates against injustice, yet also be loyal to the company.

Candor. A leader is direct and forthright in all dealings.

Fairness. The leader must always be fair and impartial. Work loads must be evenly distributed, and workers treated alike, without prejudice or favoritism.

Patience. Some workers must be told, shown, and instructed again and again; patience in such instances is absolutely essential.

HOW TO MAKE DECISIONS

Men are advanced to management positions only when they have the technical knowledge and ability to make sound decisions. A skilled executive displays imagination, technical knowledge, and sound judgment. Although major decisions cannot be based on an absolute formula, certain principles should always be adhered to:

1. Gather all facts before making a decision
2. Avoid undue delay in making decisions
3. Keep your doubts to yourself
4. After making a decision, follow through to see that each person carries out his assigned part of the task
5. When assigning tasks, delegate authority to carry them out

6. Base decisions on facts, not prejudices
7. Disagree with superiors if you know you are right.

HOW TO COMMUNICATE

No matter how sound his decisions, the man who fails in communication will fail as an executive. A successful leader of any activity—government, education, business—is necessarily a skilled communicator.

Order Giving (Oral Communication). An executive's success varies with the ability of his subordinates to carry out instructions. To improve the ability to communicate orders: (1) make the orders clear and understandable; (2) choose an employee who has the experience, intelligence, and ability to carry out the assignment; (3) if an order is very complicated, write it out; (4) do not over-burden subordinates; (5) avoid sarcasm, profanity, and other abuses, which are barriers to communication; and (6) be certain your orders do not conflict with previously issued orders.

Written Communication. Effective written communication is perhaps the most important factor influencing the success and growth of an organization. In many companies, writing of poor quality is losing money for management. Writing shows thinking ability. Every report, memorandum, or business letter has one primary purpose—to communicate. For clear, accurate, and complete communication, this eight-step formula should be followed:

1. Have a specific purpose in mind
2. Gather all the facts before beginning to write
3. Outline the material
4. Direct the message to a specific readership
5. Make a rough draft of the message
6. Revise and edit the rough draft
7. Rewrite the edited copy
8. When it will add meaning, illustrate the message with graphs, charts, etc.

HOW TO DELEGATE WORK

A successful leader must be able to increase the work load of employees without antagonizing them. Although there is no foolproof plan for accomplishing this, the following principles are recommended:

Maintain Incentives. A leader can most effectively increase work loads by creating new rewards for his personnel. Work inevitably grows monotonous if there is no incentive for doing better.

Develop the Right Man for the Right Job. A leader must study his personnel and determine what can and cannot be expected of each worker. Employees will assume new duties more capably if they have been intelligently trained.

Encourage Self-Improvement. Most employees have weaknesses that can be corrected. By studying employees carefully, the leader can determine how to enlarge the capacities of each.

Recognize Good Work. Average workers can be developed into people of outstanding merit, if given proper recognition. Praise them honestly.

Allow Margin for Error. Mistakes are bound to occur when employees assume new job assignments. The leader should offer only tactful, constructive criticism.

HOW TO GAIN ADMINISTRATIVE SKILLS

No blueprint for successful administrative skills is feasible; nevertheless, certain administrative responsibilities are common to all business operations:

Planning implies looking ahead, developing in advance comprehensive programs to meet all contingencies. The successful administrator analyzes his own work day, week, and month for maximum efficiency, and does the same for his staff.

Organizing implies the handling of people, money, materials, and equipment to carry out plans. Effective organizational plans take into consideration the nature of the product or service, the size of the operation, the type of activity, etc.

Directing implies actually "getting the job done," seeing that money, people, and equipment are properly utilized. Directing is the end of which planning and organizing are the means.

To improve the overall operation of an organization and enable it to meet competition more effectively, the manager must: (1) know exactly his responsibilities and long-range objectives; (2) maintain a capable staff, hiring and training people who can share capably in administrative responsibilities; (3) allot definite hours for specific work activities, while keeping the schedule flexible enough to meet unexpected eventualities; (4) have assistants screen all matters and pass on only those demanding executive attention; and (5) listen to the "grapevine"—the fastest means of communication known—in . order to squash false rumors through formal communications, such as bulletins, memoranda, etc.

HOW TO DEAL WITH PEOPLE

The leader should strive always to know his workers better. He cannot judge their potentialities without definite knowledge of them as individuals. Next to performing his own work assignment, a leader's most important duty is to prepare others for advancement. The good leader never neglects a chance to help a skilled worker advance. He must know the training and work experience of all his employees. Records of workers coming from other organizations or departments should be carefully examined. Also, the leader should know something of his employees' home life, physical condition, and personality. Three methods of acquiring such information are personnel records, on-the-job contacts, and outside contacts. Personnel records are usually available to supervisory officials. On-the-job contacts can help to build better personal understanding between worker and supervisor. Encouragement of outside activities such as extension courses, night school, athletic activities, can enhance this understanding. Knowledge of one's employees leads to increased effort and cooperation on their part; the greatest accomplishments in leadership can be obtained through congenial leader-subordinate relationships.

As important as knowing one's workers is the task of making their work meaningful to them. Many people work only for the obvious reason of making money. Their jobs become meaningful to them only if they feel their work is valuable and worthwhile. The leader, therefore, must relate the workers' daily routine to the part it plays in the final product or service—its part in "the big picture."

WHAT MAKES A GOOD SUPERVISOR

Although a good supervisor develops his own rules to meet particular situations, certain basic rules generally make for efficient operation. The good supervisor: (1) is considerate of his workers' feelings; (2) asks and accepts suggestions from subordinates and superiors alike; (3) strives to eliminate personal hostility among his workers; (4) is able to train his staff and thoroughly explain new procedures; (5) maintains efficient work flow and keeps abreast of work progress in his section; (6) has a knowledge of overall operations and of jobs unrelated to his own, to achieve successful communication between departments; (7) can take and maintain an unpopular stand, if necessary; and (8) accepts responsibility without trying to pass the buck.

Training for Supervision. The complexities of modern business and industrial management require the best and most comprehensive training possible. Such training takes various forms, among which are:

Orientation Programs. In most businesses, new employees undergo an orientation program. Such programs range from a few hours devoted to outlining the main features and objectives of the company, to weeks or months of specialized technical training.

O.J.T. Programs. Directly opposite to orientation programs are on-the-job-training programs, in which training occurs under actual working conditions. The outstanding value of on-the-job training is the confidence derived from learning "under fire."

Field Training. This technique trains employees during the course of their work. Particularly well adapted to sales-training programs, this method brings personnel together at convenient locations for training sessions.

Continuous Training. Much of the knowledge necessary to a supervisor is constantly changing. To meet the challenges of the modern business world, continuous training is imperative. Continuous training is varied, but usually originates in an orientation program, continues (perhaps) with correspondence training, and is finally supplemented by field or seasonal training. A well-planned continuous training program includes consideration of: (1) who will be trained and who will train; (2) what will be taught; (3) why it should be taught; and (4) when, where, and how the program should be organized.

CONCLUSION

Opportunities in management today are boundless. Those who want to succeed cannot justly complain "The times are against me!" To assure advancement in management:

1. Develop oral and written communication skills
2. Strive to win the confidence and trust of superiors and subordinates alike
3. Remember that genuine accomplishment results from real leadership and teamwork
4. Welcome challenging work assignments
5. Develop full potentialities by "getting the big picture," acquiring technical knowledge not only of your own job, but of the jobs around you.

BUSINESS MACHINES

The businessman should consider well the various ways in which he may attain increased efficiency, as well as economy, by the use of modern machines to save time and labor. Many routine office jobs formerly done by hand are now quickly and easily done by machines, at considerable saving in time, money, and manpower—*e.g.*, mail stamping (postage meters), document sorting (collators), envelope stuffing (inserters), pen-and-ink bookkeeping (accounting machines). Data-processing machines make it possible to assemble all the facts relating to a business, giving its management a complete, accurate, and timely picture of the company's operations and making possible skillful planning for the full utilization of men and machines. Personnel and inventory records also are economically handled by machines.

The value of a machine to any given business can be calculated by balancing the estimated depreciation of the machine plus its cost in operators and maintenance against the cost of the same operations performed by hand over a fixed period. If increased efficiency is attained without an out-of-balance increase in costs, the machine will be worth while. The purchase of elaborate equipment might be a definite liability for some businesses; in such cases, machines may be rented instead of purchased. Some operations can be done with relatively simple machines which will produce a common language by-product and this in turn can be economically processed by a service bureau, as described below. Some businesses find it advantageous to use certain data-processing equipment on their own premises and to use other more sophisticated equipment at a service bureau. The cost of equipment should therefore be carefully weighed against the size and complexity of the operations to be performed.

Some of the principal types of business machines now available, the jobs they perform, and their relative values are described below. Such machines as adding machines, cash registers, and typewriters are not included, as their usefulness has long been recognized.

STANDARD OFFICE MACHINES

Addressing Machines. Addressing machines range from simple, hand-operated stencil devices to complex machines equipped with various automatic attachments, such as daters, numerators, and selectors that will choose certain types of addresses by means of a code. In most of the simple machines, address plates (of fiber, plastic, or metal) are fed either manually or automatically into the machine, which inks the plates, presses them against the envelopes or post cards, and then disposes of the printed envelope and the used plate and receives the next. Such machines are valuable to any business that maintains a mailing list for the sending of sales letters, accounts, bills, and similar materials.

Billing Machines. Billing machines, of which there are several kinds, are basically a combination of typewriter and calculating machine. They can add, subtract, divide, and multiply, and thus permit the operator to post ledger entries along with other information, as on invoices. These save much time and labor for any business which needs to prepare monthly or periodic bills.

Bookkeeping Machines. Like billing machines, these are a combination of computer and typewriter. The operator can insert an old balance, post new transactions, and automatically obtain a new balance. The machines can also compute debit and credit balances, and accumulate and automatically print proof totals. These machines are useful for preparing inventory records, payroll records, customers' bills, etc.

Calculating Machines. These machines, which automatically add, sub-tract, multiply, and divide, are of three basic kinds:

1. The key-driven type, on which calculations are made by expert stroking of keys on a full keyboard. This type gives only end results; there is no proof of calculations

2. The rotary calculator, which may have either a full keyboard or a combination of full keyboard and 10 keys. Results and proofs appear on, and are copied from, dials; when the dials are cleared there is no proof

3. The 10-key printing calculator, which shows the proof of all calculations on paper, to be filed if desired. A trained operator can make such calculations as figuring percentages and analyzing statistical reports quickly and efficiently.

Calculating machines are valuable aids in bookkeeping and accounting. The buyer should judge them in relation to the particular calculating and accounting problems of his business.

Collating Machines. Collators are machines which assemble, staple, and stack prepared sheets for mailing or distribution. Various models range from relatively slow machines operated by hand to electrically operated ones capable of collating as many as 12,000 sheets per hour. Such machines eliminate much tedious and wasteful hand labor, as well as the mistakes to which hand collation is liable.

Communications Equipment. There are various forms of loudspeaker and interoffice telephone equipment, the need for which depends largely on the size and general layout of the office or business. On these matters the local telephone company will be glad to consult. The business which has men constantly moving about (*e.g.*, television repair men, laundry collectors) may save time and money by providing its cars with radiotelephones.

Dictating Machines. These machines record dictation electronically on wire, plastic tape, bands, or disks, from which it is transcribed by a stenographer. The recording surface may then be electronically erased and re-used. Dictating machines are of value when the volume of correspondence is large, or when time formerly spent by the stenographer in taking dictation can be used to better advantage. Further, any good typist can transcribe machine dictation, and typists command lower salaries than skilled shorthand stenographers. The machines are also valuable for the small businessman who does not employ a fulltime stenographer; letters can be dictated at any time and transcribed later by a typist. Some modern machines are so light and compact that they can be readily carried by the businessman as he travels, thus saving time by dictating on a train or plane.

If a typing pool is maintained, equipment is available by which the businessman can dial a dictating machine in the typists' room and dictate directly to it; this will reduce the number of machines required by the firm.

Duplicating Equipment. There are various devices for making multiple copies. One of the oldest and most widely used is the *Mimeograph* (stencil duplication). Letters are cut into a waxed stencil sheet (or designs may be drawn by a stylus). This stencil is then fastened to an ink-bearing cylinder and rotated over sheets of blank paper, fed in by hand or automatically. The machine can be operated by hand or electricity. Modern high-speed electric machines can make as many as 10,000 copies per hour. Mimeograph stencils

have the advantage that they can be filed and re-used several times.

Another widely used process is *offset printing*. The matter to be duplicated is placed (by typing, drawing, or photographic reproduction) on a master plate which, like a Mimeograph stencil, is fastened to a cylinder. Rollers apply ink and an ink-repellent grease to the plate as it revolves. The inked image is transferred by contact to a rubber blanket on another cylinder, and the image on this rubber sheet is transferred to sheets of paper fed into the machine. The ease with which this process reproduces typescript, printing, and illustrations makes it especially suitable for printing bill forms, personalized bank checks, etc.

Fluid duplication is another widely used method. Here the text matter is typed or drawn on a sheet of paper equipped with a special carbon which prints the text in reverse on the back of the paper. This reversed carbon, called a master sheet, is fastened to a cylinder which revolves over fed sheets of blank paper. As the cylinder revolves, the master, moistened with a chemical, transfers the image to the blank sheets. The process is quite rapid and is one of the least expensive.

Another reproduction method coming into increasing use is *photo-copying*. Several devices are marketed for producing exact reproductions—same size, reduced, or enlarged—of any kind of reproducible matter. These are useful because of the exactness of reproduction (*e.g.*, for engineering drawings, customers' statements, etc.); there is no possibility of human or mechanical error. These devices are so self-contained that no special knowledge of photography is necessary.

Another photographic reproduction method is *microfilming*. Greatly reduced images of documents are photographed on either 16- or 35-millimeter film (a page of a standard-size newspaper will make one frame on a roll of 35-millimeter film). Because of the operating speed of the camera and the small space needed to file rolls of microfilm, this process is especially useful for the preservation of inactive or semi-inactive records (*e.g.*, bank checks and statements, personnel records, etc.). The camera requires a trained operator; but the *microfilm reader,* which enlarges the documents back to readable size, can be operated by anyone.

Duplicating equipment is marketed under various trade names. Each type of device has its own advantages.

Mail-Handling Machines. There are several kinds of mail-handling machines, which perform such operations as sealing and stamping outbound, and opening inbound, envelopes. For large firms, a machine called an inserter automatically stuffs envelopes with a variety of inserts (*e.g.*, payroll checks, invoices, bills, premium notices, punch cards, sales-promotion material) and then seals and prints postage on the envelopes. These machines can handle as many as 6,000 pieces per hour, depending on the size and bulk of the material.

Postage Meters. Postage meters are machines which weigh individual pieces of mail and print the proper amount of postage (prepaid at the local post office) on the envelopes, or on gummed stickers for packages. They thus save the inconvenience and delay sometimes caused by insufficient postage, as well as the time and effort spent on weighing individual pieces of mail and applying individual postage stamps. They also save the cost of stamps damaged by humidity or careless handling, or (in some instances) lost by pilferage. Even a relatively inexperienced operator can get the mail out several times faster by postage meter than by all-manual handling.

Time Recorders. Time-recording devices promote efficiency and economy. The familiar *time clock* tends to eliminate deliberate or accidental time loss among employees and makes possible exact calculation of labor costs. It also provides accurate and verifiable data for compliance with today's increasing number of labor laws. The *job time recorder* provides accurate records for cost accounting and for wage calculations. The *time stamp* records the date and time of incoming mail, orders, etc., and thus tends to expedite the handling of the matters involved.

Typewriters, Electric. The electric typewriter offers several advantages over nonelectric machines. As the entire mechanism is electrically powered, the machine gives greater speed, at the same time reducing operator fatigue. Although the touch can be much lighter, the power applied to the keys is uniform, thus making neater typescript and more uniform copy for duplicating purposes. Electric typewriters can also make from three to four times as many clear carbon copies as nonelectric machines. Among the newest electric typewriters are machines with interchangeable type styles, which can be removed and inserted by the typist in a few seconds. One machine can thus take the place of several in work requiring a variety of type faces.

Miscellaneous Business Machines. Many other machines are available to perform a wide variety of jobs for the businessman or office. Among them are recording door-locks, indicating clocks, check or bill endorsers, folding machines, coin changers and counters, automatic files, and electronic scanners to sort or classify papers by means of code numbers in magnetic inks (as on bank checks). The nature and size of the job to be done will determine where these, and others, may be of value.

DATA-PROCESSING MACHINES

Accounting Machines. Accounting machines are designed to add, subtract, select data for printing, obtain combinations of totals, sort, classify, and perform other similar operations. The basic record is a punch card (unit record), into which information in the form of small holes in predetermined "fields" is set up on the card. Data may be entered on the card in several ways: (1) by key-driven operation; (2) by common-language devices such as perforated paper tape, by-product of other office machines, or magnetic tape; (3) by pencil marks (mark sensing); and (4) by portable hand punches. The punched cards are separated into groups by a sorting machine, and the accounting machine proper then computes and prints the results. As the punched holes constitute a permanent and unchanging record, the cards can be used and re-used in connection with other machines for the preparation of many different reports. Various models of accounting machines are available. They are of value mainly to the business that requires a fast, economical means of preparing records, reports, and analyses for efficient management control.

Adding Machines, Punched-Tape. These machines perform all the functions of standard adding machines. In addition, however, they simultaneously punch data into a paper tape (which may then be processed by a service bureau) for record and analysis.

Automatic Writing Machines. These machines "read" punched paper tape, write documents (such as purchase orders), and punch paper tape as an automatic by-product of the document-writing. The small business may find it useful to process this by-product tape in the same machine to produce reports; or it may be simpler to have the tape processed by a service bureau. Larger companies may transfer the information on the tape to tabulating cards to be processed on their own machines.

Automatic Writing-Calculating Machines. These machines perform the same functions as automatic writing machines; in addition, however, they may also handle figurework and so provide automatic preparation of invoices and similar documents that call for simultaneous calculating and typing.

Computers. Computers are electronic devices which can accept information, apply definite quantitative decisions and/or arithmetical operations to the information, and supply the result. Computers designed for processing business information may be divided into four basic types of functional units: (1) input components; (2) file-storage components; (3) central processing components; and (4) output components. Input components provide the system with a means of receiving data to be processed through such media as punched paper tape or cards, magnetic tape, magnetic ledger cards, or keyboard entry. File storage components provide the system with a means of recording volumes of "static" file data to be used by the computer in the daily processing cycle. File data such as unit cost, unit price, employee name, etc., are recorded on magnetic tape, and are on call to the system at electronic speeds (in millionths of a second). Central processing components control all machines in the system and make the decisions and calculations in processing business transactions according to a "program," or series of instructions stored in the memory. This unit is often referred to as the logic and control unit. It performs the functions of manipulation of data, such as addition, multiplication, subtraction, division, rearrangement of information, and sorting and updating of records. Here preplanned decisions are made as a result of processing the data.

An important section of the processor or computer is the "memory." This is somewhat like an electronic filing cabinet, completely indexed and instantly accessible to the computer. Here data are received from the input or file components for processing by the system. In addition, the memory holds the program which instructs the processor in each step of the procedure. Output components provide the system with a means of producing a record resulting from calculations or from updating files. The information produced may be recorded on punched paper tape, punched cards, or magnetic tape, or it may be printed in the form of a report, check, or other business record.

The science of management takes on new meaning with the ability to relegate the routine, minor decisions to the computer. Only those items that do not fit the preplanned pattern are brought to management's attention. This form of management-by-exception is becoming more and more desirable as the economy expands.

Service Bureaus. These bureaus, maintained by most manufacturers in the larger cities, provide vital services to management by enabling it to:

1. Determine the business, accounting, and computer functions that can and should be performed by automatic data-processing methods

2. Sharply reduce operating costs while dispensing with clerical error

3. Make time available for planning through reducing clerical and administrative burdens

4. Discover opportunities for development of new techniques by using modern mathematical and computer methods

5. Obtain the full benefits of automation without the need to select, purchase, install, and implement on-premises processing systems

6. Automate specific functions which in themselves do not warrant the establishment of an on-premises processing installation

7. Obtain data-processing facilities and technical support to expedite the smooth conversion from manual to automatic procedures

8. Supplement on-premises processing capacity during peak periods

9. Provide trained office personnel on a "task force" basis to supplement the force on the premises.

By using automatic writing, automatic writing-calculating, and punched-tape adding machines, the small business can bypass the need for expensive tabulating equipment but still obtain the advantages of such equipment. The businessman simply sends the punched tape which the machines produce as an automatic by-product to the service bureau, which does the processing job and furnishes detailed accounting records and reports at nominal charge.

As a business grows in size and volume of work, more and larger machines can be employed to greater advantage. The recent rapid growth of electronic business machinery offers, and will increasingly offer, considerable advantages. The individual businessman should, however, consider fully his own needs, and how machines can serve him, before investing. Many large business-machine companies employ special representatives who will make a survey of a firm's requirements and give advice on the type of machines most likely to be useful. They will also advise whether it would be better to purchase or rent such equipment.

CARE AND MAINTENANCE

Because machines represent a definite financial investment, and because their continued operation is needed for efficiency, proper care and maintenance have a definite cash value. Broadly speaking, maintenance costs less than repairs; and, in turn, replacement of aging machines costs less than continued repairs and maintenance.

Each operator should be carefully instructed in the operation and care of his machine. For many of the more complex machines, detailed manuals are provided, or the supplying company will provide necessary training for the operators. In any office, regardless of size, it is wise to have a stand-by operator trained to take over in case of absence or emergency. Further, the office supervisor should have enough knowledge of the machines to be able to train emergency help if necessary. Generally, no machine much more complex than a typewriter or a billing machine should be operated, however briefly, by anyone not specifically trained for its operation.

Typewriters and similar machines with open, moving parts should be kept covered when not in use. Type-cleaning, ribbon-changing, and carriage-oiling are relatively simple and can be done by any trained operator. Any more extensive oiling and *all* repairs should be left to the repairman; amateur tinkering can prove to be not only inefficient but expensive. There is one exception to this rule: Almost every machine is capable of some eccentricities, foreseeable by the manufacturer (*e.g.*, a duplicating machine which may print unevenly or crinkle the paper). These possible flaws in operation, and the means for correcting them, are usually covered in some detail in the manual. But note that *anything not covered in the manual* still calls for the experienced repair or maintenance man.

Many manufacturers, or their sales agencies, provide maintenance service on a monthly or annual contract basis, with specific rates for individual service calls. It is also possible in most cities to arrange for similar contractual or semi-contractual service with local repair and service agencies.

It is also wise to keep a detailed record on each machine, showing its initial cost and the amounts spent over its useful life on maintenance and repairs. This will provide a safe and economical way of determining when to replace worn-out or obsolescent machines.

OFFICE PLANNING AND FURNISHING[1]

The automated, mechanized modern age of business and industry has fostered a need for the services of interior architects and designers to solve the new and numerous complexities involved in office planning. Elements such as air conditioning, acoustics, lighting, telephone intercommunication, television, pneumatic tubes, and conveyor belts all play a part in an ever-growing awareness of the importance of an efficient office; they are tools which, by their very nature, are handled best by the specialist in office planning.

Office Planning. The methods and procedures used by the office planner involve determination of: (1) the space requirements of each individual in the organization; (2) the relationship of individuals to one another in terms of work flow, amount of traffic, supervision, etc.; (3) the requirements for such facilities as reception rooms, board rooms, pantries, interview rooms, and conference rooms; and (4) expansion requirements anticipated for the space as a whole. In addition to the functional requirements, the factor of prestige frequently is involved, particularly where individuals are in contact with outside clientele and where the factor of corporate identity must be established.

With this information determined, the specialist proceeds with the develop-

---

[1] Prepared by G. Luss, vice president and director of design, Designs for Business, Inc.

ment of plans indicating these relationships. At this stage he brings into play certain basic tenets of space planning, such as (1) determination of size and character of reception rooms, which—as the first "face" of the organization to its public—set the tenor for the entire organization; (2) relationship of departments to this reception room in terms of traffic; (3) determination of circulation systems permitting access to departments without walking through other departments; and (4) integration of file requirements, storage needs, coat and clothes closet facilities.

Based on a preliminary plan in which all required functions are integrated, the construction or engineering drawings are then initiated, including the following items:

1. Design of lighting on an individual area basis. For example, the general illumination level of 50 to 60 foot-candles for general office work must be raised to 85 to 125 foot-candles for close work such as drafting. Corridors, however, suffice with 8 to 10 foot-candles, and reception rooms are adequately lighted on a 20 to 25 foot-candle level. Conference rooms may require lighting that graduates from zero foot-candles for projection-room facilities to 50 to 60 foot-candles for reading reports or studying data. Dimmer equipment is often supplied for this type of usage. Fluorescent lighting having a warm quality complementing the human skin is customarily used for general work areas, while a less commercial type such as recessed incandescent lighting is preferable for reception and conference rooms

2. Integration of interoffice communication and telephone systems, and study of other types of data-processing and automation devices for the movement of papers and materials

3. Integration of heating and air conditioning to provide the proper temperatures, again on an individual area basis. For example, a conference room may be normally used for eight to ten persons, but on occasion will require facilities for 10 to 20 persons; therefore, air conditioning must be adjustable. Smoke control is also advisable for areas of large personnel concentration. Electronic data-processing rooms may require additional air conditioning to offset the added radiation in such areas. See also Air Conditioning in Home and Office

4. Integration of acoustical control. For example, an executive office is normally adequately controlled by carpets and draperies common to the decoration of such areas; therefore, plaster ceilings frequently are used to avoid the commercial effect of acoustical tile ceiling. However, electronic data-processing rooms, having a high decibel level, may require additional sound absorbing mediums on walls and floors. The installation of commercial-grade carpeting is often used for additional sound absorption. The noise level has been proven by extensive testing to be a prime factor in human fatigue and thus is a vital factor in planning office efficiency

5. Planning and integrating partitions and partitioning systems for efficient division of space. Partitions should be movable according to the degree of flexibility required by the current operation and anticipated future changes. The work flow and departmental relationships influence the arrangement of partitions. For ideal flexibility, partitions are established everywhere on the same predetermined module so that they can be both movable and interchangeable. The module is determined by the space utilization that best suits the tenant's needs, keeping in mind the modules of standard materials on the market. Partition panel inserts are designed or selected in a variety of materials to serve various functions. Woods, clear and translucent glass, cork, and metals are used. Finishes vary, too, and these should be guided by function, aesthetics, and maintenance. For example, clear glass has proved valuable for creating small

private offices that give the illusion of greater size. For personnel who require a degree of privacy, this is a satisfactory solution. Translucent glass, through which light diffuses, can bring an outside, windowed feeling to interior space, thereby both upgrading and efficiently utilizing such areas. Woods are generally reserved for executive offices and areas. Cork is a useful provision for pin-up materials, enabling walls to be used as utility elements as well as dividers. Metals, too, may accommodate wall shelves, cabinets, etc., and may be finished to order to achieve a more aesthetic appearance

6. Integration of electrical outlets to provide easy and efficient access. These should be properly related to furniture placement and should be planned in anticipation of all possible requirements within the area

7. Planning of employee facilities such as water fountains, rest rooms, and lunch rooms. Lunch rooms especially have been the subject of concentrated study, particularly in urban areas where the office building boom has created a disproportionate shortage of restaurant facilities. In this respect, vending machines for soups, desserts, coffee, candy, etc., have seen increasing use in the well-planned company lunch room.

Furniture, Furnishings, and Decoration. While the preliminary plans are being prepared, the interior designer determines the furniture, furnishings, and equipment necessary to each area. In essence, of course, the final plan is a result of these functional needs. Therefore, at the time of approval of the preliminary plans, the construction and engineering plans and the program for furniture, furnishings, and decoration are also instituted.

In most cases, the tenant has many items of furniture and furnishings which can be reused. These are all measured and their condition reported at the time the requirements are first surveyed. Thus it is usually possible to reallocate or reassign furniture, permitting new expenditures to be made to the greatest advantage.

Another factor is the possibility of reducing the space required for the individual or department by use of more efficient furniture or equipment requiring less space. This often provides even greater utility, and the saving over the term of the lease may more than offset the cost of the new furniture or equipment.

Factors involved in setting up the new program of furniture, furnishings, and decoration are the following:

1. Furniture should require as little maintenance as possible; therefore, contemporary materials such as plastics, metals, oil-finished woods, composition flooring, and stain-resistant fabrics are desirable

2. Furniture should be designed and placed in such a way as to eliminate moving of pieces in order to clean floors

3. Chairs, where possible, should have a design feature which avoids scarring or scuffing of walls at back height

4. Desk surfaces in areas of heavy clerical or paper work should have minimum color contrast, to reduce eye fatigue

5. Wall surfaces, where economically feasible, should utilize permanent plastic coverings, eliminating the need for repainting

6. Telephones should be placed with regard to the hand used by the office or desk occupant; for example, a right-handed person needs the telephone on the left to leave the right hand free for writing, and *vice versa* for the left-handed person

7. Suitable storage facilities for an individual's work should be provided, as a major contribution to order and cleanliness

8. Varied types of desk design can enhance the appearance of any office. For example, a small office benefits greatly through use of the open type of

table desk instead of the closed box type, which tends to reduce the apparent size of the room. Where open desks are used, drawer storage is provided in an adjacent unit to the side or rear of the occupant. This serves also as additional work surface

9. Auxiliary seating facilities in executive offices may be of a type to permit meetings in a more informal area than that of the desk and its immediate vicinity

10. Color should be chosen on an individual area basis. For example, offices with cool northern exposures benefit from the use of warm colors such as yellow, red, brown, and orange. Southern exposures benefit from cooler colors such as green and blue. Bright, sparkling colors often enhance large general areas normally outfitted with gray steel desks; however, the same colors used in a small office will tend to have an oppressive effect. Lighter colors are usually best for small offices, since they tend to expand the apparent size of the room

11. Draperies are often thought of merely as decorative treatment for the executive office. On the contrary, however, they are important in areas needing acoustical control, since they are an effective sound-absorbing medium. Draperies should be selected with maintenance in mind, utilizing colors that will resist fading.

AIR CONDITIONING IN HOME AND OFFICE

Perhaps no single development since the end of World War II has had a greater impact on America's living and working habits—at home, in the office, the store, and the industrial plant—than has air conditioning. While in 1946 air conditioning was confined for the most part to motion-picture houses and some of the larger department stores, by 1960 it was estimated that nearly 10,000,000 United States homes had some sort of air conditioning—more than a million of them cooled by central units. Commercially, the nonair-conditioned store, shop, or office was the exception. Americans today demand air conditioning, and, entirely aside from the comfort factor, stores, shops, offices, and factories note that the increased efficiency of workers more than offsets its cost.

As an example, the United States government made a closely controlled study of two groups of workers doing identical work in identical surroundings, one group working in air-conditioned comfort and the other without this advantage. The air-conditioned group performed more than 9 per cent more efficiently than did the other. Factories, stores, and nongovernment offices, too, have found that this increased efficiency pays off. A survey of 75 industrial plants in the New York area showed that the average plant without air conditioning lost the equivalent of $108 in wages for each employee in one year because of hot-weather shutdowns.

Many industries, and the products they make, would not have come into being without a means for controlling temperature and humidity conditions. The electronics industry, for instance, produces many microscopic parts in which close tolerances are essential. Temperature and humidity must be closely controlled not only in the manufacture of these parts but in the operation of the machines of which they become a part. Much of today's quality printing would be virtually impossible if produced in nonair-conditioned plants; and many synthetic fibers —and some drugs—could not be produced in noncontrolled surroundings.

The health benefits of air conditioning, both to hospitalized patients and in the general maintenance of health in the home, have been pinpointed by observations of medical authorities as well as in studies of families living in air-conditioned homes.

Safeguarding of the healthy heart from undue overwork in hot, humid weather, as well as the weakened hearts of cardiac patients from dangerous overstrain, is but one of the contributions air conditioning makes to the nation's health. Another is the relief of sufferers from air-borne allergens—generally termed hay fever. Air conditioning already has provided relief for thousands of hay-fever sufferers, and within ten years the allergy will be virtually unknown except to those whose activities keep them outside in pollen-laden summer air. Medical tests have shown that air conditioning can reduce the pollen count in a test room by 98 per cent.

Studies of the health and other benefits of air conditioning in the home have resulted in equally positive results. In Austin Village, Tex., the National Association of Home Builders studied 22 families living in centrally air-conditioned homes, and compared them with a control group of 22 families with similar backgrounds, but without air conditioning. Those in the former group got an average of 8.1 hours' sleep per night during the summer months, compared with 6.9 hours for those without air conditioning. Children in air-conditioned homes slept 9.5 hours and napped 1.5 hours, whereas children in the other group slept 8.9 hours and napped an average of half an hour. In Levittown, Pa., a similar study was made. Though in a cooler area than that of the Texas survey, results were similar.

Air conditioning has been defined as "the process by which simultaneously the temperature, moisture content, movement, and quality of air in enclosed spaces intended for human occupancy may be maintained within required limits." On the basis of recent developments, this might be amended to read ". . . spaces intended for human occupancy or for certain industrial processes . . ." This definition covers both the cooling and heating aspects of air conditioning, as found in a year-round installation. Much of the foregoing deals primarily with the cooling function of air conditioning, but there are many varieties and types of air conditioners. They may be placed in three major categories: (1) room air conditioners; (2) unitary air conditioners; and (3) systems.

Room air conditioners, or window units, are used in homes and in some office buildings, hotels, apartments, etc., particularly those built before 1950. Most newer office buildings, hotels, and apartments have central installations. Room air conditioners may be constructed to aid in the heating function.

Unitary air conditioners are factory-assembled units—either self-contained or functioning in two separate but matched assemblies. Usually such separate assemblies, called "split systems," have the cooling coil indoors and the condensing assembly outside, where the heat taken from the conditioned space is dissipated. This type of unit, used for central residential air conditioning and certain commercial and industrial applications, also may be constructed for use as a heat pump, warming in winter and cooling in summer.

"Systems" are large, field-erected installations used in big buildings, factories, etc.; these, too, may be engineered to produce cooling in summer and heating in winter. In fact, some are installed so that heat may be removed from the interior rooms of a building and "pumped" to the exterior rooms, where additional heat is needed, in winter weather.

Installation of both unitary equipment (most of which distributes heat and cooling through ducts) and systems requires the services of an engineer to determine the heat load and other factors, and to assure proper installation. It is not a do-it-yourself job.

While window units may be installed by the layman, usually it is best to call in experts to make the installation. Certainly this becomes necessary in the installation of "through-the-wall" units, which utilize a sleeve through the building wall rather than being set in a window. Prior to installation, the purchaser should determine the capacity (in terms of British thermal units, or B.T.U.'s) of the unit he requires.

COMFORT CHART FOR STILL AIR

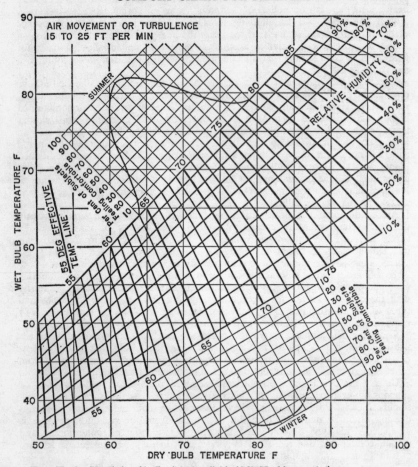

From Heating Ventilating Air Conditioning Guide 1960. Used by permission.

Both summer and winter comfort lines apply to inhabitants of the United States only. Application of winter comfort line is further limited to rooms heated by central systems of the convection type. The line does not apply to rooms heated by radiant methods. Application of summer comfort line is limited to homes, offices, and the like, where the occupants become fully adapted to the artificial air conditions. The line does not apply to theaters, department stores, and the like where the exposure is less than three hours. The summer comfort line shown pertains to Pittsburgh and to other cities in the northern portion of the United States and southern Canada, and at elevations not in excess of 1,000 ft. above sea level. Dotted portion of winter comfort line was extrapolated beyond test data

The calculation of heating and air-conditioning requirements takes into consideration the orientation of the building, glass, wall, and roof areas and their construction, as well as insulation, shading, ventilation, and internal loads such as people, lights, and equipment. Generally, the engineer or contractor has forms available to make these calculations.

Any product is judged by its workmanship and performance. The "product" here is properly installed equipment of proper size. Heating is usually somewhat oversized, in the expectation that there may be days colder than the "design temperature." To a degree, this is true of summer air conditioning, but, because of its nature, a principal concern is to maintain a reasonable level of humidity as well as cooling. This means that the capacity of an air conditioner should not exceed the requirements for the space it is intended to cool. If the equipment has too much capacity, it will cool the space quickly, then automatically cut off. When the unit is not operating, humidity is building up, and this contributes as much to discomfort as does the temperature. During hot, humid weather, it is desirable that the unit operate almost continuously, rather than cutting on and off too frequently.

When installation of a unitary air conditioner is contemplated, a prospective purchaser should obtain proposals from a number of contractors. It is likely that they will show conflicting requirements. To compare properly, one should have on hand the proposal, brochures covering the equipment proposed, and the standard ratings of the proposed units. Even though the units may not be operated at standard rating conditions, their capacity has a common basis for comparison. Proposals should include changes in existing ductwork, or, if new ducts are to be installed, how they will be installed; electrical additions including type of disconnect switch and size of wire; changes in existing outlets, or what new outlets will be needed; type of insulation to be applied to ductwork running through unconditioned space, and other factors.

Each installation is an individual problem. Purchasers must judge the installation by its workmanship and efficiency. It should be pointed out that the comfort expected should be discussed with the designer and be fully understood before proceeding with the design. It also should be pointed out that the unit controls should be set at the conditions desired and equipment should be permitted to operate at that setting continuously without toying with the controller, or the proper effect cannot be achieved.

Maintenance of a system is a matter of individual concern. Several room air conditioners, naturally, will require more attention than an equivalent unitary installation. In any event, filters must be kept clean; depending on the application, these will need attention only at two-month intervals at most. Any unit should be inspected at least once a year and coils and drain pans brushed off. In systems using a cooling tower, most contractors probably will suggest that condenser water be softened with a water softener and will recommend how frequently the sump should be cleaned.

With proper attention and periodic servicing, an installation should give many years of trouble-free service. It is next to impossible to estimate maintenance costs, since the use and treatment of air conditioners varies with each user. Even homes next door to one another may vary as much as 50 per cent in maintenance and operational costs. As already pointed out, however, properly serviced equipment should give good service without extra costs for replacement of abused parts.

FIRST AID IN THE OFFICE

Wherever there are people, there is need for a first-aid kit. Suggested contents and management are outlined here.

The legal requirements for kits, their contents, and their maintenance vary according to state, city, or other governmental regulations. Usually the departments of health or labor prescribe the requirements according to the type or size of an organization or the number of employees.

Practical requirements vary according to several conditions. It must be remembered, however, that first aid is a temporary expedient and, except for very minor injuries, represents merely the care prior to professional treatment.

An establishment close to a hospital requires only the simplest supplies. The distance to professional care might increase the complexity of a kit to some extent. The capability of the person or persons in charge of first aid; environmental conditions such as dust or splintery woodwork, and local experience with certain recurring injuries also may influence the choice of contents of the first-aid kit.

The container should be clearly identified and should be dust- and moisture-proof. It should be kept in a regular place but be portable so that it can be taken to the scene of an accident if necessary.

Responsibility for maintaining the kit in a ready condition should be established, and the responsible person should have authority to purchase or obtain replacements of supplies as needed.

Contents. The most common item is the adhesive compress or prepared bandage. A supply of individually packaged sterile gauze pads of various sizes ($3'' \times 3''$, $4'' \times 4''$) is required for both wounds and burns. The inclusion of larger gauze pads and sanitary napkins will depend on office policy; the latter are excellent for large, freely bleeding wounds, as well as burns. Sterile pads specially shaped for eye injuries may be included.

Bandages are used to hold dressings in place. Adhesive tape is a bandage; others are rolls in varying width and triangular bandages of unbleached muslin. While both roll and triangular bandages are readily improvised, it is wise to have them available.

A pair of scissors should be included. The bandage type is best, but any blunt-nosed, sharp pair will do. A single-edged razor blade is also handy.

Tweezers or forceps should be provided for removal of small foreign bodies. A magnifying glass may be useful in this operation.

At least one and preferably several good-quality woolen blankets should be on hand. These may be stored in plastic bags for protection against moths and dust. Blankets are useful in cases of shock, in handling of patients, and as splints in some cases. Other splints may be stocked if materials for improvising them are absent. Excellent splints of cardboard, packaged for convenient storage, are easily available.

Absorbent cotton also is useful for padding splints.

A flashlight and a fresh supply of batteries may prove indispensable.

Some items should be included in the kit only after discussion with a physician; these might include ointments for minor burns, oils for the eyes, and analgesics such as aspirin. While some of these are commonly used without prescription, no layman should recommend or prescribe their use. Office policy may permit their inclusion for persons who desire to use them on their own responsibility, but they should never be administered by the first aider.

Antiseptics are in a similar category. An injury serious enough to require a physician should be cleaned and treated only by him; the application of an antiseptic prior to such treatment may actually complicate it. Should an antiseptic be desired, however, a physician should suggest which one to include, as such preparations vary in strength, effectiveness, stability, and applicability.

Last but not least in the contents of the kit should be a current first-aid textbook,[1] whose contents are understood by several of the office or plant force.

---

[1] For example, the "First Aid Textbook," published by the American National Red Cross (1957).

COMMERCIAL ARITHMETIC

ROMAN NUMBERS

The Roman system of writing numbers employs the following seven letters:

I V X L C D M
1 5 10 50 100 500 1000

Here are a few simple guides for reading and writing Roman numbers.

Repeating a letter repeats its value. Thus, X=10; XX=20.

The value of a smaller letter written after a larger one is added to the larger value. Thus, X=10; XV=15.

The value of a smaller letter written before a larger one is subtracted from the larger one. Thus, X=10; IX=9.

A horizontal bar placed above a letter increases its value a thousand times. Thus, CX=110; $\overline{CX}$=110,000.

Fractions cannot be written in the Roman system. The value of the Roman system today is chiefly decorative, and its use is largely confined to ornamental numbering, as on cornerstones, clock faces, title pages and chapter headings in books, and certain semiornamental documents such as scrolls and diplomas.

Two conventional uses of lower-case Roman numerals (i, v, x, l, c; d and m almost never appear in these uses) should be noted. They are frequently used in conjunction with upper-case Roman and Arabic numerals to distinguish numbers of play-scenes from act and line numbers, *e.g.*, Act II, scene ii, line 2. They are also used to mark off pages of front-matter (prefaces, introductions) and back-matter (appendixes, indexes) in books and some magazines.

ARABIC NUMBERS

The Arabic system uses ten figures and a decimal point, as follows:

0, 1, 2, 3, 4, 5, 6, 7, 8, 9, and .

With these any number can be written.

HOW TO READ NUMBERS

6	3	7	4	9	8	5	2	3	1	4	0	6
Trillions	Hundred-billions	Ten-billions	Billions	Hundred-millions	Ten-millions	Millions	Hundred-thousands	Ten-thousands	Thousands	Hundreds	Tens	Units

The number is read, "Six trillion, three hundred seventy-four billion, nine hundred eighty-five million, two hundred thirty-one thousand, four hundred six."

In the United States, Canada, and France a billion is a thousand millions (1,000,000,000). In England and Germany a billion is a million millions (1,000,-000,000,000).

ADDITION

There are 45 combinations possible with our primary numbers, that is, the numbers from 1 to 10. The first step toward quick and accurate addition is to memorize them perfectly.

```
1 1 1 1   1   1   1   1   1
1 2 3 4   5   6   7   8   9
2 3 4 5   6   7   8   9  10
  2 2 2   2   2   2   2   2
  2 3 4   5   6   7   8   9
  4 5 6   7   8   9  10  11
    3 3   3   3   3   3   3
    3 4   5   6   7   8   9
    6 7   8   9  10  11  12
      4   4   4   4   4   4
      4   5   6   7   8   9
      8   9  10  11  12  13
          5   5   5   5   5
          5   6   7   8   9
         10  11  12  13  14
              6   6   6   6
              6   7   8   9
             12  13  14  15
                  7   7   7
                  7   8   9
                 14  15  16
                      8   8
                      8   9
                     16  17
                          9
                          9
                         18
```

Column Addition. In adding a column of figures, do not say 5 plus 6 is 11 plus 0, plus 3 is 14, etc., but simply state the result of each addition, as 11—14—23—25. It is preferable to put down the sum of each column instead of carrying from one column to another, since this method makes the correction of errors easier. In checking, begin at the left column. (Write your answers first on a sheet of scratch paper; place only the checked total result at the foot of the column.)

```
        8972
        9869
        4523
        6750
        8976
        7865
       ─────
       46955

         25   42
         33   46
         46   33
         42   25
       ─────  ─────
       46955  46955
```

Bankers' or Civil Service Addition. In adding each column the number to be carried is added into the next sum. Like column addition, of which this is a variation, this can be interrupted, and yet the one who is doing the adding can take it up at the point where he left off without having to go back to the beginning.

$$\begin{array}{r} 2679.50 \\ 188.75 \\ 2.38 \\ 5463.44 \\ 234.25 \\ \hline 22 \\ 23 \\ 28 \\ 26 \\ 15 \\ 8 \\ \hline 8568.32 \end{array}$$

Horizontal Addition. Numbers written horizontally, as in invoices, need not be rewritten in vertical columns before they are added, but it is important to be sure that the units added together are of the same order. For example:

$$654+345+13+22+1704=2738$$

SUBTRACTION

Subtraction by Addition. Instead of subtracting, add to the subtrahend the number needed to equal the corresponding number in the minuend. In the example below, 4 plus 7 equal 11. Carry 1 and 6 plus 6 equals 12, and so on through the rest of the figures. This is a good way to check a subtraction.

$$\begin{array}{r} 5\ 4\ 3\ 8\ 2\ 1 \quad \text{minuend} \\ 2\ 9\ 6\ 5\ 7 \quad \text{subtrahend} \\ \hline 5\ 1\ 4\ 1\ 6\ 4 \quad \text{answer} \end{array}$$

Subtraction and Addition Together. If a column consists of certain numbers to be added and others to be subtracted, you may find it easier to add all the negative numbers in one column and all the positive numbers in another column and then subtract to find the difference between the two.

$$\begin{array}{r} 5\ 7\ 8\ 2 \\ -4\ \ 5\ 6 \\ 4\ 4\ 1\ 4 \\ -7\ 2\ 3\ 1 \\ 1\ 5 \\ \hline 2\ 5\ 2\ 4 \end{array}$$

DIVISION

All even numbers are divisible by 2.

A number is divisible by 3 if the sum of its digits is divisible by 3. For example, 3,882. 3+8+8+2=21. Therefore 3,882 is divisible by 3.

A number is divisible by 4 if it ends in two ciphers or in two figures which are divisible by 4. For example, 8,724 is divisible by 4 but 9,862 is not, though 6+2=8 is divisible by 4.

A number ending in 0 or 5 is divisible by 5.

An even number is divisible by 6 if the sum of its digits is divisible by 3. For example, 5,424. 5+4+2+4=15. Therefore, 5,424 is divisible by 6.

7, 11, or 13 will divide 1,001 or any of its multiples, as 2,002, 6,006, 12,012, etc.

A number is divisible by 8 if it ends in three ciphers or in three digits forming a number divisible by 8, as 154,000 or 543,816.

A number is divisible by 9 if the sum of its digits is divisible by 9. For example, 2,592. 2+5+9+2=18. Therefore, 2,592 is divisible by 9.

A number ending in 0 is divisible by 10.

A number ending in 00, 50, or 75 is divisible by 25.

A number ending in 000 is divisible by 125.

A *factor* of a given number is a number by which the given number is exactly divisible. For example, 4 is a factor of 16, 3 of 27, etc. The factor of a number is also a factor of all multiples of that number. Thus, 3 is a factor of 9. It is, therefore, a factor also of 18, 27, 36, 45, etc.

MULTIPLICATION

The *multiplicand* is the number to be multiplied. The *multiplier* is, of course, the number by which it is to be multiplied.

To multiply by 10, 100, etc., add as many ciphers to the multiplicand as there are in the multiplier.

To multiply by 5, 50, 500, etc., add as many ciphers to the multiplicand as there are figures in the multiplier and divide the result by 2.

To multiply by 25, 250, etc., multiply by 100, 1,000, etc., and divide the result by 4.

To multiply by any number ending in 9, multiply by the next higher number and then subtract the multiplicand.

Example. Multiply 26×49: 26×50=1,300–26=1,274.

To multiply any number of two figures by 11, write the sum of the two figures between them.

Example. Multiply 54×11. 5+4=9. Hence 594 is the answer.

If the sum of the two numbers is 10 or over add the 1 to the left-hand figure. Thus, multiply 88×11. 8+8=16. Hence, 968 is the answer.

To square any number of 9's. Beginning at the left, write 9 as many times less 1 as there are 9's in the given number, an 8, as many ciphers as 9's less 1, and 1.

Example. The square of 99=9,801, of 999=998,001.

To multiply by 1¼, add 0 and divide by 8.

To multiply by 1⅔, add 0 and divide by 6.

To multiply by 2½, add 0 and divide by 4.

To multiply by 3⅓, add 0 and divide by 3.

To multiply by 5, add 0 and divide by 2.

To multiply by 6¼, add 00 and divide by 16.

To multiply by 8⅓, add 00 and divide by 12.

To multiply by 12½, add 00 and divide by 8.

To multiply by 16⅔, add 00 and divide by 6.

To multiply by 25, add 00 and divide by 4.

To multiply by 33⅓, add 00 and divide by 3.

To multiply by 50, add 00 and divide by 2.

To multiply by 66⅔, add 000 and divide by 15.

To multiply by 83⅓, add 000 and divide by 12.

To multiply by 125, add 000 and divide by 8.

To multiply by 166⅔, add 000 and divide by 6.

To multiply by 250, add 000 and divide by 4.

To multiply by 333⅓, add 000 and divide by 3.
To multiply by 7½, add 0 and subtract ¼ of that result.
To multiply by 11¼, add 0 and then add ⅛ of that result.
To multiply by 13⅓, add 0 and then add ⅓ of that result.
To multiply by 75, add 00, divide by 4, and multiply the result by 3.

Handy Multiplication and Division Tables

Most people find it convenient to know the multiplication tables by heart through 12×12. The pyramid shown below gives the tables in handy form through 25×25. The number in heavy type at the left is the multiplicand, the number just below the line is the multiplier, and the number just below

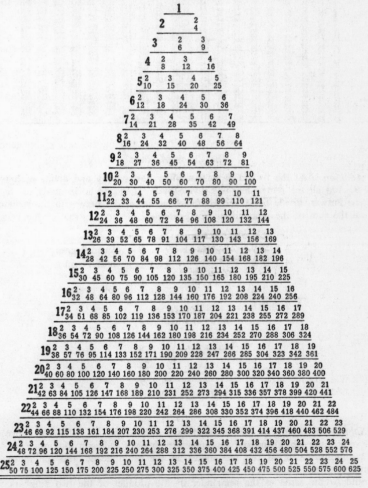

Handy Multiplication and Division Table

the multiplier is the result. For instance, 2×2=4; 3×2=6; 3×3=9; and so on through 25×25=625. Every multiplication table is also, of course, a division table, if it is read backward. To find how many times the number in heavy type at the left will go into a given number, find the number on the lower line and read the number just above it. Thus, to find how many times 24 is contained in 408, find the heavy-type 24, run along the line until you reach 408, then read the number just above it, 17.

Here is another table, much like the pyramid table, except that the arrangement is slightly different. The one to use is the one you find easier to read.

1	2	3	4	5	6	7	8	9	10
2	4	6	8	10	12	14	16	18	20
3	6	9	12	15	18	21	24	27	30
4	8	12	16	20	24	28	32	36	40
5	10	15	20	25	30	35	40	45	50
6	12	18	24	30	36	42	48	54	60
7	14	21	28	35	42	49	56	63	70
8	16	24	32	40	48	56	64	72	80
9	18	27	36	45	54	63	72	81	90
10	20	30	40	50	60	70	80	90	100
11	22	33	44	55	66	77	88	99	110
12	24	36	48	60	72	84	96	108	120
13	26	39	52	65	78	91	104	117	130
14	28	42	56	70	84	98	112	126	140
15	30	45	60	75	90	105	120	135	150
16	32	48	64	80	96	112	128	144	160
17	34	51	68	85	102	119	136	153	170
18	36	54	72	90	108	126	144	162	180
19	38	57	76	95	114	133	152	171	190
20	40	60	80	100	120	140	160	180	200
21	42	63	84	105	126	147	168	189	210
22	44	66	88	110	132	154	176	198	220
23	46	69	92	115	138	161	184	207	230
24	48	72	96	120	144	168	192	216	240
25	50	75	100	125	150	175	200	225	250
26	52	78	104	130	156	182	208	234	260

1	2	3	4	5	6	7	8	9	10
27	54	81	108	135	162	189	216	243	270
28	56	84	112	140	168	196	224	252	280
29	58	87	116	145	174	203	232	261	290
30	60	90	120	150	180	210	240	270	300
31	62	93	124	155	186	217	248	279	310
32	64	96	128	160	192	224	256	288	320
33	66	99	132	165	198	231	264	297	330
34	68	102	136	170	204	238	272	306	340
35	70	105	140	175	210	245	280	315	350
36	72	108	144	180	216	252	288	324	360
37	74	111	148	185	222	259	296	333	370
38	76	114	152	190	228	266	304	342	380
39	78	117	156	195	234	273	312	351	390
40	80	120	160	200	240	280	320	360	400
41	82	123	164	205	246	287	328	369	410
42	84	126	168	210	252	294	336	378	420
43	86	129	172	215	258	301	344	387	430
44	88	132	176	220	264	308	352	396	440
45	90	135	180	225	270	315	360	405	450
46	92	138	184	230	276	322	368	414	460
47	94	141	188	235	282	329	376	423	470
48	96	144	192	240	288	336	384	432	480
49	98	147	196	245	294	343	392	441	490
50	100	150	200	250	300	350	400	450	500

The Check of Nines

Addition. Add the figures in each number horizontally and divide each result by 9. Add all the remainders and divide by 9. Then add horizontally the figures in the answer, divide by 9, and compare the remainder here with the remainder from the sum of the remainders. For example:

$$\begin{array}{r} 2\ 6\ 8\ 1 \\ 4\ 7\ 5\ 2 \\ 8\ 3\ 3\ 9 \\ 3\ 6\ 2\ 6 \\ \hline 1\ 9\ 3\ 9\ 8 \end{array}$$

Remainders

$\dfrac{2+6+8+1=17}{9}$ 8 (Since 9 goes into 17 only once with 8 left over)

$\dfrac{4+7+5+2=18}{9}$ 0

$\dfrac{8+3+3+9=23}{9}$ 5

$\dfrac{3+6+2+6=17}{9}$ 8

$\dfrac{21=3}{9}$

$\dfrac{1+9+3+9+8=30=3}{9}$

Subtraction. Think of the minuend (see *Subtraction by Addition,* above) as the sum of the subtrahend and the remainder, and proceed as in addition.

Multiplication. Find the remainders in the multiplicand and the multiplier. Multiply these remainders and then find the remainder of the product. This should be the same as the remainder of the product of the two numbers. For example:

$$
\begin{array}{lll}
7\ 6\ 4 & 7+6+4=17 & 8 \\
\underline{3\ 5} & \overline{9} & \\
\overline{2\ 6\ 7\ 4\ 0} & 3+5=8 & 8 \\
& \overline{9} & \overline{64=1} \\
& & 9 \\
& 2+6+7+4+0=19=1 & \\
& \overline{9} &
\end{array}
$$

Division. Think of the dividend as the product of the quotient and the divisor, and proceed as in multiplication.

Fractions

A fraction is a part of a unit.

There are two ways of writing fractions: $\frac{1}{2}$ is a *common fraction;* .5 is a *decimal fraction.* In the common fraction any number may be the denominator; in the decimal fraction the denominator is 10 or some multiple of 10.

The decimal may be written .5, .6, .7, or 0.5, 0.6, 0.7, etc. The latter is safer because it shows that no whole number has been accidentally omitted before the decimal. This form is used by everyone who makes a great number of mathematical calculations.

A *proper fraction* is one which has a numerator smaller than its denominator, *e.g.,* $\frac{2}{3}$. An *improper fraction* is one with a numerator larger than the denominator, *e.g.,* $\frac{7}{4}$. A *mixed number* is a whole number and a fraction, *e.g.,* $14\frac{2}{3}$.

A fraction is said to be reduced to its lowest terms when the numerator and the denominator cannot both be evenly divided by any whole number except 1. $\frac{72}{80}$ reduced to its lowest terms=$\frac{9}{10}$. The practical value of this is that $\frac{9}{10}$ is much easier to work with than $\frac{72}{80}$.

Decimal fractions cannot usually be reduced to lower terms. As decimals, .5 and .025 cannot be reduced further; both, however, can be changed to common fractions and then reduced: $\frac{5}{10}=\frac{1}{2}$ and $\frac{25}{1000}=\frac{1}{40}$.

An improper fraction may be reduced to a mixed number by dividing the numerator by the denominator. Thus, $\frac{95}{50}=1\frac{9}{10}$.

A mixed number may be reduced to an improper fraction by multiplying together the whole number and the denominator of the fraction and adding the numerator. Thus, $3\frac{5}{8}=\frac{29}{8}$. (In each unit there are $\frac{8}{8}$. Therefore, in three units there are $3\times8=24+$the $\frac{5}{8}$ we already have$=\frac{29}{8}$.)

A common fraction may be changed to a decimal by adding ciphers to the numerator and dividing by the denominator. Thus $\frac{1}{2}=1.00\div2=.50$. If the division is not even it should be carried out two places and the fraction retained, or, for all practical purposes, four places and the fraction thrown away. Thus, $\frac{2}{3}=.66\frac{2}{3}$ or .6666.

The denominator of a decimal is always 1, with as many ciphers after it as there are places in the decimal. Thus, $.5=\frac{5}{10}$; $.00005=\frac{5}{1000000}$.

A *complex decimal, i.e.,* a decimal with a fraction, like $66\frac{2}{3}$, is changed into a common fraction in the same way as a simple decimal. It is simplest to forget the whole number and reduce the fraction as you would any ordinary fraction. Thus, $66\frac{2}{3}=66.6666$.

Mensuration

Mensuration is the process of measuring—length, area of surfaces, volume of solids—from data of lines and angles.

A *surface* is a figure which has only two dimensions, length and breadth.

A *quadrilateral* is a plane surface with four sides and four angles.

Quadrilateral

A quadrilateral with its opposite sides parallel is called a *parallelogram*.

Parallelograms

A parallelogram whose angles are right angles is a *rectangle*.

Rectangle

A rectangle with four equal sides is a *square*.

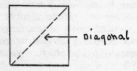

Square

A straight line drawn between opposite vertices of a quadrilateral is a *diagonal*.
The area of any parallelogram may be found by multiplying the base by the altitude.

Solid figures have three dimensions—length, breadth, and thickness.

A *prism* is a solid whose ends are congruent parallel plane figures and whose sides are parallelograms.

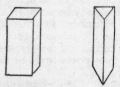

Prisms, Square and Triangular

A *cylinder* is a surface formed by one side of a rectangle rotated around the parallel side as an axis.

Cylinder

A *triangle* is a figure with three sides and three angles.

Triangles

The base of a plane figure is the side upon which it is supposed to stand. The altitude is a perpendicular line drawn from the base to the highest point on the opposite side.

The area of any triangle is one-half the base multiplied by the altitude. The volume of a prism or of a cylinder may be found by multiplying the area of the base by the altitude. The result is expressed in *cubic* units—cu. in., cu. ft., etc., which may be reduced to bushels or any other measure of capacity.

Doubling the diameter of a pipe increases its capacity four times.

A *circle* is a plane figure enclosed by a curved line which is at all points the same distance from the center. A straight line drawn from the center of a circle to the circumference is the *radius*. The radius is one-half the length of the diameter. The circumference of a circle is found by multiplying the diameter by 3.1416. If measurements need not be exact, $3\frac{1}{7}$ may be used instead. The diameter may, of course, be found by dividing the circumference by 3.1416; or it may be found by multiplying the circumference by .31831.

To find the area of a circle, multiply the square of the diameter by .7854. To find the cubic contents of a cylinder or pipe, multiply the area by the height or depth. Thus, a pipe 1 ft. in diameter and 1 ft. in length contains .7854 cu. ft. To find how many gallons are contained in a pipe or cylinder, divide the cubic contents in cubic inches by 231, which is the number of cubic inches in a United States gallon.

CIRCUMFERENCES AND AREAS OF CIRCLES

Diameter	Circumference	Area	Diameter	Circumference	Area	Diameter	Circumference	Area	Diameter	Circumference	Area
1/32	.09817	.0008	17/32	1.66897	.2217	1- 1/16	3.33794	.8866	2- 1/16	6.47953	3.3410
1/16	.19635	.0031	9/16	1.76715	.2485	1- 1/8	3.53429	.9940	2- 1/8	6.67588	3.5466
3/32	.29452	.0069	19/32	1.86532	.2769	1- 3/16	3.73064	1.1075	2- 3/16	6.87223	3.7583
1/8	.39270	.0123	5/8	1.96350	.3068	1- 1/4	3.92699	1.2272	2- 1/4	7.06858	3.9761
5/32	.49087	.0192	21/32	2.06167	.3382	1- 5/16	4.12334	1.3530	2- 5/16	7.26493	4.2000
3/16	.58905	.0276	11/16	2.15984	.3712	1- 3/8	4.31970	1.4849	2- 3/8	7.46128	4.4301
7/32	.68722	.0376	23/32	2.25802	.4057	1- 7/16	4.51604	1.6230	2- 7/16	7.65763	4.6664
1/4	.78540	.0491	3/4	2.35619	.4418	1- 1/2	4.71239	1.7671	2- 1/2	7.85398	4.9087
9/32	.88357	.0621	25/32	2.45437	.4794	1- 9/16	4.90874	1.9175	2- 9/16	8.05033	5.1572
5/16	.98175	.0767	13/16	2.55254	.5185	1- 5/8	5.10509	2.0739	2- 5/8	8.24668	5.4119
11/32	1.07992	.0928	27/32	2.65072	.5591	1-11/16	5.30144	2.2365	2-11/16	8.44303	5.6727
3/8	1.17810	.1105	7/8	2.74889	.6013	1- 3/4	5.49779	2.4053	2- 3/4	8.63938	5.9396
13/32	1.27627	.1296	29/32	2.84707	.6450	1-13/16	5.69414	2.5802	2-13/16	8.83573	6.2126
7/16	1.37444	.1503	15/16	2.94524	.6903	1- 7/8	5.89049	2.7612	2- 7/8	9.03208	6.4918
15/32	1.47262	.1726	31/32	3.04342	.7371	1-15/16	6.08684	2.9483	2-15/16	9.22843	6.7771
1/2	1.57080	.1964	1	3.14159	.7854	2	6.28319	3.1416	3	9.42478	7.0686

A *square* is a parallelogram having four equal sides and four right angles. A square is equal in area to a circle when the side of the square equals 0.88623 multiplied by the diameter of the circle, or when the diameter of the circle equals 1.12838 multiplied by the side of the square.

The surface of a ball may be found by multiplying the square of the diameter by 3.1416. The cubic inches in a ball may be found by multiplying the cube of the diameter by .5236.

The distance around any plane figure is the *perimeter*.

The extent of surface inside a plane figure is the *area*. It is expressed in square units—sq. inches, sq. yards, sq. rods, etc.

Example. Find the number of acres in a plot 36 rd. by 48 rd. How much fence would be needed to enclose it?

$$36 \text{ rd.} \times 48 \text{ rd.} = 1,728 \text{ sq. rd.}$$
$$1,728 \text{ sq. rd.} \div 160 \text{ (No. sq. rd. in one acre)} = 10\tfrac{4}{5} \text{ acres.}$$

To find the amount of fence needed we simply find the perimeter.

$$2 \times (36 + 48) = 168 \text{ rds.}$$

Squares and Cubes

The *square* of a number is the result obtained when the number is multiplied by itself. Thus, $2 \times 2 = 4$. Four is the square; two is the square root.

The *cube* of a number is the result obtained when the number is multiplied by itself three times. Thus, $2 \times 2 \times 2 = 8$. Eight is the cube, two is the cube root.

SQUARES, SQUARE ROOTS, CUBES, AND CUBE ROOTS OF NOS. 1 TO 100

No.	Sq.	Cube	Square Root	Cube Root	No.	Sq.	Cube	Square Root	Cube Root	No	Sq.	Cube	Square Root	Cube Root
0.1	0.01	0.001	0.316	0.464	23	529	12167	4.795	2.843	63	3969	250047	7.937	3.979
.15	0.022	0.003	0.387	0.531	24	576	13824	4.899	2.884	64	4096	262144	8.000	4.000
.2	0.04	0.008	0.447	0 585	25	625	15625	5.000	2.924	65	4225	274625	8.062	4.020
.25	0.062	0.015	0 500	0.630	26	676	17576	5.099	2.962	66	4356	287496	8.124	4.041
.3	0.09	0.027	0.548	0.669	27	729	19683	5.196	3.000	67	4489	300763	8.185	4.061
.35	0.122	0.042	0.592	0.705	28	784	21952	5.291	3.036	68	4624	314432	8.246	4.081
.4	0.16	0.064	0.633	0.737	29	841	24389	5.385	3.072	69	4761	328509	8.306	4.101
.45	0.202	0.091	0.671	0.766	30	900	27000	5.477	3.107	70	4900	343000	8.366	4.121
.5	0.25	0.125	0.707	0.794	31	961	29791	5.567	3.141	71	5041	357911	8.426	4.140
.55	0.302	0.166	0.742	0.819	32	1024	32768	5.656	3.174	72	5184	373248	8.485	4.160
.6	0.36	0.216	0.775	0 843	33	1089	35937	5.744	3.207	73	5320	389017	8.544	4.179
.65	0.422	0.274	0.806	0 866	34	1156	39304	5.831	3.239	74	5476	405224	8.602	4.198
.7	0.49	0.343	0.837	0.888	35	1225	42875	5.916	3.271	75	5625	421875	8.660	4.217
.75	0.562	0.421	0.866	0.909	36	1296	46656	6.000	3.301	76	5776	438976	8.717	4.235
.8	0.64	0.512	0.894	0.928	37	1369	50653	6.082	3.332	77	5929	456533	8.775	4.254
.85	0.722	0.614	0.922	0.947	38	1444	54872	6.164	3.362	78	6084	474552	8.831	4.272
.9	0.81	0.729	0.949	0.965	39	1521	59319	6.245	3.391	79	6241	493039	8.888	4.290
.95	0.902	0 857	0.975	0.983	40	1600	64000	6.324	3.420	80	6400	512000	8.944	4.308
1	1.000	1.000	1.000	1.000	41	1681	68921	6.403	3.448	81	6561	531441	9.000	4.326
2	4	8	1.414	1.259	42	1764	74088	6.480	3.476	82	6724	551368	9.055	4.344
3	9	27	1.732	1.442	43	1849	79507	6.557	3.503	83	6889	571787	9.110	4.362
4	16	64	2.000	1.587	44	1936	85184	6.633	3.530	84	7056	592704	9.165	4.379
5	25	125	2.236	1.710	45	2025	91125	6.708	3.556	85	7225	614125	9.219	4.396
6	36	216	2.449	1.817	46	2116	97336	6.782	3.583	86	7396	636056	9.273	4.414
7	49	343	2.645	1.913	47	2209	103823	6.855	3.608	87	7569	658503	9.327	4.431
8	64	512	2.828	2.000	48	2304	110592	6.928	3.634	88	7744	681472	9.380	4.448
9	81	729	3.000	2.080	49	2401	117649	7.000	3.659	89	7921	704969	9.434	4.464
10	100	1000	3.162	2.154	50	2500	125000	7.071	3.684	90	8100	729000	9.486	4.481
11	121	1331	3.316	2.224	51	2601	132651	7.141	3.708	91	8281	753571	9.539	4.497
12	144	1728	3.464	2.289	52	2704	140608	7.211	3.732	92	8464	778688	9.591	4.514
13	169	2197	3.605	2.351	53	2809	148877	7.280	3.756	93	8649	804357	9.643	4.530
14	196	2744	3.741	2.410	54	2916	157464	7.348	3.779	94	8836	830584	9.695	4.546
15	225	3375	3.873	2.466	55	3025	166375	7.416	3.803	95	9025	857375	9.746	4.562
16	256	4096	4.000	2.519	56	3136	175616	7.483	3.825	96	9216	884736	9.798	4.578
17	289	4913	4.123	2.571	57	3249	185193	7.549	3.848	97	9409	912673	9.848	4.594
18	324	5832	4.246	2.620	58	3364	195112	7.615	3.870	98	9604	941192	9.899	4.610
19	361	6859	4.358	2.668	59	3481	205379	7.681	3.893	99	9801	970209	9.949	4.626
20	400	8000	4.472	2.714	60	3600	216000	7.746	3.914	100	10000	1000000	10.000	4.641

The *root* of a number is one of the equal factors of that number. Thus, 4 is a root of 16; 3 is a root of 243.

This sign, $(\sqrt{\;\;})$, called the *radical sign,* denotes that the root of a number is to be found.

$\sqrt{196}$ indicates that the square root of 196 is to be found.

$\sqrt[3]{216}$ indicates that the cube root of 216 is to be found.

The number of times a number is to be multiplied by itself is indicated by a small number written above it to the right, thus, 10^5, 25^8, 40^{15}. This small number is called the *exponent*.

The Slide Rule

For making rapid calculations which involve multiplication, division, ratios, square roots, cube roots, squares, cubes, etc., the slide rule offers a quick and easy method. The ten-inch rule is the standard size in general use. Directions come with the rule, which can be operated after a little practice by anyone familiar with decimal fractions. Although results obtained from the slide rule are not as accurate as results obtained by hand, they are good for most practical purposes. Answers obtained with the ten-inch rule are correct to three and sometimes four figures. The rule is invaluable to engineers, mechanics, architects, etc. Estimators and accountants can make quick calculations sufficiently accurate to check all major errors. The rule furnishes an easy way to check reports and is, in fact, indispensable to anyone who makes use of any branch of applied mathematics involving the processes mentioned above. The slide rule will not add or subtract.

Multipliers for Key-Operated Machines

In making calculations with key-operated machines the following multipliers are to be used:

In converting

square inches to square feet	multiply by	0.00695
square feet to square yards	" by	0.1111
cubic inches to cubic feet	" by	0.00058
cubic feet to cubic yards	" by	0.03704
cubic feet to gallons	" by	7.48224
cubic feet to feet board measure	" by	12.0
cubic inches to gallons	" by	0.00433
cubic inches to feet board measure	" by	0.00695
cubic inches to pounds steel	" by	0.284
cubic inches to pounds iron	" by	0.261
cubic inches to pounds copper	" by	0.319

Lumber: Width in inches $\times$ breadth in inches $\times$ length in feet $\times$ 0.08333 = feet board measure.

Steel: Width in inches $\times$ breadth in inches $\times$ length in feet $\times$ 3.40 = pounds.

INTEREST

Interest is money paid for the use of money. Throughout the United States and her territories, and, indeed, in most civilized countries, the amount of interest that may be charged is regulated by law.

If more interest than the law allows is required by the money lender it is called usurious interest. Professional money lenders, however, have many ways of evading the usury laws. In some instances they charge a bonus for the loan but the bonus does not appear in the official record. In others, they demand that a certain amount of the loan remain on deposit, which means that the borrower actually gets a much smaller sum than the one upon which he is paying interest.

INTEREST LAWS IN THE UNITED STATES AND SOME OF HER TERRITORIES AND POSSESSIONS (1961)[1]

State	Interest Rate Legal Rate	Contract Rate	State	Interest Rate Legal Rate	Contract Rate	State	Interest Rate Legal Rate	Contract Rate
	Per Ct.	Per Ct.		Per Ct.	Per Ct.		Per Ct.	Per Ct.
Ala.	6	8	La.	5	8	Okla. ...	6	10
Alaska .	6	8	Maine ..	6	Any rate[2]	Ore.	6	10
Ariz. ...	6	8	Md.	6	6	Pa.	6	6
Ark. ...	6	8	Mass. ..	6	Any rate[3]	P. Rico .	6	8[6]
Cal.	7	10	Mich. ..	5	7	R. I.	6	30[7]
Col.	6	12	Minn. ..	6	8	S. C.	6	7
Conn. ..	6	12	Miss.	6	8	S. D.	6	8
Del.	6	6	Mo.	6	8	Tenn. ..	6	6
D of C ..	6	8	Mont. ..	6	10	Tex.	6	10
Fla.	6	10	Neb.	6	9	Utah ...	6	10
Ga.	7	8	Nev.	7	12	Vt.	6	6
Hawaii .	6	12	N. H. ...	6	Any rate	Va.	6	6
Idaho ..	6	8	N. J.	6	6	Virgin Is.	6	10[8]
Ill.	5	7	N. M. ...	6	12[4]	Wash. ..	6	12
Ind.	6	8	N. Y.	6	6	W. Va. ..	6	6
Iowa ...	5	7	N. C.	6	8[5]	Wis. ...	6	10
Kan. ...	6	10	N. D.	4	7	Wyo. ...	7	10
Ky. ...	6	6	Ohio ...	6	8			

[1] By contract rate is meant the maximum rate, but there are many exceptions for specific types of loans such as pawnbroker loans; small loans by licensed lenders; loans by banks, credit unions, building and loan associations; loans insured by the Federal Housing Administration, etc. In some states the penalty for charging usurious interest is forfeiture of principal and interest, in some states interest and part of principal, in others interest or a multiple thereof, and in others only interest in excess of the legal maximum. In some states usurious interest once paid can be recovered; in others it cannot. In the following states a corporation may lawfully be charged any rate of interest: Delaware, Illinois, Indiana, Kansas, Maryland, Minnesota, Missouri, New Jersey, New York (except corporations whose principal asset is a one- or two-family house, a loan made within six months of incorporation and after April 6, 1956), Pennsylvania (certain corporations), Virginia, West Virginia. In the following states the lawful maximum for a corporation differs from individual rates as follows: Florida, 15 per cent; Oregon, 12 per cent.

[2] Except on loans under $300.

[3] On loans under $1,000 maximum rate is 18 per cent.

[4] 10 per cent if secured.

[5] Cultivation loans secured by crops, 10 per cent.

[6] 9 per cent on amounts to $3,000.

[7] 5 per cent per month for six months; thereafter 2½ per cent per month under $50.

[8] 6 per cent if secured by first mortgage or real estate.

INTEREST TABLES[9]

Showing the amount of interest on $1.00 from one day to 120 days at various rates. To use the table, find the interest on $1.00 for the specified number of days, then multiply it by the number of dollars to be borrowed. For example, to find the interest on $200 for 60 days, at 6 per cent, find the interest on $1.00 at 6 per cent, for 60 days. The table shows that this is .009863. Multiply by 200 and you have $1.97, which is the amount of interest that will be charged.

[9] By permission of the Lefax Corporation, Philadelphia, Pa.

Days	2%	2 1/2%	3%	3 1/4%	3 1/2%	3 3/4%	4%	4 1/4%	4 1/2%	Days
1	.000055	.000068	.000082	.000089	.000096	.000103	.000110	.000116	.000123	1
2	.000110	.000137	.000164	.000178	.000192	.000205	.000219	.000233	.000247	2
3	.000164	.000205	.000247	.000267	.000288	.000308	.000329	.000349	.000370	3
4	.000219	.000274	.000329	.000356	.000384	.000411	.000438	.000466	.000493	4
5	.000274	.000342	.000411	.000445	.000479	.000514	.000548	.000582	.000616	5
6	.000329	.000411	.000493	.000534	.000575	.000616	.000658	.000699	.000740	6
7	.000384	.000479	.000575	.000623	.000671	.000719	.000767	.000815	.000863	7
8	.000438	.000548	.000658	.000712	.000767	.000822	.000877	.000932	.000986	8
9	.000493	.000616	.000740	.000801	.000863	.000925	.000986	.001048	.001110	9
10	.000548	.000685	.000822	.000890	.000959	.001027	.001096	.001164	.001233	10
11	.000603	.000753	.000904	.000979	.001055	.001130	.001205	.001281	.001356	11
12	.000658	.000822	.000986	.001068	.001151	.001233	.001315	.001397	.001479	12
13	.000712	.000890	.001068	.001158	.001247	.001336	.001425	.001514	.001603	13
14	.000767	.000959	.001151	.001247	.001342	.001438	.001534	.001630	.001726	14
15	.000822	.001028	.001233	.001336	.001438	.001541	.001644	.001747	.001849	15
16	.000877	.001096	.001315	.001425	.001534	.001644	.001753	.001863	.001973	16
17	.000932	.001164	.001397	.001514	.001630	.001747	.001863	.001979	.002096	17
18	.000986	.001233	.001479	.001603	.001726	.001849	.001973	.002096	.002219	18
19	.001041	.001301	.001562	.001692	.001822	.001952	.002082	.002212	.002342	19
20	.001096	.001370	.001644	.001781	.001918	.002055	.002192	.002329	.002466	20
21	.001151	.001438	.001726	.001870	.002014	.002158	.002301	.002445	.002589	21
22	.001205	.001507	.001808	.001959	.002110	.002260	.002411	.002562	.002712	22
23	.001260	.001575	.001890	.002048	.002205	.002363	.002521	.002678	.002836	23
24	.001315	.001644	.001973	.002137	.002301	.002466	.002630	.002795	.002959	24
25	.001370	.001712	.002055	.002226	.002397	.002568	.002740	.002911	.003082	25
26	.001425	.001781	.002137	.002315	.002493	.002671	.002849	.003027	.003205	26
27	.001479	.001849	.002219	.002404	.002589	.002774	.002959	.003144	.003329	27
28	.001534	.001918	.002301	.002493	.002685	.002877	.003068	.003260	.003452	28
29	.001589	.001986	.002384	.002582	.002781	.002979	.003178	.003377	.003575	29
30	.001644	.002055	.002466	.002671	.002877	.003082	.003288	.003493	.003699	30
31	.001699	.002133	.002548	.002760	.002973	.003185	.003397	.003610	.003822	31
32	.001753	.002192	.002630	.002849	.003068	.003288	.003507	.003726	.003945	32
33	.001808	.002260	.002712	.002938	.003164	.003390	.003616	.003842	.004068	33
34	.001863	.002329	.002795	.003027	.003260	.003493	.003726	.003959	.004192	34
35	.001918	.002397	.002877	.003116	.003356	.003596	.003836	.004075	.004315	35
36	.001973	.002466	.002959	.003205	.003452	.003699	.003945	.004192	.004438	36
37	.002027	.002534	.003041	.003295	.003548	.003801	.004055	.004308	.004562	37
38	.002082	.002603	.003123	.003384	.003644	.003904	.004164	.004425	.004685	38
39	.002137	.002671	.003205	.003473	.003740	.004007	.004274	.004541	.004808	39
40	.002192	.002740	.003288	.003562	.003836	.004110	.004384	.004658	.004932	40
41	.002247	.002808	.003370	.003651	.003932	.004212	.004493	.004774	.005055	41
42	.002301	.002877	.003452	.003740	.004027	.004315	.004603	.004890	.005178	42
43	.002356	.002945	.003534	.003829	.004123	.004418	.004712	.005007	.005301	43
44	.002411	.003014	.003616	.003918	.004219	.004521	.004822	.005123	.005425	44
45	.002466	.003082	.003699	.004007	.004315	.004623	.004932	.005240	.005548	45
46	.002521	.003151	.003781	.004096	.004411	.004726	.005041	.005356	.005671	46
47	.002575	.003219	.003863	.004185	.004507	.004829	.005150	.005473	.005795	47
48	.002630	.003288	.003945	.004274	.004603	.004932	.005260	.005589	.005918	48
49	.002685	.003356	.004027	.004363	.004699	.005034	.005370	.005705	.006041	49
50	.002740	.003425	.004110	.004452	.004795	.005137	.005479	.005822	.006164	50
51	.002795	.003493	.004192	.004541	.004890	.005240	.005589	.005938	.006288	51
52	.002849	.003562	.004274	.004630	.004986	.005342	.005699	.006055	.006411	52
53	.002904	.003630	.004356	.004719	.005082	.005445	.005808	.006171	.006534	53
54	.002959	.003699	.004438	.004808	.005178	.005548	.005918	.006288	.006658	54
55	.003014	.003767	.004521	.004897	.005274	.005651	.006027	.006404	.006781	55
56	.003068	.003836	.004603	.004986	.005370	.005753	.006137	.006521	.006904	56
57	.003123	.003904	.004685	.005075	.005466	.005856	.006247	.006637	.007027	57
58	.003178	.003973	.004767	.005164	.005562	.005959	.006356	.006753	.007151	58
59	.003233	.004041	.004849	.005253	.005658	.006062	.006466	.006870	.007274	59
60	.003288	.004110	.004932	.005342	.005753	.006164	.006575	.006986	.007397	60

Days	2%	2 1/2%	3%	3 1/4%	3 1/2%	3 3/4%	4%	4 1/4%	4 1/2%	Days
61	.003342	.004178	.005014	.005432	.005849	.006267	.006685	.007103	.007521	61
62	.003397	.004247	.005096	.005521	.005945	.006370	.006795	.007219	.007644	62
63	.003452	.004315	.005178	.005610	.006041	.006473	.006904	.007336	.007767	63
64	.003507	.004384	.005260	.005699	.006137	.006575	.007014	.007452	.007890	64
65	.003562	.004452	.005342	.005788	.006233	.006678	.007123	.007568	.008014	65
66	.003616	.004521	.005425	.005877	.006329	.006781	.007233	.007685	.008137	66
67	.003671	.004589	.005507	.005966	.006425	.006884	.007342	.007801	.008260	67
68	.003726	.004658	.005589	.006055	.006521	.006986	.007452	.007918	.008384	68
69	.003781	.004726	.005671	.006144	.006616	.007089	.007562	.008034	.008507	69
70	.003836	.004795	.005753	.006233	.006712	.007192	.007671	.008151	.008630	70
71	.003890	.004863	.005836	.006322	.006808	.007295	.007781	.008267	.008753	71
72	.003945	.004932	.005918	.006411	.006904	.007397	.007890	.008384	.008877	72
73	.004000	.005000	.006000	.006500	.007000	.007500	.008000	.008500	.009000	73
74	.004055	.005068	.006082	.006589	.007096	.007603	.008110	.008616	.009123	74
75	.004109	.005137	.006164	.006678	.007192	.007705	.008219	.008733	.009247	75
76	.004164	.005205	.006247	.006767	.007288	.007808	.008229	.008849	.009370	76
77	.004219	.005274	.006329	.006856	.007384	.007911	.008438	.008966	.009493	77
78	.004274	.005342	.006411	.006945	.007479	.008014	.008548	.009082	.009616	78
79	.004329	.005411	.006493	.007034	.007575	.008116	.008658	.009199	.009740	79
80	.004384	.005479	.006575	.007123	.007671	.008219	.008767	.009315	.009863	80
81	.004438	.005548	.006658	.007212	.007767	.008322	.008877	.009432	.009986	81
82	.004493	.005616	.006740	.007301	.007863	.008425	.008986	.009548	.010110	82
83	.004548	.005685	.006822	.007390	.007959	.008527	.009096	.009664	.010233	83
84	.004603	.005753	.006904	.007479	.008055	.008630	.009205	.009781	.010356	84
85	.004658	.005822	.006986	.007568	.008151	.008733	.009315	.009897	.010497	85
86	.004712	.005890	.007068	.007658	.008247	.008836	.009425	.010014	.010603	86
87	.004767	.005959	.007151	.007747	.008342	.008938	.009534	.010130	.010726	87
88	.004822	.006027	.007233	.007836	.008438	.009041	.009644	.010247	.010849	88
89	.004877	.006096	.007315	.007925	.008534	.009144	.009753	.010363	.010973	89
90	.004932	.006164	.007397	.008014	.008630	.009247	.009863	.010479	.011096	90
91	.004987	.006232	.007479	.008103	.008726	.009350	.009972	.010595	.011219	91
92	.005041	.006301	.007561	.008192	.008822	.009452	.010082	.010712	.011343	92
93	.005096	.006369	.007644	.008281	.008918	.009555	.010191	.010828	.011466	93
94	.005151	.006438	.007726	.008370	.009014	.009658	.010300	.010945	.011589	94
95	.005205	.006506	.007808	.008459	.009109	.009761	.010409	.011061	.011712	95
96	.005260	.006575	.007890	.008548	.009205	.009863	.010519	.011178	.011836	96
97	.005314	.006643	.007972	.008637	.009301	.009966	.010628	.011294	.011959	97
98	.005369	.006712	.008055	.008726	.009397	.010069	.010737	.011411	.012082	98
99	.005424	.006780	.008137	.008815	.009493	.010172	.010846	.011527	.012206	99
100	.005478	.006849	.008219	.008904	.009589	.010274	.010956	.011643	.012329	100
101	.005533	.006917	.008301	.008993	.009685	.010377	.011065	.011760	.012452	101
102	.005588	.006986	.008383	.009091	.009781	.010480	.011174	.011876	.012575	102
103	.005642	.007054	.008465	.009180	.009877	.010583	.011283	.011993	.012699	103
104	.005697	.007123	.008548	.009269	.009972	.010685	.011393	.012109	.012822	104
105	.005751	.007191	.008630	.009358	.010068	.010788	.011502	.012226	.012945	105
106	.005806	.007260	.008712	.009447	.010164	.010891	.011611	.012342	.013069	106
107	.005861	.007328	.008794	.009536	.010260	.010994	.011720	.012458	.013192	107
108	.005915	.007397	.008876	.009625	.010356	.011096	.011830	.012575	.013315	108
109	.005970	.007465	.008959	.009714	.010452	.011199	.011939	.012691	.013439	109
110	.006025	.007534	.009041	.009803	.010548	.011302	.012048	.012808	.013562	110
111	.006079	.007602	.009123	.009892	.010644	.011405	.012157	.012924	.013685	111
112	.006134	.007671	.009205	.009981	.010740	.011507	.012267	.013041	.013808	112
113	.006188	.007739	.009287	.010070	.010835	.011610	.012376	.013157	.013932	113
114	.006243	.007808	.009370	.010159	.010931	.011713	.012485	.013274	.014055	114
115	.006298	.007876	.009452	.010248	.011027	.011816	.012595	.013390	.014178	115
116	.006352	.007945	.009534	.010337	.011123	.011918	.012704	.013506	.014302	116
117	.006407	.008013	.009616	.010426	.011219	.012021	.012813	.013623	.014425	117
118	.006462	.008082	.009698	.010515	.011315	.012124	.012922	.013739	.014548	118
119	.006516	.008150	.009781	.010604	.011411	.012226	.013032	.013856	.014671	119
120	.006571	.008219	.009863	.010693	.011507	.012329	.013141	.013972	.014795	120

Days	4 3/4%	5%	5 1/4%	5 1/2%	5 3/4%	6%	6 1/2%	7%	8%	Days
1	.000130	.000137	.000144	.000151	.000158	.000164	.000178	.000192	.000219	1
2	.000260	.000274	.000288	.000301	.000315	.000329	.000356	.000384	.000438	2
3	.000390	.000411	.000432	.000452	.000473	.000493	.000534	.000575	.000658	3
4	.000521	.000548	.000575	.000603	.000630	.000658	.000712	.000767	.000877	4
5	.000651	.000685	.000719	.000753	.000788	.000822	.000890	.000959	.001096	5
6	.000781	.000822	.000863	.000904	.000945	.000986	.001068	.001151	.001315	6
7	.000911	.000959	.001007	.001055	.001103	.001151	.001247	.001342	.001534	7
8	.001041	.001096	.001151	.001205	.001260	.001315	.001425	.001534	.001753	8
9	.001171	.001233	.001295	.001356	.001418	.001479	.001603	.001726	.001973	9
10	.001301	.001370	.001438	.001507	.001575	.001644	.001781	.001918	.002192	10
11	.001432	.001507	.001582	.001658	.001733	.001808	.001959	.002110	.002411	11
12	.001562	.001644	.001726	.001808	.001890	.001973	.002137	.002301	.002630	12
13	.001692	.001781	.001870	.001959	.002048	.002137	.002315	.002493	.002849	13
14	.001822	.001918	.002014	.002110	.002205	.002301	.002493	.002685	.003068	14
15	.001952	.002055	.002158	.002260	.002363	.002466	.002671	.002877	.003288	15
16	.002082	.002192	.002301	.002411	.002521	.002630	.002849	.003068	.003507	16
17	.002212	.002329	.002445	.002562	.002678	.002795	.003027	.003260	.003726	17
18	.002342	.002466	.002589	.002712	.002836	.002959	.003205	.003452	.003945	18
19	.002473	.002603	.002733	.002863	.002993	.003123	.003384	.003644	.004164	19
20	.002603	.002740	.002877	.003014	.003151	.003288	.003562	.003836	.004384	20
21	.002733	.002877	.003021	.003164	.003308	.003452	.003740	.004027	.004603	21
22	.002863	.003014	.003164	.003315	.003466	.003616	.003918	.004219	.004822	22
23	.002993	.003151	.003308	.003466	.003623	.003781	.004096	.004411	.005041	23
24	.003123	.003288	.003452	.003616	.003781	.003945	.004274	.004603	.005260	24
25	.003253	.003425	.003596	.003767	.003938	.004110	.004452	.004795	.005479	25
26	.003384	.003562	.003740	.003918	.004096	.004274	.004630	.004986	.005699	26
27	.003514	.003699	.003884	.004068	.004253	.004438	.004808	.005178	.005918	27
28	.003644	.003836	.004027	.004219	.004411	.004603	.004986	.005370	.006137	28
29	.003774	.003973	.004171	.004370	.004568	.004767	.005164	.005562	.006356	29
30	.003904	.004110	.004315	.004521	.004726	.004932	.005342	.005753	.006575	30
31	.004034	.004247	.004459	.004671	.004884	.005096	.005521	.005945	.006795	31
32	.004164	.004384	.004603	.004822	.005041	.005260	.005699	.006137	.007014	32
33	.004295	.004521	.004747	.004973	.005199	.005425	.005877	.006329	.007233	33
34	.004425	.004658	.004890	.005123	.005356	.005589	.006055	.006521	.007452	34
35	.004555	.004795	.005034	.005274	.005514	.005753	.006233	.006712	.007871	35
36	.004685	.004932	.005178	.005425	.005671	.005918	.006411	.006904	.007890	36
37	.004815	.005068	.005322	.005575	.005829	.006082	.006589	.007096	.008110	37
38	.004945	.005205	.005466	.005726	.005986	.006247	.006767	.007288	.008329	38
39	.005075	.005342	.005610	.005877	.006144	.006411	.006945	.007479	.008548	39
40	.005205	.005479	.005753	.006027	.006301	.006575	.007123	.007671	.008767	40
41	.005336	.005616	.005897	.006178	.006459	.006740	.007301	.007863	.008986	41
42	.005466	.005753	.006041	.006329	.006616	.006904	.007479	.008055	.009205	42
43	.005596	.005890	.006185	.006479	.006774	.007068	.007658	.008247	.009425	43
44	.005726	.006027	.006329	.006630	.006932	.007233	.007836	.008438	.009644	44
45	.005856	.006164	.006473	.006781	.007089	.007397	.008014	.008630	.009863	45
46	.005986	.006301	.006616	.006932	.007247	.007562	.008192	.008822	.010082	46
47	.006116	.006438	.006760	.007082	.007404	.007726	.008370	.009014	.010301	47
48	.006247	.006575	.006904	.007233	.007562	.007890	.008548	.009205	.010521	48
49	.006377	.006712	.007048	.007384	.007719	.008055	.008726	.009397	.010740	49
50	.006507	.006849	.007192	.007534	.007877	.008219	.008904	.009589	.010959	50
51	.006637	.006986	.007336	.007685	.008034	.008384	.009082	.009781	.011178	51
52	.006767	.007123	.007479	.007836	.008192	.008548	.009260	.009973	.011397	52
53	.006897	.007260	.007623	.007986	.008349	.008712	.009438	.010164	.011616	53
54	.007027	.007397	.007767	.008137	.008507	.008877	.009616	.010356	.011836	54
55	.007158	.007534	.007911	.008288	.008664	.009041	.009795	.010548	.012055	55
56	.007288	.007671	.008055	.008438	.008822	.009205	.009973	.010740	.012274	56
57	.007418	.007808	.008199	.008589	.008979	.009370	.010151	.010932	.012493	57
58	.007548	.007945	.008342	.008740	.009137	.009534	.010329	.011123	.012712	58
59	.007678	.008082	.008486	.008890	.009295	.009699	.010507	.011315	.012932	59
60	.007808	.008219	.008630	.009041	.009452	.009863	.010685	.011507	.013151	60

Days	4 3/4%	5%	5 1/4%	5 1/2%	5 3/4%	6%	6 1/2%	7%	8%	Days
61	.007938	.008356	.008774	.009192	.009610	.010027	.010863	.011699	.013370	61
62	.008068	.008493	.008918	.009342	.009767	.010192	.011041	.011890	.013589	62
63	.008199	.008630	.009062	.009493	.009925	.010356	.011219	.012082	.013803	63
64	.008329	.008767	.009205	.009644	.010082	.010521	.011397	.012274	.014027	64
65	.008459	.008904	.009349	.009795	.010240	.010685	.011575	.012466	.014247	65
66	.008589	.009041	.009493	.009945	.010397	.010849	.011753	.012658	.014466	66
67	.008719	.009178	.009637	.010096	.010555	.011014	.011932	.012849	.014685	67
68	.008849	.009315	.009781	.010247	.010712	.011178	.012110	.013041	.014904	68
69	.008979	.009452	.009925	.010397	.010870	.011342	.012288	.013233	.015123	69
70	.009110	.009589	.010068	.010548	.011027	.011507	.012466	.013425	.015342	70
71	.009240	.009726	.010212	.010699	.011185	.011671	.012644	.013616	.015562	71
72	.009370	.009863	.010356	.010849	.011342	.011836	.012822	.013808	.015781	72
73	.009500	.010000	.010500	.011000	.011500	.012000	.013000	.014000	.016000	73
74	.009630	.010137	.010644	.011151	.011658	.012164	.013178	.014192	.016219	74
75	.009760	.010274	.010788	.011301	.011815	.012329	.013356	.014384	.016438	75
76	.009890	.010411	.010932	.011452	.011973	.012493	.013534	.014575	.016658	76
77	.010021	.010548	.011075	.011603	.012130	.012658	.013712	.014767	.016877	77
78	.010151	.010685	.011219	.011753	.012288	.012822	.013890	.014959	.017096	78
79	.010281	.010822	.011363	.011904	.012445	.012986	.014068	.015151	.017315	79
80	.010411	.010959	.011507	.012055	.012603	.013151	.014247	.015342	.017534	80
81	.010541	.011096	.011651	.012205	.012760	.013315	.014425	.015534	.017753	81
82	.010671	.011233	.011795	.012356	.012918	.013479	.014603	.015726	.017973	82
83	.010801	.011370	.011938	.012507	.013075	.013644	.014781	.015918	.018192	83
84	.011079	.011507	.012082	.012658	.013233	.013808	.014959	.016110	.018411	84
85	.011062	.011644	.012226	.012808	.013390	.013973	.015137	.016301	.018630	85
86	.011192	.011781	.012370	.012959	.013548	.014137	.015315	.016493	.018849	86
87	.011322	.011918	.012514	.013110	.013705	.014301	.015493	.016685	.019068	87
88	.011452	.012055	.012658	.013260	.013863	.014466	.015671	.016877	.019288	88
89	.011582	.012192	.012801	.013411	.014021	.014630	.015849	.017068	.019507	89
90	.011712	.012329	.012945	.013562	.014178	.014795	.016027	.017260	.019726	90
91	.011842	.012466	.013089	.013713	.014336	.014960	.016205	.017452	.019945	91
92	.011972	.012603	.013233	.013863	.014493	.015124	.016383	.017644	.020163	92
93	.012102	.012740	.013377	.014014	.014651	.015288	.016561	.017835	.020382	93
94	.012233	.012877	.013520	.014165	.014808	.015453	.016739	.018027	.020600	94
95	.012363	.013014	.013664	.014315	.014966	.015617	.016917	.018219	.020819	95
96	.012493	.013151	.013808	.014466	.015123	.015781	.017095	.018411	.021037	96
97	.012623	.013288	.013952	.014617	.015281	.015946	.017273	.018602	.021256	97
98	.012753	.013425	.014096	.014767	.015438	.016110	.017451	.018794	.021474	98
99	.012883	.013562	.014240	.014918	.015596	.016274	.017629	.018986	.021693	99
100	.013013	.013699	.014383	.015069	.015753	.016439	.017807	.019178	.021911	100
101	.013144	.013836	.014527	.015219	.015911	.016603	.017985	.019370	.022130	101
102	.013274	.013973	.014671	.015370	.016068	.016768	.018163	.019561	.022348	102
103	.013404	.014110	.014815	.015521	.016226	.016932	.018341	.019753	.022567	103
104	.013534	.014247	.014959	.015672	.016383	.017096	.018519	.019945	.022785	104
105	.013664	.014384	.015103	.015822	.016541	.017261	.018697	.020137	.023004	105
106	.013794	.014521	.015246	.015973	.016698	.017425	.108875	.020328	.023222	106
107	.013924	.014658	.015390	.016124	.016856	.017589	.019053	.020520	.023441	107
108	.014055	.014795	.015534	.016274	.017014	.017654	.019231	.020712	.023659	108
109	.014185	.014932	.015678	.016425	.017171	.017818	.019409	.020904	.023878	109
110	.014315	.015069	.015822	.016576	.017329	.017983	.019587	.021096	.024096	110
111	.014445	.015206	.015966	.016726	.017486	.018147	.019765	.021287	.024315	111
112	.014575	.015343	.016109	.016877	.017644	.018313	.019943	.021479	.024533	112
113	.014705	.015480	.016253	.017028	.017801	.018478	.020121	.021671	.024752	113
114	.014835	.015617	.016397	.017178	.017959	.018642	.020299	.021863	.024970	114
115	.014966	.015754	.016541	.017329	.018116	.018806	.020478	.022055	.025189	115
116	.015096	.015891	.016685	.017480	.018274	.018971	.020656	.022246	.025408	116
117	.015226	.016028	.016829	.017630	.018431	.019135	.020834	.022438	.025626	117
118	.015356	.016165	.016973	.017781	.018589	.019300	.021012	.022630	.025845	118
119	.015486	.016302	.017116	.017932	.018746	.019464	.021190	.022822	.026063	119
120	.015616	.016439	.017260	.018082	.018904	.019628	.021368	.023013	.026282	120

To Calculate Interest. Multiply the principal by the number of days, and

For	4 per cent, divide by 90			For	8 per cent, divide by 45
"	5 " " " 72			"	9 " " " 40
"	6 " " " 60			"	10 " " " 36
"	7 " " " 52			"	12 " " " 30

Example. Find the interest on $600 for two months and two days at 4 per cent.

$$600 \times 62 = 37,200 \div 90 = \$4.13$$

To find the interest at 6 per cent for 60 days, simply move the decimal point two places to the left. For example, the interest on $500 for 60 days is $5.00. When the time is more or less than 60 days it is easy to find the rate for 60 days and then add or subtract, as the case may be.

For 120 days, multiply by 2	For 30 days, divide by 2
" 90 " add ½ of itself	" 15 " " " 4
" 75 " " ¼ of itself	" 3 " " " 20

Example. Find the interest on $840 for 75 days.

Interest for 60 days = $8.40
Interest for 15 days = 2.10
Interest for 75 days = 10.50

The interest on any sum of money for any length of time may be calculated through the formulas below in which

P = Principal   R = Rate
I = Interest   T = Time

In order to find the interest when the principal, rate, and time are given

$$I = P \times R \times T$$

Example. Find the interest on $2,000 for three years at 6 per cent.

$$I = 2,000 \times .06 \times 3 = \$360$$

In order to find the principal when interest, rate, and time are given

$$P = \frac{I}{R \times T}$$

Example. Find the principal when the interest is $360, the rate 6 per cent, the time three years.

$$P = \frac{360.00}{.06 \times 3} = \$2,000$$

In order to find the rate when interest, principal, and time are given

$$R = \frac{I}{P \times T}$$

Example. Find the rate of interest on $2,000 for three years when interest amounts to $360.

$$R = \frac{360}{2,000 \times 3} = .06 \ (\frac{6}{100} = 6 \text{ per cent})$$

In order to find the time when the interest, rate, and principal are given

$$T = \frac{I}{P \times R}$$

Example. Find the time when the principal is $2,000, the interest $360, and the rate is 6 per cent.

$$T = \frac{360}{2,000 \times .06} = 3 \text{ years}$$

Compound Interest. If interest is withdrawn as soon as it falls due on a deposit, it is called simple interest. But if it is allowed to remain, interest and principal are added together (compounded) at regular intervals, which may be a year, six months, or any other time agreed upon. On a deposit of $100 at 6 per cent annually payable twice a year, simple interest would be $3.00 each payment; but the same amount at compound interest would bring in the first four payments $3.00; $3.09; $3.18; and $3.28 respectively. At simple interest at 5 per cent a sum of money doubles itself in 20 years; at compound interest it doubles itself in 14⅙ years. Compound interest is usually paid on savings bank deposits. Life insurance premiums are figured out on the basis of compound interest. Returns from bonds are also reckoned by compound interest.

TIME IN WHICH MONEY DOUBLES AT INTEREST

Rate	Simple Int.	Comp. Int. (Compounded yearly)	Rate	Simple Int.	Comp. Int. (Compounded yearly)
2	50 years.	35 years.	5	20 years.	14 yrs. 75 da.
2½	40 years.	28 yrs. 26 da.	6	16 yrs. 8 mo.	11 yrs. 327 da.
3	33 yrs. 4 mo.	23 yrs. 164 da.	7	14 yrs. 104 da.	10 yrs. 89 da.
3½	28 yrs. 208 da.	20 yrs. 54 da.	8	12½ years.	9 yrs. 2 da.
4	25 years.	17 yrs. 246 da.	9	11 yrs. 40 da.	8 yrs. 16 da.
4½	22 yrs. 81 da.	15 yrs. 273 da.	10	10 years.	7 yrs. 100 da.

TABLE SHOWING AMOUNT OF $1.00 AT COMPOUND INTEREST IN ANY NUMBER OF YEARS FROM ONE TO TWENTY-FIVE

Subtract $1.00 from the amount in this table to find the interest.

Yr.	2 per cent	2½ per cent	8 per cent	3½ per cent	4 per cent	4½ per cent
1	1.0200 0000	1.0250 0000	1.0300 0000	1.0350 0000	1.0400 0000	1.0450 0000
2	1.0404 0000	1.0506 2500	1.0609 0000	1.0712 2500	1.0816 0000	1.0920 2500
3	1.0612 0800	1.0768 9062	1.0927 2700	1.1087 1787	1.1248 6400	1.1411 6612
4	1.0824 3216	1.1038 1239	1.1255 0881	1.1475 2300	1.1698 5856	1.1925 1860
5	1.1040 8080	1.1314 0821	1.1592 7407	1.1876 8631	1.2166 5290	1.2461 8194
6	1.1261 6242	1.1596 9342	1.1940 5230	1.2292 5533	1.2653 1902	1.3022 6012
7	1.1486 8567	1.1886 8575	1.2298 7387	1.2722 7926	1.3159 3178	1.3608 6183
8	1.1716 5938	1.2184 0290	1.2667 7008	1.3168 0904	1.3685 6905	1.4221 0061
9	1.1950 9257	1.2488 6297	1.3047 7318	1.3628 9735	1.4233 1181	1.4860 9514
10	1.2189 9442	1.2800 8454	1.3439 1638	1.4105 9876	1.4802 4428	1.5529 6942
11	1.2433 7431	1.3120 8666	1.3842 3387	1.4599 6972	1.5394 5406	1.6228 5305
12	1.2682 4179	1.3448 8882	1.4257 6089	1.5110 6866	1.6010 3222	1.6958 8143
13	1.2936 0663	1.3785 1104	1.4685 3371	1.5639 5606	1.6650 7351	1.7721 9610
14	1.3194 7876	1.4129 7382	1.5125 8972	1.6186 9452	1.7316 7645	1.8519 4492
15	1.3458 6834	1.4482 9817	1.5579 6742	1.6753 4883	1.8009 4351	1.9352 8244
16	1.3727 8570	1.4845 0562	1.6047 0644	1.7339 8604	1.8729 8125	2.0223 7015
17	1.4002 4142	1.5216 1826	1.6528 4763	1.7946 7555	1.9479 0050	2.1133 7681
18	1.4282 4625	1.5596 5872	1.7024 3306	1.8574 8920	2.0258 1652	2.2084 7877
19	1.4568 1117	1.5986 5019	1.7535 0605	1.9225 0132	2.1068 4918	2.3078 6031
20	1.4859 4740	1.6386 1644	1.8061 1123	1.9897 8886	2.1911 2314	2.4117 1402
21	1.5156 6634	1.6795 8185	1.8602 9457	2.0594 3147	2.2787 6807	2.5202 4116
22	1.5459 7967	1.7215 7140	1.9161 0341	2.1315 1158	2.3699 1879	2.6336 5201
23	1.5768 9926	1.7646 1068	1.9735 8651	2.2061 1448	2.4647 1555	2.7521 6635
24	1.6084 3725	1.8087 2595	2.0327 9411	2.2833 2849	2.5633 0417	2.8760 1383
25	1.6406 0599	1.8539 4410	2.0937 7793	2.3632 4498	2.6658 3633	3.0054 3446

Yr.	5 per cent	6 per cent	7 per cent	8 per cent	9 per cent	10 per cent
1	1.0500 000	1.0600 000	1.0700 000	1.0800 000	1.0900 000	1.1000 000
2	1.1025 000	1.1236 000	1.1449 000	1.1664 000	1.1881 000	1.2100 000
3	1.1576 250	1.1910 160	1.2250 430	1.2597 120	1.2950 290	1.3310 000
4	1.2155 063	1.2624 770	1.3107 960	1.3604 890	1.4115 816	1.4641 000
5	1.2762 816	1.3382 256	1.4025 517	1.4693 281	1.5386 240	1.6105 100
6	1.3400 956	1.4185 191	1.5007 304	1.5868 743	1.6771 001	1.7715 610
7	1 4071 004	1.5036 303	1.6057 815	1.7138 243	1.8280 391	1.9487 171
8	1.4774 554	1.5938 481	1.7181 862	1.8509 302	1.9925 626	2.1435 888
9	1.5513 282	1.6894 790	1.8384 592	1.9990 046	2.1718 933	2.3579 477
10	1.6288 946	1.7908 477	1.9671 514	2.1589 250	2.3673 637	2.5937 425
11	1.7103 394	1.8982 986	2.1048 520	2.3316 390	2.5804 264	2.8531 167
12	1.7958 563	2.0121 965	2.2521 916	2.5181 701	2.8126 648	3.1384 284
13	1.8856 491	2.1329 283	2.4098 450	2.7196 237	3.0658 046	3.4522 712
14	1.9799 316	2.2609 040	2.5785 342	2.9371 936	3.3417 270	3.7974 983
15	2.0789 282	2.3965 582	2.7590 315	3.1721 691	3.6424 825	4.1772 482
16	2.1828 746	2.5403 517	2.9521 638	3.4259 426	3.9703 059	4.5949 730
17	2.2920 183	2.6927 728	3.1588 152	3.7000 181	4.3276 334	5.0544 703
18	2.4066 192	2.8543 392	3.3799 323	3.9960 195	4.7171 204	5.5599 173
19	2.5269 502	3.0255 995	3.6165 275	4.3157 011	5.1416 613	6.1159 090
20	2.6532 977	3.2071 355	3.8696 845	4.6609 571	5.6044 108	6.7275 000
21	2.7859 626	3.3995 636	4.1405 624	5.0338 337	6.1088 077	7.4002 499
22	2.9252 607	3.6035 374	4.4304 017	5.4365 404	6.6586 004	8.1402 749
23	3.0715 238	3.8197 497	4.7405 299	5.8714 637	7.2578 745	8.9543 024
24	3.2250 999	4.0489 346	5.0723 670	6.3411 807	7.9110 832	9.8497 327
25	3.3863 549	4.2918 707	5.4274 326	6.8484 752	8.6230 807	10.8347 059

TABLE SHOWING AMOUNT OF $1.00 DEPOSITED ANNUALLY AT COMPOUND INTEREST FOR ANY NUMBER OF YEARS FROM ONE TO TWENTY-FIVE

Periods	2 per cent	3 per cent	4 per cent
1	1.02	1 03	1.04
2	2.0604	2.0909	2.1216
3	3.121608	3.183627	3.246464
4	4.204040	4.309136	4.416323
5	5.308121	5.468410	5 632975
6	6.434283	6.662462	6.898294
7	7.582969	7.892336	8.214226
8	8.754628	9.159106	9.582795
9	9.949721	10.463879	11.006107
10	11.168715	11.807796	12.486351
11	12.412090	13.192030	14.025805
12	13.680332	14.617790	15.626838
13	14.973938	16 086324	17.291911
14	16.293417	17.598914	19.023588
15	17.639285	19 156881	20.824531
16	19.012071	20.761588	22.697512
17	20.412312	22.414435	24.645413
18	21.840559	24.116868	26.671229
19	23.297370	25 870374	28.778079
20	24.783317	27 676486	30 969202
21	26.298984	29.536780	33.247970
22	27.844963	31.452884	35.617889
23	29.421862	33.426470	38.082604
24	31.030300	35.459264	40 645908
25	32.670906	37 553042	43.311745

DISCOUNTS

Chain Discounts. A *chain discount* (called also a compound discount) is a series of discounts, like 25 per cent and 10 per cent; or 25 per cent, 10 per cent, and 5 per cent. It is quite different from the sum of the discounts. Only the first, or primary, discount is from the list price. The second, or secondary, discount is taken from what is left after the first discount has been taken. The third discount is taken from what is left after the second has been taken, and so on.

The tables on the following pages give the net amounts of $1.00 after the chain discounts most commonly used in commercial transactions have been deducted.

TABLE OF CHAIN DISCOUNTS*

Primary Discount

Secondary Discount	5	7-1/2	10	12-1/2	15	16-2/3	20	22-1/2	25	27-1/2	30	32-1/2	33-1/3	35	37-1/2
2	.93100	.90650	.88200	.85750	.83300	.81667	.78400	.75950	.73500	.71050	.68600	.66150	.65333	.63700	.61250
2-1/2	.92625	.90188	.8775	.85313	.82875	.8125	.78	.75563	.73125	.70688	.6825	.65813	.65	.63375	.60938
5	.9025	.87875	.855	.83125	.8075	.79167	.76	.73625	.7125	.68875	.665	.64125	.63333	.6175	.59375
5 2-1/2	.87994	.85678	.83363	.81047	.78731	.77188	.741	.71784	.69469	.67153	.64838	.62522	.6175	.60206	.57891
5 5	.85738	.83481	.81225	.78969	.76713	.75208	.722	.69943	.67688	.65431	.63175	.60919	.60167	.58663	.56406
5 5 2-1/2	.83594	.81394	.79194	.76994	.74795	.73328	.70395	.68195	.65995	.63795	.61596	.59396	.58663	.57196	.54996
7-1/2	.87875	.85563	.8325	.80938	.78625	.77083	.74	.71688	.69375	.67063	.6475	.62438	.61667	.60125	.57813
7-1/2 2-1/2	.85678	.83423	.81169	.78914	.76659	.75156	.7215	.69895	.67641	.65386	.63131	.60877	.60125	.58622	.56367
7-1/2 5	.83481	.81284	.79088	.76891	.74694	.73229	.703	.68103	.65906	.63709	.61513	.59316	.58583	.57119	.54922
10	.855	.8325	.81	.7875	.765	.75	.72	.6975	.675	.6525	.63	.6075	.60	.585	.5625
10 2-1/2	.83363	.81169	.78975	.76781	.74588	.73125	.702	.68006	.65813	.63619	.61425	.59231	.585	.57038	.54844
10 5	.81225	.79088	.7695	.74813	.72675	.7125	.684	.66263	.64125	.61988	.5985	.57713	.57	.55575	.53438
10 5 2-1/2	.79194	.77111	.75026	.72942	.70858	.69469	.6669	.64606	.62522	.60438	.58354	.5627	.55575	.54186	.52102
10 7-1/2	.79088	.77006	.74925	.72844	.70763	.69375	.666	.64519	.62438	.60356	.58275	.56194	.555	.54113	.52031
10 7-1/2 5	.75133	.73156	.71179	.69202	.67225	.65906	.6327	.61293	.59316	.57338	.55361	.53384	.52725	.51407	.49429
10 10	.7695	.74925	.729	.70875	.6885	.675	.648	.62775	.6075	.58725	.567	.54675	.54	.5265	.50625
10 10 2-1/2	.75026	.73052	.71078	.69103	.67129	.65813	.6318	.61206	.59231	.57257	.55283	.53308	.5265	.51334	.49359
12-1/2	.83125	.80938	.7875	.76563	.74375	.72917	.70	.67813	.65625	.63438	.6125	.59063	.58333	.56875	.54688
12-1/2 2-1/2	.81047	.78914	.76781	.74648	.72516	.71094	.6825	.66117	.63984	.61852	.59719	.57586	.56875	.55453	.5332
12-1/2 5	.78969	.76891	.74813	.72734	.70656	.69271	.665	.64422	.62344	.60266	.58188	.56109	.55417	.54031	.51953
12-1/2 7-1/2	.76891	.74867	.72844	.7082	.68797	.67448	.6475	.62727	.60703	.5868	.56656	.54633	.53958	.52609	.50586
12-1/2 10	.74813	.72844	.70875	.68906	.66938	.65625	.63	.61031	.59063	.57094	.55125	.53156	.525	.51188	.49219
12-1/2 10 5	.71072	.69202	.67331	.65461	.63591	.62344	.5985	.5798	.56109	.54239	.52369	.50498	.49875	.48628	.46758
12-1/2 10 5 2-1/2	.69295	.67472	.65648	.63824	.62001	.60785	.58354	.5653	.54707	.52883	.5106	.49236	.48628	.47412	.45589
12-1/2 10 7-1/2	.69202	.6738	.65559	.63738	.61917	.60703	.58275	.56454	.54633	.52812	.50991	.4917	.48563	.47348	.45527
12-1/2 10 10	.67331	.65559	.63788	.62016	.60244	.59063	.567	.54928	.53156	.51384	.49613	.47841	.4725	.46069	.44297
15	.8075	.78625	.765	.74375	.7225	.70833	.68	.65875	.6375	.61625	.595	.57375	.56667	.5525	.53125
15 2-1/2	.78731	.76659	.74588	.72516	.70444	.69063	.663	.64228	.62156	.60084	.58013	.55941	.5525	.53869	.51797
20	.76	.74	.72	.70	.68	.66667	.64	.62	.60	.58	.56	.54	.53333	.52	.50

*By courteous permission of the Lefax Corporation, Philadelphia.

TABLE OF CHAIN DISCOUNTS*

Secondary Discount	Primary Discount																			
	40	42½	45	47½	50	52½	55	57½	60	62½	65	66⅔	70	72½	75	77½	80	85	87½	90
2	.58800	.56350	.53900	.51450	.49000	.46550	.44100	.41650	.39200	.36750	.34300	.32667	.29400	.26950	.24500	.22050	.19600	.14700	.12250	.09800
2½	.58500	.56063	.53625	.51188	.48750	.46313	.43875	.41438	.39000	.36563	.34125	.32500	.29250	.26813	.24375	.21938	.19500	.14625	.12188	.09750
5	.57000	.54625	.52250	.49875	.47500	.45125	.42750	.40375	.38000	.35625	.33250	.31667	.28500	.26125	.23750	.21375	.19000	.14250	.11875	.09500
5 2½	.55575	.53259	.50944	.48628	.46313	.43997	.41681	.39366	.37050	.34734	.32419	.30875	.27788	.25472	.23156	.20841	.18525	.13894	.11578	.09263
5 5	.54150	.51894	.49638	.47381	.45125	.42869	.40613	.38356	.36100	.33844	.31588	.30083	.27075	.24819	.22563	.20306	.18050	.13538	.11281	.09025
5 5 2½	.52796	.50596	.48397	.46197	.43997	.41797	.39597	.37397	.35198	.32998	.30798	.29331	.26398	.24198	.21998	.19799	.17599	.13199	.10999	.08799
7½	.55500	.53188	.50875	.48563	.46250	.43938	.41625	.39313	.37000	.34688	.32375	.30833	.27750	.25438	.23125	.20813	.18500	.13875	.11563	.09250
7½ 2½	.54113	.51858	.49603	.47348	.45094	.42839	.40584	.38330	.36075	.33820	.31566	.30063	.27056	.24802	.22547	.20292	.18038	.13528	.11273	.09019
7½ 5	.52725	.50529	.48331	.46135	.43938	.41741	.39544	.37347	.35150	.32953	.30756	.29292	.26363	.24166	.21969	.19772	.17575	.13181	.10984	.08788
10	.54000	.51750	.49500	.47250	.45000	.42750	.40500	.38250	.36000	.33750	.31500	.30000	.27000	.24750	.22500	.20250	.18000	.13500	.11250	.09000
10 2½	.52650	.50456	.48263	.46069	.43875	.41681	.39488	.37294	.35100	.32906	.30713	.29250	.26325	.24131	.21938	.19744	.17550	.13163	.10969	.08775
10 5	.51300	.49163	.47025	.44888	.42750	.40613	.38475	.36338	.34200	.32063	.29925	.28500	.25650	.23513	.21375	.19238	.17100	.12825	.10688	.08550
10 5 2½	.50018	.47933	.45849	.43765	.41681	.39597	.37513	.35429	.33345	.31261	.29177	.27788	.25009	.22925	.20841	.18757	.16673	.12504	.10420	.08336
10 7½	.49950	.47869	.45788	.43706	.41625	.39544	.37463	.35381	.33300	.31219	.29138	.27750	.24975	.22894	.20813	.18731	.16650	.12488	.10406	.08325
10 7½ 5	.47453	.45475	.43498	.41521	.39544	.37567	.35589	.33612	.31635	.29658	.27681	.26363	.23726	.21749	.19772	.17795	.15818	.11863	.09886	.07909
10 10	.48600	.46575	.44550	.42525	.40500	.38475	.36450	.34425	.32400	.30375	.28350	.27000	.24300	.22275	.20250	.18225	.16200	.12150	.10125	.08100
10 10 2½	.47385	.45406	.43436	.41467	.39488	.37518	.35539	.33559	.31590	.29616	.27641	.26325	.23693	.21718	.19744	.17769	.15795	.11846	.09872	.07898
10 10 5	.46170	.44246	.42323	.40399	.38475	.36551	.34628	.32704	.30780	.28856	.26933	.25650	.23085	.21161	.19238	.17314	.15390	.11543	.09619	.07695
10 10 5 2½	.45016	.43140	.41264	.39389	.37513	.35638	.33762	.31886	.30011	.28135	.26259	.25009	.22508	.20632	.18757	.16881	.15005	.11254	.09378	.07503
10 10 10	.43740	.41918	.40095	.38273	.36450	.34628	.32805	.30983	.29160	.27338	.25515	.24300	.21870	.20048	.18225	.16403	.14580	.10935	.09113	.07290
12½	.52500	.50313	.48125	.45938	.43750	.41563	.39375	.37188	.35000	.32813	.30625	.29167	.26250	.24063	.21875	.19688	.17500	.13125	.10938	.08750
12½ 2½	.51188	.49055	.46922	.44789	.42656	.40523	.38391	.36258	.34125	.31992	.29859	.28438	.25594	.23461	.21328	.19195	.17063	.12797	.10664	.08531
12½ 5	.49875	.47809	.45719	.43641	.41563	.39484	.37406	.35328	.33250	.31172	.29094	.27708	.24938	.22859	.20781	.18703	.16625	.12469	.10391	.08313
12½ 7½	.48563	.46539	.44516	.42492	.40469	.38445	.36422	.34398	.32375	.30352	.28328	.26979	.24281	.22258	.20234	.18211	.16188	.12141	.10117	.08094
12½ 10	.47250	.45281	.43313	.41344	.39375	.37406	.35438	.33469	.31500	.29531	.27563	.26250	.23625	.21656	.19688	.17719	.15750	.11813	.09844	.07875
12½ 10 5	.44888	.43017	.41147	.39277	.37406	.35536	.33666	.31795	.29925	.28055	.26184	.24938	.22444	.20573	.18703	.16833	.14963	.11222	.09352	.07481
12½ 10 5 2½	.43765	.41942	.40118	.38295	.36471	.34648	.32824	.31000	.29177	.27353	.25530	.24314	.21883	.20059	.18236	.16412	.14588	.10941	.09118	.07294
12½ 10 7½	.43706	.41885	.40064	.38243	.36422	.34601	.32780	.30959	.29138	.27316	.25495	.24281	.21853	.20032	.18211	.16390	.14569	.10927	.09105	.07284
12½ 10 7½ 5	.41521	.39791	.38061	.36331	.34601	.32871	.31141	.29411	.27681	.25951	.24221	.23067	.20761	.19030	.17300	.15570	.13840	.10380	.08650	.06920
12½ 10 10	.42525	.40753	.38981	.37209	.35438	.33666	.31894	.30122	.28350	.26578	.24806	.23625	.21263	.19491	.17719	.15947	.14175	.10631	.08859	.07088
15	.51000	.48875	.46750	.44625	.42500	.40375	.38250	.36125	.34000	.31875	.29750	.28333	.25500	.23375	.21250	.19125	.17000	.12750	.10625	.08500
15 2½	.49725	.47653	.45581	.43509	.41438	.39366	.37294	.35222	.33150	.31078	.29006	.27625	.24863	.22791	.20719	.18647	.16575	.12431	.10359	.08288
20	.48000	.46000	.44000	.42000	.40000	.38000	.36000	.34000	.32000	.30000	.28000	.26667	.24000	.22000	.20000	.18000	.16000	.12000	.10000	.08000

To illustrate its use: Find the net amount of a bill of $345 discounted at 25–10–10–5 per cent. Look first in the horizontal column at the top for the primary discount of 25 per cent. Follow this column down until you are opposite the 10–10–5 in the column at the extreme left under the heading, Secondary Discount. You see then that the net amount of $1.00 after 25–10–10–5 per cent has been taken off is .57713. Multiply this by $345 and you have $199.11, which is the net amount of the bill.

Cash Discounts. A *cash discount* is a premium allowed by the seller of goods to the buyer on condition that the invoice is paid within a specified time. When cash discounts are higher than the rate of interest on the money would be for the same length of time, it is wise to borrow money from the bank, if necessary, and take advantage of the discount. The table below shows the ordinary discount rates and their equivalent interest rates figured on an annual basis:

½ % 10 days—net 30 days = 9% per annum
1 % 10 " " 30 " = 18% " "
1½ % 10 " " 30 " = 27% " "
2 % 30 " " 4 mos. = 8% " "
2 % 10 " " 60 days = 14% " "
2 % 30 " " 60 " = 24% " "
2 % 10 " " 30 " = 36% " "
2 % 40 " " 60 " = 36% " "
2 % 70 " " 90 " = 36% " "
2 % 10, 30X days—net 60 days = 36% per annum
2 % 10, 60X " " 90 " = 36% " "
3 % 10 days—net 4 mos. = 10% per annum
3 % 30 " " 60 days = 36% " "
3 % 10 " " 30 " = 54% " "
4 % 10 " " 4 mos. = 13% " "
4 % 10 " " 60 days = 29% " "
5 % 10 " " 4 mos. = 16% " "
5 % 10 " " 60 days = 36% " "
5 % 10 " " 30 " = 90% " "
6 % 10 " " 4 mos. = 20% " "
6 % 10 " " 60 days = 43% " "
7 % 10 " " 4 mos. = 23% " "
8 % 10 " " 4 " = 26% " "

MARKING GOODS

Most retail houses have a secret way of marking goods so that at a glance they can see both the cost price and the selling price. The usual way is to select a word or phrase containing ten different letters, like pink flower, regulation, etc., thus:

pink flower
1234 567890

Sometimes an outside letter like x or z is used where a figure is repeated. Suppose the cost of an article is $2.50 and the selling price $2.75; the mark on the goods would be, if the scheme above is used,

ifr $2.75

If the cost were 44 cents and the selling price 60 cents the mark would be

kz $.60

MARKUP

Markup[1] is that component which is added to a basic cost in order to arrive at a selling price.

A proper selling price should include a reasonable profit.

Profit is essential to successful business administration.

The importance of this subject is obvious. The following table is therefore likely to prove continuously useful to the businessman.

MARKUP TABLE

Total Deductions from Selling Price	Markup Percentage on Cost	Total Deductions from Selling Price	Markup Percentage on Cost	Total Deductions from Selling Price	Markup Percentage on Cost
1%	1.0101%	18%	21.9512%	35%	53.8461%
2%	2.0408%	19%	23.4568%	36%	56.25 %
3%	3.0928%	20%	25. %	37%	58.7301%
4%	4.1667%	21%	26.5823%	38%	61.2903%
5%	5.2632%	22%	28.2051%	39%	63.9344%
6%	6.383 %	23%	29.8701%	40%	66.6667%
7%	7.5269%	24%	31.5789%	41%	69.4915%
8%	8.6957%	25%	33.3333%	42%	72.4138%
9%	9.8901%	26%	35.1351%	43%	75.4386%
10%	11.1111%	27%	36.9863%	44%	78.5714%
11%	12.3595%	28%	38.8889%	45%	81.8181%
12%	13.6364%	29%	40.8451%	46%	85.1851%
13%	14.9425%	30%	42.8571%	47%	88.6791%
14%	16.2791%	31%	44.9275%	48%	92.3076%
15%	17.647 %	32%	47.0588%	49%	96.0784%
16%	19.0476%	33%	49.2537%	50%	100. %
17%	20.4819%	34%	51.5151%		

Explanation of Markup Table. The column headed "Total Deductions from Selling Price" refers to the various allowances to be made on the selling price, *viz.*: discount, commission, overhead, and profit desired.

For example, if the discount to be allowed is

  2% of the selling price,

  5% of the selling price is allowed to a salesman for commission,

 15% of the selling price is the estimated overhead, and

  8% of the selling price is the desired profit, then

30% is the "Total Deductions from Selling Price" (including profit).

"Total Deductions from Selling Price" of 30 per cent is equivalent to a "Markup Percentage on Cost" of 42.8571 per cent or approximately 43 per cent as shown on "Markup Table." Therefore an article costing $10 will have added to it $4.30 (43 per cent). If sold at $14.30, all of the deductions, including profit of 8 per cent, will have been considered.

    Proof:

Cost of Article	$10.00
Markup (43%)	4.30
	$14.30

[1] This information is reprinted by permission of Maurice Goldberg & Company, C.P.A., New York and Los Angeles.

Deductions:

2%	Discount	.29
5%	Commission	.72
15%	Overhead	2.15
8%	Profit	1.14
	Total Deductions (including profit)	4.30
	Cost of Article	$10.00

The deductions may be changed to accord with conditions, resulting in a fluctuation of the markup percentage. For instance, if the selling price is to take into consideration

5% Discount
5% Overhead
5% Profit

a total of 15 per cent, the markup percentage will be 17.647 per cent or $1.76, which amount added to the cost of $10 results in a selling price of $11.76.

MAKING CHANGE

Add enough pennies to the cost of the article to make even money, then add the larger coins.

The cost of the article is 31 cents, and the customer gives a 50-cent piece in payment. Begin with the number 31. Add four pennies to make 35. Add five to make 40 and ten to make 50.

READY RECKONER TABLES

Showing how to find the price of any number of units, such as pounds, yards, bushels, etc., at from two cents to $3.00 per unit. The first column gives the number of units; the columns to the right give the prices per unit. If the number required is not in the column, add together two or more numbers until it is reached. For instance, to find the price of 145 bu., add the price of 100 bu., 40 bu., and 5 bu.

Nos.	2 ct.	3 ct.	4 ct.	5 ct.	6 ct.	6-1/4 ct.	7 ct.	8 ct.	9 ct.	10 ct.	11 ct.
2	.4	.6	.8	.10	.12	.12-1/2	.14	.16	.18	.20	.22
3	.6	.9	.12	.15	.18	.18-3/4	.21	.24	.27	.30	.33
4	.8	.12	.16	.20	.24	.25	.28	.32	.36	.40	.44
5	.10	.15	.20	.25	.30	.31-1/4	.35	.40	.45	.50	.55
6	.12	.18	.24	.30	.36	.37-1/2	.42	.48	.54	.60	.66
7	.14	.21	.28	.35	.42	.43-3/4	.49	.56	.63	.70	.77
8	.16	.24	.32	.40	.48	.50	.56	.64	.72	.80	.88
9	.18	.27	.36	.45	.54	.56-1/4	.63	.72	.81	.90	.99
10	.20	.30	.40	.50	.60	.62-1/2	.70	.80	.90	1.00	1.10
11	.22	.33	.44	.55	.66	.68-3/4	.77	.88	.99	1.10	1.21
12	.24	.36	.48	.60	.72	.75	.84	.96	1.08	1.20	1.32
13	.26	.39	.52	.65	.78	.81-1/4	.91	1.04	1.17	1.30	1.43
14	.28	.42	.56	.70	.84	.87-1/2	.98	1.12	1.26	1.40	1.54
15	.30	.45	.60	.75	.90	.93-3/4	1.05	1.20	1.35	1.50	1.65
16	.32	.48	.64	.80	.96	1.00	1.12	1.28	1.44	1.60	1.76
17	.34	.51	.68	.85	1.02	1.06-1/4	1.19	1.36	1.53	1.70	1.87
18	.36	.54	.72	.90	1.08	1.12-1/2	1.26	1.44	1.62	1.80	1.98
19	.38	.57	.76	.95	1.14	1.18-3/4	1.33	1.52	1.71	1.90	2.09
20	.40	.60	.80	1.00	1.20	1.25	1.40	1.60	1.80	2.00	2.20
25	.50	.75	1.00	1.25	1.50	1.56-1/4	1.75	2.00	2.25	2.50	2.75
30	.60	.90	1.20	1.50	1.80	1.87-1/2	2.10	2.40	2.70	3.00	3.30
40	.80	1.20	1.60	2.00	2.40	2.50	2.80	3.20	3.60	4.00	4.40
50	1.00	1.50	2.00	2.50	3.00	3.12-1/2	3.50	4.00	4.50	5.00	5.50
60	1.20	1.80	2.40	3.00	3.60	3.75	4.20	4.80	5.40	6.00	6.60
70	1.40	2.10	2.80	3.50	4.20	4.37-1/2	4.90	5.60	6.30	7.00	7.70
80	1.60	2.40	3.20	4.00	4.80	5.00	5.60	6.40	7.20	8.00	8.80
90	1.80	2.70	3.60	4.50	5.40	5.62-1/2	6.30	7.20	8.10	9.00	9.90
100	2.00	3.00	4.00	5.00	6.00	6.25	7.00	8.00	9.00	10.00	11.00

Nos.	12 ct.	12-1/2 ct.	13 ct.	14 ct.	15 ct.	16 ct.	18 ct.	18-3/4 ct.	19 ct.	20 ct.	21 ct.
2	.24	.25	.26	.28	.30	.32	.36	.37-1/2	.38	.40	.42
3	.36	.37-1/2	.39	.42	.45	.48	.54	.56-1/4	.57	.60	.63
4	.48	.50	.52	.56	.60	.64	.72	.75	.76	.80	.84
5	.60	.62-1/2	.65	.70	.75	.80	.90	.93-3/4	.95	1.00	1.05
6	.72	.75	.78	.84	.90	.96	1.08	1.12-1/2	1.14	1.20	1.26
7	.84	.87-1/2	.91	.98	1.05	1.12	1.26	1.31-1/4	1.33	1.40	1.47
8	.96	1.00	1.04	1.12	1.20	1.28	1.44	1.50	1.52	1.60	1.68
9	1.08	1.12-1/2	1.17	1.26	1.35	1.44	1.62	1.68-3/4	1.71	1.80	1.89
10	1.20	1.25	1.30	1.40	1.50	1.60	1.80	1.87-1/2	1.90	2.00	2.10
11	1.32	1.37-1/2	1.43	1.54	1.65	1.76	1.98	2.06-1/4	2.09	2.20	2.31
12	1.44	1.50	1.56	1.68	1.80	1.92	2.16	2.25	2.28	2.40	2.52
13	1.56	1.62-1/2	1.69	1.82	1.95	2.08	2.34	2.43-3/4	2.47	2.60	2.73
14	1.68	1.75	1.82	1.96	2.10	2.24	2.52	2.62-1/2	2.66	2.80	2.94
15	1.80	1.87-1/2	1.95	2.10	2.25	2.40	2.70	2.81-1/4	2.85	3.00	3.15
16	1.92	2.00	2.08	2.24	2.40	2.56	2.88	3.00	3.04	3.20	3.36
17	2.04	2.12-1/2	2.21	2.38	2.55	2.72	3.06	3.18-3/4	3.23	3.40	3.57
18	2.16	2.25	2.34	2.52	2.70	2.88	3.24	3.37-1/2	3.42	3.60	3.78
19	2.28	2.37-1/2	2.47	2.66	2.85	3.04	3.42	3.56-1/4	3.61	3.80	3.99
20	2.40	2.50	2.60	2.80	3.00	3.20	3.60	3.75	3.80	4.00	4.20
25	3.00	3.12-1/2	3.25	3.50	3.75	4.00	4.50	4.68-3/4	4.75	5.00	5.25
30	3.60	3.75	3.90	4.20	4.50	4.80	5.40	5.62-1/2	5.70	6.00	6.30
40	4.80	5.00	5.20	5.60	6.00	6.40	7.20	7.50	7.60	8.00	8.40
50	6.00	6.25	6.50	7.00	7.50	8.00	9.00	9.37-1/2	9.50	10.00	10.50
60	7.20	7.50	7.80	8.40	9.00	9.60	10.80	11.25	11.40	12.00	12.60
70	8.40	8.75	9.10	9.80	10.50	11.20	12.60	13.12-1/2	13.30	14.00	14.70
80	9.60	10.00	10.40	11.20	12.00	12.80	14.40	15.00	15.20	16.00	16.80
90	10.80	11.25	11.70	12.60	13.50	14.40	16.20	16.87-1/2	17.10	18.00	18.90
100	12.00	12.50	13.00	14.00	15.00	16.00	18.00	18.75	19.00	20.00	21.00

Showing how to find the price of any number of units, such as pounds, yards, bushels, etc., at from two cents to $3.00 per unit. The first column gives the number of units; the columns to the right give the prices per unit. If the number required is not in the column, add together two or more numbers until it is reached. For instance, to find the price of 145 bu., add the price of 100 bu., 40 bu., and 5 bu.

Nos.	22 ct.	23 ct.	24 ct.	25 ct.	26 ct.	27 ct.	28 ct.	29 ct.	30 ct.	31 ct.	31-1/4 ct.
2	.44	.46	.48	.50	.52	.54	.56	.58	.60	.62	.62-1/2
3	.66	.69	.72	.75	.78	.81	.84	.87	.90	.93	.93-3/4
4	.88	.92	.96	1.00	1.04	1.08	1.12	1.16	1.20	1.24	1.25
5	1.10	1.15	1.20	1.25	1.30	1.35	1.40	1.45	1.50	1.55	1.56-1/4
6	1.32	1.38	1.44	1.50	1.56	1.62	1.68	1.74	1.80	1.86	1.87-1/2
7	1.54	1.61	1.68	1.75	1.82	1.89	1.96	2.03	2.10	2.17	2.18-3/4
8	1.76	1.84	1.92	2.00	2.08	2.16	2.24	2.32	2.40	2.48	2.50
9	1.98	2.07	2.16	2.25	2.34	2.43	2.52	2.61	2.70	2.79	2.81-1/4
10	2.20	2.30	2.40	2.50	2.60	2.70	2.80	2.90	3.00	3.10	3.12-1/2
11	2.42	2.53	2.64	2.75	2.86	2.97	3.08	3.19	3.30	3.41	3.43-3/4
12	2.64	2.76	2.88	3.00	3.12	3.24	3.36	3.48	3.60	3.72	3.75
13	2.86	2.99	3.12	3.25	3.38	3.51	3.64	3.77	3.90	4.03	4.06-1/4
14	3.08	3.22	3.36	3.50	3.64	3.78	3.92	4.06	4.20	4.34	4.37-1/2
15	3.30	3.45	3.60	3.75	3.90	4.05	4.20	4.35	4.50	4.65	4.68-3/4
16	3.52	3.68	3.84	4.00	4.16	4.32	4.48	4.64	4.80	4.96	5.00
17	3.74	3.91	4.08	4.25	4.42	4.59	4.76	4.93	5.10	5.27	5.31-1/4
18	3.96	4.14	4.32	4.50	4.68	4.86	5.04	5.22	5.40	5.58	5.62-1/2
19	4.18	4.37	4.56	4.75	4.94	5.13	5.32	5.51	5.70	5.89	5.93-3/4
20	4.40	4.60	4.80	5.00	5.20	5.40	5.60	5.80	6.00	6.20	6.25
25	5.50	5.75	6.00	6.25	6.50	6.75	7.00	7.25	7.50	7.75	7.81-1/4
30	6.60	6.90	7.20	7.50	7.80	8.10	8.40	8.70	9.00	9.30	9.37-1/2
40	8.80	9.20	9.60	10.00	10.40	10.80	11.20	11.60	12.00	12.40	12.50
50	11.00	11.50	12.00	12.50	13.00	13.50	14.00	14.50	15.00	15.50	15.62-1/2
60	13.20	13.80	14.40	15.00	15.60	16.20	16.80	17.40	18.00	18.60	18.75
70	15.40	16.10	16.80	17.50	18.20	18.90	19.60	20.30	21.00	21.70	21.87-1/2
80	17.60	18.40	19.20	20.00	20.80	21.60	22.40	23.20	24.00	24.80	25.00
90	19.80	20.70	21.60	22.50	23.40	24.30	25.20	26.10	27.00	27.90	28.12-1/2
100	22.00	23.00	24.00	25.00	26.00	27.00	28.00	29.00	30.00	31.00	31.25

Nos.	32 ct.	33 ct.	33-1/3 ct.	34 ct.	35 ct.	36 ct.	37 ct.	37-1/2 ct.	38 ct.	39 ct.	40 ct.
2	.64	.66	.66-2/3	.68	.70	.72	.74	.75	.76	.78	.80
3	.96	.99	1.00	1.02	1.05	1.08	1.11	1.12-1/2	1.14	1.17	1.20
4	1.28	1.32	1.33-1/3	1.36	1.40	1.44	1.48	1.50	1.52	1.56	1.60
5	1.60	1.65	1.66-2/3	1.70	1.75	1.80	1.85	1.87-1/2	1.90	1.95	2.00
6	1.92	1.98	2.00	2.04	2.10	2.16	2.22	2.25	2.28	2.34	2.40
7	2.24	2.31	2.33-1/3	2.38	2.45	2.52	2.59	2.62-1/2	2.66	2.73	2.80
8	2.56	2.64	2.66-2/3	2.72	2.80	2.88	2.96	3.00	3.04	3.12	3.20
9	2.88	2.97	3.00	3.06	3.15	3.24	3.33	3.37-1/2	3.42	3.51	3.60
10	3.20	3.30	3.33-1/3	3.40	3.50	3.60	3.70	3.75	3.80	3.90	4.00
11	3.52	3.63	3.66-2/3	3.74	3.85	3.96	4.07	4.12-1/2	4.18	4.29	4.40
12	3.84	3.96	4.00	4.08	4.20	4.32	4.44	4.50	4.56	4.68	4.80
13	4.16	4.29	4.33-1/3	4.42	4.55	4.68	4.81	4.87-1/2	4.94	5.07	5.20
14	4.48	4.62	4.66-2/3	4.76	4.90	5.04	5.18	5.25	5.32	5.46	5.60
15	4.80	4.95	5.00	5.10	5.25	5.40	5.55	5.62-1/2	5.70	5.85	6.00
16	5.12	5.28	5.33-1/3	5.44	5.60	5.76	5.92	6.00	6.08	6.24	6.40
17	5.44	5.61	5.66-2/3	5.78	5.95	6.12	6.29	6.37-1/2	6.46	6.63	6.80
18	5.76	5.94	6.00	6.12	6.30	6.48	6.66	6.75	6.84	7.02	7.20
19	6.08	6.27	6.33-1/3	6.46	6.65	6.84	7.03	7.12-1/2	7.22	7.41	7.60
20	6.40	6.60	6.66-2/3	6.80	7.00	7.20	7.40	7.50	7.60	7.80	8.00
25	8.00	8.25	8.33-1/3	8.50	8.75	9.00	9.25	9.37-1/2	9.50	9.75	10.00
30	9.60	9.90	10.00	10.20	10.50	10.80	11.10	11.25	11.40	11.70	12.00
40	12.80	13.20	13.33-1/3	13.60	14.00	14.40	14.80	15.00	15.20	15.60	16.00
50	16.00	16.50	16.66-2/3	17.00	17.50	18.00	18.50	18.75	19.00	19.50	20.00
60	19.20	19.80	20.00	20.40	21.00	21.60	22.20	22.50	22.80	23.40	24.00
70	22.40	23.10	23.33-1/3	23.80	24.50	25.20	25.90	26.25	26.60	27.30	28.00
80	25.60	26.40	26.66-2/3	27.20	28.00	28.80	29.60	30.00	30.40	31.20	32.00
90	28.80	29.70	30.00	30.60	31.50	32.40	33.30	33.75	34.20	35.10	36.00
100	32.00	33.00	33.33-1/3	34.00	35.00	36.00	37.00	37.50	38.00	39.00	40.00

Showing how to find the price of any number of units, such as pounds, yards, bushels, etc., at from two cents to $3.00 per unit. The first column gives the number of units; the columns to the right give the prices per unit. If the number required is not in the column, add together two or more numbers until it is reached. For instance, to find the price of 145 bu., add the price of 100 bu., 40 bu., and 5 bu.

Nos.	41 ct.	42 ct.	43 ct.	44 ct.	45 ct.	46 ct.	47 ct.	48 ct.	49 ct.	50 ct.	51 ct.
2	.82	.84	.86	.88	.90	.92	.94	.96	.98	1.00	1.02
3	1.23	1.26	1.29	1.32	1.35	1.38	1.41	1.44	1.47	1.50	1.53
4	1.64	1.68	1.72	1.76	1.80	1.84	1 88	1.92	1.96	2.00	2.04
5	2.05	2.10	2.15	2.20	2.25	2.30	2.35	2.40	2.45	2.50	2.55
6	2.46	2.52	2.58	2.64	2.70	2.76	2.82	2.88	2.94	3.00	3.06
7	2.87	2.94	3.01	3.08	3.15	3.22	3.29	3.36	3.43	3.50	3.57
8	3.28	3.36	3.44	3.52	3.60	3.68	3.76	3.84	3.92	4.00	4.08
9	3.69	3.78	3.87	3.96	4.05	4.14	4.23	4.32	4.41	4.50	4.59
10	4.10	4.20	4.30	4.40	4.50	4.60	4.70	4.80	4.90	5.00	5.10
11	4.51	4.62	4.73	4.84	4.95	5.06	5.17	5.28	5.39	5.50	5.61
12	4.92	5.04	5.16	5.28	5.40	5.52	5.64	5.76	5.88	6.00	6.12
13	5.33	5.46	5.59	5.72	5.85	5.98	6.11	6.24	6.37	6.50	6.63
14	5.74	5.88	6.02	6.16	6.30	6.44	6.58	6.72	6.86	7.00	7.14
15	6.15	6.30	6.45	6.60	6.75	6.90	7.05	7.20	7.35	7.50	7.65
16	6.56	6.72	6.88	7.04	7.20	7.36	7.52	7.68	7.84	8.00	8.16
17	6.97	7.14	7.31	7.48	7.65	7.82	7.99	8.16	8.33	8.50	8.67
18	7.38	7.56	7.74	7.92	8.10	8.28	8.46	8.64	8.82	9.00	9.18
19	7.79	7.98	8.17	8.36	8.55	8.74	8.93	9.12	9.31	9.50	9.69
20	8.20	8.40	8.60	8.80	9.00	9.20	9.40	9.60	9.80	9.80	10.20
25	10.25	10.50	10.75	11.00	11.25	11.50	11.75	12.00	12.25	12.50	12.75
30	12.30	12.60	12.90	13.20	13.50	13.80	14.10	14.40	14.70	15.00	15.30
40	16.40	16.80	17.20	17.60	18.00	18.40	18.80	19.20	19.60	20.00	20.40
50	20.50	21.00	21.50	22.00	22.50	23.00	23.50	24.00	24.50	25.00	25.50
60	24.60	25.20	25.80	26.40	27.00	27.60	28.20	28.80	29.40	30.00	30.60
70	28.70	29.40	30.10	30.80	31.50	32.20	32.90	33.60	34.30	35.00	35.70
80	32.80	33.60	34.40	35.20	36.00	36.80	37.60	38.40	39.20	40.00	40.80
90	36.90	37.80	38.70	39.60	40.50	41.40	42.30	43.20	44.10	45.00	45.90
100	41.00	42.00	43.00	44.00	45.00	46.00	47.00	48.00	49.00	50.00	51.00

Nos.	52 ct.	53 ct.	54 ct.	55 ct.	56 ct.	57 ct.	58 ct.	59 ct.	60 ct.	61 ct.	62 ct.
2	1.04	1.06	1.08	1.10	1.12	1.14	1.16	1.18	1.20	1.22	1.24
3	1.56	1.59	1.62	1.65	1.68	1.71	1.74	1.77	1.80	1.83	1.86
4	2.08	2.12	2.16	2.20	2.24	2.28	2.32	2.36	2.40	2.44	2.48
5	2.60	2.65	2.70	2.75	2.80	2.85	2.90	2.95	3.00	3.05	3.10
6	3.12	3.18	3.24	3.30	3.36	3.42	3.48	3.54	3.60	3.66	3.72
7	3.64	3.71	3.78	3.85	3.92	3.99	4.06	4.13	4.20	4.27	4.34
8	4.16	4.24	4.32	4.40	4.48	4.56	4.64	4.72	4.80	4.88	4.96
9	4.68	4.77	4.86	4.95	5.04	5.13	5.22	5.31	5.40	5.49	5.58
10	5.20	5.30	5.40	5.50	5.60	5.70	5.80	5.90	6.00	6.10	6.20
11	5.72	5.83	5.94	6.05	6.16	6.27	6.38	6.49	6.60	6.71	6.82
12	6.24	6.36	6.48	6.60	6.72	6.84	6.96	7.08	7.20	7.32	7.44
13	6.76	6.89	7.02	7.15	7.28	7.41	7.54	7.67	7.80	7.93	8.06
14	7.28	7.42	7.56	7.70	7.84	7.98	8.12	8.26	8.40	8.54	8.68
15	7.80	7.95	8.10	8.25	8.40	8.55	8.70	8.85	9.00	9.15	9.30
16	8.32	8.48	8.64	8.80	8.96	9.12	9.28	9.44	9.60	9.76	9.92
17	8.84	9.01	9.18	9.35	9.52	9.69	9.86	10.03	10.20	10.37	10.54
18	9.36	9.54	9.72	9.90	10.08	10.26	10.44	10.62	10.80	10.98	11.16
19	9.88	10.07	10.26	10.45	10.64	10.83	11.02	11.21	11.40	11.59	11.78
20	10.40	10.60	10.80	11.00	11.20	11.40	11.60	11.80	12.00	12.20	12.40
25	13.00	13.25	13.50	13.75	14.00	14.25	14.50	14.75	15.00	15.25	15.50
30	15.60	15.90	16.20	16.50	16.80	17.10	17.40	17.70	18.00	18.30	18.60
40	20.80	21.20	21.60	22.00	22.40	22.80	23.20	23.60	24.00	24.40	24.80
50	26.00	26.50	27.00	27.50	28.00	28.50	29.00	29.50	30.00	30.50	31.00
60	31.20	31.80	32.40	33.00	33.60	34.20	34.80	35.40	36.00	36.60	37.20
70	36.40	37.10	37.80	38.50	39.20	39.90	40.60	41.30	42.00	42.70	43.40
80	41.60	42.40	43.20	44.00	44.80	45.60	46.40	47.20	48.00	48.80	49.60
90	46.80	47.70	48.60	49.50	50.40	51.30	52.20	53.10	54.00	54.90	55.80
100	52.00	53.00	54.00	55.00	56.00	57.00	58.00	59.00	60.00	61.00	62.00

Showing how to find the price of any number of units, such as pounds, yards, bushels, etc., at from two cents to $3.00 per unit. The first column gives the number of units; the columns to the right give the prices per unit. If the number required is not in the column, add together two or more numbers until it is reached. For instance, to find the price of 145 bu., add the price of 100 bu., 40 bu., and 5 bu.

Nos.	62-1/2 ct.	63 ct.	64 ct.	65 ct.	66 ct.	66-2/3 ct.	67 ct.	68 ct.	69 ct.	70 ct.	71 ct.
2	1.25	1.26	1.28	1.30	1.32	1.33-1/3	1.34	1.36	1.38	1.40	1.42
3	1.87-1/2	1.89	1.92	1.95	1.98	2.00	2.01	2.04	2.07	2.10	2.13
4	2.50	2.52	2.56	2.60	2.64	2.66-2/3	2.68	2.72	2.76	2.80	2.84
5	3.12-1/2	3.15	3.20	3.25	3.30	3.33-1/3	3.35	3.40	3.45	3.50	3.55
6	3.75	3.78	3.84	3.90	3.96	4.00	4.02	4.08	4.14	4.20	4.26
7	4.37-1/2	4.41	4.48	4.55	4.62	4.66-2/3	4.69	4.76	4.83	4.90	4.97
8	5.00	5.04	5.12	5.20	5.28	5.33-1/3	5.36	5.44	5.52	5.60	5.68
9	5.62-1/2	5.67	5.76	5.85	5.94	6.00	6.03	6.12	6.21	6.30	6.39
10	6.25	6.30	6.40	6.50	6.60	6.66-2/3	6.70	6.80	6.90	7.00	7.10
11	6.87-1/2	6.93	7.04	7.15	7.26	7.33-1/3	7.37	7.48	7.59	7.70	7.81
12	7.50	7.56	7.68	7.80	7.92	8.00	8.04	8.16	8.28	8.40	8.52
13	8.12-1/2	8.19	8.32	8.45	8.58	8.66-2/3	8.71	8.84	8.97	9.10	9.23
14	8.75	8.82	8.96	9.10	9.24	9.33-1/3	9.38	9.52	9.66	9.80	9.94
15	9.37-1/2	9.45	9.60	9.75	9.90	10.00	10.05	10.20	10.35	10.50	10.65
16	10.00	10.08	10.24	10.40	10.56	10.66-2/3	10.72	10.88	11.04	11.20	11.36
17	10.62-1/2	10.71	10.88	11.05	11.22	11.33-1/3	11.39	11.56	11.73	11.90	12.07
18	11.25	11.34	11.52	11.70	11.88	12.00	12.06	12.24	12.42	12.60	12.78
19	11.87-1/2	11.97	12.16	12.35	12.54	12.66-2/3	12.73	12.92	13.11	13.30	13.49
20	12.50	12.60	12.80	13.00	13.20	13.33-1/3	13.40	13.60	13.80	14.00	14.20
25	15.62-1/2	15.75	16.00	16.25	16.50	16.66-2/3	16.75	17.00	17.25	17.50	17.75
30	18.75	18.90	19.20	19.50	19.80	20.00	20.10	20.40	20.70	21.00	21.30
40	25.00	25.20	25.60	26.00	26.40	26.66-2/3	26.80	27.20	27.60	28.00	28.40
50	31.25	31.50	32.00	32.50	33.00	33.33-1/3	33.50	34.00	34.50	35.00	35.50
60	37.50	37.80	38.40	39.00	39.60	40.00	40.20	40.80	41.40	42.00	42.60
70	43.75	44.10	44.80	45.50	46.20	46.66-2/3	46.90	47.60	48.30	49.00	49.70
80	50.00	50.40	51.20	52.00	52.80	53.33-1/3	53.60	54.40	55.20	56.00	56.80
90	56.25	56.70	57.60	58.50	59.40	60.00	60.30	61.20	62.10	63.00	63.90
100	62.50	63.00	64.00	65.00	66.00	66.66-2/3	67.00	68.00	69.00	70.00	71.00

Nos.	72 ct.	73 ct.	74 ct.	75 ct.	76 ct.	77 ct.	78 ct.	79 ct.	80 ct.	81 ct.	82 ct.
2	1.44	1.46	1.48	1.50	1.52	1.54	1.56	1.58	1.60	1.62	1.64
3	2.16	2.19	2.22	2.25	2.28	2.31	2.34	2.37	2.40	2.43	2.46
4	2.88	2.92	2.96	3.00	3.04	3.08	3.12	3.16	3.20	3.24	3.28
5	3.60	3.65	3.70	3.75	3.80	3.85	3.90	3.95	4.00	4.05	4.10
6	4.32	4.38	4.44	4.50	4.56	4.62	4.68	4.74	4.80	4.86	4.92
7	5.04	5.11	5.18	5.25	5.32	5.39	5.46	5.53	5.60	5.67	5.74
8	5.76	5.84	5.92	6.00	6.08	6.16	6.24	6.32	6.40	6.48	6.56
9	6.48	6.57	6.66	6.75	6.84	6.93	7.02	7.11	7.20	7.29	7.38
10	7.20	7.30	7.40	7.50	7.60	7.70	7.80	7.90	8.00	8.10	8.20
11	7.92	8.03	8.14	8.25	8.36	8.47	8.58	8.69	8.80	8.91	9.02
12	8.64	8.76	8.88	9.00	9.12	9.24	9.36	9.48	9.60	9.72	9.84
13	9.36	9.49	9.62	9.75	9.88	10.01	10.14	10.27	10.40	10.53	10.66
14	10.08	10.22	10.36	10.50	10.64	10.78	10.92	11.06	11.20	11.34	11.48
15	10.80	10.95	11.10	11.25	11.40	11.55	11.70	11.85	12.00	12.15	12.30
16	11.52	11.68	11.84	12.00	12.16	12.32	12.48	12.64	12.80	12.96	13.12
17	12.24	12.41	12.58	12.75	12.92	13.09	13.26	13.43	13.60	13.77	13.94
18	12.96	13.14	13.32	13.50	13.68	13.86	14.04	14.22	14.40	14.58	14.76
19	13.68	13.87	14.06	14.25	14.44	14.63	14.82	15.01	15.20	15.39	15.58
20	14.40	14.60	14.80	15.00	15.20	15.40	15.60	15.80	16.00	16.20	16.40
25	18.00	18.25	18.50	18.75	19.00	19.25	19.50	19.75	20.00	20.25	20.50
30	21.60	21.90	22.20	22.50	22.80	23.10	23.40	23.70	24.00	24.30	24.60
40	28.80	29.20	29.60	30.00	30.40	30.80	31.20	31.60	32.00	32.40	32.80
50	36.00	36.50	37.00	37.50	38.00	38.50	39.00	39.50	40.00	40.50	41.00
60	43.20	43.80	44.40	45.00	45.60	46.20	46.80	47.40	48.00	48.60	49.20
70	50.40	51.10	51.80	52.50	53.20	53.90	54.60	55.30	56.00	56.70	57.40
80	57.60	58.40	59.20	60.00	60.80	61.60	62.40	63.20	64.00	64.80	65.60
90	64.80	65.70	66.60	67.50	68.40	69.30	70.20	71.10	72.00	72.90	73.80
100	72.00	73.00	74.00	75.00	76.00	77.00	78.00	79.00	80.00	81.00	82.00

Showing how to find the price of any number of units, such as pounds, yards, bushels, etc., at from two cents to $3.00 per unit. The first column gives the number of units; the columns to the right give the prices per unit. If the number required is not in the column, add together two or more numbers until it is reached. For instance, to find the price of 145 bu., add the price of 100 bu., 40 bu., and 5 bu.

Nos.	83 ct.	84 ct.	85 ct.	86 ct.	87 ct.	87-1/2 ct.	88 ct.	89 ct.	90 ct.	91 ct.	92 ct.
2	1.66	1.68	1.70	1.72	1.74	1.75	1.76	1.78	1.80	1.82	1.84
3	2.49	2.52	2.55	2.58	2.61	2.62-1/2	2.64	2.67	2.70	2.73	2.76
4	3.32	3.36	3.40	3.44	3.48	3.50	3.52	3.56	3.60	3.64	3.68
5	4.15	4.20	4.25	4.30	4.35	4.37-1/2	4.40	4.45	4.50	4.55	4.60
6	4.98	5.04	5.10	5.16	5.22	5.25	5.28	5.34	5.40	5.46	5.52
7	5.81	5.88	5.95	6.02	6.09	6.12-1/2	6.16	6.23	6.30	6.37	6.44
8	6.64	6.72	6.80	6.88	6.96	7.00	7.04	7.12	7.20	7.28	7.36
9	7.47	7.56	7.65	7.74	7.83	7.87-1/2	7.92	8.01	8.10	8.19	8.28
10	8.30	8.40	8.50	8.60	8.70	8.75	8.80	8.90	9.00	9.10	9.20
11	9.13	9.24	9.35	9.46	9.57	9.62-1/2	9.68	9.79	9.90	10.01	10.12
12	9.96	10.08	10.20	10.32	10.44	10.50	10.56	10.68	10.80	10.92	11.04
13	10.79	10.92	11.05	11.18	11.31	11.37-1/2	11.44	11.57	11.70	11.83	11.96
14	11.62	11.76	11.90	12.04	12.18	12.25	12.32	12.46	12.60	12.74	12.88
15	12.45	12.60	12.75	12.90	13.05	13.12-1/2	13.20	13.35	13.50	13.65	13.80
16	13.28	13.44	13.60	13.76	13.92	14.00	14.08	14.24	14.40	14.56	14.72
17	14.11	14.28	14.45	14.62	14.79	14.87-1/2	14.96	15.13	15.30	15.47	15.64
18	14.94	15.12	15.30	15.48	15.66	15.75	15.84	16.02	16.20	16.38	16.56
19	15.77	15.96	16.15	16.34	16.53	16.62-1/2	16.72	16.91	17.10	17.29	17.48
20	16.60	16.80	17.00	17.20	17.40	17.50	17.60	17.80	18.00	18.20	18.40
25	20.75	21.00	21.25	21.50	21.75	21.87-1/2	22.00	22.25	22.50	22.75	23.00
30	24.90	25.20	25 50	25.80	26.10	26.25	26.40	26.70	27.00	27.30	27.60
40	33.20	33.60	34.00	34.40	34.80	35.00	35.20	35.60	36.00	36.40	36.80
50	41.50	42.00	42.50	43.00	43.50	43.75	44.00	44.50	45.00	45.50	46.00
60	49.80	50.40	51 00	51.60	52.20	52.50	52.80	53.40	54.00	54.60	55.20
70	58.10	58.80	59.50	60.20	60.90	61.25	61.60	62.30	63.00	63.70	64.40
80	66 40	67.20	68.00	68.80	69.60	70 00	70.40	71.20	72.00	72.80	73.60
90	74.70	75 60	76 50	77.40	78.30	78.75	79.20	80.10	81.00	81.90	82.80
100	83.00	84.00	85.00	86.00	87 00	87.50	88.00	89.00	90.00	91.00	92.00

Nos.	93 ct.	94 ct.	95 ct.	96 ct.	97 ct.	98 ct.	99 ct.	$1.	$2.	$3.
2	1.86	1.88	1.90	1.92	1.94	1.96	1.98	2.	4.	6.
3	2.79	2.82	2.85	2.88	2.91	2.94	2.97	3.	6.	9.
4	3.72	3.76	3.80	3.84	3.88	3.92	3.96	4.	8.	12.
5	4.65	4.70	4.75	4.80	4.85	4.90	4.95	5.	10.	15.
6	5.58	5.64	5.70	5.76	5.82	5.88	5.94	6.	12.	18.
7	6.51	6.58	6.65	6.72	6.79	6.86	6.93	7.	14.	21.
8	7.44	7.52	7 60	7.68	7.76	7.84	7.92	8.	16.	24.
9	8.37	8.46	8.55	8.64	8.73	8.82	8.91	9.	18.	27.
10	9.30	9.40	9.50	9.60	9.70	9.80	9.90	10.	20.	30.
11	10.23	10.34	10.45	10.56	10.67	10.78	10.89	11.	22.	33.
12	11.16	11.28	11.40	11.52	11.64	11.76	11.88	12.	24.	36.
13	12.09	12.22	12.35	12.48	12.61	12.74	12.87	13.	26.	39.
14	13.02	13.16	13.30	13.44	13.58	13.72	13.86	14.	28.	42.
15	13.95	14.10	14.25	14.40	14.55	14.70	14.85	15.	30.	45.
16	14.88	15.04	15.20	15.36	15.52	15.68	15.84	16.	32.	48.
17	15.81	15.98	16 15	16.32	16.49	16.66	16.83	17.	34.	51.
18	16.74	16.92	17.10	17.28	17.46	17.64	17.82	18.	36.	54.
19	17.67	17.86	18 05	18.24	18.43	18.62	18.81	19.	38.	57.
20	18 60	18.80	19.00	19.20	19.40	19.60	19.80	20.	40.	60.
25	23 25	23.50	23.75	24.00	24.25	24.50	24.75	25.	50.	75.
30	27 90	28 20	28.50	28.80	29.10	29.40	29.70	30.	60.	90.
40	37.20	37 60	38 00	38.40	38.80	39.20	39.60	40.	80.	120.
50	46.50	47.00	47 50	48.00	48.50	49.00	49.50	50.	100.	150.
60	55.80	56.40	57.00	57.60	58.20	58.80	59.40	60	120.	180.
70	65.10	65 80	66 50	67.20	67.90	68.60	69.30	70.	140.	210.
80	74.40	75.20	76 00	76.80	77.60	78.40	79.20	80.	160.	240.
90	83.70	84 60	85 50	86 40	87.30	88.20	89.10	90.	180.	270.
100	93.00	94 60	95.00	96.00	97.00	98.00	99.00	100.	200.	300.

SHOWING THE VALUE OF ARTICLES SOLD BY THE TON

.25	.60	.75	1-3/4	$2	2-1/4	2-1/2	2-3/4	Weight	$3	3-1/4	3-1/2	$4	4-1/2	$5	$6
.00	.00	.00	.01	.01	.01	.01	.01	10	.02	.02	.02	.02	.03	.03	.03
.00	.01	.01	.02	.02	.02	.03	.03	20	.03	.03	.04	.04	.05	.05	.06
.00	.01	.01	.03	.03	.03	.04	.04	30	.05	.05	.05	.06	.07	.08	.09
.01	.01	.02	.04	.04	.05	.05	.06	40	.06	.07	.07	.08	.09	.10	.12
.01	.01	.02	.04	.05	.06	.06	.07	50	.08	.08	.09	.10	.11	.13	.15
.01	.02	.02	.05	.06	.07	.08	.08	60	.09	.10	.11	.12	.14	.15	.18
.01	.02	.03	.06	.07	.08	.09	.10	70	.11	.11	.12	.14	.16	.18	.21
.01	.02	.03	.07	.08	.09	.10	.11	80	.12	.13	.14	.16	.18	.20	.24
.01	.02	.03	.08	.09	.10	.11	.12	90	.14	.15	.16	.18	.20	.23	.27
.01	.03	.04	.09	.10	.11	.13	.14	100	.15	.16	.18	.20	.23	.25	.30
.13	.25	.38	.88	1.00	1.13	1.25	1.38	1000	1.50	1.63	1.75	2.00	2.25	2.50	3.00
.14	.28	.42	.96	1.10	1.24	1.38	1.51	1100	1.65	1.79	1.93	2.20	2.48	2.75	3.30
.15	.30	.45	1.05	1.20	1.35	1.50	1.65	1200	1.80	1.95	2.10	2.40	2.70	3.00	3.60
.16	.33	.49	1.14	1.30	1.46	1.63	1.79	1300	1.95	2.11	2.28	2.60	2.93	3.25	3.90
.18	.35	.53	1.23	1.40	1.58	1.75	1.93	1400	2.10	2.28	2.45	2.80	3.15	3.50	4.20
.19	.38	.56	1.31	1.50	1.69	1.88	2.06	1500	2.25	2.44	2.63	3.00	3.38	3.75	4.50
.20	.40	.60	1.40	1.60	1.80	2.00	2.20	1600	2.40	2.60	2.80	3.20	3.60	4.00	4.80
.21	.43	.64	1.49	1.70	1.91	2.13	2.34	1700	2.55	2.76	2.98	3.40	3.83	4.25	5.10
.23	.45	.68	1.58	1.80	2.03	2.25	2.48	1800	2.70	2.93	3.15	3.60	4.05	4.50	5.40
.24	.48	.71	1.66	1.90	2.14	2.38	2.61	1900	2.85	3.09	3.33	3.80	4.28	4.75	5.70
.26	.53	.79	1.84	2.10	2.36	2.63	2.89	2100	3.15	3.41	3.68	4.20	4.73	5.25	6.30
.28	.55	.83	1.93	2.20	2.48	2.75	3.03	2200	3.30	3.58	3.85	4.40	4.95	5.50	6.60
.29	.58	.86	2.01	2.30	2.59	2.88	3.16	2300	3.45	3.74	4.03	4.60	5.18	5.75	6.90
.30	.60	.90	2.10	2.40	2.70	3.00	3.30	2400	3.60	3.90	4.20	4.80	5.40	6.00	7.20
.31	.63	.94	2.19	2.50	2.81	3.13	3.44	2500	3.75	4.06	4.38	5.00	5.63	6.25	7.50
.33	.65	.98	2.28	2.60	2.93	3.25	3.58	2600	3.90	4.23	4.55	5.20	5.85	6.50	7.80
.34	.68	1.01	2.36	2.70	3.04	3.38	3.71	2700	4.05	4.39	4.73	5.40	6.08	6.75	8.10
.35	.70	1.05	2.45	2.80	3.15	3.50	3.85	2800	4.20	4.55	4.90	5.60	6.30	7.00	8.40
.36	.73	1.09	2.54	2.90	3.26	3.63	3.99	2900	4.35	4.71	5.08	5.80	6.53	7.25	8.70
.38	.75	1.18	2.62	3.00	3.38	3.75	4.13	3000	4.50	4.88	5.25	6.00	6.75	7.50	9.00

$7	$8	$9	$10	$11	$12	Weight	$13	$14	$15	$16	$17	$18
.04	.04	.05	.05	.06	.06	10	.07	.07	.08	.08	.09	.09
.07	.08	.09	.10	.11	.12	20	.13	.14	.15	.16	.17	.18
.11	.12	.14	.15	.17	.18	30	.20	.21	.23	.24	.26	.27
.14	.16	.18	.20	.22	.24	40	.26	.28	.30	.32	.34	.36
.18	.20	.23	.25	.28	.30	50	.33	.35	.38	.40	.43	.45
.21	.24	.27	.30	.33	.36	60	.39	.42	.45	.48	.51	.54
.25	.28	.32	.35	.39	.42	70	.46	.49	.53	.56	.60	.63
.28	.32	.36	.40	.44	.48	80	.52	.56	.60	.64	.68	.72
.32	.36	.41	.45	.50	.54	90	.59	.63	.68	.72	.77	.81
.35	.40	.45	.50	.55	.60	100	.65	.70	.75	.80	.85	.90
3.50	4.00	4.50	5.00	5.50	6.00	1000	6.50	7.00	7.50	8.00	8.50	9.00
3.85	4.40	4.95	5.50	6.05	6.60	1100	7.15	7.70	8.25	8.80	9.35	9.90
4.20	4.80	5.40	6.00	6.60	7.20	1200	7.80	8.40	9.00	9.60	10.20	10.80
4.55	5.20	5.85	6.50	7.15	7.80	1300	8.45	9.10	9.75	10.40	11.05	11.70
4.90	5.60	6.30	7.00	7.70	8.40	1400	9.10	9.80	10.50	11.20	11.90	12.60
5.25	6.00	6.75	7.50	8.25	9.00	1500	9.75	10.50	11.25	12.00	12.75	13.50
5.60	6.40	7.20	8.00	8.80	9.60	1600	10.40	11.20	12.00	12.80	13.60	14.40
5.95	6.80	7.65	8.50	9.35	10.20	1700	11.05	11.90	12.75	13.60	14.45	15.30
6.30	7.20	8.10	9.00	9.90	10.80	1800	11.70	12.60	13.50	14.40	15.30	16.20
6.65	7.60	8.55	9.50	10.45	11.40	1900	12.35	13.30	14.25	15.20	16.15	17.10
7.35	8.40	9.45	10.50	11.55	12.60	2100	13.65	14.70	15.75	16.80	17.85	18.90
7.70	8.80	9.90	11.00	12.10	13.20	2200	14.30	15.40	16.50	17.60	18.70	19.80
8.05	9.20	10.35	11.50	12.65	13.80	2300	14.95	16.10	17.25	18.40	19.55	20.70
8.40	9.60	10.80	12.00	13.20	14.40	2400	15.60	16.80	18.00	19.20	20.40	21.60
8.75	10.00	11.25	12.50	13.75	15.00	2500	16.25	17.50	18.75	20.00	21.25	22.50
9.10	10.40	11.70	13.00	14.30	15.60	2600	16.90	18.20	19.50	20.80	22.10	23.40
9.45	10.80	12.15	13.50	14.85	16.20	2700	17.55	18.90	20.25	21.60	22.95	24.30
9.80	11.20	12.60	14.00	15.40	16.80	2800	18.20	19.60	21.00	22.40	23.80	25.20
10.15	11.60	13.05	14.50	15.95	17.40	2900	18.85	20.30	21.75	23.20	24.65	26.10
10.50	12.00	13.50	15.00	16.50	18.00	3000	19.50	21.00	22.50	24.00	25.50	27.00

SHOWING THE VALUE OF LIVESTOCK

The middle column gives the number of pounds and the top of each column the price per hundred weight.[1]

05	.10	2.50	2.75	3.00	3.25	Weight	3.50	3.75	4.00	4.25	4.50
.00	.00	.08	.08	.09	.10	3	.11	.11	.12	.13	.14
.00	.01	.13	.14	.15	.16	5	.18	.19	.20	.21	.23
.01	.01	.25	.28	.30	.33	10	.35	.38	.40	.43	.45
.01	.02	.38	.41	.45	.49	15	.53	.56	.60	.64	.68
.01	.02	.50	.55	.60	.65	20	.70	.75	.80	.85	.90
.01	.03	.63	.69	.75	.81	25	.88	.94	1.00	1.06	1.13
02	.03	.75	.83	.90	.98	30	1.05	1.13	1.20	1.28	1.35
.02	.04	.88	.96	1.05	1.14	35	1.23	1.31	1.40	1.49	1.58
02	04	1.00	1.10	1.20	1.30	40	1.40	1.50	1.60	1.70	1.80
02	05	1.13	1.24	1.35	1.46	45	1.58	1.69	1.80	1.91	2.03
.03	.05	1.25	1.38	1.50	1.63	50	1.75	1.88	2.00	2.13	2.25
.03	.06	1.38	1.51	1.65	1.79	55	1.93	2.06	2.20	2.34	2.48
.03	.06	1.50	1.65	1.80	1.95	60	2.10	2.25	2.40	2.55	2.70
.03	.07	1.63	1.79	1.95	2.11	65	2.28	2.44	2.60	2.76	2.93
.04	.07	1.75	1.93	2.10	2.28	70	2.45	2.63	2.80	2.98	3.15
.04	.08	1.88	2.06	2.25	2.44	75	2.63	2.81	3.00	3.19	3.38
.04	.08	2.00	2.20	2.40	2.60	80	2.80	3.00	3.20	3.40	3.60
04	.09	2.13	2.34	2.55	2.76	85	2.98	3.19	3.40	3.61	3.83
.05	.09	2.25	2.48	2.70	2.93	90	3.15	3.38	3.60	3.83	4.05
.05	.10	2.38	2.61	2.85	3.09	95	3.33	3.56	3.80	4.04	4.28
05	.10	2.50	2.75	3.00	3.25	100	3.50	3.75	4.00	4.25	4.50
.10	.20	5.00	5.50	6.00	6.50	200	7.00	7.50	8.00	8.50	9.00
.15	.30	7.50	8.25	9.00	9.75	300	10.50	11.25	12.00	12.75	13.50
20	.40	10.00	11.00	12.00	13.00	400	14.00	15.00	16.00	17.00	18.00
.25	.50	12.50	13.75	15.00	16.25	500	17.50	18.75	20.00	21.25	22.50
30	.60	15.00	16.50	18.00	19.50	600	21.00	22.50	24.00	25.50	27.00
.35	.70	17.50	19.25	21.00	22.75	700	24.50	26.25	28.00	29.75	31.50
.40	.80	20.00	22.00	24.00	26.00	800	28.00	30.00	32.00	34.00	36.00
.45	.90	22.50	24.75	27.00	29.25	900	31.50	33.75	36.00	38.25	40.50
.50	1.00	25.00	27.50	30.00	32.50	1000	35.00	37.50	40.00	42.50	45.00
.55	1.10	27.50	30.25	33.00	35.75	1100	38.50	41.25	44.00	46.75	49.50
.60	1.20	30.00	33.00	36.00	39.00	1200	42.00	45.00	48.00	51.00	54.00
.65	1.30	32.50	35.75	39.00	42.25	1300	45.50	48.75	52.00	55.25	58.50
.70	1.40	35.00	38.50	42.00	45.50	1400	49.00	52.50	56.00	59.50	63.00
.75	1.50	37.50	41.25	45.00	48.75	1500	52.50	56.25	60.00	63.75	67.50
.80	1.60	40.00	44.00	48.00	52.00	1600	56.00	60.00	64.00	68.00	72.00
.85	1.70	42.50	46.75	51.00	55.25	1700	59.50	63.75	68.00	72.25	76.50
.90	1.80	45.00	49.50	54.00	58.50	1800	63.00	67.50	72.00	76.50	81.00
.95	1.90	47.50	52.25	57.00	61.75	1900	66.50	71.25	76.00	80.75	85.50
1.00	2.00	50.00	55.00	60.00	65.00	2000	70.00	75.00	80.00	85.00	90.00
1.05	2.10	52.50	57.75	63.00	68.25	2100	73.50	78.75	84.00	89.25	94.50
1.10	2.20	55.00	60.50	66.00	71.50	2200	77.00	82.50	88.00	93.50	99.00
1.15	2.30	57.50	63.25	69.00	74.75	2300	80.50	86.25	92.00	97.75	103.50
1.20	2.40	60.00	66.00	72.00	78.00	2400	84.00	90.00	96.00	102.00	108.00
1.25	2.50	62.50	68.75	75.00	81.25	2500	87.50	93.75	100.00	106.25	112.50
1.30	2.60	65.00	71.50	78.00	84.50	2600	91.00	97.50	104.00	110.50	117.00
1.35	2.70	67.50	74.25	81.00	87.75	2700	94.50	101.25	108.00	114.75	121.50
1.40	2.80	70.00	77.00	84.00	91.00	2800	98.00	105.00	112.00	119.00	126.00
1.45	2.90	72.50	79.75	87.00	94.25	2900	101.50	108.75	116.00	123.25	130.50
1.50	3.00	75.00	82.50	90.00	97.50	3000	105.00	112.50	120.00	127.50	135.00
1.55	3.10	77.50	85.25	93.00	100.75	3100	108.50	116.25	124.00	131.75	139.50
1.60	3.20	80.00	88.00	96.00	104.00	3200	112.00	120.00	128.00	136.00	144.00
1.65	3.30	82.50	90.75	99.00	107.25	3300	115.50	123.75	132.00	140.25	148.50
1.70	3.40	85.00	93.50	102.00	110.50	3400	119.00	127.50	136.00	144.50	153.00
1.75	3.50	87.50	96.25	105.00	113.75	3500	122.50	131.25	140.00	148.75	157.50
1.80	3.60	90.00	99.00	108.00	117.00	3600	126.00	135.00	144.00	153.00	162.00
1.85	3.70	92.50	101.75	111.00	120.25	3700	129.50	138.75	148.00	157.25	166.50
1.90	3.80	95.00	104.50	114.00	123.50	3800	133.00	142.50	152.00	161.50	171.00
1.95	3.90	97.50	107.25	117.00	126.75	3900	136.50	146.25	156.00	165.75	175.50
2.00	4.00	100.00	110.00	120.00	130.00	4000	140.00	150.00	160.00	170.00	180.00
2.05	4.10	102.50	112.75	123.00	133.25	4100	143.50	153.75	164.00	174.25	184.50
2.10	4.20	105.00	115.50	126.00	136.50	4200	147.00	157.50	168.00	178.50	189.00
2.15	4.30	107.50	118.25	129.00	139.75	4300	150.50	161.25	172.00	182.75	193.50
2.20	4.40	110.00	121.00	132.00	143.00	4400	154.00	165.00	176.00	187.00	198.00
2.25	4.50	112.50	123.75	135.00	146.25	4500	157.50	168.75	180.00	191.25	202.50

[1] 100 pounds, usually abbreviated "cwt."

KEEPING ACCOUNTS

The success of a business depends largely on efficient administration. Today's businessman must have adequate financial information concerning the operation of his business. He must know how he is doing and where he stands financially in order to plan and control future operations. He must maintain a system of accounting records which will provide the necessary information. These records are frequently referred to as "books of account," and the process of maintaining them is called "keeping accounts" or bookkeeping.

Bookkeeping is the recording of business transactions in a systematic and convenient form; its purpose is to permit the determination of the amounts and the sources of profits and losses for any given period of time, as well as the determination of the financial position of the business at the end of that period. The financial position of a business depends on the nature and the value of the assets, or things owned; on the nature and amount of the liabilities, or amounts owed; and on the net worth or capital of the owner.

All things which have monetary value will be claimed by someone. Therefore the total value of the assets must equal the sum of the liabilities, or creditors' claims, and the owner's equity. This is expressed in the following equation: Assets = Liabilities and Net Worth.

This equation holds true at all times, although the nature and the value of the individual assets and liabilities are constantly changing as a result of business activity. Incomes are being earned and expenses and costs incurred; many transactions take place daily. The effects of these transactions must be recorded and summarized systematically to permit the preparation of financial statements setting forth the results of operations and the financial position of the business.

THE LEDGER

The ledger is the center of every bookkeeping system. Additional books are used primarily to summarize the effects of the transactions and to facilitate their systematic recording in the ledger.

The ledger is a book which contains a separate financial history of every asset and liability of the business, as well as one of the owner's equity. Each such history is called an account and is assigned a page in the ledger. Thus the page number becomes the account number, and it is frequently used for cross-referencing.

An account, then, is an appropriately titled, written record showing the changes in any asset or liability, or in the net worth of the business, for a given period of time. Each account shows the value at the beginning of the period, the increases and decreases during the period, and the value at the end of the period.

The owner's equity is represented by the net worth, or capital account. Incomes earned increase the balance in this account; costs and expenses incurred decrease this balance. However, if these increases and decreases are entered directly into the capital account much valuable information is lost concerning the source and the amount of the major items of income, and the amount and nature of the significant items of expense. To insure that this information is readily available, separate ledger accounts are set up for each significant type of income and expense. The number of accounts used depends on the type of business and on the nature of its operations.

Income and expense accounts are temporary subdivisions of the capital account. At the end of each accounting period, the balances in these accounts are transferred or "closed out" to the owner's capital account. This adjusts the capital account so that its new balance reflects the owner's equity at the end of the accounting period. Prior to closing out the income and expense accounts, the balances in the ledger accounts represent the incomes and expenses for the period just completed and the new values for the assets and liabilities at the end of that period. This is the information needed for the financial reports.

Account No. 1

CASH

19—			F	Debit	19—			F	Credit
Jan	1	Balance		$10,000.	Jan	4		J1	$3,000.
	8		J1	5,000.		6		J1	1,000.
	10		J1	4,400.		31		J2	12,600.
	29	Bal 9,300.	J2	6,500.					

Ledger Account

The left side of an account is called the debit side; entries on this side are called debits. The right side is called the credit side; entries on this side are called credits. Assets are recorded on the debit side of the account, liabilities and net worth on the credit side. Incomes, representing increases in net worth, are recorded on the credit side of the account; expenses, representing decreases, on the debit side. Entering an amount on the debit side of an account is called debiting the account, on the credit side, crediting the account. The rules for debit and credit are as follows:

Debit to record an increase in an asset or expense; to record a decrease in a liability, net worth, or income.

Credit to record an increase in a liability, net worth, or income; to record a decrease in an asset or expense.

The cash account illustrated here shows a debit balance of $10,000 on January 1. During the month of January cash is received, and the account is debited for these amounts to record the increases in the asset cash; payments are made, and the account is credited to record decreases in the assets. The account also shows the dates of these transactions, and the folio (F) column indicates the source of the information. The numbers J1, J2, etc., refer to the pages in the journal where the transactions were originally recorded and from which the related debits and credits are taken.

The balance in an account is found by totaling the debits and the credits and finding the difference. If the debits exceed the credits the balance is a debit balance, and vice versa. The balance is usually entered in the explanation column on the last line used on the appropriate side of the account. Since the transactions are recorded and explained in the journal, explanations are seldom entered in the ledger accounts.

THE JOURNAL

The journal is an accounting record in which all the transactions of a business are recorded chronologically. The effects of each transaction are determined and set forth clearly, expressed in terms of debits and credits to the appropriate ledger accounts. Periodically these debits and credits are transferred from the journal to the ledger. This procedure is called posting.

Careful analysis of a business transaction will disclose its twofold effect. Double-entry bookkeeping recognizes and records both effects at the same time. One of these effects represents a debit to a ledger account, the other a credit to a ledger account. These are the debit and credit elements of a journal entry, and in each case the debits must equal the credits.

Jones Sales Company

Journal   Page 1.

19--			F	Debit	Credit
Jan	2	Purchases	26	5,000.	
		Accounts Payable—Brown & Co.	11		5,000.
		To record the purchase of merchandise on account.			
	4	Fixtures and Equipment	8	3,000.	
		Cash	1		3,000.
		Purchased fixtures and equipment from the Block Manufacturing Co.			
	6	Rent Expense	38	1,000.	
		Cash	1		1,000.
		Paid rent for the month of January.			
	8	Cash	1	5,000.	
		Notes Payable	13		5,000.
		Borrowed $5,000. from First National Bank on a 60-day, 6% note.			
	10	Cash	1	4,400.	
		Sales	20		4,400.
		Sold merchandise for cash.			
	12	Accounts Receivable—Smith & Co.	2	7,600.	
		Sales	20		7,600.
		Sold merchandise on account.			

Journal

In the journal illustrated here the first transaction reflects a $5,000 increase in purchases, which is debited to the purchases account. It also represents an increase in a liability, accounts payable, of $5,000, which is credited to this account. In the next entry the asset account, fixtures and equipment, is debited to record the increase in the asset value, while cash is credited to record the decrease as the result of the payment of cash. And so on for the other transactions. In every case the debits must equal the amount of the credits.

A journal entry consists of recording the debit and credit elements of a transaction. It includes the date of the transaction, the account to be debited and the amount, the account to be credited and the amount, and a brief explanation. Periodically, the debits and credits are transferred from the journal to the appropriate accounts in the ledger, where they are summarized by account name. This procedure is called posting, and it requires the cross-referencing of the amounts in the journal with the numbers of the accounts in the ledger to which they are posted.

The cross-referencing of the amounts in the ledger with the page numbers of the journal from which they are taken, and of the amounts in the journal with the ledger account number to which they are posted, eliminates the need for explanations in the ledger and simplifies the checking of the work.

SPECIAL JOURNALS

In theory the journal and the ledger described above are the only books necessary for the operation of a double-entry bookkeeping system. In practice, however, and particularly in large business concerns, the journal is divided into several special journals, each of which is designed to simplify and facilitate the recording of a particular class of transactions. Special forms can be designed for each class, and special columns can be added to speed the recording of the transactions and to permit columnar totals rather than individual items to be posted to the ledger. Yet the procedure is essentially the same as before: the debit and credit effects of the transactions are recorded in the journals and posted to the appropriate accounts in the ledger.

Some of the special journals used are: (1) Sales Book, used to record all sales of merchandise on account; (2) Purchases Book, used to record all purchases of merchandise on account; (3) Cash Receipts Book, used to record all receipts of cash; and (4) Cash Payments Book, used to record all payments of cash.

When returned sales and returned purchases occur frequently special books are used to record such transactions. The number of special books used depends on the number and nature of the transactions to be recorded.

CONTROLLING ACCOUNTS

As a business expands, the number of accounts in the ledger grows, and eventually it becomes unwieldy and impractical. When this happens separate ledgers are set up for special groups of similar accounts, and a single controlling account is substituted for them in the ledger, which is then called the general ledger. A controlling account is a summary account in the general ledger which is explained in detail in the accounts of a subsidiary ledger.

Controlling accounts are most frequently used for amounts due from customers (accounts receivable) and for amounts due to creditors (accounts payable). Thus a single account called accounts receivable in the general ledger takes the place of all customers' accounts, which are now placed in a subsidiary ledger called the accounts receivable subsidiary ledger. Accounts payable can be handled in the same way. Controlling accounts can also be used for various other groups of accounts. Periodically the balances of the accounts should be totaled and checked against the balance in the controlling account.

BALANCING THE BOOKS

When all the transactions of a business for a given period of time have been entered in the journals and posted to the ledger, a trial balance is prepared. This is done by listing the account names in the ledger and the balance in each account. Two money columns are used; one for debit balances, one for credit balances. The total of the debit balances should equal the total of the credit balances, since for every debit recorded in the journal there is a credit of equal value.

The trial balance provides a check only on the mathematical accuracy of the work. It will not reveal postings to wrong accounts. The taking of the trial balance and the establishing of the equality of the total debit balances and total credit balances is called balancing the books. This should be done frequently, at least at the end of each month, to check on posting done during the month.

Jones Sales Company Trial Balance—December 31, 19——		
	DEBIT	CREDIT
Cash	$ 60,000.	
Accounts Receivable	19,020.	
Merchandise Inventory	70,000.	
Office Equipment	30,000.	
Accounts Payable		$ 17,400.
Notes Payable		40,000.
Arthur Jones, Capital		111,620.
Sales		250,000.
Purchases	150,000.	
Rent Expense	20,000.	
Utilities Expense	5,000.	
Wages Expense	56,000.	
Miscellaneous General Expense	9,000.	
Totals	$419,020.	$419,020.

Trial Balance

The trial balance also facilitates the preparation of the financial reports. It shows all the assets, liabilities, income, and expenses, as well as the owner's equity. From this listing it is possible to prepare reports showing the profit or loss for the period and the financial position at the end of the period.

CLOSING THE BOOKS

The income and expense accounts are set up as temporary subdivisions of the capital account. At the end of the accounting year, these are closed into the capital account. Journal entries are recorded to make these transfers, and usually the balances are summarized in a special account called the profit and loss account. From this, the net profit or net loss is transferred to the owner's capital account. At the beginning of the next year the income and expense accounts have zero balances, and the net worth account includes the profit or loss for the previous year.

THE ACCOUNTING CYCLE

Since many of these bookkeeping operations have been discussed out of their normal sequence, it may be advantageous at this point to present the steps of the accounting cycle in the order of performance.
1. The transactions are recorded in the journal as they occur
2. The debits and credits are posted from the journal to the ledger
3. The trial balance is prepared from the ledger at the end of the accounting period
4. The financial statements or reports are prepared
5. The books are closed. This is done usually at the end of the year.

GENERALIZED TYPES OF FARMING IN THE UNITED STATES

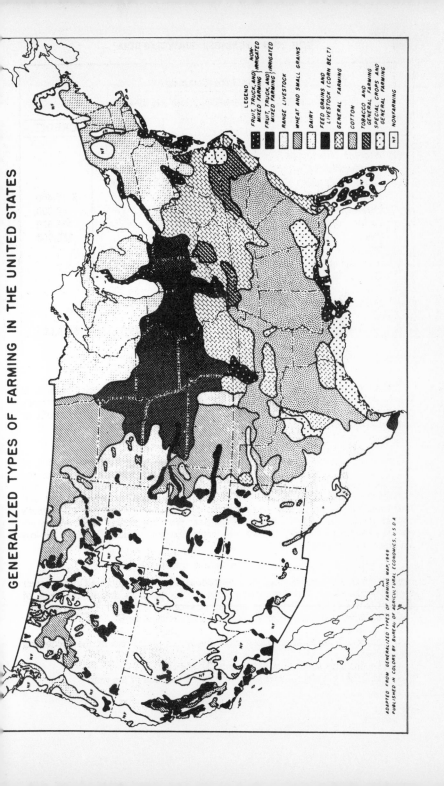

LEGEND

FRUIT, TRUCK, AND } NON-IRRIGATED
MIXED FARMING

FRUIT, TRUCK, AND } IRRIGATED
MIXED FARMING

RANGE LIVESTOCK

WHEAT AND SMALL GRAINS

DAIRY

FEED GRAINS AND
LIVESTOCK (CORN BELT)

GENERAL FARMING

COTTON

TOBACCO AND
GENERAL FARMING

SPECIAL CROPS AND
GENERAL FARMING

GENERAL FARMING

NF NONFARMING

ADAPTED FROM GENERALIZED TYPES OF FARMING MAP, 1949
PUBLISHED IN COLORS BY BUREAU OF AGRICULTURAL ECONOMICS, U.S.D.A.

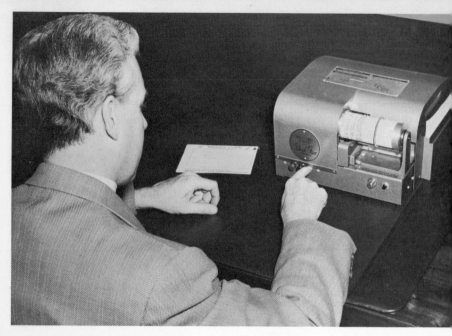

Shown in these pages are a group of business machines that have done much to revolutionize office operation, making possible the speedy handling of many formerly time-consuming tasks. The compact, desk-corner facsimile machine called Desk-Fax serves as an electronic messenger, sending and receiving messages in "picture" form at the push of a button. The outgoing message is flashed automatically to a central telegraph office *(courtesy Western Union Telegraph Company).*

The adding machine has long been an office fixture. Modern models, however, such as this 10-column listing and totaling machine, add many operations to the familiar add-and-subtract features. Among the advantages of this Burroughs P401 model is a multiple total adding-subtractor.

A money- and time-saving necessity in the modern office is the postage meter. This electrically operated Pitney-Bowes Model 4350 automatically feeds, stamps, seals, and stacks letters at a "cruising speed" of some 11,000 an hour.

The task of making copies of important papers has undergone a revolution since the days when a typist might spend hours duplicating a single document. Office copiers are available in many styles. Shown here are *(above)* the Verifax Auto-Twin Copier and *(below)* the Multilith Offset Model 1250W. Machines such as these make it possible for a secretary or other office worker to produce clean, identical copies almost at the touch of a switch.

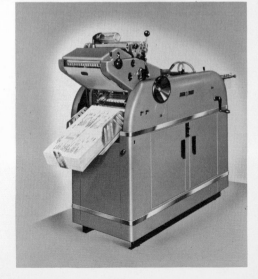

From the first office of Wells, Fargo & Co. *(left)*, the art of bank architecture led through many stages to the ultra-modern style of this San Francisco branch *(below)* of the Wells Fargo Bank American Trust Co., designed by Skidmore, Owings & Merrill. Banking "in the round" provides a spot of beauty as well as efficiency in the city's business district. The lightness and airiness of the structure, which is largely of glass, add much to its attractiveness for both clients and personnel.

This interior view *(right)* of the Wells, Fargo bank branch shown above illustrates the attractive effect of its ceiling design as it casts its shadow on the floor, and the feeling of spaciousness created by the subtle drapery arrangement. Gone are the forbidding tellers' cages, replaced by simple counters that help to establish an atmosphere of personal contact with the bank's clients.

The "miracles" made possible by well-planned store-front modernization are well illustrated in these two photographs. The original property *(top)*, old-fashioned and unattractive, was transformed into a gleaming supermarket *(below)*, with open-vision front of polished plate glass and automatically operated glass doors. Its clean, cool appearance more than doubled business for its Athens, Wisconsin, owner, as well as raising employee morale to a high level *(courtesy Pittsburgh Plate Glass Co.)*.

The design of an office can exert an enormous influence, both on the prospective customer and on the organization's personnel. The modern trend toward elimination of the traditional desk is illustrated in this executive office *(left)* of the Olin Mathieson Chemical Co. Executive secretaries of the Simmons Co. occupy this glassed-in private office *(right)*, with its businesslike banks of file cabinets and contrasting rows of potted plants *(courtesy Designs for Business, Inc.)*.

In the offices *(left)* of Designs for Business, Inc., the usefulness of the traditional "cubicle" is retained while a sense of spaciousness is achieved by adroit use of glass partitions. This area is occupied by an executive secretary and assistants. The bank of two-drawer file cabinets provides useful work space on top. Novel use of lighting is a highlight of the microfilm desk *(right)* in the editorial reference library of Time, Inc.

The trading floor of the New York Stock Exchange, despite its frantic appearance, is a place of well-organized routine where countless orders to buy and sell stocks are handled daily with accuracy and dispatch.

The use of data processing equipment, first manufactured commercially in 1951, has been phenomenal. Its uses include accounting functions and scientific and engineering research computation. In the photo above, several types of Univac systems are shown, illustrating the wide variety of styles and sizes available. In the photo below, the IBM 7090 Data Processing System is shown, with the operators control console in the foreground and magnetic tape units in the background.

FINANCIAL STATEMENTS

Financial reports are prepared to show the financial condition of a business. They provide the businessman with information which he must have in order to operate efficiently and effectively. Knowledge of the results of past operations and of the resources available is essential to good planning and effective control of future operations. The most important financial reports are the balance sheet and the statement of income. Additional statements and reports are used to supplement these and to explain certain sections of them in greater detail.

Financial statements must be prepared in accordance with generally accepted accounting principles. These principles govern methods and procedures which have evolved out of practice and have stood the test of time. Knowledge of them is required for full understanding of the information presented in the balance sheet and the statement of income of a business.

Financial statements must be prepared on a basis that is consistent from year to year so that those for any given year can be compared, with meaningful results, with those of the previous year. By using statements for a series of years, long-term changes and trends can be identified.

Material or significant information leading to a better understanding of the financial statements is usually set forth in the form of footnotes to the statements if it cannot be shown readily in the statements themselves.

FORM OF STATEMENT

The business manager and the owner are not the only persons interested in the financial well-being of a business. Banks, investors, credit organizations, creditors, suppliers of materials, employees, and unions are among those who may wish information on its financial condition. The form of a particular set of statements depends on the purpose for which they are prepared. The form varies, too, with the type of business and the nature of the business activity. Although there is no standard form, those presented below are widely used.

The usefulness of financial statements as far as management is concerned depends, to a great extent, on their being available as soon as possible after the end of the accounting period. A good accounting system will permit much of the bookkeeping work to be done during the year so that statements can be prepared promptly at the year's end. Frequently interim statements are prepared on a monthly or quarterly basis to keep the businessman better informed as to how his business is doing.

The balance sheet is a summary statement which sets forth the financial position of a business as of a specific date. It shows the dollar value of the financial properties owned as well as the claims of creditors and the equity of the owner or owners. The financial properties owned are called assets and comprise all things of monetary value owned by the business. The claims of creditors are called liabilities and are all the financial obligations to other than the owner. The owner's equity, which is equal to the difference between the assets and the liabilities, is called net worth or capital.

To make the balance sheet more meaningful, the assets and the liabilities are classified into special groups and are summarized within the groups. The reader of such a balance sheet can tell at a glance the total amount of any group and the nature of the items comprising that group. He can also compare the various groups.

The statement of income, also known as the statement of profit and loss, is a financial statement setting forth the results of operations for a given period of time. It shows the net gain or loss as well as how this gain or loss came about. The revenues are called incomes and represent increases in the owner's

JONES SALES COMPANY

BALANCE SHEET—DECEMBER 31, 19——

ASSETS

Current Assets:

Cash			$ xxx
Accounts Receivable			xxx
Notes Receivable			xxx
Merchandise Inventory			xxx
Prepaid Expenses			xxx
Total Current Assets			$ xxx

Investments:

Stocks and Bonds			xxx

Fixed Assets:

Fixtures & Equipment	$ xxx		
Less Allowance for Depreciation	xxx	$ xxx	
Building	xxx		
Less Allowance for Depreciation	xxx	xxx	xxx

Intangible Assets:

Patents & Formulas		xxx	
Goodwill		xxx	xxx
Total Assets			$ xxx

LIABILITIES AND NET WORTH

Current Liabilities:

Accounts Payable	$ xxx
Wages Payable	xxx
Taxes Payable	xxx
Notes Payable	xxx
Total Current Liabilities	$ xxx

Long-term Liabilities:

Mortgage Payable	xxx
Total Liabilities	$ xxx

Net Worth:

Arthur Jones, Capital	xxx
Total Liabilities and Net Worth	$ xxx

Balance Sheet

Note: In the case of a balance sheet for a corporation the *Net Worth* section would be comprised of accounts such as these: Capital Stock, Paid-In Surplus, Retained Earnings

JONES SALES COMPANY

STATEMENT OF INCOME FOR THE YEAR ENDED
DECEMBER 31, 19—

Sales		$ xxx
Less: Returned Sales & Allowances		xxx
Net Sales		$ xxx
Cost of Sales:		
Merchandise Inventory—Jan. 1, 19—	$ xxx	
Add: Purchases	xxx	
	xxx	
Less: Purchase Returns & Allowances	xxx	
	xxx	
Less: Merchandise Inventory—Dec. 31, 19—	xxx	xxx
Gross Profit		$ xxx
Selling Expenses:		
Advertising Expense	$ xxx	
Sales Salaries	xxx	
Delivery Expense	xxx	
Miscellaneous Selling Expense	xxx	
	$ xxx	

General and Administrative Expenses:			
Wages Expense	$ xxx		
Bad Debts Expense	xxx		
Insurance Expense	xxx		
Property Taxes Expense	xxx		
Miscellaneous General Expense	xxx	xxx	xxx
Net Profit from Operations			$ xxx
Other Income			
Divided Income	$ xxx		
Rent Income	xxx		xxx
			$ xxx
Other Expense			
Interest Expense			xxx
			$ xxx
Special Income Credit			
Profit on Sale of Assets			xxx
Net Income[1]			$ xxx

The Income Statement

[1] In the case of a corporation the Provision for Federal Income Taxes is deducted from the Net Income to get the Net Income After Taxes.

equity. The costs incurred in earning these incomes are called expenses and reduce the owner's equity.

On the statement of income, costs and expenses are classified and the groups are totaled. Amounts for gross profit and net profit from operations are significant, because they indicate the efficiency of the business operations for a period of time. The net income is the amount of net profit and represents an increase in the amount of net worth.

FINANCIAL ANALYSIS

Businessmen and analysts use the balance sheet and the statement of income to calculate many ratios in an effort to determine the strong points and the weaknesses in the financial condition of a business. However, financial analysis is not a routine procedure; ratios and averages have value only when they are used intelligently. They must be evaluated in the light of the individual circumstances and the factors peculiar to the firm being analyzed. Financial analysis requires sound judgment in assembling and appraising all the data which affect the problem at hand.

CREDIT

Since World War II the use of credit in business has increased tremendously. Indeed, without credit much of the smoothness of distribution from producer to consumer would be lost.

Two types of credit are prominent in the distribution process: *commercial* credit, and *retail*, or *consumer*, credit. Commercial credit is used by business firms in their dealings with one another. The terms of these dealings depend on the industry in which the individual firm operates and on the firm's size, economic resources, and commercial reputation. In addition, credit is extended by banks and investment houses to firms seeking capital for various purposes.

Retail, or consumer, credit is the credit extended by a department store, automobile dealer, appliance dealer, etc., to an individual purchaser. Ordinarily, the consumer uses such credit to make large purchases so as to spread the payment over a long span of time while retaining enough income to meet normal expenses, or because he wishes to avoid cash transactions and to simplify record keeping—for budgeting, tax purposes, etc. Installment buying and charge accounts meet these needs. On the retailer's side, credit selling is one of the ways in which a small business can boost its sales volume.

A specialized form of credit, related to retail credit, is that extended by physicians, dentists, and hospitals and clinics.

For each of these types of credit, certain information is necessary before the person or firm extending the credit, the *credit granter*, can make a decision on the advisability of extending it to the applicant.

Commercial Credit. Modern business is built largely upon credit, and there are many agencies which make a business of finding out just how good is the credit of various commercial organizations. The most famous is Dun and Bradstreet, Inc., which publishes quarterly rating books giving, as nearly as can be determined from signed statements of the firms, the financial ratings of business houses. The National Association of Credit Management and the Credit Clearing House are others, but nearly every house has ways of its own to find out the advisability of extending credit. One of these is to ask for a statement from the customer himself. Another is through his own ledger accounts, which, if active, tell an up-to-date and fairly accurate story. A third is through the personal knowledge of the credit manager, who should be a man with wide knowledge of human nature and tact enough to deal with it pleasantly.

A customer who is asked for a financial statement from a credit agency should furnish it promptly. Refusal is often taken as evidence of financial weakness. The signed statement should be accurate, for it must stand in law. Many houses voluntarily submit statements of their financial standing, a custom which is becoming more and more general.

Credit is extended on the basis of the character of the customer, his ability, and his capital. The length of time for which credit is extended varies in different kinds of business. Farmers go from crop to crop. Small dealers often prefer weekly or monthly statements with no discount, while larger ones prefer the chain discounts (trade discounts). Cash discounts always amount to more than the interest on the money would be, and failure to take advantage of a cash discount is considered evidence of financial weakness. Every business has its own system; the customary practices are the wise ones to follow. For examples of letters exchanged between applicants and credit granters, see *Letters* (Credit Letters). See also *Discounts*.

Of particular interest to credit granters are several publications or sources of information. Besides the already mentioned Dun and Bradstreet, Inc., these include Babson's Business Report Service, *The Wall Street Journal, The Journal of Commerce,* Moody's Investors Service, and many others. Some trade association journals are published monthly; special credit publications include *Credit and Financial Management,* published by the National Association of Credit Management, *The Credit World,* published by the National Retail Credit Association, and publications of the Associated Credit Bureaus of America, Inc.

Consumer Credit. The small businessman finds it profitable as well as necessary to use credit selling, but it is difficult for him to run his business and still have the time and staff to investigate the customer who wishes credit. To meet the needs of small business, a type of credit service—the credit bureau—has grown up. Many of these are affiliated with the Associated Credit Bureaus of America, Inc.

A credit bureau provides information from its files to business and professional people for their confidential use in extending credit. The user pays for the information on a subscription or on a single-report basis. Many sources are consulted by the bureau to obtain this information. The whole picture—good or bad—is reported. Courthouse records are checked for chattel mortgages, liens, bankruptcies, deeds, etc. Police records are noted, and newspaper items containing vital facts are clipped and placed in a permanent record.

From the permanent record, the bureau can provide such information as: (1) the customer's residence and moving habits, as a measure of his permanency; (2) a verification of his employment; (3) his approximate salary; (4) the number of his dependents; and (5) merchants' reports as to how the customer actually pays his bills. The bureau may submit the information on a standard form, or it may make a simple telephone report. Through affiliations with other bureaus, it is able to provide credit reports on newcomers to the community.

To get the best credit bureau service, the credit granter should report his own experience with his customers, thus helping keep the bureau up to date. To aid the bureau in finding the information required, the granter should obtain the following information from the credit applicant: (1) first and last name; (2) wife's or husband's name; (3) complete address; (4) place of employment; and (5) any references he can give.

Another service offered by some credit bureaus is that of a collection department to handle past-due accounts. There are several advantages to allowing the same agency to handle investigation and collection functions: the collection department of a credit bureau, for example, is in a position to point out to debtors that unless prompt payment is made, an unfavorable record will be entered in the files. Because of its access to credit records, it can work out a reasonable schedule through which a debtor can pay his bills. And, as in investigating credit applicants, use of the credit granter's staff to collect past-due accounts rather than for other duties more closely related to business is often uneconomical.

Other information on consumer credit will be found in the section *Household Money Management*. See also *Letters* (Collection Letters).

GRAPHS

A graph is a diagram showing relationships. It is drawn on graph paper or cross-section paper (which is available in stationery and school-supply stores) and consists of a series of points connected by a curve. The information in a graph could also be presented in a table, except that the graph shows at a glance what the information means, while it may take several minutes to puzzle out what the table means.

Let us see how it works. Suppose a magazine secures its only revenue from advertising and that, as with nearly all magazines, its advertising falls off during the summer. The advertising revenue falls off, but the overhead expenses remain the same. The publisher has the information in the following table:

Month	No. of Pages of Advertising	Month	No. of Pages of Advertising
January	50	July	26
February	52	August	25
March	54	September	38
April	50	October	48
May	45	November	52
June	32	December	52

To make a picture (or diagram) of this, he uses a sheet of graph paper ruled off, as indicated in the accompanying illustration, horizontally and vertically into uniform squares, which in turn are divided into smaller squares. He selects 12 of the heavy vertical lines and lets each one represent a month. Then he lets the heavy horizontal lines represent the number of pages and, for convenience, lets each heavy line represent a unit of six pages. The scale values are shown on the left-hand side of the graph.

In January the number of pages was 50, so he puts a point on the January vertical line where it crosses the horizontal 50-page line. In February he puts a point at 52 (between 50 and 56), and so on to the end of the year. Then he draws a smooth line, or curve, through all these points. This is the solid (————) line in the diagram below. The slump in his business (which looks alarming but occurs with nearly all magazines and many other businesses) is clearly evident.

Now suppose the publisher also wishes to see how his overhead compares each month with his income. He finds the cost of obtaining a page of advertising by dividing his overhead by the number of pages sold. Let us assume

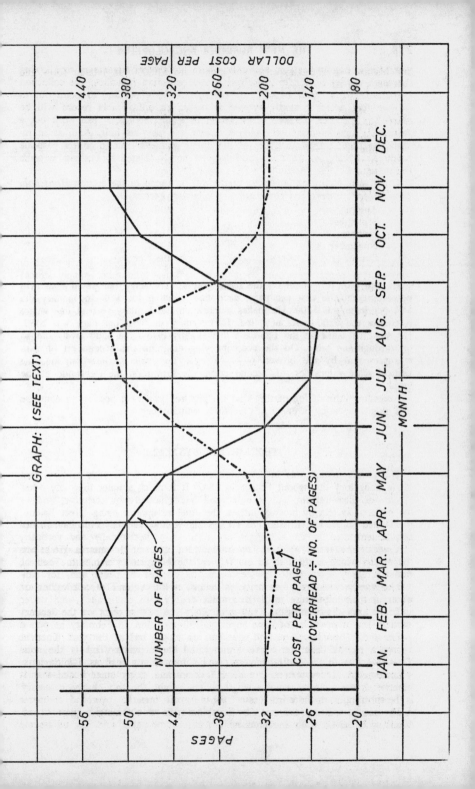

GRAPH: (SEE TEXT)

DOLLAR COST PER PAGE

440 380 320 260 200 140 80

DEC. NOV. OCT. SEP. AUG. JUL. JUN. MAY APR. MAR. FEB. JAN.

MONTH

NUMBER OF PAGES

COST PER PAGE
(OVERHEAD ÷ NO. OF PAGES)

56 50 44 38 32 26 20

PAGES

that his fixed overhead expenses per month are $10,000. In tabular form, the cost per page is:

Month	Cost per Page	
January	$200	($10,000 ÷ 50)
February	193	($10,000 ÷ 52)
March	185	etc.
April	200	
May	225	
June	312	
July	385	
August	400	
September	264	
October	210	
November	193	
December	193	

He can plot this curve on the same graph. The heavy horizontal lines will now represent the cost per page, each line standing for $60. In January the cost per page was $200. He makes a mark on the January vertical line where it crosses the $200 horizontal line. In February the cost per page was $193. He makes a mark on the February line slightly below the $200 level, and so on through the table. On the accompanying diagram, this second set of data is represented by the broken (———) line. To avoid misinterpretation, the vertical scale values for this second curve are shown on the right side of the graph paper.

Recording information of this kind in "pictures" makes it possible to compare at a glance the result of one year's activities with another.

THE METRIC SYSTEM

The metric system was invented toward the close of the 18th century, and made obligatory throughout France in 1837. It is much simpler than any other system of measurement and is now used internationally by scientists, and as the national system by most countries, the chief exceptions being Great Britain, the United States, and Russia. The United States, however, has a decimal monetary system.

Units of the Metric System. The fundamental units of the metric system are the *meter*, which is the unit of length, and the *kilogram,* which is the unit of mass.

The *liter,* a measure of capacity, is defined as the volume of a kilogram of water at the temperature of its maximum density (4° centigrade), and under standard atmospheric pressure (760 millimeters). All other units are the decimal subdivisions or multiples of these.

The meter, the kilogram, and the liter are closely related. For all practical purposes, 1 cubic decimeter equals 1 liter and 1 liter of water weighs 1 kilogram. Thus, the quantity 5,432.768 meters can be immediately read as 5 kilometers, 4 hectometers, 3 decameters, 2 meters, 7 decimeters, 6 centimeters, and 8 millimeters. If the quantity is not a length, but a weight, the only change necessary is the substitution of the word "grams" for the word "meters."

The metric tables are formed by combining the word "meter," "gram," and "liter" with the six following prefixes:

Prefixes	*Meaning*		*Units*
milli-	= one-thousandth	.001	
centi-	= one-hundredth	.01	"meter" for length
deci-	= one-tenth	.1	"gram" for weight
Unit	= one	1.	or mass
deka-	= ten	10	
hecto-	= one hundred	100	"liter" for capacity
kilo-	= one thousand	1000	"are" for land area

The *joule* is a unit of both mechanical and electrical energy. It is equivalent to the work done or the heat generated in keeping up for one second a current of one ampere against a resistance of one ohm, or in raising the potential of one coulomb by one volt. It is equal to 10,000,000 ergs or .73756 foot-pound.

The *calorie* is one of two recognized units of heat. The greater calorie is the amount of heat necessary to raise one kilogram of water 1° C.; the lesser or small calorie is the amount of heat necessary to raise one gram of water 1° C.

The National Bureau of Standards advocates use of "kilocalorie" and "calorie," respectively, for the greater and lesser calorie.

Foot-pound, horsepower, and cheval or cheval vapeur, as generally defined, vary from place to place by ½ per cent because of variations in the intensity of gravity. The relations given below are for the international standard gravity, which gives an acceleration of 980.665 centimeters per second per second.

A Comparison of Centimeters and Inches

METRIC ABBREVIATIONS

k	= kilo	h	= hecto	dk	= deka
m	= milli	d	= deci	c	= centi
g	= gram	m	= meter	c. c.	= cubic centimeter
hl	= hectoliter	kg	= kilogram	l	= liter
t	= ton metric	a	= are	s	= stere

METRIC CONVERSIONS

Millimeters × .03937	= inches
Millimeters ÷ 25.4	= inches
Centimeters × .3937	= inches
Centimeters ÷ 2.54	= inches
Meters × 39.37	= inches
Meters × 3.28	= feet
Meters × 1.094	= yards
Kilometers × .6214	= miles
Kilometers ÷ 1.6093	= miles
Kilometers × 3,280.8	= feet
Square millimeters × .00155	= square inches
Square millimeters ÷ 645	= square inches
Square centimeters × .155	= square inches
Square centimeters ÷ 6.45	= square inches
Square meters × 10.764	= square feet
Square kilometers × 247.1	= acres
Square kilometers × .3861	= square miles
Hectares × 2.471	= acres
Hectares × .003861	= square miles
Cubic centimeters ÷ 16.387	= cubic inches
Cubic centimeters ÷ 3.70	= fluid drams
Cubic centimeters ÷ 29.57	= fluid ounces
Cubic meters × 35.314	= cubic feet

Cubic meters × 1.307	= cubic yards
Cubic meters × 264.2	= gallons (231 cubic inches)
Liters × 61.025	= cubic inches
Liters × 33.81	= fluid ounces
Liters × .2642	= gallons (231 cubic inches)
Liters ÷ 3.785	= gallons (231 cubic inches)
Liters ÷ 28.317	= cubic feet
Hectoliters × 3.53	= cubic feet
Hectoliters × 2.84	= bushels (2,150.42 cubic inches)
Hectoliters × .131	= cubic yards
Hectoliters ÷ 26.42	= gallons (231 cubic inches)
Grams × 15.432	= grains
Grams (water) ÷ 29.57	= fluid ounces
Grams ÷ 28.35	= ounces avoirdupois
Grams per cubic centimeter ÷ 27.7	= pounds per cubic inch
Joule × .7373	= foot-pounds
Kilograms × 2.2046	= pounds
Kilograms × 35.27	= ounces avoirdupois
Kilograms ÷ 908.68	= short tons (2,000 pounds)
Kilograms per square centimeter × 14.223	= pounds per square inch
Kilogram meters × 7.233	= foot-pounds
Kilograms per meter × .671	= pounds per foot
Kilograms per cubic meter × .062	= pounds per cubic foot
Kilograms per cheval × 2.235	= pounds per horsepower
Kilowatts × 1.34	= horsepower (33,000 foot-pounds per minute)
Watts ÷ 746	= horsepower
Watts × .00134	= horsepower
Watts × 44.24	= foot-pounds per minute
Calories × 3.968	= B.T.U. (British Thermal Unit)
Cheval vapeur × 0.986	= horsepower
Centigrade × 1.8 + 32	= degrees Fahrenheit

Acceleration due to gravity, international standard, 980.665 centimeters per second^2, or 980.665 centimeters per second per second.

Measures of Length. The meter is the unit. It is equal to 39.37 inches, or 3⅜ feet.

1 kilometer = 1,000 meters
1 hectometer = 100 meters
1 dekameter = 10 meters
1 decimeter = 0.1 meter
1 centimeter = 0.01 meter
1 millimeter = 0.001 meter = 0.1 centimeter
1 micron = 0.000001 meter = 0.001 millimeter
1 millimicron = 0.000000001 meter = 0.001 micron
1 foot = ⅓ yard = 30.48 centimeters
1 inch = ¹⁄₃₆ yard = ¹⁄₁₂ foot = 2.54 centimeters
1 link = 0.22 yard = 7.92 inches
1 rod = 5½ yards = 16½ feet
1 chain = 22 yards = 100 links = 66 feet = 4 rods
1 furlong = 220 yards = 40 rods = 10 chains
1 statute mile = 1,760 yards = 5,280 feet = 320 rods = 1,609.35 meters
1 hand = 4 inches
1 point = ¹⁄₇₂ inch
1 fathom = 6 feet
1 span = 9 inches = ⅛ fathom
1 U.S. nautical mile ⎫ = 6,080.20 feet
1 sea mile ⎬ = 1.151553 statute miles
1 geographical mile ⎭ = 1,853.248 meters

Measures of Area. The square meter is the unit, that is, a square which is one meter long on each side.

1 square kilometer = 1,000,000 square meters
1 hectare or square hectometer = 10,000 square meters
1 are or square dekameter = 100 square meters
1 centare = 1 square meter
1 square decimeter = 0.01 square meter
1 square centimeter = 0.0001 square meter
1 square millimeter = 0.000001 square meter = 0.01 square centimeter
1 square foot = $\frac{1}{9}$ square yard
1 square inch = $\frac{1}{1296}$ square yard = $\frac{1}{144}$ square foot
1 square link = 0.0484 square yard = 62.7264 square inches
1 square rod = 30.25 square yards = 272.25 square feet = 625 square links
1 square chain = 484 square yards = 16 square rods = 10,000 square links
1 acre = 4,840 square yards = 160 square rods = 10 square chains = .4047 hectare = 40.47 are
1 square mile = 3,097,600 square yards = 640 acres = 259 hectares

Measures of Volume. The cubic meter is the unit, that is, a cube each edge of which is one meter long.

1 cubic kilometer = 1,000,000,000 cubic meters
1 cubic hectometer = 1,000,000 cubic meters
1 cubic dekameter = 1,000 cubic meters
1 stere = 1 cubic meter
1 cubic decimeter = 0.001 cubic meter
1 cubic centimeter = 0.000001 cubic meter = 0.001 cubic decimeter
1 cubic millimeter = 0.000000001 cubic meter = 0.001 cubic centimeter
1 cubic foot = $\frac{1}{27}$ cubic yard
1 cubic inch = $\frac{1}{46656}$ cubic yard = $\frac{1}{1728}$ cubic foot
1 board foot = 144 cubic inches = $\frac{1}{12}$ cubic foot
1 cord = 128 cubic feet

Measures of Capacity. The liter is the unit. The liter is 1.000027 cubic decimeters, or 61.025 cubic inches, which is equal to .264178 gallons, or 2.11342 liquid pints.

1 hectoliter = 100 liters
1 dekaliter = 10 liters
1 deciliter = 0.1 liter
1 centiliter = 0.01 liter
1 liquid quart = $\frac{1}{4}$ gallon = 57.57 cubic inches
1 liquid pint = $\frac{1}{8}$ gallon = $\frac{1}{2}$ liquid quart = 28.785 cubic inches
1 gill = $\frac{1}{32}$ gallon = $\frac{1}{4}$ liquid pint = 7.19625 cubic inches
1 fluid ounce = $\frac{1}{128}$ gallon = $\frac{1}{16}$ liquid pint
1 fluid dram = $\frac{1}{8}$ fluid ounce = $\frac{1}{128}$ liquid pint
1 minim = $\frac{1}{60}$ fluid dram = $\frac{1}{480}$ fluid ounce
1 firkin = 9 gallons
1 peck = $\frac{1}{4}$ bushel = 537.605 cubic inches
1 dry quart = $\frac{1}{32}$ bushel = $\frac{1}{8}$ peck = 67.200625 cubic inches
1 dry pint = $\frac{1}{64}$ bushel = $\frac{1}{2}$ dry quart = 33.6003125 cubic inches
1 barrel (for fruits, vegetables, and other dry commodities) 7,056 cubic inches = 105 dry quarts
Note:
A (U.S.) gallon is a unit of capacity equivalent to the volume of 231 cubic inches
A (U.S.) bushel is a unit of capacity equivalent to the volume of 2,150.42 cubic inches

Measures of Mass. The kilogram is the unit. A kilogram is the equivalent of 2.2046 pounds avoirdupois.

1 metric ton = 1,000 kilograms
1 hectogram = 100 grams = 0.1 kilogram

1 dekagram = 10 grams = 0.01 kilogram
1 decigram = 0.1 gram
1 centigram = 0.01 gram
1 milligram = 0.001 gram
1 avoirdupois ounce = $\frac{1}{16}$ avoirdupois pound
1 avoirdupois dram = $\frac{1}{256}$ avoirdupois pound = $\frac{1}{16}$ avoirdupois ounce
1 grain = $\frac{1}{7000}$ avoirdupois pound = $\frac{10}{4375}$ avoirdupois ounce = $\frac{1}{5760}$ troy pound
1 apothecaries' pound = 1 troy pound = $\frac{5760}{7000}$ avoirdupois pound
1 apothecaries' or troy ounce = $\frac{1}{12}$ troy pound = $\frac{480}{7000}$ avoirdupois pound = 480 grains
1 apothecaries' dram = $\frac{1}{96}$ apothecaries' pound = $\frac{1}{8}$ apothecaries' ounce = 60 grains
1 pennyweight = $\frac{1}{20}$ troy ounce = 24 grains
1 apothecaries' scruple = $\frac{1}{3}$ apothecaries' dram = 20 grains
1 metric carat = 200 milligrams = 0.2 gram
1 short hundredweight = 100 avoirdupois pounds (used in United States)
1 long hundredweight = 112 avoirdupois pounds (used in England)
1 short ton = 2,000 avoirdupois pounds
1 long ton = 2,240 avoirdupois pounds

WEIGHTS AND MEASURES TABLES

LINEAR MEASURE

12 inches =	1 foot	8 furlongs =	
3 feet =	1 yard	320 rods =	
5½ yards =	} 1 rod	1,760 yards =	} 1 statute mile
16½ feet =		5,280 feet =	
40 rods =	1 furlong	6,080.20 feet =	1 nautical mile = 1.1516 statute miles

Note: A "knot" is a speed of 1 nautical mile per hour.

SOME SPECIAL LINEAR MEASURES

1,000 mils = 1 inch		18 inches = 1 cubit
72 points = 1 inch		2½ feet = 1 military pace
4 inches = 1 hand		6 feet = 1 fathom
7.92 inches = 1 surveyor's link		40 yards = 1 bolt (cloth)
9 inches = 1 span		10 chains = 1 furlong

SQUARE MEASURE

144 square inches = 1 square foot	160 acres = 1 quarter section	
9 square feet = 1 square yard	4 quarter sections =	} 1 square mile
30¼ square yards = 1 square rod	640 acres =	
160 square rods = } 1 acre	36 square miles = 1 township	
43,560 square feet =		

CUBIC MEASURE

1,728 cubic inches = 1 cubic foot
27 cubic feet = 1 cubic yard
128 cubic feet = 1 cord

Note: A "board foot," used in lumber measurements, is a volume equivalent to that of a board 1 ft. × 1 ft. × 1 in., or 144 cu. in.

CIRCULAR MEASURE

60 seconds = 1 minute	4 quadrants =	} 1 circle
60 minutes = 1 degree	360 degrees =	
90 degrees = 1 quadrant		

A convenient method of finding the difference in time between two places, is to notice their distance apart, in degrees of longitude, and allow 4 minutes to each degree, based on the following calculation:

1,440 minutes = 1 day or revolution of the earth
1 revolution of the earth is
360 degrees; therefore,
1 degree = 4 minutes

PAPER MEASURE

For small papers the old measure is still in use:

24 sheets = 1 quire
20 quires = 1 ream (480 sheets)

For papers put up in cases, bundles, or frames the following measure is now used:

25 sheets = 1 quire
20 quires = 1 standard ream (500 sheets)

SURVEYOR'S MEASURE

7.992 inches = 1 link (Gunter's or surveyor's)
100 links = 1 chain (= 66 feet)
80 chains = 1 mile

SURVEYOR'S AREA MEASURE

625 square links = 1 (square) pole or square rod
16 (square) poles = 1 square chain (surveyor's)
10 square chains or 160 square rods = 1 acre
640 acres = 1 square mile
36 square miles = 1 township

MARINER'S MEASURE

6 feet = 1 fathom
120 fathoms = 1 cable length (U.S. Navy)
10 cable lengths = 1 nautical mile = 6,080 feet (Br.) = 6,080.20 feet (U.S.)
A statute mile is 5,280 feet

TIME MEASURE

60 seconds = 1 minute
60 minutes = 1 hour
24 hours = 1 day
7 days = 1 week
29 days, 12 hours, 44 minutes, 2.78 seconds (with a variation of 13 hours due to the eccentricity of the orbit) = 1 lunar month
28, 29, 30, or 31 days = 1 calendar month
30 days = 1 month (in computing interest)
52 weeks and 1 day ⎫ 1 year
12 calendar months ⎰
365 days, 5 hours, 48 minutes, and 46 seconds = 1 solar year
366 days = 1 leap year

APOTHECARIES' FLUID MEASURE

60 minims = 1 fluid dram
8 fluid drams = 1 fluid ounce
16 fluid ounces = 1 liquid pint
8 liquid pints = 1 gallon
(British measures differ from the above)

APOTHECARIES' WEIGHT

20 grains	=	1 scruple
3 scruples	=	1 dram
8 drams	=	1 ounce
12 ounces	=	1 pound

AVOIRDUPOIS WEIGHT

$27\frac{11}{32}$ grains =	1 dram		100 pounds =	1 short hundredweight
16 drams =	1 ounce		112 pounds =	1 long hundredweight
16 ounces =	} 1 pound		2,000 pounds =	1 short ton
7,000 grains =			2,240 pounds =	1 long ton

TROY WEIGHT

24 grains	= 1 pennyweight
20 pennyweights	= 1 ounce
12 ounces	= 1 pound (Troy)

Carat (for precious stones) = 200 milligrams. The carat was formerly an ambiguous term having many values in various countries.

Carat (fineness of gold) = $\frac{1}{24}$ (by weight) gold. For example, 24 carats fine = pure gold; 18 carats fine = $\frac{18}{24}$ pure gold.

MISCELLANEOUS UNIT MEASUREMENTS

12 pieces = 1 dozen	165 pounds of potatoes = 1 barrel
12 dozen = 1 gross	140 pounds of apples = 1 barrel
12 gross = 1 great gross	11.7 pounds of molasses = 1 gallon
20 units = 1 score	200 pounds of lime = 1 barrel
196 pounds of flour = 1 barrel	200 pounds of pickled fish = 1 barrel
200 pounds of beef or pork = 1 barrel	63 pounds of butter = 1 tub

In measuring iron, lead, etc.

14 pounds	= 1 stone
21½ stones	= 1 pig

LEGAL MEASUREMENTS OF VARIOUS COMMODITIES

Weights in Pounds per Bushel. The bushel commonly used in the United States is the Winchester bushel which contains 2,150.42 cu. in. This was in use both in this country and in England at the time of the Declaration of Independence and has since been approved by Act of Congress.

Commodities are sold either by the struck or level bushel or by the heaped bushel. There are no specifications as to how high the heaped bushel should be but custom decrees that it shall be "as high as may be without special effort or design." The heaped bushel is about 25 to 27 per cent larger than the struck bushel. It is often reckoned as 2,747.71 cu. in. Grain, berries, beans, peas, and small fruits are usually measured by the struck bushel; apples, pears, potatoes, onions, etc., are measured by the heaped bushel.

There are 0.8 of a level bushel in a cubic foot of space. (This is found by dividing the number of cubic inches in a foot, 1,728, by the number of cubic inches in a bushel.)

There are 0.63 of a heaped bushel in a cubic foot of space (1,728 ÷ 2,747.71 = 0.63).

To find the number of bushels a bin will hold, find the capacity of the bin in cubic inches (length × height × width) and multiply its capacity in cubic feet by 0.8 if the bushels are level; by 0.63 if they are heaped.

To find the number of bushels and odd pounds in a load of grain weighing a certain number of pounds, divide the pounds per bushel for the particular type of grain into the net weight of the grain. For example, a bushel of clover seeds legally weighs 60 lb. in most states. A load of clover seeds weighing 3,500 lb. would therefore contain 58 bu. and 20 lb. of clover seeds, or 3,500 divided by 60. If a state legal weight is not established for a particular grain, it is customary to use the following bushel measures: wheat, 60 lb. per bushel; barley, 48 lb. per bushel; oats, 32 lb. per bushel; rye and Indian corn, 56 lb. per bushel.

One of the most important points to remember in connection with measures for struck bushels is that a measure with a narrow diameter will not allow either proper settling down or proper heaping of the commodities. For this reason the Bureau of Standards has adopted the following minimum diameters of cylindrical dry measures of various capacities:

	Minimum diameter in inches		Minimum diameter in inches
½ bushel	13¾	2 quarts	6⅝
1 peck	10⅞	1 quart	5⅜
½ peck	8½	1 pint	4

Dry commodities should never be bought or sold in measures for liquids, since all liquid measures are from 14 per cent to 16 per cent smaller than the corresponding dry measures.

The British imperial bushel is about 3 per cent larger than the United States standard Winchester bushel. The imperial bushel contains 2,219.36 cu. in.

It is because of the difficulties in measuring by volume that some states have laws requiring that commodities be sold by weight. In other states only the commodities for which a standard weight has been legally established must be sold by weight. Whenever possible it is desirable to buy by weight instead of by volume.

STANDARD BARREL MEASURE

The capacity of the standard barrel for fruits, vegetables, and other dry commodities has been fixed by Act of Congress. Except for the cranberry barrel and the lime barrel, which is graded on a weight basis, the capacities of the standard barrel and its subdivisions for the commodities mentioned above are as follows:

Size	Cubic inches	Bushels[1]	Quarts[1]
Barrel	7,056	3.281	105
¾ barrel	5,292	2.461	78¾
½ barrel	3,528	1.641	52½
⅓ barrel	2,352	1.094	35

The capacities of the standard cranberry barrel and its subdivisions are as follows:

Size	Cubic inches	Bushels[1]	Quarts[1]
Cranberry barrel	5,826	2.709	86 45/64
¾ cranberry barrel	4,369.5	2.032	65 1/64
½ cranberry barrel	2,913	1.355	43 11/32
⅓ cranberry barrel	1,942	0.903	28 29/32

[1] Struck measure.

MEASURING WATER, OIL, ETC.

The unit of measurement for cisterns, tanks, etc., is the gallon, which consists of 231 cu. in. A cubic foot of space contains 1,728 cu. in. ÷ 231, which equals 7.48 gal.

To find the number of gallons which a cistern or a tank will hold, multiply the capacity in cubic feet by 7.48.

Water

1	cubic inch	.03617	pound
12	cubic inches	.434	pound
1	cubic foot	62.4	pounds
1	cubic foot	7.48052	U. S. gallons
1.8	cubic feet	112.0	pounds
35.84	cubic feet	2,240.0	pounds
1	cylindrical inch	.02842	pound
12	cylindrical inches	.341	pound
1	cylindrical foot	49.10	pounds
1	cylindrical foot	6.0	U. S. gallons
2.281	cylindrical feet	112.0	pounds
45.62	cylindrical feet	2,240.0	pounds
1	imperial gallon	10.0	pounds
11.2	imperial gallons	112.0	pounds
224	imperial gallons	2,240.0	pounds
1	U. S. gallon	8.355	pounds
13.41	U. S. gallons	112.0	pounds
268.1	U. S. gallons	2,240.0	pounds

Note: The center of pressure of water against the side of the containing vessel or reservoir is at two-thirds the depth from the surface. One cubic foot of salt water weighs 64.3 pounds.

Other Liquids (pounds per cubic foot)

Liquid	Pounds	Liquid	Pounds
Alcohol: ethyl	50.4	Oils—(cont.)	
methyl	50.5	Lard	57.4
Aniline	64.5	Lavender	54.7
Benzene	56.1	Linseed (boiled)	58.8
Bromine	199.0	Neat's foot	57.0–57.2
Carbolic acid (crude)	59.2–60.2	Olive	57.3
Carbon disul.	80.6	Palm	56.5
Chloroform	93.0	Pentane	40.6
Ether	45.9	Peppermint	56.0–57.0
Gasoline	41.0–43.0	Petroleum	54.8
Glycerin	78.6	Pine	53.0–54.0
Milk	64.2–64.6	Poppy	57.7
Naphtha (petroleum ether)	41.5	Resin	59.6
		Sperm	55.0
Oils: Amber	49.9	Soybean	57.3
Camphor	56.8	Train or whale	57.3–57.7
Castor	60.5	Turpentine	54.2
Cocoanut	57.7	Valerian	60.2
Cottonseed	57.8	Wintergreen	74.0
Creosote	64.9–68.6	Water	62.4

Note: Milk, at 68° Fahrenheit, weighs 8.60 lb. a gallon, provided it contains 3 per cent of butter fat; cream at the same temperature weighs 8.37 lb. a gallon, if it has in it 28 per cent of butter fat. When cream contains 40 per cent of fat it weighs 8.28 lb. a gallon.

TABLE OF SOLUBILITIES

(S—soluble in water. I—insoluble in water. P—slightly soluble in water.
Ia—insoluble in water and dilute acids.)

	Aluminum	Ammonium	Antimony	Arsenious	Barium	Bismuth	Cadmium	Calcium	Cobalt	Copper	Ferrous (Fe^{++})	Ferric (Fe^{+++})	Lead	Magnesium	Manganese	Mercurous (Hg^{+})	Mercuric (Hg^{++})	Nickel	Potassium	Sodium	Silver	Zinc
Acetate	S	S	—	—	S	—	S	S	S	S	S	—	S	S	S	P	S	S	S	S	S	S
Bromide	S	S	P	S	S	P	S	S	S	S	S	S	P	I	S	P	I	S	S	S	Ia	S
Carbonate	—	S	—	—	I	I	I	I	I	—	I	—	I	I	I	S	I	—	S	S	I	I
Chlorate	S	—	—	—	S	—	S	S	S	S	S	—	S	S	S	S	S	—	S	S	S	S
Chloride	S	S	P	S	S	P	S	S	S	S	S	S	P	S	S	I	S	S	S	S	I	S
Chromate	—	S	—	—	I	I	S	I	I	I	—	I	Ia	S	S	P	P	—	S	S	I	—
Hydroxide	I	S	P	S	S	I	I	S	S	I	I	I	I	I	S	I	I	S	S	S	Ia	S
Iodide	S	S	P	P	P	I	S	S	S	—	S	I	S	S	S	I	I	S	S	S	Ia	S
Nitrate	S	S	—	—	S	S	S	S	S	I	I	I	I	I	I	P	I	I	S	S	S	I
Oxide	I	I	I	P	S	I	I	I	I	I	I	I	I	I	I	P	P	I	S	S	I	I
Phosphate	I	S	—	—	I	I	S	I	I	I	I	I	I	I	I	P	P	S	I	S	I	I
Sulphate	S	S	S	—	Ia	I	S	S	S	S	S	Ia	Ia	S	S	S	P	P	S	S	P	S
Sulphide	—	S	Ia	Ia	S	Ia	Ia	P	P	I	Ia	S	P	—	Ia	S	I	—	I	S	S	Ia
Sulphite	—	S	—	—	I	—	S	P	P	I	—	—	I	S	P	—	—	—	I	S	S	P

MEASURING FUELS

Coal, Coke, and Charcoal. The estimates in the table below are according to the Bureau of Standards at Washington, D.C. Remember that a "long" ton weighs 2,240 lb. avoirdupois while a "short" ton weighs 2,000 lb. avoirdupois. The long ton is the common measure in Great Britain, the short ton in the United States and Canada.

(Weights are approximate only)

Anthracite coal (piled loose):
  1 cubic foot = 50 to 57 pounds
  1 short ton = 35 to 40 cubic feet
  1 long ton   = 39 to 45 cubic feet
Bituminous coal (piled loose):
  1 cubic foot = 23 to 32 pounds
  1 short ton = 62 to 87 cubic feet
  1 long ton   = 70 to 97 cubic feet

Coke (piled loose):
  1 cubic foot = 44 to 54 pounds
  1 short ton = 37 to 45 cubic feet
  1 long ton   = 42 to 51 cubic feet
Charcoal (of pine and oak):
  1 cubic foot = 15 to 30 pounds

The average weight of the various kinds of anthracite coal in pounds per cubic foot is as follows:

Size	White ash	Red ash
Egg	57.0	53.0
Stove	56.5	52.5
Chestnut	55.5	52.0
Pea	53.5	51.0
Buckwheat	53.0	50.5

To find how much coal a bin will hold find its volume in cubic feet (length × width × height). Divide this by the number of cubic feet in a ton (for ordinary estimates 37 is used for anthracite coal, 40 for bituminous coal), and the result is the amount of coal the bin will hold.

Example. Find the number of tons of anthracite coal that a bin 24 ft. long, 4 ft. wide and 6 ft. high will hold.

$$24 \times 4 \times 6 = 576 \text{ cu. ft.}$$
$$576 \div 37 = 15\frac{1}{2} \text{ short tons}$$

For making steam one ton of coal roughly equals two cords of wood.

Wood. Wood is measured by the cord. A cord is a pile of wood 8 ft. long, 4 ft. wide, and 4 ft. high. It contains 128 cu. ft.

To find the number of cords in a given pile of wood, find the number of cubic feet in the pile (length × width × height) and divide by 128.

Example. Find the number of cords in a pile of wood 8 ft. wide, 6 ft. high, and 12 ft. long.

$$8 \times 6 \times 12 = 576 \text{ cu. ft.}$$
$$576 \text{ cu. ft.} \div 128 \text{ cu. ft.} = 4\frac{1}{2} \text{ cords}$$

Example. A woodshed is 16 ft. long, 12 ft. wide, and 8 ft. high. How many cords of wood can be piled in it?

$$16 \times 12 \times 8 = 1,536 \text{ cu. ft.}$$
$$1,536 \div 128 = 12 \text{ cords of wood}$$

WEIGHTS OF VARIOUS SUBSTANCES[1]

Solids (pounds per cubic foot)

Material	Pounds	Material	Pounds
Asbestos	125–175	Leather: dry	54
Asphalt	69–94	greased	64
Basalt	150–190	Lime: mortar	103–111
Brick	87–137	slaked	81–87
Caoutchouc	57–62	Limestone	167–171
Celluloid	87	Litharge:	
Cement, set	170–190	artificial	580–585
Chalk	118–175	natural	490–500
Chrome yellow	374	Marble	160–177
Clay	122–162	Mica	165–200
Coal, soft	75–94	Paper	44–72
Copal	65–71	Paraffin	54–57
Emery	250	Peat	52
Feldspar	159–172	Pitch	67
Flint	164	Porcelain	143–156
Fluorite	198	Quartz	165
Gamboge	75	Resin	67
Gas carbon	117	Rock salt	136
Gelatin	180	Sandstone	134–147
Glass: common	150–175	Slag, furnace	125–240
Graphite	144–170	Slate	162–205
Gum arabic	80–85	Soapstone	162–175
Gypsum	144–145	Tallow	57–60
Ivory	114–120		

[1] Source, Smithsonian Institution.

Woods (pounds per cubic foot)

Wood	Pounds	Wood	Pounds
Alder	26–42	Hazel	37–49
Apple	41–52	Hickory	37–58
Ash	40–53	Holly	47
Bamboo	19–25	Iron-bark	64
Basswood	20–37	Juniper	35
Beech	43–56	Laburnum	57
Blue gum	62	Lancewood	42–62
Birch	32–48	Lignum vitae	73–83
Box	59–72	Locust	42–44
Butternut	24	Logwood	57
Cedar	30–35	Mahogany	41
Cherry	43–56	Mahogany, Spanish	53
Cork	14–16	Maple	39–47
Dogwood	47	Oak	37–56
Ebony	69–83	Pear tree	38–45
Elm	34–37	Plum tree	41–49
Fir or pine, American white	22–31	Poplar	22–31
Fir or pine, larch	31–35	Satinwood	59
Fir or pine, pitch	52–53	Sycamore	24–37
Fir or pine, red	30–44	Teak, Indian	41–55
Fir or pine, spruce	30–44	Walnut	40–43
Fir or pine, yellow	23–37	Water gum	62
Greenheart	58–65	Willow	24–37

RESISTANCE TO CRUSHING FOR VARIOUS MATERIALS

(Square inch)

Material	Resistance to crushing in pounds per square inch	Material	Resistance to crushing in pounds per square inch
Brick:		Granite	9,700–34,000
soft-burned	3,000– 6,000	Limestone	6,000–25,000
hard-burned	4,500– 6,500	Marble	7,600–20,700
vitrified	8,500–25,000	Sandstone	2,400–29,300
Brownstone	7,300–23,600	Tufa	7,700–11,600
Concrete	800– 3,800		

TENSILE STRENGTH OF METALS[1]

(Given in pounds per square inch. The values can be considered
only as approximations.)

Metal	Tensile Strength in lbs. per sq. in.
Aluminum wire	30,000–40,000
Brass wire	50,000–150,000
Bronze wire, phosphor, hard-drawn	110,000–140,000
Bronze wire, silicon, hard-drawn	95,000–115,000
Bronze	60,000–75,000
Cobalt, cast	33,000
Copper wire, hard-drawn	60,000–70,000
German silver	40,000–50,000
Gold wire	20,000
Iron, cast	13,000–33,000
Iron wire, hard-drawn	80,000–120,000
Iron wire, annealed	50,000–60,000
Lead, cast or drawn	2,600–3,300
Magnesium, hard-drawn	33,000
Monel metal, cold-drawn	80,000–100,000
Nickel, hard-drawn	155,000
Palladium	39,000
Platinum wire	50,000
Silver wire	42,000
Steel	40,000–330,000
Steel wire, maximum	460,000
Steel, specially treated nickel steel	250,000
Steel, piano wire, 0.033 in. diam.	357,000–390,000
Steel, piano wire, 0.051 in. diam.	325,000–337,000
Tantalum	130,000
Tin, cast or drawn	4,000–5,000
Tungsten, hard-drawn	590,000
Zinc, cast	7,000–13,000
Zinc, drawn	22,000–30,000

[1] Source, Smithsonian Institution.

MODULUS OF RUPTURE,
TRANSVERSE TESTS FOR VARIOUS WOODS[1]

Material	Modulus[2] lbs. per sq. in.	Material	Modulus[2] lbs. per sq. in.
Ash, white	10,800	Maple, silver	5,800
Basswood	5,000	Maple, sugar	9,100
Beech	8,200	Oak, red	7,700
Cedar, red	5,200	Oak, white	8,300
Cedar, white	4,200	Pine, longleaf	8,700
Cypress, bald	6,800	Pine, white	5,300
Elm, white	6,900	Spruce, red	5,700
Fir, grand	6,100	Sycamore	6,500
Hemlock, Eastern	6,700	Walnut, black	9,500
Hickory, pecan	9,800	Yew, Western	10,100

[1] Source, Smithsonian Institution.
[2] Recommended allowable working stress (interior construction): ⅙ tabular value.

SPECIFIC GRAVITY

The density of a substance compared with the density of the same amount of another substance is called its specific gravity. With solids and liquids the standard of comparison is water; with gases it is air. The quality of a substance, *e.g.,* milk, can often in large measure be determined by determining its specific gravity.

TABLE OF SPECIFIC GRAVITIES

Iridium	23.000	Diamond	3.550	Beeswax	.960
Platinum	21.500	Plate glass	2.760	Lard	.947
Gold, pure	19.258	Marble	2.720	Butter	.942
Mercury, pure	14.000	Salt	2.130	Ice	.920
Silver	10.500	Brick	2.000	Petroleum	.880
Copper	8.788	Ivory	1.870	Turpentine	.870
Brass	8.000	Sugar	1.600	Hickory, dry	.840
Steel	7.840	Honey	1.456	Alcohol	.840
Tin	7.290	Milk	1.032	White pine, dry	.400
Cast iron	7.200	Water	1.000	Cork	.240

WATER PRESSURE PER SQUARE INCH

Depth in feet	Pressure in pounds	Depth in feet	Pressure in pounds	Depth in feet	Pressure in pounds
6	2.60	45	19.49	130	56.31
8	3.40	50	21.65	140	60.64
10	4.33	60	25.99	150	64.97
15	6.49	70	30.32	160	69.31
20	8.66	80	34.65	170	73.64
25	10.82	90	38.98	180	77.97
30	12.99	100	43.31	190	82.30
35	15.16	110	47.64	200	86.63
40	17.32	120	51.98	215	93.14
				230	99.63

CONVERSION OF TEMPERATURES

Fahrenheit and centigrade temperatures may be converted by means of two simple formulas. To convert Fahrenheit to centigrade, subtract 32° from the Fahrenheit and multiply by $\frac{5}{9}$. To convert centigrade to Fahrenheit, multiply the centigrade by $\frac{9}{5}$ and add 32. For example, to convert 50° Fahrenheit, subtract 32, which leaves 18, and multiply by $\frac{5}{9}$; the result is 10° centigrade. To convert 50° centigrade, multiply by $\frac{9}{5}$; which gives a product of 90, and add 32; the result is 122° Fahrenheit.

The following is a comparison of various centigrade and Fahrenheit temperatures:

C.	F.	C.	F.	C.	F.	C.	F.
−40	−40	−5	23.	10	50.	42	107.6
−35	−31	−4	24.8	11	51.8	43	109.4
−30	−22	−3	26.6	12	53.6	44	111.2
−25	−13	−2	28.4	13	55.4	45	113.
−20	− 4	−1	30.2	14	57.2	50	122.
−15	+ 5	0	32.	15	59.	55	131.
−14	6.8	+1	33.8	20	68.	60	140.
−13	8.6	2	35.6	25	77.	65	149.
−12	10.4	3	37.4	30	86.	70	158.
−11	12.2	4	39.2	35	95.	75	167.
−10	14.	5	41.	37	98.6	80	176.
− 9	15.8	6	42.8	38	100.4	85	185.
− 8	17.6	7	44.6	39	102.2	90	194.
− 7	19.4	8	46.4	40	104.	95	203.
− 6	21.2	9	48.2	41	105.8	100	212.

MEASURING ICE

Ice weighs 57.5 pounds per cubic foot. There are 30 cubic inches in a pound. To get the weight of a block of ice multiply its length by its breadth by its thickness. If it is 16 in. long × 10 in. wide × 8 in. thick it will contain 1,280 cubic inches. Since there are 30 cubic inches in a pound there will be 1,280 ÷ 30 = 42⅔ pounds in the block.

SOME INTERESTING TEMPERATURES

	Degrees Centigrade	Degrees Fahrenheit
Freezing point of mercury	−39	−38
Freezing cold storage	{ −18 0	0 +32
Freezing point of water	0	32
Danger of frost	+4	39
Proper temperature for household refrigerator	{ 7 13	45 55
Temperature for gymnasium, or rooms where occupants are actively engaged in physical work or exercise	13	55
Temperature for rooms where occupants are not exercising {	20 21	68 70
Normal temperature of the human body determined by thermometer under the tongue	37	98.6
Melting point of tallow	52.8	127
Boiling point of alcohol	75	167
Boiling point of water at normal pressure	100	212
Melting point of common soft solder	185	365
Melting point of lead	327	621
Melting point of aluminum	659	1,220

FACTS ABOUT THE EARTH

Surface area	196,950,284 sq. mi.
Radius at the equator	3,963.338 mi.
Radius at the poles	3,949.992 mi.
One degree of latitude at the equator	68.70 mi.
One degree of latitude at the pole	69.41 mi.
Mean distance to the sun	92,897,416 mi.
Mean distance to the moon	238,857 mi.
Mean density	5.52 grams per cubic centimeter

FACTS ABOUT TIME

"Time is a great deal more than money. If you have time you can obtain money—usually. But though you have the wealth of a cloakroom attendant at the Carlton Hotel, you cannot buy yourself a minute more of time than I have, or the cat by the fire has."—ARNOLD BENNETT in *How to Live on Twenty-Four Hours a Day.*

Standard Time. Since March 19, 1918, standard time has been the legal time throughout the United States. Like the standard time in nearly every other country in the world, it is measured from the prime meridian at Greenwich, England. Eastern standard time is 75° west from Greenwich; Central standard time is 90° west from Greenwich; Mountain standard time is 105° west from Greenwich; Pacific standard time is 120° west from Greenwich; and Alaskan standard time is 150° west from Greenwich.

Eastern standard time is used from the Atlantic Ocean to a line drawn irregularly through Lake Michigan, Indiana, Kentucky, and Tennessee; down the western border of Georgia, and through the panhandle of Florida.

Central standard time is used from this first line to a line drawn irregularly down the western border of North Dakota, through South Dakota, Nebraska, and Kansas, and down the western borders of Oklahoma and Texas.

Mountain standard time is used from the second line to a line drawn irregularly down the western border of Montana, along the westward course of the Salmon River, along the western and southern borders of Idaho, through Utah, and down the western border of Arizona.

Pacific standard time is used from the third line to the Pacific Ocean.

Exact time signals, based on precise astronomical calculations, are sent out daily at 3 A.M., noon, and 3 P.M., Eastern standard time, from the United States Naval Observatory at Washington, D.C. The signals are transmitted by telegraph control lines which automatically operate the radio stations at Arlington and Annapolis. At noon the stations at Key West and at San Diego are also operated.

Daylight-Saving Time. When daylight-saving time is adopted, the clock is advanced one hour. In states observing the custom, it usually is in effect from the last Sunday in April to the last Sunday in September. In 1955 some states, particularly in the East, began extending the period to the last Sunday in October.

DIFFERENCES IN TIME BETWEEN NEW YORK CITY
AND OTHER UNITED STATES CITIES

When it is noon, Eastern standard time, in New York City, the time in various other cities of the United States is as follows:

Atlanta, Ga.	Noon	Milwaukee, Wis.	11:00 A.M.
Baltimore, Md.	Noon	Minneapolis, Minn.	11:00 A.M.
Boston, Mass.	Noon	New Haven, Conn.	Noon
Chicago, Ill.	11:00 A.M.	New Orleans, La.	11:00 A.M.
Cleveland, Ohio	Noon	Philadelphia, Pa.	Noon
Dallas, Texas	11:00 A.M.	Pittsburgh, Pa.	Noon
Denver, Colo.	10:00 A.M.	Portland, Ore.	9:00 A.M.
Detroit, Mich.	Noon	St. Paul, Minn.	11:00 A.M.
Houston, Texas	11:00 A.M.	Salt Lake City, Utah	10:00 A.M.
Indianapolis, Ind.	11:00 A.M.	San Francisco, Calif.	9:00 A.M.
Kansas City, Mo.	11:00 A.M.	Seattle, Wash.	9:00 A.M.
Los Angeles, Calif.	9:00 A.M.	St. Louis, Mo.	11:00 A.M.
Louisville, Ky.	11:00 A.M.	Washington, D.C.	Noon

DIFFERENCES IN TIME BETWEEN NEW YORK CITY
AND VARIOUS FOREIGN CITIES

When it is noon, Eastern standard time, in New York City, the time in various other cities and parts of the world is as follows:

Amsterdam	6:00 P.M.	Madrid	6:00 P.M.
Berlin	6:00 P.M.	Manila	[1]1:00 A.M.
Brussels	6:00 P.M.	Melbourne	[1]3:00 A.M.
Buenos Aires	2:00 P.M.	Moscow	7:00 P.M.
Cape Town	7:00 P.M.	Paris	6:00 P.M.
Copenhagen	6:00 P.M.	Peking	[1]1:00 A.M.
Durban	7:00 P.M.	Rome	6:00 P.M.
Havre	6:00 P.M.	Stockholm	6:00 P.M.
Istanbul	7:00 P.M.	Vienna	6:00 P.M.
Johannesburg	7:00 P.M.	Yokohama	[1]2:00 A.M.
Leningrad	7:00 P.M.	[1] Denotes next day.	
London	5:00 P.M.		

SHIP TIME

Until recently time on shipboard was marked off by bells, as follows:

Time, A.M.		Time, A.M.		Time, A.M.	
1 Bell	12:30	1 Bell	4:30	1 Bell	8:30
2 Bells	1:00	2 Bells	5:00	2 Bells	9:00
3 "	1:30	3 "	5:30	3 "	9:30
4 "	2:00	4 "	6:00	4 "	10:00
5 "	2:30	5 "	6:30	5 "	10:30
6 "	3:00	6 "	7:00	6 "	11:00
7 "	3:30	7 "	7:30	7 "	11:30
8 "	4:00	8 "	8:00	8 "	Noon

The time P.M. was the same as the time A.M.

The day commenced at noon and was divided as follows:

Afternoon Watch, noon to 4 P.M.   First Watch, 8 P.M. to midnight
First Dog Watch, 4 P.M. to 6 P.M.   Middle Watch, midnight to 4 A.M.
Second Dog Watch, 6 P.M. to 8 P.M.   Morning Watch, 4 A.M. to 8 A.M.
Forenoon Watch, 8 A.M. to noon

Recently many ships have abandoned this in favor of the system followed in ordinary civil life in which the day commences at midnight and comprises the hours which elapse before the following midnight. In some instances, the hours are counted from 0 to 24, but, generally, they are divided into two series of twelve hours each in which the hours are marked A.M. or P.M., as the case may be.

The International Date Line. The international date line is an imaginary line in the Pacific Ocean at which dates change. It runs mainly along the 180th meridian of longitude but zigzags here and there so that closely associated groups of islands will have the same calendar. This is the line upon which eastbound travelers set their calendars back one day and repeat a day, and westbound travelers set it ahead one day or skip a day. The necessity for this is caused by the rotation of the earth. A traveler going in the same direction that the earth is moving, *i.e.*, one going east, travels with respect to the sun at the rate the earth is moving, plus the rate at which he is moving over the surface of the earth. A traveler moving in the opposite direction, *i.e.*, to the west, travels with respect to the sun at the rate he is moving over the surface of the earth, minus the speed of the rotation of the earth. Without the date line there would be endless confusion all over the world.

The Watch as a Compass. If you are lost in the woods and your watch is keeping correct time you can locate the cardinal points of the compass in the following manner. Hold the watch flat in your hand like a compass with the face upward. Hold a small stick or match straight up at the edge of the watch and turn the watch until the shadow of the stick falls along the hour hand nearest to the actual hour of day. This hand will then point toward the sun. In the morning south will lie halfway between the hour hand and 12, forward. At noon south will lie along the shadow cast by the match. In the afternoon south will lie halfway between the hour hand and 12, backward. If the watch is running according to daylight-saving time, it is one hour fast by the sun, and adjustments should be made accordingly.

The Thirteen-Month Year. The 13-month year was endorsed by the League of Nations in 1926. A number of business houses would welcome it because of its greater convenience.

According to the scheme there would be 13 months of 28 days, each containing four weeks, each week beginning on Sunday and ending on Saturday. Every month would be like every other month, and days would fall on identical dates. That is, the first of every month would always be on Sunday, the second on Monday, etc.

The 13-month would come between June and July and would be like all the other months.

The last day in every year would be dated December 29, and, since it is an extra day, would be called Year Day, and would not have a weekday name, such as Monday or Tuesday.

In leap years a similar day would be inserted as June 29, to be known as Leap Day, thus providing a midsummer holiday as well as the midwinter holiday which December 29 would give.

Bankers' Time Table. For periods of less than one year the following table may be found useful. From it one can tell at a glance the number of days between any day in any month and the corresponding day in any other month for any period of time not greater than one year. To find the number of days between October 25 and April 25, take October in the first column, follow the line through to April; the number is 182. From December 10 to October 10 is 304 days. To find the number of days between uneven dates, between April 9 and August 20, for instance, find the number of days between April 9 and August 9, and add to it the number of days from August 9 to August 20. The table shows that there are 122 days between April 9 and August 9. Add to this the 11 days between August 9 and August 20 and you have 133 days.

From any day of	To the Same Day of the Next											
	Jan.	Feb.	Mar.	Apr.	May	June	July	Aug.	Sept.	Oct.	Nov.	Dec.
Jan.	365	31	59	90	120	151	181	212	243	273	304	334
Feb.	334	365	28	59	89	120	150	181	212	242	273	303
Mar.	306	337	365	31	61	92	122	153	184	214	245	275
Apr.	275	306	334	365	30	61	91	122	153	183	214	244
May	245	276	304	335	365	31	61	92	123	153	184	214
June	214	245	273	304	334	365	30	61	92	122	153	183
July	184	215	243	274	304	335	365	31	62	92	123	153
Aug.	153	184	212	243	273	304	334	365	31	61	92	122
Sept.	122	153	181	212	242	273	303	334	365	30	61	91
Oct.	92	123	151	182	212	243	273	304	335	365	31	61
Nov.	61	92	120	121	181	212	242	273	304	334	365	30
Dec.	31	62	90	121	151	182	212	243	274	304	304	365

Reckoning Time for Ordinary Interest. In ordinary interest calculations the year is reckoned as having 12 months of 30 days each, making 360 days in all. In finding time for more than a year this basis is used. For instance, find the time between June 29, 1911, and March 4, 1930.

Years	Months	Days
1929	14	34
1911	6	29
18	8	5

Since it is impossible to subtract 29 days from four days you borrow a month, which makes it 34 days but leaves you only two months in the column to the left. Six months cannot be subtracted from two and so you borrow a year, making it 14 months, but leaving you with a year less in the "Years" column.

Reckoning Time for Accurate Interest. The United States government and certain bankers compute accurate rather than ordinary interest, that is, they count on a basis of 365 days to a year. It is much more troublesome to work out than ordinary interest. There are tables for it as well as for ordinary interest, but since they are seldom used in the general run of commercial transactions they are not included here. A simple way to find out the accurate interest is to find the ordinary interest. Ordinary interest is as much greater than accurate interest as $^{360}\!/_{360}$ is greater than $^{360}\!/_{365}$, which is $^1\!/_{72}$. Therefore, to find the accurate interest subtract $^1\!/_{72}$ of it from itself. Similarly, to find the ordinary interest, add $^1\!/_{72}$ of the accurate interest to itself.

ROPE

Splicing. Rope is said to be spliced when the two ends are joined together by untwisting their strands for a short distance and threading the strands of each rope under and over the strands of the other to form a joint. To avoid increasing the thickness of the rope at the joint, the loose ends of the strands are cut to varying lengths and thinned down to points. The strands of one rope are then twisted into the vacant spaces in the other rope and the tapered ends threaded.

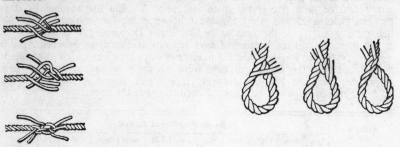

Stages in making common forms of splice. Left, short splice joining two rope ends. Right, eye splice, for making a loop.

Knots. The knot most commonly used is the overhand knot (1). A square or reef knot (2) is made by making a second overhand knot over the first. The bowline (3) forms a loop that will not draw and can be undone very quickly. The clove hitch (4) is one of the best knots for fastening a line. It is very secure. The timber hitch (5) is used for hoisting or towing heavy timbers, the sheepshank (6) for shortening a rope when neither end is free.

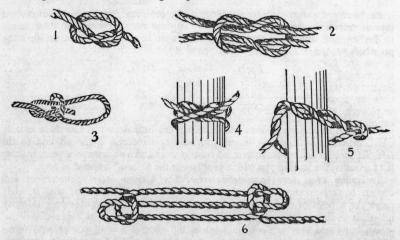

Knots in common use. 1. Overhand. 2. Square or Reef. 3. Bowline. 4. Clove hitch. 5. Timber hitch. 6. Sheepshank.

AMERICAN LABOR UNIONS

Of the American labor force, approximately 17,000,000 workers belong to labor unions; of these about 13,500,000 are in unions affiliated with the American Federation of Labor and Congress of Industrial Organizations. This organization, created in 1955 by merger of the two groups, comprises 133 national or international unions, with jurisdictions based upon occupation or industry.

Workers are organized into local unions, which are units of the national or international unions. Each national union has a charter giving it jurisdiction over a given trade or industry. There is a degree of overlapping in these charters. The federation has established machinery for settling jurisdictional disputes, but it is not fully effective. It has no direct power over its member unions and can invoke no disciplinary action except expulsion from the organization.

The A.F.L.-C.I.O. has central bodies, or geographical organizations of local unions, in all 50 states and more than 800 communities. Like the federation itself, these central bodies are chiefly concerned with political and legislative affairs affecting all workers. There are also six departments within the federation, grouping unions with common interests into a single operating unit. However, collective bargaining with employers is exclusively the function of the various national unions and their constituent locals.

A number of unions are not affiliated with the A.F.L.-C.I.O., such as the United Mine Workers, some of the Railroad Brotherhoods, and the International Brotherhood of Teamsters.

NATIONAL LABOR RELATIONS BOARD

The National Labor Relations Board (abbreviated N.L.R.B.), an independent Federal agency established in 1935, administers the nation's principal labor relations law, the National Labor Relations Act (also referred to as the Wagner Act), as amended. Application of the act generally extends to all interstate commerce except railroads and airlines. The N.L.R.B. implements national labor policy to protect the public interest by eliminating certain barriers to peaceful relations between employers and employees, encouraging collective bargaining. It also provides machinery for the resolution of labor-management disputes. The N.L.R.B. has two primary functions: (1) to prevent and remedy unfair labor practices committed by employers or by unions; and (2) to determine representatives for collective bargaining by conducting employee elections.

The original act called upon the N.L.R.B. to remedy employer unfair labor practices such as interference with employees' exercise of their right to organize and bargain collectively, domination of unions, anti-union discrimination, and refusal to bargain collectively. The Taft-Hartley Act, or National Labor Relations Act, 1947, broadened coverage of the law to bar certain unfair practices by unions, such as intimidation of employees, restraint or coercion of employers, and refusal to bargain collectively. The board of three members, appointed by the President with the consent of the Senate, was increased to five members. Appointment of a general counsel by the President, with Senate consent, also was provided. The board's judicial functions were separated from its prosecuting functions by delegating to the general counsel final authority to act for the board in issuance of complaints in unfair labor practice cases. The closed shop[1] was outlawed but the open shop[1] was permitted.

[1] The closed shop is a form of union security under which an employer may hire only union members and retain only union members in good standing; it is illegal. The union shop is a form of union security under which all employees are required to become members of the union within a specified time after hiring or after a labor agreement is negotiated, and to remain members of the union as a condition of employment; it is permissible under the law.

The Labor Reform Act of 1959 (popularly known as the Landrum-Griffin Act) again substantially amended the basic act. Restrictions were placed on organizational and recognition picketing, secondary boycott[1] provisions were tightened, hot-cargo[2] contracts outlawed, and steps taken to eliminate the "no man's land" between Federal and state jurisdiction in labor relations disputes. In 1961, in accordance with the 1959 law, the board delegated broad decision-making powers and responsibilities to its 28 regional directors, subject to review by the board on limited grounds.

FAIR LABOR STANDARDS ACT

The Fair Labor Standards Act, also known as the Federal Wage and Hour Law, has been described as providing a floor for wages, a standard for hours, and a break for children. Prior to Sept. 3, 1961, it applied to those employees who were engaged in interstate or foreign commerce, or in the production of goods for such commerce, or in a closely related process or occupation directly essential to such production. Thus, a typical employee covered by the act was one employed in a factory or wholesale establishment engaged in producing goods for, or receiving or shipping goods in, interstate or foreign commerce.

All employees to whom the act applied before Sept. 3, 1961, and who were not specifically exempt, must be paid a minimum wage of at least $1.15 an hour, effective Sept. 3, 1961, and must receive an increase to $1.25 an hour, effective Sept. 3, 1963. The overtime-pay requirement for these employees, if not specifically exempt, is at least one and one-half times their regular rates of pay for hours worked over 40 in any workweek.

Amendments to the act, effective Sept. 3, 1961, extended provisions of the original act to several million additional employees. The greater number of these employees were affected by the 1961 amendments which extended the coverage of the act to employees employed in enterprises engaged in interstate or foreign commerce or in the production of goods for such commerce. Definitions of such enterprises are part of the legislation.

Exemptions. Some employees to whom the minimum wage or overtime provisions, or both, would otherwise apply are excluded by specific exemptions. These exemptions apply only in those cases where their terms and conditions are specifically met.

Other Provisions of the Act. The minimum wage and overtime requirements of the act are not limited to employees working at an hourly wage. Pay requirements apply whatever the method of payment—hourly, weekly, monthly, piecework, commission, combination, or any other basis.

Premium pay for overtime work must be paid for each hour worked in excess of the maximum workweek applicable to the type of employment in which the employee is engaged. Overtime must be paid at a rate of not less than one and one-half times the employee's regular rate of pay. The *regular rate* may be more than the minimum wage, but it cannot be less; it includes all payments made by the employer to, or on behalf of, the employee, except for certain types of payments which are specifically excluded.

Unless specifically exempt, all covered employees must be paid at least the applicable minimum wage, regardless of the basis of payment. However, learners,

---

[1] A boycott is a concerted attempt by a union to discourage the purchase, handling, or use of products of an employer with whom the union is in dispute. When such action is extended to another company doing business with the employer involved in the dispute, it is termed a secondary boycott. A hot-cargo contract is one that includes a clause whereby an employer agrees not to handle, work on, transport, or otherwise deal in goods of an employer who has a dispute with the union.

apprentices, messengers, handicapped workers, and fulltime students employed outside of school hours, under certain circumstances, may be paid special lower minimum wage rates, *provided* that special certificates are first obtained from the administrator. Also, for employees in Puerto Rico, the Virgin Islands, and American Samoa, industry wage orders may set minimum rates below the statutory minimum.

The law applies equally to men and women; to homeworkers, factory, store, and office workers (certificates issued by the divisions are necessary for homeworkers in certain industries); and regardless of the number of employees of an employer.

Employers must maintain certain records on wages, hours, and other items listed in the record keeping regulations. No particular form of record keeping is necessary. Establishments with covered workers are required to display posters which outline the law's provisions.

Administration. The Fair Labor Standards Act establishes the Wage and Hour Division in the United States Dept. of Labor, under an administrator appointed by the President. There are ten regional offices, which cover all the states; and there is at least one field office in almost every state.

The act provides these methods of recovering unpaid minimum and/or overtime wages. The administrator may supervise payment of back wages, and, in certain circumstances, the Secretary of Labor may bring suit for back pay upon the written request of the employee. The employee may sue for back pay and an additional sum, up to the amount of back pay, as liquidated damages, plus attorney's fees and court costs. The employee may *not* bring suit if he has been paid back wages under supervision of the administrator, or if the Secretary of Labor has filed suit to collect the wages. It is a violation of the law to fire an employee for filing a complaint or participating in a proceeding under the law.

The Secretary of Labor may also obtain a court injunction to restrain an employer from violating the law, including the unlawful withholding of proper minimum-wage and overtime compensation. For willful violation, an employer may be subject to criminal prosecution and fined up to $10,000. A second conviction may result in imprisonment.

A two-year statute of limitations applies to the recovery of back wages.

See also Child Labor; Workmen's Compensation.

CHILD LABOR

Employment of children is regulated in the United States by the Federal Fair Labor Standards Act—to a certain degree—and by the child labor laws of the individual states.

Federal Regulation. No child under 16 years of age may work at a job or in the work place of a manufacturing, mining, or processing operation; or in transportation, communication, public utilities, construction, warehousing or storage; or as a public messenger; or in tending power-driven machinery other than office machinery.

Children of 14 and 15 years may work outside of school hours in a limited number of jobs, such as office and sales jobs, and for a limited number of hours. No minor under 18 years of age may work in occupations declared hazardous by the Secretary of Labor.

The Fair Labor Standards Act also provides that no producer, manufacturer, or dealer shall ship, or deliver for shipment, in interstate or foreign commerce any goods produced in an establishment in or about which any children have been employed illegally during the 30 days preceding shipment of the goods.

The prohibition against the employment of oppressive child labor in interstate or foreign commerce, or in the production of goods for such commerce, was made applicable to employment in any enterprise newly covered by the amendments of 1961.

State Regulation. Every state has a child labor law. These laws usually apply to the employment of minors up to 16 or 18 years of age. In general, they fix the minimum age at which a child may go to work, regulate the maximum daily and weekly hours that he may work, prohibit night work, require work permits or employment certificates as a condition for his employment, and prohibit work in hazardous occupations.

Although in most states a minimum age of 14 is set for employment, 22 states have now adopted laws which set 16 as the minimum age for employment during school hours or in factories at any time. Many states also prohibit employment of minors below 18 years of age in specified hazardous occupations: in mines, in work with explosives, or in operating dangerous machines. In a majority of the states, the work of children between 14 and 16 is limited to 8 hours a day and 40, 44, or 48 hours a week; and nearly all prohibit night work for children under 16. Over one-third of the states, however, have limited the maximum weekly hours for children under 16 to 40 or 44, while 9 states have established a 40- or 44-hour week also for minors of 16 and 17. Work permits are required for minors under 16 in practically all the states, with about one-half the states requiring such certificates up to 18.

See also Fair Labor Standards Act; Workmen's Compensation.

WORKMEN'S COMPENSATION

Workmen's compensation is a form of social insurance that provides monetary compensation for injuries arising out of and in the course of employment. In recent years, this compensation has been extended to cover some, but not all, occupational diseases.

In the United States, all states, Puerto Rico, the Virgin Islands, and the Federal government have enacted workmen's compensation laws. The Bureau of Employees' Compensation of the United States Dept. of Labor administers the act of Sept. 7, 1916, which provides workmen's compensation benefits for civil employees of the United States who suffer injuries in the line of duty, as well as the Federal Longshoremen's and Harbor Workers Compensation Act. Certain large groups of employees, such as railroad workers and seamen, are not covered by compensation laws, largely because these workers feel that employers' liability laws give them greater protection. Also not covered by workmen's compensation laws in general are most farm laborers, domestic servants, and employees of nonprofit institutions.

Workmen's compensation laws in the United States are characterized by the following provisions:

Waiting Time Before Compensation Becomes Payable. A waiting time has been prescribed in all states except Oregon, ranging from two to seven days.

Temporary Disability. Compensation for temporary disability is based on a percentage of the worker's wages, usually 60, 65, or 66⅔ per cent; 31 states and Puerto Rico have set a maximum time limit during which payments are allowed, ranging from 208 to 500 weeks.

Permanent Total Disability. Twenty-seven states, the District of Columbia, Puerto Rico, and the two Federal acts provide a fraction of the worker's former wage each week for the period of disability; other states limit compensation to between 330 and 550 weeks, and the total maximum compensation, where limited, ranges from $7,500 to $30,000.

Permanent Partial Disability. Special payments for permanent partial disability are made, scaled according to the member or faculty lost; payment for extra disability (*e.g.*, the loss of a second eye) out of special funds is provided by 46 states, the District of Columbia, and Puerto Rico, and under the Federal Longshoremen's Act.

Medical Care. Medical care and surgical appliances which may be necessary for injured workers are provided for in compensation laws, though in 14 of the laws the benefits are limited either as to period of time or total cost.

Death. In the case of death, all the laws except that of Oklahoma provide for payment of burial expenses subject to a specified maximum amount, in addition to compensation to the surviving dependents. Nine states, the District of Columbia, and the two Federal acts provide that the widow shall be paid a percentage of the weekly wages until death or remarriage, plus an allowance for children under a certain age; in the other states, the period of time of payment or the maximum amount of benefits is limited.

Rehabilitation. Provision for rehabilitation was first made in Massachusetts, in 1918, through surgery, re-education, and other means; the next year nine states followed with similar provisions. In 1920 Congress agreed to match with equal sums all amounts appropriated by the states for rehabilitation. At present, all states are cooperating in this program. In addition, special provisions relating to rehabilitation of injured workers are included in the workmen's compensation laws of 22 states, the District of Columbia, and Puerto Rico, and in the two Federal acts.

Occupational Diseases. Full coverage of occupational diseases is provided by 30 states, the District of Columbia, Puerto Rico, and the two Federal acts, while 18 states cover only certain specified diseases; two states make no provision for coverage of occupational diseases.

Most states have established official agencies for the administration of workmen's compensation laws. The administrative officials of these state agencies and those of the Canadian provinces, New Zealand, and the Republic of the Philippines are organized into the International Association of Industrial Accident Boards and Commissions.

FAIR EMPLOYMENT PRACTICES

There is no authoritative definition of the term "fair employment practices." Nevertheless, the United States was founded on the principle that "all men are created equal," thus it has been felt that it is the duty of men of good will to combat undermining prejudice which would deny the fruits of freedom to fellow citizens because of race, religion, color, national origin, or ancestry. To this end, since June 1941, beginning with President Franklin D. Roosevelt, each succeeding President has issued various orders designed to prevent discrimination because of race, creed, color, or national origin on the part of persons doing business with the Federal government. On March 6, 1961, effective April 7, 1961, President John F. Kennedy established a Committee on Equal Employment Opportunity, comprising 11 heads of government agencies and 14 public members. The Vice President of the United States, the Secretary of Labor, and an Assistant Secretary of Labor were included in the membership.

In addition, 19 states have enforceable fair employment practices laws: Alaska, California, Colorado, Connecticut, Delaware, Illinois, Kansas, Massachusetts, Michigan, Minnesota, New Jersey, New Mexico, New York, Ohio, Oregon, Pennsylvania, Rhode Island, Washington, and Wisconsin. Indiana also has a law which provides for public hearings with respect to fair employment practices, but which does not provide for enforcement of the state commission's recommendations.

All of these states mentioned and the Federal committee have attempted to implement the principle that all men should be permitted to advance in accordance with their ambition and ability.

SOCIAL SECURITY ACT

The Social Security Act is a national law, passed by Congress and approved by the President on Aug. 14, 1935. The purpose of the act and its subsequent amendments is to prevent and relieve the misfortunes that come when earnings are cut off by lack of work, old age, blindness, prolonged disability, or death and when children are left with no one to support them or when they lack necessary care. Most of the programs covered by the Act provide for direct cash payments to qualified individuals.

The Social Security Administration (abbreviated S.S.A.), part of the United States Department of Health, Education, and Welfare, administers the act and has responsibility for all the programs under the act except unemployment insurance, which has been administered by the United States Department of Labor since Aug. 20, 1949. (The S.S.A. also administers the Federal credit-union program under the Federal Credit Union Act; see Cooperatives.)

Old-Age, Survivors, and Disability Insurance. Old-age, survivors, and disability insurance protects most of the gainfully employed in the United States (including the self-employed) when old age, prolonged disability, or death ends their earnings. The program is wholly Federal in operation and is administered by the Bureau of Old-Age and Survivors Insurance of the S.S.A.

Monthly benefits directly related to past earnings are provided for workers who meet certain qualifications when they stop work because of age or prolonged disability and to their dependent wives or husbands and their children (under age 18 or with a disability that began before that age). The wife of such a worker must be aged 65 to qualify for a benefit (though she may receive a reduced benefit at age 62) or have a child of the worker in her care. When an insured worker dies, benefits go to his widow at age 62 or while she has the worker's child in her care, to the dependent widower, to the worker's dependent parents, and to his children under age 18 (or with a disability that began before that age). A lump-sum payment (not more than $255) is made at the death of every insured worker.

To qualify for benefits for himself and his family a worker must have been in jobs covered by the program long enough to get a specified number of quarters of coverage. A quarter of coverage is a calendar quarter in which $50 or more is earned, and the number needed varies with the age of the worker at retirement or on the date of his death or disablement if he dies or becomes disabled before he retires. A person with $400 or more of self-employment income in a year is credited with four quarters of coverage. (Under a special provision for farm workers, their earnings are also considered on an annual basis instead of quarterly.) To be fully insured a worker must have one quarter of coverage for each four calendar quarters after 1950 (or after age 21 if that is later). He must have at least six quarters of coverage; no one needs more than 40. The worker's fully insured status gives eligibility for all types of benefits except (1) the disabled worker's benefit, which requires in addition that the worker have 20 quarters of coverage out of the 10-year period before the disability occurred; and (2) those based on the woman worker's earnings—dependent husband's and dependent widower's benefits, which require that the worker be also currently, as well as fully, insured—that is, she must have one and a half years' work out of the three years before her death or retirement. Child's benefits and benefits paid to a widow with the earner's child in her care, as well as the lump-sum death payment, are payable even when the worker is only currently insured.

The employer and employee each pay the same amount toward the benefits as a fixed percentage of the worker's earnings up to $4,800. For 1962 the rate for each is 3⅛ per cent; for 1963 through 1965, 3⅝ per cent; and for 1966 through 1967, 4⅛ per cent. In 1968 and thereafter, each will pay 4⅝ per cent of the employee's wage.[1] This money goes into two Federal funds: the Disability Insurance Trust Fund, where ¼ per cent of the employee's earnings from the employee's tax and ¼ per cent from the employer's tax are deposited to pay the disabled workers' benefits; and the Old-Age and Survivors Insurance Trust Fund, from which all the other benefits are paid.

Public Assistance. The Federal government makes grants to the states to help finance their programs for four groups of needy persons—dependent children, the blind, the permanently and totally disabled, and the aged. Since October 1960 aid for the aged is provided through two programs: old-age assistance, for those with little or no income who need help with all or most of their living expenses; and medical assistance for the aged, for those who need help to pay their medical bills. The grants are administered by the Bureau of Family Services of the S.S.A. The programs are operated by the states, and the eligibility requirements and amount of the payments are determined by the states. They must meet certain requirements of the Social Security Act before Federal funds can be made available for them.

All states, the District of Columbia, Puerto Rico, the Virgin Islands, and Guam have programs of old-age assistance, aid to the blind, and aid to families with dependent children; all but three states have programs of aid to the permanently and totally disabled. The programs provide for direct monthly payments to the needy individual (and to the parents or to one other adult relative, in aid to families with dependent children); for payments in their behalf for medical care; and for rehabilitative and other social services designed to prevent or reduce dependency. The Federal government shares in the monthly payments according to a formula related in part to state per-capita income and in the cost of services and other administrative expenses.

Half the states maintain programs for medical assistance for the aged. As in the other programs, state plans must meet certain requirements to qualify for Federal funds, but the states have wide latitude in determining the scope of medical services offered and eligibility qualifications. Services the state may pay for under the law include inpatient and outpatient hospital services, physicians' services, private-duty nursing services, skilled nursing-home services, home health-care services, and a broad range of other types of medical care. Federal sharing in the costs ranges from 50 per cent to 80 per cent under a formula based chiefly on per-capita income.

Maternal and Child Health and Child Welfare. The Social Security Act provides for Federal grants to states to help them develop and improve three programs: maternal and child health services, services for crippled children, and child welfare services. The programs are operated by the state health and welfare agencies, and the Federal grants are administered by the Children's Bureau of the S.S.A. Successive amendments to the Social Security Act have increased the amount of Federal funds authorized for these programs.

Most of the maternal and child health services provided are preventive services, designed to keep mothers and children well, and include maternity clinics, child-health conferences, health services for school-age and pre-school children, immunizations, dental and mental health services, and nutrition education.

Services for crippled children include diagnostic clinics and the provision of medical, surgical, and corrective services, hospitalization, and aftercare.

Child welfare services are designed to meet the problems of dependent, neglected, and delinquent children and children in danger of becoming delinquent. See also Children.

Employment Security. The Social Security Act provides for a state-Federal

[1] The self-employed pay 1½ times these rates.

program of unemployment insurance that pays benefits to jobless workers. Each state has its own law and operates its own program; the Bureau of Employment Security of the United States Department of Labor administers the Federal part of the program. Employers are taxed a percentage of the employees' wages, and in a few states employees are taxed also.

This program is joined in the states with the employment-service program to provide a twofold service—insurance against loss of pay and help in finding a job. When a man loses his job, he is required to file a claim at the local employment office. Public employment offices register unemployed workers, whether or not they are insured under the state law, and try to find work for them free of charge. For the insured worker, if no job is found, his benefit payments begin after a waiting period—in most states, one week. The amount of his weekly payment and the length of time he may receive it vary from state to state.

During recent recession periods, the Federal government authorized temporary programs under which Federal funds were lent to states to help them extend unemployment insurance benefits for workers who had exhausted their benefit rights but were still unemployed.

Because the programs under the Social Security act are broadened and revised from time to time through amendments to the Act, the reader is advised to seek the most recent information from the nearest office of the Social Security Administration.

WOMEN'S BUREAU

The Women's Bureau, first established as the Woman in Industry Service in 1918, and made permanent by a congressional act of June 5, 1920, is part of the United States Department of Labor. It is charged with formulating standards and policies for promoting the welfare of wage-earning women, improving their working conditions, increasing their efficiency, and advancing their opportunities for profitable employment. It investigates and publishes reports on matters pertaining to the welfare of working women.

The bureau is concerned with all women at work, or seeking work, and with their training and skills; with women in all fields of employment; with the girl on her first job and the older woman worker; and with women who are both homemakers and wage earners.

Continuous research is carried on by the bureau's technical experts to help it formulate policies and programs. Some studies provide information on trends in the employment of women and on demand and supply in selected occupations and professions. Others are concerned with employment opportunities, wages, and conditions of work in individual occupations or industries. The bureau also plans to collect information on how automation and mechanization affect women workers, who account for more than two-thirds of all clerical workers. Another area of interest relates to the day-care needs of children of working mothers, a problem important because of the increase in the number of working mothers.

The bureau makes analyses of, and recommendations on, existing and proposed labor laws and regulations covering women, on administrative procedures, and on laws affecting women's civil and political status. It administers no laws. The major types of legislation on which the bureau compiles data and provides technical advisory services are equal pay, minimum wage, hours of work, and family and property law.

In cooperation with other Labor Department bureaus, the Women's Bureau assists in programs for Labor Department officials and trade-union leaders and members from other countries, and provides to these leaders and to labor departments abroad information and publications on questions affecting employed women. Bureau staff members provide technical materials to international agencies and act as advisers to United States delegates to international conferences of such agencies and commissions as the International Labor Organization, the United Nations Commission on the Status of Women, and the Inter-American Commission of Women of the Organization of American States.

The "Handbook on Women Workers," a biennial publication prepared by the bureau, provides basic information on women's employment and occupations; it is designed as a source book for the use of employers and persons interested in facts about the employment of women.

FARMING AND AGRICULTURE IN THE UNITED STATES

The agriculture of any area depends primarily on *climate, soil, topography,* and *markets.*

Perhaps the two most important *climatic features* which determine the type of farming in a given area are the length of the frost-free season and the rainfall. The southern part of the United States has 200 days or more between frosts, which is sufficient time for the growth of cotton. The northern fringe of the country, as well as much of the Rocky Mt. area, has less than 140 days of frost-free season, which is insufficient for the growth of corn, but long enough for small grains.

The eastern half of the country has more than 20 in. of rainfall per year. Most of the western half has less than 20 in., although the northern Pacific coast

TABLE I

CASH RECEIPTS FROM THE SALE OF FARM PRODUCTS
(AVERAGE 1959 AND 1960)

Item	Cash Receipts (in millions)	Per cent of Total
Cattle and calves	$ 7,615	22.6
Dairy products	4,670	13.8
Hogs	2,820	8.4
Eggs	1,637	4.9
Chickens, including broilers	1,085	3.2
Turkeys and other poultry	413	1.2
Sheep and lambs	332	1.0
Other	336	1.0
Total livestock and products	*$18,908*	*56.1*
Feed Crops	2,845	8.4
Cotton and cottonseed	2,498	7.4
Food grains	2,366	7.0
Vegetables	1,710	5.1
Fruits and tree nuts	1,589	4.7
Oil-bearing crops	1,316	3.9
Tobacco	1,108	3.3
Other	1,392	4.1
Total crops	*$14,824*	*43.9*
Total cash receipts	*$33,732*	*100.0*

has a very high rainfall. Twenty inches is about the minimum rainfall required to produce crops without irrigation or special procedures to conserve moisture.

The areas with a heavy concentration of farming are those which have a favorable combination of climate, soil, topography, and markets. Most such areas are in the eastern half of the country. The exceptions to this are the irrigated valleys of the Pacific coastal states. The largest concentration of farming is in the corn belt—a strip of land, about 250 mi. wide and 800 mi. long, extending from western Ohio to eastern Nebraska.

Another area with concentrated agriculture is the northern Atlantic seaboard. This area has excellent markets, and in many parts is also favored with respect to climate, soil, and topography. The central valley of California has excellent soil and topography and excellent climate for fruit growing, but irrigation must be practiced.

Because of the widely varying conditions in different parts of the United States, farmers grow many different crops. The most important crop is corn; it occupies about one-fourth of the crop area. Hay occupies about one-fifth and wheat a little less. A large proportion of the total crop area is devoted to crops which are used for livestock feed: corn, hay, oats, barley, and sorghums. Together they account for about two-thirds of the total crop area.

Table I indicates the sources of farm income in the United States. A little more than half of the total is from livestock and livestock products.

TYPES OF FARMS

The general tendency in all business in the United States is toward increased specialization. Such specialization permits a division of labor, with each person becoming skilled at one job. Specialization is common in agriculture also—not so much on the worker level, but on the farm-unit level. Here, specialization continues to increase. Production of broilers and eggs is now almost entirely in the hands of specialized producers. Milk, fruits, vegetables, cotton, wheat, rice, tobacco, cattle, and hogs are important products in which specialization is common. In fact, general farms are the exception rather than the rule. In 1959 the Bureau of the Census reported the following breakdown of farms by type:

TYPE OF FARM	PER CENT OF ALL FARMS
Cash-grain	10.7
Tobacco	5.1
Cotton	6.5
Other field crops	1.0
Vegetables	.6
Fruit and tree nuts	1.6
Poultry	2.8
Dairy	11.6
Livestock, other than dairy and poultry	18.5
General farms	5.7
Unclassified (part-time, retirement, etc.)	35.9
	100.0

There were 3.7 million farms counted by the 1959 Census of Agriculture. To be classified as a particular type, a farm had to have sales of a particular product or group of products amounting in value to 50 per cent or more of the total value of all farm products sold during the year.

Dairy farms are located largely in the Northeast and in the states bordering the Great Lakes. Most of the hog farms are in the corn belt. Beef-cattle and sheep ranches utilize most of the land in the Rocky Mt. states. Fruit and vegetable farms are located chiefly in the states bordering the Atlantic and Pacific oceans and the Great Lakes.

The present type of farming in each region is the result of years of experimentation. A newcomer should not try a "new" type of farming until he is certain that his new idea is not merely one that farmers in the area tried out years ago and discarded when they found it did not pay.

SIZES OF FARMS

The average farm size for the entire United States in terms of acres was 302 in 1959; it varied from 83 acres per farm in North Carolina to 5,542 acres per farm in Arizona. (Farms in Arizona are not necessarily large businesses, however; a very large area is required to support a family where the topography is rough and the rainfall is low.) The average acreage per farm in the northern states was 246, in the southern states 217, and in the western states 997.

The 1959 Census of Agriculture classified the farms of the United States according to economic classes. The classification was based primarily on the total value of the farm products sold in 1959. With this as a basis, the farms were divided into several groups, as indicated in Table II.

TABLE II

FARMS BY ECONOMIC CLASS

Type of Farm	Thousands of Farms	Per cent of All Farms
Commercial farms	2,412	65.2
Farms with sales of:		
$40,000 or more	102	2.8
$20,000 to $40,000	210	5.7
$10,000 to $20,000	482	13.0
$ 5,000 to $10,000	653	17.6
$ 2,500 to $ 5,000	617	16.7
$ 50 to $ 2,500	348	9.4
Other farms[1]	1,289	34.8

[1] Part-time and part-retirement farms, with sales of $50 to $2,500, and institutional farms.

In 1954 the top 10 per cent of the farms, ranked according to the value of farm products sold, accounted for 54 per cent of the total value of all farm products sold. The top 20 per cent of the farms accounted for 71 per cent of the products sold, while the bottom 50 per cent of the farms accounted for only 6 per cent of the products sold. Hence the contribution of the vast majority of our farms is small.

By most business standards, all the small and medium-sized farms were "small business," producing not over $20,000 worth of goods in a year; even some of the large farms would be so considered. Some of the large farms were owned by corporations, but most of them were operated by individual farm families. Many of the corporate farms were family farms whose owners had incorporated for tax or inheritance purposes or for other reasons.

KINDS OF FARM ORGANIZATION

There are many kinds of farm organization, and it is important to understand the differences between them and the place in the economy of each kind. Farms may first be divided into *family farms* and *large-scale farms*. On family farms, most of the work is done by the farmer and his family. Most of the farms in the United States are family farms, even though they may require hired help at one or more times during the year.

Family Farms. Family farms may be divided into four groups: (1) subsistence; (2) residential; (3) commercial; and (4) part-time.

A *subsistence farm* is one which emphasizes production for home use, with only small amounts produced for sale, and little or no nonfarm income. Thus, there is little cash and, therefore, little in the way of modern conveniences.

A *residential farm* is primarily a place to live. Farm production is slight, and little is sold; the family depends largely on nonfarm income.

A *part-time farm* is a combination of a residential farm and a commercial farm, the owner of which is a man with two jobs, one of them farming. The part-time farmer makes farming a business, but the income he receives from his farming operations is usually less than he receives from his nonfarm employment.

A *family-commercial farm* is one owned by a family and operated as a business. Most of the agricultural production of the United States is from such farms; they include units with sales of up to $20,000 to $25,000. Family-commercial farms emphasize production for sale. Most of the products are sold, and all or most of the family income is from farming. Some labor may be hired, depending on the amount of family help available.

Large-Scale Farms. Large-scale farms are those with a number of workers under one manager or operator, whose time is taken up almost completely with management. There are relatively few such farms in the United States. Farm-management studies have shown that for most of the different types of farms, the most efficient size of operation is capable of being run by a single family. Studies indicate that significant economies of size are achieved in moving up the scale to the point at which a "line of equipment" is fully utilized, which is well within the size limits of family farms.

Although family-operated farms continue to predominate in American agriculture, the farms themselves have changed greatly. There is a rising trend in the size of farm, the value of products sold per farm, and the investment required for successful farming. These changes can be attributed to such technological changes as mechanization, improved cultural practices, and the introduction of better varieties of plants and breeds of animals. These advances have greatly increased the efficiency (output per hour) of the farm worker and have made it possible for the farm family to operate successfully far larger farms than was possible 30 or 40 years ago.

Although the family farm is likely to remain the strongest and most important element in United States agriculture, there have been, and there will be, if present trends continue, a transfer of some of the farm-management functions from the farmer to a "higher authority." This authority might be, for example, the operator of a large integrated broiler-producing enterprise; or it might be the Secretary of Agriculture, acting under one or more programs to control the marketing of certain farm products. In either case, the decision of how much of each commodity to produce will be influenced by how much of certain products the higher authority will allow or wants the farmer to produce.

COSTS AND RETURNS

Farming is an expensive business to enter. Unless a person inherits farm property, he must be prepared to invest many thousands of dollars if he wishes to farm as an owner. Table III shows the value of capital assets of typical family-operated farms in a number of farming areas, the average size of farms, and the

TABLE III

SELECTED DATA ON FAMILY-OPERATED FARMS, BY TYPE, 1959

Type of Farm	Land in Farm	Value of Land and Buildings	Value of Machinery & Equipment	Value of Livestock & Crops	Gross Farm Income[1]	Operating Expenses[2]	Net Farm Income	Charge for Capital[3]	Return to Operator & Family Labor	Return per Hour
	Acres	Dollars	Dollars	Dollars	Dollars	Dollars	Dollars	Dollars	Dollars	Dollars
Northeast dairy	221	20,440	6,370	11,860	12,124	7,611	4,513	2,127	2,386	.67
Coastal plains tobacco-cotton	100	20,300	3,100	1,460	7,333	4,615	2,718	1,426	1,292	.52
Delta cotton (small)	58	9,310	2,940	750	4,438	2,415	2,023	688	1,335	.53
Kansas winter wheat	738	74,540	9,860	8,060	14,935	5,902	9,033	4,690	4,343	2.16
Corn belt cash grain	236	93,930	7,700	10,880	13,464	7,756	5,708	5,626	82	.02
Corn belt hog-beef fattening	212	46,850	7,270	19,930	23,144	15,253	7,891	3,702	4,189	1.14
Eastern Wisconsin dairy	140	23,620	7,180	9,930	9,348	6,459	2,889	2,036	853	.23
Northern plains cattle	4,340	48,520	7,820	26,570	12,139	6,967	5,172	4,146	1,026	.32
Northwestern wheat-pea	566	155,000	17,450	4,670	26,260	10,106	16,154	8,998	7,156	2.60
New Jersey poultry	10	45,150	1,930	7,490	24,860	26,195	-1,335	3,001	-4,336	-.88

[1] Includes an allowance for food produced and consumed on the farm and for the rental value of the farm dwelling.
[2] Does not include an allowance for operator and family labor.
[3] Return to operator on the value of capital based on current interest rates.
Note: Net income is subject to abrupt changes from year to year as weather and price changes affect the quantity and value of farm products sold.

returns from farming. One important point to remember when studying this table is that the returns to capital which go to the operator are based on the current value of land, buildings, etc., rather than on the money the operator actually has invested in the farm. Prices for land are at record or near-record levels, and so are prices for machinery and equipment. Additional capital (working capital) is required for livestock and day-to-day expenses. After allowing for a return on capital at current interest rates, the returns per hour which can be expected for the labor of the operator and his family are, with few exceptions, lower than wages paid in off-farm employment.

Viewed as an investment, the rate of return to capital in agriculture in 1959, according to a Dept. of Agriculture report, was 3.5 per cent. In this computation, the work of operator and family labor was valued at a wage rate of about 80¢ per hour.

If returns are so low, why do farm operators continue to farm? Of course, many of them do not. The census reported a decline of nearly 1 million farms in the five years 1954–59. Most of the farmers who left agriculture found better-paying jobs elsewhere. Their farms were purchased mainly by other farmers, who could run them without much, if any, additional investment in machinery, thus increasing the efficiency of the buyers' operations. Others turned to off-farm work to supplement their income. In 1959, 44 per cent of farm operators reported working off their farms, and 31 per cent reported 100 or more days of such work.

Most farm operators own their farms and have owned them for a long time, and most of these owner-operator farms are free of debt. While returns on the basis of current values of property and equipment are unattractive to the prospective farmer, to the owner-operator of a mortgage-free farm, returns on his actual investment in his farm look good. Furthermore, his property is an appreciating asset. The average value of land and buildings, per acre, in 1959 was $121, compared with $84 in 1954 and $32 in 1940. Ownership of farm land has provided a great deal of protection against the inflation following World War II.

FACTORS IN SUCCESS OF A FAMILY-COMMERCIAL FARM

The actual reasons for success or failure stand out more clearly after a study of the records of many farm businesses. The discussion which follows proposes to summarize the findings from thousands of farm records for many different years.

Size of Business. Records indicate that farms large enough to require 1.5 to 2 man-years of labor are more successful than those which furnish work for less than that number, primarily because of economy in the use of labor, equipment, and capital.

With a very small business, a considerable proportion of the time is spent in getting ready for a job and in finishing up after it—it does not take five times as long to clean up the milking machine for 50 cows as it does for ten. It is also difficult for a man to do many farm operations alone. Thus, a farm which actually has too little business to keep two men profitably employed often has a second man because it is impossible to do some of the work without him.

Greater efficiency in the use of equipment is another advantage. It takes almost as much equipment to run a 100-acre dairy farm as it does to run one twice that size. Very little farm equipment, even on a large farm, is used to full capacity. As more equipment is invented, it becomes increasingly important to have a business of sufficient size to use it economically.

Rates of Production of Crops and Animals. Over the years, farm-management records have indicated that, within the limits of the actual practice of farmers, the higher the yield of crops or the production of animals, the higher the labor income of the farmer. With yields much below average, a farmer usually makes less than a hired man's wages.

Many factors must be considered to obtain good rates of production. One of the most important is to secure good land and good animal breeds. A farmer should be a good judge of both.

The farmer's problem is to adjust his crop yields and the production per animal to the conditions with which he works. It is a mistake to suggest that every farmer should get 15,000 lb. of milk per cow, or 300 eggs per hen, or 900 bu. of potatoes per acre. These fixed goals are too high for some and too low for others. The most profitable adjustment of yields depends on many factors. These include the price of land, the quality of the animals, the cost of labor, the price of fertilizer, and the price of the product. It is not desirable that every farmer should attempt to get the maximum possible crop yields or production per animal. There is plenty of evidence that good yields are profitable, while extremely high yields are usually obtained at a high cost.

Selection and Combination of Enterprises. In deciding on the best combination of enterprises for any one farm, there are also many factors to be considered. The most important are listed below:

1. Relative profits of different enterprises—because of differences in climate, soil, topography, and markets, certain areas have definite advantages in the production of some products

2. Labor distribution—it is desirable to choose a group of enterprises which require labor throughout the year, in preference to a selection which causes seasonal peaks in labor requirements

3. Relative amounts of tillable and untillable land—where considerable untillable land is available, the enterprises chosen should provide a use for this land, such as grazing livestock

4. Use of by-products

5. Maintenance of productivity

6. Rotation

7. Risk

8. Distribution of income throughout the year

9. Use of buildings and machinery

10. Capital available

11. Type of farming done by neighbors

12. Personal preference.

One of the common errors in advising farmers in the selection of enterprises is overemphasizing some one of the above factors at the expense of the others. For example, much has been said concerning the risk involved in one-crop farming; yet, most one-crop areas have chosen to operate in this manner because they have found it pays best. On the other hand, wherever there is a situation in which two or three enterprises are about equally profitable, a diversified agriculture is almost certain to result.

Labor Efficiency. Labor is the most expensive item in the cost of farm operation, whether the farmer hires help or not. The farmer's own time is valuable, because he usually has the alternative of taking another job.

Labor is used most efficiently on a moderately large farm with good yields of crops and production per animal and with enterprises so combined that the labor requirements are spread out during the year. The use of well-tested labor-saving machines is always important, but some farmers buy so much machinery that they lose money. Changes in the layout of the farm or the arrangement of the buildings offer possibilities of increased efficiency on many farms.

Planning the work ahead will help on many farms, though a farmer's plans are always subject to change without notice because of a change in the weather. It is important to keep a list of jobs which need doing, in order that when the weather changes the farmer can know immediately which is the most pressing job in the changed situation. Doing work on time is one way to save labor and do a better job. This is particularly true of weed control. If weeds are killed when they are small, it will take less time than if the job is postponed.

Efficiency in the Use of Farm Equipment. Few, if any, farm businesses are large enough to justify ownership of all the modern equipment. If a farm business is not large enough to make efficient use of a particular piece of machinery, the farmer has several possible courses to follow. Among them are to:

1. Buy the machine, but use it inefficiently

2. Do without the machine, but attempt to compete with the man who has a business large enough to use it

3. Buy the machine, and make full use of it by doing custom work for others in addition to doing his own work

4. Go in with the neighbors on cooperative ownership of the machine

5. Hire someone who owns the machine to do the job

6. Enlarge his farm business to the point where it justifies ownership of the machine.

The first two choices listed above are not good. Each of the last four choices has its value, and it is not uncommon for one farmer to practice all of them at once—for different machines.

PRICES

The importance of a farmer's producing the right combination of products as efficiently as possible is only half the story of profitable farming—the half over which the individual producer has a large measure of control. The other half—prices—is something over which the individual has no control whatever, but which influences greatly the right combination of products. Farmers as a group sell in two different markets: a controlled market and a free market. In the former, the controls are imposed by the government.

The effects of government farm programs, enacted by the Congress, are felt by almost every segment of agriculture. So pervasive and important have these programs become, that farm prices and incomes are determined to a larger degree by decisions made in Washington than by competitive conditions in the market place. Farmers, acting individually, adjust their operations to maximize their incomes within the price-and-control framework laid down by the government.

The government supports prices for food grains, feed grains, oilseeds, milk for manufacturing, cotton, wool, mohair, tung nuts, dry beans, tobacco, honey, and naval stores. For all of these commodities, except wool and mohair, the government stands ready, in effect, to buy any amount offered to it which cannot be sold at the support prices announced by the Dept. of Agriculture prior to the planting season. Wool and mohair are sold on the open market, and the difference between the market price and the higher support price is paid directly to growers by the government. For sugar beets and sugar cane, producer prices and incomes are protected by a combination of government payments and quantity limitations on imports of sugar. About 45 per cent of the cash receipts from the sale of farm products come from price-supported products. This includes receipts amounting to 17 per cent of the total from products whose production is restricted by the government. Marketing-agreement and order programs, which establish orderly marketing conditions for commodities moving in interstate commerce, are authorized for fluid milk, certain fruits, vegetables, tobacco, and tree nuts. Under these programs, various controls over quality, quantity, and rate of shipment from specified production areas act to increase the prices producers receive for these items. Not all producer groups have taken advantage of the provisions of these programs.

Finally, funds are available for the removal of temporary surpluses of perishable products. The government will buy meat, vegetables, etc., to alleviate the effects of temporary market gluts. Quantities purchased are distributed through welfare organizations and the school-lunch program.

Support prices are reflected not only in higher incomes to producers of the supported products, but also in higher costs to producers of livestock products (feed-grain prices are supported) and in higher costs of entering the business of farming. The benefits of some support programs have been capitalized into the value of farm land, *e.g.,* for tobacco, the value of the acreage allotment (the right to produce tobacco) is worth more than the value of the land on which the tobacco is produced.

The security of knowing in advance the minimum price at which one's products will sell is obviously an enormous benefit to a producer. With the price risk removed, the decision as to how much to produce is much easier.

For those products sold on the free market, the decision is very difficult. Here the farmer's ability as a price forecaster may spell the difference between profit and loss. To the farmer, price is a matter of almost daily concern. He must follow current developments closely if he is to sell his products at a time when they will yield the greatest return. He must also be a student of production and price trends, so that his products are ready for market at the most opportune time.

Price and supply are intimately related. The supply of a commodity on the market affects the price farmers receive. And the price the farmer gets affects the quantity he will produce in the future, and thus the price he will receive in the future. When the price of a commodity is good, compared with prices for alternative products, farmers as a group tend to produce more of it. They tend to cut down on output of commodities for which prices are relatively low.

The shrewd operator will try to plan his production and marketings to take advantage of these cyclical ups and downs in prices. To assist him in this, there is a substantial volume of price and production "outlook" material published by the Dept. of Agriculture and by the farm magazines.

In certain fields, farmers have been able to minimize price risks by contracting for the delivery of specified quantities of certain products, principally fruits and vegetables for processing, at specified prices. This arrangement has obvious benefits for both farmers and processors.

GETTING STARTED ON A FAMILY-COMMERCIAL FARM

Personal Qualifications. Some persons who may succeed in specialized jobs in a city are not qualified for farming, because farming calls for versatility. A good farmer is a combination of businessman, mechanic, naturalist, and laborer.

On a modern farm, most of the products are sold, and most of the necessities for the family are purchased. The farm is a business, and sound business principles must be applied if it is to succeed. Mechanical ability has always been important in farming, and the great increase in the use of complicated machines in recent years has made this ability much more important than formerly.

The farmer's job is growing plants and raising animals. He must know the scientific principles of crop and animal production. He must also know the practical application of these principles to his own farm. Good health and physical strength are important for both the farmer and his wife; running a farm is no job for either the physically or the mentally handicapped.

Education and Experience. In preparing for farming, one should consider both education and experience. One alone is not enough, nor can either substitute for the other. Farm-management records indicate that the farmers with higher education, on the average, run larger businesses, do a better job of farming, and make more money than those with less. Some college graduates have made spectacular failures, and some men who can hardly read and write have been very successful farmers. Records, however, indicate that these are exceptions rather than the rule.

Education is not a guarantee of success in farming. It cannot overcome the handicaps of lack of ability, inexperience, or poor soil. For any individual farmer, education improves the chances of achieving financial success. As farming becomes more of a science and less of an art, the greater is the importance of education and the willingness to accept new ideas. In a competitive economy, it is the innovator who reaps the greatest returns from the adoption of new techniques, which most farmers ultimately accept.

Farm experience is very important. The knowledge required for success in any business is largely gained by practical experience, and farming is no exception, something people who have never tried to run a farm often fail to realize.

Getting Control of Capital. A big problem in starting farming is capital. To finance an average farm, including stock and tools, requires an enormous amount of money, as indicated in Table III. To acquire the use of this capital is naturally a considerable problem. Farmers have done this by a number of different methods. Some of these are: (1) working at some job other than farming to save money; (2) working on the home farm, gradually working into the business, and eventually buying all or part of the farm; (3) using the "hired-man-tenant" method of saving money and getting established in farming; and (4) inheriting or being given a farm or financial backing.

In using the traditional "hired-man-tenant" route to farm ownership, a young man works as a hired man until he has obtained some experience, saved a little money, and established a good reputation in the community. Next, he may have an opportunity to rent a farm, with the landlord furnishing most of the capital. He will then gradually accumulate some livestock and equipment. After he has accumulated enough livestock and equipment to run a farm, he may have an opportunity to buy one, borrowing all or most of the purchase price. Unfortunately, the rate of capital accumulation required to own and operate a farm of sufficient size in these times makes the traditional "agricultural ladder" inadequate.

Opportunities to enter farming are limited and promise to become even more restricted. The relatively few persons entering farming are primarily farm-reared boys, many of whom receive a great deal of assistance from their families. In fact, it is extraordinarily difficult to begin farming without family help, usually long-term financial assistance in buying land; the use of family-owned machinery and equipment; partnership arrangements; and/or gifts, or inheritance. Sometimes this kind of help is provided by a benevolent landlord—a retired farmer or a city businessman with farming interests—who finds a promising young man and backs him financially.

Many young men, even those with strong family ties, start farming as renters. There are four major types of leases: cash; crop-share; livestock-share; and labor-share. Cash leases are least frequently used, because of the higher capital requirements.

Under the crop-share lease, the landowner shares in the production risk, taking one-third to one-half of the crop as his rent. The young farmer furnishes all the labor, machinery, equipment, fuel, etc., and a proportionate share of such costs as seed, fertilizer, pesticides, etc.

Livestock-share leases provide for a joint ownership of livestock and the sharing of income from both crops and livestock, often on a 50-50 basis. The landowner furnishes the farm and permanent facilities for livestock and part of the investment in livestock, feed, etc.

In a labor-share lease, the operator provides only his labor; the landowner provides the capital items. Often the operator is guaranteed a minimum return equal to a hired man's wages.

Part-time farming may be a goal in itself, or it may be an important step in the transition between a start in farming and a full-time operation. Part-time farming helps the young man in accumulating sufficient operating capital to make efficient use of available labor, and, while working at his nonfarm job, he can watch for opportunities to buy or rent an acreage he can operate in his spare time.

Most young men who start farming need to borrow money. An important question is where to borrow it. For financing a farm mortgage, the most common single source of credit is private individuals. Credit from banks and government agencies are not the main sources of farm-mortgage credit. A common method of financing the purchase of a farm is to get a first mortgage from the Federal Land Bank, a local bank, or a life insurance company, and a second mortgage from a local individual. Often the second mortgage is held by the person who sells the farm. In this method of financing, the confidence of the local individual is of the utmost importance.

Another method of financing a farm which is rapidly rising in importance is the land contract. In this agreement, the buyer promises to pay the purchase price in installments over a period of years. The seller promises to transfer possession of the land at the time the contract is made. However, title to the land is usually retained by the seller until the final installment has been paid. The advantage of this form of purchase from the buyer's standpoint is the low down payment compared with that required by a conventional mortgage. This means the buyer can hold a greater portion of his net worth in the form of operating capital, returns on which are usually greater than on land capital. Disadvantages to the buyer are the higher interest charges, the risk of losing the farm in case of a default, and increased vulnerability to declines in farm-product prices or land values in the early years of the contract, when the unpaid balance is still large.

CAPITAL REQUIREMENTS

A Dept. of Agriculture research bulletin reports widely varying capital requirements, depending on the type of farm, in order to provide operator earnings of $2,500 and $3,500 per year. These requirements are summarized in Table IV (values refer to 1956 prices).

TABLE IV

INVESTMENT REQUIRED FOR SPECIFIED RETURNS, BY TYPES OF FARM

| Type of Farm | Dollar Investment Required for Earnings of | | | |
| | $2,500 | | $3,500 | |
	Land and Buildings	Total	Land and Buildings	Total
Piedmont S.C. cotton-beef	14,595	26,910	17,515	34,430
West. Tenn. dairy-cotton	15,180	24,050	15,755	25,050
East. Okla. cotton	10,760	14,320	13,510	17,130
East. Wis. dairy	21,760	37,660	26,810	45,390
Central Kans. wheat-beef	54,135	80,360	81,900	102,820
Mont. wheat	79,270	89,150	109,205	121,960

Labor requirements vary from a low of 1,113 man-hours on the Montana farm to a high of 7,450 man-hours on the Oklahoma cotton farm.

CHOOSING A FARM

A check list of points to consider when buying a farm is included with this article. Of all the points in the check list, climate is one of the most likely to be overlooked. Any person on any day of any year can see the topography of a farm. A well-trained person can see the soil any day when it is not frozen. With respect to climate, however, a person might be wrong, even after several years' observations or after "asking the neighbors." Climate is weather over a period of years, and the only way to choose a climate with any degree of certainty is to look at the records of the United States Weather Bureau. Even the Weather Bureau records, however, do not give all the information needed. There are many local variations in climate not shown by the records; there are even differences on individual farms.

Of all the various features of soils, drainage is the most likely to be limiting in the United States. While some well-drained soils are so infertile as to be practically worthless, most of them are good soils; poorly drained soils are, of course, generally difficult to farm profitably.

Good buildings can usually be bought cheaper than they can be built. For this reason, a farm with good buildings in good repair is likely to be a better "buy" than a similar farm with buildings which are inadequate or run-down. The difference in price of two such farms is seldom enough to cover the cost of reconditioning the poor buildings.

What to Consider Before Buying a Farm

Acreage

Crops
Pasture
Woods
Farmstead, roads, waste, etc.
Potential cropland
Total

Location

Kind of road
Amount of travel on road
Proximity to markets
Accessibility in all seasons
Distance to, and quality of, school
Churches, community organizations
Quality of neighborhood farms
Type of neighbors
Potential for future real estate development

Climate

Annual rainfall
Growing-season rainfall
Average days between killing frosts
Frequency of drought, hail, flood, etc.

Topography

Elevation at the buildings
Effect on ease of cultivation
Effect on air drainage
Effect on erosion
Effect on hauling in and out of barn

Layout

Size and shape of fields
Convenience to farmstead
Obstructions in fields
Condition and adequacy of fences

Building Layout

Location with respect to highway
Location with respect to each other
Site of farmstead

Water Supply

House
Barn
Pasture
Spray
Irrigation

Timber

Species
Condition

House

General condition, appearance, and
 size
Foundation
Roof
Running water
Bathroom
Furnace

Soils

Names of types of soil
Acreage of each type
Texture
Lime
Drainage
Natural productivity
Present productivity
Stones
Weeds

Orchard

Acres

Age
Varieties of fruit
Condition

Barns

General condition, appearance, and
 size
Foundation and roof
General arrangement
Lights
Running water
Concrete floor

Taxes

Tax rate
Financial condition of the community

Productive Capacity

Acreage and expected yield of the
 different crops
Number of each kind of stock that
 can be carried

WHERE TO GO FOR ADVICE ON FARM PROBLEMS

The best persons to give advice on how to get started in farming or on living in a given rural community are the successful farmers in that community. In every community, there are some who are both qualified and willing to give advice and suggestions about farms for sale or rent, about opportunities for jobs as hired men on successful farms, and about opportunities for residential farming for persons who may wish to live in the country and work in town.

The County Agricultural Agent. Each agricultural county has a county agricultural agent, who is employed jointly by the extension service of the state agricultural college, the United States Dept. of Agriculture, and the farmers of the county. This agent is a trained agricultural specialist who is in a position to give much helpful advice to persons interested in farming or living in the country. His office is usually at the county seat.

State Agricultural Colleges. These institutions offer free of charge a large number of bulletins and circulars on the techniques of farming and ranching, the marketing of farm products, and on other aspects of agriculture. The United States Dept. of Agriculture, Washington 25, D.C., provides a list of the names and addresses of the agricultural colleges, as well as a catalogue of its own publications. See also The Department of Agriculture.

FACTS FOR FARMERS

The sections below offer facts which may help farmers plan their work. Dates for planting seeds and harvesting crops, average temperatures, average precipitation, and information about dairy cows are offered, with additional information regarding estimating barbed wire and the capacity of silos.

SEEDTIME AND HARVEST

Crop and State	Main Plantings From	To	Bulk of Harvest From	To
Winter wheat				
Kansas	Sept. 15	Oct. 15	June 25	July 20
Ohio	Sept. 25	Oct. 15	June 25	July 15
Spring wheat				
North Dakota	April 10	April 30	July 25	Aug. 15
Oats				
Minnesota	April 1	May 31	July 5	Aug. 31
Spring oats				
South Carolina	Jan. 15	Feb. 15	June 5	June 25
Corn				
Iowa	April 25	May 31	Oct. 20	Dec. 15
Alabama	April 1	May 31	Oct. 1	Nov. 30
Cotton				
Texas	March 1	May 20	July 15	Nov. 15
Mississippi	April 10	May 10	Sept. 1	Nov. 10
Tobacco				
North Carolina	April 10	June 15	July 1	Sept. 25
Kentucky	May 15	June 20	Aug. 10	Sept. 25
Soybeans				
Illinois	May 15	June 25	Sept. 20	Oct. 31
Arkansas	April 15	June 10	Oct. 1	Nov. 30
Potatoes				
Maine	May 10	June 10	Sept. 10	Oct. 15
Idaho	May 10	June 10	Sept. 1	Oct. 31
Florida	Sept. 10	Dec. 10	May 5	June 5
Rice				
Louisiana	April 10	May 31	Aug. 25	Oct. 15
California	April 10	June 20	Sept. 20	Dec. 10
Oranges				
Florida	[1]Feb. 25	March 5	Jan. 15	Feb. 1
California	[1]March 5	March 30	Nov. 15	May 15
Apples				
New York	[1]May 10	May 30	Sept. 1	Oct. 25
Washington	[1]April 10	May 10	Sept. 10	Oct. 25
Peaches				
South Carolina	[1]March 5	March 25	June 15	Aug. 1
California	[1]March 1	March 25	June 25	Sept. 5
Tomatoes				
Texas	Jan. 1	March 15	April 25	July 15
New Jersey	April 25	June 15	July 1	Oct. 15
Lettuce				
California	All year		All year	
Snap beans				
Florida	Nov. 1	March 15	Jan. 1	May 15
″	Sept. 1	Oct. 31	Oct. 15	Dec. 31
New York	May 1	July 15	July 1	Oct. 31

[1] Usual dates of full bloom.

GROUND ELEVATION OF WEATHER STATIONS
AND DATES OF OCCURRENCE OF FREEZE (32° F.)
FOR SELECTED CITIES[1]

STATION	Ground elevation (feet)	OCCURRENCE OF FREEZE			
		Spring date		Fall date	
		Mean	Latest	Mean	Earliest
Alabama............Mobile............	10	Feb. 20	Mar. 20	Dec. 5	Nov. 15
Alaska............Juneau	15	Apr. 27	June 8	Oct. 19	Sept. 22
Arizona............Phoenix	1,083	Jan. 30	Mar. 2	Dec. 5	Nov. 4
Arkansas............Little Rock	257	Mar. 16	Apr. 13	Nov. 15	Oct. 23
California............Los Angeles	312	Jan. 17	Jan. 21	....	None
Sacramento	25	Jan. 23	Mar. 14	Dec. 5	Nov. 4
San Francisco	52	Jan. 17	Jan. 21	Dec. 12	Dec. 11
Colorado............Denver	5,221	May 2	May 28	Oct. 14	Sept. 18
Connecticut............Hartford	169	Apr. 22	May 10	Oct. 19	Sept. 27
Delaware............Wilmington	72	Apr. 18	May 9	Oct. 26	Sept. 27
District of Columbia............Washington	73	Apr. 10	May 12	Oct. 28	Oct. 2
Florida............Jacksonville	18	Feb. 15	May 14	Nov. 30	Nov. 9
Miami	8	....	....	....	....
Georgia............Atlanta	1,054	Mar. 20	Apr. 15	Nov. 19	Oct. 24
Hawaii............Honolulu	12				
Idaho............Boise	2,842	Apr. 29	May 23	Oct. 16	Sept. 20
Illinois............Chicago	610	Apr. 19	May 13	Oct. 28	Sept. 25
Peoria	654	Apr. 22	May 25	Oct. 16	Sept. 29
Indiana............Indianapolis	718	Apr. 17	May 11	Oct. 27	Oct. 1
Iowa............Des Moines	807	Apr. 20	May 11	Oct. 19	Sept. 28
Kansas............Wichita	1,321	Apr. 5	Apr. 21	Nov. 1	Sept. 27
Kentucky............Louisville	457	Apr. 1	Apr. 19	Nov. 7	Oct. 15
Louisiana............New Orleans	9	Feb. 15	Mar. 20	Dec. 8	Nov. 13
Maine............Portland	61	Apr. 29	May 30	Oct. 15	Sept. 17
Maryland............Baltimore	146	Mar. 28	Apr. 16	Nov. 17	Oct. 20
Massachusetts............Boston	15	Apr. 16	May 19	Oct. 25	Sept. 26
Michigan............Detroit	619	Apr. 25	May 12	Oct. 23	Sept. 29
Sault Ste. Marie	721	May 18	June 8	Oct. 3	Aug. 22
Minnesota............Duluth	1,162	May 13	June 1	Oct. 3	Sept. 13
Minneapolis	830	Apr. 30	May 24	Oct. 13	Sept. 18
Mississippi............Jackson	305	Mar. 10	Apr. 13	Nov. 13	Oct. 17
Missouri............Kansas City	741	Apr. 5	Apr. 17	Oct. 31	Oct. 6
St. Louis	465	Apr. 2	May 2	Nov. 8	Oct. 14
Montana............Great Falls	3,664	May 14	June 8	Sept. 26	Sept. 7
Nebraska............Omaha	978	Apr. 14	....	Oct. 19	....
Nevada............Reno	4,397	May 14	June 25	Oct. 2	Aug. 30
New Hampshire............Concord	339	May 11	May 26	Sept. 30	Sept. 13
New Jersey............Atlantic City	8	Apr. 10	....	Nov. 5	....
New Mexico............Albuquerque	5,310	Apr. 16	May 18	Oct. 29	Oct. 11
New York............Albany	19	Apr. 27	May 20	Oct. 13	Sept. 23
Buffalo	693	Apr. 30	May 24	Oct. 25	Sept. 23
New York	10	Apr. 7	Apr. 24	Nov. 12	Oct. 19
North Carolina............Charlotte	727	Mar. 21	Apr. 16	Nov. 15	Oct. 15
Raleigh	400	Mar. 24	Apr. 20	Nov. 16	Oct. 29
North Dakota............Bismarck	1,650	May 11	May 30	Sept. 24	Sept. 6
Ohio............Cincinnati	761	Apr. 15	May 25	Oct. 25	Sept. 28
Cleveland	787	Apr. 21	May 14	Nov. 2	Sept. 29
Columbus	815	Apr. 17	May 9	Oct. 30	Oct. 7
Oklahoma............Oklahoma City	1,254	Mar. 28	Apr. 17	Nov. 7	Oct. 23
Oregon............Portland	30	Feb. 25	May 4	Nov. 26	Oct. 30
Pennsylvania............Philadelphia	26	Mar. 30	Apr. 20	Nov. 17	Oct. 19
Pittsburgh	749	Apr. 16	May 4	Nov. 8	Oct. 10
Rhode Island............Providence	55	Apr. 13	Apr. 24	Oct. 27	Oct. 3
South Carolina............Columbia	217	Mar. 14	Apr. 13	Nov. 11	Nov. 1
South Dakota............Sioux Falls	1,420	May 5	May 29	Oct. 3	Sept. 12
Tennessee............Memphis	263	Mar. 23	Apr. 15	Nov. 12	Oct. 17
Nashville	577	Mar. 28	Apr. 19	Nov. 7	Oct. 17
Texas............Dallas	487				
El Paso	3,920				
Houston	41	Feb. 5	Mar. 26	Dec. 11	Oct. 25
Utah............Salt Lake City	4,260	Apr. 12	Apr. 30	Nov. 1	Sept. 25
Vermont............Burlington	331	May 8	May 23	Oct. 3	Sept. 13
Virginia............Norfolk	26	Mar. 18	Apr. 14	Nov. 27	Nov. 7
Richmond	162	Apr. 2	Apr. 20	Nov. 8	Oct. 21
Washington............Seattle	14	Feb. 23	Apr. 3	Nov. 26	Oct. 19
Spokane	2,357	Apr. 20	May 16	Oct. 12	Sept. 18
West Virginia............Charleston	950	Apr. 18	May 11	Oct. 28	Sept. 29
Wisconsin............Milwaukee	672	Apr. 20	May 9	Oct. 25	Sept. 24
Wyoming............Cheyenne	6,181	May 20	June 18	Sept. 27	Sept. 5
Puerto Rico............San Juan	47				

[1] Taken from U.S. Weather Bureau records; date of freeze based on standard 30-year period (1921-50).

NORMAL MONTHLY AVERAGE TEMPERATURE IN FAHRENHEIT DEGREES, FOR SELECTED CITIES[1]

STATION		Jan.	Feb.	Mar.	Apr.	May	June	July	Aug.	Sept.	Oct.	Nov.	Dec.	Annual
Alabama	Mobile	53.1	55.5	60.1	67.4	74.3	80.5	81.9	82.0	78.7	69.9	59.4	54.1	68.1
Alaska	Juneau	29.5	29.9	34.4	40.4	47.3	54.5	56.0	55.9	50.8	44.0	36.2	30.6	42.5
Arizona	Phoenix	51.3	55.7	60.9	68.2	76.6	85.0	90.5	88.9	83.6	72.1	60.1	53.4	70.5
Arkansas	Little Rock	41.8	45.6	52.8	62.5	69.8	78.5	81.9	81.3	74.8	64.1	51.5	43.9	62.4
California	Los Angeles	55.0	56.4	58.9	61.5	64.8	67.8	72.5	72.9	71.0	66.6	62.1	57.3	63.9
	Sacramento	45.2	50.6	54.9	59.2	65.0	71.2	75.3	74.0	71.3	63.8	54.3	46.7	60.9
	San Francisco	50.1	53.0	54.9	55.7	57.1	59.1	58.9	59.3	61.6	61.0	57.2	51.9	56.7
Colorado	Denver	31.4	34.5	39.3	48.6	57.3	67.3	73.7	72.4	63.7	53.0	41.3	34.1	51.4
Connecticut	Hartford	27.0	27.5	36.9	47.4	58.9	67.7	72.7	70.4	63.1	52.6	41.7	30.1	49.7
Delaware	Wilmington	33.3	33.7	42.5	51.3	62.3	71.5	75.9	73.8	68.0	56.2	45.5	35.1	54.2
District of Columbia	Washington	36.5	37.5	45.7	54.7	65.2	73.9	77.3	75.3	69.9	58.4	48.0	38.2	56.3
Florida	Jacksonville	57.3	58.7	63.4	69.1	75.2	80.2	81.7	81.5	79.1	71.3	62.7	57.7	69.8
	Miami	68.5	68.7	70.8	74.1	77.1	80.3	81.6	82.1	81.0	77.6	72.3	69.5	75.3
Georgia	Atlanta	44.6	46.6	53.1	61.5	69.5	76.9	78.7	78.1	73.9	63.5	62.1	45.3	62.0
Hawaii	Honolulu	72.0	72.0	72.2	73.3	75.1	76.9	77.9	78.5	78.3	77.5	75.2	73.3	75.2
Idaho	Boise	27.3	34.0	41.3	49.9	58.1	65.1	74.3	72.5	62.4	52.6	39.6	31.0	50.3
Illinois	Chicago	24.9	27.4	37.0	48.1	59.2	69.4	74.6	72.7	65.6	54.1	39.5	28.0	50.1
	Peoria	25.0	28.3	38.3	50.5	61.0	70.9	76.7	73.7	66.3	54.7	39.7	28.6	51.0
Indiana	Indianapolis	31.1	33.1	41.9	52.7	63.5	73.5	78.0	75.9	69.2	58.2	43.6	33.2	54.5
Iowa	Des Moines	22.8	26.7	37.6	51.0	62.0	71.5	77.1	74.5	66.5	55.0	39.1	27.0	50.9
Kansas	Wichita	32.0	37.2	45.3	56.2	64.9	75.3	80.9	79.9	71.7	60.2	45.1	35.5	57.0
Kentucky	Louisville	35.6	37.8	46.1	56.5	65.9	74.9	78.6	76.9	71.1	59.8	46.7	37.6	57.3
Louisiana	New Orleans	55.9	58.5	63.0	69.3	76.1	81.9	83.1	83.4	80.3	72.8	62.5	57.1	70.4
Maine	Portland	20.7	21.5	31.5	41.9	52.3	61.8	67.3	66.4	58.6	48.4	37.5	25.1	44.5
Maryland	Baltimore	36.6	37.3	45.3	54.3	65.3	74.3	78.5	76.4	70.4	59.3	48.7	38.8	57.1
Massachusetts	Boston	29.1	29.2	37.6	47.2	57.8	67.2	72.2	71.5	64.3	55.0	44.4	32.3	50.7
Michigan	Detroit	26.2	26.7	35.1	46.4	57.8	68.1	73.1	71.3	64.3	52.9	40.1	29.5	49.3
	Sault Ste. Marie	13.8	13.5	23.0	36.8	48.9	58.1	63.9	62.9	55.2	44.4	31.5	19.9	39.3
Minnesota	Duluth	10.3	13.3	24.6	38.3	49.3	58.7	65.8	64.8	56.1	45.2	28.6	15.0	39.2
	Minneapolis	14.6	18.2	30.9	46.0	58.5	68.2	74.1	71.5	62.2	50.4	33.0	19.4	45.6
Mississippi	Jackson	48.3	51.0	56.8	64.9	72.3	79.9	82.1	81.4	76.7	66.4	55.2	49.0	65.4
Missouri	Kansas City	30.0	34.6	43.3	55.8	65.5	75.4	80.9	79.0	70.6	59.6	44.3	33.7	56.1
	St. Louis	33.3	36.7	45.3	56.5	66.2	75.8	80.6	78.6	71.4	60.6	46.0	36.2	57.3
Montana	Great Falls	22.7	24.6	32.5	44.3	53.8	60.7	69.6	67.1	56.9	48.1	35.2	26.5	45.1
Nebraska	Omaha	23.0	27.2	38.2	52.2	62.7	72.6	78.5	75.7	67.0	55.5	38.9	27.4	51.8
Nevada	Reno	31.2	36.3	40.6	47.7	55.3	61.5	69.6	67.4	60.5	50.7	40.2	33.2	49.5
New Hampshire	Concord	20.1	21.2	31.8	43.0	54.8	64.1	69.0	66.5	55.8	43.0	36.7	24.0	44.8
New Jersey	Atlantic City	35.8	36.4	41.5	49.4	59.1	68.7	73.6	73.1	68.3	58.0	48.1	38.2	54.1
New Mexico	Albuquerque	33.7	39.5	46.0	55.5	65.3	74.9	79.0	76.9	69.9	58.2	44.0	36.0	56.6
New York	Albany	25.2	25.6	35.8	47.3	59.4	68.7	73.1	71.3	63.8	52.5	41.4	29.1	49.4
	Buffalo	25.5	24.7	33.0	43.8	55.4	65.5	70.6	68.9	62.4	51.2	39.9	29.0	47.5
	New York	32.9	32.7	40.7	49.8	60.8	69.8	74.6	73.2	67.3	57.0	46.3	35.7	53.4
North Carolina	Charlotte	42.3	44.4	51.0	59.7	68.3	76.6	78.6	77.3	72.6	61.5	50.4	43.0	60.5
	Raleigh	42.7	44.4	51.3	59.7	68.5	76.6	79.3	78.0	73.4	62.6	52.1	44.0	61.1
North Dakota	Bismarck	9.2	12.7	26.7	43.1	54.8	64.3	72.1	69.3	58.5	45.7	28.4	15.5	41.7
Ohio	Cincinnati	33.1	34.8	43.3	53.6	63.6	72.3	76.6	74.8	68.9	57.4	44.6	35.0	54.9
	Cleveland	29.5	30.1	37.7	48.0	59.1	69.3	73.7	72.2	66.3	55.5	43.8	32.9	51.5
	Columbus	31.1	32.6	41.1	51.4	62.2	72.0	75.3	73.8	67.8	56.1	43.2	33.3	53.4
Oklahoma	Oklahoma City	37.8	42.5	50.3	60.9	68.6	78.0	82.5	82.2	74.6	63.8	49.7	40.9	61.0
Oregon	Portland	39.5	43.8	48.4	53.6	59.1	63.8	68.5	68.4	63.9	56.1	47.2	42.4	54.6
Pennsylvania	Philadelphia	34.9	35.1	43.5	52.7	63.7	72.6	77.2	75.2	69.3	58.5	47.8	37.4	55.7
	Pittsburgh	33.0	33.6	41.6	51.8	62.6	71.7	75.4	73.1	67.9	55.9	44.6	35.2	53.9
Rhode Island	Providence	30.3	30.3	38.9	48.1	59.0	68.1	73.5	71.8	64.8	54.5	44.2	33.2	51.4
South Carolina	Columbia	47.9	49.4	55.9	63.8	71.5	79.2	80.9	79.7	75.9	65.5	54.9	48.1	64.4
South Dakota	Sioux Falls	14.2	19.5	32.0	46.4	58.1	68.0	74.8	72.4	62.4	50.0	32.2	19.4	45.8
Tennessee	Memphis	41.9	44.5	52.4	62.2	70.5	78.7	81.3	80.3	74.8	65.0	52.1	44.4	62.4
	Nashville	39.9	42.3	49.8	59.7	68.2	76.9	80.0	78.7	73.2	61.8	49.3	41.6	60.1
Texas	Dallas	45.7	49.8	57.4	66.3	73.7	81.9	85.5	85.8	78.9	68.8	55.8	48.3	66.5
	El Paso	43.4	49.1	54.5	63.1	71.6	80.2	81.3	79.8	74.9	65.2	52.0	44.8	63.3
	Houston	53.8	57.7	62.6	69.5	75.9	81.8	83.8	84.2	80.0	72.6	61.9	55.8	70.0
Utah	Salt Lake City	26.5	33.4	41.1	50.1	58.9	67.1	76.6	74.4	64.3	52.9	39.3	31.5	51.3
Vermont	Burlington	17.9	18.1	29.3	42.3	55.4	65.5	70.4	68.1	59.9	48.2	36.4	22.3	44.5
Virginia	Norfolk	43.1	43.5	50.5	57.9	67.3	76.0	78.7	77.8	73.4	63.0	53.2	44.5	60.7
	Richmond	39.6	40.9	48.2	56.8	66.5	74.7	77.9	76.3	71.2	60.0	49.8	40.8	58.6
Washington	Seattle	40.7	43.5	47.0	51.8	57.3	61.8	65.6	65.2	61.0	54.4	47.0	43.1	53.2
	Spokane	24.9	29.7	38.1	46.3	54.7	61.4	69.6	67.9	59.2	48.6	35.7	29.1	47.1
West Virginia	Charleston	36.4	38.2	44.9	55.3	63.7	72.0	75.4	73.6	68.6	57.4	45.8	38.1	55.8
Wisconsin	Milwaukee	23.0	25.1	34.0	44.8	54.8	65.4	72.3	70.9	63.8	52.6	38.5	26.8	47.7
Wyoming	Cheyenne	25.5	27.7	31.8	41.1	50.1	60.3	68.1	66.8	57.4	46.4	35.1	23.7	44.9
Puerto Rico	San Juan	74.9	74.9	75.6	76.6	78.7	79.5	80.0	80.5	80.5	80.1	78.4	76.5	78.0

[1] Taken from U.S. Weather Bureau records; based on standard 30-year period (1921-50).

NORMAL MONTHLY AND ANNUAL PRECIPITATION
IN INCHES, FOR SELECTED CITIES[1]

(T DENOTES TRACE)

STATION		Jan.	Feb.	Mar.	Apr.	May	June	July	Aug.	Sept.	Oct.	Nov.	Dec.	Annual
Alabama	Mobile	5.02	4.81	7.62	5.10	4.64	6.00	8.97	6.31	5.78	3.75	4.07	5.41	67.57
Alaska	Juneau	4.48	3.35	3.47	2.98	3.19	3.18	4.65	5.16	6.92	8.47	5.92	4.17	55.94
Arizona	Phoenix	0.60	0.79	0.66	0.35	0.17	0.06	0.70	0.99	1.00	0.40	0.47	0.97	7.16
Arkansas	Little Rock	5.12	4.06	4.85	5.16	4.85	3.43	3.10	3.15	2.85	2.81	3.92	4.03	47.38
California	Los Angeles	2.38	3.37	2.36	1.17	0.26	0.07	T	0.02	0.27	0.50	1.03	3.11	14.54
	Sacramento	2.86	3.31	2.23	1.43	0.57	0.14	T	T	0.03	0.92	1.59	3.19	16.32
	San Francisco	4.03	3.91	2.73	1.49	0.59	0.15	0.01	0.01	0.13	1.07	2.27	4.07	20.51
Colorado	Denver	0.50	0.53	1.19	2.05	2.20	1.64	1.36	1.43	1.08	1.01	0.70	0.51	14.20
Connecticut	Hartford	3.15	2.57	3.81	3.56	3.66	3.62	3.50	3.54	3.44	2.80	3.43	3.29	40.48
Delaware	Wilmington	3.56	2.98	3.61	3.64	3.81	4.02	4.49	5.28	3.80	2.99	3.33	2.99	44.50
District of Columbia	Washington	3.24	2.44	3.03	3.06	3.93	3.41	4.26	4.75	4.12	2.85	2.73	2.61	40.48
Florida	Jacksonville	2.68	2.66	3.42	3.34	3.43	6.82	7.64	6.43	6.96	4.71	1.62	2.37	52.08
	Miami	2.06	1.78	2.25	3.99	5.55	6.82	6.73	6.61	8.33	8.23	2.41	1.65	56.41
Georgia	Atlanta	4.67	4.82	5.87	4.42	3.82	4.02	4.41	3.81	2.96	2.60	3.41	4.55	49.16
Hawaii	Honolulu	4.31	2.49	2.30	2.05	1.01	0.63	0.86	1.09	1.34	2.28	2.08	3.48	23.92
Idaho	Boise	1.33	1.35	1.34	1.10	1.09	0.84	0.18	0.21	0.46	0.94	1.35	1.29	11.48
Illinois	Chicago	1.84	1.41	2.85	2.82	3.66	4.15	2.73	3.19	3.23	2.56	2.33	1.95	32.72
	Peoria	1.97	1.91	2.79	3.44	3.94	3.88	3.70	2.99	3.73	2.44	2.35	2.04	35.18
Indiana	Indianapolis	3.15	2.08	3.89	3.85	3.85	4.21	3.03	3.52	3.67	2.52	3.13	2.79	39.69
Iowa	Des Moines	1.23	1.08	2.03	2.45	3.60	4.99	2.94	3.76	3.64	2.20	1.68	1.14	30.74
Kansas	Wichita	1.05	0.98	1.74	3.52	3.79	4.99	3.43	2.96	3.23	2.13	1.73	1.10	30.70
Kentucky	Louisville	4.10	2.99	4.67	4.01	3.93	4.06	3.08	3.06	2.70	2.45	3.12	3.30	41.47
Louisiana	New Orleans	4.73	4.18	6.56	5.45	5.43	5.57	7.09	6.41	5.52	3.66	4.01	4.53	63.54
Maine	Portland	4.43	3.83	4.03	3.75	3.36	3.32	2.83	2.59	3.08	2.98	3.79	3.79	41.78
Maryland	Baltimore	3.66	2.99	3.63	3.72	4.01	3.52	3.94	4.38	3.46	3.37	2.96	2.95	42.59
Massachusetts	Boston	3.50	2.93	3.43	3.46	2.91	3.48	3.18	3.23	2.99	2.79	3.49	3.37	38.76
Michigan	Detroit	2.08	2.02	2.53	2.91	3.61	2.90	2.91	2.62	2.78	2.29	2.18	2.20	31.03
	Sault Ste. Marie	2.16	1.52	1.85	1.95	2.55	3.02	2.49	2.62	3.49	2.98	3.26	2.30	30.19
Minnesota	Duluth	1.23	1.22	1.78	2.50	3.17	4.83	3.64	3.45	3.22	2.22	1.78	1.20	29.72
	Minneapolis	0.80	0.89	1.43	1.91	3.12	4.26	2.67	2.79	2.35	1.65	1.44	0.85	24.71
Mississippi	Jackson	5.09	5.09	6.23	4.82	4.09	3.72	4.61	3.23	2.10	2.13	4.05	5.60	50.66
Missouri	Kansas City	1.43	1.16	2.51	3.61	4.41	5.02	2.83	3.89	3.35	2.93	2.17	1.50	35.31
	St. Louis	1.92	1.66	3.42	3.93	4.02	4.37	2.58	3.55	3.54	3.08	2.57	2.09	36.73
Montana	Great Falls	0.55	0.57	0.99	0.95	1.93	2.96	1.35	1.20	1.44	0.72	0.67	0.70	14.03
Nebraska	Omaha	0.85	0.87	1.32	2.15	2.75	4.51	3.34	3.12	3.16	1.73	1.29	0.81	25.90
Nevada	Reno	1.04	1.05	0.70	0.46	0.48	0.42	0.23	0.23	0.22	0.55	0.64	0.94	6.96
New Hampshire	Concord	2.91	2.30	3.04	3.08	3.04	3.62	3.57	3.10	3.39	2.80	3.27	2.81	37.23
New Jersey	Atlantic City	3.78	3.24	3.58	3.40	2.98	2.99	3.78	4.72	3.51	3.21	3.32	3.31	41.77
New Mexico	Albuquerque	0.28	0.33	0.44	0.53	0.57	0.72	1.43	1.38	1.05	0.84	0.42	0.59	8.68
New York	Albany	2.27	2.03	2.83	2.61	2.80	3.37	3.30	2.89	3.15	2.21	2.69	2.17	31.82
	Buffalo	2.78	2.59	2.72	2.55	2.47	2.70	2.43	2.54	3.01	2.49	3.09	2.92	32.29
	New York	3.46	3.13	3.56	3.22	3.51	3.70	4.24	4.34	3.67	3.04	3.09	3.07	42.03
North Carolina	Charlotte	3.68	3.55	4.09	3.17	2.98	3.51	4.67	4.86	3.65	2.99	2.65	3.79	43.09
	Raleigh	3.34	3.27	3.60	3.53	3.40	4.09	5.45	4.96	4.49	2.82	2.85	3.29	45.09
North Dakota	Bismarck	0.86	0.43	0.76	1.89	1.94	3.33	2.33	1.50	1.43	1.00	0.53	0.40	15.40
Ohio	Cincinnati	3.44	2.55	4.07	3.64	3.54	4.05	3.70	3.38	2.88	2.19	3.06	2.84	39.34
	Cleveland	2.38	2.12	2.89	2.73	2.73	3.05	3.04	2.64	3.13	2.42	2.66	2.29	32.08
	Columbus	2.94	2.35	3.43	3.44	3.97	4.33	3.85	3.21	2.91	2.18	2.86	2.49	37.96
Oklahoma	Oklahoma City	1.50	1.24	2.09	3.17	4.25	3.93	2.15	2.50	3.43	2.66	1.82	1.43	30.22
Oregon	Portland	5.43	4.87	4.15	2.43	1.87	1.62	0.42	0.61	1.33	3.53	6.05	7.10	39.91
Pennsylvania	Philadelphia	3.37	3.02	3.32	3.38	3.58	3.87	4.20	4.53	3.46	2.60	3.08	2.67	41.13
	Pittsburgh	2.77	2.37	3.20	3.19	3.77	4.07	3.91	3.13	2.97	2.44	2.59	2.51	36.92
Rhode Island	Providence	3.75	2.84	3.58	3.87	3.02	3.17	3.06	3.63	3.19	2.83	3.74	3.45	39.63
South Carolina	Columbia	3.14	3.63	3.79	3.54	3.23	4.05	6.56	5.53	4.42	2.42	2.25	3.59	46.15
South Dakota	Sioux Falls	0.72	0.74	1.85	2.35	3.38	4.25	3.00	3.23	2.93	1.46	1.11	0.67	26.24
Tennessee	Memphis	5.55	4.59	5.59	4.80	3.92	3.33	3.23	2.94	2.55	2.27	4.56	5.09	49.42
	Nashville	4.93	4.16	5.28	3.69	3.73	3.19	3.96	3.31	2.74	2.52	3.41	4.06	45.03
Texas	Dallas	2.47	2.62	2.81	3.87	4.97	3.45	1.97	1.83	2.71	2.67	2.43	2.62	34.42
	El Paso	0.42	0.36	0.23	0.27	0.41	0.62	1.32	1.32	1.13	0.83	0.38	0.49	7.83
	Houston	3.98	2.81	3.10	3.40	4.84	4.08	4.45	3.09	3.65	3.39	3.95	4.63	45.37
Utah	Salt Lake City	1.20	1.23	1.66	1.76	1.56	0.91	0.61	0.97	0.74	1.84	1.42	1.34	14.74
Vermont	Burlington	1.89	1.53	2.19	2.63	2.89	3.57	3.75	3.01	3.14	2.89	2.85	1.88	32.22
Virginia	Norfolk	3.17	3.06	3.27	3.16	3.45	4.16	6.05	5.93	3.86	2.45	2.67	2.88	42.26
	Richmond	3.64	2.76	3.42	3.23	3.64	3.27	6.54	5.05	3.65	2.61	2.49	2.89	42.89
Washington	Seattle	4.49	3.74	3.06	1.94	1.61	1.25	0.52	0.87	1.58	3.08	4.46	5.34	31.92
	Spokane	1.72	1.46	1.34	0.99	1.04	1.17	0.36	0.49	0.93	1.83	1.88	2.21	14.92
West Virginia	Charleston	3.99	3.50	4.16	3.74	3.78	3.93	5.45	4.55	2.94	2.81	3.17	2.98	45.00
Wisconsin	Milwaukee	1.58	1.27	2.19	2.39	2.93	3.22	2.43	2.62	3.33	1.97	2.11	1.43	27.57
Wyoming	Cheyenne	0.56	0.65	1.22	2.14	2.46	2.10	1.96	1.61	1.20	1.18	0.70	0.52	16.25
Puerto Rico	San Juan	4.69	2.67	2.42	3.80	6.51	5.16	6.02	6.26	6.00	5.27	6.37	4.33	60.00

[1] Taken from U.S. Weather Bureau records; based on standard 30-year period (1921–50).

BREEDS OF DAIRY COWS

There are five major breeds of dairy cattle kept in the United States. The fat and the total solids content of the milk of each breed is given below. The average production of fat per cow per year is about the same for all five breeds, assuming equal care and quality of animals. For example, in comparing Holsteins and Jerseys, the total amount of milk produced by one cow will be higher for Holsteins, in about the same proportion as the fat content of the milk is lower. There are good and poor cows in each breed. The choice of breed depends primarily on the premium which the market pays for milk with a high fat content. If the premium is small, Holsteins are kept. If it is large, Jerseys or Guernseys are kept.

MILK YIELD OF DAIRY COWS IN THE UNITED STATES

Breed	Fat content of milk (per cent)	Other solids in milk (per cent)	Total solids in milk (per cent)
Jersey	5.4	9.5	14.9
Guernsey	4.9	9.6	14.5
Brown Swiss	4.1	9.3	13.4
Ayrshire	4.0	9.0	13.0
Holstein	3.5	8.8	12.3

ESTIMATING BARBED WIRE FOR FENCES

The following table shows the estimated number of pounds of barbed wire required to fence the space or distances mentioned, with 1, 2, or 3 lines of wire, based upon each pound of wire measuring 1 rod (16½ ft.).

	1 Line	2 Lines	3 Lines
1 square acre	50⅔ lb.	101⅓ lb.	152 lb.
1 side of a square acre	12⅔ lb.	25⅓ lb.	38 lb.
1 square half acre	36 lb.	72 lb.	108 lb.
1 square mile	1,280 lb.	2,560 lb.	3,840 lb.
1 side of a square mile	320 lb.	640 lb.	960 lb.
1 rod in length	1 lb.	2 lb.	3 lb.
100 rods in length	100 lb.	200 lb.	300 lb.
100 feet in length	6¹⁄₁₆ lb.	12⅛ lb.	18³⁄₁₆ lb.

APPROXIMATE CAPACITY OF CYLINDRICAL SILOS
(FOR CORN SILAGE)

Depth of silage after settling 2 days	Diameter of the silo in feet					
	10	12	14	16	18	20
(feet)	(tons)	(tons)	(tons)	(tons)	(tons)	(tons)
5	4	6	9	11	14	17
10	10	15	20	26	33	41
15	18	25	34	45	57	70
20	26	38	51	67	85	105
25	36	52	70	92	116	143
30	47	67	91	119	151	187
35	58	84	114	149	188	232
40	70	101	138	180	229	280
45	82	118	160	213	271	334
50	94	137	186	248	319	389
55		155	212	283	365	444
60			240	319	415	500

A ton of timothy hay in a well-settled mow occupies approximately 450 cu. ft. A ton of clover hay in a well-settled mow occupies approximately 550 cu. ft.

THE DEPARTMENT OF AGRICULTURE

On May 15, 1862, President Abraham Lincoln signed the bill establishing what is now the United States Department of Agriculture as a separate agency, with bureau status and headed by a commissioner. On Feb. 9, 1889, the department was raised to cabinet rank.

The primary functions of the department are to compile and distribute useful information concerning agriculture, and to conduct research and educational programs. In addition, the department directs the conservation, marketing, and regulation of farm products, including crops and livestock, for the purpose of protecting both the farmer and the consumer.

Toward this end the department maintains a number of specialized agencies. The functions of the most important of these are listed below.

Agricultural Research Service

The Agricultural Research Service (abbreviated A.R.S.) was established in 1953 to consolidate most of the physical, biological, chemical, and engineering research of the department within a single organization. Such functions had previously been performed in a number of department bureaus and agencies.

The A.R.S. conducts studies relating to the production and utilization of agricultural products and has responsibility for regulatory programs that involve plant and animal quarantines, meat inspection, control of diseases and insect pests of animals, and related work. Both the research and regulatory work are carried on at locations in all 50 states, the Commonwealth of Puerto Rico, the Virgin Islands, and a number of foreign countries. Most of the research is in cooperation with state agricultural experiment stations and other public and private agencies. Special A.R.S. pioneering laboratories conduct basic research to advance knowledge in specific areas of the agricultural sciences. Other basic studies are done as an integral part of the regular program of each of the several A.R.S. research divisions.

Aid in selecting the most urgent agricultural problems requiring research, in coordinating the work, and in avoiding duplication of effort comes from representatives of the major segments of United States agriculture and the consuming public—the groups that use research findings.

A.R.S. activities are organized into six main areas of work, as follows:

Human Nutrition and Home Economics. The Institute of Home Economics is concerned with developing new knowledge about nutrition, improved consumer use of food, fiber, and other farm products, and improved household management.

Farm Research. Such research is conducted to improve methods of soil and water management; to improve field and horticultural crops and the control of crop diseases, nematodes, and weeds; to develop superior strains of beef and dairy cattle, swine, sheep, goats, and poultry and to improve dairy husbandry; to control livestock diseases and pests; to study the biology and habits of insects and to develop methods for controlling insects harmful to man, animals, and crops; and to develop safe and efficient use of farm power, machines, structures, and materials.

New Uses for Farm Products. Utilization research seeks new and expanded uses for agricultural products. It includes investigations in chemistry and other sciences and technological and engineering research to develop new and improved foods, feeds, drugs, fabrics, industrial chemicals, and other products from farm commodities. Four A.R.S. Utilization Research and Development Divisions have headquarters in Albany, Calif.; Peoria, Ill.; New Orleans, La.; and Philadelphia, Pa.

Foreign Research. The Foreign Research and Technical Programs Division administers department research at institutions in foreign countries aimed at developing new and expanded uses for United States commodities and in the areas of farm, marketing, and forestry research. The program is financed with foreign currencies received from the sale abroad of United States surplus commodities.

Regulatory Programs. These programs include: (1) Federal meat inspection; (2) animal disease eradication; (3) animal inspection and quarantine; (4) plant pest control; and (5) administration of plant-quarantine programs to prevent entry of foreign agricultural pests into the United States.

Experiment Stations. The Experiment Stations staffs administer Federal-grant funds for research in agriculture and rural life made available to agricultural experiment stations in the states and Puerto Rico. They also plan and coordinate research done by the department in cooperation with various state stations and supervise Federal research in Puerto Rico and the Virgin Islands and a Federal-state research program in Alaska.

Other Specialized Agencies

Agricultural Marketing Service. The agency administers the marketing, distribution, and related programs and activities of the Department of Agriculture. These programs include marketing research; standardization, inspection, grading, and classing of agricultural commodities; market news; matching-fund programs with state departments of agriculture; marketing regulatory programs; freight rate services; food trades; direct distribution; food-stamp programs; surplus removal, export, and diversion; school lunch and school milk programs; marketing agreements and orders on fruits, vegetables, nuts, and hops; and related defense production and mobilization activities of the department.

Commodity Credit Corporation. The C.C.C. is the financing agency through which a number of commodity programs of the department are carried out. These programs include price support; storage, sales, donations, and barter of commodities acquired through price-support operations; and farm storage facility loans. It also is responsible for United States operations under the International Wheat Agreement.

Commodity Exchange Authority. This agency administers the Commodity Exchange Act. Its functions are primarily to prevent price manipulation and to prevent dissemination of false and misleading crop and market information affecting prices.

Commodity Stabilization Service. This service is responsible for programs relating to price supports; soil and water conservation; foreign supply; foreign purchases; stabilization and marketing of sugar production; the International Wheat Agreement; procurement, handling, payment, and similar services on assigned purchase and export programs; adjustments which include allotments of acreage and marketing quotas; milk-marketing agreements and orders; and assigned defense food activities.

Economic Research Service. Created on April 3, 1961, the service conducts research on agricultural prices and income; commodity outlook and situation; food demand, supply, and consumption; market cost, structure, and development; market potentials; distribution and merchandising of farm products; efficient use of farm labor, land, buildings, and equipment; and adjustments to technological developments and changing market outlets. It also analyzes and interprets conditions affecting foreign markets for United States farm products.

Farmer Cooperative Service. The service performs research, educational, and service functions for farmers who are members of cooperatives.

Farmers Home Administration. The agency provides small farmers with credit to improve farming operations or to become owners, and supplements its loans with individual guidance in sound farm and home management.

Federal Crop Insurance Corporation. The corporation was created to enable farmers to strengthen their financial position by insuring money spent to produce crops against loss from unavoidable destruction by weather, insects, and disease. It does not insure a profit or cover losses due to neglect.

Federal Extension Service. This is the cooperative educational agency under which the Department of Agriculture and the state agricultural colleges carry on educational programs on agriculture and homemaking among people in rural areas. It encourages membership in the 4-H clubs and emphasizes health, nutrition, and sanitary standards as important considerations in efficient agricultural production. The service also fosters group study and discussion of broad agricultural problems and policies.

Foreign Agricultural Service. This agency represents the department in foreign matters and develops foreign markets for United States agricultural surplus.

Forest Service. This service is responsible for promoting the conservation and wise use of the nation's forest lands, which comprise one-third of the total land area of the United States.

Rural Electrification Administration. This agency finances the construction of electric power facilities in the unserved rural areas and administers the extension and improvement of rural telephone services. Cooperatives are the principal borrowers, but the administration also lends to public power districts and commercial power companies.

Soil Conservation Service. The service is responsible for the development and prosecution of a national program to bring about physical adjustments in land use that will further human welfare, conserve natural resources, establish a permanent and balanced agriculture, and reduce the hazards of floods and siltation.

Statistical Reporting Service. Established on April 3, 1961, the service reviews, coordinates, and improves statistical methods and techniques throughout the department. In its estimating and forecasting program, it collects, summarizes, and evaluates data from which it prepares and issues reports on crops, livestock, and prices. The service also issues reports on farm employment, farm wages, cold-storage holdings, and naval stores.

Staff and Service Agencies

Office of Budget and Finance. This agency is responsible for the financial affairs of the department, including the acquisition and distribution of funds.

Office of Information. The office plans, coordinates, and directs the informational activities of the department.

Other staff agencies include the *Office of Personnel,* the *Office of Plant and Operations,* and the *Office of the Solicitor.*

FARM CREDIT ADMINISTRATION

The activities of the Farm Credit System date back to legislation passed in 1916 and various subsequent acts. The Farm Credit Administration was established as an independent agency in 1933, and operated on this basis until 1939, when it was made a part of the Department of Agriculture. Under the Farm Credit Act of 1953 the administration again became an independent agency of the United States government.

The administration supervises and coordinates a cooperative credit system for agriculture, providing long- and short-term credit to farmers and their cooperative marketing, purchasing, and business service organizations. The United States is divided into 12 farm-credit districts, each of which has a Federal land bank, a Federal intermediate credit bank, and a bank for cooperatives. The activities of the three banks are coordinated through a district farm credit board.

PLANNING A HOME GARDEN

Home gardening can be an important source of flowers and fresh vegetables for the family, as well as an excellent form of outdoor exercise and recreation. From a financial standpoint, a well-planned and well-managed garden can consistently yield crops that more than repay the relatively low cost of seeds, tools, fertilizer, and other necessary materials. It is important, however, that the garden be carefully planned.

Choosing a Proper Site. The following rules are generally accepted in choosing a garden site:

1. The plot should receive at least six hours of direct sunshine each day, and should be protected from the wind

2. The ground should be level and well drained, although some sloping plots can be utilized, provided that the rows of plants can be terraced to avoid erosion

3. The garden should be located near a convenient water supply

4. The soil should be rich enough to show a good crop of weeds or grass; marshy ground, soil consisting of gravel and subsoil fill, and soil contaminated by chemical wastes should not be utilized

5. The plot should be located in an area not likely to receive excessive storm drainage or stream overflow.

The site of a flower garden should receive special attention. A study should be made of the landscape around the home, and a site should be chosen that will fit in with this and make the most attractive addition to the scene. The gardener should consider how the garden will appear from all sides, and try to visualize it in bloom. It is an excellent plan to plot the garden on paper.

Making a Good Plot. Once a good location has been chosen, the garden plot should be planned and a seed bed prepared according to the following directions:

1. Remove all rubbish, stones, weeds, and grass

2. If the soil is excessively sandy or clayey, add manure or compost, which should be spread evenly over the soil before spading

3. Spade or plow the soil to a depth of 8 to 10 in. until the soil is dry and level, and all clods have been worked down

4. Rake the surface of the soil until the ground is smooth enough to permit making shallow trenches for the seeds.

Berry and Herb Gardens. Strawberries and similar perennial herbs can be grown successfully by the home gardener. Plots and seed beds should be prepared in the same manner as for vegetable gardens. Any soil in which potatoes grow well is suitable for this type of plant. Good surface drainage is essential; and care should be taken not to set the plants too close together.

Planting. Only a small quantity of seeds is required for planting the average garden; and in the long run the best brands are the cheapest. The types of vegetables to be planted depend mainly on the time of year and weather conditions. The following table lists some of the most common vegetables, grouped according to the approximate times they can be planted, and their relative requirements for cool and warm weather.[1]

---

[1] From the United States Department of Agriculture publication, "Growing Vegetables in Town and City."

APPROXIMATE PLANTING TIME FOR VEGETABLES

Cold-hardy plants for early spring planting		Cold-tender or heat-hardy plants for late spring or early summer planting			Hardy plants for late summer or fall planting except in the North (plant 6 to 8 weeks before first fall freeze)
Very hardy (plant 4 to 6 weeks before frost-free date)	Hardy (plant 2 to 4 weeks before frost-free date)	Not cold-hardy (plant on frost-free date)	Requiring hot weather (plant 1 week or more after frost-free date)	Medium heat tolerant (good for summer planting)	
Broccoli Cabbage Lettuce Onions Peas Potatoes Spinach Turnips	Beets Carrots Chard Mustard Parsnips Radishes	Beans, snap Cucumbers Okra New Zealand spinach Soybeans Squash Sweet corn Tomatoes	Beans, lima Eggplant Peppers Sweet potatoes	Beans, all Chard Soybeans New Zealand spinach Squash Sweet corn	Beets Collards Kale Lettuce Mustard Spinach Turnips

The principal planting errors of most inexperienced gardeners are: (1) sowing seeds too deep; (2) sowing too many seeds; (3) sowing seeds too close together; and (4) failing to properly thin out excess plants. In vegetable gardens, care should also be taken to plant perennial plants, such as asparagus and rhubarb, at one side of the plot where they can be handled conveniently without interfering with the annual spading and plowing of other parts of the garden. The following table gives a ready guide to the proper spacing of plants and seeds in the vegetable garden when grown intensively for hand culture.*

SPACING OF VEGETABLE PLANTS OR SEEDS

Crop	Distance between—		Depth to cover seeds or roots	Seeds or plants required for—		
	Rows	Plants or hills in rows		1 ft. of row or per hill	100 ft. of row	1 acre
	In.	In.	In.	No.		Lb.
Asparagus[1]	30	18	8	....	70 plants	3
Beans, lima (bush)	28	4	1½	4	¾ pound	100
Beans, lima (pole)[2] ...	36	24	1½	24	½ pound	60
Beans, snap (bush)	28	3	1½	5	¾ pound	100
Beans, snap (pole)[2] ...	36	24	1½	24	¼ pound	40
Beets	16	3	¾	6	1 ounce	12
Broccoli, sprouting[3] ...	30	18	½	3	1 packet	¼
Brussels sprouts[3]	30	18	½	3	1 packet	¼
Cabbage[1]	30	18	....		70 plants	¼
Cabbage, Chinese[3]	24	10	½	4	1 packet	¼

* From the United States Department of Agriculture publication, "Growing Vegetables in Town and City."

[1] Plants or sets.

[2] Hills of about 4 plants each.

[3] Four or 5 seeds planted in 1 spot where plants are to stand; later thinned to 1 plant.

| Crop | Distance between— | | Depth to cover seeds or roots | Seeds or plants required for— | | |
	Rows	Plants or hills in rows		1 ft. of row or per hill	100 ft. of row	1 acre
	In.	In.	In.	No.		Lb.
Carrots	16	1½	½	20	¼ ounce	4
Cauliflower[1]	30	18			70 plants	¼
Celery and celeriac[1]	24	6		2	200 plants	¼
Chard	24	6	¾	4	1 ounce	12
Chervil	16	2	½	15	¼ ounce	4
Chives	16	2	½	15		
Chicory, witloof	20	4	½	10	1 packet	2
Collards[3]	30	18	½	3	1 packet	¼
Corn salad	16	10	½	5	1 packet	2
Corn, sweet	36	12	1½	2	¼ pound	15
Cress, upland	16	3	¼	20	1 packet	2
Cucumbers[2]	72	72	1	[2]12	½ ounce	2
Dandelion	16	8	¼	10	1 packet	2
Eggplant[1]	36	30			40 plants	¼
Endive	20	10	½	10	1 packet	2
Florence fennel	20	4	½	20	¼ ounce	3
Garlic[1]	16	3	1½	4	1 pound	325
Horseradish[1]	30	18	2		70 roots	
Kale[3]	24	10	½	4	1 packet	4
Kohlrabi	16	4	½	10	¼ ounce	4
Leeks	16	3	½	20	¼ ounce	4
Lettuce, head[1]	16	12			100 plants	¼
Lettuce, leaf	16	6	½	10	1 packet	2
Mustard	16	6	½	10	1 packet	2
Okra	36	18	1	3	1 ounce	8
Onions, seed	16	3	½	20	¼ ounce	4
Onions[1]	16	3		4	{ 1 qt. sets { 400 plants	600 3
Parsley	16	4	¼	20	¼ ounce	2
Parsnips	16	3	½	15	½ ounce	3
Peas, garden (dwarf)	18	1	1½	12	1 pound	120
Peas, garden (tall)	24	1	1½	12	1 pound	120
Peas, black-eye	28	3	1½	5	½ pound	60
Peppers[1]	30	18			70 plants	¼
Potatoes	30	12	4	1	7 pounds	1,200
Radishes, spring	12	1	½	15	1 ounce	12
Radishes, summer or winter	20	3	½	10	½ ounce	6
Rhubarb[1]	42	42	4		30 roots	
Rutabagas	20	4	½	20	¼ ounce	2
Salsify	20	2	½	15	1 ounce	12
Shallots[1]	16	2			600 plants	
Sorrel	20	6	½	10	¼ ounce	2
Soybeans	24–36	3	1½	5	½–1 pound	45–90
Spinach	12	4	½	12	½ ounce	10
Spinach, New Zealand	30	12	1	3	1 ounce	4
Squash, bush[2]	48	48	1	10	½ ounce	3
Squash, trailing[2]	96	48	1	10	½ ounce	2
Sweet potatoes[1]	36	12			100 plants	
Tomatoes,[1] not staked	48	48			26 plants	⅛
Tomatoes,[1] staked	36	24			51 plants	¼
Turnips	16	3	½	20	¼ ounce	2

[1] Plants or sets.

[2] Hills of about 4 plants each.

[3] Four or 5 seeds planted in 1 spot where plants are to stand; later thinned to 1 plant.

Flower Garden. Special attention should be given to the arrangement of plants in the flower garden. If the garden is against a hedge or wall, the taller flowers should be planted in the rear, then the intermediate sizes, then the low plants, at the front. Color schemes should be considered when planting, in order that the garden in bloom may present an artistic blend of colors. Seeds should be planted about 2 to 4 in. apart in rows or in circles. Flower seeds should not be planted too deep and should be sprinkled lightly after planting. The following table gives the principal characteristics of some popular annual flowers.[1]

PRINCIPAL CHARACTERISTICS OF SOME ANNUAL FLOWERS

Common name	Height of plant in feet	Color	Preference for sun or shade	Hardiness to cold
Aster, China	2	purple, rose, and white	sun	half hardy
California poppy	1	yellow, orange	sun	very hardy
Cape marigold	1	yellow, orange	sun	hardy
Chrysanthemum, summer	2	yellow, white	sun	tender
Cornflower	2½	blue, rose, and white	sun or shade	very hardy
Dahlia	3	red, yellow, and white	sun	tender
Forget-me-not	1	blue	partial shade	hardy
Four-o'clock	1½	crimson, yellow, and white	sun	tender
Larkspur	2½	blue, pink, and white	sun	very hardy
Marigold, Aztec	2	yellow, orange	sun	hardy
Marigold, dwarf	1	golden yellow	sun	tender
Mignonette	1½	greenish	sun	half hardy
Nasturtium, dwarf	1	scarlet, orange, and yellow	sun	tender
Pansy	1	purple, yellow, and blue	sun or shade	hardy
Petunia	1	rose, purple, and white	sun	tender
Phlox, Drummond	1	red, lilac, buff, and white	sun	hardy
Pink	1	scarlet, pink, and white	sun	hardy
Poppy	2	scarlet, pink, and white	sun	very hardy
Rose, everlasting	1½	pink and white	sun	half hardy
Snapdragon	2	scarlet, yellow, and white	sun	very hardy
Sorghum	4	green	sun	tender
Strawflower	2½	lemon yellow	sun	hardy
Sunflower	4	yellow	sun	hardy
Zinnia	2½	rose, scarlet, yellow, and orange	sun	hardy

Transplanting. Many types of flowers and vegetables can be grown more successfully if they are first planted in a protected place, to prevent damage by unfavorable weather conditions. They are transplanted to the open garden later, when they have developed a sturdy root growth. This procedure is simple for

[1] From the United States Department of Agriculture bulletin, "Growing Annual Flowering Plants."

some types of flowers that can be planted indoors in boxes. Other flowers and vegetables, however, require special hotbeds and cold frames; the small gardener will find it advisable to buy these plants from nurseries rather than to try to grow them from seed.

Making a Rock Garden. A rock garden is easy to build and can be an attractive addition to the home landscape. The following make excellent sites: (1) natural banks of rocks; (2) slopes or banks of earth; (3) natural rises in the ground, or excavated piles of earth; and (4) depressions in the ground, or old excavations. The rock garden should be in the open sunlight, away from trees but protected from the wind.

The preparation of the plot depends largely on the site chosen. If a natural bank of rocks has been selected, it is only necessary to make paths between the rocks for plants and to fill in with pockets of good soil. If rocks are to be brought to the site the directions below should be followed:

1. Select weather-beaten stones or rocks in various sizes and shapes, avoiding the use of too many small rocks

2. Place stones in the soil, starting at the bottom of the mound, slope, or depression, and gradually work upward

3. Slant stones toward the ground to form pockets for soil and rain. Cover three-fourths of each stone with earth

4. Place good top soil or sand and gravel, depending on the type of plants to be used, in the pockets. Use ample soil and allow it to settle for several days before planting.

Native perennial plants make the best choice for a rock garden. Low plants are best for the main part of the garden, but somewhat taller plants may be used for the borders and background. The general recommendations for planting and care of the rock garden are the same as those given for other types.

Care of the Garden. After it is planted, a garden requires constant care. Some of the necessary routines are described below:

1. The garden should receive a good watering at least once a week. This is preferable to light sprinklings at frequent intervals. The best method is to apply water along the length of the furrows between the rows of plants

2. Weeds, which rob the cultivated plants of nutrients and water, should be pulled or hoed under whenever they appear

3. In nonirrigated soils with a low moisture content, a mulch of straw, dry grass, leaves, or similar material should be applied over the soil to help conserve water

4. The constant danger of insects and plant diseases should be controlled. Every gardener should have a duster or sprayer for applying fungicides or insecticides.[1]

HOME DESIGN AND CONSTRUCTION

The information on construction details given in this section refers mainly to an individual home, in order that in either building or buying a house the reader may have a general knowledge of construction and be able to discriminate between good and bad quality. A large structure is only an enlargement of a home; the information given here can, therefore, be utilized for constructions of any type.

Building a house falls into two parts, namely, planning and construction. If an architect is employed the house will be made to order; if stock plans, which are available from both private and governmental sources, are used the house

[1] Information concerning the control of insects and diseases in the home garden can be obtained for a nominal fee from the United States Department of Agriculture.

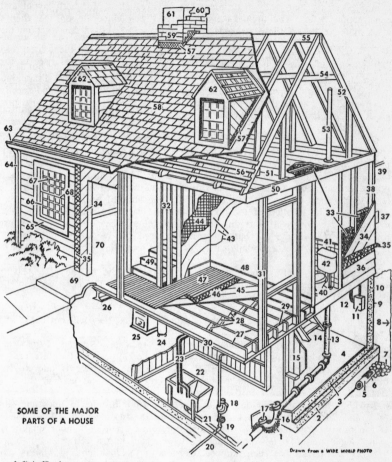

**SOME OF THE MAJOR
PARTS OF A HOUSE**

Drawn from a WIDE WORLD PHOTO

1. Cinder fill under cellar floor
2. Footing of foundation
3. Concrete cellar floor
4. Cement finish floor
5. Open joint drain tiles
6. Burlap over joints
7. Crushed rock
8. Soil
9. Membrane waterproofing
10. Concrete foundation
11. Electric fuse box
12. Electric conduit
13. Sewer line
14. Cellar stairs
15. Cellar partition
16. Sewer trap
17. Cleanout plugs

18. Water meter
19. Water shut-off
20. Water supply line
21. Laundry drain
22. Laundry tubs
23. Hot and cold water
24. Hot water storage tank
25. Heating plant
26. Steel I-beam
27. Floor joists
28. Bridging
29. Firestops
30. Sill
31. Studs doubled
32. Single studs
33. Insulation in walls and ceiling
34. Diagonal sheathing

35. Building paper
36. Clapboards or siding
37. Electric meter
38. Corner post
39. Electric lead in
40. Bathroom fixtures
41. Bathroom tilework
42. Flush tank
43. Three coats of plaster
44. Metal lath
45. Diagonal sub-flooring
46. Building felt
47. Finish flooring
48. Baseboard
49. Staircase
50. Plate
51. Attic floor
52. Rafters

53. Sewer pipe ventilator
54. Collar beams
55. Ridgeboard
56. Shingle lath
57. Flashing
58. Shingled roof
59. Chimney
60. Chimney cap
61. Flue lining
62. Dormer windows
63. Gutter or eaves trough
64. Leader or down spout
65. Window frame
66. Window stiles
67. Muntins
68. Meeting rail
69. Doorstep
70. Entrance

will be of ready-made design. Without deprecating the function of an architect, it may be stated that ready-made plans are often excellent, for both layout and construction detail. The architect may interpret and elaborate on the client's ideas, but the greater the divergence from simple and standard construction, the greater the cost.

Architect. The function of the architect is to indicate on prepared plans his and the client's ideas on the way the house should be built. Briefly, he builds on paper and tears down with an eraser, thus saving the expense and disappointment of preventable errors. His plans show the layout of the rooms and specify the method of construction and the materials to be used. The architect also prepares *specifications* which prescribe in detail the quality of material and the workmanship.

General Contractor. The general contractor receives the architect's plans and specifications and prepares an estimate of the cost of construction. If the estimate submitted is satisfactory to the owner, a contract is prepared. It consists of plans, specifications, and the contract document. The contract document need not be prepared by an attorney; the forms can be obtained at a stationer's or a legal-supply shop, or directly from the American Institute of Architects.

Location. The location of the house should be carefully considered for view, privacy, and exposure. It is traditional to place the service portions of the house toward the rear of the lot; but this tradition need not be followed if, for example, the street is exceptionally noisy, or if the prevailing summer winds blow from the rear.

Generally, the house should not be set in the middle of the plot, leaving several small areas of grass at the sides, front, and rear. The open area should be localized, to permit a garden or other plantation.

Foundation. The foundation walls, which support the house, should extend at least 6 in. below the frostline and above ground, so that they will not heave and crack during freezes and thaws.

Vertical cracks in concrete foundations usually indicate a settling of the structure; they should not occur. Hairline cracks are not important; they are caused by volume changes in the concrete. If, however, the concrete is uneven, has holes in it, and broken corners, probably too little cement was used or the concrete was placed carelessly in the forms.

Brick or masonry foundation walls should be smooth, true to lines and surface, and fairly uniform. To test them, pick at the mortar with a knife blade. If the mortar crumbles easily, too much sand was used, or a poor quality of cementing material. It is a good idea to drive a nail into a vertical joint to see whether the mortar has been skimped. Corners of the building and window and door openings should be vertical and even. Wooden jambs and trim around doors and windows should fit snugly against the masonry. Joints between wood and masonry should be carefully filled with mortar. The sills of all windows, particularly the cellar windows, should drain outward. Areaways under windows should have a drainage outlet for rain water and snow.

Check the wall thickness through a cellar window. The minimum for concrete is 8 in., for brick or concrete blocks 12 in. Examine the joint between the top of the wall and the sill to make sure that there are no air spaces.

Walls. The side walls of the upper structure may be covered with wood siding, shingles, brick, stucco, or stone, or may be built entirely of brick, stone, concrete, or a combination of such materials. When used properly they are all good.

A *wood-framed house* is one in which the vertical supporting members are wood studs at least 2 × 4 in. in size and usually spaced 16 in. on centers. On the outside of these studs are nailed boards or sheathing, laid diagonally for maximum rigidity and strength in the walls. The exterior surface is applied in the form of wood siding, shingles, stucco, a layer of brick (veneer), or an enclosure of stone. Some houses are *framed with steel*. Light steel sections, bolted together as a skeleton frame, permitting variation in design, take the place of the wood frame; the companion materials used in the walls are changed very little.

If *wood siding* has been used, examine the condition of paint on the siding; particularly notice whether the paint film is dense and opaque, and whether the wood is showing through. If it is, repainting should be done immediately. Repainting is also indicated for painted surfaces which are dull and chalky. Run your hand over some of the boards to see that the painted surface is fairly free from blisters or scales; if these are present, they should be sanded down before repainting is done. It is a good rule to paint wood houses every three to five years.

The siding should be laid evenly, with overlapped and tight butt joints. At the house corners, the siding may be mitered or fitted snugly against vertical corner boards.

The woods most in use today are red cypress, western red cedar, redwood, southern yellow pine, Douglas fir, West Coast hemlock, Ponderosa pine, spruce, yellow poplar, and several others. If you are lucky enough to own a century-old New England landmark, the wood is probably white pine. By scraping off some of the paint you can determine the type of wood—if you are an expert.

Shingle-covered walls may be stained for the sake of appearance or treated with some kind of creosote oil for greater durability. Shingles should be fastened with noncorroding nails, *i.e.*, zinc, copper, zinc-coated, or cement-coated. The shingles should be at least ⅜ in. thick at the bottom. For side walls, shingles 24 in. long should be exposed not more than 11 in. to the weather; 18-in. shingles not more than 8½ in.; and 16-in. shingles not more than 7½ in. Smaller exposures require more shingles but make a thicker wall covering.

If side walls are *stuccoed,* look for signs of cracking or of mortar spalling off. Outside stucco is usually a mixture of portland cement and sand, applied to a metal base, which should be furred out ¼ in. or so from the sheathing so that the stucco can be forced through the mesh and form a tight bond. Heavy, waterproof building paper is applied over the sheathing, either separately or as an integral part of the mesh. One requirement for a permanent stucco finish is that no water shall seep behind it. Flashing strips (noncorrosive metal) over tops of windows and at other horizontal projections covering the edges of stucco work will prevent seepage. Window sills should have a groove or drip underneath, so that water will drip clear of the wall and not run down over the face. Incidentally, the stucco should start from a water table several inches above the finished grade to prevent staining and disintegration of the mortar on account of ground moisture or splashing rain. No matter what the material, look it all over carefully for defects or careless workmanship.

If the house has a *brick exterior,* the walls may be of solid brick or of brick veneer (a layer 4 in. thick) to serve as an outside finish to a frame wall. Varied effects can be obtained with either common brick or face brick. The latter is more decorative but also more costly.

Exposed brickwork should be built of hard, well-burned brick. Such walls are extremely durable if the mortar joints between the bricks are laid carefully. Joints should be *filled,* not merely closed up at the outer edge of the brick. If the joints are pointed (finished) so that a ledge is left at the edge of every brick, opportunity is afforded for water to collect and seep through the walls of the building.

Headers are bricks laid lengthwise into the wall. In a solid brick wall, 13 in. thick, the headers are commonly concealed. In an all-brick wall, header courses should occur at least once to every 6 regular "stretcher" courses or the equivalent

of 2 header bricks to every square foot of wall. Brick veneer should be well tied
to the framework by metal bonds, well-spiked to the framework; this feature
should be concealed. Copper ties are preferred for durability.

A white deposit appearing on the surface of brickwork is called efflorescence.
This is usually caused by moisture penetrating the interior of the masonry, where
it dissolves the soluble salts in the materials and carries them to the surface,
where they are deposited by evaporation. It can be removed by washing or by a
good driving rain. Efflorescence seen on older houses or recurring on newer
houses is a sign of defective construction, such as faulty roof drainage or open
joints in masonry or around windows and doors, with resultant leakage.

Gutters and Flashing. Provision should be made for carrying rain water and
melting snow from the roof of the house to the ground without damage to the
house or its foundation. Rustproof gutters, without any sag, should be placed at
all eaves. Downspouts, preferably of copper, zinc, or aluminum, should extend
to the ground, where they should be cemented into an upright cast-iron or
glazed-clay pipe protruding above the ground, and thence should drain into the
sewer. If the downspouts are not connected to a drainage system, they should
be fitted at the bottom with a curved elbow and discharge onto a flat stone or
slab, leading well away from the foundation. There should be strainers over the
inlets from the gutters to the downspouts, to keep leaves, etc., from clogging the
pipes. The strips and fittings holding the downspouts in place should also be of
nonrusting metal. (Iron painted to resemble copper or bronze can be detected
with a magnet; zinc, copper, or other nonferrous metals will not be attracted.)

Above each window, in frame construction, there is a joint between the outside trim and the wall. This should be "flashed" or protected by a sheet of copper
or other noncorrosive metal. Window frames in masonry walls should be well-
caulked to stop up all air spaces between the frame and the wall. Unfortunately,
this is not common practice.

Chimneys from the Outside. The chimney should be plumb and erected on a
substantial masonry foundation, constructed to prevent cracking or settling. If it
is an exterior chimney the vertical joints between the chimney and the side walls,
in frame construction, should be tight, to shut out the elements.

The chimney should be high enough to be above air currents which may
interfere by blowing directly down the flues. Winds, at times, swoop up one slope
of a peak roof and then swirl downward into a low chimney on the other side.
A chimney at the peak will draw well, and so will a high chimney on the slope,
provided, of course, that the fireplace and flues are correctly designed. There is
no certainty possible, but try to judge whether the top of your chimney is safely
above a draft down-zone. It should be 3 ft. above a flat roof, at least 2 ft. above
the ridge of a sloping roof, and preferably capped; but capping should not decrease the required flue area.

Blinds. Blinds or shutters are nowadays used more for appearance than for
utility. On colonial-type houses they suit the décor; on other types they frequently are merely incongruous. Workable blinds, however—*i.e.*, hinged shutters
that move, as distinct from imitation shutters nailed to the walls—can add protection in severe climates and provide security during your absence.

Screens. Copper screens, although they customarily cost somewhat more than
other types, last longest. The frames should be fitted tightly and firmly together.
If they are of the sliding type, see that the tongues which slide in the grooves
are unbroken and straight and that each screen is numbered for the opening in
which it belongs. It is a good idea to screen the bottom of doors, and to have
such screening reinforced, to prevent scuffing.

Structural Features. The framework is the backbone of the house. Scrutinize the *inside basement walls* even more carefully than you did the outside. They should be free from unduly large bulges. Be sure that the masonry where it supports the floor beams and girders has not been crushed. Look for indications of leaks; the best time to look for these is after a rainy spell. *Joints* around windows should be tight, to prevent entrance of air or moisture.

The *basement floor* should be dry; look for water stains along the angles between floor and walls. If drainage has been taken care of outside, so that the water is carried away from the foundation walls, you will be fairly safe on this score. If it has not, the builder may have obtained a watertight cellar by mopping hot pitch on the outside of the wall, or by using, below ground, a rich cement mortar. You can determine this by digging down a little on the outside of the wall. Since it is difficult and expensive to waterproof a building satisfactorily from the inside, this should be a careful inspection on your part. All holes where pipes come through the foundation wall should be cemented. Tap all around the floor to be sure there are no bubbles in the finish or hollow spaces beneath to cause the floor to crack. A floor drain is an advantage. It permits washing down the floors and provides for an overflow from the tubs, but it is no indication of watertightness. Some cities prohibit floor drains. If present, they should never be connected directly with the sewer, for the water which seals the trip in the drainpipe is likely to dry up and admit sewer gas. In some localities, danger from sewers backing up may necessitate a backwater valve in the drainpipe. Some builders slope the cellar floor toward a drain so that water runs off quickly.

The concrete floor should have a hard, smooth, troweled, uncracked surface. Check *cellar-entrance steps,* which should be sound and sturdy, and without projections which can be easily broken. See whether there is danger of rain or snow accumulating on these steps or at the bottom of the area. If so, there should be an area drain. The *basement door* should be large enough to permit carrying in furniture or parts of a new boiler.

Floor Beams. The floor beams or joists support the load on the first floor. These in turn are supported at one end by the basement wall and at the other end by a steel or wood girder, or by the opposite wall. In the average house the floor beams are of *wood,* although *steel beams* and also *reinforced concrete beams* have been recently introduced in residential construction. Wood joists should be evenly spaced about every 16 in. and be "bridged" about every 8 ft. of their length with snugly fitted cross braces securely nailed with 2 nails at the top of one joist and the bottom of the next. The bridging stiffens the joists and helps to distribute the heavy loads.

Examine the joists for sagging and warping and for cracks, especially vertical cracks. Look carefully at any joists which have been cut to permit piping. Small holes along the middle of a beam for piping or electric wiring can have a weakening effect. The presence of knots is not a serious defect, unless there are a great many toward the center of the span or near the edges.

The *size of the joists* will depend on several factors: distance between the supports, the assumed load, and the kind and grade of lumber used.

Between the floor joists you should see the rough or *subfloor* of nominal 1-in. boards, not over 8 in. wide (shrinkage in wider boards may distort the finished floor), preferably laid diagonally to the joists. Diagonal flooring stiffens the house in a horizontal plane against heavy winds. It should extend to the outside edge of the vertical studs, in frame construction, and be fitted tightly against the inside of masonry walls. The subfloor should never be omitted in the first floor of a house. It makes the floors stronger and stiffer and helps to prevent squeaking, is an excellent insulator, and serves as a working platform during the building of the house. Look through the cracks between adjacent boards and make sure that a heavy-coated or *waterproof building paper* has been laid on the sub-floor. A waterproof paper will not only cut off drafts and dust from the cellar but will also prevent possible cellar dampness from getting into and warping the finished floor.

Numerous knots are permissible in the subfloor, provided the knots are sound. A No. 2 common grade of lumber is suitable for this purpose. Do not condemn the house if you observe *blue-stained lumber;* the stain is a harmless fungus which does not affect the strength of a beam or floor. You can test the soundness and hardness of the wood by sticking a penknife into it. However, blue-stained lumber would be objectionable in paneling or woodwork that is to have a natural, unpainted finish.

Floor beams resting directly on basement walls should have at least 3 in. of support. Make sure there is *ventilation* around the ends of all wood beams resting on masonry. If the ends of the joists are sealed into the wall, they cannot dry out and may even absorb moisture from the wall. In such event decay is to be expected. When wood beams frame into a masonry wall, the ends should be beveled with a "fire cut," so that in case of a fire burning through one or two joists before it can be controlled, the joists can fall down without destroying the wall. With masonry walls, every fourth joist should be anchored to the wall with wrought-iron pin anchors.

In most frame houses the floor beams rest on wood sills laid around the top of the basement wall and set in a full mortar bed. This still provides a level, even support for the vertical framing pieces called studs, and the mortar insures a weatherproof and verminproof joint between the bottom of the sill and the masonry. See that the wood sill is *bolted to the masonry* every 8 ft. along the wall. During hurricanes many homes are blown off their foundations simply because these anchor bolts have been omitted.

Stick the point of your knife into the sill at various spots to see whether the wood is sound. Occasionally, the sills absorb an excessive amount of moisture; in such cases they are likely to decay. This danger can be avoided by the use of sills chemically treated with either creosote or salts, or by the use of heartwood.

Termites. Termites are prevalent in certain sections of the country, more particularly in the South. They will not attack wood that has been given proper chemical treatment. Termites live mostly in the ground, are blind, and avoid light. They build slender shelter tubes up the walls of a house, from the ground to the sills and joists, to obtain moisture. Destruction of these tubes will kill all termites. In a termite-infested district, look for signs of these tubes and for the white pellets deposited by termites; insist upon termite shields. These are metal sheets placed on top of the foundation walls and bent down at a 45-degree angle for 2 in. or so on each side of the wall. It is also a wise precaution to have the lumber for sills, joists, and studs treated chemically. All-heart California redwood also offers considerable resistance to termites. Creosoted material, because of its odor, is seldom used above the foundations.

Floor Beams of Steel or Concrete. Examine all joists that have had holes punched in them for piping. Holes less than 3 in. in diameter, if on the center line, have little weakening effect. Similar holes near flanges, however, may be dangerous.

Unless the ceiling is plastered, the concrete slab will be visible between the beams. The concrete should be smooth and fit snugly against the beams at all points. Good concrete work is of vital importance in such floor systems.

Inside the Walls. You may be able to see, near the basement ceiling and in the attic, the rough boarding or sheathing which, in the wood-framed house, is nailed to the outside of the studs. In certain sections of the country insulating boards are employed as sheathing. Since these boards vary in quality, thickness, efficiency, and strength, the product of each manufacturer should be given separate consideration. Lumber sheathing should be nailed diagonally unless the house is stuccoed, in which case horizontal sheathing has been found the better; diagonal bracing, however, must be used at all corners of the house to provide against high-wind pressures. Heavy building paper should always be used between the sheathing and the outside wall covering; it will prove invaluable in shutting out the wind, even though it is negligible as an insulator.

Fire Stops. Spaces between studs or openings for pipes should be blocked off or "fire stopped" at all floor levels, but especially at the first floor. Even a 1-in. board helps somewhat (one reason for extending the subflooring to the outside face of the studs), but incombustible filling is better. It should completely occupy the hollow space between floor joists and studs to a height of 3 in. above the floor level. Loose material should be held in place with a rust-resistant wire mesh or wood strips at least 2 in. thick. Without fire stops these spaces may act as veritable flues in case of fire. Unblocked spaces permit warm air in the cellar to pass up to the top of the house and escape, thus increasing the fuel bill. They also permit the passage of rats and mice from the basement to the upper part of the house. The house built by speculators seldom has fire stops; but if you are building your own house insist upon them. It is good and cheap insurance.

It is also a wise precaution to have the entire basement ceiling, or at least the area over the heating plant, protected with metal lath and plaster or some fire-resistant material. There should be at least 15 in. overhead clearance. This also applies to wood framing at the sides of the furnace or boiler.

Test the various basement windows to be sure that they are securely hinged and that the hardware works, and see that the windows are not broken or warped to permit air leaks. If there is a coal chute opening, it should preferably have a heavy metal frame to withstand hard service.

Basement partitions should also be carefully examined, to see that they are fastened at both top and bottom and are not mere makeshifts.

Chimneys. If your house has a potential fire hazard, the chances are that it lies in the details of the chimney construction. Make sure there is a good fire-clay flue lining ¾ in. thick inside the brickwork or masonry and extending from below the flue opening to 2 in. above the cap. Under certain circumstances the flue lining may be omitted, but then the chimney walls must be 8 in. thick, if of brick, with a special firebrick lining; or 6 in. thick, if of reinforced concrete. But insist upon a flue lining for the ordinary chimney.

Have no wood within 2 in. of any chimney wall, and no wood within 4 in. of the back wall of the fireplace. The violation of this rule causes countless fires. Make sure that:

1. Chimneys shall not rest upon or be carried by wooden floors, beams, or brackets, or be hung from wooden rafters

2. Chimneys shall be built upon concrete or masonry foundations properly proportioned to carry the width imposed without danger of settlement or cracking

3. All spaces between chimneys and wooden joists or beams shall be filled with loose cinders, loose mortar refuse, gypsum block, or other porous incombustible material to form a fire stop

4. The incombustible material shall be supported by strips of sheet metal or metal lath set into the brickwork and nailed to the wooden beams, forming a buckled, flexible joint between, or by similar strips of metal nailed to the woodwork with the inner edge close to the chimney

5. No wooden studding, furring, lathing or plugging shall be placed against

any chimney or in the joints thereof. Wooden construction shall either be set away from the chimney or the plastering shall be directly on the masonry, or on metal lathing, or on incombustible furring material. Wood furring strips, placed around chimneys to support base or other trim, shall be insulated from the masonry by asbestos paper at least ⅛ in. thick, and metal wall plugs or approved incombustible nail-holding devices attached to the wall surface shall be used for nailing

6. All fireplaces and chimney breasts shall have trimmer arches or other approved fire-resistive construction supporting hearths. The arches and hearths shall be at least 20 in. wide, measured from the face of the chimney breast. The arches shall be of brick, stone, or hollow tile, not less than 4 in. thick. A flat stone or a reinforced concrete slab may be used to carry the hearth instead of an arch, if it be properly supported and a suitable fill be provided between it and the hearth. The length of trimmer arches and hearths shall be not less than 24 in. longer than the fireplace opening. Hearths shall be of brick, stone, tile, or concrete, as may be specified.

Flooring. Entirely satisfactory finished flooring may be had in various materials, although wood is the one most commonly used. The most beautiful wood flooring is probably a clear grade of quarter-sawed (*i.e.,* sawed at right angles to the annual rings of the tree) hardwood, such as white oak, although plain-sawed material is also attractive and durable. Strips are carefully matched for color and grain in the best floors. Since a price difference of about 30 per cent exists between first- and second-grade oak, it is often wise to use the lower grade in bedrooms and upper-story rooms, where it is not objectionable to have a few defects in the wood.

Quarter-sawed (also called edge-grain or vertical-grain) southern pine and Douglas fir are two good choices for floor woods. Edge-grain western larch and West Coast hemlock are other good woods.

Be sure that the wood floors, and also the interior finish or woodwork, are installed after the plaster has dried out. Although flooring is carefully dried in a kiln by the modern manufacturer, if it is laid in a damp house it will absorb moisture. This will cause expansion and, probably, warping. When the house is heated, the wood dries out, the flooring shrinks, and cracks appear; the result is squeaky floors. Wide flooring strips, though attractive and used in colonial-type houses, will expand or contract more than narrow strips. The remedy here is to delay the finished flooring until plaster is thoroughly dried out—at least two to three weeks after the last coat is applied.

As you walk over a floor, notice whether it squeaks, or seems to deflect or spring under your weight. If the floor joists are adequate and a subfloor has been included, neither of these things should happen. You can tell whether the floors are level by stretching a string across them.

Tile Work. The best indication of good workmanship in tiled floors, walls (particularly bathrooms), wainscots, or mantels is a clean-looking over-all job.

Tile floors should be smooth, without raised tiles or depressed areas. Joints should be regular and uniform throughout. If white tile has been used, the floors should appear white all over; numerous discolored tiles indicate soft, inferior material. The pattern should be carried out accurately. Fittings around fixtures should be done neatly. There should be no visible opening between the tile floor and the threshold.

Tile work on walls—*e.g.,* in baths or kitchens—should be smooth, have neat, uniform joints, and be free from chipped or broken tiles. The top, or cap, course of the tile wall or wainscot should be level and neatly returned into the plaster surface above. Slight stains in the center of wall tile are due to the wetting of tile for proper setting. They disappear after a short time as the work dries. In colored tile, some variations in shade are typical.

Plastic tile and colored aluminum tile are being increasingly used. These are, in general, somewhat less costly than regular tiles. They have the additional advantage that they can be laid (or repaired) without difficulty by the adept home craftsman.

Trim and Millwork. This is the woodwork around doors and windows, paneling, moldings, staircases, and similar features. It may be painted or stained, or finished in a natural grain. Do not be misled by imitation graining. Most woods are more attractive in their natural grain than when finished to imitate a more expensive wood. Different woods lend themselves to different treatments. Your own judgment and taste should be your guide, but bear in mind the relation of trim and woodwork to flooring and the room as a whole. Narrow trim is popular today because it is neater-looking and more economical. Hardwood trim, such as birch, red gum, or oak, is attractive when given a natural, varnished, lacquered, waxed, or oil finish. So are the softer pines in the knotty grades that are selected especially for paneling. Other softwoods are generally painted to suit the room decorations. Be sure there are no open joints, hammer marks, warped pieces, or signs of nailing.

Woodwork manufacturers kiln-dry their various products to prevent shrinkage after installation. Unless this dry millwork is protected from dampness, before as well as after it is installed in the house, it will absorb moisture and lose the benefits of this drying. Millwork should be painted on the back with a good paint primer before it is installed. Although this is an inexpensive method of protection, it is not common practice. Many of the more careful builders actually measure the humidity in the newly plastered house and, by means of the heating plant, in cold or continued wet weather dry out the house properly before installing the kiln-dried woodwork. After that it remains for the home owner to avoid excessive dryness (with further shrinkage) during the long winter heating season. Usually this calls for humidifiers, or at least the use of water pans on radiators and hot-air registers, to maintain a relative humidity of from 40 to 60 per cent. (Hot-air heating systems, unless equipped with built-in humidifiers, are a major cause of excessive drying.) Natural dampness, even during a rainy period in midsummer, is seldom detrimental to woodwork. It is the excessive drying out in overheated rooms, through several weeks or months, that causes glued joints to open.

Over the door, where the side casings meet the horizontal "header," the trim is often mitered, that is, fitted at an angle. If this joint is tight, as all joints should be, it is an indication of careful workmanship. If the joint has opened at the bottom, however, the wood has shrunk after installation; if the joint has opened at the top, it has taken on too much moisture and expanded—it was probably installed before the wet plaster had dried out. Many doors have the trim applied with square-cut butt joints, without molding, which are more economical and less likely to open.

The baseboard should fit snugly against the floor and the wall at all points. Make sure that walls have been plastered back of the baseboard. Cracks between the baseboard and the floor are favorite retreats for waterbugs and other insects. Why baseboards? To cover the joint between wall and floor, to protect walls from furniture and vacuum cleaners, and to add to the appearance of solidity. A chair rail—a molding which encircles a room at a height of about 3 ft.—is sometimes added to protect the wall from the backs of chairs.

Some builders avoid a crack between the floor and the base molding by nailing the shoe mold to the subfloor, stopping the finished floor at the inner face of the base mold. Then, even if the baseboard shrinks, it will not pull the shoe mold away from the floor, nor will any shrinkage of the finished floor pull the molding away from the baseboard.

Wainscoting and paneling seem somewhat mysterious to most of us, particularly with reference to the methods of making plywood panels out of veneer, or thin sheets of wood. For the better class of plywood, 5-ply construction is usually preferred. This is the result of skillful laying together and gluing under high pressure of 5 thin sheets of wood. The wood in the outer layers is carefully selected for appearance and for ease of finishing. Simpler and cheaper plywood, designated 3-ply, is made with 3 sheets.

The core for workmanlike plywood must be chosen for strength, stability, and minimum variation under atmospheric conditions. The face wood is selected for appearance and durability. The idea that veneer covers an inferior base does not apply to well-manufactured plywood. Color and grain of wood should be matched in the different panels, if the wood is finished in natural grain.

Doors. Doors should swing freely and close tightly without sticking. They should be high enough to admit large pieces of furniture, as well as tall people. If there is a threshold under the front-entrance door, there should be no opening for the admittance of cold, snow, and bugs. Be sure that the back and side doors remain in position. Interior doors should be hung so that they clear the rugs and should not interfere with other doors or electric-light wall brackets. They should latch readily and stay latched.

Outside doors, which are subject to rain and cold on one side and warm, dry air on the other, should be at least 1¾ in. thick at the edges, and the panels considerably thinner. Inside doors are usually only 1⅜ in. thick. Doors may be of either solid wood or plywood, of either hardwood or softwood. The solid door has stiles and rails (the thicker vertical and horizontal framework) of one piece; the veneered or plywood doors have veneer applied over a built-up core. In hardwood designs for certain styles of architecture, specially planed or flush plywood doors are occasionally required, but generally such doors are too heavy and costly.

Door panels are set in grooves in the stiles and rails; enough clearance is allowed for expansion of the panels under abnormal conditions. However, the panels should fit snugly in the grooves so as not to rattle.

No wood patches or wedges should be present; they indicate a second-grade door. Large panels are nearly always built up of 3 or 5 plies of veneer, glued together. Small panels may be solid. Various methods are used to join the different parts of a door. Examine the joints for neatness and workmanship. Glazed doors should be set in putty; and in a veneered exterior door it is good practice to have a beveled strip along the lower edge of the opening before it is glazed, in order that water running down the glass shall not get in between the veneer and the core.

Windows. The exposed portions of the frame and sash should preferably be of hardwood, from such species as red cypress, genuine white pine, and redwood, although less durable woods may often be used.

In most cases window sash will be the common double-hung type. The choice, however, between double-hung sash and casements is largely a matter of the most appropriate window for the house. With casements, a full window opening for ventilation can be utilized. The advantage of double-hung windows lies in the ease with which ventilation can be had on bad days. Also, such windows are easily screened and fairly weathertight. Since, however, there is always a certain amount of play between windows and frames, it is economical to have them weather-stripped. This also applies to doors, more particularly to casements. Interlocking metal weather strips should be placed around the edges. Weather stripping should not interfere with the opening of doors or windows.

The meeting rails, where the upper and lower sash are locked together, may have a joint that is straight, beveled, or stepped. The latter two bring the sash together when the window is locked and give the most weathertight joints. The underside of the lower sash should be thoroughly puttied and painted, to exclude moisture. When looking at windows, also test shades and be sure there are no cracked panes of glass.

In casement windows, notice whether they are hung to swing inward. These windows are extremely hard to make watertight, so look for signs of leaks. Outswinging casements require a special type of inside screens. Wood casements are preferably 1¾ in. thick, as are exterior doors.

Examine wood sash for signs of decay and steel sash for signs of rust. Notice whether there is a draft around windows and look for crevices in window framing. Also examine the glass, to see whether it is flawless or wavy and distorted.

Examine metal sash for signs of springing. Aluminum sash is slightly more flexible than steel and tends to get out of alignment more easily. Sprung sash can cause leakage and, by faulty or difficult closing, can also cause expensive glass breakage.

Partitions. The house is divided into rooms by walls or partitions. A well-built wall has double studs at the sides of door openings, and across the top a double header, with the pieces set on edge for maximum stiffness. If the studs rest on floor joists, any shrinkage in the joists will cause a corresponding settling in the partition, and probably a plaster crack at the ceiling.

Lath. There are three general types of lath: *wood lath, metal lath,* and *plaster lath.* Also, *insulation boards* are widely used as lath substitute.

In partition walls and in side walls of wood-framed houses the lath is nailed, usually horizontally, across the vertical 2 × 4 in. studs, spaced 16 in. on centers. Plaster is then applied over the lath in 2 or 3 coats. In masonry walls furring or nailing strips are usually nailed to the wall, and the lath is then nailed to these strips and plastered. Since it is not possible to see the lath, except perhaps in attic or basement, it should be judged from the general appearance and solidity of the plaster applied as a covering.

Plaster. Miscellaneous, random plaster cracks probably mean poor plaster or lath, or inferior workmanship. In a new house an outline of the lath should never show through the plaster; if there is such an outline it means thin, skimped plaster.

Examine the walls to see whether they are smooth, without valleys and hills. The joints between trim and plaster should be tight. Tap on the walls to see whether they are of plaster or composition wallboard. Such wallboards are used to replace both lath and plaster when costs are being held down.

If plaster is exposed on walls or ceilings, see whether there are any chalky, light-colored spots; these spots indicate "dry-outs" where the water in the plaster evaporated before the plaster was set. These places will always be soft and subject to cracking. If *damp* spots have occurred, these can be cured by supplying heat and ventilation immediately, unless the dampness has come from a leaky roof or wall.

If the plaster has a sandy appearance and the sand can be brushed off by rubbing your hand over it, the plaster is oversanded, weak, and easily destroyed.

Painted Walls and Wallpaper. Interior flat finishes using the oil type of paint present a pleasing matte appearance. If the paint finish shows streaks and hair cracks, it indicates that the priming coats were not properly designed and that a refinishing coat should be applied.

In recent years paints with a latex (rubber) base have become increasingly popular for interior finishing. These have three great advantages. They are quick-drying; they are virtually odorless; and they can be readily applied by anyone. Thus soiled walls can be repainted, or a whole décor can be changed, in a matter of hours by the housewife herself, if she so chooses.

In wallpaper, your personal taste, as well as the condition of the paper, should be your standard.

Closets. There is more "to" a closet than just the size. The walls should be completely plastered—or, if of wallboard, should have tight joints—because unfinished openings may admit vermin. Some builders raise the closet floors to a level with the threshold so that they can be easily cleaned.

Kitchen. Beech, birch, or maple flooring, or linoleum, make excellent floors for the kitchen. Wooden flooring should be coated with waterproof varnish. Linoleum flooring in the kitchen (or bathroom) should be flush with the baseboards and firmly cemented down to prevent water leakage to the underlying wood, and subsequent rotting.

The sink should be about 35 in. above the floor and be fitted tightly against the wall at the back. Examine the enameled surface of the sink; if it is rough and the iron is beginning to show through, it will be difficult to keep clean. Sink cabinets should also be fitted firmly against the wall, with some backing to prevent splashed water from getting down behind. Flooring under, and walls behind, sink cabinets and storage cabinets should be complete and tight, to prevent the entrance or harboring of vermin. Drainboards should be made of, or at least covered with, sound waterproof material, and be so slanted that they actually drain into the sink.

Avoid a range that has too many corners to clean and too much metal to shine. Figure burner and oven capacity in relation to the size of your family and the size of the meals you normally serve. (A four-burner "apartment" range is obviously not suitable for a family of six or eight.) An insulated oven is an advantage.

Avoid an electric refrigerator that makes too much noise or that makes the lights blink sharply as it goes on; also avoid a gas refrigerator that seems to smell (unless you can get positive assurance from the gas company that a *minor* adjustment will remedy the trouble).

Ideally, there should be some sort of cross-ventilation. Vent fans, now increasingly used, are an asset.

Bathroom. A tile floor should be of unglazed, ceramic mosaic, glazed, faience, or plastic floor tile. The edges should be cut evenly and the pieces should be snugly fitted against the base. A linoleum floor should be firmly cemented down and fitted flush against all walls and fixtures. (Watch for curled linoleum near the tub and toilet bowl.)

Wall tile should be installed wherever water may be splashed. If the walls appear to be tiled, tap the tiles so that you may know whether they are real or imitation. There is no serious disadvantage to modern plastic or tinted-aluminum tiles; but you should at least know what you are buying.

Examine plumbing fixtures, which should be modern. The last 20 years have produced many changes in design and use. Be sure the fixtures, such as bathtub and medicine cabinet, are of adequate size for your family.

Lighting fixtures should be so placed as to provide ample mirror light for shaving and makeup. The bathroom should contain no exposed wiring, and all light switches should be safely out of the normal reach of persons with wet hands or feet.

Staircase. See that the staircase is easy to walk up and down and is not squeaky. The railings should be secure. Balusters should be firmly mortised into holes in the steps. Steps should not bend under your weight, and there should be sufficient clearance overhead so that a tall person can descend with safety.

Roof Anchorage. Rafters should be notched over and spiked to the side wall plate over the studs. With masonry walls this plate should be fastened to the walls by means of anchor bolts embedded securely in the masonry. Proper anchorage is extremely important, but it is often overlooked in a house.

In examining side walls see whether the outside sheathing has been carried up to the roof boarding. Note also whether *fire stops* have been inserted between the studs, to shut off drafts and prevent the rapid spread of fire.

Over the rafters is laid the *roof sheathing,* which should be of a good grade of lumber. Look at the undersurface for stains or signs of leakage. Shingle roofs are better laid on solid sheathing than on shingle lath. Although the latter permits ventilation for the shingles, it lessens roof insulation and has less fire resistance.

Some building codes, especially in areas of booming speculative building, permit the use of plywood for roof sheathing. This should be watched out for, except in the Southwest and similar areas of little rainfall. If you must accept plywood roof sheathing, be sure that the shingles overlap the edge far enough to prevent the entry of wind-driven rain upon the plywood edges; otherwise you invite rotted sheathing, rotted walls beneath, and damaged wallpaper or paint on interior walls.

Roof. The roof is usually of wood shingles, slate, tile, sheet metal, or asbestos shingles.

Inspect as much of the roof surface as possible. For any shingle roof the slope should be at least 1:2; that is, the roof should rise 6 in. in every foot, measured horizontally. For tile or slate a slightly steeper pitch should be used. For sheet metal, a nearly flat roof is permissible, if it has enough slope to take care of drainage.

Be sure that *flashing* of rustproof material is used around chimneys, vent pipes, and skylights, and at the channels for water formed at the intersection of roof surfaces. This flashing should extend far enough upward to prevent water from backing up over the top of the flashing. Copper and aluminum are the most durable and trouble-free materials. Some older houses have flashing of sheet tin or galvanized iron; such materials are sound enough, but note that they require periodic repainting to prevent rust.

Ascertain for how long a period the roof is guaranteed.

Garage or Carport. The garage deserves the same careful inspection as the rest of the house. It should have adequate fire protection and be adequately lighted and, if possible, heated. (An unheated attached garage separated from the house proper only by an interior-type wall can cause serious heat losses.) The floor should be fireproof and greaseproof (preferably concrete). There should be an adequate supply of water and a floor drain. Examine the doors to see whether they work properly and smoothly. In climates where snows are heavy, lift doors are preferable to outward-opening doors. Be sure that both garage and driveway are large enough for your car.

A carport (a roofed but only partially enclosed shelter, increasingly popular today) should, ideally, be on the side of the house away from the prevailing directions of wind-blown rain or snow. (If it is not, there should be some provision for fastening shelter curtains.)

Hardware. Finished hardware comprises such articles as door handles, locks, bolts, hinges, window lifts and pulleys, casement latches and levers, and shutter fasteners. These may be of cast iron, wrought iron, wrought steel, cast or wrought brass, bronze, or cast aluminum. Plated hardware of good quality may be satisfactory; but on doorknobs and on surrounding plates and escutcheons the plating may wear off. All hardware in bathrooms should be of bronze or brass with nickel or chromium finish as proof against rust. The best criterion for hardware is that it be reliable for its purposes.

Plumbing. A detailed explanation of plumbing and heating systems would be too technical for our present purposes. If the house itself is satisfactory the purchaser should retain a competent engineer or contractor to check over carefully the plumbing and heating installations.

A good plumbing system is never obtrusive. It supplies water whenever desired and takes care of all household drainage in a sanitary and efficient manner.

The water-supply system consists simply of a cold-water pipe from the source of supply, with a connection to each of the plumbing fixtures requiring water. To provide hot water, one branch of pipe is usually run in coils through a heating apparatus, frequently a special gas or electric heater. For storage purposes there is usually a hot-water tank; the hot water, being lighter than the cold, rises, and the cold water falls, thus maintaining by gravity a constant circulation.

A hot-water supply must have not only proper-sized piping but also a satisfactory hot-water heater. The hot-water storage tank should have a capacity, for even a small family, of 30 gal.; for a larger family a capacity of at least 7 gal. per person is needed.

Water may be heated in many ways and with different fuels. Today, many gas companies, bottle-gas suppliers, fuel-oil companies, and electric companies furnish expert advice on all phases of hot-water heating.

Drainage and Sanitation. The drainage or waste system carries off various kinds of household wastes. It also protects against gas entering the house from the sewer and provides air pipes or vents necessary for the successful operation of the system.

Observe the general character of the plumbing as to both materials and workmanship. See whether flanges are installed to cover any holes where piping comes through the floors. Look for signs of corrosion, particularly at joints.

It is wise also to follow the house sewer line to the street or main sewer connection to see if there are adjacent trees whose roots may work their way into the joints of the pipes and so cause backwater damage or expensive digging up of pipes.

Cesspools and Septic Tanks. If the house is in a rural district it has its own sewage-disposal system. The *cesspool* is obsolete and unsanitary and has long been banned in many communities. (Older houses sometimes have abandoned cesspools on the property. These should be either filled in or solidly cemented over, as continuing menaces to the unwary, particularly children.)

A properly installed *septic tank,* underground and watertight, is the safest and most satisfactory method of rural sewage disposal. A septic tank can be tested for watertightness by filling it with water in the afternoon and noting the water level the next afternoon. A drop of more than half an inch during 24 hours indicates a leaky tank. Most communities, except perhaps in very remote areas, now have one or more experts in the installation, care, and repair of septic tanks.

Heating. Your house may be heated by coal, oil, gas, or electricity, through the medium of steam, hot water, or warm air. Electric heating is not yet widespread except in certain areas of inexpensive power but has been gaining much acceptance in recent years. If you are building a new house, it might be worth while to consider radiant heating, a system by which pipes or electric wires are buried in the floors or walls; this provides uniform, draft-free heating and resultant economies of operation.

In any heating unit, check the workmanship, especially around connections. Watch out for any obviously defective material (metal, asbestos, etc.). If everything seems to be in good condition, and the boiler or furnace is of reputable make, you can call in the expert. Without wishing to emphasize brand names unduly, it should be pointed out that a brand of equipment not commonly sold in your own locality can mean an absence of qualified repair workers or, worse still, of replacement parts.

The entire question of the heating system to be selected depends on the initial cost and the upkeep in relation to the comfort and satisfaction to be derived. Be sure that the heating system is operated correctly; if the manufacturers' directions are not followed, you can have trouble even with a perfect system. Ideally, do not consider a heating system that is not thermostatically controlled, unless such controls can be applied without too much trouble and expense; the resulting comfort, as well as economy of operation, will amply reward this precaution.

Electric Wiring. The connecting link between the feed wires and the electric lights and appliances in your house is the electric wiring. Most of it is concealed, but some parts may be visible, such as those in the cellar or the attic. In many communities electric wiring is inspected by a municipal or a fire insurance inspector, who issues certificates of inspection. Such certificates are the best possible evidence that the requirements of good workmanship and the necessary technical requirements have been met; these certificates should be checked on.

These certificates, of course, do not indicate the number or the location of circuits and outlets; the purchaser must decide for himself whether they are adequate. The purchaser should also examine switches and lighting fixtures.

As with heating and plumbing, an expert should be called in to examine electric wiring, and cables, conduits, fuses, and circuits.

LUMBER

Kinds of Lumber. Lumber is divided into three kinds: (1) *Yard lumber,* meaning lumber that is less than 6 in. thick; (2) *Structural timbers,* meaning lumber that is 6 in. or more in both thickness and width; and (3) *Factory* or *Shop lumber,* meaning lumber that will be cut up and used in manufacturing.

Yard lumber less than 2 in. thick and less than 8 in. wide is called *strips.* Yard lumber less than 2 in. thick but 8 in. or more wide is called *boards.* All yard lumber except strips, boards, and timbers is called *dimension lumber.* Dimension lumber is therefore 2 in. but less than 7 in. thick, and any width. When it is 2 in. and less than 4 in. thick and 8 or more in. wide it is called *planks.* When it is 2 in. but less than 6 in. thick and less than 8 in. wide it is called *scantlings.* When it is 4 in. but less than 6 in. thick and 8 in. or more wide it is called *heavy joists.*

Framing lumber is a common lumber called technically dimension and heavy joist lumber. It is 2 in. or more in thickness and 4 to 12 in. wide. From it the frameworks of buildings are made. The most important subdivisions of the framework are: the *posts,* or *stanchions,* which form the main interior support for the building; the *sills,* which form the lowest part of the structure, resting as they do on the foundation walls, and furnish a nailing base for the studs and joists; the *girders,* or *sleepers,* which form the main horizontal supports for the floors and partitions; the *joists,* which are the horizontal timbers directly supporting the floor or ceiling; the *studs,* which are uprights to which sheathing boards or laths are nailed; the *plates,* which are the horizontal timbers which support the trusses or rafters of a roof; the *ribbons,* which are narrow strips framed into the studs to support the floor or ceiling joists; the *collar ties,* which are boards to keep the roof from sagging or spreading; the *rafters,* which are the sloping timbers which support the roof; and the *lookouts,* which are bracket-like pieces which support the overhanging part of a roof.

Lumber as it comes from the saw is called *rough. Surfaced lumber* has been planed. *Worked lumber* has been matched (dressed so as to make a close tongue-and-groove joint at the edges or ends when laid together), or shiplapped (dressed so as to make a close rabbeted or lapped joint), or patterned (made into a pattern or mold).

TABLE OF BOARD FEET

Size in inches	Length in Feet							
	10	12	14	16	18	20	22	24
1x2	1-2/3	2	2-1/3	2-2/3	3	3-1/3	3-2/3	4
1x3	2-1/2	3	3-1/2	4	4-1/2	5	5-1/2	6
1x4	3-1/3	4	4-2/3	5-1/3	6	6-2/3	7-1/3	8
1x5	4-1/6	5	5-5/6	6-2/3	7-1/2	8-1/3	9-1/6	10
1x6	5	6	7	8	9	10	11	12
1x7	5-5/6	7	8-1/6	9-1/3	10-1/2	11-2/3	12-5/6	14
1x8	6-2/3	8	9-1/3	10-2/3	12	13-1/3	14-2/3	16
1x10	8-1/3	10	11-2/3	13-1/3	15	16-2/3	18-1/3	20
1x12	10	12	14	16	18	20	22	24
1x14	11-2/3	14	16-1/3	18-2/3	21	23-1/3	25-2/3	28
1x16	13-1/3	16	18-2/3	21-1/3	24	26-2/3	29-1/3	32
1x18	15	18	21	24	27	30	33	36
1x20	16-2/3	20	23-1/3	26-2/3	30	33-1/3	36-2/3	40
1-1/4x4	4-1/6	5	5-5/6	6-2/3	7-1/2	8-1/3	9-1/6	10
1-1/4x6	6-1/4	7-1/2	8-3/4	10	11-1/4	12-1/2	13-3/4	15
1-1/4x8	8-1/3	10	11-2/3	13-1/3	15	16-2/3	18-1/3	20
1-1/4x10	10-5/12	12-1/2	14-7/12	16-2/3	18-3/4	20-5/6	22-11/12	25
1-1/4x12	12-1/2	15	17-1/2	20	22-1/2	25	27-1/2	30
1-1/2x4	5	6	7	8	9	10	11	12
1-1/2x6	7-1/2	9	10-1/2	12	13-1/2	15	16-1/2	18
1-1/2x8	10	12	14	16	18	20	22	24
1-1/2x10	12-1/2	15	17-1/2	20	22-1/2	25	27-1/2	30
1-1/2x12	15	18	21	24	27	30	33	36
2x4	6-2/3	8	9-1/3	10-2/3	12	13-1/3	14-2/3	16
2x6	10	12	14	16	18	20	22	24
2x8	13-1/3	16	18-2/3	21-1/3	24	26-2/3	29-1/3	32
2x10	16-2/3	20	23-1/3	26-2/3	30	33-1/3	36-2/3	40
2x12	20	24	28	32	36	40	44	48
2x14	23-1/3	28	32-2/3	37-1/3	42	46-2/3	51-1/3	56
2x16	26-2/3	32	37-1/3	42-2/3	48	53-1/3	58-2/3	64
2-1/2x12	25	30	35	40	45	50	55	60
2-1/2x14	29-1/6	35	40-5/6	46-2/3	52-1/2	58-1/3	64-1/6	70
2-1/2x16	33-1/3	40	46-2/3	53-1/3	60	66-2/3	73-1/3	80
3x6	15	18	21	24	27	30	33	36
3x8	20	24	28	32	36	40	44	48
3x10	25	30	35	40	45	50	55	60
3x12	30	36	42	48	54	60	66	72
3x14	35	42	49	56	63	70	77	84
3x16	40	48	56	64	72	80	88	96
4x4	13-1/3	16	18-2/3	21-1/3	24	26-2/3	29-1/3	32
4x6	20	24	28	32	36	40	44	48
4x8	26-2/3	32	37-1/3	42-2/3	48	53-1/3	58-2/3	64
4x10	33-1/3	40	46-2/3	53-1/3	60	66-2/3	73-1/3	80
4x12	40	48	56	64	72	80	88	96
4x14	46-2/3	56	65-1/3	74-2/3	84	93-1/3	102-2/3	112
6x6	30	36	42	48	54	60	66	72
6x8	40	48	56	64	72	80	88	96
6x10	50	60	70	80	90	100	110	120
6x12	60	72	84	96	108	120	132	144
6x14	70	84	98	112	126	140	154	168
6x16	80	96	112	128	144	160	176	192
8x8	53-1/3	64	74-2/3	85-1/3	96	106-2/3	117-1/3	128
8x10	66-2/3	80	93-1/3	106-2/3	120	133-1/3	146-2/3	160
8x12	80	96	112	128	144	160	176	192
8x14	93-1/3	112	130-2/3	149-1/3	168	186-2/3	203-1/2	224
10x10	83-1/3	100	116-2/3	133-1/3	150	166-2/3	183-1/3	200
10x12	100	120	140	160	180	200	220	240
10x14	116-2/3	140	163-1/3	186-2/3	210	233-1/3	256-2/3	280
10x16	133-1/3	160	186-2/3	213-1/3	240	266-2/3	293-1/3	320
12x12	120	144	168	192	216	240	264	288
12x14	140	168	196	224	251	280	308	336
12x16	160	192	224	256	288	320	352	384
14x14	163-1/3	196	228-2/3	261-1/3	294	326-2/3	359-1/3	392
14x16	186-2/3	224	261-1/3	298-2/3	336	373-1/3	410-2/3	448

Smoothly finished lumber with very few defects, suitable for natural finishes or paint, is called select lumber. Lumber which contains defects but is still good for structural purposes is called common lumber. Each of these divisions has many subdivisions. The United States Bureau of Standards under the auspices of the United States Chamber of Commerce and the National Lumber Manufacturers' Association have worked out a table of blemishes and defects indicating the kinds and quantities that will be allowed in the various grades of wood.

Grading of Lumber. Grading of wood, however, cannot in the nature of things be an exact science. Dimensions can, of course, be measured exactly, but one man's summing up of the quality of a plank may not be the same as another's. Five per cent is the variation allowed for differences in judgment.

It is possible today to buy grade-marked lumber. More than 7,000,000,000 ft. of grade-marked pine and fir are produced annually by American mills. The National Lumber Manufacturers' Association guarantees the integrity of such wood and if the customer is dissatisfied he can call for a reinspection of the lumber. The Association will send an inspector and will allow only the five per cent margin for human fallibility mentioned above. Grade marking is simply a guarantee which protects the customer.

Lumber is graded from the better side, and if lumber is surfaced on one side only it is graded from that side.

It is also possible to buy short lengths instead of the customary long lengths. Farmers, for example, and small builders can save from 15 per cent to 25 per cent by using short lengths.

Board Measurement. Lumber is measured in board feet. A board foot is a square foot of board one inch, or less than one inch, thick. If no thickness is mentioned, it is understood to be one inch. Each of the following diagrams represents a board foot of lumber.

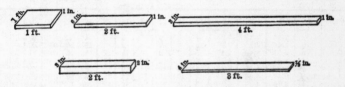

Various forms of a board foot of lumber

To find the number of board feet in a piece of lumber multiply the length in feet by the width in inches and the thickness in inches and divide by 12. Lumber-yard practice, however, is as follows:

To find the board feet in a piece of timber one inch thick and

4 in. wide, take ⅓ of the length
6 in. wide, take ½ of the length
8 in. wide, take ⅔ of the length
9 in. wide, take ¾ of the length

10 in. wide, take ⅚ of the length
12 in. wide, take the length
14 in. wide, add ⅙ to the length
15 in. wide, add ¼ to the length

If the lumber is

2 in. by 4 in. (2 × 4 = 8), take ⅔ of the length
2 in. by 8 in. (2 × 8 = 16), take ⅓ of the length, etc.

To ascertain the board measure contents of a number of pieces of lumber of the same width and thickness and of various lengths, multiply the number of pieces of each length by their respective lengths and treat as one piece. For example, to find the number of feet in ten pieces of lumber 2 in. × 4 in. thick and 10 ft. long and ten pieces of the same width and thickness 12 ft. long and ten pieces of same width and thickness 16 ft. long, multiply the different lengths separately (10 × 10 = 100; 10 × 12 = 120; 10 × 16 = 160), add the results (100 + 120 + 160 = 380). Since it is all 2 in. by 4 in., take two-thirds of the length. This will give 253 ft., which is the total board measure of the pieces of lumber in question.

Doubling any one dimension of a piece of lumber doubles its volume; doubling two dimensions makes the volume four times as much; doubling all three dimensions makes the volume eight times as much. Thus, a piece of lumber 1 in. thick × 2 in. wide, 12 ft. long contains 2 bd. ft. A piece of lumber 1 in. thick × 4 in. wide, 12 ft. long contains 4 bd. ft. A piece of lumber 1 in. thick × 4 in. wide, 24 ft. long contains 8 bd. ft. A piece of lumber 2 in. thick × 4 in. wide, 24 ft. long contains 16 bd. ft.

In practically all transactions in the United States lumber is stocked and sold at so much per thousand board feet.

Moldings, screening strips, splines, etc., are bought and sold by the linear foot. The unit is usually 100 linear feet.

To Estimate Cubic Feet in a Log. If the diameter of the log is the same all the way along, measure it in inches and then square it (*i.e.*, multiply it by itself). Multiply the result by .7854 and then multiply by the length of the log in feet. Divide by 144 and the result will be the number of cubic feet in the log. If the log is tapering, find the diameter at each end and divide by two to get the average diameter. Then proceed as above.

To Estimate Cubic Feet in a Standing Tree. Find the circumference of the tree in inches. Divide by 3.1416. This gives the diameter. From this point proceed as in estimating the cubic feet in any other log (see preceding paragraph).

TABLE SHOWING CUBICAL CONTENTS OF ROUND TIMBER

Length in feet	Diameter in inches															
	6	7	8	9	10	11	12	13	14	15	16	17	18	19	20	21
8	1.57	2.14	2.79	3.53	4	5	6	7	8	10	11	12	14	16	17	19
9	1.76	2.40	3.14	3.97	5	6	7	8	9	11	12	14	16	18	20	22
10	1.96	2.67	3.49	4.42	5	7	8	9	10	12	14	16	18	20	22	24
11	2.16	2.94	3.84	4.86	6	7	8	10	12	13	15	17	19	22	24	26
12	2.35	3.20	4.19	5.30	6	8	9	11	13	15	17	19	21	24	26	29
13	2.55	3.47	4.54	5.74	7	9	10	12	14	16	18	20	23	26	28	31
14	2.75	3.74	4.89	6.19	7	9	11	13	15	17	19	22	25	28	31	34
15	2.94	4.05	5.24	6.63	8	10	12	14	16	18	21	23	26	30	33	36
16	3.14	4.27	5.58	7.07	9	11	12	14	17	20	22	25	28	32	35	38
17	3.33	4.54	5.93	7.51	9	11	13	16	18	21	24	27	30	33	37	41
18	3.53	4.81	6.28	7.95	10	12	14	16	19	22	25	28	32	35	39	43
19	3.73	5.07	6.63	8.39	10	13	15	17	21	23	27	30	33	37	41	45
20	3.92	5.34	6.98	8.84	11	13	16	18	21	25	28	31	35	39	44	48

TABLE SHOWING CUBICAL CONTENTS OF ROUND TIMBER (*Cont.*)

Length in feet	Diameter in inches																
	22	23	24	25	26	27	28	29	30	31	32	33	34	35	36	37	38
8	21	23	25	27	29	32	34	37	39	42	45	48	50	53	57	60	62
9	24	26	28	31	33	36	38	41	44	47	50	53	57	60	64	67	70
10	26	29	31	34	37	40	43	46	49	52	56	59	63	67	71	75	79
11	29	32	35	37	41	43	47	50	53	57	61	65	69	73	77	82	86
12	32	34	38	41	44	47	51	55	58	62	67	71	76	80	85	90	94
13	34	37	41	44	48	51	56	60	63	68	72	77	82	87	92	97	102
14	37	40	44	48	52	55	60	64	68	73	78	83	88	94	99	105	110
15	40	43	47	51	55	59	64	69	73	78	84	89	95	100	106	112	118
16	42	46	50	55	59	63	68	73	78	83	89	95	101	107	113	119	126
17	45	49	53	58	63	68	73	78	83	89	95	101	107	114	121	127	135
18	48	52	57	61	66	72	77	82	88	94	100	106	114	120	128	134	142
19	50	55	60	65	70	75	81	87	93	99	106	112	120	127	135	142	151
20	53	58	63	68	74	79	85	91	98	105	112	118	126	134	142	149	159

Standard Dressed Sizes of Lumber. The standard yard board is $^{25}\!/_{32}$ in. thick; the standard industrial board is $^{26}\!/_{32}$ in. thick.

The standard yard dimension of 2-in. stock not more than 12 in. wide shall have in finished sizes a thickness of 1⅝ in., whether it is surfaced on one side or both sides. The standard industrial dimension shall be 1¾ in. thick.

The finished widths of a finish surfaced on one or two edges shall be ⅜ in. off on standard lumber 3 in. wide; ½ in. off on standard lumber 4 to 7 in. wide; ¾ in. off on standard lumber 8 to 12 in. wide. The finished widths of boards and dimension, surfaced on one or two edges, shall be ⅜ in. off on lumber of standard widths less than 8 in., and ½ in. off on lumber of standard widths of 8 to 12 in.

The abbreviations S1S, S2S, S1E, S2E, mean surfaced (or dressed or planed) one side, surfaced two sides, surfaced one edge, and surfaced two edges respectively. S4S means surfaced on all four sides.

TABLES SHOWING THICKNESSES AND WIDTHS OF FINISHED LUMBER, S1S OR S2S AND/OR S1E OR S2E

FINISH, COMMON BOARDS AND STRIPS, AND DIMENSION
(The thicknesses apply to all widths and the widths to all thicknesses)

Product	Size, board measure		Dressed dimensions at standard commercially dry shipping weight and moisture content		
	Thickness	Width	Standard thickness, yard	Standard thickness, industrial	Standard width
	Inches	Inches	Inches	Inches	Inches
Finish	...	3	5/16	...	2-5/8
	...	4	7/16	...	*3-1/2
	...	5	9/16	...	*4-1/2
	...	6	11/16	...	*5-1/2
	1	7	25/32	26/32	*6-1/2
	1-1/4	8	1-1/16	...	*7-1/4
	1-1/2	9	1-5/16	...	*8-1/4
	1-3/4	10	1-7/16	...	*9-1/4
	2	11	1-5/8	1-6/8	*10-1/4
	2-1/2	12	2-1/8	...	*11-1/4
Common boards and strips	3	...	2-5/8	...	...
	1	3	25/32	26/32	2-5/8
	1-1/4	4	1-1/16	...	3-5/8
	1-1/2	5	1-5/16	...	4-5/8
	...	6	...	...	5-5/8
	...	7	...	...	6-5/8
	...	8	...	...	7-1/2
	...	9	...	...	8-1/2
	...	10	...	...	9-1/2
	...	11	...	...	10-1/2
	...	12	...	...	11-1/2
Dimension	2	2	1-5/8	1-6/8	1-5/8
	2-1/2	4	2-1/8	...	3-5/8
	3	6	2-5/8	...	5-5/8
	4	8	3-5/8	...	7-1/2
	Over 4	10	Off 3/8	...	9-1/2
	...	12	...	...	11-1/2

* Based on kiln-dried lumber. Other figures were obtained by measuring the wood at standard commercially dry shipping weight, with moisture content allowed for each species.

SIDING, FLOORING, CEILING, PARTITION, SHIPLAP, AND DRESSED AND MATCHED

(The thicknesses apply to all widths and the widths to all thicknesses except as modified by the last footnote below)

Product	Size, board measure		Dressed dimensions at standard commercially dry shipping weight and moisture content	
	Thickness	Width	Standard thickness	Standard face width
Bevel siding	· · ·	4	*7/16 by 3/16	3-1/2
	· · ·	5	10/16 by 3/16	4-1/2
	· · ·	6	· · ·	5-1/2
Rustic and drop siding (shiplapped)	· · ·	4	9/16	3-1/8
	· · ·	5	3/4	4-1/8
	· · ·	6	· · ·	5-1/16
	· · ·	8	· · ·	6-7/8
Rustic and drop siding (dressed and matched)	· · ·	4	9/16	3-1/4
	· · ·	5	3/4	4-1/4
	· · ·	6	· · ·	5-3/16
	· · ·	8	· · ·	7
Flooring..........................	· · ·	2	5/16	1-1/2
	· · ·	3	7/16	2-3/8
	· · ·	4	9/16	3-1/4
	1	5	25/32	4-1/4
	1-1/4	6	1-1/16	5-3/16
	1-1/2	· · ·	1-5/16	· · ·
Ceiling..........................	· · ·	3	5/16	2-3/8
	· · ·	4	7/16	3-1/4
	· · ·	5	9/16	4-1/4
	· · ·	6	11/16	5-3/16
Partition..........................	· · ·	3	3/4	2-3/8
	· · ·	4	· · ·	3-1/4
	· · ·	5	· · ·	4-1/4
	· · ·	6	· · ·	5-3/16
Shiplap...........................	1	4	25/32	3-1/8
	· · ·	6	· · ·	5-1/8
	· · ·	8	· · ·	7-1/8
	· · ·	10	· · ·	9-1/8
	· · ·	12	· · ·	11-1/8
Dressed and matched	1	4	25/32	3-1/4
	1-1/4	6	1-1/16	5-1/4
	1-1/2	8	1-5/16	7-1/4
	· · ·	10	· · ·	9-1/4
	· · ·	12	· · ·	11-1/4

* Minimum, 7/16.

In tongued and grooved Flooring and in tongued and grooved and shiplapped Ceiling 5/16", 7/16", and 9/16" thick, board measure, the tongue or lap shall be 3/16" wide, with the over-all widths 3/16 inch wider than the face widths shown above.

In all other patterned material, 11/16", 3/4", 1", 1¼", and 1½" thick, board measure, the tongue shall be ¼" wide in tongued-and-grooved lumber, and the lap 3/8" wide in shiplapped lumber, with the over-all widths ¼" and 3/8" wider, respectively, than the face widths shown above.

The standard dimensions of rough lumber, commercially dry, shall be enough larger than the standard dimensions of finished lumber of the corresponding size to allow the surfacing of one or both sides and one or both edges to standard finishes.

FACTORY FLOORING, HEAVY ROOFING, DECKING, AND SHEET PILING

(The thicknesses apply to all widths and the widths to all thicknesses)

Size, Board Measure		Dressed dimensions at standard commercially dry shipping weight and moisture content			
			Standard Face Width		
Thick-ness	Width	Standard Thickness	D&M	Ship-lapped[1]	Grooved[1] for Splines
Inches	*Inches*	*Inches*	*Inches*	*Inches*	*Inches*
2	4	1⅝	3⅛	3	3½
2½	6	2⅛	5⅛	5	5½
3	8	2⅝	7⅛	7	7½
4	10	3⅝	9⅛	9	9½
. . .	12	. . .	11⅛	11	11½

[1] In patterned material 2 in. thick and thicker, the tongue shall be ⅜ in. wide in tongue-and-grooved lumber and the lap ½ in. wide in shiplapped lumber, with the over-all widths ⅜ in. and ½ in. wider, respectively, than the face widths shown above.

Odd Lengths. With the following exceptions which are permissible in grades of building lumber, odd lengths of yard lumber and structural timbers are not considered in American Lumber Standards:

2 by 4 in., 6 and 8 in.—9 and 11 ft. long
2 by 8 in. and 10 in.—13 ft. long
2 by 10 in.—15 ft. long
8 by 8 in., 10 by 10 in., 10 by 12 in., 12 by 12 in., 14 by 14 in., 16 by 16 in., 18 by 18 in.—11 and 13 ft. long
6 by 16 in., 6 by 18 in., 8 by 16 in., 8 by 18 in.—15 and 17 ft. long

Structural Material. Structural material has three basic grades: dense select, select, and common. All grades shall be sound except where decay is specifically allowed.

According to its uses it is separated into the divisions indicated by the following tables:

JOIST AND PLANK

Joists, Rafters, Scaffold Plank, Factory flooring, etc.

Nominal thicknesses: 2 to 4 in.
Nominal widths: 4 in. and wider
Standard thicknesses, S1S or S2S: ⅜ in. off
Extra standard thickness, 2 in., S1S or S2S: ¼ in. off
Standard widths, 4 to 7 in., S1E or S2E: ⅜ in. off; ⅜ in. and wider: S1E or S2E: ½ in. off
Standard lengths, multiples of 2 ft.

BEAMS AND STRINGERS

Beams, Girders, Stringers, etc.

Nominal thicknesses: 5 in. and thicker
Nominal widths: 8 in. and wider
Standard lengths: Multiples of 2 ft.
S1S, S1E, S2S, or S4S: ½ in. off each way

POSTS AND TIMBERS
Posts, Caps, Sills, Timbers, etc.

Nominal sizes: 6 by 6 in. and larger
Standard lengths: Multiples of 2 ft.
S1S, S1E, S2S, or S4S: ½ in. off each way.

Softwood Factory and Shop Lumber. Softwood factory planks are graded from the poorer side, although both sides are taken into consideration.

The standard dressed thicknesses of such lumber are shown in the table below. All other thicknesses are special. The standard lengths are 6 ft. and over in multiples of 1 ft.

Size, board measure in inches	Finished thicknesses, S1S or S2S, at commercially dry shipping weight and moisture content	
	Standard	*Extra standard*
	Inches	*Inches*
1	$^{25}/_{32}$	$^{26}/_{32}$
1¼	1 $^{5}/_{32}$	—
1½	1$^{13}/_{32}$	—
2	1$^{26}/_{32}$	—
2¼	2⅛	—
2½	2⅜	—
3	2⅝	—
4	3⅝	—

Note: It is to be understood that any association which publishes and administers rules for factory lumber under the American Lumber Standards, will not be required to furnish 1-in. factory lumber in both the standard and extra-standard thicknesses.

There are two grades of cuttings in factory plank. No. 1 cuttings are free from defects on both sides. No. 2 cuttings shall admit any of the following defects:

Light blue stain on one side, not larger in extent than one-half the area of one side.

Medium brown kiln or heart stain covering half the surface on one face, or a greater area of lighter stain, or a proportionate amount on two sides.

A small, sound, and tight knot which does not exceed ⅝ in. in diameter.

A small pitch pocket not over ⅛ in. wide nor over 1 in. long in Western pine and California pine.

One or more small season checks whose combined length does not exceed 8 in.

Light pitch or small pitch streaks that do not form a pronounced defect.

Slightly torn grain on one side.

SIZES OF CUTTINGS

Stiles shall be 5 and 6 in. wide by 6 ft. 8 in. to 7 ft. 6 in. long. They may be either No. 1 or No. 2 in quality.

Bottom rails shall be 9 and 10 in. wide by 2 ft. 4 in. to 3 ft. long. They may be either No. 1 or No. 2 in quality.

Muntins shall be 5 and 6 in. wide by 3 ft. 6 in. to 4 ft. long. They may be either No. 1 or No. 2 in quality.

Top rails shall be 5 and 6 in. wide by 2 ft. 4 in. to 3 ft. long. They must be of No. 1 cutting quality, but shall be considered as No. 2 cuttings.

Sash cuttings shall be 2½ and 3½ in. in width by 28 in. and over in length.

Laths.[1] Wood laths may be of pine, spruce, Douglas fir, hemlock, or other soft woods. (Many other types of laths are made of metal, gypsum, or special composite materials.) A good standard size is 1½ in. wide, ⅜ in. thick, and 4 ft. long. Dealers often estimate laths at the rate of two to each square foot. This gives plenty of margin for waste. A more accurate measurement is shown on the table below:

WOOD LATHS

Size of lath in.		Laths per square yard	Pounds of nails per 1,000
1 in. × 2⅔ ft.		26.0	9
1	× 2⅔	26.0	7
1	× 4	19.5	14
1	× 4	19.5	10
1⅛	× 4	19.0	14
1⅛	× 4	19.0	10
1½	× 4	14.5	14
1½	× 4	14.5	10
1⅝	× 4	14.4	14
1⅝	× 4	14.4	10

Clapboards. Clapboards are four feet long and are sold by the thousand. Laid four inches to the weather, one clapboard will cover 1⅓ sq. ft. Generally clapboards are laid over sheathing paper.

In estimating the number of clapboards needed, openings are, as a rule, disregarded unless they amount to 4 sq. ft. or more.

Roofing. The pitch or slant of a roof is determined by the angle of its rise. To determine the pitch, divide the height at the highest point by the distance (measured horizontally) required to reach this height. Thus, if the height of the ridge-

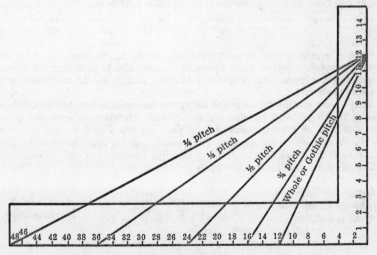

A Diagram Showing How Roof Pitches Are Determined

[1] See also Plastering.

pole is equal to one-fourth of the distance from the edge of the roof to the center, the pitch of the roof is stated as being one-fourth pitch. This rule is for simple roofs only, and does not consider roofs containing two slopes before reaching their highest point. The diagram below shows how carpenters determine some of the more common pitches.

The area of a roof may be found by getting the area on the level of the plates on which the rafters rest. Then, for the different pitches, add the following percentages:

One-fourth pitch, add to area on square	12 per cent
One-third pitch, add to area on square	20 per cent
One-half pitch, add to area on square	42 per cent
Three-eighths pitch, add to area on square	25 per cent
Five-eighths pitch, add to area on square	60 per cent
Three-fourths pitch, add to area on square	80 per cent

Cornice projections must be added to the above dimensions.

The length of the *rafters* for the various pitches can be found as follows:

Pitch	Rafter Length		Pitch	Rafter Length	
	W ×	L ×		W ×	L ×
¼	0.56	1.12	½	0.71	1.42
⅓	0.60	1.20	⅝	0.80	1.60
⅔	0.63	1.25	¾	0.90	1.80

W = Width of building over plates,
or, if rafters extend into
cornice, over cornice.
L = ½ of W.

The rise in inches per foot for the various pitches is as follows:

¼	6		⅜	9		⅝	15
⅓	8		½	12		¾	18

Roofing is generally estimated in units of 100 sq. ft. The materials most frequently employed are shingles (wood or composition), slate, tin, aluminum, tarred paper, gypsum, etc. Many city building ordinances demand the use of fireproof material.

Shingles are sold by the thousand or by the bundle. The standard bundle contains 250 shingles and bundles are not divided. Ordinary shingles are 16 in. long and have an average width of 4 in. They are laid with 4 in., 4½ in., 5 in., or 5½ in. exposed to the weather. The amount exposed depends upon the pitch of the roof; the steeper the pitch, the greater the amount of shingle exposed. The following table shows the usual estimate per 100 sq. ft.:

Length (in Inches) of Shingle Exposed to the Weather	Number of Shingles per 100 Sq. Ft.	Pounds of Nails Required
4	1,000	4
4½	900	3.9
5	800	3.5
5½	700	3.3

There are many other sizes of shingles. Manufacturers will be glad to furnish information as to the number needed with various exposures. Manufacturers of slate and other special roofings will also be glad to furnish specifications.

In estimating shingles openings are disregarded, as a rule, unless they amount to 4 sq. ft. or more, in which case they are subtracted.

Preparation of Wood Shingles.[1] If shingles are not to be stained, wet them thoroughly with water before applying. If stain is to be used, dip, when thoroughly dry, two-thirds of their length in stain and dry them in a loose pile. Do not soak shingles in stain. To secure very uniform color, give them a brush coat after laying, as a second coat. Avoid the use of cheap stains, especially those mixed with kerosene or benzene.

Shingle Nails. Do not use an ungalvanized nail. A hot-dipped, zinc-coated, cut-iron nail or a hot-dipped, zinc-coated, copper-bearing steel-wire nail is preferable, as such nails are covered with a 6 per cent to 10 per cent coating of pure zinc and in themselves are remarkably resistant to rust. Insist on carpenters' using either of these nails, as they will double the life of your shingle roof. Aluminum, pure copper, or pure zinc nails are excellent but expensive. For shingles measuring 5 butts to 2 in. or thinner, use 3d nails. For thicker shingles, use 3½d or 4d nails.

Metal Work. Use old-style I.C.C. hand-dipped and heavily coated tin for flashing around chimneys. For ridge roll and valleys, use either copper or at least 20-gauge heavily galvanized iron, or 14-in. best quality old-style tin, heavily coated.

Laying Shingles. Starting at eaves, lay first course, two-ply, allowing 1¼ in. projection over crown mold and 1 in. projection at gables; 16-in. shingles that measure 5 butts to 2 in. or thicker should be laid 4½ in. or 5 in. to the weather; 18-in. shingles should be laid 5½ in. to the weather; 24-in. shingles should be laid 7½ in. to the weather. All shingles should be spaced at least ⅛ in. apart.

Break all joints 1⅛ in. (side lap), seeing that no break comes directly over another on any three consecutive courses. This covers all nails and is extremely essential for a serviceable roof.

Use a straight edge to insure straight courses. Nail 16-in. shingles 6 in. or 6½ in. from butt; 18-in. shingles 7 in. from butt; and 24-in. shingles 9 in. from butt. Nail ⅝ in. to ¾ in. from sides, with only two nails in each shingle. Do not drive nail heads into shingles.

Flooring. To estimate the amount of regular tongue-and-groove flooring needed, 2¼ face, add one-third of the total number of square feet in the room. For example, if a room is 10 ft. wide by 12 ft. long, it contains 120 sq. ft. To get the amount of flooring needed, add one-third, which is 40. You will, therefore, need 160 sq. ft. to cover the entire room.

For wider flooring add about one-fourth to the total number of square feet in the room.

For underflooring add one-fourth. Different widths change this figure a little but it is practically right for any underflooring.

In laying diagonal underflooring, add one-fourth for squared-edged flooring, one-third for matched flooring.

The final flooring should be laid as late as possible in building operations to avoid damage.

_____

[1] The information on shingling which follows is by courtesy of the Red Cedar Shingle Bureau, Chicago, Ill.

QUANTITY OF FLOORING AND NAILS NEEDED TO COVER 100 SQUARE FEET

Hardwood Floors

Thickness	Face	Materials: Board Feet	Materials: Nails (pounds)
3/8	1½	145	1.2
13/16	2¼	134	3.3

Pine Floors

Thickness	Face	Materials: Board Feet	Materials: Nails (pounds)
13/16	2¼	134	4.3
13/16	3¼	128	3.4
13/16	5¼	120	2.2
1 1/16	2¼	168	6.8
1 1/16	3¼	160	5.3
1 1/16	5¼	150	3.5
1 5/16	2¼	200	10.0
1 5/16	3¼	192	7.7
1 5/16	5¼	180	4.9
1 5/8	5 1/8	246	8.9
2 5/8	5 1/8	369	18.4

Subfloors

Thickness of Subfloors	Stock Sizes	Materials: Board Feet	Materials: Nails (pounds)
1″	1 × 6	120	3.0
	1 × 8	114	2.3
	1 × 10	113	2.7
	1 × 12	112	4.5
2″	2 × 6	240	. . .
	2 × 8	228	. . .
3″	3 × 6	360	. . .
	3 × 8	342	. . .

Plywood. Plywood is the name given to boards made up of plies or thin veneers of wood cemented or glued together with the grain of each layer placed at right angles to the layer on either side of it. It has numerous advantages in comparison with solid timber, including lightness combined with strength, and great width without a joint, as much as 2½ yd. in width being possible. Plywood is much less likely to warp or split than solid wood. It is used for paneling walls and for making boxes, furniture, chair seats, etc.

Preserving Lumber. Lumber can be preserved by treating it with coal-tar creosote or zinc chloride. Ideally, the liquid should be forced into the pores of the wood by pressure, but this demands fairly elaborate equipment; and where such facilities are not available, reasonably satisfactory results may be obtained by spraying, brushing, or dipping.

One gallon of creosote oil will give two coats for every 100 sq. ft. of lumber unless there are defects which make the surface absorb a larger amount than this. Creosote oil makes an excellent paint for farm buildings, fences, etc., and for houses where a rustic finish is desired, because in addition to providing an attractive brown color it greatly increases their resistance to decay.

To treat lumber with zinc chloride, use a 2 per cent to a 5 per cent solution.

Steep the lumber in this solution, one day for each inch of thickness and an extra day for luck at the end.

NAILS

Approximate number to a pound of various kinds and sizes

COMMON NAILS AND BRADS

Size	Length and Gauge	Approx. Number to Pound
2d	1 inch No. 15	876
3d	1¼ inch No. 14	568
4d	1½ inch No. 12½	316
5d	1¾ inch No. 12½	271
6d	2 inch No. 11½	181
7d	2¼ inch No. 11½	161
8d	2½ inch No. 10¼	106
9d	2¾ inch No. 10¼	96
10d	3 inch No. 9	69
12d	3¼ inch No. 9	63
16d	3½ inch No. 8	49
20d	4 inch No. 6	31
30d	4½ inch No. 5	24
40d	5 inch No. 4	18
50d	5½ inch No. 3	14
60d	6 inch No. 2	11

SHINGLE NAILS

Size	Length and Gauge	Approx. Number to Pound
3d	1¼ inch No. 13	429
3½d	1⅜ inch No. 12	345
4d	1½ inch No. 12	274
5d	1¾ inch No. 12	235
6d	2 inch No. 12	204

FENCE STAPLES
Made of No. 9 wire

Length	Number to Pound	Length	Number to Pound
¾	132	1¼	87
⅞	120	1½	72
1	108	1¾	65
1⅛	96	2	58

JOINTS

Lapped Joint. A lapped joint is one formed when one beam overlaps another.

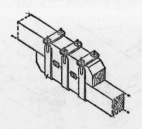

Fished Joint. A fished joint is formed when two beams meet end to end. The cover plates are called fish plates.

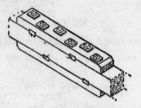

Scarfed Joint. A scarfed joint is made by cutting away two pieces of wood to make them fit into each other. Scarfed joints are secured by bolting, nailing, riveting, etc. Wedges are often used to tighten up the joint.

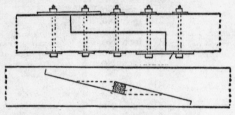

Keyed Joint. Keys are pieces of hard wood which are used either to join two pieces of wood together or to keep them from sliding over each other.

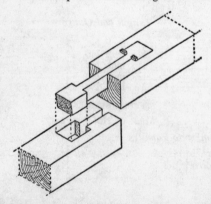

Halved Joint. In making a halved joint the two pieces of timber are cut to half their depth and secured with bolts, nails, screws, or wooden pegs. This is one of the simplest and most useful of joints.

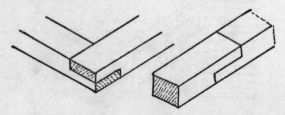

Housed Joint. A housed joint is one in which the end of one piece is let down into the body of the other. A post, for example, may be housed in a bottom cross rail, etc.

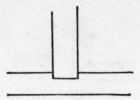

Mortise and Tenon Joint. A mortise and tenon joint is formed by fitting a projection from a piece of wood, *i.e.*, a tenon, into a hole in another piece of wood called a mortise.

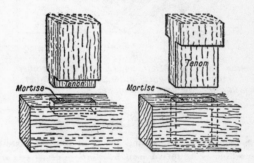

Dovetail joints are forms of mortise and tenon joints, so called because the tenon flares like a dove's tail.

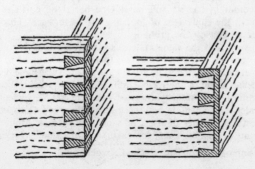

Miter Joint. A miter joint is formed by the junction of two similar blocks or moldings, the meeting ends of which are equally beveled. The following illustrations will make this clearer.

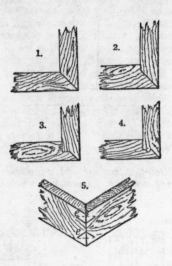

Miter. 1. Common form. 2. Miter where wooden members are of different widths. 3. Greek miter. 4. Tongued miter. 5. Keyed miter, i.e., wooden keys glued and driven into the saw cuts at an angle.

CONCRETE

Concrete is a compound of sand and gravel or crushed stone bound together by cement, the whole being mixed with water. *Reinforced concrete* is like ordinary concrete except that metal is embedded in it to make it capable of taking tensile loads. *Prestressed concrete* is concrete which is subjected to an initial precompression by any of several means to such an extent that the member itself will not be forced into tension regardless of the forces acting upon it.

Various types of cement are manufactured for use in construction work, the most commonly used being portland cement. Before the invention of portland cement in 1824 the adhesive agent was lime mortar of one kind or another. Portland cement comes in barrels and bags. One barrel of portland cement weighs 376 lb. net and is the equivalent of four bags of 94 lb. each. This material should not be allowed to rest on the ground.

All cement work uses the same materials but proportions vary. The proportions are expressed thus: 1:2:4, which means 1 part of the cement to 2 parts of sand and 4 parts of gravel. The materials are always listed in the same order.

How to Make Good Concrete.[1] Until the fairly recent discovery that the strength, durability, and watertightness of concrete are dependent upon the proportion of water to cement it was customary to specify mixtures as one part cement to a certain number of parts of sand and pebbles. Modern practice is to state the amount of mixing water for each sack of cement, varying according to

[1] By permission of the Portland Cement Association.

the class of work. For example, the recommended mixture for sidewalks and that class of work is 4¼ gal. of water per sack of cement, when the sand and pebbles are moist. As moisture in the aggregates is free to act on the cement, less water is needed than if the aggregates were absolutely dry. If these are dry, the correct amount of water would be 5½ gal. for each one-sack batch.

Cement Binds Particles Together. In a concrete mix, cement and water form a paste which, upon hardening, acts as a binder cementing the particles of sand and pebbles together into a permanent mass. The use of too much mixing water thins or dilutes the paste, weakening its cementing qualities. To get the best results, it is important that cement and water be used in proper proportions. These proportions depend upon the nature of the work.

The accompanying tables give recommended quantities of water for different kinds of concrete work and also suggest proportions of cement to sand and pebbles to use in trial batches. The trial batch for sidewalks is 1 part cement to 2 parts sand and 3 parts pebbles (1:2:3 mix). It may be necessary to change the amounts of sand and pebbles (as described below) to obtain a smooth, plastic, workable mix. Under no conditions vary the amount of water from the quantity shown.

RECOMMENDED MIXTURES FOR SEVERAL CLASSES OF CONSTRUCTION

Intended primarily for use on small jobs

Kind of Work	Gallons of Water to Add to Each One Sack Batch			Trial Mixture For First Batch			Maximum aggregate size
	Dry sand and pebbles	Moist sand and pebbles	Wet sand and pebbles	Cement	Sand	Pebbles	
				Sacks	Cu. ft.	Cu. ft.	In.
Foundation walls which need not be watertight, mass concrete for footings, retaining walls, garden walls, etc.	7-1/2	6	5	1	3	5	2
Watertight basement walls and pits, walls above grounds, dams, lawn rollers, hand tamper, shoe scrape, hotbeds, cold frames, storage and cyclone cellar walls, etc.	6-1/2	5	4-1/4	1	2-1/2	3-1/2	1-1/2
Water storage tanks, well curbs and platforms, cisterns, septic tanks, watertight floors, sidewalks, stepping stone and flagstone walks, driveways, porch floors, basement floors, garden and lawn pools, steps, corner posts, gate posts, piers, columns, chimney caps, concrete for tree surgery, etc.	5-1/2	4-1/4	3-3/4	1	2	3	1
Fence posts, clothes-line posts, grape-arbor posts, mailbox posts, etc., flower boxes and pots, benches, bird baths, sundials, pedestals and other garden furniture, work of very thin sections.	4-1/2	3-3/4	3-1/2	1	2	2	3/4

The trial proportion (1:2:3) suggested for sidewalks may result in a mixture that is too stiff, or too wet, or which lacks smoothness and workability. This is remedied by changing slightly the proportions of sand and pebbles, *not the water.* If the mix is too wet, add sand and pebbles slowly until the right degree of wetness is obtained. If the mix is too stiff, cut down the amounts of sand and pebbles in the next batch. In this way the best proportions for any job may be determined.

How to Obtain Workable Mixture. A workable mixture is one of such wetness and plasticity that it can be placed in the forms readily, and that with spading and tamping will result in a dense concrete. There should be enough cement-sand mortar to give good smooth surfaces free from rough spots, and to bind pieces of coarse aggregate into the mass so they will not separate out in handling. In other words the cement-sand mortar should completely fill the spaces between the pebbles and insure a smooth plastic mix. Mixtures lacking sufficient mortar will be hard to work and difficult to finish. Too much sand increases porosity and cuts down the amount of concrete obtainable from a sack of cement.

A workable mix for one type of work may be too stiff for another. Concrete that is to be deposited in thin sections like fence posts must be more plastic than for more massive construction such as walls. A good rule to follow is to proportion the sand and pebbles to obtain the greatest volume of concrete of correct plasticity for the work to be done.

Aggregates. Sand and pebbles or crushed rock are usually spoken of as "aggregate." Sand is called "fine aggregate" and pebbles or crushed stone "coarse aggregate." Fine aggregates such as rock screenings include all particles from very fine (exclusive of dust) up to those which will pass through a screen having meshes ¼ in. sq. Coarse aggregate includes all pebbles or broken stone ranging from ¼ in. up to 1½ or 2 in. In thin walls or slabs the largest pieces of aggregate should never exceed one-third the thickness of the thinnest section. Maximum sizes of aggregate for different classes of work are shown in the table.

Sand should be clean and hard, free from fine dust, loam and clay, and vegetable matter. These foreign materials prevent bond between the cement and sand and thereby reduce the strength of the concrete. Concrete made with dirty sand hardens very slowly and often will not harden sufficiently to be used for its intended purpose.

Sand should be well graded. The particles should be not all fine nor all coarse, but should vary in size from fine up to that which will just pass through a ¼-in. mesh screen. If the sand is well graded the finer particles help to fill the spaces between the larger ones.

Pebbles or crushed stone should be tough, fairly hard, and free from foreign matter. Stone containing considerable numbers of soft, flat, or elongated particles should not be used.

Bank-Run Gravel. Bank-run gravel is the natural mixture of sand and pebbles taken from a gravel bank. In this material fine and coarse aggregates are seldom present in proper proportions; it usually contains too much sand. Money can be saved by screening out the sand and recombining the sand and pebbles in proportions suitable to the class of work being done.

Water. Water used in mixing concrete should be clean, free from oil, alkali, and acid. In general, water that is fit to drink is good for mixing concrete.

Measuring Materials. All materials, including water, should be accurately measured. A pail marked on the inside at different heights to indicate quarts and gallons will be found handy for measuring water. A pail may also be used for measuring cement, sand, and pebbles. In mixing one-sack batches it is not necessary to measure cement, as one sack holds exactly 1 cu. ft. Sand and pebbles are then most conveniently measured in bottomless boxes made to hold 1 cu. ft., 2 cu. ft., or other volumes desired.

Mixing the Concrete. Although machine mixing is generally preferable, first-

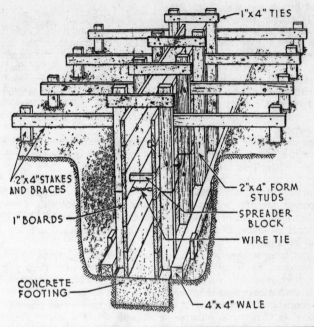

1"x4" TIES

2"x4" STAKES
AND BRACES

1" BOARDS

2"x4" FORM
STUDS

SPREADER
BLOCK

WIRE TIE

CONCRETE
FOOTING

4"x4" WALE

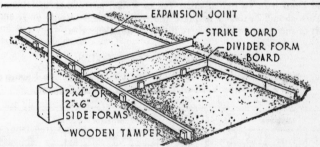

EXPANSION JOINT

STRIKE BOARD

DIVIDER FORM
BOARD

2"x4" OR
2"x6"
SIDE FORMS

WOODEN TAMPER

TOP: *Forms for a concrete foundation*
BELOW: *Sidewalk construction*
By the Portland Cement Association

class concrete can be mixed by hand. Whichever way is used, mixing should continue until every pebble is completely coated with a thoroughly mixed mortar of cement and sand.

If a tight floor is not available for mixing concrete, make a watertight mixing platform. This should be large enough for two men using shovels to work upon at the same time. A good size is 7 × 12 ft. If possible, this platform should be made of matched lumber, so that the joints will be tight. Nail strips along three sides to keep materials from being pushed off during the mixing.

Spread the measured quantity of sand out evenly on the platform. On this, distribute evenly the required quantity of cement. Turn the cement and sand with square-pointed shovels to produce a mass of uniform color, free from streaks of brown and gray. Such streaks indicate that cement and sand are not thoroughly mixed. Then measure out the required amount of coarse aggregate and spread this in a layer on top of the cement-sand mixture. Continue mixing until the pebbles have been uniformly distributed throughout the mass. Now form a depression or hollow in the middle of the pile and add the correct amount of water, while the materials are being turned. Continue the mixing until the cement, sand, and pebbles have been thoroughly and uniformly combined.

The concrete should be placed in the forms within 30 minutes after mixing. It should be well tamped or spaded as it goes into the forms. This operation forces the coarse aggregate back from the face, making a dense concrete with smooth surfaces.

Extreme care should be taken to avoid excessive handling or working of concrete once it is placed in the form. Such "puddling" causes water in the mix to rise to the surface, thus producing a weakened material.

Curing. Do not permit newly placed concrete to dry out. Protect it from the sun for a week or 10 days; otherwise the water necessary for proper hardening will evaporate, and this will in turn produce a loss of strength. Floors, walks, and similar surfaces can be protected by covering with earth or straw kept moist by occasional sprinkling as soon as the concrete has hardened sufficiently so that it will not be injured.

Walls and other sections which cannot be conveniently covered by this method can be protected by hanging moist canvas or burlap over them and wetting down the work frequently for 10 days or so after placing. In cold weather concrete work should be protected but need not be kept moist.

Reinforcement. Reinforcement is the term used to describe the steel rods or mesh placed in concrete to increase its strength where it is subjected to forces tending to bend it or to pull it apart (as in walks, pavements, and load-bearing walls). Care should be taken to place the reinforcement in correct position and in the part of the concrete mass where it will be most effective.

HOW TO FIGURE QUANTITIES

Quantities of Cement, Fine Aggregate and Coarse Aggregate Required
for One Cubic Yard of Compact Mortar or Concrete

Mixtures			Quantities of Materials				
				Fine aggregate		Coarse aggregate	
Cement	F. A. (Sand)	C. A. (Gravel or stone)	Cement in sacks	Cu. Ft.	Cu. Yd.	Cu. Ft.	Cu. Yd.
1	1.5	....	15.5	23.2	0.86	......	......
1	2.0	....	12.8	25.6	0.95	......	......
1	2.5	....	11.0	27.5	1.02	......	......
1	3.0	....	9.6	28.8	1.07	......	......
1	1.5	3	7.6	11.4	0.42	22.8	0.85
1	2.0	2	8.3	16.6	0.61	16.6	0.61
1	2.0	3	7.0	14.0	0.52	21.0	0.78
1	2.0	4	6.0	12.0	0.44	24.0	0.89
1	2.5	3.5	5.9	14.7	0.54	20.6	0.76
1	2.5	4	5.6	14.0	0:52	22.4	0.83
1	2.5	5	5.0	12.5	0.46	25.0	0.92
1	3.0	5	4.6	13.8	0.51	23.0	0.85

1 sack cement = 1 cu. ft.; 4 sacks = 1 bbl. Based on tables in Taylor and Thompson's "Concrete, Plain and Reinforced."

C. = Cement in sacks

F.A. = Fine aggregate (sand) in cu. ft.

C.A. = Coarse aggregate (pebbles or broken stone) in cu. ft.

(Quantities may vary 10 per cent either way depending upon character of aggregate used. No allowance made in table for waste.)

Materials Required for 100 sq. ft. of Surface for Varying Thicknesses of Concrete or Mortar

Pro-portion	1:1-1/2			1:2			1:2-1/2			1:3		
Thickness in inches	C.	F. A.	C. A.	C.	F A.	C. A.	C.	F.A.	C. A.	C.	F. A.	C. A.
3/8	1.8	2.7		1.5	3.0		1.3	3.2		1.1	3.4	
1/2	2.4	3.6		2.0	4.0		1.7	4.3		1.5	4.4	
3/4	3.6	5.4		3.0	6.0		2.5	6.3		2.2	6.8	
1	4.8	7.2		4.0	7.9		3.4	8.4		3.0	8.9	
1-1/4	6.0	9.0		4.9	9.9		4.2	10.5		3.7	11.1	
1-1/2	7.2	10.8		5.9	11.9		5.1	12.7		4.4	13.3	
1-3/4	8.4	12.6		6.9	13.9		5 9	14.7		5.2	15.7	
2	9.6	14.4		7.9	15.8		6.8	16.9		5.9	17.7	
	1:2:2			1:2:3			1:2-1/2:3-1/2			1:3:5		
3	7.7	15.4	15.4	6.5	13.0	19.3	5.5	13.6	19.1	4.3	12.8	21.3
4	10.2	20.4	20.4	8.6	17.2	25.8	7.3	18.1	25.4	5.7	17.0	28.4
5	12.8	25.6	25.6	10.8	21.6	32.2	9.1	22.6	31.8	7.1	21.3	35.5
6	15.4	30.7	30.7	12.9	25.8	38.6	10.9	27.2	38.2	8.5	25.6	42.6
8	20.6	41.0	41.0	17.2	34.4	21.6	14.6	36.4	51.0	11.4	34.1	57.0
10	25.6	51.2	51.2	21.5	43.2	64.4	18.2	45.3	63.5	14.2	42.5	71.0
12	30.7	61.4	61.4	25.8	51.6	77.2	21.8	54.5	76.3	17.0	51.1	85.1

CONDENSED SPECIFICATIONS FOR SIDEWALKS[1]
One-Course Sidewalks

Cement. Shall meet the requirements of the Standard Specifications of the American Society for Testing Materials (Serial Designation C150–49).

Fine Aggregate. Shall consist of natural sand or screenings from hard, tough, crushed rock, gravel, or slag. Must be clean and well graded. All fine aggregate shall pass a ¼-in. screen and 95 per cent shall be retained on a 100-mesh screen.

Coarse Aggregate. May be pebbles, broken stone, or blast-furnace slag. Must be clean, hard, durable, and uncoated. All coarse aggregate shall pass a 1-in. screen and 95 per cent shall be retained on a ¼-in. screen.

Water. Shall be clean enough to drink.

Joint Filler. Shall be premolded strips of bitumen-filled fiber or mineral aggregate, ½-in. thick, as wide as the thickness of the sidewalk, and at least 2 ft. long.

Forms. Shall be of lumber 2 in. thick or of steel of equal strength. Flexible strips may be used on curves. They shall be rigidly held to line and grade by stakes or braces.

Division Plates. Shall be of ⅛-in. steel as wide as the depth of the slab and as long as the width of the walk.

Subgrade. Shall be well drained and compacted to a firm surface with a uniform bearing power.

Drains. Where necessary, 4-in. concrete tile drains shall be laid to protect the walk from damage by frost action.

Sub-base. On poorly drained soil, where drains are impracticable, a 5-in. sub-base of cinders, gravel, or other porous material shall be constructed. It shall be thoroughly tamped and drained into the street gutter.

Thickness and Proportions. The walk shall never be less than 5 in. thick. Concrete shall be mixed in the approximate proportions of 1 part cement, 2 parts fine aggregate, and 3 parts of coarse aggregate with a maximum of 6¼ gal. of water per sack of cement, including the moisture in the aggregates.

Concrete. Shall be mixed until each particle of fine aggregate is coated with

[1] By the Portland Cement Association.

cement and each particle of coarse aggregate is coated with mortar, and not less than one minute.

Placing and Finishing. Concrete shall be placed immediately after mixing. It shall be tamped and struck off with a template and shall be floated with a wood float until the surface has a true contour. Care shall be taken not to bring to the surface an excess of water and fine sand by overfinishing.

Jointing. The walk shall be cut into separate rectangular slabs not greater than 6 ft. on any one side. The surface edges of each slab shall be rounded to a ¼-in. radius. Markings shall be exactly at cuts between slabs.

Expansion Joints. Shall extend from the surface to the subgrade and shall be at right angles to the sidewalk surface, and completely filled with compressible material. A ½-in. expansion joint shall be made across the walk at approximately 50-ft. intervals. At all places where the walk intersects a curb line or another walk, 1-in. expansion joints shall be made.

Curing. Finished concrete shall be kept wet for seven days.

Two-Course Sidewalks[1]

Same as specifications for one-course sidewalks, except the following paragraphs which should be substituted for those of corresponding headings in One-Course Sidewalk Specifications.

Thickness and Proportions. Two-course walks shall never be less than 5 in. thick. They shall consist of a base 4¼ in. thick, composed of concrete in the approximate proportions of 1 part cement, 2½ parts fine aggregate, 4 parts coarse aggregate, and a maximum of 6¼ gal. of water per sack of cement; and a top coat ¾ in. thick, composed of mortar in the proportions of 1 part cement and 2 parts fine aggregate.

Placing and Finishing. The base shall be thoroughly compacted by tamping and shall be struck off with a template which shall leave it ¾-in. below the finished surface. The top coat shall be placed within 45 minutes after the base course is laid. It shall be struck off and finished with a wood float until the surface has a true contour.

FORMS AND CURING

A great deal of concrete must be set in *forms*. It is economy to buy new wood for forms, since nail holes, etc., in old wood must be closed up to prevent imperfections in the concrete. White pine and spruce, being light and strong, are excellent for forms. One-inch slabs are used for small jobs; for beam sides, etc., 2-in. slabs are used. The wood must be dressed on one side and the edges; it is better to have it dressed all around. Forms should be simply made so that they can be used again. Most of them are put together with cleats. Forms should be thoroughly cleaned and oiled before the concrete is placed, to keep the concrete from sticking to the wood and to keep the wood from warping under the influence of the water from the concrete. Forms are also made of metal. Several commercial makes of prefabricated forms (wood, metal, and combinations of wood and metal) are available.

Newly placed concrete should be protected until it has thoroughly hardened. The water in the mixture begins a slow chemical action, and if the mixture is exposed to the sun this water, so necessary for the proper hardening of the concrete, will evaporate. The concrete, especially if the surface is large, should, therefore, be protected by moist sand, canvas, etc., which should be placed as soon as the mixture has hardened sufficiently to prevent surface injury. In cold weather the materials should be heated to begin with and the finished work should be protected from frost.

---

[1] One-course walks are recommended.

Bonding, in the event that there are more courses than one, can be done with a heavy wire brush if the forms are removed as soon as the concrete can bear its own weight. Otherwise a sharp instrument must be used.

Forms should never be removed until the concrete has hardened enough to resist whatever pressure may immediately be brought to bear upon it. Records should be kept of the dates of pouring and removing forms. The following table, taken from the Engineering Regulations of the Building Code of the District of Columbia, shows the length of time which the work should remain undisturbed:[1]

	No. of Days	
	April 1 to Nov. 1	Nov. 1 to April 1
For slabs less than 3-ft. span	3	6
For slabs more than 3 ft. and less than 8 ft.	7	10
For slabs more than 8 ft. and less than 15 ft.	12	15
For slabs more than 15 ft. and all 15 beams	15	21
For columns and walls	3	12

Concrete expands and contracts with heat and cold at practically the same rate at which steel expands and contracts, thus making it possible to combine the two materials. Concrete is a poor conductor of heat; steel is an excellent one. Steel at high temperatures softens; this is why a casing of concrete is placed around nearly all structural steel.

Reinforced concrete is one of the most adaptable of all building materials. Concrete has great resistance to compression; steel has great tensile strength. This, combined with the equal rate of expansion and contraction of the two materials, the plasticity of the mixture, and its great lasting qualities make this a building material almost without equal.

STUCCO

CONDENSED SPECIFICATIONS FOR PORTLAND CEMENT STUCCO[2]

GENERAL

Preparation of Surface. All hangers, fasteners, trim, or other fixed supports or projections of any kind shall be in place before the application of stucco. In masonry backing the surface shall be cleaned thoroughly before stucco is applied and shall be sufficiently rough to provide a good mechanical bond for the first coat.

Flashing. Flashing shall be in place before the application of stucco in the following locations: at the top and along sides of all openings wherever projecting trim occurs; across the wall and under coping, cornices, or brick sills with mortar joints, flashing to project beyond upper edge of stucco; under built-in gutters and around roof openings; at the intersection of walls and roofs; and at all other points where flashing would prevent water from getting behind the stucco.

Water Protection. All horizontal exposed surfaces, which are of stucco, such as copings, cornices, belt courses, shall be given sufficient fall to prevent water from accumulating on such surfaces. In general, the construction shall protect the surface against excessive concentrated water flow, all horizontal projections

---

[1] Table applies to the District of Columbia only. Generally, the length of time depends upon climatic and weather conditions.
[2] By courtesy of the Portland Cement Association.

being provided with overhanging drips and watertight joints. Stucco wall surfaces shall be stopped 6 in. above grade line.

MATERIALS

Cement. Portland cement shall conform to the current standard specifications of the American Society for Testing Materials.

Fine Aggregate. Fine aggregate shall consist of clean sand, screenings from crushed stone or pebbles, graded from fine to coarse, passing when dry a No. 4 screen, with not more than 20 per cent through a No. 50 screen, free from dust or other deleterious materials.

Water. Water shall be clean, free from oil, acid, strong alkali, or vegetable matter.

Coloring Materials. Only permanent mineral oxides that are fully guaranteed by the manufacturer to be unaffected by lime, cement, or weathering shall be used in coloring.

Hydrated Lime. Hydrated lime shall meet the requirements of the standard specifications of the American Society for Testing Materials and when used shall not exceed one-fifth the volume of the cement.

Reinforcement. The principle to be followed is to create a continuous metal-mesh reinforcement over the entire surface to be stuccoed, and to have this of a character similar to the reinforcing system of reinforced concrete. To meet such a requirement demands that the reinforcement have large enough openings to allow the mortar to fill the space back of the mesh reinforcement completely.

Metal lath if used as a reinforcement (without back-plastering) should have as large mesh openings as possible, be furred out ¼ in. from sheathing, and weigh not less than 3.4 lb. per sq. yd. Special care must be used to encase the lath completely by pushing the mortar through so that the mortar is "keyed" over the lath. Unless this is done the purpose of having the lath act strictly as a reinforcement is defeated.

CONSTRUCTION

Proportions. Mortar for all coats shall be mixed in the proportions of 1 part by volume of portland cement to not less than 3 nor more than 5 parts by volume of damp, loose aggregate. Hydrated lime may be added up to 25 per cent by volume of the portland cement. The final coat should be similarly mixed, except that the color of the cement should be selected and any desired coloring matter added.

Mixing. Ingredients shall be thoroughly mixed before water is added. It is positively essential that a definite system be used which will produce uniform mixes for all coats. The quantity of water shall be determined by trial and thereafter used in the proper proportions. The use of a machine mixer is advocated for uniformity of mixing if the work is of sufficient size to warrant its use. Ordinarily a mortar box will suffice.

Framing. Spacing of studs shall not exceed 16 in. Studding shall run from foundation to rafters without intervening horizontal members, tied together below 2nd-floor joists with 1 × 4-in. boards let into the inner faces of the studs. In open construction without sheathing the spacing of studs shall not exceed 12 in. The corners of all walls shall be braced diagonally to secure the necessary rigidity of the structure. Bridging of studding with 2 × 4-in. braces shall occur at least once in each story height.

Sheathing. Sheathing boards shall not be less than 6 in., nor more than 8 in. wide, dressed to a uniform thickness, laid horizontally, and fastened securely to each stud. Over the sheathing shall be laid, horizontally, beginning at the bottom, any standard asphalt-saturated roofing felt weighing 15 lb. per square, the bottom layer lapping the baseboard and each strip lapping the strip below and all flashing at least 2 in.

Application of Reinforcement. Reinforcement shall be placed horizontally and fastened with approved furring devices not more than 8 in. apart over the surface. Vertical laps shall occur at supports. The sheets shall be returned around corners at least 6 in. for sheathed construction and 16 in. for open construction. Corner beads shall not be used.

Furring. All reinforcement shall be furred out from the studs, sheathing, or base ¼ in. by any device which will not reduce the effective section of the scratch coat.

Half-Timbering. Embedded trim or half-timbering shall be securely nailed directly upon sheathing or studs, and shall have the inside corners of vertical members grooved into which the mortar of the first coat shall be forced, forming a watertight joint. All joints on horizontal members shall be flashed.

Masonry Walls. Concrete, concrete block, brick, hollow tile, and similar walls shall be rigid and constructed upon solid footings, all units being set in portland cement mortar. The surface on which stucco is to be applied shall be clean, free from all dust, dirt, or loose particles, preferably rough and of coarse texture. Wood lintels over wall openings shall not be used. Monolithic concrete walls shall be roughened by hacking, wire brushing, or other effective means. Concrete block, tile, or brick units shall have the joints cut back even with the surface. Clay tile shall be hard burned with dovetail or heavy, ragged scoring. Clay brick walls shall be composed of rough, hard-burned clay brick, and if painted or waterproofed shall be covered with reinforcing fabric before overcoating with stucco.

Wetting the Surface. Immediately preceding the application of the stucco, the surface of the wall shall be evenly wetted but not saturated. Water shall not be rapidly absorbed from the plaster, nor remain standing on the surface.

Retempering. Retempering by the addition of water shall not be permitted.

Consistency. Only sufficient water to produce a workable consistency shall be used.

Application of Stucco Coats on Frame Construction. The application shall be carried on continuously in one general direction without allowing the stucco to dry at the edges. If it is impossible to work the full width of the wall at one time, the joining shall be at some natural division of the surface, such as a window or door. The scratch coat shall be shoved thoroughly through the metal reinforcement, forming a solid mass against the sheathing paper, thus completely encasing the metal. This coat shall be ⅜ in. thick, fully covering the face of the reinforcement, and shall have its surface heavily cross-scratched to provide a strong mechanical key or bond. Allow this coat to become thoroughly dry. It shall be wetted down but not saturated before applying the second coat. The second, or browning, coat shall be at least ⅜ in. thick over the face of the first coat; it shall be rodded straight and true in every direction, or left untrue, giving a wavy effect, as the desired finish would suggest. If the finish is to be a float-type finish, the second coat shall be brought to a good even surface with wood floats. This coat shall be wet down for at least three days and allowed to become thoroughly dry before the finishing coat is applied. The finish coat shall be applied not less than one week after the application of the second coat and shall vary in thickness from ⅛ in. to ¾ in., depending upon the texture of the finish coat.

Scratch Coat on Masonry Walls. Mortar shall be troweled on to a thickness of approximately ⅜ in., heavily cross-scratched, and allowed to become thoroughly dry before the browning coat is applied. (From this point on use specification covering "Application of Stucco Coats on Frame Construction.")

Freezing. Methods shall be employed to keep the stucco above 50° F. during application and for 48 hours thereafter.

Curing. Each coat shall be protected from drying rapidly from effects of intense sunlight or wind until it has sufficiently hardened to permit sprinkling. Each coat shall be kept moist by sprinkling for at least two days following its application.

Back-Plastered Construction. In back-plastered construction, the metal lath shall be furred out from the face of the studs by an approved furring device and the mortar of the first, or scratch, coat applied with sufficient force to push it through the openings of the metal lath forming keys behind. The back-plastering coat shall not be applied until the scratch coat has hardened sufficiently to prevent injuring the keys of the scratch coat. The back-plastered coat shall not be less than ½ in. thick back of reinforcement, composed of the same proportions and materials as the scratch coat, and shall be applied from side to side of the hollow space between studs. The application of the browning and finish coats on back-plastered construction is identical with other methods as previously given.

Open Construction. In open construction the studs shall have parallel strands of No. 18 W & M gauge or heavier soft-annealed wire stretched tightly across their faces at 6-in. intervals to serve as a backing for the standard 15-lb. asphalt-saturated roofing felt. Metal reinforcement shall be applied over the entire surface held in place by approved furring devices, lapping at least 2 in. on all horizontal laps and at least 6 in. on all vertical laps. All metal reinforcement shall be returned around corners at least 16 in. Corner beads will not be permitted.

Finish Coat. The finish coat should be any color selected. Color can be varied by the admixture of cement coloring material, and can also be varied by the choice of light, medium, or very dark cement.

Prepared Portland Cement Stucco. Although to the average plasterer the preparation, proportioning, mixing, and application of portland cement stucco is a simple operation, it is possible to obtain a more uniform quality of stucco by using prepared portland cement stucco. This may be obtained from retail stores, completely mixed, in properly proportioned packages, ready for the addition of water. This prepared stucco gives the advantage of factory-measured and -proportioned materials, machine mixing, and grinding of the coloring pigment with the cement and selected materials.

Application of Stucco Coats. Portland cement stucco shall be applied in three coats. The first base (or scratch) coat, ⅜ in. thick, shall be cross-scratched and allowed to damp-cure from a fine water spray for not less than 48 hours after setting. The second base (or brown) coat, ⅜ in. thick, shall be applied over a dampened and cured first coat, rodded level, broomed to a rough surface, and damp-cured for at least 48 hours. The third (finish) coat shall be applied over the dampened and cured second coat, to a thickness of ⅛ in. to ¼ in., steel-troweled to a smooth even surface, and when set shall be damp-cured for not less than 72 hours.

Back-Plastered Construction. In back-plastering, care should be taken that complete embedment of the reinforcement is accomplished without injury to the first plaster coat already in place.

Hair or Fiber. Hair or fiber should be used only in the first coat of mortar in back-plastered metal lath construction, or for the underside of horizontal surfaces.

Finishing. The architect should bring to his client's attention the possibilities in portland cement stucco colors and textures. In the choice of these, samples may be submitted by competent stucco contractors and in every case a definite sample of texture and color should be furnished by the architect for the basis of bids.

The application of the finish is a distinct craft and the plastering contractor should endeavor to use only experienced workmen to obtain good results. Many variations of color and texture are possible.

Materials Required for 100 Square Feet of Surface for Various Thicknesses of Stucco

Thickness	Proportions			
	1:3		1:3-1/2	
	Cement (sacks)	Sand (cubic feet)	Cement (sacks)	Sand (cubic feet)
1/8 inch	.36	1.10	.33	1.15
1/4 inch	.73	2.20	.65	2.29
3/8 inch	1.10	3.30	.98	3.44
1/2 inch	1.47	4.40	1.31	4.59
3/4 inch	2.22	6.60	1.91	6.87
1 inch	2.94	8.80	2.62	9.18
1-1/4 inches	3.68	11.00	3.28	11.45

These quantities may vary 10 per cent in either direction due to the character of the sand and its moisture content. No allowance is made for waste.

If hydrated lime is used (20 per cent by volume of cement) decrease these quantities 12 per cent.

Overcoating Old Houses with Stucco. "Overcoating" is the term generally applied to the method of using portland cement stucco as a covering for the exterior surfaces of old houses. The structural framework of such houses invariably possesses useful life, usually being built of staunch, seasoned timber. The problem which this rejuvenation process solves is how to preserve and utilize the value of this worth-while structure, while eliminating the dilapidated appearance. The preparation of the surface of the old wall to receive the stucco overcoat requires but a minimum of treatment.

In adding an inch or more of stucco to this surface it is of course necessary that all the original projections or trim, such as window and door frames, be extended or built out proportionately to this depth. The majority of houses which are overcoated are of frame construction, with siding boards. After the extension of the trim a layer of some substantial, waterproof building paper should be applied directly on the siding, which should be renailed if found loose. The sheet of reinforcement is attached over this paper and furred out ¼ in. so that it will be in the approximate center of the stucco slab and so insure its positive and complete embedment in the mortar.

When the old surface is of masonry it should be sufficiently rough to give the first coat of mortar a good mechanical bond. If the wall is painted or otherwise glazed, reinforcement should be fastened over it and standard procedure followed.

The advantages of overcoating an old house with portland cement stucco may be summarized as follows: Increased property value is assured by better appearance; upkeep in painting and repairing has been cut; the house has been insulated against temperature changes, resulting in a saving in the cost of heating; and the fire safety of the structure has been increased.

BRICKWORK

Bricks. The standard dimensions for building brick, established by the United States Bureau of Standards, are as follows:

8 in. in length
3¾ " " width
2¼ " " height

Though these dimensions are still considered standard, the dimensions in all building products are currently being coordinated on multiples of 4 inches when placed in the finished wall. Under this system of dimensional standardization, brick instead of being 8 in. in length would be 7½ in. where made for ½-in. mortar joint, and 7⅝ in. where made for ⅜-in. mortar joint, thus giving an over-all length of brick and joint of 8 in., or two (2) 4-in. modules. Similar dimensional differences are made in width and height.

SOLID BRICK WALLS IN RUNNING BOND

Sq. Ft. Wall Area	4" Wall No. of brick	8" Wall No. of brick	12" Wall No. of brick
1	6.16	12.32	18.48
10	62	124	185
20	124	247	370
30	185	370	555
40	247	493	740
50	308	616	924
60	370	740	1,109
70	432	863	1,294
80	493	986	1,479
90	555	1,109	1,664
100	616	1,232	1,848
200	1,232	2,464	3,696
300	1,848	3,696	5,544
400	2,464	4,928	7,392
500	3,080	6,160	9,240
600	3,696	7,392	11,088
700	4,312	8,624	12,936
800	4,928	9,856	14,784
900	5,544	11,088	16,632
1000	6,160	12,320	18,480

Mortar. One barrel of lime, 1 cu. yd. of sand, and 4 bags of cement will lay about 1,200 standard-size bricks with the standard ⅜-in. joint. If the joint is thicker more mortar will be needed; if thinner, less will be needed. Lump lime is better if properly slaked, but hydrated lime can also be used. For the above mixture six 50-lb. bags of hydrated lime will be needed. Bricks should be dipped in a soft-soap solution to keep mortar drippings from adhering to them.

In ordinary work one man should be able to lay about 800 bricks a day, but there are many factors which may cause variations from this figure. Odd sizes, corners, projections, etc., make a difference in time. And it takes longer to lay press bricks (the kind used in fireplaces) than to lay ordinary bricks.

Masonry Tools.[1] Masonry requires few special tools; many common to other trades are used. The major masonry tools are illustrated and described below:

---

[1] From "Home Repairs Made Easy" by Training-Thru-Sight Associates: Lee Frankl; copyright 1949, by Lee Frankl.

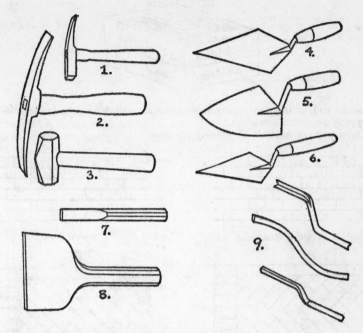

1. *Brick hammer* to plumb corners, cut brick to size and break brick.
2. *Scrutch* to cut away and finish broken edges.
3. *Lump* to cut large holes and channels.
4. *Brick trowel* to spread mortar.
5. *Buttering trowel* to butter bricks and to make small joints.
6. *Pointing trowel* to point up joints.
7. *Cold chisel* to cut holes, steel wire and other metal.
8. *Blocking chisel* to cut brick to size.
9. *Joint finishers* to smooth and compact mortar joints.

Bonding. Bricks are laid in a number of different patterns. The beauty and soundness of the work depend upon these patterns or "bonds," as they are called by bricklayers. Bricks laid without bonding would present an appearance like this:

A wall laid in this fashion would depend upon the strength of the mortar; in a bonded wall each brick helps to resist downward pressure.

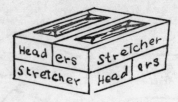

Bricks laid so that the shorter face shows are called *headers;* bricks laid the long way are called *stretchers*.

Other popular methods of bonding are these:

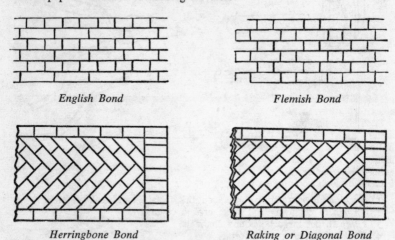

English Bond   Flemish Bond

Herringbone Bond   Raking or Diagonal Bond

For thick walls a bonding like the one below gives great strength:

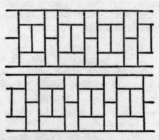

Bond for Thick Walls

In nearly all cities brickwork is regulated by laws which prescribe the use of good, well-burned bricks and a firm mortar or cement. Damp courses are prescribed to keep down moisture which might rise through the bricks which, being porous, might form good conductors.

When the wall has progressed 4 or 5 ft. a scaffold should be built to carry on the upper part of it. Since the safety of the workman depends upon this scaffold and since it can be used again and again, it is simple economy to build a good one.

To Make a Rounded Arch of Brick or Stone. First, measure the width of the arch. This is the distance covered by a straight line drawn from A to B. Then describe from each point a half-circle, each half-circle having the same radius. The point where the half-circles intersect is equidistant from A and B. Next divide the two lines AC and AB into equal parts (the number of equal parts does not particularly matter) and connect as indicated in the diagram. The curve at the base is an exact part of a circle.

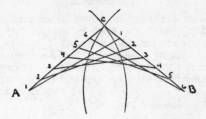

Scaffolding. Any kind of temporary structure for seating spectators at a parade or show is called a scaffold, but the scaffold most commonly met with is the elevated platform used by workers, *e.g.*, bricklayers, in building.

Such a scaffolding is made of poles placed horizontally, vertically, and obliquely, and fastened securely together. The main part of the structure is formed by the vertical poles, or standards, and the horizontal poles, which may be either ledgers or putlogs. The oblique poles, or braces, are for the purpose of strengthening the structure. The putlogs are short timbers placed at right angles to the ledgers, or long horizontal timbers.

In bricklayers' scaffolds the putlogs are allowed to rest one end against the brickwork; but in masons' scaffolds the whole structure must be independent of the wall in order to avoid disfiguring it.

In setting up a bricklayers' scaffold the first step is to place the standards singly or in pairs, 6 ft. to 8 ft. apart in a straight line with one another, parallel with the walls of the building and 4 ft. to 6 ft. in front of it. They should be sunk 2 ft. or more into the ground.

When the standards are placed the ledgers are lashed to them at a distance of from 5 ft. to 6 ft. from the ground. Three-strand Manila cords may be used for the lashing, tied generally with the "builders' knot" or clove hitch (see *Rope*). Wire ropes are sometimes substituted. There are also patented systems of fastening which do away with the ordinary lashing. After the ledgers are lashed the putlogs are placed about 5 ft. apart. One end of the putlog rests on the ledger, the other on the wall, where it is given a bearing of some 6 in. The platform is laid across the putlogs, the planks falling the long way, parallel with the building. No plank should project more than 6 in. beyond the putlog. A guard rail is erected about 3 ft. 6 in. from the platform.

Rising standards are lashed to those embedded in the ground. A putlog which touches a standard may form the base for the next rising standard. When double uprights are used they are paired in uneven lengths and the shorter timber, or puncheon, forms the base for the standard, which is lashed to the longer timber.

Scaffolding poles are made generally of pine or spruce. They are from 30 ft. to 50 ft. long and between 6 in. and 9 in. in diameter. Putlogs are about 6 ft. long and 4 in. square except at the end which enters the wall. Here they are cut down to about the size of a brick end, 2½ in. × 3½ in. Platform planks are between 12 ft. and 14 ft. long, about 8 in. wide, and from 1½ in. to 2 in. thick. The ends are often bound with strap iron to keep them from splitting.

When a tall scaffolding is not needed a series of horses or trestles may answer the purpose. These should be 5 ft. wide and 5 ft. high and placed on six or seven 2 in. × 10 in. planks laid close together. This should be kept sufficiently far back from a green wall as not to throw it out of plumb.

Metal scaffolding is coming into increasing use, both for economy (long-term re-usability) and for safety.

STONEWORK

The ordinary unit in estimating stonework is the perch, which is equal to 24.75 cu. ft. The cubic yard is also used. Percentages vary but on an average one-ninth is allowed for mortar and filling, that is, 2.75 cu. ft. to each perch.

To find out the amount of stone needed find the dimensions of the wall in feet (width × height × thickness) and divide by 22. The figure 22 is obtained by subtracting the amount allowed for mortar from the whole amount of the perch. To find the number of perches divide the number of cubic feet in the wall by the number of cubic feet in a perch (24.75).

METALWORK

Welding. Welding is a method of joining two pieces of metal together by the application of heat, with or without the application of pressure and with or without the addition of filler metal in the form of welding rods or electrodes.

There are some 30 different welding processes in commercial use today. Many of these processes lend themselves to high-production rates only. Others are equally suitable for low-rate production, job shop repairs, and even minor home repairs or work projects. Among the latter processes are *shielded metal-arc welding, oxyacetylene* (or other fuel gas such as *propane, butane,* etc.) *welding,* and *torch brazing.*

Except for the brazing processes, the difference between the welding processes is in the method of heating. In the brazing processes a lower-melting-point filler metal is used and capillary attraction is a factor in distributing the molten metal through the joint.

All commonly used metals can be welded by the use of the proper processes, proper joint preparation, proper filler metal, and proper technique. When correctly welded, the joint will be equal in service properties to the parts joined.

Knowledge and experience are necessary for good welding. Before one attempts any welding job, it is advisable to consult the American Welding Society, 345 East 47th Street, New York, N.Y., for information regarding specific applications.

Soft Soldering. Soft soldering is a means of joining two pieces of metal together with another metal melted into the joint. Solders are generally made of tin, lead, or a tin-lead alloy, with or without additions of antimony, silver, arsenic, or bismuth, to impart special properties. These solders may be used in the form of wire (or string) bars, powders, or ingots. A common solder is a 50-50 mixture of tin and lead; a 60-40 solder is also used widely.

The parts to be soldered should be mechanically or chemically cleaned and a flux should always be used. The flux serves to clean the joint, prevent oxidation, and lower the surface tension of the solder, thus increasing its melting properties. Fluxes may be composed of rosin or rosin alcohol, citric acid in water, zinc chloride, ammonium chloride, and muriatic acid. Glycerine is added to some fluxes to increase wettability. Lactic acid, levulinic acid, sulfonated alcohol, and turpentine are added for different metals. Soldered joints should be thoroughly cleaned to prevent corrosive action by a flux residue.

Solder is applied with a soldering "iron" made of a short, stout copper bar pointed at the working end and fitted at the other end into an iron shank, which is in turn fitted into a wooden handle. The iron may be heated electrically or over a gas flame. Care must be taken not to allow it to become red-hot. When the proper temperature is reached the end should be filed on an ordinary file, dipped in the flux, and pressed against the solder, which spreads over and "tins" the end. The end is then applied to the joint which has been already covered with the flux.

Brazing, which employs higher-melting-point alloys and more involved methods of heating, is sometimes erroneously referred to as hard soldering, but should not be confused with the above process.

PLASTERING

Plaster is made of gypsum, plus an aggregate—sand or one of the lightweight aggregates, such as perlite or vermiculite. The plaster may be fibered or unfibered. Either two or three coats of plaster are necessary for a well-finished wall, depending upon the type of lathing used.

Plastering is generally estimated by the square yard. Suppose the problem is to plaster a room 10 ft. long, 8 ft. wide, and 8½ ft. high. It has two windows, 3 ft. × 6 ft., and one door, 3 ft. × 7 ft. Find the cost of plastering the walls and ceiling at 50 cents per sq. yd.

The area of the walls of a room is found by multiplying the perimeter (the distance around the room) by the height. Therefore:

$$10 + 8 + 10 + 8,$$

or, as it may be more easily expressed,

2 × (10 + 8) = 36 ft. perimeter of room
8½ × 36 = 306 sq. ft. in the walls
8 × 10 = 80 sq. ft. in the ceiling
306 sq. ft. + 80 sq. ft. = 386 sq. ft. in both ceiling and walls
2 × 3 × 6 = 36 sq. ft. in windows
3 × 7 = 21 sq. ft. in the door
36 + 21 = 57 sq. ft. in both doors and windows
386 − 57 = 329 sq. ft., net area of walls and ceiling
329 sq. ft. ÷ 9 sq. ft. = 36½ sq. yd.
36½ × .50 = $18.25, cost of plastering the room.

Plastering Bases and Lathing. Plastering bases are those materials or constructions which receive the base coat of plaster. These bases are usually divided into two classes, lathing bases that are secured to the structure to provide a relatively smooth and level surface, and masonry bases. Gypsum lath is frequently used as a plastering base. It may be nailed to wood framing or furring, and may be secured to wood or metal furring with special clip attachments. Generally, it is used in sheets ⅜ in. thick × 16 in. wide × 48 in. long, although other sizes are available. The usual requirements for nailing gypsum laths call for 4 nails per lath on each stud on the sidewalls, and 5 on the ceiling. Lath nails should be of 13-gauge wire, be 1⅛ in. long, and have a ⅜-in. head. They should be driven home so that the head is just below the paper surface, without breaking the paper. Gypsum lath should be applied with the long dimension horizontal, and with vertical joints staggered. All lath ends must have bearing on wood framing, headers, or nailing blocks, and be securely nailed. Metal corner lath on inside corners helps to reinforce the joints.

Metal lath makes a strong plastering base because the steel becomes embedded in the plaster and so produces a reinforced plaster slab. The following table gives the various types and weights of metal, wire, and wire fabric laths.

TYPES AND WEIGHTS OF METAL LATH, WIRE LATH, AND WIRE FABRIC, AND SPACING, CENTER TO CENTER OF SUPPORTS[1]

Type of lath	Minimum weight of lath, lb. per sq. yd.	Maximum allowable spacing of supports, in.				
		Vertical supports			Horizontal supports	
		Wood	Metal		Wood or concrete	Metal
			Solid partitions	Others		
Flat expanded metal lath	2.5	16	16	12	0	0
	3.4	16	16	16	16	13-1/2
Flat rib metal lath	2.75	16	16	16	16	12
	3.4	19	24	19	19	19
3/8-in. rib metal lath[2]	3.4	24	...	24	24	19
	4.0	24	...	24	24	24
Sheet metal lath	4.5	24	24	24	24	24
Wire lath	2.48	16	16	16	13-1/2	13-1/2
V-stiffened wire lath	3.3	24	24	24	19	19
Wire fabric[3]	....	16	0	16	16	16

(Reprinted from the "Manual of Gypsum Lathing and Plastering")

Wood lath is also an important lathing material. No. 1- or No. 2-grade wood lath of white pine, spruce, or other soft wood, free of knots, sap, and bark should be used. This lath should be spaced ¼ in. to ⅜ in. apart. The lath should be fastened to each stud with a 3d, 16-gauge wire nail. Wood lath should be soaked in water overnight before application and made wet again before the plaster is applied. Soaking is necessary to prevent the wood from absorbing water from the plaster, then swelling and causing the plaster to loosen. See also Laths, in the section on Lumber.

Plastering Methods. A three-coat application of plaster is required over metal or wood laths. This consists of a first coat, or scratch coat, of plaster which is applied directly to the plastering base, cross-raked, and allowed to set and to dry partially; a second coat, or brown coat, of plaster which is surfaced out to the proper grounds, left rough, and allowed to set and to dry partially; and a third, or finish, coat of plaster. The two-coat application of plaster is similar in every respect, except that the cross-raking of the first coat is omitted and the second coat of plaster is applied within a few minutes to the unset first coat. This two-coat method is generally accepted practice in applying plaster to masonry and gypsum lath, except in certain localities where the three-coat method predominates. The three-coat method is often preferred since it develops a harder and stronger base coat. The set and partially dried first coat has a strong suction which draws much of the excess water from the second coat. The second coat is thereby densified because the water-to-gypsum ratio is reduced, thus producing a stronger plaster.

---

[1] Lath may be used on any spacings, center to center, up to the maximum shown for each type and weight.

[2] Rod-stiffened or V-stiffened flat expanded metal lath of equal rigidity and weight is permissible on the same spacings as ⅜-in. rib metal lath.

[3] Minimum weight: paper-backed wire fabric, No. 16-gauge wire, 2 × 2 in.-mesh, with stiffener.

CONDENSED SPECIFICATIONS FOR THREE-COAT PLASTERING

1. The first coat is made of sand and lime in a 2:1 mixture.[1] Enough clean water should be added to make the mixture hold together well. This coat should be about ¼ to ½ in. thick, depending on the type of lath used, and should be scratched or roughened to form a key for the next coat.

2. The second coat should be applied not sooner than 48 hours after the application of the first coat, and should have a thickness of about ⅜ in. It should be a 3:1 mixture of sand and lime, to which hair may be added. Strips of plaster 4 or 5 in. wide, carefully plumbed and leveled, should be laid at intervals to serve as a guide for the rest of the coat. The space between these strips should then be filled and the surface scoured with a wooden float. If the plaster shows a tendency to dry, water should be sprinkled on with a brush. This scouring should be done two or three times with an interval of 6 to 24 hours between. Small inequalities should be leveled at this time. The coat is then ready to be keyed for the next coat. This is done by going over it with a wire brush or a nail float.

3. The final, or surface, coat is made of lime putty. When putty made from finishing hydrated lime is used the proportions should be 4½ parts of putty to at least 1 part of good gauging plaster. This is equivalent, approximately, to 3 lb. of dry hydrated lime to 1 lb. of dry gauging plaster. When putty made from high calcium quicklime is used the proportions should be 4 parts of lime putty to at least 1 part of good gauging plaster. The ingredients should be mixed together thoroughly and applied by first covering all of the second-coat surface. This should be followed up immediately with another coat to form an even surface. This final coat should be troweled, and brought to a true, even, smooth surface, free from checks, cracks, and other blemishes.

4. Plaster should be protected until it is thoroughly dry. In the hot summer months doors and windows should be kept closed to prevent it from drying before it has crystallized. In winter it should not be allowed to freeze, and in very wet weather artificial means of drying should be provided. Local building specifications often call for the temporary closing of a building and other measures to insure the proper drying of plaster.

Many varieties of base-coat and finish-coat plaster are manufactured; they require only the addition of water at the job site. It is important to follow the manufacturer's specifications for these carefully. Small repairs are generally made with plaster of Paris or a prepared patching plaster.

PAINTING

Materials. Painting could be much cheaper for the home owner and hours could be much better for the painter if painting were not practically confined to the spring and fall of the year. There is no need for this. Outside painting can be done at any time of the year when the atmosphere is dry and the thermometer 40 or more degrees Fahrenheit, and there is no danger of a sudden drop in temperature. Interior painting can be done at any time of the year; it is better not to do it in the rush seasons, but in the winter. The ideal temperature for inside work is between 60 degrees and 70 degrees Fahrenheit.

In painting as in most other fields the most economical way to begin is to *buy the best materials.* There are many manufacturers today whose names are guarantees of the soundness of their products. It is important not only to choose good paint but suitable paint. Exterior paints should be used only for exteriors; interior paints only for interiors. Chemists have for many generations been studying the qualities of paints; they know now what kinds will stand exposure and what kinds will not, what kinds will give a glossy coat and what kinds will

---

[1] The use of cattle or goat hair is optional. If hair is used, it should be in the proportion of 1 lb. of hair to every 2 or 3 cu. ft. of the mortar.

give a dull finish, what kinds are good for undercoats and what kinds should be used on the surface. Continued research work has led to the development of new paint products such as rubber-base paints, one-coat exterior paints, mildew-resistant and fire-retardant paints, and many others which add to the quality or life of paint on a surface.

Mixing Paints. In mixing paints a clean flat wooden paddle is used. It is best to have two pails so that the paint can be poured from one to the other during the mixing process. With ready-mixed paints the pigment is stirred thoroughly and the liquid added a little at a time. For the final coat these paints should not, as a rule, be thinned. If, however, they have been left uncovered (and no paint should ever be left uncovered when not in use) thinning may be necessary.

For mixing paste paints the paste should be put in a mixing keg that will hold at least twice the amount of paste needed. A very small quantity of oil should be added until the mixture becomes easily workable. If the paint is to be tinted, the tint is now added, having first been mixed with oil or turpentine. The tint should be added slowly since it takes only a little to color a white paint. The tint should be tested by brushing it on a sample surface. After the color has been thoroughly mixed in, the turpentine is added and stirred in, then the final amount of linseed oil. Last of all the drier is added.

Paint formulas vary, but for ordinary work the following estimate has been given: For each 100 lb. of white lead or paste use between 6½ and 7 gal. of linseed oil. Turpentine may be added to thin out the mixture. Turpentine should never be added before at least a part of the oil has been added, since it makes mixing difficult.

The proportions of linseed oil and turpentine vary according to the kind of surface desired. For a full-gloss finish the proportions are about one-fifth turpentine and four-fifths linseed oil. For a semigloss, about one-third turpentine and two-thirds linseed oil; for a flat finish, about three-fourths turpentine and one-fourth linseed oil. If a dead flat effect is desired, as for enamel undercoats and certain other interior work, turpentine alone should be used. It is best in this case to mix the paint and allow it to stand overnight. The small amount of oil that is in the paste will rise to the top. All the liquid on top should be poured off and the paint mixed with fresh turpentine. Paint mixed in this way will dry entirely without gloss. If the paint is to be exposed to the sun more turpentine should be added to prevent blistering and only boiled linseed oil should be used. For unexposed work raw linseed oil may be used.

Paint should be mixed so that it is thin enough to brush out freely, but not too thin to hide the surface upon which it is to be used.

Brushes. After one has bought the best and most suitable paint, the next step is to buy a good brush. Once more it is economy to buy the best. The finest paint in the world will not give good results if it is streaked with bristles and if it is spattered or spread on unevenly. The best brushes are bound in leather or metal and set in cement or vulcanized rubber. Bristles set in vulcanized rubber will not come out in any kind of paint.

The size and style of a brush is a matter for each painter to decide for himself, but the size most commonly used for outside walls is a 4-inch flat brush with bristles about 4¾ in. long. Shorter bristles wear out more quickly and make the brush less easy to handle. A wall-stippling brush to eliminate brush marks should have bristles about 3½ in. long. Oval paint and varnish brushes are useful for certain kinds of work and wear out less quickly than flat brushes.

Paint brushes not in use should be kept suspended in linseed oil. The paint should first be thoroughly wiped out. The oil should cover the bristles entirely and come about an inch above the ferrule. The bristles should not touch the bottom of the container or they will become bent. As a makeshift the brush may be cleaned by wiping it with rags and washing out the remainder of the paint in a container of benzene, gasoline, or kerosene.

Varnish should never be allowed to dry on a brush. If it does, it may be removed with alcohol mixtures or turpentine. Varnish brushes may be kept in linseed oil or varnish but all the oil should be wiped out before the brush is used.

Shellac brushes may be kept suspended in shellac but the best treatment is to clean them with alcohol immediately after using.

Lacquer brushes should be cleaned with lacquer thinner.

Brushes used in bronze paints should be washed clean with turpentine as soon as they have been used.

Brushes should never be cleaned near a fire or flame, and painters should not experiment with new cleaners. Ammonia, for example, added to some of the lacquer varnishes, creates a poisonous gas which may result in an extremely sore throat or even more serious consequences.

New brushes must be broken in, and they should be broken in on a priming coat, not on a finish coat. Loose bristles should first be worked out and the brush dipped into the paint (a brush should never be dipped in more than two or three inches) and wiped several times across the mixing paddle. An old brush is more satisfactory for poking into corners and for grille work.

Surface Preparation. The surface to be painted should be properly prepared. This is usually a very simple matter. New wood should be gone over with a duster and a putty knife to remove dirt, plaster, etc. Knots and sappy places should be brushed with turpentine, solvent naphtha, or a coat of aluminum knot primer applied about 20 minutes before the application of the priming coat. Otherwise the pitch in the lumber will be drawn out by the sun and the surface will be discolored.

Moisture is at the bottom of most paint difficulties. It is not enough for the surface only to be dry; the structure must be dry through and through or the paint will blister when the sun draws the moisture to the surface. A blistered surface may be scraped clean with a putty knife and painted over. The scraped patches should be touched up with paint before the whole job is gone over.

When paint has cracked or scaled it is best to remove it with a blowtorch before applying new paint, but the blowtorch should be handled only by a professional painter because of the fire hazard.

Priming Coats. If any one coat of paint is more important than any other, it is the priming coat, which is the foundation. The application of this coat should not be delayed too long. It forms a protective coat which keeps out moisture from fogs, rains, etc.; yet, if it is thin enough, it allows the moisture within to escape.

The formula for the priming coat must be varied to suit the kind of wood to which it is applied. Porous woods which absorb oil readily, such as bass, cedar, white pine, and boxwood, require an extra amount of oil in the priming coat. Woods with an oily fiber, like cypress, yellow pine, fir, hemlock, spruce, and gum, require an excess of turpentine for the priming coat. In case any one of these woods has an excess of gum it is advisable to add one pint of solvent naphtha 160 degrees, to each gallon of the priming coat. The priming coat should be allowed to dry thoroughly. The length of time necessary will depend upon the weather conditions, the paint formula, and the wood; but it should not be allowed to remain so long that it becomes chalky or badly weathered. Otherwise the finish will appear faded.

Estimating Coverage. It is difficult to give an estimate of the amount of paint required for a surface, for so much depends upon the surface—whether it is rough or smooth, exposed or protected, painted or unpainted, porous or hard. Under average conditions a gallon of good paint will cover 300 sq. ft., and sometimes even as much as 500 sq. ft. An expert painter can cover nearly 25 per cent more surface than an inexperienced one. Dark-colored paints have a greater coverage than light because they can be spread thinner. It takes more paint to cover a dark surface with light paint than to cover a light surface with dark paint, since the paint must be spread more thickly.

Painting Shingles. New shingles should be dipped in paint or stain a few days before they are laid. The best method is to use a barrel containing stain or paint and to dip a dozen or so shingles at a time, butt end down, to a depth of 6 or 8 in., and to stand them in a trough to catch the drippings. After the shingles are laid, a second coat should be applied with an old paint brush which will go into all the cracks and joints.

Painting Cement and Stucco. Cement and stucco surfaces should be clean and thoroughly dry. Freshly formed cement needs a treatment to neutralize the free lime present; otherwise oil paints will be damaged. This treatment consists of a neutralizing wash made of two or three pounds of zinc sulphate crystals dissolved in a gallon of water, brushed or sprayed on the surface and allowed to dry before the paint is applied. This treatment is unnecessary on stucco that has been allowed to age. Since the priming coat must bind the loose particles of cement on the surface and at the same time supply a good foundation for the succeeding coats, it is advisable to add an extra quantity of oil or varnish to the formula. Any good house paint is suitable for the finishing coats.

Painting Brick. In painting bricks an excess of oil is used in the priming coat. The application of paint to a brick wall is an excellent way to seal the pores and prevent the penetration of moisture, which often causes dampness and decay.

Painting Interiors. For doing interior painting, good ventilation is desirable; an electric fan may serve the purpose. All dust should be removed, and the floor and such furniture as cannot be readily moved out should be carefully covered with light duck, heavy muslin, or old sheets.

The plan of painting should be figured out before the brush is dipped into the pail. Floor painting should begin in the far corner of the room so that the painter will end up at the door. Wall painting should begin in the upper left-hand corner of the room.

New plaster, like new stucco, should be treated for free lime to keep the surface from "burning." The treatment is a solution of zinc sulphate crystals in the proportions of 2 lbs. to a gallon of water. The solution is applied with a brush. Next, the wall is sandpapered and the small cracks are filled with plaster of Paris or a crack filler. When the surface is entirely smooth it is ready to be sized and primed. *Old plaster* in good condition needs only to be dusted. Particles of paint must be wiped off with a wire brush. Grease may be washed off with a solution of sal soda or ammonia and water. Old calcimine, if in bad condition, should be washed off. Cracks should be filled as in the case of new plaster and the whole surface sanded smooth.

Wallboard should be smoothed before it is sized and primed. This operation involves the filling in of all joints, cracks, etc.

Wallpaper which is still tight to the walls and in good condition may be dusted and painted over, but work done under such circumstances cannot be guaranteed.

A good *sizing* for plaster or wallboard is a coat of first-class interior varnish, thinned with turpentine and colored with a little of the wall paint.

The best *primer* is a coat of flat wall paint which contains an excess of linseed oil. Wallboard is more porous than plaster and therefore requires a greater proportion of oil.

Wall paint is usually faster drying than exterior paint and the brushing is somewhat more difficult. If the paint is too thin it will run and if it is improperly applied it will not be smooth. The general rule is to begin in the upper left-hand corner, working from left to right and from ceiling to floor in strips a foot or two wide. Narrow strips are painted so that the edge of each painted area can be smoothly joined to the one that has preceded it before it has had a chance to set. The brush should never be pressed down too hard. Small brush marks disappear as the paint dries if the paint is properly flowed on. Too much brushing should be avoided since it brings the oil to the surface and gives a gloss. Once an area has been left it will not help but injure it to go over it again with the brush.

Stippling. Stippling is done with a regular stippling brush. Paint for this coat should be quite thick and the stippling should be done while it is still wet. Usually two painters work together, the second following the first with the stippling brush.

Sponging. A novel finish is sometimes applied with a sponge cut flat on one side. The flat side is used to apply the paint. The sponge is dipped into a little paint which has been poured into a shallow container and tapped on the surface. The sponge should be pressed against the wall and pulled away straight without twisting the hand. It is advisable to soak the sponge in benzene or water before beginning and also every five or ten minutes while working in order to keep it fluffy and remove the accumulations of paint. A small sponge should be used for corners.

A wad of cheesecloth, crepe paper, muslin, or burlap may be used in the same way, except that the hand is twisted in using these materials instead of being held straight as with the sponge.

Scumbling. For scumbling a wall, a harmonizing or contrasting color is applied over the dry ground color. Then, while it is still wet, a wad of newspaper is placed firmly against the wall and rolled downward and over, thus allowing the ground coat to show through.

Starching. For starching a wall, a handful of starch is dissolved in just enough cold water to cover it and boiling water is added until it has reached a thick, jellylike consistency. It is then thinned with cold water until it has a consistency about like that of milk and brushed on with an ordinary flat wall brush. A pinch of dry color may be added. If the wall has a gloss finish, it is best to wipe it down with vinegar or alcohol before applying the starch coat.

Only new walls should be starched, because the process merely serves to bring out defects in old ones.

Pasteurized buttermilk may be used instead of starching to produce much the same effect. It is brushed on and then stippled with a wall-stippling brush.

When it becomes desirable to freshen the wall, this starch or buttermilk coat is simply washed off.

Washing Walls. A painted wall can be satisfactorily washed only when the entire wall is washed. Washing small patches leaves rings.

A good solution for washing a wall is prepared by shaving a small cake of pure white soap or soap flakes into a quart of water. Dissolve about 2 oz. of glue in another quart of water and mix the two liquids together. A little flour may be added to make a thicker solution, or a little sal soda or washing powder to make a stronger solution. The whole mixture is applied with a soft sponge, working from the bottom up. The wall is then wiped down with a chamois skin. If the wall is badly soiled the solution should be allowed to stand for two or three minutes to loosen the dirt and then be washed off with a clean sponge and a pail of clean water.

Walls coated with a thin film of grease may be treated with the same solution, except that an extra amount of sal soda or ammonia should be added.

Another recommended mixture for cleaning walls is made by dissolving 1 oz.

of soap flakes in 16 oz. of water and adding about 3 oz. of turpentine. The mixture is kept agitated and is applied with a brush or a sponge.

Varnishing. Both the varnish and the room in which it is used should be warm. In very cold weather the varnish should be placed near a radiator or in a pail of warm water (*never before an open fire*) for an hour or two before using.

Painting Radiators. Bronze and aluminum paints should not be used on radiators because they reduce the emission of heat by as much as 20 per cent. A white or light-colored wall paint protects the metal and retards heat emission practically not at all. When it is desired to reduce the heat given out by pipes, as in a furnace room or basement, bronze or aluminum paints serve very well; but when it is desired to increase the heat a light or white paint should be used.

Sizing. Size is any one of a number of gelatinous materials used to give glaze to a surface. Ordinary painter's size is glue with too much water in it to allow it to harden, usually 5 qt. of water to 1 lb. of glue. To prepare the sizing, add 1 lb. of glue to 2 qt. of boiling water. Stir until the glue is thoroughly mixed, and then add 3 qt. of water.

Whitewash. Whitewash is made of slaked lime mixed with water to form a thin paste and applied with a brush. The surface to be whitewashed should be rough. It is excellent for use on fences, barns, brickwork, etc.

Government specifications for a whitewash which is almost as good as paint are as follows:

Slake ½ bu. of lime with boiling water, keeping it covered during the process. Strain it and then add a peck of salt dissolved in warm water, 3 lb. of rice which has been boiled to a thin paste, ½ lb. of Spanish whiting, and 1 lb. of clean glue which has been dissolved in warm water. Mix thoroughly and let stand for three days. Then heat and apply with a brush while still very hot.

PAPER HANGING

Wallpaper is sold by the roll. Most American papers are 18 in. wide. A single roll is 24 ft. long; a double roll is 48 ft. long. If the paper has to be matched it is best to use a double roll to reduce waste to a minimum.

To estimate the amount of wallpaper needed, find the distance around the room and subtract the width of the doors and windows. Divide the result in feet (which is the net perimeter of the room) by 1½ ft. (the width of one strip of standard American paper). This gives the number of strips of paper needed. To find the number of strips in a roll of paper, divide the length of the roll by the height of the wall.

New walls are prepared by sanding the surface to make it even and by washing and sizing to make the paper stick.

For ordinary papers a stiff paste made of wheat or rye flour is generally used, with a little formalin or carbolic acid added to prevent decomposition and attacks from insects. For heavy embossed or leather papers a glue paste is used and thin tacks are driven in lightly so that they can be taken out when the paper is dry.

In hanging figured paper great care should be taken to keep the pattern perfect. In covering projecting or recessed corners the paper should be cut so that only half an inch or so turns the corner. The paper hanger should work away from a window rather than toward it, so that the overlapping edges do not face the light. This makes them much less conspicuous.

For medium-weight paper something more than a pint of paste will be needed for each roll. Light papers will need less and heavy papers will need more.

EXCAVATIONS

Estimates for excavations are usually figured in cubic yards or cubic feet. If there is any doubt as to the nature of the underlying surface the owner or architect should have borings made to determine how deep one has to go before a firm foundation can be secured and to find out whether shoring and pumping will be necessary. If the job is a large one this should in any case be done. Costs depend upon all these items and also upon whether the excavated material is to be removed from the site, or redistributed for grading. Bids can usually be obtained for removal of earth in accordance with plans, with rock excavation as an "extra" at a unit price per yard. The unit price will vary for general rock or rock for piers. Be sure to include excavation for sewer and water trenches. Great care in the beginning may save much trouble later on.

DAMS

Earth dams should never be more than 100 ft. high. *Masonry dams* may be of any height; dams more than 100 ft. high are practically always of masonry.

The area to be covered by a dam should first be cleared of trees, top soil, and other organic matter which would soften in water. A trench should then be dug where the center of the dam is to be, deep enough to reach a solid base. The center of the trench should be filled with a core wall of concrete or puddled clay. This wall is built up with the banks, which are made of earth, the excavated material being used for this purpose. The inside slope should be protected from the waves by slabs of concrete or something which answers the same purpose. The core wall should be somewhat higher than the high-water mark of the reservoir. This is a safety factor.

The largest earth dam in the world is the one which impounds Gatun Lake on the Isthmus of Panama. It is more than a mile long, has a base width of nearly half a mile and contains more than 20,000,000 cu. yd. of material. The water which it holds in check covers 171 sq. mi.

ADVERTISING

Advertising is any paid form of nonpersonal presentation or promotion of ideas, goods, or services by an identified sponsor. It is done today in various ways—by announcements in newspapers and magazines, by radio and television, by mail, billboards, car-cards, electric signs, or any other medium that will carry the advertiser's selling message to the public.

Mass production, typical of present-day business, depends upon large-scale distribution. Advertising is one of the tools employed to achieve wide distribution of a product or service. In some instances, advertising is expected not only to attract attention and arouse interest but also to stimulate desire and get action. This is true with lower-priced and convenience items. With higher-priced goods and technical products, advertising is used primarily to attract attention and to interest prospects. Completion of the sale is left to regular salesmen.

Much confusion has arisen concerning the merits of advertising. Consumer groups, in particular, often condemn advertising as an unnecessary and wasteful charge added to the purchase price. They contend that it stimulates desire for many unnecessary products and services, tends to standardize consumer goods, and makes it difficult for the small nonadvertising competitor to remain in business. The proponents of advertising argue that it lowers prices to consumers by making possible large-scale distribution, which in turn results in lower-cost production. They claim that if advertising were eliminated, the over-all cost of marketing would go up substantially and prices would necessarily be much higher.

Both these points of view are extreme; examples can be given to uphold both sides. Practically, advertising is an important sales tool. As such it may be efficient or inefficient, good or bad, depending upon the way it is employed.

When used properly, it is an unusually effective implement for distributing large quantities of mass-produced goods at the lowest possible cost. When used improperly, it may maintain artificially high prices or persuade people to purchase items for which they have little need. An intelligent view of advertising sees it as an important adjunct to personal selling which promotes sound products and services at the lowest possible cost.

An analysis of advertising indicates that it is especially effective in: (1) introducing new products and services by familiarizing potential consumers with the uses of the offerings; (2) helping to obtain desirable wholesale and retail dealers by making it easier for them to sell; (3) paving the way for the salesman by acquainting prospects with his company and the nature of its products; (4) informing potential customers of new developments and new applications of existing products; and (5) making it possible under certain conditions to complete sales even in the absence of salesmen.

In another sense, advertising is used in three distinct ways to promote the sales of a product. When a product is first introduced, it must be explained to potential consumers. They must be educated regarding its merits. When other firms begin to offer similar products, advertising is used to fight off competition and to capture the largest possible share of the market. This is done by explaining why a particular product is better than that of the competitor. A third problem stems from the desire to retain customers. This entails an advertising program designed to keep the product's benefits constantly in the minds of users. This accounts for the heavy use of repetitive advertising. At the retail level, advertising is used to build up store traffic. The alert retailer never stops seeking to create an image of his business in the public's mind to attract a specific clientele, one suited to the particular lines he carries.

Effective advertising must be based on a sound product. Misrepresentation may sell goods, but it also builds ill will. Since the advertiser who misrepresents his product harms not only the public but the whole industry as well, organized efforts have been made to prevent objectionable advertising. One of these was the model statute against fraud in advertising drafted in 1911 by the magazine *Printers' Ink*. This statute has since been enacted by 43 states, in either the original or a modified form, and covers 95 per cent of the population of the United States.

Further government control over advertising was achieved by the Federal Trade Commission Act (1914), as amended by the Wheeler-Lea and other acts. These gave the Federal Trade Commission[1] (abbreviated F.T.C.), among others, the power to prosecute for unfair methods of competition and unfair or deceptive acts and practices, including false advertising. Another protection for the consumer against fraudulent advertising is the National Better Business Bureau,[2] with offices throughout the United States and Canada. A protection to the advertiser against misrepresentation by publications is the Audit Bureau of Circulations; its function is to determine the net paid circulation of newspapers and magazines. Practically all magazines and newspapers which accept advertising submit audited accounts to the A.B.C.

Most firms turn over the entire problem of advertising to advertising agencies. This practice generally costs the advertiser nothing because the agency receives a commission from the medium in which the advertisement appears. The medium returns to the agency 15 per cent of the cost of space or time sold to the advertiser. With this return the agency can offer its clients many services in addition to preparing advertisements, and still make a profit. In recent years, serious questions have been raised regarding this method of agency compensation. The F.T.C. has intimated that it might be in violation of Federal statutes.

---

[1] See the article on Federal Trade Commission.
[2] See the article on Better Business Bureaus.

The entire subject is being intensively studied by advertising media and agencies and their clients in an effort to clarify the situation; so far, however, few changes in method of compensation have taken place.

Agencies are usually equipped to handle every phase of the program. They may help with research, prepare the advertisements and select the media in which the ads are to be run, and they may also assist in other phases of marketing and even in product development.

Market Research. It is easy to lose money in advertising. The best prevention lies in market research, which provides a careful study of the product and the market. Expert research staffs eliminate "blind" advertising. Such a staff will (1) find out how the product compares with others in the same field and suggest improvements, if any are needed; (2) study the market and determine the potential buyers of the product; and (3) make a study of advertising media, to determine which will produce the greatest returns.

Many considerations enter into this work. The market for the product may consist of men, or women, or both: different groups require different appeals. The woman of wealth, for instance, will not be induced to buy through the kind of advertising that will interest the less wealthy woman; and different parts of the country require different types of approach.

In order to shed light on these and similar questions, newer techniques borrowed from the field of psychology are utilized. Studies designed to reveal the underlying reasons *why* people buy are being stressed to an ever-increasing degree. Such studies, generally known as motivation research, help advertisers to avoid pitfalls and to adapt their appeals more closely to the underlying interests of consumers.

To avoid possible errors in advertising, larger advertisers pretest their campaigns. Many techniques have been developed for this purpose. Some firms try out their program first in small selected test markets. Others use "split-run" techniques, in which two different advertisements are tested in alternate markets simultaneously. Still others measure coupon response in test advertisements before deciding on the final campaign.

Preparing the Advertisement. In planning advertising, it is not necessary to have a detailed knowledge of the highly technical skills involved in preparing an advertisement. However, an understanding of the components of an advertisement, of their functions and preparation, and of how they are combined into usable form is essential.

The customary parts of an advertisement are (1) heading or headline, (2) illustration, (3) copy, and (4) company or product identification. These may be arranged in many ways. Headlines may appear anywhere in the advertisement. Copy may vary from a few words to a detailed description of the offering. The illustration may be very simple, it may be a reproduction of a fine painting or there may be no illustration at all. In any case, the four basic ingredients noted above *must* be considered in preparing an advertisement. The first step is to visualize the idea. Headlines and copy must then be considered, and a decision made on the illustration and the type. Finally, these must be assembled in finished form for reproduction.

The first rule in preparing an advertisement is to capture attention. If the ad does not "stop" the prospect, it cannot make sales. Attention should be arrested by an effective layout, a telling headline, or by both. That is why the first step in preparing an advertisement is to visualize its appearance.

First, a rough sketch or layout is prepared in which headline, illustration, copy, company identification, and any other features are drawn to scale to indicate in what manner the various components are to appear.

The layout should have two important characteristics—it should be interesting to look at and it should convey a feeling of movement and action.

The layout should observe the principles of design. It should be balanced properly. A lopsided advertisement will interfere unpleasantly with the desired effect. The materials that go into the layout should be harmonious in shape, color, and tone. They should be knit together logically and should stress ideas according to their relative importance. Emphasis is secured through contrast; the contrast may be in color, type, size, or many other features.

Another desirable characteristic is distinctiveness. This may be achieved by emphasis or exaggeration, by unusual use of white space, by action pictures, by striking type- or border-treatment, or even by sheer simplicity.

The size of the space to be used is an important factor and will depend on the type of advertisement planned and the purposes behind it. There are many natural advantages in the use of large space, but often this is unnecessary and wasteful. When comparatively little money is available for advertising, it is usually an error to spend it all on one or two large ads. The same amount spent on a series of smaller advertisements may be far more effective.

Headlines and copy are developed after the advertisement is laid out. The headline is used to capture attention and to arouse interest. It should appeal to the reader's self-interest. A good headline holds out a specific promise to do something that people want done. It should be exciting, and as clear and concise as possible. It may be informative, may create a desire for further information, or may have news value. The headline carries the heaviest burden of attracting desirable readers. No other part of the copy is worked over more thoroughly by experienced advertising men.

A headline is often used as a caption for a picture; but it should do more than simply describe the picture. Good headlines often combine a number of functions. They are particularly effective in appealing to the desired type of reader.

A weakness of many headlines is that they are neither specific nor vivid. They utter dull platitudes, and fail to challenge the reader's curiosity. The headline should express a worth-while idea in the fewest possible words. Some ideas require more words than others; but the headline should be kept short.

Sometimes a secondary or subordinate headline, called a subcaption, helps to round out the idea in the headline. It may clarify the headline, introduce the product, or present the idea in a different light. The headline and sub-headline are usually considered together; they provide the cue to the copy which follows.

The Copy. The text or reading matter in the advertisement is called advertising copy. (In radio or television programs the "commercials" are the copy.) In most advertisements, the major burden of delivering the message falls upon the copy. It is the function of copy, supported by illustrations, to express the message in such a way that it will leave both a favorable and a lasting impression.

It is absolutely essential that the copy be adapted to the prospects who are to be influenced and to the media in which it is to appear, as well as to the product. Copy aimed at factory purchasing agents is written very differently from that expected to influence housewives. Copy published in trade papers is quite unlike that printed in newspapers and magazines.

The first job of the copywriter is to get at the facts. Good copy involves preliminary research, study, and analysis. Every product or service has unsuspected or unexploited angles. Market research and product research uncover many concrete facts which the copywriter may use imaginatively and convincingly. Often a good source of copy information is a competitor's advertising.

The copywriter must know the basic principles of good writing. He must be able to write clearly and convincingly and to convey the exact shade of meaning the advertisement requires. Artificiality and superficial cleverness will

PROOFREADERS' MARKS

Mark	Meaning	Mark	Meaning	Mark	Meaning
∧	Make correction indicated in margin.		close up.	*ital.*	Change to Italic.
Stet	Retain crossed-out word or letter; let it stand.	ℓ	Line drawn through. a cap means lower case.	≡	Under letter or word means caps.
••••	Retain words under which dots appear; write "Stet" in margin.	9	Upside down; reverse.	=	Under letter or word, small caps.
Stet		⌒	Close up; no space.	—	Under letter or word means Italic.
x	Appears battered; examine.	#	Insert a space here.	～	Under letter or word, bold face.
=	Straighten lines.	⊥	Push down this space.	9/	Insert comma.
∨∨∨	Unevenly spaced; correct spacing.	⊔	Indent line one em.	;/	Insert semicolon.
//	Line up; i.e., make lines even with other matter.	[	Move this to the left.	:/	Insert colon.
run in	Make no break in the reading; no ¶	]	Move this to the right.	⊙	Insert period.
no ¶	No paragraph; sometimes written "run in."	⌐	Raise to proper position.	/?/	Insert interrogation mark.
out see copy	Here is an omission; see copy.	⌐	Lower to proper position.	(!)	Insert exclamation mark.
¶	Make a paragraph here.	////	Hair space letters.	/=/	Insert hyphen.
tr	Transpose words or letters as indicated.	w.f.	Wrong font; change to proper font.	∨	Insert apostrophe.
	Take out matter indicated; dele.	Qu?	Is this right?	∨∨	Insert quotation marks.
	Take out character indicated and	l.c.	Put in lower case (small letters).	e/	Insert superior letter or figure.
		s.c.	Put in small capitals.	⊓	Insert inferior letter or figure.
		caps	Put in capitals.	[/]	Insert brackets.
		c.&s.c.	Put in caps and small caps.	(/)	Insert parenthesis.
		rom.	Change to Roman.	1/m	One-em dash.
				2/m	Two-em parallel dash.

not hold the reader; common sense and sincerity are far more convincing. Trickery in copy more often distracts from the real message than it attracts attention to the advertisement. It should never be forgotten that the function of advertising is to sell, not merely to entertain.

In preparing copy, it is important that the proper types of advertising appeals be used. These are the buying motives, or the "reasons why" prospects should purchase the product. The appeals will vary with the type of product and the type of prospects to whom the advertising is directed. The best results are obtained when the appeals of the seller meet the wants of the buyer. Therefore, a thorough knowledge of how and why people buy a product is necessary for the preparation of successful advertising.

Certain rules have been found effective in enhancing the selling power of copy. These are:

1. Dramatization of the facts
2. Presentation of the facts from the consumer's point of view
3. Use of specific details
4. Use of local testimonial material whenever possible
5. Use of performance evidence whenever possible
6. Use of statements that ring true
7. Presentation of good reasons when advertising reduced prices.

Copy is often classified on the basis of action desired from the reader or listener as (1) institutional, or good-will and (2) selling, or immediate-action. The first is intended to build up friendship for and confidence in the company, its policies and products. Selling copy, on the other hand, looks for quick response in the form of purchases or inquiries.

Another classification of copy is by the style employed or the method of approach. These are (1) news or editorial, (2) "reason why," (3) explanatory, (4) humorous, (5) testimonial, (6) conversational, (7) "teaser," (8) human-interest, (9) "trick," and others. Obviously, these groups are not at all mutually exclusive. The important thing is to employ the type of motivation and mode of expression consonant with the product or service being advertised.

The Use of Illustrations. The primary functions of illustration are to attract attention and to convey part of the message. It is not necessary (or possible) to illustrate all types of advertisement, but it should be done whenever possible because of the strong psychological effect. The illustration simplifies the problem of presenting a mental image of the product.

Certain types of pictures attract more attention than others. Pictures of children and animals are particularly effective. A large, simple picture gets more attention than several small pictures. In the last analysis the pictures utilized will depend upon the advertisement under consideration.

Study has demonstrated that the product pictured in the advertisement gets more attention if it is shown in use, especially when it is accomplishing something for the user. For example, a hat or shirt that is being worn, making a man look neat and successful, is superior to a picture of a single hat or shirt. Seeing the product in use stimulates desire in the reader.

Illustrations are used to emphasize the truthfulness of claims. Photographs are particularly convincing. Most people believe what they see. Illustrations are also used to show, even to dramatize, details of a product. Drawings or "close-up" photographs can show special features.

The illustration should be integrated with the rest of the advertisement and be closely related to the product or service advertised. If the illustration is used solely because of its attention-getting power, it may distract the reader from the copy, and much of the total impression-value is lost.

There are five major types of illustrative material used in advertising: (1) photographs; (2) original drawings; (3) original paintings; (4) charts; and (5) technical drawings. Of these the most commonly used is the photograph. Original paintings by outstanding artists are so expensive that they are beyond the reach of the average small advertiser. They are effective, but must be used in relation to the product or service being advertised. Original drawings, on the other hand, are heavily employed, especially in newspaper advertising. "Line" and "wash" drawings are very effective, and seldom approach good paintings in cost.

Charts are unusually effective in presenting facts or reasons for buying; they make it easy to grasp the essential points. Technical drawings are often employed in trade papers and in direct advertising to explain the workings of complicated products.

Choice of Type. The selection of type is a technical matter which must relate to the over-all theme and purpose of the advertisement. Here the type expert must decide. The problem requires an artistic sense in addition to "visual psychology." Type should be chosen for its ability to express the exact shade of feeling intended. Hand lettering may add further distinction.

Italic or bold-face type may be used for emphasis or for contrast. Borders are sometimes used to enhance the effect of unity or to support enclosed material, but their use is decreasing. Type should be suited to the subject and the audience and should take into consideration the kind of paper and illustration to be used and the amount and purpose of the copy.

Advertising Production. The final stage in preparing the advertisement for production is the assembly of the elements. The various components and the layout are sent to the printer, who sets up the ad in accordance with the layout; he should be required to follow instructions meticulously. When he has finished, proofs are made and submitted to the advertiser. These are carefully examined for possible needed corrections and returned to the printer. He makes the necessary changes, if any, and returns final proofs to the advertiser. When these have been approved, the advertisement is ready to be run.

Media Selection. Approximately $12,000,000,000 is spent for advertising annually. This sum is apportioned among the various media, which include newspapers, magazines, television and radio, direct mail, business and trade papers, and others.

The selection of media to reach the largest number of potential customers per dollar spent can be made intelligently only after careful study of each medium. Large advertising agencies have a media expert, whose primary duty is to suggest the best media in the best combinations for the advertiser. A brief examination of the leading media follows.

Newspapers have always been considered very effective for local advertising. In the past decade their value in nationwide advertising has been recognized. Today they dominate the scene, absorbing 32 per cent to 35 per cent of all advertising expenditures. Newspapers offer heavy coverage at comparatively low cost, in localized areas. They can be utilized on short notice, which makes them particularly effective for most types of retailing. They are strong "traffic builders" and are depended upon heavily by retailers.

Magazines account for another 8 per cent of all advertising expenditures. They are particularly effective in developing national recognition for a firm and its products. The circulation of the larger magazines runs into many millions and each copy is read by many people. The cost of magazine advertising, however, precludes its use by smaller firms.

Television and radio account for close to 20 per cent of advertising budgets, with television absorbing 14 per cent and radio taking the balance. The growth of television advertising has been spectacular, but in recent years its growth has leveled off, showing a pattern similar to that of other media. After sagging badly with the advent of television, radio advertising has regained considerable stature. It is now recognized that there are many prospective customers who either are not in a position to watch television or simply prefer radio. Radio broadcasting on frequency modulation (FM), which is static-free, has grown rapidly. This has been especially true with the increase of interest in classical music. Multiplex FM broadcasting, which has been approved by the Federal Communications Commission, makes possible high-quality stereophonic broadcasting and should accelerate this trend.

Direct mail has grown very rapidly in recent years. Over 14 per cent of advertising funds are spent on this medium. It is very effective in achieving selective contacts with potential buyers; experts claim it to be a form of personal selling. Retailers, especially department stores and home-furnishings firms, use it very successfully. Direct mail is a somewhat expensive medium, but there is comparatively little waste.

This medium is also unusually adaptable to the needs and requirements of different advertisers. It may be employed for large campaigns or small ones and in various forms and shapes; it may be used nationally or locally. For these reasons it is depended upon heavily by small businessmen with relatively little money to spend. They can achieve high local coverage by printing inexpensive circulars, handbills, leaflets, announcements, etc., and distributing them quickly, either by mail or in person.

Mailing lists can be purchased at reasonable fees from firms which specialize in this business. Virtually any group or geographic area of prospects in the country can thus be approached.

Outdoor advertising, a comparatively small medium, is growing in importance. Expenditures for it are about 2 per cent of the total. Outdoor advertising has been held back somewhat because it has been esthetically abused, but correction of this misuse has eliminated much of the feeling against it. The importance of this medium lies in its ability to increase the local intensity of a marketing campaign. Coverage can be adapted to meet the requirements of any situation. The medium is flexible enough to be used either by the storekeeper who wants only one sign posted or by the large concern selling nationally, which supplements its advertising in other media with the outdoor form. The ads may range from small placards to very large signs electrically lighted.

The remainder of the advertising budget is spent largely for promotional material, such as point-of-sale displays, samples, premiums, contests, and consumer education. These are employed to tie in with both advertising and personal selling. Their use has been growing rapidly in recent years and may be expected to grow further. These are very flexible devices; they may be used to initiate, maintain, or bolster a campaign.

From a practical standpoint, the advertiser wants returns; but there are other aims, such as higher standards of art and higher forms of public service. The trend has been "Truth in Advertising," a motto that should govern advertising in future years because it is a guarantee that business will reach "the possible attainment of that ideal state in which the fact that an article is advertised through any medium will be alone a guarantee of its worth."

SALESMANSHIP

Salesmanship is the art of persuading people to buy specific goods and services. It has also been defined as the art of helping people to buy intelligently. It is a personal process, as distinguished from advertising, which is impersonal.

Selling is a threefold operation. The first step is to uncover the needs or latent desires of prospective customers. The second is to win their confidence by reflecting a knowledge of their problems and by offering a helpful solution. The third is to persuade them to buy.

Selling concepts have changed very much in the past few decades; however, present-day sales principles are not too well understood by most people. In spite of the service which salesmanship has rendered to our economic system, many people still consider selling a necessary evil rather than a creative skill. So much criticism is voiced about the heavy costs of distribution that many persons think of salesmanship as a wasteful and questionable pursuit. Even salesmen often share this point of view. For these reasons, this occupation has had difficulty in achieving professional status.

High-pressure selling,[1] in which people are sold by improper tactics, is universally condemned. This should not be confused, however, with aggressive selling, in which the salesman takes the initiative and seeks out potential customers who should buy his product or services but who, perhaps because of inertia, tend not to call on him. Relatively few people, for example, call on insurance salesmen.

It is true that many years ago salesmen did engage in questionable practices. The old concept of selling demanded that the salesman get the order by fair means or foul. Current thinking is very different. Today a salesman is definitely expected to help the customer buy. The salesman must so win over the customer that he will regard the salesman as a friend and buy from him again and again. This type of selling requires thorough training of the salesman, in order that he may fully understand the needs of his "prospects" and may give them valuable assistance. The modern, trained salesman does not consider his job finished when the item has been sold and delivered. He will follow up the purchase by seeing that his customer knows how to use the product properly. If the sale is to a dealer, the salesman will help him promote the item. Such a salesman is truly a merchandise counselor, whose visits are looked forward to by his customers.

Formerly it was the practice to hire salesmen rather haphazardly and, if they failed, to let them go. Seldom did the executive in charge consider the possibility that his methods were responsible for the failure of his men. Today, however, the duties of the selling job are analyzed very carefully; men are selected to meet the requirements of specific positions and are carefully trained and supervised. Then, if the salesman falls down, the executive in charge bears the brunt

---

[1] See also chapter on Dishonest Salesmanship.

of criticism. This approach developed because more and more businessmen came to the conclusion that poor salesmen were a serious liability to their firms.

For the remainder of this article we will examine modern salesmanship methods primarily from the point of view of the wholesale salesman, because wholesale selling necessarily includes most of the techniques employed in retail and specialty selling. A little thought will convince the reader that no dealer will buy a product for resale unless he is first persuaded that the product is a good buy. Therefore, the wholesale salesman must face the dual problem of "selling" the dealer as a potential user of the product and of selling to him as a businessman who must see a profit in the resale of the item.

Requirements for Salesmanship. A good salesman should have an agreeable personality as well as thorough training and should enjoy meeting people. Firms expect their salesmen to be loyal, honest, dependable, and courteous. Men with these characteristics plus thorough training should be very effective in their jobs.

Before the novice undergoes regular sales training, it is important that personality deficiencies be ironed out. Irritating characteristics must be eliminated. Speech defects must be corrected and the vocabulary enlarged to include a firm grasp of the terms needed for the types of selling involved. The appearance and dress of novices must pass muster; here again constructive suggestions are of great benefit. Besides having a pleasant attitude and the ability to get along with people, in some types of selling the salesman must be able to write a good sales letter.[1] This is a more difficult ability to develop.

The properly equipped salesman must be fully trained in every phase of the sales presentation. He must have thorough knowledge of his industry, his firm, and the product it manufactures or the service it sells. He must be trained in the psychology of selling as well as in effective presentation. His training should include the techniques of finding prospects, getting interviews, and giving complete, convincing demonstrations which will result in sales. He should also be able to describe clearly any additional promotional services that the firm expects him to render. With such training, plus the usual selling equipment, the salesman should be ready to do a satisfactory job. These factors in sales training will now be discussed in detail.

Factors in Sales Training. Familiarity with his industry as a whole is a prime requisite for a salesman if he is to meet competition successfully. His customers will expect him to be familiar with competing firms and their products, typical practices in the industry, and its business methods. He should know what trends are significant and should be able to pass on this information to his customers.

Thorough knowledge of his own firm and its business organization is even more important; it is customary to give new men this information in detail. They should be told of the firm's history and of its current activities and objectives. They should be introduced to all executives with whom they may expect to come in contact and to the work of those departments which will have a direct bearing on their sales. These departments include packing, shipping, scheduling, record-keeping, and especially credit-granting.

In this connection it should be noted that a major area of conflict usually exists between salesmen and credit men. Salesmen naturally tend to sell every prospect they can, but sometimes customers are poor credit risks. Credit men, on the other hand, have to see that losses are held to a minimum and often refuse to approve sales on credit to such customers. The natural reaction of salesmen working on a commission basis is to feel that they are being injured by persons who fail to understand the complexities of selling. Conflict is bound to develop between credit men and salesmen unless the work of each is carefully explained to the other. Introducing salesmen to credit men tends to eliminate this

[1] For information on Sales Letters, see Letters.

friction, for once individuals get to know each other it is much easier to lessen conflicts.

A knowledge of the firm includes many other areas. Distribution policies should be explained to the salesman; he should be taught how and why the marketing channels utilized by the firm have been selected. Contracts in use, price schedules, terms of sales, advertising campaigns, and any other features of the marketing program should be outlined in detail. A salesman should also be familiar with the transportation and delivery methods of his firm. This information should include the time required for production and shipment, the cost of transportation, and the problems of damage in transit; it should also cover the difficult subject of returns and allowances.

The salesman should also know the firm's method of production, the manufacturing processes, the raw materials entering into the product, the workmanship, patent rights, etc., and be thoroughly grounded in the physical characteristics of the product. These include sizes, shapes, styles, colors, packaging, and any other aspects which might be of value in selling. All too often a salesman fails to stress desirable features built into the product by the firm's engineering department; these features possess valuable sales appeal. This neglect is discovered so often that many firms make strong efforts to keep salesmen abreast of new features. They are often required to go through a modified factory-training course, or at least to demonstrate the uses of the new devices in special-training meetings. All such information is taught in terms of interest to distributors, dealers, and users.

Salesmen often fail because of an inadequate knowledge of their product. Obviously, unless the salesman thoroughly understands the uses and values of his products or services he cannot do an effective job of selling; thorough knowledge of the offering is a prerequisite for sound sales demonstration. Such knowledge enables the salesman to guide and control the sales interview and to meet objections effectively. Most important, it enables him to suit the offerings to the specific needs of his prospects.

Psychology of Salesmanship. A knowledge of sales psychology is absolutely essential to salesmen. Training in psychology of salesmanship deals primarily with the motives of human behavior. All people want goods and services. However, their reasons for wanting various items differ, and in many instances the desire for the product must be deliberately aroused. The art of salesmanship consists largely in showing prospective buyers how certain goods may satisfy their wants.

Recent studies in consumer buying psychology, especially in consumer motivation research, are of value to salesmen. As more is learned about why people buy and what influences their ultimate decisions, the more effectively can sales presentations be made.

There are many lists of desires (needs or wants) and motivations common to all people; the following is typical:

1. Food and drink—all people eat and drink
2. Comfort—pleasant and relaxed surroundings
3. Affection—doing things for loved ones
4. Pride—the desire to excel
5. Need for amusement and entertainment (including vacations)
6. Imitativeness—the desire to keep up with the neighbors
7. Sense of ownership—borrowing or renting is not sufficient for many people
8. Fear or caution—we take care of ourselves and others
9. Desire for gain or profit—people like bargains
10. Wish to construct—people like to make things with their own hands.

By utilizing such information the salesman can adapt his approach to specific types of prospects. While most wants are common to all people, it is very important that the salesman fit his offering to the specific needs of each prospect by playing up the most effective type of motivation. The sales presentation should fulfill the special desires of the prospect. In this connection it should be noted that most things are sold on the basis of ideas rather than on the basis of physical properties alone. Care should be taken to distinguish between emotional and rational buyers. Most consumers are considered to be in the former category because of their tendency to "buy with the heart" rather than with the head. Industrial and business buyers, on the other hand, are noted for their scientific approach to purchasing and can be convinced more easily with facts and figures than with frills and fancies.

Psychological training should include information regarding the personality and character traits of prospects. This should be helpful in overcoming sales resistance. The salesman should develop the faculty of keen observation and sensitivity to the reactions of prospects. He must be flexible—he must not only know his prospect but also be able to adjust to him quickly.

Sales Presentations. After the salesman has received training in psychological fundamentals, he may be taught how to make a sales presentation. It is agreed that instruction in the preparation of a selling talk is essential for most men. There is considerable disagreement, however, as to how much of the selling talk should be memorized. For many products, sales managers insist that sales presentations be memorized and given without change. These are known as "canned" presentations. Most sales executives, however, prefer more or less standardized extemporaneous presentations. This does not mean that the salesman may say anything he pleases. He has been trained in selling techniques and is expected to memorize detailed outlines of necessary selling information; but he is given leeway in his use of language and method of presentation.

The decision on whether to use memorized or extemporaneous presentations usually depends upon the type of offering and the salesman; also upon the type of prospect and the number of times he will be visited. The memorized presentation is effective in selling comparatively simple or inexpensive items, especially when the prospect is not a technical buyer and will be called upon only once, or at long intervals. When this is the situation, comparatively poor salesmen may be employed and trained in a technique which will give the highest ratio of sales per dollar of expense. The extemporaneous presentation is effective in selling products and services which require a number of visits and which are purchased only after careful consideration. Usually a higher type of salesman is required—one who can adjust rapidly to changing situations. In most sales situations the extemporaneous rather than the memorized talk is preferable.

The selling talk should be carefully planned and prepared. It crystallizes all that the salesman knows about the offering in terms of the prospect's needs. It should be developed around the basic buying motives. When properly presented it has a number of major advantages over the unprepared approach. It covers all the ground, leaving no gaps. It insures logical order. It not only saves time for the salesman and the prospect; it is especially valuable for the novice. When he might fail if left to his own devices, with such preparation he can sell effectively from the beginning. The prepared talk stimulates the salesman's confidence in his ability to conduct the sales interview and helps him to present his case more convincingly. Most sales managers believe that a salesman with a pleasant personality, who has taken the trouble to digest the standard sales presentation thoroughly, is well on his way to success.

TECHNIQUES OF SELLING

Now the salesman is ready to begin selling. The first problem is to find potential customers; this is known as prospecting. Sometimes it is simple, sometimes quite complicated. While the firm will usually give the salesman as much assistance as it can, in most cases he must rely on his own ingenuity.

Prospects may be culled from various directories, such as the telephone book, membership lists of trade associations and clubs, city directories, and various other listings. For many types of selling, however, these are less effective than some of the well-known prospecting systems. These include:

1. Endless-chain system
2. Center-of-influence technique
3. Personal observation technique
4. Direct-mail sales
5. "Cold turkey" canvassing

The *endless-chain system* is predicated upon the simple idea that you can use each customer or prospect as a "lead" to other prospects. Some time during the sales presentation, usually at or near the end, the salesman asks the prospect to suggest any other persons who might be interested in the offering. The *center-of-influence technique* is based upon the idea that if a key person in a community or group can be convinced of the merit of the offering, he will suggest a number of other prospects. The name of the influential person may be very effective in getting the next interview. *Personal observation technique* is one of the simpler prospecting techniques. Simply by being alert, the salesman can spot prospects for many types of products, even items as varied as automobiles and home furnishings. *Direct-mail leads* usually result from advertising campaigns in which readers request further information. *"Cold turkey" canvassing* is the simplest of all prospecting methods. Without any preliminary contact, the salesman works from door to door or office to office, hoping to stimulate interest in his proposition. Most salesmen object to this type of selling, but experience has proved that it brings results if the salesman perseveres.

Before a salesman makes contact with the prospect he should find out as much as he can about him. This is known as the pre-approach. Every bit of pertinent information the salesman can unearth may be helpful during the presentation. It is desirable to learn the best time for interviewing the prospect. His needs and interests are also very important to know. With this information the salesman can best adapt his offering to the prospect's requirements. Pre-approach analysis is helpful because it conserves time that might otherwise be wasted on poor leads. It also helps give the salesman enthusiasm and confidence.

Information about prospects is often available at the salesman's home office; old records and reference material may be of great value. The information should also include an analysis of the territory. Additional sources of information are government reports, marketing surveys, trade-association compilations, surveys by salesmen, leads from correspondence, and salesmen carrying related lines. Initiative and imagination are necessary for successful pre-approach work.

Although it is important for salesmen to be able to size up prospects rather quickly, there is danger in this practice. While a good salesman wastes little time on weak potential customers and, consequently, maintains a high record of sales, there is the possibility of over-reaching himself by belittling or avoiding a prospect because the initial impression does not promise a sale. Every salesman can cite instances in which unassuming prospects and questionable leads resulted in surprisingly easy sales. The study of prospects prior to making contact with them helps greatly in developing sound sales strategy. Salesmen often mistakenly cut down on this phase of the work because it seems to be a waste of time; but the lack of basic information on the prospective customer actually makes the ultimate sales presentation more difficult.

Contact with the Prospect. The salesman is now ready to make contact with the prospect. His first problem is to obtain the interview. This difficulty has been exaggerated unduly. In most cases the salesman need only present his card, or ask to see the prospective buyer. What occurs once he makes the contact is a different problem.

If, however, the interview is not readily granted, other methods must be tried. A simple device employed by many firms is to send out advance announcements. Cards or letters timed to precede the call of the salesman are mailed to prospects in order to break the ice. These may be quite effective. Often, sending in the salesman's card with a message on it which should appeal to the buyer will result in an interview. Sometimes an appeal to good fellowship, self-interest, or curiosity will induce the prospect to see the salesman. Psychologically, the salesman should expect to get the interview.

Various other devices and maneuvers are employed to make contact with the prospect. Some firms offer free services—for example, polishing furniture or checking up on an oil burner or radio free of charge. Once contact is made the salesman may work into his presentation. A number of cooking-utensil firms hold parties in the home of a prospect, supplying the food and doing the necessary work. All they ask is an opportunity to show the guests how efficiently their utensils perform. A sales practice frequently considered questionable has developed in many parts of the country. Salesmen will claim that they are making a survey, but once they are in the home or office will launch into the sales demonstration. The best technique for getting interviews, as was outlined in the discussion on prospecting, is that which is developed from preceding contacts.

A crucial stage in selling is the initial phase of the sales interview. The salesman must secure favorable attention quickly or he may find it impracticable to continue. If the prospect is not immediately interested or favorably impressed, he may dismiss the salesman at once. For this reason, he must be very careful in his approach. First, the salesman's appearance and attitude should of themselves insure a friendly reception. Second, great care should be given to the opening statements, which should refer to the prospect's problems and focus his full attention upon the salesman and his offering. Different devices are used to accomplish this end. The salesman may show the customer samples, models, manuals, or pictures which may be of interest; the salesman may also refer to mutual friends, or give concrete facts which will interest the prospect.

During the initial stage of the interview, in addition to winning favorable attention, the salesman must check the information he acquired concerning the prospect prior to the interview. Once he is sure of his facts, the salesman can go on to create interest. Certain cautions are in order. The salesman should proceed slowly in utilizing his information and in presenting his samples or models. He should wait for responses in order to gauge attention. He should see that the prospect is comfortable, to make sure that he will listen to the proposition in detail.

Many salesmen follow a standard procedure in building up interest. They begin with selling points that bear directly on the prospect's problems, hoping to capture his attention, then quickly tie in the prospect's problems with the selling points of the offering. They next emphasize the way in which the offering will supply his needs or solve his problems. In presenting these points, salesmen are on the alert for the dominant buying motive. Usually certain points or features stimulate a prospect more than others; these selling points, when stressed, become the key to the sale.

All buyers have inhibitions which must be overcome. Either they have been buying from sources which they consider satisfactory, or they do not wish to try something new. These are major hurdles in any sales presentation. Buyers do not like to be high-pressured; a shrewd salesman lets the prospect feel that he is making the decision. In this respect suggestions are more effective than high pressure. The basic problem is to arouse the feeling of need and to show how the offering solves the need. The salesman must adjust the speed of his presentation to the mind of the prospect. Genuine enthusiasm is contagious.

Even if the prospect indicates a desire to own the product, the sale may be far from made. Conflicts with older desires in the mind of the buyer may tend to postpone decision. At this stage it is necessary to solidify desire into conviction. This may be done by the use of tests, guarantees, facts, statistics, and testimonials from satisfied users.

With certain products it is possible to prove to the prospect by tests that they will meet his needs. For example, if it is stated that a ladder will support a certain number of pounds, weights can be placed on the ladder to prove it. With fabrics, in which tensile strength is an important asset, a simple, small hand device can make the test on the spot. It is easy to prove that a ball-point pen will make carbon copies by having the prospect write on manifold paper forms.

Guarantees may be used to clinch sales, especially of technical merchandise and equipment. Any doubts regarding quality must be resolved. If the salesman's firm guarantees the product, the prospect is more likely to buy. Sometimes, unfortunately, salesmen make statements which are not backed up by the contract. Such improper practices result in much ill will.

Facts and statistics are effective in selling to technical buyers. Proof of this nature will often convince them when descriptions of the product seem to get nowhere.

Testimonials are useful in selling consumer goods. The average person tends to believe what he reads or hears, especially if it is said by someone of importance or someone he knows. If a satisfactory trial has been made by some well-known person, the implication is that it will also be satisfactory to the prospect. That is why many salesmen find the name of a local purchaser effective in selling to others.

At this stage of the sales demonstration it is suggested that the salesman use positive expressions, avoiding neutral or negative statements. The prospect likes to hear what the offering will do for him, not, as a rule, what it will not do. In this connection, many sales managers caution their men against mentioning competitors' products unless forced to do so by the prospect.

"Objections" Techniques. At any stage of the sales presentation the prospect is likely to raise objections. These may be simple and unimportant or they may be serious. Some salesmen are irritated by objections, but that is the wrong attitude. Objections are guideposts to the prospect's reactions, and a good salesman is on the alert for them and makes the most of them. He listens carefully before answering. Perhaps he repeats the question, so that both he and the prospect understand it exactly. Then he answers it, for he knows full well that unless he meets it adequately the sale will not be made.

A number of techniques are used to answer objections. First there is the "reverse English" or "boomerang" technique. Sometimes the question raised by the prospect can be turned into a strong selling point. For example, the prospect may object to a light-colored automobile. The salesman then points out that a light-colored car is safer than a dark-colored one because the former can be seen more easily at night.

A second technique is to "reverse positions." If the prospect's objections as to quality are unfounded, the salesman may suggest that the prospect tell exactly what is wrong with the item; he will have difficulty finding specific warranted complaints. The salesman will then examine each feature with the prospect, at the same time making the necessary selling points.

In some cases the salesman agrees that the objection of the prospect is well founded; the salesman then stresses a superior feature which compensates for the lack. For example, if, in the sale of a ball-point pen, the prospect objects that such pens eliminate individuality in handwriting, the salesman agrees, but points out that only a ball-point pen can make carbon copies or write on all types of surfaces under a wide variety of conditions.

Once in a while a salesman will answer an objection with a direct denial, but the utmost caution should be used in employing this type of answer. Under most circumstances it will alienate the prospect and preclude any possibility of a sale. In certain cases, however, it is necessary to deny a statement made by the prospect. This is especially true when the reputation or business practices of the salesman's firm are impugned unfairly.

Never magnify an objection. A poor salesman may build up a simple objection into so complex a discussion that a sale is impossible. Avoid arguments in handling objections; no one wins, and the atmosphere is not conducive to a sale. Many salesmen anticipate possible objections and forestall them by working both the objection and the answer into the regular prepared presentation.

Getting the order is the acid test in selling; some salesmen seem able to do everything but complete the sale—they cannot bring themselves to ask for the order. Various techniques may be used for the closing. There is no reason why this should not be done at the right time. In this respect it should be noted that it is not always necessary to go through the complete presentation before trying to close. A "trial close" is tried by a good salesman at different points along the way. Quite often the sale can be completed in short order, especially when the prospect asks for a certain type of item. Sometimes a lengthy presentation will do more harm than good. Some firms employ an "up-the-sleeve offer," in which an additional item or a discount is offered by way of inducement. When the product is in short supply, the "standing-room-only" technique is usually effective. The prospect is advised that unless he buys immediately, he may not be able to buy at all. The simplest type of closing is that in which there is implied consent. As the salesman finishes the presentation, having eliminated any objections, he takes out his order book and begins to write up the order. Naturally, unless the prospect stops him, it is taken for granted that the sale is being consummated.

The modern salesman is expected to do more than merely take an order. He must cooperate with other departments within the marketing division, especially with advertising and sales promotion. He is expected to assist the dealer in every way possible—by showing him how the product can be sold, pointing out different selling methods, instructing the dealer's salespeople, and assisting in setting up point-of-sale displays.

The salesman may be expected to perform service work on the product both before and after the sale, and to assist in credit and collection duties. Usually he will be asked to submit reports and records of his activities. He will also be expected to attend sales meetings, conventions, exhibits, and demonstrations which may help him to improve his techniques or at which he can meet prospects.

From the foregoing it is evident that the modern salesman's work is far from simple; yet a man who acquires the necessary training and maintains a pleasant and cooperative attitude is usually successful.

Promotion may be accelerated by the alert salesman. Self-evaluation is the basis for improvement. Every salesman has at his finger tips the tools for self-analysis. These lie in the reports he submits to management or in the information that can be culled from his salesbook. When sales reports are not required, the salesman can prepare them for his own use.

Any alert man is interested in seeing whether or not he is making satisfactory progress. This becomes clear when sales figures are studied. Many kinds of analyses can be made of sales data. Some of the most valuable analyses are the following:

1. Total sales volume for the period, compared to total sales volume in similar preceding periods
2. Sales made per day, week, month
3. Average size of order
4. Composition of order received
5. Number of accounts today as compared with same time a year ago
6. Number of prospects contacted daily
7. Average time spent per call
8. New accounts gained for period
9. Number of accounts lost and why lost
10. Analysis of returns, cancellations.

TALKING

One of the most common human activities is talking. Even as infants we begin to express our desires and convey our thoughts by word of mouth. We want other people to understand what is on our minds, and we transmit these ideas by speech.

Talking is also one of our most revealing habits. It gives a strong insight into the speaker's personality. Over 2,000 years ago, Demosthenes said that "as a vessel is known by the sound whether it is cracked or not, so men are proved by their speeches whether they be wise or foolish." This statement is every whit as true today. When a person begins to speak, our impressions of him tend to change for better or worse. His speech, coupled with his appearance, makes a lasting impression. For this reason, if for no other, the way in which a person talks should be given serious attention.

Communication with others is most commonly carried on by word of mouth. This is as true in business as in other walks of life. Business executives must be skilled in communicating with others, for failure to develop this ability results in misunderstandings. Effective speech is an incalculable aid toward attaining social or business success.

Effective speakers are made, not born. Speech may be improved in many ways. It is necessary to build a good vocabulary, because words are the tools of speech. Grammatical errors must be eliminated consciously until correct speech becomes natural. Enunciation and pronunciation must also be cultivated to make sure that listeners can easily grasp what is being said.

Various techniques may be employed to correct speech deficiencies. Speaking in front of a mirror, for instance, is very helpful. It will quickly reveal mannerisms which are distracting or unattractive. The speaker can observe his facial expressions and improve upon them. Another technique is the use of a voice recorder. A record of the voice should be made and listened to critically. While the first reaction to the playback will probably be shock, after one overcomes this initial reaction, he can readily distinguish and correct speaking defects.

Think before you speak. Do not talk just to make conversation. If you are in doubt about what to say, listen. One of the basic principles of salesmanship is that most people enjoy talking much more than listening. A customer will sometimes talk himself into a sale when the best unaided efforts of the salesman might fail.

An intelligent speaker adjusts his way of talking to his listeners. Do not talk "over the heads" of people, nor as if you were superior to them. Either attitude is irritating. Use language and expressions which befit the situation. Be pleasant and natural. Everyone dislikes artificiality, but respects sincerity. If you talk in an interesting, engaging manner, people are bound to like you and look forward to seeing and hearing you again.

SLANDER AND LIBEL

Slander and libel are different forms of defamation; *slander* is defamation by spoken word, whereas *libel* is defamation by writing, print, picture, effigy, sign, or otherwise than by speech. Some courts have held that the reading of a defamatory letter or a broadcast over the radio from a script is libel and not slander.

No defamation can constitute the basis of an action to recover damages unless it is "published." In the law of defamation, "publication" has a special meaning. It is the communication of the defamatory matter to another person. A libel is not published if it is read *only* by the person defamed; and a slander is not published if it is heard *only* by the person defamed. However, no person defamed can recover damages when he himself communicates or by his conduct is responsible for the communication of the defamatory matter, or if he authorizes its publication. To illustrate, when a person who receives a defamatory letter exhibits it to another, the publication is not actionable.

There are *two classes of defamation;* one is defamatory per se, the other is not. A defamation is slander per se or libel per se if the words on their face, without other proof, are recognized as injurious; but if the words on their face are not injurious, but become so only as a result of the surrounding circumstances, the defamation is not per se. In the former case damage is presumed to follow from the language used, whereas in the latter case damage must be alleged and proved.

Generally, words are libelous per se, *i.e.,* no special damage need be alleged and proved, if they expose or even tend to expose a person to public hatred, shame, disgrace, or contempt.

Some words may constitute libel per se but not slander per se. The distinction has an ancient origin. It rests on the fact that a libel is a more permanent form of defamation than a slander and can, therefore, be more readily circulated with greater possibility of causing damage to the person defamed.

Words are slanderous per se if they impute the commission of a crime or the possession of a loathsome or contagious disease, or if they prejudice a person in his profession, trade, or business.

When the words are libelous per se or slanderous per se the person defamed is entitled to recover damages without regard to the motive with which the publication was made. Such motive is unimportant. If malice is proved the person defamed can recover *exemplary damages,* that is, damages greater than the actual loss, and imposed for punishment.

In all actions of slander or libel, whether per se or not, the words must be *false.* Falsity is presumed; it need not be proved. Truth must be established by the person who published the defamation.

Under some circumstances a person who is sued for defamation may plead *privilege.* The privilege grants immunity for what is otherwise defamatory, whether per se or not. Privilege may be *absolute* or *qualified.* It rests on public policy. Generally, a privileged communication is one made in good faith by some person to another when both have an interest in the subject matter of the communication. For example, defamatory statements, even if malicious, made in a judicial proceeding which are material and relevant to the issues there involved are absolutely privileged.

Derogatory statements by an employer concerning a former employee constitute a qualifiedly privileged communication if made in answer to inquiries by a prospective employer.

Newspapers have no special privilege in the absence of statute. Fair and impartial reports by newspapers of judicial, legislative, or executive proceedings are privileged. Comment or criticism that is fair and reasonable gives immunity to newspapers. Public welfare requires that newspapers shall have the right of making such criticism and comment. However, actual malice defeats the defense of fair comment and criticism.

All persons who either cause or participate in the publication of defamations are liable. A newspaper owner is liable for a libel printed in his newspaper, even though it was made without his knowledge or consent; the author is also liable.

Libel is also a crime, usually a misdemeanor. The statutes defining the crime usually require that the publication be malicious; however, malice is presumed unless justification or excuse is shown. In some states, threat to publish a libel is also a misdemeanor. Generally the publication is excused with respect to criminal prosecution when the statement is honestly made in the belief of its truth and upon reasonable grounds for the belief, but in some jurisdictions truth is only admissible to show intent and not as an excuse.

ORGANIZATION OF CLUBS AND PARLIAMENTARY LAW

A club is a group of people organized for a purpose—generally social, business, political, or educational, but not for profit.

One or more persons usually start to organize a club after informal discussions. They invite other interested persons to come to the first meeting. When they convene, one person generally "takes the chair" and explains the purposes for which they have met. This person may retain the chairmanship during the meeting, or he may suggest that another be chosen as a temporary chairman. Someone may then rise and say, "I move that Mr.—— retain the chairmanship for this meeting," and someone else may say, "I second the motion." The chairman then announces to the group, "You have heard the motion: That Mr.—— retain the chairmanship for this meeting. Are there any other nominations?" If there are none, he calls for a vote by saying, "All those in favor, say 'aye,' all those against say 'no.'" He then counts the votes, and says, "The ayes have it, and Mr.—— retains the chair during this meeting."

The chairman appoints a temporary secretary, or one is elected from those present. Both temporary officers serve until their successors are elected in accordance with rules the club will later adopt. A committee should be selected by the chairman to draft a constitution and bylaws. The meeting is then adjourned.

At the next meeting a copy of the proposed constitution and bylaws is given to the chairman, who reads it and moves "for the adoption of the constitution and bylaws as read." When this motion is seconded, he reads the constitution, section by section, permitting time for discussion and amendments, if any are proposed, before putting each section to a vote. When the constitution has been adopted, the bylaws are taken up in the same manner. Since the future activities of the club will be governed by these rules, and conditions may change, flexibility is desirable. It is advisable to provide that the constitution and bylaws may be amended.

CONSTITUTION OF —— CLUB[1]

ARTICLE I: NAME

The name of the club shall be ——.

ARTICLE II: PURPOSE

The purpose of this club is ——.

[1] This is a basic constitution; the actual text of a specific constitution depends on the purpose of the group, and other special circumstances.

ARTICLE III: MEMBERSHIP

Membership in this club shall be granted to those over ——— years, and ——— (state prerequisites).

ARTICLE IV: OFFICERS

The officers of the club shall be a president, a vice president, a secretary, and a treasurer.

ARTICLE V: MEETINGS AND QUORUM

Section 1. Regular meeting shall be held (fix time and place).

Section 2. The annual meeting shall be held (fix time and place).

Section 3. Special meetings may be called by the president; or, on request of ——— members, the president shall call such meeting.

Section 4. ——— members of the club in good standing shall constitute a quorum for transacting business.

ARTICLE VI: AMENDMENT

This constitution may be amended at any meeting of the club by a two-thirds vote, a quorum being present.

Bylaws

ARTICLE I: DUTIES OF THE OFFICERS

Section 1. It shall be the duty of the president to preside at all meetings of the club and perform all duties pertaining to his office.

Section 2. In the absence or disability of the president, the vice president shall perform the duties of the president.

Section 3. The secretary shall keep and record the minutes of club proceedings. He shall send notice of meetings, notify officers of election, and perform such other duties as his office may require.

Section 4. The treasurer shall receive and keep the club's funds in ——— bank, and pay out the same only on order of the president. He shall make an annual report of receipts and disbursements.

ARTICLE II: ELECTION OF OFFICERS

Section 1. All officers shall be elected by ballot at the annual meeting and shall assume office at the close of that meeting.

Section 2. No member shall be eligible to office who has not been a member of the club for (state requirement).

Section 3. No member shall hold the same office more than ——— years in succession, and filling an unexpired term shall be considered as a term in office.

Section 4. Should an officer resign before new elections are held, the president shall appoint some member in good standing to assume the office temporarily and direct the secretary to send notice of a special meeting at the next regular meeting, when the vacancy can be filled.

ARTICLE III: MEMBERSHIP

Section 1. Candidates must be proposed by a member and must be seconded by another member, and the vote shall be held at the meeting following that at which membership was proposed. ——— negative votes shall exclude a candidate, and the same name may not be proposed more than once during a club year.

Section 2. The secretary shall notify the treasurer of the election of new members, whereupon he shall notify the elected members, with instruction to send dues to the treasurer. Failure to pay such dues within ——— days shall forfeit membership.

Section 3. Resignation from membership shall be in writing. Members in arrears for one year shall be dropped.

ARTICLE IV: DUES

Section 1. The annual dues shall be $——, payable at the first regular meeting after the annual meeting.

Section 2. When an election to membership takes place within —————— months of the expiration of the fiscal year, the dues shall be credited to the following year.

ARTICLE V: COMMITTEES

Section 1. At the regular meeting next previous to the annual meeting, the president shall appoint the following committees to report at the annual meeting: a nominating committee to present a list of candidates for election to office for the following year; an auditing committee to report on the correctness of the treasurer's accounts.

Section 2. The president shall appoint such special committees as he considers necessary at any time, or, on the majority vote of the members present at any meeting, he shall appoint committees as they direct.

ARTICLE VI: AMENDMENTS

These bylaws may be amended at any meeting by a two-thirds vote, a quorum being present.

ARTICLE VII: PARLIAMENTARY AUTHORITY

Cushings' *Manual of Parliamentary Practice* shall be the parliamentary authority on all matters not covered by the constitution and bylaws of the club.

ARTICLE VIII: SUSPENSION OF BYLAWS

These bylaws may be suspended in case of emergency by unanimous vote of all those present at a meeting at which a quorum is present.

Conduct of a Meeting

Order of Business. The customary conduct of a meeting is as follows:
1. Call to order by the presiding officer
2. Reading of minutes of previous meeting by the secretary; corrections, if any; vote of acceptance
3. Treasurer's report (as necessity requires at annual meeting)
4. Committee reports
5. Unfinished business
6. New business
7. Program of the day
8. Good and welfare
9. Adjournment.

When the constitution and bylaws have been adopted, the permanent officers are elected. The candidates for office may be chosen and presented by a nominating committee, or the presiding officer may call for nominations from the floor. Nominations from the floor do not have to be seconded.

Nominating and voting must be held in the manner set forth in the bylaws. When officers have been elected, the newly elected president takes the chair; the temporary secretary retains his office until the end of the meeting, when he turns over his records and the minutes of all meetings to his successor.

The club is then fully organized to function. It can decide to apply for a state charter by incorporating as a nonprofit organization, so that the individual members shall not be personally liable for any debts the club may contract. The laws of the states vary; an attorney should be consulted concerning proper incorporation.

Motions. Matters of interest to the organization which require approval by the membership are brought before the club by motion. A member who desires to make a motion rises and addresses the presiding officer by title, as "Mr. Chairman" or "Madam Chairman." This officer grants recognition by calling the member's name. If two members rise, the officer should recognize the one whose voice he first heard. Not until one is recognized may the motion be made. The proper way to make a motion is to introduce the substance of the motion by saying, "I move that ——," or "I move to ——."

The motion may not be discussed or voted upon before approval is obtained by another member. Approval is accomplished by that member saying, "I second the motion," but only after recognition has been granted to him by the presiding officer.

The member who made the motion has the privilege of withdrawing it at any time before it is put to a vote. The motion to withdraw need not be seconded, unless objection is made, in which event a motion to withdraw must be made, seconded, and carried by majority vote of the members present.

If the motion is not thus withdrawn, the presiding officer restates the motion and discussion ensues. If there is no discussion, the matter is put to a vote. While the motion is pending no other unrelated business may be introduced; however, certain other motions may be made with reference to the main motion. These are:

Motion to amend. The member who introduced the motion may accept a proposed amendment after it has been regularly made and seconded. If he refuses to accept it, the members first vote upon the amendment, and in the event it is carried, the motion as amended is brought to a vote. The proposed amendment must relate to the subject matter of the main motion; otherwise it may not be entertained. An amended motion may be further amended only once.

Motion to refer to a committee. At times it may be advisable to obtain the benefit of the view of a committee before putting a motion to a vote, in which event it may be referred to such committee by motion regularly made, seconded, and carried.

Motion to postpone or lay on the table. When it is deemed advisable to defer putting the motion to a vote, it can be postponed by motion regularly made, seconded, and carried to a certain future time, in which case it can only be considered at that time; or it can be laid on the table, in which case it may be considered at any time.

Motion to close debate or to call the previous question. After some discussion and in order to force a vote, a motion is made to call for the previous question; if such motion is carried, the main motion must be voted upon.

Voting. The action of the membership is reflected by vote. There are several methods of voting:

By voice vote (viva voce) or by show of hands. The presiding officer calls for a vote by requesting those in favor to say "aye," and after they have responded he requests those opposed to say "no." He judges the responses by ear and announces the result. Sometimes the voting is by show of hands.

By rising. If there is any doubt as to the result of the previous method of voting, the presiding officer requests those in favor of the motion to rise and remain standing until counted. When the count is reported, these members are seated and those opposed rise. They are counted, and after they sit down the vote is announced.

By unanimous consent. In routine and minor matters, when it is obvious that there is no difference of opinion, the presiding officer may say, "There being no objection, the motion to —— will stand approved as read."

By roll call. When the motion is put to a vote each member's name is called; he or she answers "yes" or "no" and the votes are recorded. When the entire roll has been called, the "yes" and "no" votes are totaled, and the result is announced.

By ballot. The voting methods previously discussed reveal how the members voted. At times members may not wish to disclose how they voted; if ballots are used the voting is secret.

A member may change his vote at any time before the result is announced, except when the ballot method is used, for then there is no way of identifying the voter.

Quorum. A quorum is the number of members fixed by the bylaws as the number that must be present to transact business which will bind the entire membership.

Committees. Committees are small groups of members with special duties. The officer authorized by the bylaws appoints members to the committees. Such designees must accept or decline promptly. If a member accepts, he can resign only by notifying such officer. The committees function under the authority of a chairman appointed by the president or by the entire board of officers.

There are *standing* and *special* committees. A standing committee is one which continues, while a special committee ceases to exist when it completes the work for which it was formed. Each committee has its own secretary, who records the work of the group and prepares reports, which are signed by the chairman. When the chairman renders the report to the membership he does not say, "I wish to report," but "Your committee wishes to report."

Amendments. Amendments to the constitution and bylaws should be submitted in writing. They should be voted upon by the greatest number of members possible, after appropriate deliberation. For this reason, a copy of the proposed amendment should be mailed to each member with a notice stating the date of the meeting when voting thereon will take place.

Adjournment. An adjournment for a short period during the meeting is a recess; a continuation of the meeting to another time is an adjournment.

A motion to adjourn must be seconded; it may not be debated or amended, and after it has been voted, it cannot be reconsidered.

Unfinished Business. Business left unfinished at a meeting must be disposed of as old business at the next succeeding meeting before any new business may be called for discussion.

The Minutes. The operations of the club are recorded in permanent form in a minute book. The minutes are kept and signed by the secretary. After a meeting is called to order, it is customary for the presiding officer to request the secretary to read the minutes of the previous meeting; if the minutes as read require amendment by deleting or adding thereto, a motion to such effect is made and seconded. If no amendment is made, the minutes are approved as read by appropriate motion to that effect. These minutes need not be detailed, but should recite the names of the officers who were present and absent, and contain a summary of committee reports and a record of all motions and their disposition, together with a brief statement of other matters that were discussed at the meeting.

Resolutions. A resolution is a formal expression of opinion by the club as a body. It is generally adopted after motion by a majority vote of those present at the meeting. It is in writing and dated; a copy is made part of the minutes of the meeting at which it was adopted, and the original is transmitted to the person or body affected by its subject matter. The nature and purpose of the resolution will determine to what extent it is publicized. A sample resolution follows:

RESOLUTION AGAINST TOLL ROADS

Whereas: The free use of the public highway is a fundamental principle of government;

Whereas: Motor vehicle owners of the United States through special taxes are today largely meeting the costs of the construction of these highways; *and*

Whereas: So-called express highways are simply a step in the further improvement of our public highway system which will be found necessary in those localities where traffic is heavy and congestion great,

Be It Resolved: That the National Automobile Chamber of Commerce opposes any effort to place control of any part of the public highways in the hands of private promoters, and

Be It Further Resolved: That the National Automobile Chamber of Commerce emphatically supports the principle that **the public highways shall be kept forever free to the general public.**

(*Voted by directors of National Automobile Chamber of Commerce, February 1, 1928.*)

If it is decided to incorporate the club, the following form of resolution might be used. Most banks, however, have their own form of resolution for such a purpose.

RESOLUTION AUTHORIZING CLUB TO OPEN A BANK ACCOUNT

Resolved: That the treasurer of ———— be and he is hereby authorized to open an account in the ———— bank at its branch located at ————, City of ————, in the name of such club, and that said bank be, and hereby is, authorized to honor checks drawn against funds deposited in the said bank by this club, when they are signed by the treasurer and the president.

Program. The program of a club will, of course, be dictated by its aims and purposes. The specific purpose for which the club is organized constitutes its over-all program.

Most clubs have a special committee, known as the program committee, whose function is to arrange the program of activities to be held under the auspices of the club at stated intervals during the club year. The committee might decide to sponsor a series of lectures or debates, or a musical program, or a series of concerts. If the organization does not have members with special talents to present such programs, the committee generally looks outside the group. If they decide on a lecture series, for instance, they can consult with an organization to obtain speakers or lecturers. There are many such organizations. The American National Red Cross, local and Federal district attorneys' offices, local police and Federal narcotics agents, the National Federation of Business and Professional Women's Clubs, and many others will be glad to send speakers, usually free of charge, to speak on their special topics to interested groups. Debates may often be arranged through a local debating society.

In the event that a subject of importance to the club arises with which the members are not particularly well acquainted, it may be advisable to organize a special committee which would first conduct an investigation for the purpose of ascertaining all relevant facts and then report to the membership. Proper resolutions could be adopted on the basis of their findings. The committee might then be directed to meet with governmental agencies, or other authorities, to urge that they act in a way to alleviate or help solve the particular problem. Civic and business groups would probably be most interested in this type of program activity. Other groups might find other types of programs more suitable.

MARRIAGE

Legally, marriage is a relationship founded on contract. It is also a status to which the state is a party and, therefore, the legislative bodies of *each state* have jurisdiction to prescribe the qualifications of the parties; to declare how marriages are to be solemnized and who may perform the marriage ceremony; to define the rights, duties, and obligations of the parties; to determine the effect of the marriage on property rights; and to enumerate the causes for its annulment or permanent or limited dissolution. Congress has similar power in the District of Columbia and in the territories of the United States.

The general laws of the state as to marriage apply to the residents or citizens of the state, and to those who are subject to its jurisdiction; and each state has the right to determine the marital status of its citizens under its laws. The general rule is that the validity of a marriage is determined by the law of the place where it was contracted. If valid there it will be valid in all states, unless both parties left the state of their domicile to evade its law. Such departure would have rendered the marriage invalid if the statute expressly provides that such a marriage is invalid: if the statute does not so expressly provide, then the general rule applies. This general rule, however, has no application if such marriage is contrary to the public policy of the state which the parties left—in cases, for instance, of polygamy, incest, or miscegenation.

Statutes in the various states require the procurement of a *marriage license* from an authorized person designated by statute. Many states require a physical examination and a blood test to show that the parties do not have venereal disease. The *solemnization* of a marriage is necessary, except in those states which recognize common-law marriages.

A *common-law marriage* is a marriage without formal solemnization. It is based upon an actual and mutual agreement between parties having legal capacity to marry, consummated by their living together as husband and wife openly and publicly; and it must contemplate a permanent union. In states where such marriages are recognized, they are as fully valid as ceremonial marriages, and the parties may not voluntarily change their status. Where parties contract a valid common-law marriage, it will be considered valid after removal by the parties to another state where such marriages are not recognized. If such a marriage is recognized by a state, a subsequent statute declaring such marriages invalid shall not affect any previous common-law marriage. Such statutes are constitutional if they have no retroactive effect.[1]

In order to contract a valid marriage each party must have *legal and mental capacity* at the date of the marriage. Although it is difficult to define the necessary degree of such mental capacity, the general test is whether the person understands the duties and responsibilities which are involved in such relationship. No particular form or degree of insanity invalidates a marriage. At common law, and in some states, the marriage of a person who lacks sufficient mental capacity, and, therefore, cannot give free consent, is absolutely void, and such marriage will be declared invalid in any legal proceeding whenever the question arises, whether during the lifetime of the parties or after the death of either or both of them. However, in some states, the statutes provide that such a marriage is only voidable, so that the marriage is valid until set aside in a proceeding for that purpose during the lifetime of the parties. Either the insane or the sane person, when the latter did not know of the other's insanity, can bring the proceeding.

[1] Common-law marriages are recognized in the following states: Alabama, Alaska, Colorado, Connecticut, Florida, Georgia, Idaho, Iowa, Kansas, Ohio, Oklahoma, Pennsylvania, Rhode Island, South Carolina, Texas, and the District of Columbia. In Kentucky they are recognized for Workmen's Compensation purposes. In Montana and South Dakota they are recognized if the parties file a joint declaration. They are also recognized in the following states if entered into before the date specified: California, 1895; Indiana, 1958; Michigan, 1957; Minnesota, April 26, 1941; Missouri, April 5, 1956; Nebraska, March 31, 1921; Nevada, 1923; New Jersey, March 29, 1943; New York, April 29, 1933; Mississippi, April 29, 1933. If recognized by the state where entered into, the marriage is recognized by the United States for Social Security purposes.

Physical capacity is also necessary. The marriage of one physically incapable of sexual intercourse is not void but voidable; it is valid until set aside in a legal proceeding by the person who does not suffer from the disability. Such person may, however, ratify the marriage. The impotency must be permanent and incurable. Barrenness or sterility or mere sexual weakness or frigidity will not render a person incompetent to marry.

Generally, an infant is not permitted to marry until he or she has attained the *age of legal consent* (see following table). Some statutes fixing the marriage age expressly or by clear inference provide that a marriage of a person below such age shall be absolutely void. In the absence of such express or implied declaration, such marriages are voidable. In some states, one who marries before reaching the age of consent may avoid the marriage before reaching such age, but in most states he or she may do so only on reaching the age of consent. Once such person attains the age of consent and elects to affirm the marriage, he or she may not thereafter disaffirm. Continued cohabitation will give rise to a presumption of an election to affirm. Where only one of the parties is under the age of consent at the time of the marriage, the other may not avoid the marriage on such ground.

Persons of different races or color may *intermarry*, unless such intermarriage is prohibited by statute. Many states absolutely prohibit marriages between whites and Negroes; between whites and mulattoes; between whites and Indians; between whites and Mongolians; and between whites and Japanese. Such a prohibited intermarriage is void, and either party may disregard it; its invalidity may be shown at any time, either before or after the death of one party or both parties. Such statutes have no retroactive effect; marriages contracted before the enactment of such statutes remain valid.

A person who has already contracted a valid marriage is incapacitated from contracting another marriage while the former remains in existence. All states prohibit *bigamous marriages*.

Imprisonment does not disqualify a person from marrying. In those states that declare a person imprisoned under a death or a life sentence to be civilly dead, the spouse of such person may remarry, even though no decree dissolved the earlier marriage.

Consent is the basis of marriage; it must be mutual, free, and voluntary. Where the consent is induced by *duress* or *fraud* which goes to the essence of the relationship, the marriage is voidable. Not every fraud affords ground for dissolution. Fraudulent representation of willingness to have children, fraudulent promise to have a religious ceremony, deceptive concealment of serious physical defects which will endanger the health of the other party or of the children of the marriage, or deceptive concealment of mental disease will furnish a basis for dissolution. Cohabitation with full knowledge of the fraud, not merely living together under the same roof, prevents the invalidation of such marriage. Ratification may also be established in other ways. Oral or written forgiveness will suffice, provided it was given after full knowledge of the fraud. However, fraudulent representations as to character, wealth, or social position do not constitute fraud that will invalidate the marriage.

Marriage is an executed contract and is distinguished from the *engagement to marry*. Contracts to promote marriage through *marriage brokers* are against public policy; a contract to pay a fee or commission to another to negotiate a marriage is void and unenforceable.

When a valid contract to marry has been made and is subsequently repudiated and disavowed, or there is a failure to go through with the marriage, there is a breach which gives rise to a cause of action for breach of promise. However, many states have outlawed such actions.

MARRIAGEABLE AGES AND OTHER REQUIREMENTS FOR MARRIAGE IN THE UNITED STATES[1,9]

Alabama: Age of consent: male 17; female 14. Personal or written consent of parents is required, with $200 bond when male is under 21 or female is under 18, unless such minor has been previously married.

Alaska: Age of consent: male 19, female 18. Consent of parents or guardian required for males 18 to 19, females 16 to 18.[2]

Arizona: Males under 18 and females under 16 may not marry. Consent of parents is required when male is under 21 or female is under 18.

Arkansas: Age of consent: male 18, female 16. Written consent of parents or guardian is required when male is under 21 or female is under 18.[2]

California: No age under which persons may not lawfully marry, but verified written consent of parent or guardian is required and must be filed with licensing clerk when male is under 21 or female is under 18; approval by court order is required when male is under 18 or female is under 16.

Colorado: Marriages of persons under 16 are void unless a court order is obtained, and consent of parent or guardian is required when male is under 21 or female under 18.

Connecticut: Age of consent: 16; written consent of guardian signed in presence of a witness and acknowledged before a notary must be filed with registrar; if either party is a minor a similar consent is required of the parent or guardian; court order is also required if either party is under 16.[2a]

Delaware: Age of consent: male 18, female 16. Written consent of parents or guardian, signed in presence of two witnesses, is required when male is under 21 or female is under 18.[4]

District of Columbia: Age of consent: male 18, female 16. Oral or written consent of parent or guardian attested by witnesses is required when male is under 21 or female is under 18, unless such minor has been previously married.[5]

Florida: No license will be granted to male under 18, nor to female under 16, with or without consent, unless they acknowledge under oath that they are parents or expectant parents of a child, in which case granting of license is discretionary with the judge. If either party is under 21, written, acknowledged consent of parents is required, unless both parents are dead or infant has been previously married.[2]

Georgia: Age of consent: male 17, female 14. If female is under 18 the consent of parents is required.

Hawaii: Age of consent: male 18, female 16.[2] Consent of parents is required if either is under 20.

Idaho: License will not be issued to a person under 15, except to a female upon order of court after hearing; no license will be issued to a person under 18 unless written, acknowledged consent of his or her father, mother, or guardian is obtained.

Illinois: Age of consent: male 18, female 16. Personal appearance and affidavit of consent of parents are required when male is under 21 or female is under 18.

Indiana: Age of consent: male 18, female 16. Consent of parent is required when male is under 21 or female is under 18 unless she has lived in the county where license is sought for one month before making application, and has no parent living within the state.

Iowa: Age of consent: male 16, female 14. Consent of parents is required when male is under 21 or female is under 18.

Kansas: Age of consent: male 18, female 16. Consent of parent is required when male is under 21 or female is under 18, evidenced by written certificate if not given personally; approval of judge is also required when male is under 18 or female is under 16.[2]

Kentucky: Age of consent: male 18, female 16. When either party is under 20 and has not been previously married, written consent of father is required, or if father is dead or absent from state, consent of mother is required, attested by two subscribing witnesses and proved by oath of the witnesses.[2]

Louisiana: Age of consent: male 18, female 16, unless evidence of extraordinary circumstances is presented to judge. Minors must have parents' consent, or, if both be dead, the consent of their tutor.

Maine: Age of consent: male 16, female 16. Consent of parents is required when male is under 21 or female is under 18; if either is under 16 consent of judge is required.[3]

Maryland: Age of consent: male 18, female 16. Consent of parents is required when male is under 21 or female is under 18; and they must swear or affirm that the person to be married is of age at which marriage is lawful. A license may be issued by court to persons under these ages if parties are actual or expectant parents.[7]

Massachusetts: Marriages of males under 14 and females under 12 are void. Age for license: male 18, female 16. Parents' consent is required for males under 21 and females under 18.[2]

Michigan: Age of consent: male 18, female 15. Consent of one parent is required when female is under 18.[2]

Minnesota: Age of consent: male 18, female 16; or male 16, female 15 if parents consent and judge approves. Consent of parents is required when male is under 21 or female is under 18.[3]

Mississippi: No minimum legal age of consent; no license can be obtained for males under 17 or females under 15. Consent of parents is required when male is under 21 or female is under 18.[2]

Missouri: No license can be granted to person under 15 except on court order. Written, sworn consent of either parent is required when male is under 21 or female is under 18.[2]

Montana: Age of consent: male 18, female 16. Consent of either parent is required when either party is a minor.

Nebraska: Age of consent: male 18, female 16. Written consent in affidavit form of either parent is required when either party is a minor.

Nevada: Age of consent: male 18, female 16. Parent's consent is required when male is under 21 or female is under 18. Consent must be either personal or in writing, attested by two witnesses, one of whom must appear personally and swear that he either saw the parent sign the consent or acknowledge that it was signed.

New Hampshire: Age of consent: male 20, female 18. Judge may grant permission if special circumstances warrant when male is not less than 14 or female is not less than 13.[3]

New Jersey: At common law age of consent of female is 12; no other statutory age of consent. Consent of parent is required when male is under 21 or female is under 18, but approval by judge is required when male is under 18 or female is under 16. In special circumstances (if female is pregnant) no consent of parent or court is required.[8]

New Mexico: Age of consent: male 18, female 16. Written consent of parents is required when male is under 21 or female is under 18. In special circumstances the court may authorize marriage.

New York: Age of consent: male 16, female 14. Written consent of parents

For footnotes, see page 413.

is required when male is under 21 or female is under 18; but written approval by judge is required where female is under 16.

North Carolina: Age of consent: male 16, female 16. Written consent of either parent by both parties is required when either party is under 18. A license may be issued by court if female is under age and parties are actual or expectant parents.

North Dakota: Age of consent: male 18, female 15. Consent of parents of male is required when he is under 21, or of parents of female when she is under 18. Consent must be given before judge personally or by certificate attested by two witnesses, one of whom must personally appear and testify to the signatures on the written consent.

Ohio: Age of consent: male 18, female 16. Consent of parents is required when either party is under 21. Consent may be given personally or in writing.[3]

Oklahoma: Age of consent: male 18, female 15. Court may authorize marriage of persons under such age if the female is pregnant or has an illegitimate child; written, acknowledged consent of parents is required when male is under 21 or female is under 18.

Oregon: Age of consent: male 18, female 15. Consent of parent is required when male is under 21 or female is under 18, unless no parent lives in the state and female has lived in the county for six months.[2]

Pennsylvania: Age of consent: male 16, female 16; but marriage may be authorized by court if persons are under such age. Consent of parents is required by minor; it may be given personally, or in writing attested by two witnesses and properly acknowledged.

Rhode Island: Age of consent: male 14, female 12. Written consent of parents is required when either is under 21.[12] No license may be applied for unless male is 18 and female 16, and

then with consent of parents and of Director of Public Welfare.

South Carolina: Age of consent: male 14, female 12, but no license can issue unless male is 16 and female is 14. Males 16 to 18 and females 14 to 18 require parents' consent.

South Dakota: Age of consent: male 18, female 15. Consent of parent is required when either is a minor.

Tennessee: Age of consent: male 16, female 16. Judge may authorize marriage regardless of age for good cause. Consent of parents is required when male is under 21 or female is under 18.[2]

Texas: Age of consent: male 16, female 14. Consent of parents is required when male is under 21 or female is under 18.

Utah: Age of consent: male 16, female 14. Consent of either parent is required if male is under 21 or female is under 18.

Vermont: Age of consent: male 18, female 16. Written consent of parent is required when male is under 21 or female is under 18.

Virginia: Age of consent: male 18, female 16. If a physician certifies that female is pregnant and parent consents, license may be issued. Infants, unless previously married, must have personal or written, acknowledged consent of father, if living, or else of mother; if both be dead, court may authorize license.

Washington: Age of consent: male 14, female 12 (common law). Consent of parent is required when male is under 21 or female is under 18; no consent may be given when female is under 15.[2]

West Virginia: Age of consent: male 18, female 16. Consent of parents is required when either is under 21.

Wisconsin: Age of consent: male 18, female 15. Consent of parent is required when male is under 21 or female is under 18.[3]

For footnotes, see page 413.

Wyoming: Age of consent: male 18, female 16. Consent of parents is required when either party is a minor.

Puerto Rico: Age of consent: male 18, female 16. Parents' consent is required if either party is under 21.

Virgin Islands: Age of consent: male

16, female 14. Personal, or attested, written consent of father, or if dead, mother, or if both are dead, guardian, is required when the male is under 21 or when the female is under 18 and has not been previously married.[11]

RIGHTS AND DUTIES OF HUSBAND AND WIFE

Modern legislation has altered the old common-law rule that regarded husband and wife as one legal unit with the husband having all the rights. The trend is to give equality, although this has not yet been fully accomplished.

Because the husband is head of the family, his name becomes the family name, not by law but by custom. He has the right to determine the place of residence, and the wife must follow him when he changes the residence. This right is not unlimited. He must act reasonably and have proper regard for her comfort, health, safety, and general welfare. He must provide an independent home in which his wife is mistress. He may not compel her to live in a home with members of his family where she is subjected to unwarranted interference in the control and management of the household. Her refusal without proper cause to move to a new domicile selected by him may constitute abandonment or desertion. However, his misconduct may give her the right to establish a different and separate domicile. The circumstances which will give her this right vary in the different states, and her rights depend upon statute.

The husband is under a duty to protect his wife, and has no right to inflict punishment on her.

Both spouses are under a duty to cohabit. Cohabitation includes not only the right to sexual intercourse, but also the right to each other's society, companionship, and affection.

Both parties have the right to complete religious freedom and worship in accordance with their respective beliefs.

---

[1] Wassermann or other standard laboratory blood tests are required for marriage for both applicants in all but the following states: District of Columbia, Maryland, Minnesota, Nevada, South Carolina, Washington (but men must file an affidavit), Puerto Rico (but medical certificate is required), Virgin Islands.

[2] Applicants must wait three days to obtain license to marry.

[2a] License issued fourth day after application.

[3] Applicants must wait five days to obtain license to marry.

[4] Nonresident applicants must wait 96 hours to obtain license to marry. When one party is a resident, they must wait 24 hours. No wait necessary after obtaining license.

[5] Applicants must wait three clear days for license to marry (not counting either day of application or day of issuance).

[6] No waiting period for license if both applicants are 21; if under 21, they must wait five days.

[7] Applicants must wait 48 hours to obtain license to marry.

[8] Applicants must wait 48 hours to obtain license, which should be obtained 24 hours prior to the ceremony. License valid for 30 days.

[9] It is not necessary to wait for any length of time after license is obtained except in New Jersey, where a 24-hour wait is required; in New York, where a 24-hour wait is required and three days must elapse from time of examination and blood test; in Rhode Island, where a five-day wait is required if the woman is a nonresident; and in Vermont, where a five-day wait is required.

[10] Twenty-four-hour wait.

[11] Eight-day wait.

[12] Five-day wait for nonresident woman.

Support; Property Rights; Earnings. The husband has the duty to adequately support and maintain his wife in accordance with his ability, regardless of her own financial means, or of her independent ability to support herself. This duty is a continuing one while the relationship exists, although by statute a husband may be absolved from such responsibility if the wife commits certain statutory matrimonial offenses such as abandonment of him without cause, or adultery.

No like duty rests on the wife. In some states, however, by statute the husband and wife may contract for mutual support, and under some statutes the wife may be chargeable with the support of her husband, if he is destitute and she has financial means.

At common law a wife's earnings belonged to her husband, unless he agreed or consented that she should retain them. In most states this rule has been modified so that in certain cases the wife may retain her earnings without his consent. It is, however, the duty of the wife to render household services to her husband, for which she is not entitled to be paid by him.

Notwithstanding the statutory right to dower and inheritance that a wife may have in some states, at common law the husband's property that he acquired before or after marriage belonged to him and the wife acquired no interest whatever thereto.

Household goods belong to the husband unless the couple has agreed to the contrary. In some states the wife may not remove any household goods without her husband's consent, even if she leaves him because of his misconduct. He may sell his personal property without her consent and may also do the same with his real estate, except in states where the wife has dower rights. In such states her written consent must first be obtained.

At common law the husband acquired the right to his wife's property. In some states, as a result of constitutional or statutory provision, married women retain their rights to the property which they owned before marriage.

In Arizona, California, Idaho, Louisiana, New Mexico, Nevada, Texas, and Washington there are community property laws which in essence provide that all property acquired during marriage by the husband or wife, or both, belongs beneficially to both during the continuance of the marriage relationship.

Liabilities of Husband. The husband is liable for *necessaries* supplied and furnished to the wife. Food, clothing, and medical expenses are necessaries. He is also liable in some states for her *debts* contracted before marriage. However, in some states his liability for such debts is limited to the value of the property received by him from her; in others, statutes expressly release him from all liability for such debts.

Under modern statutes married women are solely liable for *torts* they may commit or have committed. At common law neither may sue the other for torts; but by statute, in some states, such actions may be maintained.

Wills and Inheritance. In most states a married woman may make wills. In some states she may disinherit her husband, in others she may not. In many states the husband cannot completely disinherit his wife, nor may he during his lifetime fraudulently transfer his property in a way that will deprive her of her dower rights or of any other statutory right she may have in his property.

Citizenship Rights. Formerly, in the absence of statute, an alien woman who married a citizen of the United States acquired citizenship automatically. This is no longer the law. It is now provided by Federal statute that "any alien who, after September 21, 1922, and prior to May 24, 1934, has married a citizen of the United States, or any alien who married prior to May 24, 1934, a spouse who was naturalized during such period, and during the existence of the marital relation may, if eligible to naturalization, be naturalized" upon compliance with certain requirements of the naturalization laws but need not file a declaration of intention and must have resided continuously in the United States for at least

one year. "Any alien who on or after May 24, 1934, has married or shall hereafter marry a citizen of the United States, or any alien whose husband or wife
was naturalized on or after May 24, 1934, and during the existence of the marital
relationship or shall hereafter be so naturalized may, if eligible for naturalization, be naturalized" upon compliance with certain requirements of the naturalization laws, but need not file a declaration of intention and must have resided
continuously in the United States at least three years. "The naturalization of any
woman on or after May 24, 1934, by any naturalization court, upon proof of
marriage to a citizen or the naturalization of her husband and proof of but one
year's residence in the United States is validated only so far as relates to the
period of residence required to be proved by such person under the naturalization laws. The naturalization of any male person on or after May 24, 1934, by
any naturalization court, upon proof of marriage to a citizen of the United States
after Sept. 21, 1922, and prior to May 24, 1934, or of the naturalization during
such period of his wife, and upon proof of three years' residence in the United
States is validated only so far as relates to the period of residence required to be
proved by such person under the naturalization laws."

DIVORCE AND SEPARATION

A *divorce* is a dissolution of a marriage for a cause arising after the marriage
was entered into. An *annulment* of a marriage is for a pre-existing cause. A
separation does not dissolve nor annul the marriage; it only separates the parties,
either permanently or temporarily, for a cause arising after the marriage. Separation is sometimes called a limited divorce, or divorce from bed and board.

Since the state has an interest in every marriage, the parties have no right to
dissolve it by themselves. Therefore, an *agreement for a divorce* is invalid on
grounds of public policy.

A divorce or annulment can be obtained only through legal proceeding. A
separation may be obtained by legal proceeding, or, if the parties are living apart,
they may enter into a separation agreement. However, an agreement to separate
in the future made while the parties are living together is void. In no event may
the agreement completely absolve the husband from his obligation to properly
support his wife and children in accordance with his financial ability.

There is *no national law of divorce* or separation in the United States. Each
state by statute has prescribed the grounds for divorce and separation as well as
the residence requirements and forms of procedure.

The right of the guilty party to *remarry* during the lifetime of the former
spouse is regulated by statute. In the absence of statute restricting or prohibiting
remarriage, the guilty party may remarry. In many states, the statute prescribes
a minimum time which must elapse before the guilty party may remarry. A
statute which either completely prohibits remarriage of the guilty party or fixes
a minimum length of waiting time has no extraterritorial effect. To illustrate:
A husband is divorced in a state which prohibits remarriage before the expiration
of a three-year period and leaves the state before the time is up, and remarries
in another state. Then, if the marriage in that state is valid according to the laws
of that state, the marriage is legal, although it is in contravention of the laws of
the state where the divorce was obtained.

Although in most civil actions a judgment by default may be obtained against
the defendant, in matrimonial actions of divorce, annulment, and separation the
plaintiff must establish his or her case before the court even though the defendant fails to contest the action.

A woman who obtains a judgment of divorce may resume her *maiden name*
if she chooses. The court will usually award custody of minor children to the
wife, whether she is plaintiff or defendant, unless she is found not fit, and it may

grant right of visitation to the party who is not awarded custody. In most states, when a wife is granted a judgment of divorce the court will direct the husband to pay her *alimony*, which is an allowance for support and maintenance; generally, the court will not award a wife alimony if the husband obtains such a judgment. In many states, however, the court has discretionary power to award the wife alimony even when it was the husband who obtained the divorce judgment. Such power will be exercised only if circumstances warrant. In all states the court will require the husband to pay for the support and maintenance of minor children, no matter who obtains the judgment of divorce.

The amount of alimony for the wife and/or minor children which the court may require the husband to pay rests on the court's discretion; it will depend on the circumstances of each case. The amount may be increased or decreased on application to the court if changed circumstances warrant.

After divorce the minor children continue to *bear the father's name*. However, under some circumstances, on notice to the father and for good cause shown, the court may permit the name of such minors to be changed, even over the father's objection. This relief is rarely granted. If the mother remarries after obtaining a judgment of divorce and the father fails to pay support for the minors as directed, or otherwise fails to act as a dutiful father, the court may permit the minors to assume the name of the wife's second husband, particularly when children have been born from the second marriage.

The judgment of divorce may be set aside for good cause upon timely application to the court and notice to whichever party obtained the judgment. Fraud or imposition on the court is always a proper ground for obtaining such relief. If the court did not acquire jurisdiction because the plaintiff was not a bona fide resident of the state, or if such plaintiff was a bona fide resident but the defendant was not properly served as required by statute, the judgment will be set aside, even in the absence of fraud. The right to have such judgment vacated may be lost through failure to make timely application to the court, or as a result of affirmative misconduct which would make it inequitable to grant such relief. If parties who have been divorced or separated become reconciled, they may apply to the court to set aside the judgment of divorce or separation. This right, however, is statutory and the procedure is governed by the applicable statute, which must be followed.

In most states a valid judgment of divorce does not become effective until after a statutory period of time, generally fixed in the judgment, has elapsed.

The United States Constitution, Article IV, Section 1, requires each state to give full faith and credit to the judicial proceedings of every other state. This is known as the Full Faith and Credit Clause. In obedience to it, a valid judgment of divorce or separation is valid in every other state, even though the ground for which such judgment was granted is not recognized in such other state.

However, since each state is sovereign, with power to determine whether the state in which such judgment was obtained had proper jurisdiction, another state may refuse to recognize such judgment if it determines that the plaintiff was not in fact a bona fide resident of the state in which it was granted. To illustrate: If a husband, married and matrimonially domiciled in New York, went to Florida or any other state and resided there for whatever period of time the law of that state required before commencing a divorce action there, then served the summons and complaint on the wife in New York, where she had continued to reside, the judgment of divorce in that state would not be recognized in New York if the husband's residence was not bona fide. The wife, however, would have to prove that the husband's residence in the granting state was not bona fide. Determination of such questions by a New York court will depend upon the facts in each case. Temporary sojourn or mere duration of time will not suffice to confer jurisdiction on the granting state. It is the intent to acquire a *permanent* domicile that controls. However, even if the granting state did not have jurisdiction because the plaintiff had not in fact become a bona fide resident of that state, the judgment would be entitled to recognition if the defendant either filed an appearance in that action or otherwise participated as a litigant.

In a recent decision of the United States Supreme Court, the facts were as follows: The wife sued her husband in New York for separation in 1943: after trial she was granted a judgment of separation and he was directed to pay alimony. In January 1944 he went to Nevada, where he started an action for divorce in 1945. The wife did not appear in that action and the husband obtained a final judgment of divorce which did not require him to pay alimony. The husband paid alimony as directed by the New York judgment of separation until he obtained his judgment in Nevada, when he stopped making payments. The wife then sued the husband in New York to recover the arrears. The question to be decided was whether the judgment of separation survived the Nevada judgment for divorce. The majority of the New York court concluded that the Nevada judgment was valid in so far as it affected the marital status of the parties, but that it was invalid with respect to alimony. New York did not have to give full faith and credit to that part of the Nevada judgment because of the interest of the state of New York in abandoned domiciliaries of the state. An abandoned spouse might be left destitute, and so become a public charge.

The grounds for legal separation by court action are usually the same as the grounds for divorce, and in addition cruelty and nonsupport in states which do not recognize these as grounds for divorce.* An annulment is a cancellation of the marriage as if it had never taken place. The grounds are usually those which are the essence of the relationship; see the article on Marriage.

GROUNDS FOR DIVORCE IN THE UNITED STATES

Abandonment. Puerto Rico, Virgin Islands, and all states except New York and North Carolina.[1]

Adultery. All states, Puerto Rico, Virgin Islands.

Alcoholism. Puerto Rico, Virgin Islands, and all states except District of Columbia, Louisiana,[1] Maryland, New Jersey, New York, North Carolina, Pennsylvania, Texas, Vermont, Virginia.

Attempt on Life of Spouse. Illinois, Iowa, Kentucky, Louisiana,[1] Montana, Pennsylvania, Tennessee.

Attempt to Prostitute Wife. Puerto Rico.

Attempt to Prostitute Sons or Daughters. Puerto Rico.

Conviction of Felony. Puerto Rico, Virgin Islands, and all states except Florida, Maine, New Jersey, New York, North Carolina, South Carolina.[2]

Crime (Charged with Infamous Crime and Fled Jurisdiction). Louisiana[1] (proof of guilt required).

Cruel Behavior. Kentucky.

Cruelty. Puerto Rico, Virgin Islands, and all states except Alabama, Louisiana,[1] Maryland, New York, North Carolina, Virginia.

Defamation (Public). Louisiana.[1]

Desertion. See Abandonment.

Disappearance. Connecticut, New Hampshire, New York, Vermont.

Drug Addiction. Alabama, Alaska, Colorado, Hawaii, Maine, Massachusetts, Mississippi, Rhode Island, West Virginia, Puerto Rico.

Falsely Charging Wife Unchaste. Montana.

Force or Duress to Marry. Georgia, Kentucky, Pennsylvania, Washington.

Fraud to Induce Marriage. Connecticut, Georgia, Kansas, Kentucky, Ohio, Oklahoma, Pennsylvania, Washington.

Gross Misbehavior or Wickedness. Rhode Island.

Impotency. Puerto Rico, Virgin Islands, and all states except California,

---

* Some few states do not have any such action.

For footnotes, see page 419.

Connecticut, Delaware, District of Columbia, Hawaii, Idaho, Iowa, Louisiana, Montana, New Jersey, New York, North Dakota, South Carolina, South Dakota, Texas, Vermont, West Virginia.

Incest. Florida, Georgia, Mississippi, Pennsylvania, Rhode Island.

Incompatibility. Alaska, New Mexico, Oklahoma, Virgin Islands. (Also Chihuahua, Mexico.)

Indignities. Alaska, Arizona, Arkansas, Missouri, Oregon, Pennsylvania, Tennessee,[3] Virginia, Washington, Wyoming.

Insanity.[4] Alabama (3), Alaska (1½), Arkansas (3), California (3), Colorado (3), Connecticut (5), Delaware (5), Georgia (3), Hawaii (3), Idaho (6), Indiana (5), Kansas (5), Kentucky (5), Maryland (3), Minnesota (5), Mississippi (3), Montana (5), Nebraska (5), Nevada (2), New Mexico (5), New York (5),[5] North Carolina (10), North Dakota (5), Oklahoma (5), Oregon (3), South Dakota (5), Texas (5), Utah (5), Vermont (5), Washington (2), Wyoming (2), Puerto Rico (7), Virgin Islands (after marriage).

Joining Religious Order Not Believing in Cohabitation. Kentucky, New Hampshire.

Leprosy. Hawaii, Kentucky.

Malformation Preventing Intercourse. Kentucky.

Mental Incapacity. Georgia, Mississippi.

Mental Suffering.[6] Montana, Hawaii.

Nonsupport. Alabama, Alaska, Arkansas, Arizona, California, Colorado, Delaware, Hawaii, Idaho, Indiana, Kansas, Louisiana,[1] Maine, Massachusetts, Michigan, Missouri, Montana, Nebraska, Nevada, New Hampshire, New Mexico, North Dakota, Ohio, Oklahoma, Rhode Island, South Dakota,

Tennessee, Utah, Vermont, Washington, Wisconsin, Wyoming.

Out-of-State Divorce by Other Party. Florida, Michigan.[7]

Pregnancy of Wife at Marriage (Not Known or Caused by Husband). Alabama, Arizona, Georgia, Kansas, Kentucky, Mississippi, Missouri, New Mexico, North Carolina, Oklahoma, Tennessee, Virginia, Wyoming.

Prior Marriage Existing.[8] Arkansas, Colorado, Delaware, Florida, Illinois, Kansas, Mississippi, Missouri, Ohio, Oklahoma, Pennsylvania, Rhode Island, Tennessee.

Refusal to Cohabitate. New Hampshire.

Refusal of Wife to Move to New Residence. Tennessee.

Separation after a Decree of Separation.[9] Alabama (4), Colorado (3), District of Columbia (2), Louisiana (1), Minnesota (5), Utah (3), Wisconsin (5).

Separation (No Cohabitation).[9] Arizona (5), Arkansas (3), Delaware (3), District of Columbia (5), Kentucky (5), Louisiana (2), Maryland (3), Minnesota (5), Nevada (3), North Carolina (2), Rhode Island (10), Texas (7), Vermont (3), Washington (5), Wisconsin (5), Wyoming (2), Puerto Rico (7), Virgin Islands (3).

Under Age of Consent.[10] Rhode Island.

Unnatural Behavior. Alabama, North Carolina, Tennessee.

Willful Neglect. Alaska, Arizona, California, Connecticut, Idaho, Kansas, Kentucky, Maine, Massachusetts, Michigan, Montana, Nebraska, Nevada, North Dakota, Ohio, Oklahoma, Rhode Island, South Dakota, Tennessee, Utah, Vermont, Washington, Wisconsin, Wyoming.

RESIDENCE REQUIREMENTS FOR DIVORCE

Six Weeks. Idaho, Nevada, Virgin Islands.

Sixty Days. Wyoming.
Three Months. Utah.

For footnotes, see page 419.

Six Months. Florida, Georgia, Maine, North Carolina, Oklahoma.

One Year. Alabama,[1] Alaska, Arizona, California, Colorado,[2] Illinois, Indiana, Iowa, Kansas, Kentucky, Louisiana, Maryland, Michigan, Minnesota, Mississippi, Missouri, Montana, New Hampshire, New Mexico, North Dakota, Ohio, Oregon, Pennsylvania, South Carolina, South Dakota, Tennessee, Texas, Vermont, Virginia, Washington, Wisconsin, Puerto Rico.[3]

Two Years. Delaware, District of Columbia, Hawaii, Nebraska, New Jersey, Rhode Island, West Virginia.

Three Years. Connecticut.

Five Years. Massachusetts.

No Time Requirement. New York;[4] Chihuahua, Mexico.[5]

CHILDREN

Both parents are legally liable for the support of their young children. While a father has a primary obligation to support, courts recognize increasingly that both parents share this responsibility. Where the father is incapacitated or deceased, the mother has the primary support duty. If she is unable to support her children, she may apply for financial assistance to her local or state welfare office.

The mother of a child born out of wedlock may institute paternity proceedings in a court of competent jurisdiction, and, if paternity is established, the father can be compelled to support or to contribute toward the child's support. Where paternity has not been judicially determined, a father may voluntarily support his out-of-wedlock child. Sometimes contracts for support are entered into by supposed fathers. Where paternity has not been established and the

[1] Unless one party is domiciled in state and court has jurisdiction of both. Courts of this state have now held that even a party who has appeared and defaulted may question whether the other party was actually domiciled in state.

[2] Except adultery or extreme cruelty committed in the state.

[3] Unless grounds arose in Puerto Rico or while one spouse resided there.

[4] Court has jurisdiction if both parties were resident when offense was committed, or parties were married in the state, or plaintiff was a resident when offense was committed and action brought, or offense was committed in state and injured party was a resident when action commenced.

[5] In this state of Mexico, residence is established by signing the proper Municipal Roll. While in states of the United States residence in divorce statutes means domicile (place of home), residence in Chihuahua means merely residence. Divorces obtained in Chihuahua where one party is actually present and has signed the roll and the other party appears by attorney are recognized in some states of the United States, including New York.

FOOTNOTES TO LISTING OF GROUNDS FOR DIVORCE IN THE UNITED STATES

[1] In Louisiana these are grounds for separation, and if parties are not reconciled within one year divorce can be entered automatically.

[2] Some states require certain minimum sentence and/or minimum service in penitentiary.

FOOTNOTES TO LISTING OF RESIDENCE REQUIREMENTS FOR DIVORCE

[3] Discretionary with court.

[4] Number in parentheses indicates years insanity must have existed before suit commenced. Party claimed insane must be confined to institution or adjudicated. The insanity must be incurable.

[5] Called annulment.

[6] In some states, mental suffering constitutes cruelty.

[7] Discretionary.

[8] In other jurisdictions this is ground for annulment.

[9] Number after name of state indicates years of separation necessary.

[10] In other states marriage absolutely void or ground for annulment.

alleged father does not voluntarily support the child, the mother remains liable for the child's support.

If any parent neglects to furnish necessaries to a minor child,[1] a stranger who supplies such necessaries may compel payment from the parent by legal action. The parent's obligation to pay will be implied.

Ordinarily the parental obligation for child support is limited to minors who are living in the parent's household. However, the liability for child support extends to a child living in foster care. Moreover, the duty may continue even though the other parent has custody and the child is living in the other household. When a child voluntarily leaves the parent's home to make his own way in the world, the parental duty of support would continue if the child in fact could not achieve self-support. Where such a child becomes a public charge or is in danger of becoming a public charge, welfare officials may institute court action to compel parental support. Then the question would arise in the individual case as to whether the child would be expected to return to the parental home.

The duty to support rests only upon the natural parents. A stepfather is not legally bound to pay for the support of his stepchildren, except where statute imposes such obligation.

Generally, an adult child whose parent is a public charge or is likely to become a public charge has a legal obligation imposed by statute to support or contribute toward the support of that parent.

The earnings of a minor child generally belong to the father, but infants who receive gifts, or acquire property by will, retain them; the parent has no right to such property except by inheritance.

Adoption. In the United States adoption is achieved by judicial decree. The proceedings are governed by statutory provisions, and courts generally hold that these statutes are to be strictly construed. Traffic in babies is frequently referred to as "adoption black markets." It is advisable for persons who wish to adopt children to consult with local welfare departments. Many social agencies exist for the purpose of helping to effect valid adoptions.

The natural parents are relieved from their legal obligation to support a child who is adopted by others; the obligation is assumed by the adopting parents. In many states an adopted child may inherit from his adoptive parents.

Children Born Out of Wedlock. Children of an unmarried mother may be legitimized in several ways. Public acknowledgment by the father is sufficient in some states; in others adoption is necessary. In some states legitimacy may be established through judicial proceedings. The subsequent marriage of the child's parents to each other often results in legitimation. In many states, by statute, birth certificates need not contain the statement that an infant is illegitimate, and need not contain the marital status of the mother. The name of the supposed father of a child born out of wedlock may not be entered without his consent.

Guardianship. In most states guardianship proceedings are regulated by statute. In some states infants over a certain age may choose their guardians, subject to the court's approval. The relationship between the guardian and his ward is personal and sacred. Trust and a confidential relationship occur between the ward and his guardian, who owes the ward the highest degree of fidelity. The guardian is expected to act in his ward's best interest.

All states have statutory provisions regarding the welfare of children who are deprived of parental care. Specific courts are given jurisdiction over such children.

---

[1] A minor child or infant, as prescribed by law, is a child who has not attained the age of majority. The age of majority varies in the several states. At common law, the infant reaches majority at age 21, except where a different age is prescribed by statute.

Children Affected by Divorce of Parents. In divorce actions, the court has broad discretionary power to award custody of an infant to either party. Courts are likely to grant custody of young children to the mother unless there is substantial proof of her unfitness. The primary consideration in determining to whom custody is awarded is the best interest and welfare of the child. The child's preference will be considered if he or she is of sufficient age and intelligence; however, the child does not control the decision. Custody and support provisions in divorce decrees are considered as temporary. If subsequent events prove that the child's best interests require a change, the court, after taking testimony, will make other custodial provision.

For aid to dependent children, see Social Security Act.

WILLS

A will expresses a person's desire concerning the guardianship of his children, the administration of his estate, and the distribution of his property after his death. It is called a testamentary instrument.

A *codicil* is also a testamentary instrument which modifies a prior will in some particular, as by revoking a prior disposition of some or all of the property, or by enlarging or reducing a legacy, by making an entirely new legacy, or by changing the guardian, the trustee of any trust, or the executors.

A male person making a will is called a *testator,* a female a *testatrix.*

The person charged by the testator or testatrix with the responsibility of carrying out the terms of a will is called an *executor,* if male, and an *executrix,* if female.

A will can be made by any competent person of sound mind. No special mental capacity is required. A person is competent if he has the capacity to understand the nature and extent of his property, to know the relationship of those who would naturally be the object of his bounty, and to know and understand what he is doing.

Generally, statutes in the various states provide that persons over 18 may make wills relating to personal property and those over 21 wills relating to real property.

Wills must be executed in the form and manner prescribed by statute. In most states a will must be in writing, and subscribed at the physical end of the document, and signed in the presence of witnesses[1]; if it is not subscribed in the presence of such witnesses, the testator must acknowledge the will.[2] The witnesses must sign their names in the presence of the testator.

Oral wills, called *nuncupative wills,* are valid as to personal property only if made by a soldier while in actual military service, or by a mariner while at sea.

The number of witnesses required is fixed by statute—either two or three. They need not know the terms of the will. Their signatures merely attest to the fact that the testator was then of sound mind. In some states a witness cannot be a legatee.

A will may be printed, typed, or handwritten. No special language need be used. Statutory formalities must be strictly complied with and the testator's wishes must be clearly stated. A lawyer should be consulted before a will is made; he should prepare it and attend to its proper execution. Thousands of

---

[1] The testator must also declare to the witnesses that he is signing a will and request them to sign as witnesses. In some states a clause setting forth the signing, the declaration, the fact that the witnesses heard the declaration and saw the testator and other witnesses sign is required for the will to be valid to affect real property. It is always safest that such a clause, called an attestation clause, be added.

[2] Such acknowledgment is not acceptable in many states.

wills have been declared invalid because they were not prepared by lawyers. Lay persons cannot be expected to know the necessary statutory provisions.

Wills and codicils may be executed on any day, including Sundays and legal holidays.

Upon the death of the testator the will must be *probated, i.e.,* proved in a special court, in some states called a surrogate's court, in others a probate court. When proof is submitted that the will was executed with all legal requirements, a decree is made admitting the will to probate. The person designated as executor, after duly qualifying to act, marshalls the assets of the estate and, after first paying all debts and administration expenses (including Federal and state inheritance taxes) distributes the estate in accordance with the terms of the will. In some cases the inheritance tax is not payable from estate assets, but from individual legacies. After attending to all this, the executor files his account, which must be judicially approved.

The will should dispose of all property of the testator. When a will does not make specific disposition of particular property it is advisable to have a *residuary clause* to provide for disposition of such property. If there is no such clause the residue of the estate will be disposed of as if the person had died without a will.

A person may make any disposition of his property he wishes, except that in some states he may not completely disinherit his wife and children.

If a testator does not wish to give outright his wife or children complete control of money or property, but wishes to regulate the use of such property, a *trust* should be set up. It is often advisable to have a corporate trustee, because if an individual is designated his death would unnecessarily delay the administration of the estate. A trustee must also file his account and have it judicially settled.

Estate tax laws must be carefully considered in the preparation of wills. Failure to take advantage of the provisions thereof can result in the payment of taxes that might be avoided. See the chapter on Taxes.

WILL[1]

I, JOHN DOE, of (city) ———, (state), ——— being of sound and disposing mind and memory, do hereby make, publish and declare this to be my Last Will and Testament, and hereby revoke all Wills and Codicils by me at any time heretofore made.

First: I direct all my just debts, funeral and testamentary expenses be paid by the executrix hereinafter named as soon as conveniently may be after my decease.

Second: I give, devise and bequeath unto my son, JAMES DOE, Ten Thousand Dollars ($10,000).

Third: All the rest, residue and remainder of my estate, both real and personal, of whatsoever kind and nature, and wheresoever the same may be situate, of which I shall be seized or possessed, or to which I may in any way be entitled at the time of my death, I give, devise and bequeath unto my beloved wife, MARY DOE, to be hers absolutely.

In the event that my said wife shall predecease me, or that we shall die in the same accident, then in either of such events, I hereby give, devise and bequeath my entire residuary estate to my son, JAMES DOE.[2]

---

[1] This is only a suggested form. The reader is advised to secure a form, valid in his state, from a lawyer or legal stationer for use on a specific occasion.

[2] In some states statutes provide that in the event of simultaneous death the testator is presumed to have survived unless the will provides otherwise. Some-

In the event that my said wife shall predecease me, or that we shall die simultaneously or under such circumstances as to render it difficult or impossible to determine who died first, and in the event also that my son, JAMES DOE, shall not survive me, then I give, devise and bequeath my entire residuary estate as aforesaid to my brother, CHARLES DOE, of the city of ———, state of ———.

Fourth: I hereby nominate and appoint my wife, MARY DOE, to be executrix of this, my Will, and I direct that she be permitted to qualify as such without the giving of a bond or other security, in any jurisdiction. In the event that my wife, MARY DOE, shall fail to qualify, or cease to act as such executrix, then I nominate and appoint the A. B. C. TRUST COMPANY OF NEW YORK, or its successors, to be executor of this my Will, it also to be permitted to act without bond or other security. I authorize said A. B. C. TRUST COMPANY or its successors, to sell and convey, at public or private sale, all or any of my real estate, on such terms, prices, considerations and conditions as it shall deem to be for the best interests of my estate.

In witness whereof, I have hereunto subscribed my name and affixed my seal this ——— day of ———, 19–.

Witnesses: *John Doe* (seal)

   John Jones
   Henry Smith
   Charles Green

The foregoing instrument was subscribed by the above named testator, JOHN DOE, at the city of ———, county of ———, state of ———, on this ——— day of ———, in the year one thousand nine hundred and ——— in our presence, and was at the same time and place published and declared by him to us to be his Last Will and Testament, and thereupon we, at his request, and in his presence, and in the presence of each other, did subscribe our names thereto as attesting witnesses, this attestation clause having first been read aloud to us in the presence of said testator.

Names		*Residences*
John Jones	No. ———,	——— Street, (city), (state)
Henry Smith	No. ———,	——— Street, (city), (state)
Charles Green	No. ———,	——— Street, (city), (state)

CODICIL.[1]

I, JOHN DOE, of the city of ———, county of ———, state of ———, having made my Last Will and Testament bearing date the ——— day of ———, in the year one thousand nine hundred and ———, do now make and publish this Codicil thereto which is to be taken as an addition to and a part of my Last Will and Testament.

First: I revoke the legacy of Ten Thousand Dollars ($10,000) to my son, JAMES DOE, and give him in lieu thereof 100 shares of common stock in the X. Y. Z. Corporation, now in my safe deposit vault in the A. B. C. Trust Company in New York.

---

times for tax reasons or otherwise it is preferable that the named beneficiary be presumed to have survived.

[1] This is only a suggested form. The reader is advised to secure a form, valid in his state, from a lawyer for use on a specific occasion.

Second: I hereby give, devise, and bequeath Ten Thousand Dollars ($10,000) to the D. E. F. Foundation, Inc.

And I hereby ratify and confirm my Last Will and Testament in every respect save so far as any part of the same is inconsistent with this Codicil.

In witness whereof at the end of this Codicil to my Last Will and Testament I have subscribed my name and affixed my seal this ———— day of ————, one thousand nine hundred and ————.

John Doe (seal)

Subscribed by the above mentioned testator in the presence of each of us and at the same time declared by him to be a codicil to his Last Will and Testament, and thereupon we, at his request, and in his presence, and in the presence of each other, signed our names as subscribing witnesses.

Witnesses:

John L. Jones	No. ———, ———— Street, (city), (state)
Charles Green	No. ———, ———— Street, (city), (state)

PUBLIC SCHOOLS

The public school system of the United States is both new and unique. It is a product of the past century; and the secondary portion, the American high school, is chiefly the product of the past 60 years. American schools have shown, more than most others, a concern for the student's personal development and have tried to adjust their work to the interests and needs of individuals. The length of the publicly offered program is greater than in most other countries; elementary school is available to all in most nations, but in few others are so many students—currently, some 9,500,000 annually—offered secondary education as in the United States.

The standard portion of the school program consists of 12 grades. For administrative purposes, this is often divided into an eight-grade elementary school and a four-year high school. In thousands of districts, however, there are three divisions: a six-grade elementary school, a three-year junior high school, and a three-year senior high school. An impressive start has also been made toward extending the school system downward, to include the kindergarten and sometimes the nursery school. Also, the movement to establish two-year community colleges as part of the public school system is well under way.

The most recent trends in public education include the use of automated devices and television in teaching and of teaching teams rather than individual instructors. An emphasis, since 1958 particularly, on more and better teaching of science, mathematics, and foreign languages in both elementary and high schools has been notable. Earlier emphases have continued, however, among them:

1. Increased attention to the so-called "three R's"
2. An improved program of citizenship education
3. Safety education and driver training
4. Instruction in family living
5. Increased attention to cultural and spiritual values
6. Cultivation of international understanding
7. Consumer education and thrift
8. Greater use of audio-visual materials and devices in education
9. Education for the conservation and wise use of natural resources.

Currently attending the nation's schools are some 38,000,000 students, 28,-500,000 of them in elementary schools. Annual enrollment has continued to increase; by 1962 it had risen for the 17th consecutive year.

EDUCATION AS A STATE FUNCTION

Operation and Control. Each state is in charge of education within its borders. The public schools are operated and controlled, therefore, according to *state* law.

In practice, most of the states delegate much of their authority to local school districts. These districts are of many sizes and types, ranging from small communities with a single one-teacher school to the largest cities and counties. Sometimes school districts cut across county and city boundaries, to take in part or all of two or more units of local government. The trend to reorganize and consolidate the small school districts, however, continues year by year.

The governing body for the local school system is a board of education of three or more members. Boards with five or seven members are common; they are usually the recommended type for districts other than the very smallest and the very largest. Authority is given to the local school board to determine school expenditures in the district, employ the school staff, and generally oversee the local schools. Although its powers and duties are subject to state law, this board has much to do with the scope and quality of education in its district. The administrative officer who carries out the policies and directives of the board is usually known as the superintendent of schools, almost always a professionally trained person.

Because education is a state function rather than a Federal responsibility, practices, as one would expect, vary from one state to another. The sizes and types of school districts vary. The amount of state aid may range from almost none to more than four-fifths of the total school expenditures. Requirements are far from uniform for the certificates or licenses of teachers and other professional employees. Different textbooks and teaching materials are recommended, and different standards for schoolhouse construction are approved. Yet in spite of these and other differences, the general pattern of schooling is strikingly similar in the various states. In general, all children who are physically and mentally able to do so are required to attend an approved school, either public or private, from the ages of about six to 16 years.

Public education in the United States continues to grow more expensive year by year. The increase in enrollments and the rising prices for professional services and goods have raised the cost of the public elementary and high-school system to more than $15,000,000,000 annually. In only one category of expense has there been a recent decrease: in capital expenditures by local school systems for land, school buildings, and teaching equipment; in 1959–60 it went down from the previous year for the first time since 1945.

With reference to average daily attendance, the annual expenditure per pupil in 1959–60 was $376, an increase of 10 per cent over the cost of $341 in 1957–58.

The sources of funds for the public schools during the 1959–60 period were: local government, 54.1 per cent; state government, 39.4 per cent; Federal government, 4.4 per cent; and county and other intermediate school districts, 2.1 per cent. These funds included school taxes and legislative appropriations, but not receipts from loans and sales of bonds.

Requirements for Teachers. Except in rare instances, teachers are not employed under civil service but can enter their profession only after obtaining a teaching certificate, or license. In nearly all cases, this certificate is now issued by state departments of education, after the applicant has completed certain required professional preparation. Requirements vary greatly from state to state, also within a state, for different kinds of work; for instance, 37 states grant a regular certificate to beginning teachers in elementary schools only if they have a bachelor's degree.

Teachers are usually employed under written contracts, often with standard contract forms issued by the state departments of education. As a rule, initial contracts are valid for one year. After a specified probationary period of about two years, the contracts in many states become continuous and can be breached only for good cause sustained in public hearings or in the courts. Where such contracts are authorized, teachers are said to have "tenure." The form and duration of contracts, as with teaching certificates or licenses, are determined by state law, varying widely from state to state.

The number of public-school teachers, principals, supervisors, and superintendents went up from 1,340,000 in 1957–58 to an estimated 1,526,000 during 1960–61. The average annual salary of classroom teachers in 1960–61, according to the National Education Association, was $5,215. For the entire staff of professional persons employed in the public schools, the average salary was $5,389.

The average age of teachers is about 41 years, while that of superintendents is 52 years. The average age of beginning teachers is estimated at 24. Most of the teachers, 70 per cent of the men and 62 per cent of the women, are married.

ADULT EDUCATION

Continuing education is one of this nation's best wealth-producing resources. It is an essential force for meeting the challenges posed by the explosive growth of knowledge, the increasing complexity of society, and the changing needs of each individual. The world is changing at a staggering rate. Each scientific and technical "breakthrough" seems to produce a chain reaction of new knowledge and new opportunities. Today we must learn to meet these challenges of modern living in order to insure our security, productivity, and adaptability in a society facing changing conditions. The growth in knowledge and the frequent and continuous change it engenders means that man must learn new ideas, new facts, new skills, new attitudes, and new patterns of living to keep up with the flow of life.

Lifelong learning for all adults is essential in the modern complex society. The pace of living has become faster and the world is shrinking, thus requiring better and faster decisions. Informed, dynamic leadership and vision are essential to strengthen the relations between industry, labor, government, and the consuming public.

Another factor in the need for lifelong learning is the continuous change in the individual. At each stage in the life cycle, one feels the need for further learning because of greater opportunities. The urge to learn becomes more intense to qualify for promotion, to contribute more to family and community life. A person who quits learning is surrendering to an idea of limited usefulness, limited satisfaction, and limited happiness. He is contributing to his own bewilderment and adding to the feeling of insecurity in a fast-moving world. The real purpose of continuing education is self-realization, improvement in the quality of living. This requires a concern for good human relations, economic efficiency, effective family living, and civic responsibility. Lifelong learning can engender a feeling of significance, a sense of creativeness, intellectual curiosity, and knowledge of one's purpose as a citizen in a free society.

More adults are engaged in trade, business, professional, and technical adult education than in any other one type of education. The training currently offered includes management development for top executives, such as the Institute of Humanistic Studies for Executives at the University of Pennsylvania and the Creativity Conference for Heads of Leading American Corporations at the University of California; foreman and supervisory training; labor education programs at many universities; studies in international affairs and in great books; as well as the study of typing, store management, and machine-shop practice for technicians. An estimated 5,000,000 adults took part in face-to-face class-room work in 1961. This estimate does not include correspondence study, on-the-job training, education by radio and television, or educational programs that are primarily social, religious, or recreational. In addition to group instruction, more than 6,000 companies are using employee correspondence courses. Most such courses are in vocational or professional subjects that can be translated directly into increased earning power. Universities, government agencies, business and industry, and more than 500 independent correspondence schools are in the business of individual instruction. Further expansion by this method is expected because people can study at their own convenience and pace, progress according to ability, and learn to become more self-reliant and systematic by doing something on their own.

About 53 per cent of the participants in all types of adult education are women. In the area of trade, business, or technical courses, females account for about 34 per cent of the participants. By occupation, the highest number of participants are in professional, technical, clerical, and sales positions; these groups account for about half the total participants. The next highest occupational groups are craftsmen, foremen, and operative employees, who account for one-fourth of the total participation in face-to-face adult education.

More and more business and industrial corporations adopt the philosophy of providing initial and continuing training and other educational opportunities for their employees. Business firms are assigning larger staffs and increasing facilities to provide a greater variety of educational opportunities. Programs are offered in the plants, and in many cases employees are sent to training centers. The American Management Association trains more than 75,000 persons a year, and private technical institutes reach an equal number.

Recognizing the shortage of trained professional engineers, technicians, and other workers, business and industry have expanded their training programs. A spot check in 1956 showed that more post-doctoral training was going on in programs under business and industrial sponsorship than in all the universities. This was substantiated in 1957 by the study of educational programs of 500 leading American corporations by Harold F. Clark and Harold S. Sloan in their book, "Classrooms in the Factories." Programs in job training, supervisory training, management development, technical and professional training, special educational activities, and general education continue to grow. Many business, industrial, and professional groups use closed-circuit television to present new information, new products, and new developments.

At least 20 universities maintain residential continuation centers for adults. These centers are designed primarily for men and women who wish to spend relatively short periods of time in intensive and serious study of problems related to their professional, civic, or cultural interests by means of conferences, seminars, workshops, and other educational experiences. Follow-up meetings are encouraged. Among the largest users of these continuing education centers are groups of business and industrial employees, who become fulltime students for short periods in such fields as banking, insurance, legislation, economics, international relations, engineering, mining, missiles, analysis of food additives, liberal arts, and many others.

The most widely used source of information about adult education is probably the local library. Larger libraries will have books, pamphlets, magazines, and films on the subject. Many agencies such as public schools, evening colleges, university extension divisions, and state departments of education have staff members who provide information about adult education. Sources of information on the national level are: Adult Education Association of the U.S.A., 743 North Wabash Avenue, Chicago, Ill.; the U.S. Office of Education, Adult Education Section, Department of Health, Education, and Welfare, Washington 25,

D.C.; the National University Extension Association, University of Minnesota, Minneapolis; and the Council of National Organizations, 303 Lexington Avenue, New York 16, N.Y.

Adult classes are one of the least expensive forms of education. Where public school boards of education pay the cost of supervision and overhead, studies show that some courses are free while others cost the enrollee from $3 to $7, although the fee for a few highly specialized courses may range from $15 to $30. Individuals taking college-credit courses toward a degree for three semester hours may pay from $30 to $90. Institutes and training conferences may run from $5 to $50, depending on the length of time involved and the complexity of the material. Some courses, however, may run as high as $1,000 a month. The in-service training offered by business and industry is probably the largest single type of adult education program, and because of the great value both to employer and employee, there is generally no cost to the trainee.

The 1960's present a challenge which, if met with foresight and intelligent planning, can result in the most prosperous period the nation has ever known. This will require a program for improving the skills of the nation's work force. The fact that women will constitute more than half of the expected 10,000,000 increase in the labor force during this decade demands provision of more opportunities to acquire skills and of plans to utilize more women in the many occupations in which relatively few are employed today.

Lifelong learning for all requires many approaches, and the swift pace of modern life creates both urgent and continuing needs for knowledge that will serve the American people in the years to come.

INVITATIONS

Noteworthy events in the course of business are often celebrated by formal receptions, luncheons, banquets, etc. In such cases the invitations should be in keeping with the occasion; that is, they, too, should be formal. The examples shown below indicate the general style which should be followed.

The Retail Lumbermen's Association of Philadelphia

requests the pleasure of your company

at its Twenty-fifth Anniversary

on Wednesday, the thirtieth of April

at half after six o'clock

in the Rose Garden of the Bellevue-Stratford

R.s.v.p.
Charles P. Maule
2500 South Street

Reproduced by courtesy of the Bailey, Banks & Biddle Company of Philadelphia, Pa.

First National Bank of Philadelphia
requests the pleasure of your company at a
Luncheon to be served at the Banking House
Tuesday, January the twelfth, 19
between twelve o'clock noon and one o'clock P.M.

Livingston E. Jones
President

R.s.v.p.

(SEAL)

The Officers and Directors

of the

Federal Reserve Bank of Cleveland

and the

Waterville Branch

invite you to

attend the official opening of the new

Waterville Branch Building

Friday afternoon, October seventeenth

nineteen hundred and _____

at three o'clock

Five hundred fifteen Julia street

VISITING CARDS

A man's social cards should always have "Mr." in front of the name, and the name should always be written out in full. The address may be added, but nothing else.

The rule for business cards is somewhat different. The title is usually omitted, its place being taken by an announcement of the company represented in the lower left-hand corner. Examples of good practice in business cards are shown below.

Charles M. Kinsolving

Rhoades & Company
Members of the New York Stock Exchange

27 William Street
New York City

NATIONAL FOLDING BOX COMPANY

CHAMPE S. ANDREWS
DIRECTOR OF SALES

MAIN OFFICE AND FACTORY
NEW HAVEN, CONNECTICUT

MR. FRANK BRADLEY HARDER

Reproduced by courtesy of the Bailey, Banks & Biddle Company of Philadelphia, Pa.

HARVEY WILSON

REPRESENTING
THE BABCOCK & WILCOX TUBE CO.
PACKARD BUILDING
PHILADELPHIA, PA.

W. WALTER WILSON

PRESIDENT
FIRST MILTON NATIONAL BANK   MILTON, PA.

Reproduced by courtesy of the Bailey, Banks & Biddle Company of Philadelphia, Pa.

LETTERS

Business letters give the writer a valuable opportunity to multiply his personal efforts in dealing with customers and others. Consequently, no letter should be looked on as routine. Each letter should reflect the same positive attitude a businessman would use in dealing in person with an important individual.

The majority of business letters can be written effectively if the writer will adopt a few simple rules: (1) know what you want to say; (2) reveal the subject of the letter to the reader as quickly as possible; (3) always remember that the most important person to the reader is himself, so present the subject from the viewpoint of the reader's self-interest.

Certain types of letters, such as letters of application, adjustment letters, and sales letters, require special handling because of the attitude of the recipient. Such letters are often written by experts, but the ordinary business letter is a fairly simple matter. Simply follow the three rules stated above.

Beginning a Letter. The first sentence of a letter usually indicates whether or not the writer has a clear idea of what he is driving at. In order to let his correspondent know at once, the writer may place a line by itself at the right between the heading and the body of the letter, reading: "Subject: Your order of December 16"; or if the letter, though addressed to a firm, should go to a specific person or department: "Attention of Mr. Brownell," or "Mail Order Department."

The openings given below are good examples of brief but clear and definite ways to begin a letter:

Thank you for your letter of April 21.

Your letter of May 5 was very helpful.

Upon receipt of your letter of July 9 concerning the sale of the lot on the northeast corner of Hulton and Franklin streets, I discussed the title fully with Messrs. Mann and Graham.

We appreciate your request for a copy of our catalog.

The information you requested in your letter of June 20 is enclosed. I believe you will find the specifications on page 3 of particular interest.

It is a pleasure to enclose the information you requested.

Your comments about the burglary insurance on the laboratory are very pertinent. I agree that . . .

I enjoyed our telephone conversation of this morning. This letter will confirm our verbal agreement about . . .

In this letter I would like to take up a number of points regarding the title closing:

1. . . . . .
2. . . . . .
3. . . . . .
4. . . . . .

The reason I may seem insistent about making an appointment with you for October 2 is that I believe you cannot afford to remain without . . .

I am enclosing a copy of a letter I wrote you on December 9. As I have not received an answer to it, I assume that the original never reached you.

So much has been written about phrases to be avoided in the beginning of a letter that it ought not to be necessary to say anything about them here. "Yours of the 31st ult. to hand and contents noted" does exactly what the beginning of a letter should do, but there are two objections to it: it is old-fashioned, like "Your esteemed favor"; it is not personal and, therefore, lacks individuality.

Ending a Letter. The middle of an ordinary letter should present no special difficulties if the writer exercises the usual care, but the ending he may find awkward. It is hard to take leave gracefully. The main thing to avoid is trailing dimly off into space. Always end with a complete sentence. Do not write:

> Hoping to hear from you soon,
> Sincerely yours,

but:

> May we hear from you soon?
> Sincerely yours,

If the letter is long, there should be a summary of its main points at the end. Above all, the ending, like the beginning, should be clear-cut and definite. Such endings are the following:

Let me thank you for your splendid cooperation in this matter.

Will you give me all this information as soon as you get it?

Let us get together one day next week—I suggest Thursday at my Fifth Avenue office at two o'clock—and talk the whole matter over.

I hope you can see me on Wednesday.

I hope the delay has caused you no inconvenience.

I am sure that with your cooperation we shall be able to handle this sale in a way that will be profitable to all of us.

May I hear from you about this?

If you are willing to do this, I think we can demonstrate to your satisfaction that it will be a profitable plan for you.

I await further word from you.

Thank you for all the trouble you have taken in the matter.

Will you please let me know just what the situation is?

I trust your judgment and leave the matter entirely in your hands.

If you will send a duplicate sheet, I think we can straighten out the whole matter.

If we can be of any further help in the matter, please let us know.

Please send us the above information at the earliest possible moment so that we may avoid delay in delivering the material.

Form of Letters. There are very few standard rules for the arrangement of the letter on the page.

The margins should be regular, with a little more space at the bottom than at the sides. Either the block style or the indented style illustrated on the following pages is good. If the letter is short, it should be placed a little above the center of the page, with generous side margins. Ordinarily the side margins should be from an inch to an inch and a half wide, with indentations of an additional inch. If the letter is more than one page long, the margin at the bottom should be almost one and a half times those at the sides.

For the sake of clearness, it is a good general rule to give each idea a separate paragraph, but simple ideas of kindred sorts may be considered and treated as one idea and grouped in a single paragraph. Too many paragraphs make a letter choppy in appearance and give equal stress to important and unimportant ideas.

Use a double space between paragraphs, a single space between lines. This sets off the paragraph effectively and keeps the expression of a single idea compact within a small area.

Emphasis may be obtained by underlining, by typing in capitals or red letters, or through other similar devices which are good as long as they are used sparingly. Do not try to gain emphasis through startling variations from the conventional form. A good letter does not attract too much attention to itself. Arrange your material naturally. If you have to state facts and make comments, begin with the facts. If your letter contains a résumé of events or transactions, the chronological arrangement is the natural one.

The only safe rule in business correspondence is: *One letter, one subject.* It is probable that the different topics of a letter may require the attention of different persons or departments in the organization. Also, the filing system may demand that a letter on two subjects be filed in two different places.

Very few business letters need be more than one page long, though, of course, there is no definite rule. No letter is complete until it has given all the necessary information. This may take half a page or it may take 20 pages.

It is not good practice to use more than one printed letterhead. Subsequent pages should be of plain paper of the same quality and size as the first.

Never send a letter that is blurred, blotted, or disfigured with erasures.

If you have forgotten something, do not add it in a postscript. Rewrite the letter.

Fold the letter so that it will be easy to open. Do not bring the edges exactly together.

The envelope is the last part of the letter to receive your attention but it is the first to attract that of your correspondent. Insufficient postage, irregular punctuation, awkward spacing, the omission of "Mr.," strongly colored paper or ink may prejudice the recipient against the letter even before he opens it.

There are certain essentials of every letter, whether it be long or short. They are:

1. *Heading.* In most business houses the heading is printed on the stationery; but whether printed, typed, or written by hand, the heading consists of the name and address of the firm and the date. Of course if an individual is writing, it consists simply of his address and the date. The day of the month and the complete number of the year (not just '62) should be given.

2. *Address.* This consists of the name and address of the person to whom the letter is written and should be the same both outside and inside the letter. It is the modern custom to use as little punctuation as possible. The address should be clear. If house numbers immediately precede street numbers, the shortest number should be written out in full. Not 117 7 Street, but 117 Seventh Street. The state abbreviation approved by the Post Office Department (see Abbreviations) should be used. The name of the state should never be omitted. There are a dozen Bostons, a dozen and a half Brooklyns, and two dozen Washingtons in the United States. "City" is not sufficient, even if the sender lives in New York, Chicago, or Boston. The name of the city should be written out in full, and the postal zone number should be designated.

The title of respect should never be omitted before the name of the addressee, and, if possible, it should be the right one. Many men with thoroughly illegible handwritings have been offended when their scrawls have been misread and replies have come addressed to "Miss" instead of "Mr." So and So. Other titles in good use besides the ordinary "Mr.," "Mrs.," and "Miss" are the Reverend, Doctor, Professor, Honorable (abbreviated to the Rev., Dr., Prof., Hon.), but no name should be preceded by more than one title. If the name is followed by "Esq.," use no title before it; *e.g.:*

John B. Reynolds, Esq.

In the United States a woman should not be addressed by her husband's title. The wife of a physician is not Mrs. Dr. Hubbard, but simply Mrs. Hubbard.

If you are writing to a person in a special position or department, the letter will be delivered more promptly if a line is added designating the position or department. For instance:

Mr. Frank D. Whitney
Manager, Collection Department
Mallory, Barret and Co.
119 Peachtree Street
Atlanta 3, Ga.

3. *Salutation.* This varies with the type of letter. "Dear Sir:", "Dear Mr. Roe:", and "Gentlemen:" are all good for most purposes. In addressing women the corresponding forms are "Dear Madam:", "Dear Miss Roe:", and "Ladies:". For special types of salutation see the section on official letters later in this article. In business communications the salutation is usually followed by a colon.

In some fields of business an effort is being made to eliminate the word "Dear" in the salutation. A common substitute is "Good morning, Mr. Jones:"

4. *Body of the letter.*

5. *Complimentary close.* In business the following forms are commonly used:

> Yours sincerely,
> Sincerely yours,
> Very truly yours,
> Yours truly,
> Faithfully yours,

Such a closing as "Yours respectfully" should not be used unless the letter is addressed to someone in a position that commands respect, such as a Senator or a governor. "Yours gratefully," or "Yours cordially," should not be used unless there is a genuine reason for it. "Earnestly yours," "Cooperatively yours," and the like are sometimes recommended, but it is better for a beginner to stick to "Yours sincerely."

If you are asking for a favor, do not send thanks in advance. To do so takes the favor for granted and destroys the receiver's pleasure in conferring it.

6. *Signature.* The signature of a letter, like all business signatures, should be legible. It should be written with black or blue ink, not with pencil nor with a rubber stamp. Business women often put "Mrs." or "Miss" in parentheses before their names in order to avoid embarrassment. When a letter is signed for a business firm, the name of the firm is typewritten first, then the handwritten signature is placed just below it. No title such as "Mr." or "Dr." should be used in the signature. If the person who wrote the letter cannot be on hand to sign it and the letter needs to go out at once, he may delegate this task to his stenographer, who writes his name in full with her initials beneath it.

Some examples of correct signatures are the following:

NATIONAL BANKING COMPANY

Russell H. Walker
Cashier

Charles J. Hopkins
a.w.P.

If the letter has been dictated to a stenographer there should be some means of identifying it. This is usually done by placing the initials of the dictator followed by a colon and the initials of the stenographer on the left-hand side of the page about two or three lines below the signature:

RC:EM

If there are enclosures with the letter this fact should be indicated on the letter. This makes it possible for the one who receives the letter to know whether he has everything he is supposed to have. Enclosures are usually indicated by writing the word "Enclosure" just below the identification initials:

RC:EM
Enclosures 2

The name of the firm

Address

Date

Salutation:

The body of the letter comes in these lines. In this letter it is printed block style. The heading is not at the "head" but at the bottom of the page. This position is suitable in letters that may be classified as either personal or official.

In most instances the name of the firm and the address are already printed on the stationery. The date line is, of course, always filled in with the typewriter.

The complimentary close always begins in the middle of the page whether the letter is typed in indented or block style.

Complimentary close,

Handwritten signature

Typewritten name of signer

Name of Addressee
No. and Street
City, Zone, State

Identification initials

The name of the firm

Kind of business

Address

Date

Name of Addressee
No. and Street
City, Zone, State

Salutation:

     The body of the letter comes in these lines. It may be printed with indentations as in this letter or in the block style as in the letter above.

     The date might have been put below the address of the firm at the top of the page. It should be put wherever it looks best.

Complimentary close,

Name of company

Handwritten signature

Title

Identification initials

Letters of Application. Many factors besides the letter itself enter into the result that a letter of application may produce. General business conditions and particular business conditions in the firm applied to are sometimes such that the finest possible letter will not even arouse an expression of interest; but an outstandingly good letter may live through a period of depression and bring a response long after it was written. Business houses do—occasionally, at least—consult their application files; a letter in one of them is, in a sense, a permanent record of your qualifications.

Letters of application should never be written on social stationery. Plain white paper of standard business size (8½ × 11 in.) with a standard-sized envelope (6½ × 3½ in. or 9½ × 4 in.) is best. Freak envelopes are occasionally used, sometimes with good effect, but on the whole tricks like this are not well received in business.

In large firms where no one is known to you by name, address the personnel manager.

Do not enclose a stamped, self-addressed envelope with a letter of application. There are, however, three enclosures which may be of real service:

1. Samples of your work, if its nature permits
2. Letters of recommendation (*copies*)
3. A photograph of yourself.

The letter should be typewritten unless it is in answer to an advertisement which especially requests that it be in handwriting.

The letter of application must shoot for a definite mark. The person who writes that he will take almost anything at whatever salary he can get advertises that he is not much good. To ask for a job at the bottom in order to learn the business from the ground up is a different matter, and may be an excellent way for a young person to get a foothold in business.

The letter must be concrete. A lot of words, however gracefully and neatly strung together, will not do if the essential information is lacking. The human tendency to run off the track and talk about something irrelevant is one reason why so many big houses have standard application blanks with just room enough after each question for a short answer.

The letter should be short. Its main object is to secure an interview for the applicant (very few jobs are given without this); it should, therefore, awaken the reader's interest in the writer. This can be done in a few paragraphs. It might almost be laid down as an ironclad rule that a letter of application should never be more than a page long.

What is the essential information which a letter of application should contain? Let us look at an application card. There will be variations, but the one given below is a fair sample of what the prospective employee will be asked to fill out:

Name in full
    (The name should be printed, not written, and the last name should be written first, followed by a comma, then by the first name)
Address   Street   Town
Telephone number
Date of birth   Married or single
Position applied for
Salary
Last employer   Address
How long employed
Were you ever employed here before   Dept.
Remarks

Photographs are sometimes asked for, in which case a small, unmounted picture (about 3 in. square) is sufficient.

If you have special equipment, you should make a point of mentioning it. If you are filling out a blank and there is no other place for it, include it under "Remarks."

If you can refer to someone known to the firm to which you are applying, do so. The kind of letter of recommendation that you can carry around with you is practically worthless, but if you can indicate that you would be very happy to have your prospective employer talk confidentially with your former employer or with the person who is recommending you, that will help. Letters from former school teachers, relatives, and old friends of the family carry little weight. In any case the letter of recommendation should, like the letter of application, be specific. If the position applied for is in a bank, the officials will want to know whether the applicant is honest. In such a case the letters of recommendation should be from men of proven integrity. If the position is in an advertising office, the letter should be from an advertising man, if possible. If the position is in engineering, the letter should be from someone familiar with your work in this field.

Original letters of recommendation should never be sent. They should be copied on the typewriter with COPY in capital letters at the top. In brackets just before the signature should be the word (Signed).

In applying for an executive position, you should emphasize your ability to handle men; for salesmanship, personality is the important factor; with stenographic work, it is speed, accuracy, and dependability. All items should point in the same direction.

An application blank may ask for the reason you are applying. Among reasons that should never be given, no matter how true they are, is the fact that you need the job. That is not of interest to the employer. What he wants to know is how well you can do the job. If you are asked why you left your former employer, do not take the opportunity to state your opinion of him, particularly if it is unfavorable. Simply say that you felt that you would find better opportunity for advancement elsewhere, or that you were getting into a rut and wished to develop yourself along some other line, or something else of this sort. Employers place high value on loyalty and may judge what your attitude toward them might be by your attitude toward your former employer.

The question of salary, unless specifically asked in the application blank, might better be saved for the interview. It is easier to come to terms face to face. Sometimes a letter is so high-flown that the prospective employer, while interested, feels that he cannot afford such a man. Sometimes a man who would be glad to get a position at $50 a week describes himself so grandiloquently (and, it may be added, so inaccurately) that those to whom he is applying think they have a $50,000-a-year man to deal with. Honesty is the best policy, here as elsewhere.

A word might be said about applying for a job which you think ought to exist but does not. Most of us hold jobs that someone else has made for us, but the most fortunate and brilliant people in business create jobs for themselves. It is hard to apply for a job that is not there, and the letters applying for it demand very special attention. The first letter should indicate that the applicant has something to talk over which he believes will interest the firm. He should ask to see a specific person—if not by name, at least by job, such as the publicity director or the supervisor of machinery. An interview should follow this letter; during the course of it the applicant may be asked to set forth his ideas in writing. Even if he has convinced the supervisor, he must remember that the supervisor also has people to convince, for instance, vice presidents and directors and super-supervisors. This letter should be a model of brevity and conciseness.

It is sometimes easier to act indirectly in applying for a job, that is, to act through an agency. Sometimes the agency writes the letter to be sent out; sometimes the applicant writes it. The following is an example of the kind of letter an agency might send:

PELHAM NASH AND CO.
Agents for High Grade Positions
101 Belton Street
New York 16, N.Y.

Please use Ref. 2981-B

James Howard Cook
Editor of *Radio Gazette*
333 Tenth Avenue
New York 24, N.Y.

Dear Sir:

We know a well-educated young man who is interested in finding a permanent position as publicity director, house-organ editor, or in sales-promotion work with a corporation associated with the radio industry or a closely allied field. He has asked us to address you in his behalf.

This man has had nine years of editorial experience with radio publications and is capable of assuming complete management of a publicity department or house organ for a manufacturer or advertising agency. He has a broad knowledge of present conditions in the radio industry, he is thoroughly familiar with radio from the technical viewpoint, and he has a wide acquaintance in this field. In his various positions and in free-lance publicity work he has also become well known as a writer of feature articles on radio and other subjects. This work has included both technical and popular articles for magazines and newspapers.

In addition to all this, our client has a valuable knowledge of all phases of editorial work. He has had actual experience in editing copy, planning and directing art work, laying out pages, ordering engravings, selecting proper type faces, making up at stones and with dummy, contracting with authors, making surveys, and preparing statistics. These qualifications together with his complete understanding of radio problems should render his services invaluable in the position suggested.

It will be a privilege to send you further information regarding him. This will involve no obligation on your part. His record cannot fail to convince you of his ability.

May we send the details?

Very truly yours,

PELHAM NASH AND CO.

Pelham Nash
President

N:T

Letters of Recommendation. All letters of recommendation should be dated, and the information as to when and where the person writing the letter knew the person about whom the letter is written should be very definite. You can never tell what a person's career may be after he leaves you.

The "To-Whom-It-May-Concern" letter does not, except under unusual circumstances, carry a great deal of weight, nor do the letters which a person carries around with him. The letters of real value are usually those addressed by one person to another in behalf of a third and those sent confidentially through the mails. The first letter below is an example of the first type.

Dear Mr. Blanton:

This letter is in behalf of a young man, Robert Howell, who has just completed a cruise around the world as chief radio operator on the *President Lincoln* and is now ready to settle down.

Your new short-wave station at Milbrook is very attractive to him, and he would like a position with you if you have an opening. He worked with me at 2GY for a year and a half before he sailed, and I found him an excellent operator. I would take him back, only, as you know, 2GY is temporarily suspended. He has a letter from the captain of the *President Lincoln,* a copy of which I am enclosing.

If you are interested, will you let me know when it will be convenient for you to see him?

Sincerely yours,

The captain's letter follows. It is a "To-Whom-It-May-Concern" letter, but the circumstances give it much more value than this type of letter generally has. Robert Howell wants a new job, and his new employer will be sure to wish to consult his former employer. But by the time Howell applies for the job, the captain of the ship will be far out at sea; hence, what he said before he left must be taken at face value.

To Whom It May Concern:

This is to certify that Robert Howell was chief operator on the *President Lincoln* on her around-the-world voyage which began on July 2, 19—. I found him at all times quick and reliable. In my opinion he is a good operator, and I think any station which secures his services will be fortunate. He left me entirely of his own accord.

Sincerely yours,

The letter given below is an example of the kind which is sent by mail. Such letters should be treated as entirely confidential and the writer of one should speak honestly. It is not wise, however, to make bald derogatory statements. You do not know what the person may be like now. Simply say, "My experience was . . ." or "My feeling is . . ." or something else of the sort.

Dear Mr. Smith:

Richard Allen, whose letter you sent me, worked for us during our first year in business. Before that time he had been a salesman for our friend, John Roe. What success he had with Roe I do not know. With us however, he was not a great success, although I always liked him personally. After he left us he got the idea of a specialty shop dealing in fine metalwork. I never went into the idea with him fully and so can give no opinion as to whether it is sound or not. What he has in mind now I have not the least idea. I am sorry not to be more helpful.

Sincerely yours,

Letters of Introduction. It is a fortunate man who at one time or another has not been asked for a letter of introduction which he would rather not write. When one has been so asked it may be necessary to send a separate sealed letter by mail to the person to whom the introduction is addressed, but this should be done only in extreme cases. Letters that you would rather not write should be kept formal and noncommittal; of course, if you can help it, they should not be written at all. No letter of introduction or any other letter which is to be delivered by hand should be sealed. The letter of introduction should bear on the outside, "Introducing Mr. John Jones," or a similar legend. This enables the one to whom the letter is addressed to speak to his caller at once by name and thus prevents embarrassment. The full name of the one who is being introduced should also be incorporated in the body of the letter, so that if the envelope is thrown away the person addressed can refer to the letter.

Jones may present the letter in person or, if he prefers, may enclose it with a note of his own to the addressee asking when it will be convenient for him to call. The tone of a letter of introduction depends upon the degree of intimacy the writer has with the person to whom he is writing. The two examples that follow illustrate both an informal and a formal letter of introduction.

Dear Jim:

This is to introduce an old friend of mine, John Jones. You've heard me talk about him before now. I'm sorry to have to introduce him by letter because it's one of those things I'd especially like to do in person. John is going to cover the Lawrence County territory for the Balkson people from now on and will be in your neighborhood about once a month. I think he can be of use to you and you to him. Anyway, I think you will enjoy knowing each other.

Sincerely yours,

Richard

Dear Mr. Allen:

I am sending you this letter by a young man, John H. Jones, who has been with us four years. He has worked out a selling plan for Babson pumps which seems practical to me. I wonder how it will strike you. He can explain it for himself better than I can explain it for him, and whether you approve it or not I think you will find it interesting.

Sincerely yours,

Richard Smith

Do not ask a man, except in a sealed letter, to see another man as a favor to you, unless the letter is a favor to him; do not write it, except, as was indicated above, when you can find no way out of doing so. There should be a reason behind every letter of introduction (and behind every other letter, especially in business), and the reason should be given in the body of the letter itself.

A letter of introduction should be acknowledged by the person to whom it is addressed. A brief note assuring the writer of the letter that it was a pleasure to receive it is all that is necessary:

Dear Mr. Grant:

It was a great pleasure to meet Mr. Simmons, who came to the office yesterday with your letter. I look forward to seeing him again.

Sincerely yours,

Letters of Congratulation. Friendliness in business is as heart-warming a quality as it is in other departments of life. It is a gracious thing to let a person who has had a piece of good fortune know that you are rejoicing with him.

Dear Mr. Moffitt:

It made me very happy to read in the *News* this morning that you have been made manager of the Springfield office. It is work which I know from experience you are admirably fitted to do, and I am not the only one of your friends here in your old home who will rejoice to see you back where you belong.

Most cordially yours,

Order Letters. In writing an order letter, be sure that you give an exact description of what you want. State size, quantity, color, price (approximate, if exact price is unknown), and, if you are ordering from a catalog, the catalog number. Most mail-order houses provide special blanks for their customers. These should be used when they are available.

If you are ordering several different items, arrange them in table form, making a separate paragraph of each.

State how payment is to be made. It is no longer considered good form to say "Enclosed please find check," but simply, "You will find check enclosed," the reason being that in the first instance the recipient is not doing you a favor by finding the check, and there is no sense in asking him as if he were. "Please charge this to my account" is entirely correct.

State how delivery is to be made unless it is perfectly obvious, as in the case of a department store with a regular system for delivering everything.

Be sure that your address and your name are on the order.

All these rules may seem like instructions for a child in the first grade, but every one of them is violated hundreds of times a day by presumably intelligent men and women.

143 HAMPTON BOULEVARD
SILVER SPRINGS, NEW YORK

October 14, 19—

National Screw Co.
543 West 86th Street
Chicago 18, Ill.

Gentlemen:

Please send me by express the following screws as listed in your revised price list of January 4, 19—:

Iron wood screws

2 gross	¼ in.,	No.	4	@	.24	$	.48
2 gross	½ in.,	No.	7	@	.32		.64
2 gross	⅞ in.,	No.	14	@	.70		1.40
10 gross	1¾ in.,	No.	16	@	1.20		12.00

Brass wood screws

4 gross	½ in.,	No.	4	@	.40	1.60
8 gross	¾ in.,	No.	9	@	.90	7.20
2 gross	2 in.,	No.	10	@	2.05	4.10
						$27.42

I am enclosing a check for $27.42.

Sincerely yours,

B:N

Letters of Confirmation. For the sake of record it is advisable to put into writing the substance of a conversation, especially if the conversation was in the nature of a contract. Such a letter is the following:

I am very glad to put into writing the agreement which we have made with you by which we are to have the benefit of your help and experience in scouting for new accounts, advising us on current problems, and helping us in other ways as occasion may arise.

It is understood that we are to pay you $1,200 a year, beginning November 1, payments of $100 monthly to be made by check.

Mr. French and I are looking forward to a very happy and profitable relationship. I know that it will be pleasant for us and I hope it will be for you.

Often the letter may be shorter, such as:

This is to confirm our telephone conversation of this morning, at which time it was agreed that you would send us immediately by parcel post ten gross of pencils, No. 2, Blenkinsop.

Reminders. A good many reminder letters display anger or rudeness. There is no excuse for this. One like the following gets prompter attention and leaves a better feeling behind:

Please consider this just a reminder that your company has not as yet returned the receipts for the dies we sent you about two weeks ago.

Will you please give this matter attention so that our records can be properly closed?

Stop-Gap Letters. If for any reason a letter cannot be answered at once, it should be acknowledged and the reason given for the delay. Such delay often occurs when information is requested that will take some time to assemble, or when the person to whom the letter is addressed is away from the office.

1. This is to acknowledge the pictures which you sent Miss Bancroft, who is away from the office for a few days. You will hear from her as soon as she returns.

2. It may take us several weeks to assemble all the information for which you ask in your letter of November 1, since the greater part of it must come from our office in Springfield. As soon as we get it, however, I will send it on to you. Please be patient with us.

Form Letters. In some businesses identical situations occur many times and each time demand exactly the same treatment. When a satisfactory method of handling has been found, it is unnecessary to try to vary it. For example, in a publishing house where 15 to 30 unsolicited book manuscripts come in each day, all that is necessary is a polite notice to each author that his manuscript has been received and will be given careful attention. Such notices may take the form of letters; often printed cards are used. When the manuscript has been read, the situation varies. The author may have given instructions for the return of the manuscript and have enclosed stamps for the purpose, or the publisher may wish to make suggestions for revision, in which case a personal letter must be written. Frequently there are form paragraphs which may be used, with slight variations, in many letters. But form letters must be used with discretion; if a form letter is sent in answer to another letter, it must really answer the questions asked.

Letters of Resignation. Most resignations are given orally, but some firms prefer or even demand them in writing. The conventional form is to express regret at leaving, to give some reason for it, to express pleasure (if any) at the associations which the connection has afforded, and to suggest a time at which the resignation shall become effective. The following letter was written by a young man resigning a position in the suburbs for one in the city:

> I am sorry to have to tell you that I am obliged to sever my connection with Bennett, Inc., but there are personal reasons why it is advisable for me to have a position in town rather than in West Gardens.

> If possible, I should like to leave at the end of the week. Will you let me know whether this will be convenient?

Letters of Complaint. The first rule for letters of complaint is: *Be sure you are right;* the second is: *Then go ahead;* and the third is: *Watch your step,* which means *Be courteous.*

The following letter brought immediate response. The fact that the receipt was enclosed so that the company did not have to ask for more information may have had something to do with it.

> On April 29 I bought from you two desk chairs. The enclosed receipt will give you a record of the transaction. The salesman said that one was in stock and that the other would be in a day or so and that both would be delivered before the end of the week. Ten days have passed and I have heard nothing.

> Will you please look into the matter at once and see whether you can find out what the difficulty is?

Letters of Adjustment. The way a letter of complaint is answered can determine whether a customer is lost or becomes even more loyal. A suitable tone and approach to the above complaint is illustrated in this letter:

> You are certainly entitled to an explanation why you did not receive your desk chairs within a few days of your order, as our salesman promised.

> The new shipment arrived on schedule, but our Quality Control Department rejected it because of minor defects. We have wired the manufacturer to forward us a special delivery to meet your needs and expect to be able to make shipment within a few days.

> We are proud of our reputation for keeping delivery promises and are very much concerned by the inconvenience you were caused. But I am sure you will agree that you will enjoy greater satisfaction and assurance of quality from our policy of careful quality control.

If, in the meantime, the one chair will help ease your situation, please telephone me at MAin 3-7900, Ext. 234, and I will have it delivered to you immediately.

Letters of adjustment need not be in answer to letters of complaint. The following, for instance, is about a mistake in deductions. Notice that the letter contains no hint that there was any intent to defraud on the part of the one paying the bill. It is simply a statement of facts with a polite request that proper adjustment be made.

In regard to your remittance of $1,564.98 received January 18, we note that you deducted a 2 per cent discount before you deducted the 15 per cent agency commission. In other words, from our charge of $1,602.69, you are entitled to $32.15 discount, not $37.71, as you have it. There is a difference of $5.56 in our favor.

In order that we may keep our records in check we ask that you kindly remit this difference at your earliest possible convenience.

In letters of adjustment words with unpleasant associations like "failure," "complaint," "trouble," "neglect," and "refuse" should be avoided. "Your complaint of April 1" might just as well be simply "Your letter of April 1." "Your failure to send a check" might just as well be "By some oversight the check which you mentioned in your letter was not enclosed." Do not use the words "You say" in this manner: "You say that the shipment was four crates short." This seems to imply that you believe the person to whom you are writing is not telling the truth. "The customer is always right" is a slogan that can be practiced only up to a certain point. It makes an excellent beginning policy, but there are unfair customers, who must be dealt with firmly. Politeness can be overdone and this in itself is a form of discourtesy. Fair dealing is the keystone of good business relations.

Many times letters of adjustment can be avoided by writing a letter of the kind shown below. This was written in connection with a certain kind of plumbing that was to be installed in an office building. In this instance, the extra cost did reach a fairly important total, but it was a contingency for which the house that had ordered it was prepared, and there was no angry interchange of letters when the bill was presented.

We are making the changes for which you asked in your letter of November 10. If the extra cost involved does not reach an important total, you will hear no more from us about it. If, on the other hand, it assumes such proportions, we are quite sure that you will give us consideration and help meet the extra expense.

Sales Letters. Every letter is at least glanced at by the person who receives it. If it is a sales letter, a glance may be all it gets, for sales letters as a class are not welcomed. More time and money and more expert attention are lavished upon them than upon any others, and yet more of them go into the waste basket.

Form is important in all letters but more so in sales letters than in others, for it is the form that determines whether it will get a second glance. A sales letter is not, strictly speaking, an advertisement. An advertisement is impersonal, while a sales letter, even though it be mimeographed, is directed to you because the sender has some connection with your name that makes him believe you will be interested in his product. The good salesman knows who his customers are; he does not write his letters "blind."

A point which may be worth adding is that the easier names are to get, the less likely they are to be of value as prospects for sales letters. The very fact that they are easy to get probably means that they are already on many lists and receiving letters from all of them.

Sales letters are often planned in campaigns, the number of letters running as high as ten or twelve. In such cases the article to be sold is an expensive one. Less costly articles will stand only one letter; it must, therefore, be a good one.

There is only one way to find out how good a sales letter is—try it. The usual practice is to try it first on a small group of people. Where the mailing list is very long, six and seven trial letters are sometimes sent before a final one is selected.

High-pressure compulsion in sales letters is going out. Never club your prospect into insensibility. Do not try to make him believe that the advantage is all on his side. He knows better.

Make buying a pleasure. Appeal to your prospect's pride, to his sense of comfort or economy, to his desire for efficiency, to his hope for a better social position than he now occupies.

In cases where you expect the customer to do the ordering, make it easy for him. Enclose a card with business reply postage on it. Urge him to act at once.

Many devices are used to attract attention. The most radical of these are usually not desirable. They get attention, but it is the same kind a man would get by walking around balancing a pencil on the end of his nose.

Sometimes letters are written by hand in the hope that they will win more notice than the typewritten letter. If such letters are long and if the handwriting is at all difficult to read, no one will bother with them. There is a belief that farmers and women have time enough to read all the mail they get; even if this is true, they will not read it unless it is lively and interesting. Everybody wants facts in a sales letter, not promises and glittering generalities. The tendency is to group the facts in a series of short paragraphs, the reason being that short paragraphs are easier to read than long ones.

If you state that your article is lower in price than any other in its class, give the reason, or it will be assumed that it is also inferior in quality.

Timeliness is of enormous value in a sales letter. Special Christmas and holiday appeals, if well done, bring good returns. Letters sent to a bride placing oneself at her service for invitations, flowers, trousseau, silver, etc., are likely to command attention. Alert companies see hundreds of opportunities that sleepier ones pass by. A sign painter, for example, on learning that a certain radio-supply house was to open a shop in a new location, at once wrote the following letter:

When you move to Nassau Street who will make your signs? How much will they cost? How soon can they be delivered? Will they be distinctive?

These are some of the questions that you have no doubt been asking yourself during the last week. May we offer our services? We have every modern facility for doing excellent work at a reasonable cost. The best way for you to judge is to see for yourself.

Phone Nicholson 7623 and our representative will call.

The following letter was written by the manager of a country inn to a prospective guest who was obliged to cancel a reservation:

I have your letter of April 30 saying that you cannot come to Glenfield on Friday, and I have accordingly canceled your reservation. I am very sorry you cannot be here. Glenfield is more than usually beautiful this spring. I hope you will be able to come later.

The letter below is a good example of the kind a nurseryman might send out at the end of the season:

The following are some of the surplus stock on our hands now, which we are selling at greatly reduced prices because we do not wish to carry it over until another season. All are good healthy plants, as you can easily see for yourself if you will visit our nurseries on Martin Boulevard at the Merrick Crossing. The prices are f.o.b. nursery.

Assorted evergreens	1 to 2 feet high @	$1.00 each
Rhododendrons	1½ to 2 feet high @	2.00 each
Rhododendrons	2 to 3 feet high @	3.00 each
Cedars	4 to 5 feet high @	.50 per foot
Oriental arborvitæ	4 to 5 feet high @	5.00 each
English juniper	5 to 6 feet high @	6.00 each
American holly	2 to 3 feet high @	4.00 each
Golden arborvitæ	4 to 5 feet high @	6.00 each

Assorted flowering shrubs, extra heavy, 6 years old,
50 cents to $1.00 each
Assorted French lilacs, all colors, 2 to 4 feet high
@ $2.00 each

We have also a good many other varieties, which will be sold at very attractive prices. Pay us a visit and we will save you money.

It is always a good plan to try to put yourself in the place of the person to whom you hope to make the sale. If what you have to offer is a trucking service, these are some of the questions a sensible customer will wish to have answered:

Is this trucking concern responsible in case of fire or collision in transit?

Are its men courteous and competent?

Will they be careful?

Will they arrive at the house when they say they will or must I wait for them an hour or two?

How much insurance per van load will I get?

What will be the total cost?

Can I get a better service than this?

Other points which a trucking service used with effect were the fact that they owned outright every van they operated so that the responsibility was entirely theirs, and the further fact that their men were employed by the year rather than by the season, thus enabling the company to employ competent workers.

Credit Letters.[1] As discussed elsewhere, credit is an essential part of modern business. Letters requesting or supplying credit information should be written carefully, and inquiries from credit agencies should be answered promptly. The information supplied should be accurate, because it may have to stand in law. The letters offered below are self-explanatory:

Gentlemen:

I wish to establish an account with you, beginning at once with an order for 100 pairs of black Boy Guide shoes, No. 14, C. Will you please let me know what credit information you desire so that I can send it immediately?

Sincerely yours,

---

[1] Consumer credit applications are rarely made in letter form, but by filling out a standard form. The customary procedure is to request one of these forms from the store with which one wishes to open an account and then follow whatever instructions the store includes.

Dear Mr. Bush:

It is a great pleasure to grant you the credit for which you asked in your letter of March 8. The goods are ready and will go forward at once. Our terms are three per cent, ten days; net, 30 days for the amount of your order.

We hope that this is the beginning of a long and happy relationship.

Sincerely yours,

Gentlemen:

Thank you very much for your order of June 17 for turpentine barrels amounting to $267.85. We are now preparing the barrels for shipment and are anxious to deliver them promptly. However, we cannot find on our records that we have previously furnished you with barrels, and we therefore lack the information which our credit department demands before we can open an account. Will you be so good as to fill out the enclosed form and return it to us at once so that we can make shipment? The information will, of course, be treated as confidential.

Again let us thank you for your order. We hope it will be the first of many.

Sincerely yours,

Gentlemen:

In answer to your letter of February 10 inquiring as to the credit standing of the Standard Cotton Company of Eastville, we are pleased to inform you that we have always found them entirely satisfactory as customers. They always discount our bills promptly. The highest amount of credit they have ever asked from us was about $800.

Sincerely yours,

Gentlemen:

We are very sorry to be obliged to refuse the credit for which you asked in your letter of January 9, but the information which we have been able to obtain does not seem sufficient to warrant it. As soon as further information is available, we shall be glad to go into the matter again. In the meantime we shall be very glad to send the goods C.O.D., if you will authorize us to do so.

Sincerely yours,

Collection Letters. Most letters have one purpose; collection letters have two purposes—to get the money and to keep the customer.

Collection letters usually run in series, though it is sometimes useless to prolong the series beyond five or six letters.

The first should be simply a formal reminder. This may be a statement of the bill with "Overdue" or "Please remit" stamped upon it. Better still, it may be a formal printed statement somewhat like "May we call your attention to this overdue account?" Or it may be a printed or multigraphed form with the dates and the amount of the debt filled in by hand in the blank spaces: "This is to call your attention to your account for March amounting to $540, a bill for which was sent you on April 1."

The series to follow should be carefully planned but should not be routine.

The personal element often will bring about payment when nothing else will. For this reason, some of the best collection men, even in large companies, have no form collection letters. If a man does not pay his bill there must be a reason. He may be temporarily under financial pressure; if this is true he should write frankly to his creditor stating the reasons. If his character is good and his reasons are valid, he should have no difficulty in getting an extension of time. The following letter, which was sent in response to a formal reminder attached to the bill, is an example:

> Will you give me a little time on this: My mother has just died after an illness of four months, and I am at the end of my reserves. I will certainly take care of it and would have done so long ago were it not for the heavy expenses I have had to carry.

Once an account is overdue, the debtor must not be let alone. The older the account the harder it is to get a settlement. But there should always be time between letters for a reply. It is wise, too, in some cases, to suggest partial payment instead of waiting longer for full payment. Thus:

> Thank you for your reply to my letter of April 7 regarding an outstanding account of $97.30.
>
> I suggest that you do not wait until you are in a position to remit the full amount. Send us something on account and try to have it in our hands before the close of the present month. We should then be willing to give you a reasonable length of time in which to pay the balance.

Even small accounts must be treated with firmness. One item of less than five dollars is not much, but a hundred or more of them begin to make inroads on almost anybody's business.

> Gentlemen:
>
> Again we must remind you of a little account of $3.45. It is of long standing. We are not in the least worried about the size of the bill, but we are disturbed over the fact that you seem to ignore our letters pertaining to it. The account is apparently correct, and we can see no reason why it should not be cleared up right now.
>
> Please grant us the courtesy of a reply by return mail.
>
> Very truly yours,

> Gentlemen:
>
> With regard to your small but long-standing account with us of $3.45, we regret to be obliged to inform you that our credit department has decided the item is worthless and we are charging it off to profit and loss.
>
> Perhaps in the near future you may conclude that it is to your interest to reinstate your credit with us and will decide to pay this small item.
>
> Very truly yours,

The following series of letters was used with great success in connection with a national campaign for selling a set of travel books:

> 1. Please accept our thanks for your order of "Pocket Travels." Your set is being shipped today, all charges prepaid.
>
> In accordance with our special offer, you are to examine these books thoroughly, and if you find that they are not all that you believed them to

be, or wished them to be, return them to us within the examination period, and you will owe us nothing.

But if when you have completed your examination of "Pocket Travels" you feel that you will enjoy reading them (and we are sure that this will be the case) mail us $3.50, and $3 a month each month thereafter until the full amount is paid—and the complete set is yours.

The majority of our customers take the cash discount rather than be bothered with the installment payments, and you may do so if you prefer.

Yours very truly,

The following statement of the account, properly filled in, was printed on the lower margin of the above letter:

STATEMENT OF ACCOUNT:

Amount of order .... $————
Amount paid .... $————
Balance due .... $————
Installments now due .... $————

$23.27 pays in full, if remitted within ten days.

2. We are very glad that you have decided to keep the complete set of "Pocket Travels."

Undoubtedly, your interest in searching out the hidden treasures of this invaluable work has caused you to overlook sending us your first remittance of $3.50.

Now that your attention has been directed to the matter, won't you let us have your check by return mail?

Thank you!

Yours very truly,

STATEMENT OF ACCOUNT:

Amount of order .... $————
Amount paid .... $————
Balance due .... $————
Installments now due .... $————

3. We are somewhat surprised that the first payment on your account has not been received by us.

The books were sent you, at your request, on a seven-day approval basis, with the understanding that you would return them within that period if they were not satisfactory. The seven days have long since elapsed, and we must now ask you to send us the first payment of $3.50 at once.

A business reply envelope is enclosed for your convenience.

Very truly yours,

STATEMENT OF ACCOUNT:

Account number .... ————
Amount of order .... $————
Installments now due .... $————

P.S. When you forward your remittance or write us about this, be sure to attach this letter.

4. Again I must remind you that the first payment on the books you ordered has not been received.

I am sure this is an oversight occasioned by carelessness or the pressure of time. Won't you justify my faith in your integrity by attaching a check or money order to this letter for the payment now due and mail it to me in the enclosed envelope?

Very truly yours,

STATEMENT OF ACCOUNT:

      Account number .... ——
      Amount of order .... $——
      Installments now due .... $——

P.S. If you write us about this account, be sure to attach this letter.

5. Fifteen days ago we called your attention to the fact that your account was in arrears. Up to this date we do not find that we have received remittance to bring the account up to date.

When we offered these books to you on the installment plan, we were confident that you would live up to the schedule of payments regularly and punctually. Your agreement to do so is confirmed by your signature on the original order that we hold.

We are very anxious to bring your account up to date and must request that you promptly forward your remittance for the amount now due.

Yours very truly,

STATEMENT OF ACCOUNT:

      Account number .... ——
      Amount of order .... $——
      Amount paid .... $——
      Balance due .... $——
      Installments now due .... $——

P.S. If you write us about this account, be sure to attach this letter to yours.

Account No.——
Amount——

6. Please understand that in calling your attention to the above account, no action concerning your credit standing is contemplated at this time. It generally suffices to send this final notice to bring a settlement by return mail.

7. Any good reason for not paying this account should be reported to this office *immediately*. THIS IS FOR YOUR OWN PROTECTION.

We have been exceptionally lenient in your case, in hope of reaching an amicable settlement.

Regretfully, we must now abandon this policy. Our claim against you will be sent to our attorneys for legal action unless you respond to this last notice within five days.

Yours truly,

It is useless to keep on further threatening an account. If the maker was not frightened the first two or three times he will not be frightened the next two or three. If you say you are going to place the matter in the hands of a lawyer, either do so or, if the account is too small to bother with any longer, write it off the books.

Another type of collection letter is written by a collection agency:

Dear Mr. Black:

In re: (Name of creditor and amount due)

The above account has been placed with our office and is automatically shown and must stay on your credit record until paid.

Our responsibility is to start collection procedure immediately, but in our desire to be helpful, we shall wait seven days for your reply.

It is to your interest to get in touch with us before that time, either with payment in full or for the purpose of making satisfactory arrangements.

This is a courtesy to you—please give the matter prompt attention.

Sincerely,

Further letters follow—at least one—if the account is not paid in answer to the initial letter; for example:

Dear Mr. Black:

In re: (Name of creditor and amount due)

We have written you before about this account. Surely you did not mean to ignore this bill. This credit was given to you by the credit granter as an accommodation. He shows his faith in your integrity by accepting your promise to pay.

Won't you arrange to take care of the bill at once and show that you appreciate the courtesy extended to you?

Sincerely,

Inter-Office Correspondence. It is easy for a person who is not very busy to delude himself into thinking he has a great deal to do by sending numerous long memorandums to people in his own office; in a well-regulated office, however, it should not be necessary to exchange many written messages.

Memorandums should be sent to save time. Even the simplest requests may be put into writing for this reason; *e.g.,* "Please let me have the profit-and-loss cards for July." But if the man who has the profit-and-loss cards sits only about two feet from you, ask him for them.

Memorandums may be sent as reminders.

Most important of all, memorandums may be sent as records of items of importance.

The length of a memorandum depends upon its subject. The confirmation of an order may require only three lines while the presentation of an idea for a new magazine or for some other entirely new or complicated project may require more than 100 pages.

All memorandums should be dated; it is a good plan to initial them in ink for identification.

Memorandum

From: Mr. Bennett
To: Mr. Patterson

This confirms verbal instructions to run 10,000 copies of "Green Branches." Orders are coming in far beyond our expectations and we shall want these as quickly as possible.

These books are to be absolutely uniform with the first edition.

Please let me know how soon they can be delivered.

(Date)

Large business houses have special memorandum forms. Personal forms may be supplied to individuals whose word carries special weight or whose memorandum volume is unusually large. For instance, the president of a firm might send a memorandum thus:

BALCH, INCORPORATED
654 Fifth Ave.

Memorandum from
The President

For various reasons I have an idea that June sales will be practically nil. They will certainly approach this point in the regular trade department, where publications have been postponed.

Under these circumstances it becomes necessary to curtail all advertising expenses—if not to eliminate them entirely. Will you, therefore, see that this is done?

Discussion of further advertising, promotion, etc., that will be appearing in the month of July will be had during the month of June.

(Date)

One should be very careful about putting a reprimand in the form of a memorandum. It may be more difficult, but in general it is much better to do this kind of thing by word of mouth. What is said may be forgotten and forgiven, but what is written continues to rankle.

The same holds true of letters of dismissal. Even if such a letter is sent (and often it goes, as a matter of routine, with the final pay check) it is far kinder to say to the departing employee that you are sorry it is necessary that he leave and give him your best wishes for good luck elsewhere. This seems easy, but many strong men shrink from it. The dismissed employee, however, who is so spoken to goes away with a much warmer feeling than if he had merely received a printed pink or blue slip. Employees who leave with a grudge, especially if there is something to warrant it, can do the firm a great deal of harm. See also Techniques of Management.

Official Letters. Official letters are more formal than general letters. The salutation is "Sir:" or "Sirs:" as the case may be; there are no abbreviations and all titles of respect are written out in full. Such letters are addressed to the editors of magazines and newspapers for publication, to men in official positions, and to committees or boards.

Officer	Letter Address	Letter and Verbal Salutation (1) Formal and (2) Informal
The President	The President of the United States	(1) Mr. President (2) Dear Mr. President
The Vice President	The Hon. John Smith, Vice President of the United States	(1) Sir (2) Dear Mr. Vice President
Ambassadors (American)	The Honorable John Smith	Your Excellency
Ambassadors (Foreign)	His Excellency the Italian Ambassador	Your Excellency
Cabinet Officers	The Honorable John Smith; or Mr. John Smith, Secretary of State	(1) Mr. Secretary (2) Dear Mr. Secretary
Senators	Senator John Smith	(1) Sir (2) Dear Mr. Senator; or Dear Mr. Smith
Representatives	The Honorable John Smith; or Rep. John Smith	(1) Sir (2) Dear Mr. Representative; or Dear Mr. Smith
Governors	The Honorable John Smith, Governor of Georgia	(1) Sir (2) Dear Governor Smith
Mayors	The Honorable John Smith, Mayor of Albany	(1) Dear Sir (2) Dear Mayor Smith
Supreme Court Justices	The Chief Justice of the United States; or, The Honorable John Smith, Associate Justice of the United States	(1) Mr. Justice (2) Dear Mr. Justice
Judges	The Honorable John Smith, United States District Judge	(1) Dear Sir (2) Dear Judge Smith
Cardinals	His Eminence John Cardinal Smith	Your Eminence
Archbishops (Roman Catholic)	The Most Reverend John Smith, Archbishop of New York	Your Excellency
Archbishops (Protestant)	His Grace John Smith, Archbishop of Chicago	Your Grace
Bishops (Protestant or Roman Catholic)	The Right Reverend John Smith, Bishop of Delaware	(1) Right Reverend Sir (2) Dear Bishop Smith
Clergyman (Protestant)	The Reverend John Smith	(1) Dear Sir; or Reverend Sir (2) Dear Mr. Smith
Priest (Catholic)	The Reverend John Smith	(1) Reverend Father (2) Dear Father Smith
Rabbi	Rabbi John Smith; or The Reverend John Smith	(1) Reverend Sir (2) Dear Rabbi Smith

LAW OF LETTERS

Be sure that everything you write will bear reading before a jury. Pay careful attention to syntax, for if the meaning is doubtful your letter will be interpreted according to the laws of grammar. Indecent, fraudulent, or seditious matter is unlawful, and letters of an abusive or libelous nature will subject the sender to punishment if he shows them to or allows them to be seen by a third person. In letters answering questions as to a man's financial or personal standing, do not assume too much responsibility. Do not flatly say that the man is not reliable, but that your experience with him will not warrant your endorsing him.

Many letters are permanent records of contracts and they should be so written that there will be no loophole for the man you are dealing with, should he happen to be dishonest. In accepting a contract, follow the exact conditions imposed. If the offer is made by mail and no other method is specified, accept by mail, by return mail if possible. If there is a request for acceptance by telegraph or telephone, or if a time limit is set, comply absolutely, or the contract is not binding. If you make the slightest change in the original terms of the contract it is not binding until it has been accepted by the other party. A contract holds good if the acceptance is made in the prescribed way, even if the acceptance is delayed or completely lost in transit. A man has the right to revoke an offer any time before it is accepted; but the acceptor has no right to revoke unless he makes provision for it in his acceptance.

Agreements made on Sundays and on legal holidays are not valid.

The law of the state where the acceptance is made governs the transaction.

It may be worth adding that a letter is the property of the person who writes it, not of the person to whom it is written, and no letter can be legally published without permission from the author. This does not apply to letters that are introduced into court as evidence.

A carbon copy of a letter is legally considered a duplicate of the original.

WANT ADS

"Situation wanted" ads should be brief and definite. Here is an example of the kind not to write:

Man (45) wishes position at anything; has had 20 years' business experience; can furnish references. K657 *Times.*

All that anyone knows from this advertisement is that the man is 45 years old. No clue whatsoever is given as to the kind of business experience scattered over those 20 years. He offers references, but almost anyone can produce references of one kind or another. Contrast this advertisement with the one below:

Mechanic, 37, locksmith, carpenter, electrician; own tools; steady; reasonable. *Times* 15A.

The second ad tells briefly what the man can actually do and states that he owns his own tools. He might have added something about references, but no doubt has them where they can be produced.

The "Help wanted" advertisement should follow the same rules. Here is a good example:

WANTED.—Clerical worker, young man, by fire insurance company. Must be good at figures; fire insurance experience preferred. Reply in own handwriting, stating experience and salary desired. *Herald* S17.

THE BUSINESSMAN'S REFERENCE SHELF

A program of planned reading can be of immeasurable aid to the business-man not only in helping him gain additional information but in stimulating his creative thinking. The following list includes books for the businessman who wishes either to broaden his over-all perspective or to gain specialized knowledge and skills.

"Accountant's Handbook," edited by Rufus Wixon; staff editor, Walter G. Kell; 4th ed., illus., Ronald Press Co., 1956.

Presents in compact form the principles and procedures of commercial and financial accounting.

"Accounting for Non-accountants; Key to an Understanding of Accounting," John Nicholas Myer, illus., New York University Press, 1957.

Helps the reader understand the "how" and "why" of accounting.

"Art of Window Display," Lester Gaba, illus., Thomas Y. Crowell Co., 1952.

Shows how to create shop windows with "customer pull" and offers examples of seasonal displays from leading U.S. stores.

"Credit and Collection Letters: New Techniques to Make Them Work," Richard H. Morris, 1960, sponsored by the National Assn. of Credit Management, Channel Press, Inc.

Authoritative advice on credit and collection from a business correspondence consultant.

"Foreman's Handbook," edited by Carl Heyel, 3rd ed., illus., McGraw-Hill Book Co., Inc., 1955.

Detailed data on the major elements of the foreman's job, as presented by 24 experts.

"Help Yourself to Better Mail Order," Robert A. Baker, illus., Printers' Ink, 1953 (Printers' Ink Business Books).

A guide to the basic elements of mail-order advertising by one experienced in the field.

"How to Establish and Operate a Retail Store," by O. Preston Robinson and Kenneth B. Haas, drawings by J. R. Hales, 2nd ed., Prentice-Hall, 1952 (Prentice-Hall Retailing Series).

Broad treatment is geared to the needs of the inexperienced retailer; bibliographies included.

"How to Supervise People," Alfred Morton Cooper, McGraw-Hill Book Co., Inc., 1958.

Helpful techniques for handling typical hiring and supervision problems, with examples and specific solutions currently in general practice. Questions for conference training included.

"Industrial Management," William R. Spriegel, 5th ed., illus., John Wiley & Sons, Inc., 1955 (revision of earlier work by Richard H. Lansburgh).

Describes how major business departments are related and interdependent and presents principles of successful management, with suggestions for application.

"Inventories and Business Health," Roy A. Foulke, Dun and Bradstreet.

Presents policies for sound management of inventories; includes financial ratio tables.

"Office Building and Office Layout Planning," Kenneth Ripnen, illus., McGraw-Hill Book Co., Inc., 1960.

How to make the physical plan and diagnose layout; with several complete floor plans.

"Marketing and Distribution Research," Lyndon Osmond Brown, 3rd ed., illus., Ronald Press Co., 1955.

Comprehensive view of the science of marketing and distribution research, embodying practices of outstanding practitioners in the field, plus discoveries and experience of research departments in numerous leading United States corporations.

"Personnel Interviewing," James D. Weinland and Margaret V. Gross, Ronald Press Co., 1952.

Detailed treatment of the objects and methods of modern business interviews, with examples.

"Principles of Marketing," Theodore N. Beckman, Harold H. Maynard, and William R. Davidson, 6th ed., illus., Ronald Press Co., 1957.

Down-to-earth presentation of all phases of marketing.

"New Art of Selling," Elmer G. Letterman, Harper & Brothers, 1957; also in paper, Bantam Books.

Today's salesmanship described by an outstandingly successful insurance salesman.

"Purchasing; Principles and Applications," Stuart F. Heinritz, illus., 2nd ed., Prentice-Hall, 1951.

Principles and procedures of purchasing reviewed in detail.

"Retail Advertising for the Small Store," Philip Ward Burton, illus., Prentice-Hall, 1951 (Prentice-Hall Retailing Series).

Designed for the small or medium-sized store in a small or medium-sized community.

"Secrets of Closing Sales," Charles B. Roth, illus. by John Eugene Coulter, 3rd ed., Prentice-Hall, 1953.

Various methods for closing sales.

PAPERBACK VOLUMES

"Basic Administration," J. E. Walters, Littlefield, Adams and Co.

"Business Law," Hugh W. Babb and Charles Martin, Littlefield, Adams and Co.

"Business Letter Writing Made Simple," Irving Rosenthal and Harry W. Rudman, Made Simple Books, distributed by Doubleday & Co.

"Business Organization," Wayne L. McNaughton, Littlefield, Adams and Co.

"How to Be a Successful Executive," Irving Goldenthal, Chilton Co.—Book Division.

"Practical Guide to Bookkeeping and Accounting," Ralph J. Falling, Grosset and Dunlap.

GOVERNMENT PUBLICATIONS

In the field offices maintained by the Dept. of Commerce in 33 cities, librarians and other experienced personnel will help the businessman. Publications relating to business—both domestic and foreign trade—are for sale in their publications sections, and libraries containing periodicals, directories, privately published materials, and reports from official sources are maintained. See also The Businessman and the Census Bureau.

WORDS OFTEN MISPRONOUNCED

Bad grammar betrays all language; bad spelling betrays written, and bad pronunciation spoken, language. From a person's accent we can usually tell what section of the country he comes from, and how far up the ladder of education he has climbed. Correct usage varies in different localities; and if you grew up saying *tomāto,* there is no reason why you should change now to *tomäto.* Snobbishness in speech is almost as despicable as it is in character. It is nearly always the half-educated man who says *ither* and *nīther* to impress other people in his community, if they all happen to say *ēēther* and *nēēther.* Many words admit of two pronunciations. Choose the one that attracts least attention to yourself. Other words have *only one correct pronunciation.* Read the following list carefully. You probably accent some of these words wrongly without realizing it.

accept—ăk-sĕpt′, *not* ĕk-sĕpt′.
accurate—ăk′-ū-rĭt, *not* ăk′-kĕr-ĭt.
across—à-krŏs′, *not* à-krŏst′.
address—ă-drĕs′, *not* ăd′-drĕs.
à la carte—ä-lä-kärt′, *not* ä-lä-kärt′-ĕ.
alias—ā′-lĭ-ăs, *not* ā-lī′-ăs.
aviation—ā-vĭ-ā′-shŭn, *not* ăv′-ĭ-ā-shŭn.
aviator—ā′-vĭ-ā-tẽr, *not* ăv′-ĭ-ā-tẽr.

bona fide—bō′-nà fī′-dē, *not* bō′-nà fĭd.

chasm—kăzm, *not* kă′-zŭm.
chef—shĕf, *not* chĕf.
chic—shēk, *not* chĭck.
chiropodist—kĭ-rŏp′-ô-dĭst, *not* chĭ-rŏp′-ô-dĭst.
column—kŏl′-ŭm, *not* kŏl′-yŭm.
contribute—kŏn-trĭb′-ūt, *not* kŏn′-trĭb-ūt.
corps (*military*)—kōr; *pl.*, kōrz.

data—dā′-tà, *not* dä′-tà.
deficit—dĕf′-ĭ-sĭt, *not* dē-fĭ′-sĭt.
digest—dī′-jĕst (*n.*—, *Reader's Digest; v.*—, dĭ-jĕst′).
diplomacy—dĭ-plō′-mà-sĭ, *not* dĭ-plō′-mà-sĭ.
discipline—dĭs′-ĭ-plĭn, *not* dĭ-sĭp′-lĭn.
drowned—dround, *not* droun′-dĕd.

exquisite—ĕks′-kwĭ-zĭt, *not* ĕks-kwĭz′-ĭt.
extempore—ĕks-tĕm′-pō-rē, *not* ĕks-tĕm-pōr′.

fellow—fĕl′-ō, *not* fĕl′-ẽr.

government—gŭv′-ẽrn-mĕnt, *not* gŭv′-ẽr-mĕnt.

habeas corpus—hā′-bĕ-ăs kôr′-pŭs, *not* hăb′-ĕ-ăs kôr′-pŭs.
Hawaii—hä-wī′-ē.
Hawaiian—hä-wī′-yàn.
hoof—hŏŏf, *not* hŏŏf. See *roof*.

inquiry—ĭn-kwīr′-ĭ, *not* ĭn′-kwĭ-rĭ.
interesting—ĭn′-tẽr-ĕs-tĭng, *not* ĭn-tẽr-ĕst′-ĭng.
iron—ī′-ûrn, *not* ī′-rŭn.

library—lī′-brẽr-ĭ, *not* lī′-brĭ.

mediocre—mē-dĭ-ō′-kẽr, *not* mĕd′-ĭ-ō-kẽr.
mischievous—mĭs′-chĭ-vŭs, *not* mĭs-chēē′-vŭs.

natatorium—nā′-tà-tō-rĭ-ŭm, *not* năt′-à-tō-rĭ-ŭm.
New Orleans—nū ôr′-lĕ-ănz, *not* nū or-lēēnz′.
news—nūz, *not* nŏŏz.

partner—pärt′-nẽr, *not* pärd′-nẽr.
penalize—pē′-năl-īz, *not* pĕn′-ăl-īz.
posse—pŏs′-ĕ, *not* pŏs.
pro rata—prō rā′-tà, *not* prō răt′-à, *nor* prō rät′-tà.

recognize—rĕk′-ŏg-nīz, *not* rĕk′-ẽr-nīz.
roof—rŏŏf, *not* rŏŏf.

salmon—săm′-ŭn, *not* săm′-ŭn.
sort of—sôrt ŏv, *not* sôrt′-ẽr.
speedometer—spĕd-ŏm′-ĕ-tẽr.
stupid—stū′-pĭd, *not* stŏŏ′-pĭd.

suburb—sŭb′-ûrb, *not* sū′-bûrb.
suite—swēt, *not* sōōt.

table d'hôte—tȧ′-blē dōt′, *not* tä′-bl-dō-tĕ.
theater—thē′-à-tēr, *not* thē-ā′-tēr.

used—ūsd, *not* ūst.
ultimatum—ŭl-tĭ-mā′-tŭm, *not* ŭl-tĭ-mä′-tŭm.

verbatim—vēr-bā′-tĭm, *not* vēr-băt′-ĭm, *nor* vēr-bȧ′-tĭm.

what, when, where, and which are pronounced hwŏt, hwĕn, hwâr, hwĭch, *instead of* wŏt,
wĕn, wâr, and wĭch.

WORDS OFTEN CONFUSED

Accept. All of us *except* John *accepted* the invitation.

Except. I *except* no one when I say he is the greatest man living.

Advice (noun). That is not good *advice*.

Advise (verb). Let me *advise* you. (This word is abused in business correspondence. Don't use it unless you are really giving advice.)

Affect, to influence or change something which already exists. Ignorant people believe that the moon *affects* crops.

Effect (verb), to cause or produce something. The new law *effected* a political reform.

Altar. He knelt at the *altar*.

Alter. The coat was *altered* to fit.

Beside, by the side of. He sat *beside* the manager.

Besides, in addition to. *Besides* all this, we have eight more coming.

Canvas. A *canvas* tent.

Canvass. A *canvass* for votes.

Capacity, power of receiving. He has the *capacity* to learn the work.

Ability, power to do. He has the *ability* to do this work.

Capital. Albany is the *capital* of New York. There is strife between *capital* and labor.

Capitol. State house. The national *capitol* is at Washington.

Censor, one who examines. Moving pictures pass a board of *censors* before they appear before the public.

Censure, to blame. The stenographer was *censured* severely for her carelessness.

Continual, often repeated. The morning was broken into by *continual* interruptions.

Continuous, never stopping. The *continuous* noise of a dozen typewriters is distracting to one unaccustomed to it.

Credible, believable. A *credible* yarn.

Creditable, praiseworthy. A *creditable* performance.

Emigrant. The *emigrant* from Russia settled on the East Side of New York.

Immigrant. The *immigrant* to the United States found himself among people who could not speak his language.

Expect, to look forward to. I *expect* the shipment tomorrow morning.

Suspect, to distrust. The robber was *suspected* of murder.

Export. We *export* supplies to other countries.

Import. We *import* sugar from abroad.

Few refers to number. Very *few* of the bolts were defective.

Less refers to quantity. There is *less* cotton produced in the South since the advent of the boll weevil.

Finally, at last.

Finely, adverb derived from *fine.*

Find, to discover. He *found* the leak.

Locate, to place. *Locate* Tasmania on the map. The store will be *located* in New York.

Invent. Edison *invented* the phonograph.

Discover. Columbus *discovered* America.

Lay, to put down. *Lay* the book on the desk.

Lie, to recline. I shall *lie* down for a while.

Miner. Many *miners* have to spend their working hours underground.

Minor. A *minor* is one who is not yet 21.

Practicable, capable of being put into practice. That is a *practicable* scheme.

Practical, pertaining to, or governed by, actual use and experience. He has *practical* ideas about management.

Precede, to go before. The marshal will *precede* the parade.

Proceed, to go forward. The meeting will now *proceed.*

Principal, chief, leader; sum on which interest accrues.

Principle, general truth, information, or belief.

Quiet. At last the children are *quiet.*

Quite. He lay *quite* still.

Respectfully, with respect. *Respectfully* submitted.

Respectively, singly considered. When the teacher called the roll the boys answered *respectively* to their names.

Set (transitive).

Sit (intransitive). Set the basket there and then sit down over here by me.

Stationary, not movable. The desk is *stationary.*

Stationery. Often the character of a firm is judged by the *stationery* on which its letters are written.

Therefor, for this or that or it, etc. We bought 17 cases and paid *therefor* $60.

Therefore, for that reason. We liked the idea and *therefore* submitted it to you.

To (preposition).

Too (adverb).

Two (adjective). I gave *two* rabbits *to* my brother but they were *too* heavy for him to carry.

WORDS OFTEN MISSPELLED

Rules for spelling are so complicated and are qualified by so many exceptions that it is almost useless to bother with them. But this is one worth remembering, for it holds true in practically all cases where *ei* or *ie* are found after *l* or *c.* (Believe, lieutenant; receive, conceit.) *Leisure* is an exception.

> When the letter *c* you spy
> Place the *e* before the *i*
> When the letter *l* you see
> Place the *i* before the *e*

A good speller is a good visualizer. Often he can tell which of two spellings is correct by writing them both on a slip of paper and seeing which one "looks right." Cultivate this faculty. Try to remember how the word looks on the printed page.

If there is still doubt, consult an unabridged dictionary. You will find it profitable to memorize the following list. These words are responsible for more errors than any others.

acceptable	expense	parcel
accidentally	feasible	partner
accommodate	February	picnicking
accuracy	financial	planning
achievement	fiscal	policy
across	foreclosure	prejudice
address	foreign	privilege
adequate	forty-four	promissory
advertisement	governor	publicity
all right	guarantee	pursue
apparent	incidentally	quietly
auditor	indispensable	quite
balance	insistent	recommend
bankruptcy	intelligible	reliability
benefited	inventory	remittance
business	label	replies
calendar	ledger	salable
column	liquidate	salary
committee	manageable	secretary
commodity	meant	security
communicate	miscellaneous	separate
computation	momentary	similar
consignment	mortgage	since
correspondence	necessary	stenographer
credentials	negotiable	stopped
debtor	nickel	subscription
deficit	notary	surprise
delinquent	noticeable	tariff
describe	occasion	tenant
develop	occurring	truly
disappear	omission	Tuesday
embarrassing	opportunity	twelfth
enclose	parallel	wholesale
erroneous		

MISTAKES TO AVOID IN GRAMMAR

A. Don't say, *that kind of a man,* but *that kind of man.*

Accept. Don't say, *accept of. Accept* is sufficient.

Again. Don't say, *Do it over again,* or *Return back again,* but *Do it over, Return.*

Ain't. This word has had a long life and shows no sign of dying, but it has never been used by careful writers and speakers.

And. *And* connects only words, phrases, or clauses of equal rank. *Be sure and come,* therefore, should be, *Be sure to come.* It is incorrect to write *and etc.,* for etc. means *and so forth.* Be careful not to use too many *ands;* they destroy clearness.

Anywheres. This is a vulgarism for *anywhere. Any place* is incorrect. So are *everywheres* and *every place.* Use *anywhere* and *everywhere.*

As. Don't say, *He as did it,* for *as* is never a pronoun. Substitute *who* or *that.* Don't say, *Not as I know of,* but *Not that I know of.*

At. *Where am I at?* is not good English except for humorous emphasis.

Badly. *He looks bad* is correct unless you are referring to his manner of looking out of his eyes. Similarly, *The rose smells sweet* instead of *sweetly,* for the rose has no sense of smell. Always use the adverb when you are describing the verb, the adjective when you are describing the noun.

Balance. Don't say *balance* when you mean *rest* or *remainder. Balance* has reference to the difference between the credit and the debit columns of an account.

Between. Don't say, *divided between five men,* but *divided among five men. Between* refers to two.

Don't say, *between you and I,* but *between you and me,* since the pronouns form the compound object of the preposition, *between.* You would never say *between I and you and the gatepost.*

Can. Don't say, *Can I go to the ball game?* unless you are asking your physician about your physical ability. *May* is the proper verb to use to ask permission.

Cooperate. Don't say, *cooperate together. Cooperate* means to work together.

Complected. Use *complexioned.*

Dangling participles. Never introduce a participle into a sentence unless you are sure there is something there for it to modify. *Walking into the room his eye lighted on a stranger* is inexcusable because it might so easily have been, *When he walked into the room he saw a stranger.* Keep special guard over *replying, hoping, answering, trusting,* etc.

Date. A thing does not date *back* to 1888; it dates *from* 1888.

Different is followed by *from,* never by *than.*

Do. This is one of the most abused words in the language.

Don't say, *He done it. Done* is the past participle and should always be preceded by some part of the verb *to have.*

He don't like it is as incorrect as *He do not like it.*

Don't tack *I don't think* on the end of what you say. Most of the time you say exactly the opposite from what you mean. *We won't get to Philadelphia this week, I don't think,* means, *I don't think we won't get to Philadelphia this week.*

Each. *Each, any, every one, any one, either, neither,* etc. require a singular verb. Not *Each are here,* but *Each is here,* because you are talking about only one person.

Foot. Don't say, *ten foot high,* but *ten feet high.* A *ten-foot pole* is correct, however.

Funny. *It's a funny thing. When one member of that family gets sick they all get sick.* Use *singular, odd,* or *strange,* and save *funny* for the places where it is really needed.

Gent. This is a vulgarism. Don't use it, and don't use the other word that is equally objectionable, *pants*.

He. It is correct to say, *"This is he"* when you acknowledge over the telephone that you are John Smith. The verb *to be* has the value of the sign of equality (=) and should always be followed by the nominative case. A pronoun is always a substitute. Be sure that you have made perfectly clear what it stands for. Don't use pronouns unnecessarily, as in this sentence: John, *he* began the fight, but Bill, *he* was ready for it, and pretty soon the whole crowd, *they* all pitched in. This construction is allowable when it is used for emphasis, *e.g.*, Jones, the organizer and promoter of this company, *he*, I say, is the man we want.

Here. Don't say, *this here letter* or *that there book,* but simply *this letter* or *that book.*

Its, it's. *Its* is a possessive pronoun. *It's* is a contraction for *It is.* The child loves *its* dog. *It's* very warm today.

Let. This verb is followed by the objective case. *Let John and me do it,* not *Let John and I do it.*

Like. *Like* is a preposition, *as* is a conjunction. It is ungrammatical to say, *Do like I do.* Say either *Do as I do* or *Do like me.*

Myself. Don't say, *John and myself are here,* but *John and I are here. Myself* is used reflexively or for emphasis, as *I cut myself* or *I, myself, will do it.*

Neither . . . nor, either . . . or. These conjunctions are used in pairs, always *nor* with *neither* and *or* with *either.* Place them as near as possible to the terms they connect. Don't say, *We shall either go Thanksgiving Day or Christmas,* but *We shall go either Thanksgiving Day or Christmas.*

Negatives. Avoid the double negative as you would influenza. Never say, *I don't hardly know, I ain't got none, not by no means, I did not see no one,* but *I hardly know, I have none, by no means, I saw no one.*

Nights. Don't say, *I work nights,* but *I work at night* or *every night.*

Of. Don't say, *I would of, should of,* or *could of done it. Of* is never a verb.

Off of. *Of* is unnecessary.

Ought. Don't say *had ought. Ought* should never be preceded by a helping verb.

Overly. It is a vulgarism to say, *I am not feeling overly well.*

Pair. Don't say *a new pair of shoes,* but *a pair of new shoes.*

Party. Except in legal parlance, *party* is not correctly used to refer to one person. *Party to a contract,* but not *the party with the tortoise-shell spectacles.*

Rather. *I would rather* is better form than *I had rather.*

Say. It is crude to say, *I want a say in this matter.* Better, *I want to say something about this matter.*

Don't say, *It said,* or *They said,* for *The Tribune said,* or *The people said.*

Seldom. *Seldom ever* should be *seldom, if ever.*

Size. Don't say, *A good size order,* but *A good-sized order.*

Some. Don't say, *He is some better,* but *He is somewhat better.*

Subject. The agreement between subject and predicate is very troublesome, especially when they are separated by some other part of the sentence. *The cost of necessities are constantly increasing* should be *is constantly increasing* because you are talking about the *cost,* not the *necessities. The captain, as well as the crew, were present* should be *was present,* for it is the captain whose presence you are interested in. *We shall all go to Boston, John, you and me,* should be, *We shall all go to Boston, John, you and I. John, you,* and *I* are explanatory modifiers of *we* and should therefore be in the nominative case.

Suspicion. *Suspicion* is often improperly used for *suspect*. *I suspected something was wrong,* not *I suspicioned something was wrong.*

Tense. Be sure that your verb refers exactly to the time when the action took place, and don't switch awkwardly from the past to the present in the same sentence.

Them. *Them* is a pronoun and should not be used for an adjective. Don't say, *them boys,* but *those boys.*

This, that, these, those. Don't say *these kind,* because *kind* is singular and should be modified by a singular adjective. *This kind* or *these kinds, that sort* or *those sorts.*

Up. Don't tack *up* on at the end of a verb. Not, *He divided up his work,* but *He divided his work.*

Was. Never say, *You was,* but always *You were.* Don't say, *If I was you,* but *If I were you,* for you are expressing an impossibility, and the subjunctive mode is needed.

Without. Distinguish from *unless.* Don't say, *Without you go,* but *Unless you go.*

Will. Don't say, *What will I do?* but *What shall I do? Will* with the first person denotes determination on the part of the speaker. Hence, *Shall I close the door?* and *Will I do it? I will not!* are both correct.

When. Don't say, *Good English is when you speak and write well,* because *when* is used to express time. See *where.*

Where. Don't say, *Typewriting is where you use the typewriter,* because *where* is used to express place.

Who. *Who* refers to persons, *which* to things, *that* to either persons or things. Be careful to use the objective case, *whom,* when the pronoun is the object of a preposition or a verb. *To whom did you give it? Whom do you wish to see?* are correct.

PUNCTUATION

Carelessness in punctuation is likely to cause trouble. Compare, "The office boy says the boss is a fool" with "The office boy," says the boss, "is a fool." The fashion in punctuation, as in words, changes from time to time and the best way to acquire good habits of punctuation is to notice the usage of standard magazines. The following rules, however, will cover most ordinary cases:

1. The *period* is placed at the end of a declarative or an imperative sentence, and after all initials and abbreviations. It is not placed after 1st, 2nd, 3rd, 10th, etc.

2. The *comma* indicates the smallest degree of separation of thought in the sentence, but it is the most troublesome of all the marks of punctuation. It is better to use it too little than to use it too much. It is used:

    a. To separate words, phrases, or clauses in a series.
       He laid his coat, hat, umbrella, and cane on the table.

    b. To set off "Yes," "No," and words of direct address.
       Come here, John. Yes, sir.

    c. To set off explanatory modifiers.
       The last day, Friday, was very rainy.

    d. To set off words which interrupt the regular grammatical flow of the sentence.
       Let the conference close, I beg you, as soon as the speech is over.

    e. To clarify the meaning of a long involved sentence, especially when there is danger of misinterpretation.

When the heat of midsummer made the boys irritable and lessened their efficiency, practical economy directed the manager to install electric fans and other devices for making them as comfortable as possible.

f. To separate the members of a short compound sentence.

Be square with your workers, but make them realize that you are square.

g. To show an omission.

Industry is the key to success; idleness, the bolt that bars the door. Macon, Georgia, June 16, 1920.

h. To give emphasis.

He worked hard, and won success.

i. Before *not* when it introduces a contrasting phrase or clause.

Acquire the habit of questioning everything you read, not to find fault with it, but to learn the truth from it.

j. To separate a direct quotation from the rest of the sentence except when it is very long.

Then Jackson said, "Let me hear from you."

3. The *semicolon* is placed between the members of a compound sentence when either contains a comma, when a comma is insufficient, or when the conjunction is omitted.

When he hands in his report, his power ceases; he has no authority to enforce his decisions.

What I tell you is of no consequence; what I do—behold!

4. The *colon* is used to introduce. It is placed after *as follows,* after the salutation of a business letter, and before a long quotation or an enumeration of details.

It is also used in writing the time of day in figures.

Here was the proposition: Twenty men were to work for eight days—

My dear Sir:

The statement is as follows: He works from 8:45 to 5:30.

5. The *dash* is wrongly used by many people when they are in doubt as to what other mark of punctuation to use. It is properly used to indicate an abrupt break in the thought, to replace marks of parenthesis, or to emphasize some part of the sentence.

Just at that moment the door opened slowly and—but you had better finish the story for yourself.

If you decide to keep it—and you surely will—send five dollars today.

You have everything to gain—nothing to lose.

6. The *hyphen* should be used when it is absolutely necessary to divide a word at the end of a line. Always divide words according to pronunciation.

The hyphen is used with many compound words about which no rules can be given and about which even the dictionaries disagree.

7. *Marks of parenthesis* are used to enclose a word or group of words strongly subordinate to the rest of the sentence.

The last epidemic caused 500,000 deaths (these facts can be verified) and a total economic loss of nearly four billion dollars.

8. *Brackets* are used to enclose supplementary or explanatory matter not originally found in the text.

Then he [Neal] signed the paper.

9. *Quotation marks* are used to enclose a direct quotation.

Stevenson said, "The difficulty is not to write but to write what you mean."

The title of a book, play, or magazine article may be enclosed in quotation marks or may have a line drawn under it. A single line drawn underneath a word, or a group of words, denotes that it is to be printed in italics.

I was reading *The Voice of the City* when Fred asked me to go to *Twelfth Night*.

10. The *apostrophe* is used to indicate the possessive case, to indicate omitted letters, and to form the plural of letters, figures, and symbols.

Scott's ambition was the result of his mother's teaching.

I'll see about it.

Dot your i's and cross your t's.

It is not used in the following pronouns: *its, hers, his, ours, theirs, yours.* Please read the above sentence again. This is a very common mistake.

11. The *exclamation point* is used to show strong or sudden feeling.

Oh! Fine!

12. The *question mark* is placed at the end of a direct question. It is used in parentheses to indicate doubt.

Who is there?

It happened twice, once in 1819 (?) and again in 1901.

CAPITALIZATION

Capital letters are used to begin every sentence, every line of poetry, every direct quotation, every important word in the title of a book, and every proper noun or adjective.

The pronoun "I" and the exclamation "O" are always capitalized.

The words North, East, South, and West are capitalized when they refer to sections of the country but not when they merely indicate direction.

All titles of persons begin with capital letters.

All names of the Deity should be capitalized.

Any particularly important word may be capitalized, and if special emphasis is desired the entire word may be typed in capitals.

MISCELLANEOUS ABBREVIATIONS AND SIGNS

abstr., Abstract
a.c., Alternating current
acc., acct., a/c, Account
A.D., Anno Domini, literally, In the year of our Lord
ad, adv., advt., Advertisement
adm., Administrator
agt., Agent
A.M., Before noon, (ante meridiem)
Amer., American
amt., Amount
anon., Anonymous
A1, First class
ans., Answer
Assn., Association
asst., Assistant, assorted
av., avdp., avoir., Avoirdupois
ave., Avenue

B.A., Bachelor of Arts
bal., Balance
bbl., Barrel

bdl., Bundle
b.e., B/E, Bill of exchange
bkt., Basket
b.l., B/L, Bill of lading
bldg., Building
b.p., B/P, Bills payable
b.r., B/R, Bills receivable
B.S., Bachelor of Science
b.s., Balance sheet
b.s., B/S, Bill of sale
bt., Bought
bu., Bushel
bx., Box

C., Centigrade
ca., Circa, about
cap., Capital
caps., Capital letters
c.c., Cubic centimeter
cf., Compare
chgd., Charged
c.i.f., Cost, insurance, and freight

c.l., Carload
cm., Centimeter
cml., Commercial
c.o., Carried over
c/o, Care of
c.o.d., C.O.D., Cash on delivery
col., Column
com., Commercial, commission
C.P.A., Certified public accountant
cr., Credit, creditor, crate
cs., Cases
C.S.T., c.s.t., Central standard time
ct. (pl., cts.), Cent
ctge., Cartage
cu., Cubic
c.w.o., Cash with order
cwt., Hundredweight

d.c., Direct current
D.D., Doctor of Divinity
D.D.S., Doctor of Dental Surgery
dept., Department
dft., Draft
dia., diam., Diameter
dir., Director
disct., Discount
div., Dividend
do., Ditto, the same
doz., Dozen
Dr., Doctor; dr., Debtor, dram

E., East
ea., Each
e.e., Errors excepted
e.g., For example (exempli gratia)
Eng., England, English
E.S.T., e.s.t., Eastern standard time
et al., And elsewhere; and others
etc., And so forth
ex., Example; exchange; extract
exp., Export; express; expense

F., Fahrenheit
f.a.s., Free alongside ship
fcp., Foolscap
ff., Following
fig., Figure
f.o.b., Free on board
frt., Freight
Fr., French
ft., Foot, feet; fort

g., Gram
gal., Gallon
G.M.T., g.m.t., Greenwich mean time

govt., Government
gr. gro., Great gross
gro., Gross
G.T.C., Good till canceled
guar., Guarantee

HE, High explosive
hhd., Hogshead, hogsheads
h.p. or hp, Horsepower

ib., ibid., In the same place (ibidem)
id., The same
i.e., That is (id est)
i.h.p., Indicated horsepower
imp., Imported
in., Inch
inc., Incorporated
incog., Incognito
ins., Inches; inspector; insurance
int., Interest
inv., Invoice
invt., Inventory
I O U, I owe you

lat., Latitude
lb., Pound
LL.B., Bachelor of Laws
LL.D., Doctor of Laws
long., Longitude
l.t., Long ton
Ltd., Limited

M, Thousand
M.A., Master of Arts
max., Maximum
mdse., Merchandise
mem. or memo., Memorandum
mfd., Manufactured
mfg., Manufacturing
mfr., Manufacturer
mgr., Manager
mo., Month(s)
m.o., Money order
MS., ms., MSS., mss., Manuscript, manuscripts
M.Sc., Master of Science
M.S.T., m.s.t., Mountain standard time
mun., Municipal

N., North
N.B., Note carefully (nota bene)
n.l., Not permitted (non licet)
no., nos., Number, numbers
N.P., Notary public

o/a., On account of
O.K., All correct
oz., Ounce

p., Page
p.a., per annum, By the year
pat., Patent
p. & l., Profit and loss
payt., Payment
pc., Piece
p.c., Per cent. See also *per ct.*
pd., Paid
per an., By the year
per ct., Per cent
Ph.D., Doctor of Philosophy
pk., Peck
pkg., Package
P.M., Afternoon (post meridiem)
P.O., Post Office
pop., Population
pp., Pages
p.p., Postpaid
pr., Pair
pref., Preferred
pres., President
P.S., Postscript
P.S.T., p.s.t., Pacific standard time

q.v., quod vide, which see
qr., Quarter
qt., Quart

Rd., rd., Road
recd., Received
rect., Receipt
reg., Registered
ret., Returned
R.F.D., Rural Free Delivery
R.R., Railroad

Ry., Railway

S., South
sec., sec'y, Secretary
s.d., S/D, Sight draft
ser., Series
shpt., Shipment
sq., Square
S.S., Steamship
St., Street
stge., Storage
str., Steamer
super., Superfine
supt., Superintendent

t.b., Trial balance
temp., Temporary
tr., Transpose
treas., Treasurer

v., vs., Versus; against
ves., Vessel
via, By way of
viz., Namely

W., West
W/B, Way bill
whlsle., Wholesale
wt., Weight

yd., Yard
yr., Year

&, And
$, Dollar
%, Per cent
#, Number
@, At, at the rate of

A BUSINESS DICTIONARY

Abbr. = abbreviated
A. D. = Anno Domini (Year of our Lord)
adj. = adjective
adv. = adverb
A.M., A.M., a.m. = before noon (ante meridiem)
B. C. = before Christ
Colloq. = colloquial
Eng. = England, English
etc. = et cetera (and so forth)
F. = Fahrenheit
fem. = feminine
Fr. = France, French
i. e. = id est (that is)
interj. = interjection
masc. = masculine
n. = noun
pl. = plural
P.M., P.M., p.m. = afternoon (post meridiem)
prep. = preposition
pron. = pronoun
sing. = singular
sq. = square
U.S. = United States
v. i. = verb intransitive
v. t. = verb transitive

A

A1, a registry mark denoting that a ship is in first class condition; first-rate.

a-bey-ance, a temporary holding back, as the settlement of an estate.

ab-scond, to flee in haste from one's home or duty; disappear to avoid arrest.

ab-stract (ăb′străkt), *n.,* a summary comprising the principal parts of a larger work; *v. t.* **(ăb-străkt′),** to take secretly or dishonestly; steal.

ac-cept-ance, an agreement to terms; an agreement to pay a note.

ac-cept-er, the one who receives or promises to pay a bill of exchange or draft. Also, ACCEPTOR.

ac-ces-so-ry, one who aids or abets; a confederate.

ac-com-mo-da-tion, that which fills a want or desire; the loan of money as a favor.

ac-com-mo-da-tion pa-per, a note made or endorsed by one person for another as a favor, as distinguished from a note given for value received.

ac-com-plice, a companion in crime; a confederate.

ac-count, *v. t.,* to reckon; compute; *n.,* a statement or memorandum of business transactions; bill.

ac-count-a-ble, answerable for one's actions; punishable.

ac-count-an-cy, the art or practice of keeping books or accounts.

ac-count-ant, an expert bookkeeper, especially one skilled in keeping financial records.

ac-count cur-rent, a running account showing the amount due at the present time.

ac-count ex-ec-u-tive, an advertising agency employee who handles the business of a particular advertiser or group of advertisers.

ac-count sales, the statement of a broker or salesman showing the amount of sales, freight, commission, expenses, etc.

ac-cred-it, *v. t.,* to accept as true; give credit to; to authorize; to vouch for.

ac-knowl-edg-ment, the legal admission of a fact; an avowal; a receipt; a certificate issued by the public officer before whom an acknowledgment has been made.

ac-quit, to set free; release; exonerate.

ac-quit-tal, the act of setting free; the judicial verdict of "Not guilty."

ac-quit-tance, a release from debt or other liability.

ac-tion, motion; deed; achievement; feat; battle; suit at law.

ac-tion-a-ble, giving grounds for a lawsuit.

ac-tive ac-count, an account showing many deposits and withdrawals.

a-cu-men, keenness of perception; sharpness.

ad-den-dum, *n.* (*pl.,* **addenda),** something added.

ad-dress, *v. t.,* to speak or write to; direct; *n.,* speech; bearing; residence.

ad-dress-ee, the person to whom anything is addressed.

ad-dress-o-graph, a machine for directing letters, etc.

ad-duce, to bring forward in proof; cite; quote.

ad-journ, v. t., to postpone to another time; v. i., to leave off for a future meeting.

ad-ju-di-cate, to determine in court.

ad-junct, an addition; a thing joined to another.

ad-ju-ra-tion, an oath or solemn charge.

ad-jure, to entreat earnestly; charge upon oath.

ad-just-er, one who settles claims, etc.

ad-just-ment, settlement of a legal claim or a disputed account; arrangement.

ad lib, *Slang,* from the Latin *ad libitum;* to insert material in text or music; to speak without a written script.

ad-min-is-ter, to manage; dispense; settle, especially the estate of one who dies without a will.

ad-min-is-tra-tor, one who manages, directs, or governs affairs, especially one who manages the estate of one who has died intestate.

ad-min-is-tra-trix, a woman appointed by law to settle the estate of a deceased person.

ad va-lo-rem, according to value; said of a tax or duty upon goods as distinct from a specific charge for a certain number or quantity.

ad-vance, an increase in price or value; payment beforehand.

ad-vo-cate, a lawyer or counselor in court; a pleader.

af-fi-da-vit, a sworn declaration in writing.

af-fil-i-ate, v. t., to adopt; to receive into a club or society; v. i., to associate oneself.

af-fir-ma-tion, ratification; confirmation.

af-flu-ence, wealth.

a-gen-cy, person or company carrying on business for another; the place where such business is carried on.

a-gent, one authorized to act for another; a substitute; one who handles the business of another.

ag-gra-va-tion, in law, anything which increases a crime or damages.

ag-gres-sion, unlawful infringement upon another's rights.

ag-i-o (ăj′ĭ-ō), n., the difference in value between various kinds of money; an exchange premium; discount.

a-gra-ri-an, adj., pertaining to land; n., an advocate of redistribution of land.

a-gra-ri-an-ism, the principles of those who believe in a redistribution of land.

a-gree-ment, a contract; mutual understanding; concord of opinions or feelings.

à la carte, according to the bill of fare.

a-la-mode, adv., in the fashion; adj., fashionable. Also, À LA MODE.

al-der-man, n., a city official next in rank to the mayor.

a-li-as, an assumed name.

al-i-bi, the plea of having been elsewhere when a crime was committed.

al-ien, a foreigner; adj., strange; foreign; different.

al-ien-ate, to estrange; transfer.

al-i-mo-ny, an allowance made by court to a divorced woman from her husband's estate.

al-le-ga-tion, positive assertion or declaration.

al-lege, v. t., to assert positively but without proof.

al-li-ance, a union; partnership; compact; coalition.

al-low-ance, an admission; a definite amount granted for some purpose; a deduction from the gross weight or amount of goods.

al-loy, n., any metallic compound; v. t., to mix or combine metals.

al-ter-a-tion, a change.

a-mal-gam, a mercurial compound; union.

a-mal-ga-mate, to mix or blend, as two races.

a-mal-ga-ma-tion, the union of mercury with another metal; a consolidation; union.

a-man-u-en-sis (pl., amanuenses), one who writes from dictation; a secretary.

am-a-teur, a non-professional.

am-big-u-ous, capable of being understood in two or more ways.

a-mend-ment, an alteration or change in a document, usually for the better, and usually by means of an addition.

a-merce, to punish by fine or deprivation of a right.

am-nes-ty, a general pardon for political or other offenders.

a-mor-tize, to clear off or liquidate, as a debt, by a sinking fund.

a-mount, *n.,* the sum total; *v. i.,* to reach; be equal to. AMOUNT GROSS, the total sum. AMOUNT NET, the total sum minus deductions for expenses, discounts, etc.

am-pere, unit in measuring the strength of an electric current.

an-nals, a record of events as they happen, year by year.

an-nex, *v. t.,* to add; to unite a smaller thing to a greater; *n.* an'nex, a supplementary building.

an-no Do-mi-ni, in the year of our Lord; *abbr.,* A. D.

an-no-tate, to supply with notes.

an-nu-al, yearly.

an-nu-i-tant, one who is entitled to receive a certain sum of money each year.

an-nu-i-ty, a yearly allowance or income.

an-nul, to make void; invalidate.

an-swer-a-ble, liable; responsible.

an-te-date, to date before the actual time; to occur before.

an-te me-rid-i-em, before noon; *abbr., A. M.* or *a. m.*

an-ti-quat-ed, obsolete; old-fashioned.

a-poth-e-ca-ries' weight, the system used in weighing drugs in which a pound equals 12 ounces.

ap-pel-lant, one who appeals to a higher court.

ap-pel-late, pertaining to appeals.

ap-per-tain, to belong by right.

ap-pli-ance, an article of equipment.

ap-pli-ca-ble, suitable.

ap-pli-cant, one who applies for a certificate, passport, position, etc.

ap-pli-ca-tion, a request; the act of demonstrating the practical use of.

ap-point-ment, the act of assigning or being signed to an office or trust.

ap-por-tion, to assign in right proportion; allot; divide.

ap-prais-al, valuation.

ap-praise, to estimate the value of.

ap-prais-er, one who sets a value on goods or merchandise, especially that subject to duty.

ap-pre-ci-a-ble, perceptible; sufficient in quantity to be estimated.

ap-pre-ci-a-tion, an increase in market value; a just valuation of the worth of.

ap-pre-hen-sion, arrest; comprehension; anxiety.

ap-pren-tice, a beginner; one placed in the hands of another for instruction in a trade or craft.

ap-prise, to notify, inform. Also, AP-PRIZE.

ap-pro-pri-a-tion, that which is set aside for a specific purpose, as money by the government.

ap-prox-i-mate, *v. t.,* to bring near; *v. i.,* to come close to; *adj.,* nearly but not quite accurate.

ap-pur-te-nance, that which belongs to something else; an accessory.

a pri-o-ri, from the former.

ar-bi-ter, a judge; an umpire.

ar-bi-trage, the buying and selling of stocks, etc., for the profit arising from the difference in price of the same commodity in different markets at the same time.

ar-bit-ra-ment, a decision by chosen judges.

ar-bi-tra-ry, not governed by law; discretionary; unreasonable.

ar-bi-tra-tion, the settling of a dispute by an arbitrator.

ar-bi-tra-tion of ex-change, the process of comparing and adjusting the difference in money values or rates of exchange among various countries for the purpose of international business transactions.

ar-bi-tra-tor, one chosen to settle a dispute. Also, ARBITER.

ar-che-type, the original pattern or model.

ar-chi-pel-a-go, a sea containing many islands; a body of islands.

ar-chive, more often in *pl.,* **ar-chives,** records kept for evidence or historical purposes.

a-re-a, any surface inclosed within a given space.

ar-ro-ga-tion, the taking of more than belongs to one by right.

ar-son, a malicious setting fire to a building.

ar-ti-cle, an item; a single piece of goods; a distinct division of a contract or other document.

ar-ti-cles of part-ner-ship, a written agreement defining the powers and purposes of an association for the promotion of a joint enterprise.

ar-ti-san, a trained workman; mechanic.

as-perse, to slander.

as-per-sion, calumny; slander.

as-sas-sin, one who kills by surprise assault.

as-sault, *n.*, a violent attack; *v. t.*, to attack violently.

as-say, *n.*, the act of testing; *v. t.*, to ascertain the components of; to appraise.

as-say-er, one who tests the purity of metals and coins.

as-sem-blage, an audience; the fitting of various parts together, as of an automobile.

as-sem-ble, *v. t.*, to collect; gather together; *v. i.*, to meet; convene.

as-sess, to value for taxation; to set a charge upon; fix damages.

as-sessed tax-es, taxes on income, houses, etc.

as-sess-ment, an official estimate of value for taxation; a tax on property; a share of expenses.

as-sets, *n. pl.*, property which may be used in the payment of debts; all that one owns. AVAILABLE ASSETS, assets on which there is no lien or claim, so that the owner is free to dispose of them as he wishes.

as-sign-ment, the transference of a right or title to another; the thing transferred; an allotment to some particular person or for some special use.

as-sign-or, one who transfers an interest or right; one who sets aside something for a special person or use. Also, ASSIGNER.

as-size, a court for the trial of civil or criminal cases.

as-so-ci-ate, *n.*, a colleague, companion; *v. t.*, to join; accompany; *v. i.*, to unite.

as-so-ci-a-tion, a union; confederation; combination of persons for the promotion of a business undertaking.

as-sur-ance, an agreement to pay on a contingency almost certain to occur; a pledge; confidence; insurance.

as-ter-isk, a mark (*) used in printing to indicate references.

at-las, a collection of maps in a volume.

at-tach-ment, the legal seizure of property to force compliance with a judicial decision.

at-tain-der, deprivation of the civil rights of persons outlawed or sentenced to death.

at-test, to bear witness to; certify; give proof.

at-tes-ta-tion, testimony under oath; an official declaration.

at-tor-ney, a legal agent. POWER OF ATTORNEY, a written authority for one person to transact business for another.

at-tor-ney gen-er-al, the chief law officer of a state.

auc-tion, a public sale in which the article falls to the highest bidder.

auc-tion-eer, one licensed to conduct a public sale in which the property falls to the highest bidder.

au-dit, *n.*, an official examination of accounts or claims; *v. t.*, to examine or adjust, as accounts or claims; *v. i.*, to act as an examiner.

au-di-tor, one appointed to examine accounts.

aus-pi-ces, *n. pl.*, guidance; support; patronage.

aus-pi-cious, favorable.

au-then-tic, genuine; trustworthy.

au-then-ti-cate, to establish as correct or genuine.

au-then-ti-ca-tion, in law, the verification of a document; the act of proving genuine or true.

au-thor-i-ta-tive, having due authority.

au-thor-i-ty, power or right; testimony; a person or agency in power.

au-to-graph, one's signature in his own handwriting.

au-to-ma-tion, the use of machines to do work previously performed by human beings.

au-ton-o-mous, self-governing.

au-ton-o-my, self-government; political independence.

au-top-sy, a post-mortem examination to find out the cause of death.

aux-il-ia-ry, *adj.*, aiding; *n.*, an assistant.

av-er-age, *adj.*, ordinary; midway between two extremes; *n.*, the mean value; an estimate; the general type; *v. t.*, to reduce to a mean. GENERAL AVERAGE, a proportionate contribution levied on a ship or cargo to cover loss or damage at sea. PARTICULAR AVERAGE, the compensation paid by an underwriter for damage to a part of a ship or its cargo from ordinary wear or mishaps. PETTY or PETIT AVERAGE, allowance for incidental expenses on a voyage, shared by ship and cargo.

av-o-ca-tion, a secondary occupation; a diversion.

av-oir-du-pois, a system of weights in which one pound equals 16 ounces.

B

back, *n.,* the hinder part; *v. t.,* to furnish with a back; support; *adj.,* toward the rear; overdue.

back-er, a supporter.

back-door fi-nanc-ing, provision of capital for a venture by other than the accepted means.

bad debts, uncollectible accounts.

bail, *v. t.,* to liberate on security; *n.,* surety.

bail-ee, one to whom goods are committed in trust.

bail-iff, a sheriff's deputy.

bail-ment, *n.,* in law of contracts, the delivery of goods by one person to another in trust for a special purpose; the provision of bail for an arrested person.

bal-ance, *n.,* a pair of scales; poise; the difference between two sums or weights; *v. t.,* to adjust; equalize; weigh.

bal-ance of trade, the difference between the money value of exports and imports.

bal-ance sheet, a statement of open accounts in tabular form to show assets and liabilities, profit and loss.

bank, *n.,* an establishment for the custody, exchange, or issuing of money; *v. t.,* to put in a bank. See *State Bank; Federal Reserve Bank.*

bank-a-ble, receivable at a bank.

bank bill, a banker's draft.

bank book, a depositor's pass book containing a record of credits and charges.

bank cred-it, the amount which one is allowed to draw from a bank with, or without, security.

bank dis-count, a deduction equal to the interest at a given rate on the principal of a note from the time of discounting until it becomes due.

bank draft, a bill of exchange drawn by one bank on another.

bank-er, one engaged in the custody, exchange, or issuing of money.

bank note, a promissory or other note payable at a bank.

bank-rupt, *n.,* a debtor (person or corporation) who is legally declared unable to meet his obligations in full, and whose estate is to be liquidated for the benefit of creditors; *adj.,* insolvent; *v. t.,* to impoverish.

bank-rupt-cy, failure in business; the state of being legally declared unable to pay one's debts.

bar-gain, *n.,* an agreement; a contract; a gainful transaction; *v. i.,* to haggle.

bar-ris-ter, Eng., a member of the legal profession who pleads cases in court; distinguished from solicitor, who may not appear in court.

bar-ter, to traffic; bargain.

bear, one who sells stocks, etc., for future delivery in the hope that the market price will fall.

bear-er, one who holds a note, draft, or bill of exchange.

bench, a body of judges.

bench war-rant, a legal paper providing for the arrest of an offender given out by the judge instead of the magistrate.

Ben Day proc-ess, a photographic method of preparing a printing plate, making possible the reproduction of shadings and tints: named for Benjamin Day.

ben-e-fac-tion, the act of benefiting; a gift of charity.

ben-e-fac-tor, one who confers a benefit.

ben-e-fi-ci-ar-y, one who is benefited or assisted, as by a will.

be-queath, to hand down by bequest, will, or testament.

be-quest, a legacy.

berth, *n.,* a bed in a ship or railway carriage; enough room for a ship to anchor; *v. t.,* to allot an anchorage to.

bi-an-nu-al, twice a year.

bi-as, *n.,* prejudice; *v. t.,* to prejudice; influence.

bib-li-og-ra-phy, a list of books relating to a special subject; the science which deals with the history and description of books.

bid, *v. t.,* to offer; to propose as a price; to command; *v. i.,* to make an offer; *n.,* a price offered at auction.

bi-en-ni-al, occurring once in two years; continuing for two years.

big-a-my, the act of marrying when one already has a husband or wife.

bill, *n.,* an account for goods sold, services rendered, or work done; a copy of a proposed law; a printed advertisement; negotiable paper; *v. t.,* to make a list of; to advertise by bills.

bill book, a book in which a record is kept of notes and drafts issued or received.

bill do-mes-tic, a bill of exchange or draft payable in the country in which it is drawn. Also, BILL INLAND.

bill for-eign, a bill of exchange or draft payable in a country other than the one in which it was drawn.

bill-head, a printed form for bills, etc., with the business address at the top.

bil-lion, in the United States and France, one thousand millions; in England and Germany, one million millions.

bill of en-try, a memorandum of goods entered at the custom house whether for import or export.

bill of ex-change, a written order or request from one person or house (the drawer) to another (the acceptor) to pay to the person named a certain sum at a specified future time.

bill of health, a statement given to the master of a vessel, signed by the consul or other official, giving an account of the sanitary conditions and general health of the ship and crew.

bill of lad-ing, a paper acknowledging receipt of goods to be shipped and promising to deliver them safely to the designated person or place.

bill of sale, a formal paper given by the seller to the buyer of property to declare and establish the title of the latter.

bills pay-a-ble, bills of exchange, drafts, or promissory notes issued by ourselves and payable to others.

bills re-ceiv-a-ble, bills of exchange, drafts, or promissory notes, issued by others and payable to ourselves.

bi-me-tal-lic, consisting of, or relating to, the use of two metals in a system of coinage, as gold and silver.

bi-month-ly, occurring every two months.

birth rate, the increase of population in a given district within a certain period as shown by the percentage of registered births within a specified period.

bi-sect, to cut into two equal parts.

bis-sex-tile, *n.,* leap year; *adj.,* pertaining to leap year.

bi-week-ly, fortnightly; also semiweekly.

black, in the, in bookkeeping, showing a profit.

black-leg, a swindler; a gambler who cheats.

black list, a list of persons considered deserving punishment, or a list of those regarded as undesirable in business transactions; *v. t.,* to enroll as undesirable or culpable.

black-mail, *v. t.,* to secure money by threats; *n.,* extortion of money by threats.

blank, an unfilled space in a written or printed document or such a document itself; a disk of metal before it is stamped; the bull's-eye of a target.

bleed, to print an illustration so that it extends to the edge of the paper without margin.

block-ade, *n.,* the shutting up of a place, as a port; *v. t.,* to surround and shut up.

block sys-tem, the system which provides for the safety of a railway line by dividing it into short sections and allowing only one train on a section at a time.

blood mon-ey, money obtained at the cost of another person's life; the reward paid for the capture or discovery of a murderer; money paid to the next of kin of a person slain by another.

blow-up, an enlargement of a picture or page of printed material.

blue laws, severely strict laws, especially those which relate to matters of personal conscience.

blue rib-bon, a mark of distinction or success; the highest award in a competition.

board, *n.,* a council; a group of people selected to manage a public or private affair; *pl.,* the stage.

board foot, a measure equal to the volume of a piece of timber one foot long, one foot wide, and one inch thick.

board meas-ure, measurement in board feet.

bod-y-guard, one or those who defend the person of another, usually some high official.

bod-y pol-i-tic, the people living under an organized government considered collectively.

bod-y type, the type used in the main part of a publication: distinguished from heads and other special types.

bo-gus, not genuine.

bold-face, a printing type that is heavy in tone; for instance, the type in which the entries in this listing are printed: opposite of light-face.

bo-na fi-de, genuine.

bo-nan-za, a rich vein of ore; anything which brings wealth or fortune.

bond, *n.*, a tie; an obligation; a formal deed issued by a government or corporation as a money security; *v. t.*, to mortgage.

bond cred-i-tor, a creditor whose debt is secured by bonds.

bond debt, a debt secured under bond.

bond-ed, held under pledge for payment of duties secured by bonds.

bond-ed goods, goods held in a bonded warehouse.

bond-ed ware-house, a warehouse under guarantee for strict observance of the revenue laws.

bond-hold-er, one who owns or holds bonds.

bonds-man, one who stands responsible for the payment of another's debt.

bo-nus, a premium; a special allowance beyond what is strictly due.

boo-dle, graft; bribe money.

book, *n.*, a volume; register; record; a list of race horses and the bets made on them; *v. t.*, to register; record.

book debts, accounts charged on the books of a business.

book-keep-er, one who keeps accounts; an accountant.

book-keep-ing, the keeping of a record of business transactions in systematic order. SINGLE ENTRY, the system which requires only one entry for each transaction. DOUBLE ENTRY, the system which requires two entries for every transaction, one on the debit, and one on the credit, side of the ledger.

book-mak-er, a professional betting man.

boom, *n.*, a sudden advance in prices; *v. t.*, to push forward with great energy.

booth, a temporary structure at fairs, markets, polling places, etc.

bor-ough, a municipality organized into a self-governing body under a mayor and other officials; one of the administrative units of New York City.

boun-ty, generosity; a special allowance or premium given to encourage some branch of trade or manufacture.

bourse, an exchange, especially the stock exchange of Paris.

boy-cott, *v. t.*, to combine against a person so as to hinder his trade or profession; *n.*, the act or state of combining against a person; the combination.

brand, *n.*, a burning piece of wood; any kind of trademark; a mark of infamy; *v. t.*, to mark by burning with a hot brand or by other means.

breach, the breaking of any obligation; a quarrel.

breach of trust, violation of a legal trust or duty.

break-age, allowance made by a shipper for goods broken by accident.

break-wa-ter, any structure to lessen the force of waves.

brib-er-y, the act or practice of corrupting or influencing another through gifts.

brief, *adj.*, short; condensed; *n.*, abridged statement for the instruction of a lawyer; a condensed argument.

brief-less, without clients.

broad-side, a printed or oral attack upon some public person; a political or advertising message, usually printed on one side of a large poster.

bro-chure, a pamphlet or booklet dealing with a subject of current interest.

bro-ker, one who acts as an agent for another; a buying and selling agent; a middleman who works for a commission.

bro-ker-age, the business of a broker; his commission.

buck-et shop, an office for gambling in stocks, grains, etc., in small amounts organized in such a way that it is difficult to distinguish between it and a legitimate stockbroker's establishment.

budg-et, a statement of the financial needs of the year to come of a nation, organization, etc.

buf-fer, any contrivance which serves to deaden the shock of two bodies striking together.

build-ing and loan as-so-ci-a-tion, an organization to aid its members in buying or improving real estate with money lent or subscribed by the other members.

bull, a speculator who buys in expectation of a rise in price, or to bring about a rise: opposed to *bear.*

bul-le-tin, *n.,* an official report; *v. t.,* to publish by bulletin.

bul-lion, uncoined gold or silver in bars or ingots.

bun-co, a swindling game.

bun-combe, anything said or done for mere show.

bunk, *Slang,* nonsense.

bu-reau, an office; a governmental department.

bu-reauc-ra-cy, a government by bureaus.

bur-sar, a treasurer, as of a college; a purser.

buy-er's op-tion, a purchaser's privilege of taking something within a certain period.

by-law, a private rule framed by a corporate body.

C

ca-bal, a secret combination of a few persons for carrying out a special design, usually evil.

cab-a-ret, a restaurant where the patrons are entertained by music, dancing, vaudeville acts, etc.

cab-i-net, a committee of the heads of the government departments.

ca-ble, a submarine telegraph line.

ca-ble-gram, a message sent by cable.

cal-cu-late, to compute; reckon.

cal-cu-la-tion, an estimate; computation; forecast; caution; care.

cal-cu-la-tor, one who or that which reckons.

cal-en-dar, a register of the days, weeks, and months of the year; a list.

call, *n.,* a summons; a demand for payment of money due; a request to a stockholder to pay an instalment on his subscription; a request from a government or corporation to the holders of redeemable bonds to present them for payment; a contract demanding the delivery of a certain amount of stock or goods at a stipulated price within a specified time; *v. t.,* to summon.

call loan, a loan of money subject to payment on demand.

ca-lor-ic, of or pertaining to heat.

cal-o-rie, the small calorie is the amount of heat necessary to raise one gram of water 1° centigrade. The great calorie is the amount of heat necessary to raise one kilogram of water 1° centigrade, in other words, 1,000 small calories. Also, CALORY.

ca-lum-ni-ate, to accuse falsely and maliciously.

cam-ou-flage, the art of disguising or deceiving by false appearances; any variety of concealment.

can-cel, to mark out writing by drawing lines across it; destroy; annul; revoke.

can-dle pow-er, the illuminating power of a standard candle taken as a unit to measure the power of any other light.

can-vass, *n.,* solicitation; inspection; *v. t.,* to examine; *v. i.,* to solicit.

cap-i-tal, accumulated wealth; property of a corporation or individual at a stated time; wealth or goods used in production.

cap-i-tal-ism, an economic system based on capital employed by capitalists; a system of which the operation is chiefly effected by private enterprise under competitive conditions.

cap-i-tal-ist, one possessing great wealth, which is or may be used in business.

cap-i-tal-ize, to convert into money which may be used in production; apply to the purposes of business.

cap-tion, a heading, as of a chapter, or the legend accompanying a picture.

car-at, a unit of weight for precious stones, etc. Also KARAT.

car-di-nal points, north, east, south, and west.

card in-dex, an index in which each item is listed on a separate card.

carte blanche, absolute freedom; a

signed paper given to another to fill in as he chooses.

cash, ready money; coin.

cash-book, a book containing an account of money received or paid out.

cash-ier, one in charge of the receiving and paying out of money in a bank or trading establishment.

cash-ier's check, a check drawn upon a bank by itself and signed by its cashier.

cash sale, a sale of goods for cash or payment within 30 days.

cast-ing vote, the deciding vote cast by a president or chairman.

cas-u-al-ty, an accident; in war, losses by death, disease, etc.

cat-a-log, *n.,* an arranged list; *v. t.,* to enter in such a list; to make a register of. Also, CATALOGUE.

cat-e-go-ry, a class.

Cel-si-us, see *Centigrade.*

cen-sor, an inspector with power to suppress or forbid publication; a critic.

cen-sus, an official enumeration of population.

cen-ti-grade ther-mom-e-ter, a thermometer having 0° as the freezing point, and 100° as the boiling point, of water.

cen-time, a French coin equal to one hundredth part of a franc.

cer-tif-i-cate, a written testimony or declaration of truth.

cer-tif-i-cate of de-pos-it, a statement issued by a bank that a person has on deposit a certain sum of money.

cer-ti-fi-ca-tion, the act of testifying through a written statement.

cer-ti-fied check, a check guaranteed good by the bank upon which it is drawn.

cer-ti-fy, to testify in writing.

chair-man, the presiding officer of an assembly.

cham-ber of com-merce, an association of merchants or traders for the promotion of their business interests.

chap-ter, an organized branch of a fraternity or other organization.

char-gé d'af-faires, one who transacts business for an ambassador in his absence or at a court where no ambassador is appointed.

char-la-tan, an impostor.

chart, a map, especially for the use of sailors; any tabular list of instructions or facts.

char-ter, *n.,* an official grant of certain rights, as to an association or corporation; *v. t.,* to establish by charter; to hire for one's own use.

char-tered, granted by charter; protected by charter.

char-ter par-ty, a mercantile lease for a vessel or a part thereof.

chas-sis, the frame of an automobile or airplane.

chat-tel, usually in *pl.,* movable personal property. CHATTEL MORTGAGE, a mortgage on personal property. See *Mortgage.*

check, *n.,* a restraint; hindrance; small mark used to show that an item has been attended to; an order on a bank for payment of money on demand; ticket; *v. t.,* to stop; curb; reprove; verify.

check-book, a book containing blank checks.

check-mate, *n.,* the winning move at chess; defeat; *v. t.,* to defeat utterly.

chit, a memorandum; a voucher. India, China, etc.

chron-o-log-i-cal, relating to the order of time.

chro-nol-o-gy, the science of time and dates; a chronological listing.

chro-nom-e-ter, an instrument for measuring time accurately.

ci-pher, *n.,* zero; the symbol, 0; naught; a person or thing of extremely small value; a secret code or the key to it; *v. i.,* to write in code; to work with arithmetical figures.

cir-cu-lar, a printed or written letter addressed to the public or to a group of people.

cir-cu-lar note, a note issued by bankers for travelers so that they may obtain money from correspondents at various places.

cir-cum-stan-tial, pertaining to, or inferred from, the circumstances; incidental.

cir-cum-stan-ti-ate, to describe exactly or minutely.

ci-vil-ian, one engaged in civil as opposed to military affairs.

civ-il serv-ice, the service of the government; not military or naval.

claim, *v. t.,* to demand; assert as true; *n.,* a title; a demand.

claim-ant, one who demands a thing as his by right.

clear-ance, a cleaning out; the passage of negotiable paper through the clearinghouse; settlement of claims, etc.; a customhouse certificate that a ship is free to leave.

clear-ance pa-pers, certificates issued by a customhouse stating that a vessel has complied with the law and is ready to leave.

clear-ing, the settlement of balances against each other by banks and other business agencies, carried on at a clearinghouse.

clear-ing-house, the place where banks send their representatives daily to exchange drafts, bills of exchange, etc.

clerk, a salesman; an office correspondent, or keeper of records.

cli-ent, the patron of a lawyer, architect, or other professional person.

cli-en-tele, the clients or customers of a professional person or business establishment.

closed shop, a shop closed to nonunion workers.

clo-sure, the act of closing; stopping a debate by the vote of the majority. Also CLOTURE.

co-a-lesce, to unite; fuse; combine.

co-a-li-tion, a union; combination.

c. o. d., collect on delivery, a call for payment for merchandise at the time of its delivery.

code, a system of laws or rules; a system of symbols used for brevity and secrecy.

cod-i-cil, an addition; postscript to a will.

cod-i-fy, to systematize.

cof-fer-dam, a watertight enclosure for the protection of workmen.

cog, a notch or tooth, as on a wheel.

col-lat-er-al, additional security.

col-league, an associate in a professional or civil office.

col-lec-tor, one authorized to collect money for another.

col-lu-sion, a secret and unlawful agreement.

com-men-su-ra-ble, having a common measure.

com-men-su-rate, equal in measure or extent; proportionate.

com-men-ta-ry, a series of explanatory remarks.

com-merce, extended trade; business intercourse.

com-mer-cial, *adj.,* pertaining to trade. COMMERCIAL PAPER, notes, drafts, bills of exchange, and other negotiable paper used in business transactions.

com-mis-sion, *n.,* an agent's allowance or percentage for transacting business; a document investing one with authority or rank; a duty; trust; a body of men joined to perform some duty; *v. t.,* to empower, authorize. COMMISSION BROKER, one who buys and sells for a commission.

com-mis-sion-er, an officer in charge of some branch of public service.

com-mit-ment, the act of committing; a sending to prison; a promise or pledge of action.

com-mit-tee, persons appointed to deal with some matter; **com-mit-tee′,** in law, a person to whom someone or something is given in charge.

com-mod-i-ty, an article of commerce; *pl.,* merchandise; goods.

com-mon car-ri-er, a public conveyer of persons or goods for compensation and for all persons without discrimination.

com-mon law, the unwritten law which has grown out of custom and usage.

com-mon sense, sound, practical judgment in ordinary affairs.

com-mon-weal, the general public welfare.

com-mon-wealth, the people of a state considered as a group; hence, a state.

com-mu-ta-tion, change; substitution of something less severe; the changing of an electric current by means of a commutator.

com-mu-ta-tion tick-et, a transportation ticket sold at a reduced rate, to be used during a certain period of time.

com-mute, *v. t.,* to exchange; substitute; lessen the severity of; *v. i.,* to travel regularly by use of a commutation ticket.

com-mut-er, one who changes or exchanges; one who buys a railroad ticket at a reduced rate to be used during a limited period of time.

com-pact, an agreement; contract.

com-pa-ny, an association for industrial or commercial purposes; assembly.

com-pen-di-um, an abridgment; a brief summary.

com-pen-sate, to atone; make amends for; to pay.

com-pen-sa-tion, recompense; remuneration; requital.

com-pe-tence, a sufficiency; fitness; ability.

com-pe-tent, capable; fit; qualified.

com-pet-i-tor, a rival.

com-plain-ant, a plaintiff or petitioner in a legal action.

com-ple-ment, a full number; something which completes; the amount by which a given angle or arc falls short of 90 degrees.

com-ple-men-ta-ry, forming or pertaining to the completing part.

com-plic-i-ty, a partnership in guilt.

com-po-nent, *adj.,* constituent; composing; *n.,* a necessary portion or part.

com-pos-i-tor, one who sets type.

com-pound in-ter-est, interest on both principal and interest.

com-pro-mise, *n.,* the settlement of a dispute by certain concessions from both parties; *v. t.,* to adjust or settle by mutual agreement; *v. i.,* to make an adjustment by concessions.

comp-trol-ler, a public officer who has charge of the accounts of officials under him. See *Controller.*

com-pute, to calculate; reckon.

con-cede, to grant; admit.

con-cern, a business.

con-ces-sion, a grant; the act of yielding.

con-ces-sion-aire, a person holding a concession or having a special privilege.

con-cur-rence, agreement; consent; happening together in time or place.

con-cur-rent, acting in conjunction; existing or happening together; coincident.

con-fed-er-a-cy, a league; alliance.

con-fed-er-ate, *v. i.,* to unite; *adj.,* leagued together; *n.,* an ally; an accomplice.

con-fer, *v. t.,* to bestow; *v. i.,* to consult together.

con-fer-ence, a meeting for consultation; a gathering.

con-fi-dence, trust, reliance, assurance; belief in one's own ability; something told in secret.

con-fi-den-tial, secret.

con-fir-ma-tion, ratification; corroboration; proof; additional evidence.

con-niv-ance, failure to oppose known wrongdoing.

con-nive, to pretend not to see wrongdoing; to aid secretly.

con-nois-seur, a critical judge, as of any work of art.

con-sen-sus, general agreement of opinion.

con-ser-va-tion, preservation.

con-serv-a-tism, the tendency to adhere to existing conditions and institutions and to oppose radical change.

con-serv-a-tive, one opposed to radical changes.

con-sid-er-a-tion, careful thought; deliberation; something to be considered in making a decision; regard for others; a fee.

con-sign, to deliver formally to another.

con-sign-ee, the person to whom goods are sent for sale or superintendence.

con-sign-ment, the act of delivering formally; the thing sent.

con-sign-or, one who sends goods to another. Also, CONSIGNER.

con-sol-i-date, to make solid; combine.

con-stit-u-en-cy, the voters in the district of a member of Congress or other public official.

con-stit-u-ent, an adherent; a component element.

con-sti-tu-tion, fundamental laws, as of a nation or society.

con-straint, repression; compulsion.

con-struc-tive, having the power or tendency to help or improve.

con-strue, to interpret.

con-sul, a nation's commercial agent in another country.

con-sul gen-er-al, the chief consul.

con-su-lar, pertaining to the consul.

con-su-late, the office or term of residence of a consul.

con-sum-er, one who makes ultimate use of a product.

con-text, the parts of writing which immediately precede or follow a part quoted.

con-tin-gen-cy, a possible occurrence.

con-tin-gent, *adj.,* accidental; dependent; possible; *n.,* a possibility; quota.

con-tra-band, *adj.,* illegal; *n.,* forbidden goods.

con-tract (kŏn-trăkt′), *v. t.,* to draw together; shorten; bargain; become affected with; *n.,* **(kŏn′-trăkt),** a written agreement.

con-trac-tor, one of the parties to a contract; one who undertakes to supply or construct.

con-trol-ler, an officer who oversees and verifies accounts.

con-vene, *v. i.,* to assemble; *v. t.,* to cause to meet together.

con-ven-tion, an assembly; a covenant; an arbitrary social custom.

con-ver-sant, familiar.

con-vey, to carry; transmit; cede.

con-vey-ance, the act of transmitting; a vehicle; the change of property from one owner to another.

con-vey-anc-er, one who draws up deeds, etc.

con-vo-ca-tion, the act of calling together, especially formal assemblies.

con-voy (kŏn-voi′), *v. t.,* to go with as protector; *n.,* **(kŏn′-voi),** an escort, as of a ship.

coop-er-age, the business of making barrels, etc.; the charge for such work.

co-op-er-a-tion, the act of working together.

co-or-di-nate, *v. t.,* to harmonize; *adj.,* equal in rank; of the same order.

co-or-di-na-tion, the state of being in harmony or working together.

co-part-ner, an equal partner.

cop-y, manuscript to be set in type.

cop-y-right, the exclusive right to reproduce, publish, or sell a literary or artistic work for a number of years.

cord, a measure for wood (128 cu. ft.).

co-re-spond-ent, a second person charged with guilt in a divorce suit.

cor-ner, to drive into a position from which escape is impossible. CORNER THE MARKET, to buy up a controlling interest in property or stock.

cor-ner-stone, a stone laid to symbolize the beginning of construction of a building; hence, something of basic importance.

cor-o-ner, an officer who investigates the causes of sudden or violent death.

cor-po-rate, united in a body.

cor-po-ra-tion, a body of persons legally authorized to act as a single person and having distinct rights and liabilities.

corps *(pl.,* **corps),** a body of troops; any body of persons associated in a common work.

cor-re-late, *v. i.,* to be related by parallelism, etc.; *v. t.,* to connect; to create a mutual relationship.

cor-re-spond-ence, agreement; communication by means of letters.

cor-re-spond-ent, one with whom communication is carried on by mail; one who sends communications to another by mail.

cor-rob-o-rate, to confirm; strengthen; to make more certain.

cos-mo-pol-i-tan, *n.,* one who is at home anywhere in the world; *adj.,* free from local prejudices.

cost, *n.,* price; expense; outlay; *v. t.,* to be the price of; to cause to bear or suffer.

coun-cil, an assembly for consultation; a municipal body.

coun-cil-man, a member of the council of a township, borough, etc.

coun-ci-lor, a member of a council.

coun-sel, *n.,* advice; adviser; *v. t.,* to give advice to.

coun-se-lor, *n.,* one who gives advice, especially a lawyer.

coun-ter, *adv.,* in opposition; prefix meaning contrary.

coun-ter-act, to oppose; neutralize.

coun-ter-bal-ance, *v. t.,* to offset; *n.,* a force or weight equal to another.

coun-ter en-try, an entry in an opposite sense.

coun-ter-feit, *v. t.,* to copy or imitate with the purpose of deceiving; *n.,* a forgery; an imitation made to deceive; *adj.,* false; spurious.

coun-ter-mand, *v. t.,* to change, contradict, or revoke an order; *n.,* a contrary order.

coun-ter-mine, *n.,* any means by which an enemy's plans are defeated; *v. i.* and *v. t.,* to dig an underground passageway in order to meet and destroy similar works of the enemy; to defeat by secret means.

coun-ter-sign, *v. t.,* to sign with an additional signature; *n.,* a password.

coup, a master stroke of strategy.

cou-pon, an interest certificate, attached to bonds, etc., to be torn off when due; the detachable part of a theater ticket, etc.

cov-er-ture, a cover; the legal status of a married woman.

co-work-er, a fellow worker.

craft, ability; manual art; a guild; vessels.

crafts-man, a skilled worker; artisan.

cre-den-tial, a testimony of one's ability or right to act. Usually in *pl.*

cred-it, *v. t.,* to believe; ascribe; to enter on the credit side of an account; *n.,* belief; honor; reputation; balance due; the amount which a person can obtain from a bank or other business house.

cred-i-tor, one to whom another owes money or goods.

cri-sis, a turning point; an emergency.

cri-te-ri-on, a standard by which something can be measured.

crop, to cut; to trim an illustration before printing, in order to make it fit the available space or to eliminate unwanted parts of the picture.

cross-ex-am-i-na-tion, the questioning of a witness by the opposing party.

cross-pur-pose, a contrary purpose.

cross-ques-tion, to cross-examine; question closely.

cul-de-sac, a passageway open at only one end; a blind alley.

cul-mi-nate, to reach the apex; to come to the final result.

cul-mi-na-tion, summit; climax.

cu-mu-la-tive, becoming larger by additions.

cur-ren-cy, circulation; that which is used for money.

cus-to-di-an, a keeper; guardian.

cus-to-dy, guardianship.

cus-tom-house, the place where duties are paid, and vessels are entered and cleared.

cus-tom-house bro-ker, an agent who attends to the clearing of goods and vessels for another.

cus-toms, government-levied duties payable on goods imported from abroad.

cut, *n.,* an engraved printing plate; the illustration printed from such a plate.

D

dam-ag-es, compensation paid for a specified injury, loss, or wrong.

da-ta, *n. pl., (sing., datum),* a collection of facts.

day-book, a book in which business accounts of the day are kept.

day la-bor-er, a workman who is paid by the day.

day let-ter, a telegram sent at special rates with the understanding that regular telegrams shall have precedence in time of sending.

days of grace, the time allowed for the payment of a note after it falls due.

dead let-ter, a letter which cannot be delivered and is sent to the dead-letter office to be opened and returned to the sender; anything which has lost its authority.

dead-lock, inability to reach agreement; a complete standstill.

deal, *n.,* quantity; part; division; trade; bargain; *v. t.,* to distribute; divide; *v. i.,* to conduct business.

deal-er, one who buys and sells.

de-base, to lower.

deb-it, *n.,* a recorded account of a debt; *v. t.,* to charge with debt.

debt, that which is due from one to another; obligation.

debt-or, *n.,* one who owes something to another.

dec-ade, a period of ten years; a group of ten.

dec-i-mal, *adj.,* pertaining to, or reckoned upon, the number ten; *n.,* a decimal fraction.

de-cree, *n.,* an edict; law; command; *v. t.,* to ordain; determine by law.

de-duct, to take away; subtract.

deed, *n.,* a written document for the transfer of land or other real property; an instrument; *v. t.,* to transfer by deed.

de-face, disfigure; blemish.

de fac-to, actually existing or done.

de-fal-cate, to embezzle.

de-fame, to slander; libel.

de-fault, neglect; failure; *v. i.,* to fail to perform or appear; *v. t.,* to make a failure in.

de-fault-er, an embezzler; one who fails to pay or to do.

de-fend-ant, one who is sued in a court of law.

de-fense, *n.,* a protection; excuse; bulwark; plea.

de-fer, to delay; postpone; give in to the judgment of another.

de-fi-cien-cy, a falling short; deficit.

def-i-cit, a shortage, as of money.

de-fraud, to cheat.

de-fray, to pay; bear the expenses of.

de ju-re, by right of law, distinguished from *de facto.*

de-le, *v. t.,* to erase; cancel; take out: the mark (δ) indicating that a word, etc., is to be deleted.

del-e-gate, *n.,* a representative; agent; *v. t.,* to send as a representative; to entrust.

del-e-ga-tion, a body of delegates; the act of authorizing an agent or a group of agents.

de-lete, to take out; erase. See *Dele.*

de-lin-quent, *adj.,* failing in duty; *n.,* one who falls short in the performance of duty.

de luxe, unusually fine, as an edition *de luxe* of a book.

de-mon-e-tize, to deprive of standard value, as money; to withdraw from circulation.

de-mur-rage, the delay of a vessel, railroad car, etc., after the time allowed for loading, etc.; money paid for such a delay.

de-mur-rer, one who objects; in law, a pleading against proceeding further.

de-port, to banish; exile.

de-pose, to testify, usually in writing; to remove from office.

de-pos-it, *v. t.,* to put in place of security; put in a bank; entrust; *n.,* that which is laid or set down; money in the bank. DEPOSIT SLIP, a dated slip which a depositor leaves with a deposit stating the character and amount of the funds deposited.

de-pos-i-tar-y, one to whom something is entrusted; a storehouse; guardian. Also, DEPOSITORY.

dep-o-si-tion, testimony under oath, usually written.

de-pos-i-tor, one who places in trust; one who places money in a bank.

de-pot, a warehouse; a railway station.

de-pre-ci-ate, *v. i.,* to fall in value; *v. t.,* to reduce the value of; to disparage.

de-pre-ci-a-tion, a fall in value or market price.

de-pres-sion, a period of commercial dullness.

dep-u-ta-tion, the sending of a deputy or representative; a person or a group of persons sent to represent another.

dep-u-ty, a delegate; a substitute.

de-sid-er-a-tum, anything desired as essential.

de-vise, *v. t.,* to contrive; invent; bequeath; *n.,* a will or clause of a will.

dev-i-see, one to whom a legacy has been left.

de-vis-er, one who invents or contrives; one who bequeaths property.

de-vis-or, one who bequeaths.

dic-ta-phone, an instrument like a phonograph, used for dictating material to be transcribed by a stenographer.

dic-tate, to express orally for another to take down in writing; to declare with authority; order.

dic-ta-tion, the act of speaking words which are to be taken down; words so spoken.

dic-tum, a positive assertion.

dil-a-to-ry, tending to cause delay; late.

di-rec-tor, *n.,* one who, or that which, guides or directs; *pl.,* a body of persons appointed to manage the affairs of a corporation or other organization.

di-rec-to-rate, *n.,* the office of a director; a body appointed to manage the affairs of an organization.

di-rec-to-ry, a guidebook; a book of names and addresses; a board of managers or directors.

dis-burse, to pay out; expend.

dis-burse-ment, money expended.

dis-charge, *v. t.,* to unload; free; dismiss; *n.,* the act of unloading; the thing unloaded; performance, as of duty; an explosion; dismissal.

dis-count, *n.,* a deduction made for prompt payment; the deduction made on money lent; *v. t.,* to deduct for prompt payment; lend at a discount; to allow for exaggeration in.

dis-crim-i-na-tion, discernment; an unfair distinction.

dis-par-i-ty, inequality; disproportion.

dis-pen-sa-ry, a place where medicines are given away.

dis-pen-sa-tion, distribution; dealing out in portions; relaxing of the laws or canons in special cases.

dis-pense, to deal out; **dispense with,** to do without.

dis-play, *n.,* in printing, large type of varying styles and heaviness; in advertising, a layout designed to draw attention by use of various types, illustration, and white space.

dit-to, the same thing as before.

di-ur-nal, daily; pertaining to the daytime.

div-i-dend, a share of the profits from a business, etc.; a number to be divided.

div-i-dend war-rant, a formal paper through which a shareholder obtains his dividend.

dock-age, a cutting down or off; accommodation at a dock; money paid for it.

dock-et, a summary; list; schedule; label; ticket; *v. t.,* to ticket.

doc-u-ment, an official paper giving evidence or proof.

doc-u-men-ta-ry, pertaining to official records and papers.

dol-drums, *n. pl.,* the calm equatorial zone; dullness.

do-main, territory governed; dominion.

do-mes-tic, pertaining to the household; native, not foreign.

dou-ble-faced, dishonest; deceitful.

dou-ble name pa-per, a note, draft, bill of exchange, or other negotiable paper which is additionally indorsed by some one approved by the bank which accepts or discounts it.

dow-ry, *n.,* the property a bride brings to her husband at the time of her marriage; gift; possession.

draw, *v. t.,* to obtain from a deposit; *v. i.,* to write a formal demand.

draw-ee, one on whom an order, bill of exchange, or draft is drawn.

draw-er, one who draws a draft, bill of exchange, etc.

droit, legal right.

drudge, *v. i.,* to labor at mean or unpleasant tasks; *n.,* a slave; menial.

drudg-er-y, slavish work.

dry goods, textile fabrics, etc.

due, *adj.,* owed; owing; payable; *n.,* that which belongs or may be claimed by right; *pl.,* money payable at regular intervals for membership in a club, etc.

due bill, an informal acknowledgment of a debt in writing.

dum-my, blank pages cut and folded to indicate the size and shape of a proposed publication; a pasted-up plan of the contents of such a publication. DUMMY CORPORATION, a corporation established to conceal the identity of the true principals.

du-plex, double; twofold.

du-pli-cate, *v. t.,* to make an exact likeness of; *n.,* copy; facsimile.

dur-ance, imprisonment; custody.

du-ress, constraint; compulsion; imprisonment; durance.

du-ty, tax levied by the government on certain exports, imports, or other articles.

E

ear-nest, a token; something given or done in advance as a pledge.

earn-ings, *n. pl.,* money received for services; wages.

ease-ment, in law, any of several rights, short of ownership, which one may have in the land of another, the right of passage, for instance.

e-co-nom-ic, concerning the management or administration of the income and expenditures of a household, business, community, or government.

e-co-nom-i-cal, thrifty; frugal.

e-co-nom-ics, the science that treats of the production and distribution of wealth.

e-con-o-mist, one who studies the theory of the production, etc., of wealth.

e-con-o-my, management of income, expenditures, production, etc., of a household, business, community, or government; thriftiness; a judicious use of wealth.

ed-it, to revise, correct, or adapt for publication.

e-di-tion, the whole number of the copies of a work published at a time; a literary work in its published form.

ef-fects, personal estate.

ef-fi-cien-cy, production of the desired effect with minimum effort.

e-lec-tro-type, a printing plate made from another plate, usually from a wax impression, for the purpose of providing several identical plates.

em-bar-go, a restraint imposed by law upon commerce; the act of stopping vessels or transportation by railway.

em-bez-zle, to steal that which has been entrusted to one's care.

em-bez-zle-ment, the theft of property that has been entrusted to one's care.

e-men-da-tion, correction; an improvement in a text.

e-mer-gen-cy, a crisis; an event that occurs suddenly and unexpectedly.

em-i-grate, to leave one country or state to reside in another.

em-is-sar-y, a person sent on a mission.

e-mol-u-ment, profit; compensation; salary; wages.

em-ploy-ee, one who works for another.

em-ploy-er, one who hires another to work for him.

em-ploy-ment, occupation; business.

en-clo-sure, see *Inclosure.*

en-dorse, to authorize; write on the back of, as a check. Also, INDORSE.

en-dow, to enrich; furnish with a fund.

en-dow-ment, property or income appropriated to any object; gifts of nature.

en-grav-ing, the act of producing a pattern upon metal or other hard material by cutting or etching; the plate so prepared; the impression produced by printing from an engraved plate.

en-tail, *v. t.,* to fix an estate inalienably upon certain heirs; *n.,* the act of entailing; an estate left to a particular heir or heirs.

en-trée, an entrance; freedom of access; a dish served between the chief courses at the table. *Fr.*

en-trust, *v. t.,* to place in faithful keeping; confide. Also, INTRUST.

en-try, the act of recording in a book; the thing so recorded; the act of taking possession; the giving an account of the arrival of a ship in port.

en-vel-op, to cover by wrapping, etc.; hide.

en-ve-lope, that which infolds or covers, usually sealed for safe conveyance by post, etc.; a covering.

eq-ui-ty, in finance, the difference between the actual value of a property and the total of all claims against that property.

eq-ui-ty of re-demp-tion, the time allowed a mortgagor to reclaim property by paying the obligation due.

er-ra-tum, (*pl.,* **errata**), an error in writing or printing.

er-rors and o-mis-sions ex-cept-ed, usually abbr. E. and O. E., a mark used on bills, etc., to denote that corrections will be made later on.

es-ca-la-tor clause, a provision in a union contract for automatic increases and decreases in wages according to the rise and fall in the cost of living.

es-cheat, *v. t.,* to forfeit; take possession of, as of property to which there are no heirs; *v. i.,* to revert; *n.,* property which falls to the state by forfeiture or failure of heirs.

es-crow, a deed, bond, or other written agreement given over to a third person, to be given up to the grantee only when certain conditions are fulfilled.

es-prit de corps, a spirit of common devotedness, sympathy, interest, etc., existing among persons of the same profession, society, etc. *Fr.*

et-i-quette, conventional rules of society; good breeding.

e-ven-tu-al-i-ty, a possible result.

e-vict, to put out or dispossess by legal process; expel or remove by force.

ev-i-dence, proof; testimony.

ex-cep-tion, something omitted or excluded; objection.

ex-cess, an undue amount; over-abundance; an added charge.

ex-cess prof-its tax, a tax imposed on business profits which exceed "normal" or "standard" profits.

ex-change, a trading place; a central office for the transaction of business; the settling of accounts between parties at some distance from each other.

ex-change bro-ker, one who deals in the exchange of money, especially foreign bills of exchange and money.

ex-cheq-uer, a public treasury.

ex-cise, *n.,* a tax levied upon goods within a country; a tax upon certain trades; duty; *v. t.,* to levy a tax or duty upon; to cut out.

ex-clu-sive, restricted to a privileged few.

ex-e-cute, to carry out; make valid by signature or seal; put to death under sentence of law.

ex-e-cut-ed, carried out according to law.

ex-ec-u-tive, one charged with administrative work.

ex-ec-u-tor, one appointed by a testator to carry out the terms of a will; *fem.,* **ex-ec-u-trix.**

ex-hib-it, *v. t.,* to display; *n.,* a collection of objects shown before the public; something shown in court and held to be used for further evidence.

ex-hi-bi-tion, a display; demonstration.

ex-i-gen-cy, a pressing need; an emergency.

ex of-fi-ci-o, by right of office but without other special authority.

ex-on-er-ate, to free from blame; justify; acquit.

ex-or-bi-tant, excessive.

ex par-te, one-sided, as *ex parte* evidence.

ex-pec-ta-tion of life, in insurance, the probable length of a person's life as determined by averages shown in mortality tables.

ex-pe-di-ent, advantageous; convenient; conferring a special advantage.

ex-pe-dite, to quicken the progress of.

ex-pend, to spend; use.

ex-pend-i-ture, the act of laying out time, money, energy, etc.

ex-pense, cost; the paying out of money.

ex-pen-sive, costly.

ex-pert, one specially qualified by study and practice; a specialist.

ex-ploi-ta-tion, the act of making use of or obtaining profit by, especially by unfair means.

ex-port, *v. t.,* to send out of a country, as merchandise, etc.; *n.,* goods sold and sent to another country.

ex-po-sé, an undesirable or an embarrassing disclosure. *Fr.*

ex post fac-to, happening or enacted after the deed is done; retrospective.

ex-pur-gate, to cleanse; remove offensive parts, as from a book.

ex-tem-po-re, without previous study or preparation.

ex-tem-po-rize, *v. i.,* to speak without notes on the spur of the moment; improvise; speak extempore, *v. t.,* to compose on the spur of the moment.

ex-tend, *v. t.,* to stretch out; expand; continue; *v. i.,* to reach; be prolonged.

ex-ten-sion, the allowance of additional time to a debtor by a creditor; enlargement; expansion.

ex-tort, to obtain by illegal compulsion or force.

ex-tor-tion, the act of obtaining by force, threats, or injustice.

ex-tor-tion-ate, unreasonable; excessive; oppressive.

ex-tor-tion-er, one who demands and obtains by unjust means.

ex-tra-dite, to deliver or surrender a person, usually a prisoner, under an extradition treaty or special agreement.

ex-tra-di-tion, the surrender under treaty or special agreement of a fugitive from justice by one government to another.

eye wit-ness, one who sees an event or act.

F

face, the surface of anything; hence, the printing surface of type. TYPE FACE, the style of type.

face val-ue, the nominal value which appears on a bond, coupon, piece of money, or other financial instrument.

fa-cil-i-tate, to make easy.

fac-sim-i-le, an exact reproduction.

fac-to-ry, a place where goods are made; a manufactory.

fac-to-tum, one who does all kinds of work.

Fah-ren-heit ther-mom-e-ter, the name of a thermometer having 32° as the freezing point, and 212° as the boiling point, of water.

fail-ure, bankruptcy.

fake, *v. t.,* to deceive; *n.,* a scheme for swindling; a hoax; false report of news.

fak-er, a fraud; a swindler; street peddler.

false pre-tense, a willful misrepresentation of facts with the purpose of cheating another.

fea-si-ble, practicable.

fed-er-al, pertaining to league or treaty; pertaining to a country made up of states, as the United States and Switzerland, or its government.

Fed-er-al Re-serve Bank, a system of banks organized by the United States government, to act as an agent in maintaining reserves, issuing money in the form of bank notes, and lending money to other banks.

fee, *n.,* a charge for services; an inherited estate.

feel-er, something put forth to obtain information.

fee sim-ple, an estate held in one's own right without restrictions.

fel-o-ny, a serious crime punishable by death or imprisonment.

fi-as-co, a complete or ignominious failure.

fi-at, a decree; a command; an order of court authorizing certain proceedings.

fi-du-ci-ar-y, *n.,* a trustee; *adj.,* held in trust.

fig-ure-head, a person only nominally important.

file, *n.,* an orderly arrangement of letters or papers; any device for so arranging them; a series; line; tool; *v. t.,* to arrange in order.

fi-nance, *n.,* the science of handling money, especially with regard to its investment; revenue or income of an individual, corporation, or government; *v. t.,* to manage the monetary affairs of; raise or supply money for.

fi-nan-cial, pertaining to money; pecuniary; fiscal.

fin-an-cier, one who is skilled in conducting matters of finance.

fine, *n.,* money exacted as penalty; *v. t.,* to punish by imposing a money penalty upon.

fi-nesse, skill; subtlety; stratagem.

first-hand, obtained direct from the source.

first-rate, of the highest excellence.

fis-cal, financial; pertaining to the public treasury.

fixed charg-es, charges which become due at stated intervals, such as rent, taxes, etc.

fix-ture, any fixed appliance.

float, to start a company, scheme, etc., by furnishing money.

flot-sam, wreckage of a ship or of a ship's cargo found floating on the sea.

fluc-tu-ate, to rise and fall; waver, hesitate.

fly-leaf, a blank leaf at the beginning or end of a book.

fold-er, a circular or time table, etc.

fo-li-o, the page number in a book.

font, a complete assortment of printing types of one size and style. WRONG FONT, type from one font mixed with another; *abbr., w.f.*

forced sale, a sale under legal compulsion.

fore-close, to take away the right of redeeming mortgaged property.

fore-clo-sure, the act of cutting off from further chance to redeem property: said of a mortgage.

fore-gone, determined beforehand; unavoidable.

for-eign bill, a draft or bill of exchange payable in a foreign country.

fore-man, the spokesman of a jury; a chief workman; overseer; a supervisor.

fore-sight, the power of seeing beforehand; provident care.

forge, to counterfeit.

forg-er, one who counterfeits handwriting with the intent to deceive.

forg-er-y, the act of criminally imitating the handwriting of another.

form, *n.,* a page of type locked into place in a metal frame, ready for printing.

for-mat, the size, shape, and general layout of a publication.

for-mu-la, a prescribed rule or model; an expression of chemical composition; expression of a mathematical problem by means of symbols; a prescription.

for-mu-late, to reduce to a definite statement; to put in terms of a prescription, rule, or recipe.

foun-da-tion, the base or lowest part of a structure; basic principles; an endowed institution.

foun-dry, a place where metals are cast.

fran-chise, liberty; freedom; right; privilege; right of suffrage.

frank, *n.,* free postage; *v. t.,* to send or carry a letter free of charge.

frank-ing priv-i-lege, the right of sending letters, packages, telegrams, etc., free of charges.

fra-ter-ni-ty, a brotherhood; a secret society.

free a-long-side ship, free delivery of merchandise to the side of an outgoing vessel; *abbr., f. a. s.*

free lance, *n.,* a writer or artist who works for publications without being regularly employed; *v. i.*, to work on such terms.

free list, a list of goods or merchandise admitted to a country free of duty; a list of those entitled to something free of charge.

free on board, free delivery of goods to the conveyance by which they are to be transported; *abbr., f. o. b.*

free port, a port where merchandise may pass duty free.

free trade, trade or commerce free from tariffs or customs duties.

freight, *n.,* the cargo of a ship; goods loaded on a vessel, car, etc.; the charge for the transportation of goods; *v. t.,* to load with goods; to hire for carrying goods.

freight-age, charge for freight; cargo; act of freighting.

freight-er, one who charters or loads a ship or car; a cargo vessel which carries no or few passengers.

func-tion, *n.,* duty; office; event; action; public or official ceremony; a mathematical quantity connected with and varying with another; *v. i.,* to act.

func-tion-ar-y, *n.,* an official; one who fills an important position.

fund, *n.,* stock; capital; money set apart for some special purpose; *v. t.,* to provide a fund; to place in a fund.

fun-da-men-tal, basic; essential; pertaining to the foundation.

fund-ed, in the form of bonds bearing regular interest; invested in public securities.

fund-ed debt, a public debt which has been put in the form of bonds bearing regular interest.

funds, quick capital; available financial resources.

fu-tures, merchandise, commodities, or securities bought or sold for future delivery.

G

gage, *n.,* security; pledge; defiance, challenge. See *Gauge.*

gain, *n.,* advantage; winnings; *v. t.,* to obtain; earn; *v. i.,* to make progress; increase.

gain-ful, advantageous; profitable.

gar-nish-ee, *n.,* one who controls the property of another until the claims

of a third party are settled; *v. t.,* to attach property by law for the payment of debt.

gauge, a standard of measure; the distance between the rails of a railway line; *v. t.,* to measure; to find out. Also, GAGE.

gaug-er, one who gauges; an official whose business it is to ascertain the contents of casks.

gav-el, a small mallet used by a presiding officer or chairman.

gen-er-al-ize, *v. t.,* to make general in scope or meaning; to reduce to a general law or statement; *v. i.,* to draw general inferences.

gold brick, a swindle.

goods, movable property; merchandise; wares.

goods and chat-tels, movable property.

good will, the established popularity of a business house or trade.

graft, unlawful acquisition of money, especially from the government; a bribe; *v. i.,* to practice grafting; to accept bribes.

graft-er, one who through position or business is able to accept public money without having rendered service for it.

grand ju-ry, a jury which inquires into an offense to see if there is sufficient evidence to bring an indictment. See *Jury; Petit Jury.*

grant, *n.,* the act of conferring; a gift; bestowal; privilege; *v. t.,* to give; confer; admit; concede; transfer; impart.

grant-ee, the person to whom property is transferred by law.

grant-or, the person who transfers property by law.

graph, a diagram showing a system of interrelations by points, often connected by lines.

gra-tu-i-ty, a free gift.

green-back, a U.S. note with a green back.

gross, twelve dozen; the entire amount.

guar-an-tee, *n.,* a surety; a promise; a pledge; *v. t.,* to be responsible for; warrant; secure the performance of.

guar-an-tor, one who gives a guarantee.

guar-an-ty, a legal surety; a guarantee.

guard-i-an, one who has charge of the property or person of another, as of a minor or other person incapable of managing his own affairs.

guild, a fraternity; an association.

H

ha-be-as cor-pus, Latin, meaning "you have the body"; a writ or order to bring a person into court.

hab-er-dash-er, a dealer in small wares; usually, in U.S., a dealer in men's furnishings.

half-tone, a printing plate prepared by photographing an illustration through a screen of dots, making possible reproduction of shadings as in a photograph.

hall-mark, a mark of genuineness or purity.

hand-bill, a loose printed sheet circulated for advertising purposes.

hand-book, a guidebook or manual.

har-bor mas-ter, an official whose duty is to see that the regulations of the government are observed in a harbor.

head, the title of an article or section in a publication, usually set in large type. Also HEADING.

head-quar-ters, the center of authority.

hear-ing, a judicial trial.

heir, one who inherits or is named to inherit property devised by will.

high seas, the open sea, beyond the waters owned by certain nations.

hire, *v. t.,* to engage for a stipulated reward; to rent; *n.,* a consideration paid for the use of anything; wages.

hire-ling, one who serves for pay; a mercenary person.

hol-o-caust, destruction, especially by fire, of many persons.

hon-o-rar-i-um, a fee paid for professional services on which no price is customarily set.

hon-or-ar-y, conferring or possessing something as a token of high esteem.

horse-pow-er, the power of a horse, estimated at 33,000 pounds raised one foot in one minute.

hun-dred-weight, the twentieth part of a ton; 100 pounds avoirdupois.

hy-poth-e-cate, to pledge, as life insurance, as a security for a debt or other obligation.

I

i-bi-dem, a Latin word meaning "in the same place"; *abbr., ib., ibid.*

il-le-gal, unlawful.

il-leg-i-ble, difficult to read; badly written.

il-le-git-i-mate, unlawful; unauthorized; born out of wedlock.

im-peach, to accuse; to charge with wrongdoing, especially a public official.

im-peach-ment, the act of calling to trial; charges of maladministration brought against public officials.

im-pe-cu-ni-ous, without money; poor.

im-pli-ca-tion, an entanglement; a tacit inference.

im-plic-it, to be understood, though not expressed in words.

im-port (ĭm-pōrt'), *v. t.,* to bring into one's country; (ĭm'pōrt), *n.,* merchandise brought into a country from abroad.

im-port-er, a merchant who brings in goods from abroad.

im-post, a tax, especially duty levied on goods brought into a country.

im-pos-tor, one who imposes on others; one who deceives under false character or pretensions.

im-print (ĭm-prĭnt'), *v. t.,* to stamp on paper; to fix in the mind or memory; *n.* (ĭm'-prĭnt), the name of the printer or publisher of a book with the time and place of publication; an impression.

im-pro-bi-ty, lack of integrity or principle.

im-promp-tu, offhand; without preparation.

in-ca-pac-i-tate, to deprive of capability or natural power.

in-cen-di-a-rism, the act of maliciously burning property.

in-cen-di-ar-y, *n.,* one who maliciously sets fire; one who inflames the passions, or excites violence; *adj.,* relating to arson; tending to arouse sedition.

in-ci-den-tal, *adj.,* casual; accidental; *n. pl.,* small expenses.

in-close, to shut in or surround; fence in; encompass. Also, ENCLOSE.

in-clo-sure, a space or thing surrounded; that which surrounds;

something included in the envelope with a letter. Also ENCLOSURE.

in-clu-sive, inclosing; comprehensive.

in-cog-ni-to, *adj.,* in disguise; *adv.,* under an assumed name; *n. (fem.,* **incognita**), one who travels under an assumed name.

in-come, the yearly receipts of a business or of a person; salary; revenue. GROSS INCOME, the entire receipts from a business. NET INCOME, the part of an income which remains after expenses are paid.

in-come tax, a tax levied upon the receipts of an individual or a business.

in-com-pat-i-bil-i-ty, the state of not being able to live together in harmony.

in-com-pe-ten-cy, inability. Also, INCOMPETENCE.

in-com-pe-tent, incapable; not admissible or allowable.

in-cor-po-rate, *v. t.,* to combine into one body or corporation; embody; *v. i.,* to unite so as to become a part of another body; *adj.,* united in one body; incorporated.

in-cre-ment, increase; gain; produce. UNEARNED INCREMENT, the accumulation of interest on money without effort on the part of the owner.

in-cum-ben-cy, the state of holding an office or benefice.

in-cum-bent, *adj.,* obligatory; resting upon as a duty; *n.,* one who holds an office or benefice.

in-cur, to encounter; to become subject or liable to; contract.

in-debt-ed, being under monetary or other obligation.

in-de-fea-si-ble, that cannot be made null or void, as a title.

in-dem-ni-fi-ca-tion, reimbursement for loss or damage; reparation.

in-dem-ni-ty, security against loss, injury, or damage; repayment for loss.

in-dent-ed, held by agreement, especially as an apprentice.

in-den-ture, *n.,* a mutual legal agreement; *v. t.,* to bind by written agreement, as an apprentice.

in-dex (*pl.,* **indexes, indices**), a pointer or an indicator; a table of contents; the figure or symbol showing the power or root of a quantity, as 4^a, 4^2.

in-dict, to charge with, as crime.

in-dict-a-ble, liable to be charged with crime or misdemeanor.

in-dict-er, one who charges another with crime. Also, INDICTOR.

in-dict-ment, a formal charge against a person; a written accusation against a prisoner.

in-dig-e-nous, native.

in-di-gent, destitute.

in-dis-pen-sa-ble, necessary.

in-dorse, to write on the back of, as a check, etc.; guarantee; approve; ratify. Also, ENDORSE.

in-dor-see, the person to whom a check, etc., is made payable.

in-dorse-ment, approval.

in-dors-or, one who signs over a check; one who approves, ratifies, or recommends.

in-dus-tri-al-ism, a state of society founded upon the development of manufacturing industries.

in-dus-tri-ous, hard-working.

in-dus-try, assiduity; habitual diligence; a particular branch of manufacture or trade.

in-ef-fi-cien-cy, want of power or skill.

in-ef-fi-cient, incapable; not proficient.

in-ex-pe-ri-ence, a want of personal trial and practice with life; lack of practice of any kind.

in-fant, in common law, any person under the age of twenty-one. The statute law varies in different states.

in-for-mal, unceremonious; unofficial.

in-her-it-ance, property transmitted to an heir; a legacy.

in-i-ti-a-tion, the act of introducing, as into a society, club, etc.; the rites by means of which one is introduced into such an organization.

in-i-ti-a-tive, the power of taking the lead; the energy which dares new enterprises.

in-junc-tion, legal restraint on certain proceedings.

in-no-va-tion, the introduction of a novelty; a change.

in-op-por-tune, unseasonable; untimely.

in-quest, a judicial or official inquiry into the causes of sudden death; the jury making the inquiry.

in re, concerning.

in-scribe, to write; to address formally; to dedicate.

in-scrip-tion, the act of printing or engraving for publication; the dedication of a book or a poem to a person; that which is written or engraved, as an inscription on a monument.

in-sol-ven-cy, the state of being unable to pay all debts.

in-sol-vent, *adj.,* unable to pay all debts; bankrupt; *n.,* one who is not able to pay all his debts.

in-spect, to examine carefully, so as to ascertain quality, errors, etc.

in-spec-tion, a careful survey; an official examination.

in-spec-tor, one who examines.

in-stall, to invest with office or rank; to set up for use.

in-stal-la-tion, the act of investing with office or rank.

in-stall-ment, a part payment; a part of anything produced at one time, as a serial in a magazine.

in-stall-ment plan, the system of paying a debt or price due in payments.

in-stan-ter, without delay.

in-sti-tu-tion, an organized group for promoting a particular object.

in-stru-ment, the means by which anything is accomplished; a document containing the terms of a contract.

in-sub-or-di-nate, not submitting to authority; mutinous; riotous.

in-sub-or-di-na-tion, rebellion against authority.

in-sur-a-ble, capable of being insured against loss or damage.

in-sur-a-ble in-ter-est, a right or title to a person or property insured to sustain a contract in the event of the loss insured against.

in-sur-ance, *n.,* the act or system of insuring against loss, damage, accident, etc.; the system by which a person pays a *premium* to protect himself against a specific loss or *risk.*

in-sur-ance bro-ker, an agent who handles insurance.

in-sur-ance pol-i-cy, the written contract between the insurer and the insured.

in-sur-ance trust, a trust created by a life insurance policyholder who directs that the amount of the policy shall be paid at his death to a trustee, who shall invest and administer it for the beneficiary.

in-ter-course, reciprocal dealings between individuals, nations, etc.; commerce; fellowship.

in-ter-est, premium paid for the use of money.

in-ter-im, the meantime.

in to-to, in general; in the whole.

in tran-sit, on the way.

in-val-id, having no force or effect.

in-val-i-date, to destroy the force of; cancel; nullify.

in-va-lid-i-ty, a want of legal force.

in-ven-to-ry, a list of goods, as of a merchant's stock.

in-vest, *v. t.,* to clothe, as with office or dignity; to lay out money so as to obtain interest; *v. i.,* to put money into.

in-vest-ment, the act of placing money so that it will draw interest; the money so placed.

in-ves-tor, one who lays out money for profit.

in-voice, a written account of merchandise and prices, delivered to the buyer; a bill.

in-voice book, a book in which a record of invoices is kept.

ip-so fac-to, as a result of the act itself.

ip-so ju-re, by the law itself.

ir-re-deem-a-ble, not convertible: said of paper money; not reclaimable.

i-tem, a separate article; a bit of news.

i-tem-ize, to state by separate entries.

i-tin-er-ar-y, a guide book; a diary of an extended trip; the plan of a long journey.

J

jet-sam, goods thrown overboard to lighten a ship's cargo in time of danger. Also, JETTISON.

jet-ti-son, *n.,* the act of throwing goods overboard to relieve a ship; *v. t.,* to throw overboard.

jet-ty, a structure extending into the water to influence the tide, current, etc.; a wharf.

job-ber, a middleman; an agent who does odd pieces of work.

job lot, an odd assortment of merchandise.

join-er, a skilled woodworker.

joint note, a promissory note signed by two or more persons, each of whom is responsible for a proportionate share of its payment.

joint and sev-er-al note, a promissory note signed by several persons, each of whom is liable for the whole amount in the event the others fail to make payment.

joint stock, stock that is held in common with another or others.

joint stock com-pa-ny, a group of people organized to conduct business with capital held in common.

joint ten-an-cy, tenure of property with others in such a way that when one of the joint owners dies his share goes to the others to the exclusion of his heirs.

jour-nal, a daily paper or other periodical; a diary; a ship's logbook; an account of daily transactions and events; in bookkeeping, a daybook or book of original entry.

jour-ney-man, a workman who has fully learned his trade.

judge, *n.,* an arbiter; a referee; *v. t.,* to pass sentence upon; *v. i.,* to pass sentence; estimate.

judg-ment, the decision of a court; opinion; discretion.

judg-ment note, a promissory note containing a power of attorney authorizing a judgment without process in case of nonpayment when due.

ju-di-ca-ture, a court of justice, and the extent of its jurisdiction.

junc-tion, the place where railroads, rivers, etc., meet; point of union.

ju-ror, one who serves on a jury.

ju-ry, a body of men, or women, usually twelve, selected according to law, and sworn to examine and declare truth on the evidence in a legal case before them. See *Grand Jury; Petit Jury.*

jus-ti-fi-ca-tion, vindication; in printing, arrangement of type so that each line is of equal length with the others.

K

kar-at, see *Carat.*

kil-o-gram, 1,000 grams or 22 lb. avoirdupois.

kil-o-li-ter, 1,000 liters or 264.18 gallons.

kil-o-me-ter, 1,000 meters or 3,280.8 feet.

kil-o-watt, a unit for measuring the power of an electric current; 1,000 watts.

L

la-bel, *n.,* a slip of paper, etc., attached to anything stating contents, destination, ownership, etc.; *v. t.,* to mark with such a slip.

la-bor, *n.,* toil; exertion; work; pain; *v. i.,* to toil.

lab-o-ra-to-ry, a place for scientific research.

la-bor-er, one who does work which requires little skill.

land-ed, possessing, or consisting of, land.

land-hold-er, a holder or proprietor of land.

land-la-dy, a woman who lets houses, apartments, etc., to tenants; the mistress of an inn or hotel.

land-lord, the owner of lands or buildings which he rents to others; the master of an inn, hotel, etc.

land-poor, owning unprofitable land.

lapse, *v. i.,* to pass or slip away; to fail in moral conduct or duty; to pass from one to another by some omission; *n.,* a slight failure in duty.

lar-ce-ny, theft.

lar-gess, a liberal gift. Also, LARGESSE.

lathe, a machine in which articles are held and rotated while being shaped and polished by means of a tool.

law, *n.,* a rule prescribed by authority or custom; statute; the legal profession; a principle deduced from practice or observation; a scientific statement of facts observed in natural phenomena; an established principle.

law-ful, legal; just.

law-less, unruly, not restrained by authority.

law-suit, an action in court for the recovery of a right or the settlement of a claim.

law-yer, one who practices law.

lay-out, the act of planning; the make-up of a book, advertisement, or other publication.

lead-ing (lĕd′dĭng), a strip of type metal inserted to separate lines of type; the process of inserting such strips.

leak-age, allowance made for the quantity of anything that passes in or out; the quantity which leaks.

leap year, a year of 366 days; a year divisible by 4, as 1920.

lease, *n.*, the time for which property is rented; a written contract for the renting of property; *v. t.*, to let or grant by lease; take possession of by contract.

lease-hold, tenure by contract for a certain time; property so held.

ledg-er, the principal account book of a mercantile or other business house.

leg-a-cy, a bequest by will; anything handed down by an ancestor.

le-gal, lawful; pertaining to law.

le-gal-i-ty, lawfulness.

le-gal ten-der, currency or coin authorized by the government for the payment of debts.

leg-a-tee, the person to whom property is left by will.

le-git-i-mate, lawful; born of wedded parents; reasonable.

les-see, one to whom a lease is given.

les-sor, one who grants a lease.

let-ter-head, the heading printed or engraved at the top of a sheet of writing paper.

lev-y, *v. t.*, to raise or collect by authority; to seize for unpaid rent, etc.; *n.*, the act of raising troops or collecting taxes; the number or amount raised.

li-a-bil-i-ty, the state of being subject to or responsible for; *pl.*, debts, opposed to *assets*.

li-a-ble, responsible; exposed to something unpleasant, as danger, damage, etc.

li-ai-son, a bond or link; an illicit intimacy between a man and woman.

li-bel, *n.*, defamation; slander; *v. i.*, to lampoon; defame.

li-bel-ous, defamatory.

li-cense, legal permission; *v. t.*, to permit by law; to authorize. Also, LI-CENCE.

li-cen-ti-ate, one with the authority to preach or practice a profession.

li-en, a legal claim; security held until a claim is settled.

light-er-age, the unloading of a cargo into a lighter for conveyance to or from the shore; cost of such work.

lim-i-ta-tion, stat-ute of, a period established by law after which a claim

or prosecution in law may not be made.

line en-grav-ing, a printing plate in which the pattern is produced by lines or masses, without the use of a screen. See *Halftone.*

lin-go, language; a contemptuous term for a particular language or dialect.

liq-ui-date, to pay off; clear up; settle.

liq-ui-da-tion, the act of settling or adjusting debts.

lit-i-gant, one engaged in a lawsuit.

lit-i-ga-tion, the act of carrying on a lawsuit; a lawsuit.

Lloyd's, an association of insurance underwriters in London.

loan, money made available for a set period, in consideration of payment of interest; loans may be payable in full on a certain date or in preestablished installments.

lob-by, to try to influence the members of a legislative body.

lob-by-ist, a person who tries to influence the members of a legislative body of which he is not a member.

lock-out, the shutting out of workmen from a shop or factory by their employer.

lodge, a place where members of a society hold their meetings; the members themselves; *v. t.*, to shelter temporarily; deposit; *v. i.*, to live in temporarily.

lodg-ing, a temporary dwelling place; a room or apartment hired in the house of another.

long-hand, ordinary handwriting.

loss, in bookkeeping, the excess of expenses over income.

lot, a portion of something, as land.

lu-cra-tive, profitable.

M

mag-is-trate, a civil officer with public authority.

mag-nate, a man of high rank, distinction, or influence; industrialist.

mail-a-ble, lawful or suitable to be sent by mail.

mail-ing list, a list of names and addresses of persons who may be prospects for purchase of a product or service.

main-tain, to support; keep up.

main-te-nance, means of support; the upkeep of property or equipment.

ma-jor-i-ty, the state of being greater; numerical excess; the full legal age.

make-up, the way in which the parts of anything are assembled; arrangement of printed matter in a newspaper, etc.

mal-prac-tice, a wrongful manner of conducting any profession.

man-da-mus, a command or writ from a superior court directing an inferior court or person to perform some public duty or act.

man-date, an order; an official command.

man-da-to-ry, *adj.*, pertaining to, or expressing, an official command; obligatory; *n.*, one who acts for another; a country chosen to administer or govern a certain colony or territory. Also, MANDATARY.

ma-nip-u-late, to operate or manage skillfully with the hands; to falsify.

man-u-al, *adj.*, pertaining to, or performed by, the hands; *n.*, a handbook.

man-u-fac-to-ry, a place where goods are made from raw materials; a factory.

man-u-fac-ture, *v. t.*, to make from raw materials; *v. i.*, to be occupied in making goods from raw materials; *n.*, the operation of changing raw material into useful articles; the thing made from raw material.

mar-gin, a reserve sum or quantity; an excess of time or money over that which is actually needed or used; money or other security given to a broker to guard him from loss in advancing funds on an investment.

mar-i-time, relating to the sea.

mar-ket, *n.*, a trading place; the state of trade; the region where there is a demand for a certain commodity; *v. t.*, to offer for sale in a market; to sell; *v. i.*, to deal in a market; to buy or sell provisions or goods.

mar-ket-a-ble, salable.

mar-ket re-search, see *Sampling.*

ma-tu-ri-ty, a coming due, as a note or other obligation.

max-i-mum, *n.*, the utmost; *adj.*, highest or greatest possible.

mean, *adj.*, average, as *mean tempera-*

ture; n., the middle point between two extremes; *pl.*, resources.

me-di-ate, to interpose between parties to bring about a reconciliation; to bring about by friendly interposition.

me-di-a-tion, the act of trying to reconcile.

me-di-a-tor, one who seeks to bring about friendly relations.

me-di-um, *pl.*, **me-di-a,** the method used for publicizing an advertisement, such as newspaper, radio, television, billboard.

mem-o-ran-dum, a note to help the memory; a brief entry in a diary.

men-su-ra-tion, the art or practice of measuring.

men-u, a list of dishes to be served at a meal; bill of fare.

mer-can-tile, commercial, pertaining to merchandise or trade.

mer-can-tile a-gen-cy, an organization which ascertains and furnishes information on the financial standing, business reputation, or credit rating of individuals, or firms engaged in mercantile or commercial enterprises.

mer-can-tile pa-per, commercial paper.

mer-chan-dise, goods, wares, etc., bought and sold.

mer-chant, *n.*, a trader; retailer; *adj.*, relating to trade or commerce; mercantile.

mer-chant-man, a trading vessel, as distinguished from a warship.

mer-chant ma-rine, a nation's facilities for carrying on trade on the ocean.

merg-er, the legal combination of two estates, corporations, or interests.

me-rid-i-an, the highest point reached, as by a heavenly body; the height of prosperity, etc.

me-ter, *n.*, an instrument for measuring and recording; the unit of linear measure in the metric system, 39.37 inches. Also, METRE.

met-ric sys-tem, a system of weights and measures first adopted in France, by which things are measured or numbered by tens or fractions of tens.

mid-dle-man, the dealer between producer and consumer; a broker.

mile, 5,280 feet.

mile-age, aggregate miles; an allowance for traveling expenses at the rate per mile; the charge per mile on railroads.

mil-len-ni-um, a period of 1,000 years, especially the thousand years during which it is supposed that Christ will reign on earth.

mil-li-gram, 1/1000 of a gram.

mil-li-li-ter, 1/1000 of a liter.

mil-li-me-ter, 1/1000 of a meter.

mim-e-o-graph, *n.,* a stencil device for copying written or typewritten letters; *v. t.,* to copy with such a machine.

min-i-mum, the least possible quantity or degree.

mi-nor, a person not yet twenty-one.

mi-nor-i-ty, the smaller of two numbers; opposed to *majority;* the state of being under age.

mi-nu-ti-ae, minor or unimportant details.

mis-cel-la-ne-ous, varied; consisting of several kinds.

mis-cel-la-ny, a mixture.

mis-de-mean-or, a crime less serious than a felony.

mis-rep-re-sent, to represent falsely either through intention or ignorance.

mis-tri-al, a trial in court which comes to nothing because of some error in the course of it.

mit-ti-mus, a warrant for committing to prison.

mod-el, a pattern; standard; one who poses for an artist; one who tries on costumes to display them to customers.

mon-e-ta-ry, pertaining to money.

mon-e-tize, to convert into money.

mon-ey, coin; medium of exchange; currency. See *Legal Tender.*

mon-ey mar-ket, the market for the exchange of loanable money or capital; the sphere of financial operations.

mon-ey or-der, an order demanding the payment of money.

mon-o-met-al-lism, the use of only one metal as the standard value of currency.

mo-nop-o-ly, control of any industry; the person or group of persons exercising exclusive control of any industry.

mon-sieur, a French title of courtesy equivalent to Mr.; *abbr., M.*

month-ly, *adj.,* happening once a month; continuing for a month; *adv.,* once a month; *n.,* a periodical published once a month.

mort-gage, a conveyance of property as security for debts; the legal paper by which the conveyance is made; *v. t.,* to pledge, as property as security.

mort-ga-gee, the person to whom property is given as security.

mort-ga-gor, the person who gives property as security.

mort-main, possession of lands or tenements by an organized body, ecclesiastical or otherwise.

mo-ti-va-tion re-search, a survey to establish the public's reasons for buying or not buying a given product, or its reasons for purchasing habits in general.

mulct, *v. t.,* to fine; *n.,* a fine.

mu-nic-i-pal, pertaining to a city or town.

mu-nic-i-pal-i-ty, a town or city having local self-government.

mu-tu-al, interchanged between two persons or among a group.

N

na-tion-al bank, an institution organized under a special act of Congress, for lending or custody of money.

na-tion-al debt, the aggregate of obligations of the United States government.

nat-u-ral-ize, to grant (to a foreigner) the rights and privileges of citizenship.

nav-i-ga-ble, capable of being traveled over by a boat, etc.

nav-i-ga-tion, the act of traveling on the water in ships; the art or science of managing ships.

nav-i-ga-tor, one who travels in ships; one who manages a ship.

née, born. *Fr.*

neg-li-gence, neglect; in law, failure to do or not to do a certain thing, as to exercise proper care.

ne-go-ti-a-ble, capable of being transferred or exchanged.

ne-go-ti-a-ble pa-per, bills of exchange, notes, drafts, checks, etc., which are made payable to bearer or order.

ne-go-ti-ate, *v. t.,* to trade; sell; *v. i.,* to treat with others on political or business affairs.

night let-ter, a telegram sent at reduced rates at night, to be delivered the next morning.

nom-i-nal, in name only.

non-un-ion, not belonging to, or not favoring, trade unions.

nor-mal, natural; usual.

no-ta be-ne, note well; *abbr., N. B.*

no-ta-ry, an official who attests deeds, contracts, etc. Also NOTARY PUBLIC.

no-ti-fi-ca-tion, a written or printed document by which warning, announcement, or information is sent.

no-ti-fy, to make known; inform.

nou-veau riche, one who has recently become rich. *Fr.*

nov-ice, a beginner.

null, of no legal force.

nul-li-fy, to annul; cancel.

O

o-bit-u-ar-y, a notice of death; a brief account of a person or persons deceased.

ob-li-ga-tion, the binding power of a contract, promise, or sense of duty; a written document by which one binds himself under penalty to do a thing.

ob-lig-a-to-ry, binding.

oc-cu-pan-cy, the act of having in possession, as a house.

oc-cu-pant, one who has possession of, or lives in.

oc-cu-pa-tion, the act or state of having in possession or dwelling in; business.

of-fer, *n.,* a proffer; *v. t.,* to present for acceptance or refusal; bid.

of-fi-cial, *n.,* one invested with a public office; *adj.,* pertaining to a public duty or an office; authorized.

of-fi-ci-ate, to act in a public service or capacity.

o-mis-sion, something left out.

o-pen, *adj.,* free; public; unsealed; *v. t.,* to reveal; begin; *v. i.,* to unclose itself; lead into.

o-pen ac-count, a running or unsettled account.

o-pen pol-i-cy, an insurance policy in which the insurer has to prove the value in case of loss.

op-er-ate, *v. i.,* to work; *v. t.,* to cause to work.

op-er-at-ing ex-pens-es, the costs of conducting business exclusive of fixed charges.

op-por-tune, well-timed.

op-por-tun-ism, a quickness in taking advantage of chances with little regard for ethics.

op-ti-mism, the belief that all is for the best; the expectation of a favorable outcome.

op-tion, a privilege, given to one of the parties to a time contract, which may be taken advantage of on any day within a certain specified time limit.

op-tion-al, left to one's choice.

op-u-lent, rich.

or-der, instruction to buy or sell.

or-gan, house or-gan, a paper published by an organization for circulation among its own members.

or-gan-i-za-tion, a body of persons united for some common end.

or-gan-ize, to set in working order; regulate; to persuade workers to become members of a labor organization.

out-fit, *n.,* equipment; *v. t.,* and *v. i.,* to furnish with everything necessary for an undertaking.

out-lay, expenditure in money, energy, etc.

o-ver-cap-i-tal-ize, to place a nominal or "face" value on the capital of a corporation above that of the cost or market value; to capitalize more heavily than is warranted by the business or by probable profits.

o-ver-draw, to make bank drafts, checks, etc., greater than the amount on deposit.

o-ver-due, past the time for payment.

o-ver-head, or OVERHEAD CHARGES, the expenses not included in the actual running of a business, as rent, insurance, etc.

o-ver-pro-duc-tion, supply greater than the demand.

o-ver-se-er, a superintendent; an inspector.

o-ver-time, time worked beyond the regular hours.

P

par-a-mount, superior to all others.

par-cel post, the system of the government of carrying packages by mail.

par ex-cel-lence, beyond comparison. *Fr.*

par-lia-men-ta-ry, pertaining to, or according to, the rules and usages of public assemblies.

part-ner, an associate; a sharer; one of joint principals in a business.

part-ner-ship, the state of being associated in a common undertaking or firm.

pass, permission to go and come; the right to free use or admission, as in a railroad or theater.

pass-book, a depositor's bank book; a book listing articles bought on credit.

pass-key, a master key.

pass-port, an official paper giving one permission to travel in a foreign country.

pass the buck, *Slang,* to shift the responsibility to someone else.

pat-ent, *n.,* a grant of exclusive privilege by the government; *v. t.,* to grant or secure the exclusive right to; *adj.,* secured by government protection.

pat-ent-ee, one who has secured from the government the sole right to make, use, or sell an invention for a certain number of years.

pa-tron, regular customer.

pa-tron-age, guardianship; support; clientele.

pa-tron-ize, to support; favor; act as guardian toward.

pawn, *v. t.,* to pledge as security for a loan; *n.,* something given as security for the payment of a debt.

pawn-bro-ker, a person legally licensed to lend money on goods left with him.

pawn-shop, a place where money is lent on goods deposited.

pay, *v. t.,* to give money, etc., for goods delivered or services rendered; reward; recompense; discharge; *v. i.,* to make recompense; discharge; be worth-while; *n.,* money, etc., given for goods or services rendered.

pay-a-ble, that may or should be paid; justly due.

pay-ee, one to whom money is paid.

pay-mas-ter, one who gives out money for wages.

pay-ment, the act of giving money, etc., for service done; reward.

pec-u-late, to embezzle.

pec-u-la-tion, embezzlement.

ped-dler, one who goes about selling small wares.

pe-nal, pertaining to punishment.

pe-nal-ize, to subject to penalty.

pen-al-ty, punishment; forfeiture; fine. See *Fine.*

pen-ny-weight, 24 grains troy weight.

pen-ny-wise, saving small sums at the hazard of larger.

pen-sion, *n.,* an allowance for past services; *v. t.,* to grant a pension to.

pen-sion-er, one who receives a regular allowance, because of past services or present disability.

pe-on-age, the hiring of gangs of laborers to employers, often in bondage, as for debt.

per cap-i-ta, by heads; for each individual.

per cent, by the hundred.

per-cent-age, the rate per hundred; a part or proportion.

per-en-ni-al, enduring; lasting, as a plant that lives from year to year.

per-func-to-ry, done mechanically; without interest.

pe-ri-od-ic, occurring regularly.

per-jure, to swear falsely.

per-ju-ry, willful swearing to what is false.

per-mit, a written permission or authorization to do something.

per-pe-tu-i-ty, the state of lasting forever; that to which there is no end. IN PERPETUITY, forever.

per-qui-site, an extra profit or allowance; income; gratuity.

per se, by itself.

per-son-al, pertaining to an individual; peculiar to an individual.

per-son-al-i-ty, the sum of one's qualities and characteristics; that which makes one different from all others; an offensive remark made about one's person or private affairs.

per-son-al-ty, personal belongings; movable property.

per-son-nel, a body of persons, especially, a body engaged in a certain business.

per-son-nel man-ag-er, one whose job it is to take on employees and see that they are properly placed.

pes-si-mist, one who believes that the world is bad rather than good; one who expects an unfavorable outcome.

pet-it, petty; insignificant; used only in law.

pe-ti-tion, *n.,* a supplication; a formal request; *v. t.,* to entreat, supplicate.

pet-it ju-ry, a trial jury, as distinct from a grand jury.

pet-ti-fog-ger, a petty lawyer, often one who uses dishonest methods.

pet-ty cash, money received or paid out in small amounts.

pet-ty cash book, a book in which a record is kept of money received or paid out in small amounts.

pho-to-en-grav-ing, a printing plate made by the use of photography in which the printing surface is in relief; a print made from such a plate.

pi-ca, in printing, the unit measure of width of type: there are 6 picas to the inch; a size of type.

pidg-in Eng-lish, the broken English used by the Chinese in their commerce with foreigners.

piece-work, work done by the job: opposite to time-work, or work paid by the hour, etc.

pi-geon-hole, *n.,* a small compartment in a desk; *v. t.,* to lay aside; shelve.

pin mon-ey, money settled on a wife by her husband for her private expenses; money for small personal expenses.

pit-tance, a small allowance.

plain-tiff, one who begins a lawsuit.

pledge, *n.,* anything placed as a security; guarantee; pawn; promise; *v. t.,* to give as security; promise; toast.

plu-ral-i-ty, the majority; excess of votes over those of any other candidate for an office.

plu-to-crat, one powerful on account of his wealth.

pock-et, to take unlawfully; to accept without protest.

pock-et mon-ey, money for occasional expenses; spending money.

point, in printing, the unit measure of depth of type; there are 72 points to the inch.

pol-i-cy, course of action or conduct; a certificate of insurance.

poll, *n.,* the casting or recording of votes; *pl.,* the place where voting is done; the number of votes cast; *v. t.,* to deposit or call forth a vote.

poll tax, a tax on each person; literally, a head tax.

pool, putting together of the interests of various persons for the purpose of promoting a joint undertaking; the persons themselves; a combination of interests in a common fund for the purpose of manipulating the prices of grain, cotton, securities, etc.

por-tage, a carrying of goods, etc., from one waterway to another; the cost of such carriage.

port-fo-li-o, a case for papers, etc.

post, *n.,* a station; mail; *v. t.,* to affix to a wall, etc.; mail; inform fully; transfer an entry from the first to the final record, as from a journal to a ledger.

post-age, the cost of sending letters, packages, etc., by mail.

post-al, pertaining to the post office.

post-al card, a card with a postage stamp officially printed on it.

post card, a private card, as a picture, etc., which may be sent through the mail.

post-date, to date after the actual time of writing.

post me-rid-i-em, after noon; *abbr., P. M.* or *p. m.*

post-mor-tem, an examination of a dead body.

post-script, an addition to a letter, book, etc. See *Codicil.*

po-ten-tial, capable of being; possible but not actual; latent.

pow-er of at-tor-ney, legal written authority from one person to another to act for him.

prac-ti-cal, pertaining to, or derived from, actual use and experience; useful; not merely theoretical.

prac-ti-tion-er, one who pursues any profession.

pre-am-ble, a preface or short introduction.

pre-cau-tion-ar-y, intended to prevent damage or loss; advising caution.

prec-e-dent, something done or said that may serve as a model in similar cases; an example.

pre-cinct, a district; a place marked by boundaries; *pl.,* surrounding regions.

pre-empt, to establish a prior claim.

pre-emp-tion, the act or right of buying before others.

pre-ferred stock, generally speaking, stock which gives its holders a right to receive dividends before the holders of common stock can share them.

pre-mi-um, reward; bonus; money paid for an insurance policy; a sum above face value.

pre-pay, to pay in advance.

pre-side, to direct or control, as the proceedings of a meeting; have the place of authority.

pres-tige, influence derived from past reputation, achievements, etc.

pri-ma fa-ci-e, at first view.

pri-mo-gen-i-ture, the right of the first-born to inheritance.

prin-ci-pal, one who employs another to act as agent; one primarily liable for an obligation; a capital sum drawing interest.

pri-or, previous; former.

pri-or-i-ty, the state of going before in time, place, or rank.

pro-bate, a document constituting legal proof of a will.

pro-ba-tion, period of trial; release under suspended legal sentence.

pro bo-no pu-bli-co, for the public good.

pro-ce-dure, course of action; manner of conducting a legal case.

pro-ceed-ings, a published record of the actions of a society or other organization.

proc-ess, a proceeding; legal writ.

proc-ess print-ing, a method of color printing in which separate colored plates are successively imposed over one another to produce the desired shade.

proc-la-ma-tion, an official public announcement.

prod-uce, that which is brought forth, especially farm products.

pro-duc-er, one who manufactures goods or raises farm products.

prod-uct, the result; that which is yielded, brought forth, or produced.

pro-fes-sion-al, *adj.*, pertaining to an occupation which requires superior education; *n.*, one who makes his living by arts, sports, etc., as distinct from an amateur.

prof-it, gain.

prof-it-a-ble, bringing benefit or gain.

prof-it-eer, one who takes advantage of an abnormal economic situation such as that produced by war to make undue profits on necessities.

pro-gram, a regular plan of action.

prom-i-sor, one who makes a legal agreement.

prom-is-so-ry, containing an agreement.

prom-is-so-ry note, a written agreement to pay a certain sum of money at a certain time to a certain person or bearer.

pro-mot-er, one who forwards new undertakings.

proof, test; trial; the result of evidence; in printing, a preliminary impression taken for purposes of examination and correction.

prop-a-gan-da, any organization or method for propagating a doctrine; the doctrine itself.

prop-er-ty, a thing owned. PERSONAL PROPERTY, movable property. REAL PROPERTY, land, houses, etc.

prop-o-si-tion, an offer; formal statement of a topic to be debated.

pro-pri-e-tar-y, *adj.*, pertaining to an owner; *n.*, an owner; a body of owners.

pro-pri-e-tor, owner.

pro ra-ta, in proportion.

pros-e-cute, *v. t.*, to pursue; bring legal suit against; *v. i.*, to sue; carry on a lawsuit.

pros-e-cu-tion, the act of persisting in or carrying on; the carrying on of a court proceeding, especially criminal.

pros-e-cu-tor, one who initiates a proceeding before a court.

pro-spec-tus, an outline or a plan of a proposed undertaking.

pro-test (prō-tĕst′), *v. i.*, to remonstrate; *v. t.*, to assert; to declare that payment of a bill has been refused; **(pro′-test),** *n.*, a solemn declaration of opposition; a formal declaration of nonpayment or nonacceptance of a bill.

prov-i-den-tial, effected by divine care or foresight; fortunate.

pro-vi-sion-al, temporary; subject to change.

pro-vi-so, a conditional clause in a will, etc.

pro-vi-so-ry, conditional.

prox-y, an agent; substitute.

pru-den-tial, proceeding from, or characterized by, careful thought.

pub-li-cist, one who writes on current political topics.

pub-lic-i-ty, state of being known to the public; notoriety; advertising.

pub-lic spir-it-ed, interested in the general welfare of the community.

punc-til-i-o, formality; exactness in conduct or ceremony.

punc-tu-al, prompt; exact.

pur-chase, *n.,* buying; the thing bought; leverage; *v. t.,* to buy; to move by mechanical power.

pur-port, meaning.

purs-er, a ship's clerk; paymaster.

pur-su-ant, according.

pur-vey-ance, the act of supplying provisions.

pur-vey-or, one who supplies provisions.

Q

quar-an-tine, *n.,* a time of stoppage of travel or intercourse on account of disease; *v. t.,* to place under restraint on account of disease.

quar-ter-ly, once every three months.

ques-tion-naire, a series of questions asked of a large number of people.

quire, twenty-four sheets of paper.

quit-claim, a full release of claim. QUIT-CLAIM DEED, an instrument for the conveyance of property without warranty of title.

quit-rent, a fixed rent paid by a tenant which releases him from other obligations.

quit-tance, a release; acquittance; repayment.

quo-rum, a sufficient number of persons to transact business.

quo-ta, a share or proportion from each to make up a certain quantity; a goal in sales or production of merchandise; the number of immigrants permitted to enter a country annually.

quo-ta-tion, the current price of merchandise, securities, or other commodities.

quo-tient, the result of division.

quo war-ran-to, a judicial writ commanding a person to show by what authority he exercises an office or power.

R

ral-ly, *n.,* a mass meeting; *v. t.,* to arouse to action; *v. i.,* to recover.

rate, *n.,* amount, degree, value, grade, etc., estimated according to a fixed standard; price; *v. t.,* to estimate.

rat-i-fi-ca-tion, confirmation.

ra-ti-o, the relation of one number or quantity to another; rate.

read-y-made, made beforehand; kept in stock.

re-al es-tate, lands, houses, etc.; immovable property.

re-al-ty, real estate.

ream, twenty quires of paper.

re-bate, *n.,* a discount; deduction; *v. t.,* to allow a discount to; give back a part of a sum already paid.

re-ceipt, *n.,* a written acknowledgment that something has been received; *pl.,* that which is taken in; *v. t.,* to sign in acknowledgment of receipt or payment; *v. i.,* to give a written acknowledgment of something paid.

re-ceipt book, a book of printed forms for receipts; a book in which receipts are kept.

re-ceiv-a-ble, capable of, or suitable for, reception when offered.

re-ceiv-er, one appointed by a court to manage property or funds pending judicial decision on them; a trustee; a creditor's representative.

re-ces-sion, a period of mild economic slackness. See *Depression.*

re-cip-ro-cal, mutual.

re-cip-ro-cate, *v. t.,* to give and take from one another; exchange; *v. i.,* to move backward and forward; interchange.

rec-i-proc-i-ty, equal commercial rights or benefits mutually enjoyed; free interchange.

reck-on-ing, a calculation; settlement; statement of accounts with another.

re-claim, to recover.

rec-om-men-da-tion, that which brings one into favorable notice; a favorable introduction.

re-com-mit, to send back.

rec-om-pense, *n.,* compensation; *v. t.,* to compensate; repay.

rec-ord (rĕk′-ŏrd), *n.,* a register; a written or printed report of facts or proceedings; *v. t.* (rē-kôrd′), to register; chronicle; enroll.

re-cord-er, one who keeps official public records.

re-coup, to counterbalance loss; make good.

re-course, a source of aid or protection.

re-cov-er, *v. t.,* to win back; make good; restore; *v. i.,* to win a judgment in a lawsuit.

re-cov-er-y, the obtaining of one's right to something by legal procedure.

re-crim-i-nate, to return a charge with another.

re-crim-i-na-tion, the act of accusing in return.

rec-ti-fy, to correct.

re-cur-rent, coming back at intervals.

red, in the, in bookkeeping, showing a loss.

re-deem, to buy back; make good.

red tape, official formality causing delay.

re-duce, to make lower; lessen.

re-duc-tion, the act of decreasing, degrading, or changing.

re-fer, *v. t.,* to assign; appeal; *v. i.,* direct attention.

ref-er-ee, an umpire; an arbitrator.

ref-er-ence, *n.,* the act of submitting a matter to another; a written statement of the qualifications of a person; the one who gives such statement.

ref-er-en-dum, the submitting of a proposed law to a vote by the people.

reg-is-ter, *n.,* an official list or record; that which records; *v. t.,* to enroll; record; show clearly; *v. i.,* to write one's name in a record.

reg-is-ter and re-cord-er, an officer authorized by law to record business transactions.

reg-is-trar, one who keeps lists or records.

reg-is-tra-tion, enrollment.

reg-is-try, a record; the place where an official record is kept.

re-im-burse, to pay back; refund.

re-in-sur-ance, a second insurance on something already insured; an insurance on the insurer's risk.

re-join-der, an answer to a reply; in law, the defendant's answer to the plaintiff's statements.

re-lease, *n.,* a deed by which one person who owns with another a piece of property releases to the second all of his claims; a news item set free for publication; *v. t.,* to set free; deliver from penalty, debt, etc.

rel-e-vant, pertinent to the case in hand; appropriate; applicable.

re-li-a-ble, trustworthy; dependable.

rel-ict, a widow or widower.

re-lief, help; financial aid to the indigent.

re-miss, neglectful; careless.

re-mis-sion, a canceling of a debt; pardon.

re-mit, to forgive; send, as money, etc.; lessen; relax.

re-mit-tal, a canceling; discharge.

re-mit-tance, the sending of money, etc., in payment; the money sent.

rem-nant, a remainder; fragment.

re-mu-ner-ate, to recompense; compensate; reward.

re-mu-ner-a-tion, a compensation; salary; reward.

re-mu-ner-a-tive, profitable.

re-new-al, the giving of a new note for an old.

rent, *n.,* periodic payment for the use of property; *v. t.,* to use in consideration for periodic payments; *v. i.,* to be leased.

rent-al, money paid periodically for the use of property.

re-plev-in, *n.,* a writ to recover goods; the act of recovering goods wrongfully seized; *v. t.,* to recover by writ or order of court.

re-plev-y, to get back through an order issued by a court.

rep-li-ca, a copy.

re-port, *n.,* an official statement; *v. t.,* to relate, make a statement of; *v. i.,* to present or prepare a statement.

re-port-er, one who gathers news and writes an account of public events for a newspaper.

re-pos-i-to-ry, a depository; storehouse.

rep-re-hen-si-ble, deserving reproof.

rep-re-sent-a-tive, *adj.,* acting for others; typical; *n.,* one with power to act for others; a delegate.

re-prieve, *n.,* a temporary suspension of the sentence of a criminal; *v. t.,* to delay the punishment of; free temporarily from pain or danger.

rep-ri-mand, *v. t.,* to reprove; censure; *n.,* a severe reproof.

re-pris-al, a repayment of injury with injury; retaliation.

re-pu-di-ate, to cast off; disclaim.

re-pu-di-a-tion, refusal to pay.

rep-u-ta-ble, creditable; honorable.

rep-u-ta-tion, character attributed; honor; credit.

re-pute, *n.,* reputation.

req-ui-site, *adj.,* necessary; *n.,* a necessity.

req-ui-si-tion, *n.,* an authoritative demand or claim; *v. t.,* to demand or claim by authority.

re-scind, to annul; cancel; make void.

re-search, a careful investigation of sources.

re-serve, that which is kept in store.

re-sid-u-al, remaining after part has been taken away.

re-sid-u-ar-y, pertaining to the part remaining.

res-i-due, that which remains.

re-sign, *v. t.,* to give up; *v. i.,* to withdraw from.

re-source, *n.,* that on which one relies in an emergency or difficulty; *pl.,* money, etc., means.

ré-su-mé, a summary.

re-sume, to take up again.

re-sump-tion, the act of taking up again.

re-tail, *n.,* the sale of goods in small quantities directly to consumers, as distinguished from wholesale; *v. t.,* to sell in small quantities to consumers; to tell again; *v. i.,* to sell goods in small quantities.

re-tain, to keep; hire.

re-tain-er, the act of engaging the services of a lawyer or other adviser; the fee paid for such service.

re-un-ion, a meeting of persons who have been separated.

rev-e-nue, income, especially government income; proceeds.

re-voke, *v. t.,* to annul; repeal.

rid-er, a section added to a legislative bill.

ri-par-i-an, pertaining to the banks of a river.

rod, sixteen and a half feet.

Ro-tar-i-an, a member of any one of a number of clubs having the same constitution and affiliated under the International Association of Rotary Clubs.

ro-ta-tion, the act of turning around, as on an axis; recurrence.

rote, mere repetition with little attention to the meaning.

round rob-in, a letter or petition with signatures in a circle.

route, *n.,* way; journey; *v. t.,* to send by a certain way.

rou-tine, regular practice.

S

sab-o-tage, malicious injury of property by workmen during labor troubles; destruction of property during war.

sal-a-ry, regular payment for services rendered.

sales-man, one who sells commodities.

sales-man-ship, the art or practice of selling.

sal-vage, the saving of a ship or goods from a wreck or other danger; property thus saved; payment for saving it.

sam-ple, a specimen; *v. t.,* to test by a specimen.

sam-pling, a method of studying part of a selected market to determine the probable value of the entire area for purposes of sales.

sat-is-fac-tion, payment; redress.

sat-is-fac-to-ry, meeting requirements.

sat-is-fy, to pay in full.

sav-ings, sums of money laid by.

sav-ings bank, an institution where money may be deposited at interest.

scab, a nonunion worker; a strikebreaker.

sched-ule, a list or inventory; a timetable.

scru-ple, *n.,* twenty grains; a minute quantity; hesitation for fear of doing wrong; *v. t.,* and *v. i.,* to hesitate from a sense of right and wrong.

sea-far-ing, traveling by sea; following the sea.

seal, an engraved design which may be imprinted in a soft substance, such as wax; the impression so made; *v. t.,* to place a seal upon, hence, ratify, confirm.

sea lev-el, the level of the surface of the sea at mean tide.

sea-port, a town or harbor on the coast.

search war-rant, a warrant giving a police officer the right of search.

sea-son-able, opportune; in good time.

sea-son-al, pertaining to one of the four divisions of the year.

se-cure, *v. t.,* to make safe; protect; obtain; *adj.,* safe.

se-cu-ri-ty, a pledge; guarantee; collateral.

sed-en-tar-y, stationary; accustomed to sitting a large part of the time.

sem-i-week-ly, occurring twice a week.

sen-ior, *n.,* one before others in age, rank, etc.; *adj.,* older in name or office; superior in rank, etc.

se-quent, *adj.,* following; *n.,* a result; sequel.

se-ri-al, *n.,* a tale, etc., issued in successive parts; *adj.,* periodical; occurring in regular succession.

se-ri-a-tim, in regular order.

se-ries, a regular succession, sequence.

serv-ice, employment; duty; the operation of a system which supplies a public need.

serv-ice-a-ble, useful.

ses-sion, the time during which a body holds its meetings.

set-tle-ment, a payment or adjustment of an account.

shad-y, questionable.

share, a portion; *v. t.,* to divide; partake of; *v. i.,* to have a part in.

share-hold-er, one who owns one or more parts of a property.

sharp-er, a swindler.

ship-ment, a consignment of goods for transportation.

ship-ping, the act or business of transporting goods.

ship-shape, in good order.

shod-dy, material made from refuse woolen or cotton fabrics.

shop, *n.,* a store; *v. i.,* to visit shops for the purpose of looking over and buying goods.

shop-keep-er, a storekeeper; tradesman.

shop-lift-er, one who steals goods from a shop under pretense of buying.

shop-worn, worn or soiled from having been in a shop for a long time.

short, in finance, concerning the sale of securities or commodities which the seller does not own.

short-age, a deficit.

short-hand, stenography.

show-case, a case, usually glass, in which goods are placed for display.

show-room, a place where goods to be sold are displayed.

sig-na-ture, the name of a person written by himself.

si-lo, a pit or tower for preserving green fodder.

si-mul-ta-ne-ous, happening or existing at the same time.

si-ne-cure, a position having a salary but little duty or responsibility.

si-ne di-e, Latin, meaning "without day"; without definite day for reassembling.

sink-ing fund, a money reserve to be used, with its accumulated interest, to pay off a debt.

sit-ting, a session, as of a court; also its duration.

sit-u-a-tion, location; condition; employment.

slan-der, in law, oral defamation or injurious statement about another. See *Libel.*

slo-gan, formerly, a rallying cry or a battle cry; today, a compelling phrase, used in advertising, etc.

slot ma-chine, a vending machine in which a coin may be inserted for candy, gum, etc.

slump, *n.,* a sudden dropping off; *v. i.,* to fall suddenly, as a price.

so-ci-e-ty, people in general considered as a united body; an association.

so-lic-it, *v. t.,* to ask for earnestly; *v. i.,* to seek, as votes, orders, etc.

so-lic-i-tor, an attorney; a legal counsel who does not plead cases in open court. See *Barrister.*

sol-ven-cy, ability to pay debts; capability of being dissolved.

sol-vent, able to pay debts.

spe-cial-ty, a special pursuit, product, or characteristic.

spe-cie, coined money.

spe-cif-ic, definite. SPECIFIC DUTY, a tax definitely fixed: opposite to *ad valorem* duty.

spec-i-fi-ca-tion, a detailed statement; one item in the statement; an item.

spec-i-fy, to state explicitly.

spec-i-men, a sample.

spe-cious, apparently but not actually fair; plausible.

spec-u-late, to gamble in stocks, etc.

spec-u-la-tion, any hazardous business enterprise.

spec-u-la-tive, theoretical; reflective.

spu-ri-ous, not genuine.

square, *n.,* a figure with four equal sides and four right angles; the result of multiplying a number by itself; *v. t.,* to multiply by itself; balance; *v. i.,* to accord; *adj.,* true; balanced.

square root, the number or quantity which when multiplied by itself produces a given number or quantity.

sta-bi-lize, to make steady; to prevent fluctuation, as in prices.

stag-gered hours, the system whereby one group of people goes to business earlier than another to relieve congested traffic.

stake, *n.,* that which is hazarded, as in gambling; *v. t.,* to wager.

stand-ard, *n.,* a rule; model; *adj.,* established.

stand-ard-ize, to make conform to rule, model, etc.

stand-ing, reputation.

sta-ple, the principal product or industry; raw material.

state bank, in the United States, a bank chartered under the laws of a state. See *Bank.*

stat-ed, fixed; regular.

state-ment, an account; a list of bills due or monies owed, sent periodically to customers.

state's ev-i-dence, testimony presented by the government or prosecution in a criminal case, especially that presented by an accomplice to the crime.

sta-tion-er-y, paper, pen, ink, and other writing materials.

sta-tis-tics, *n. pl.,* a classified collection of facts pertaining to a nation, industry, etc.; the science of collecting facts and tabulating them numerically.

sta-tus, legal condition of a person; rank.

sta-tus quo, a condition in which a person or thing has been or is.

stat-ute, a law.

stat-u-to-ry, enacted by law.

ste-nog-ra-pher, one who writes and transcribes shorthand.

ste-nog-ra-phy, the taking in shorthand and transcription of dictation.

ster-ling, genuine; of high value; standard.

stet, let it stand: used in proofreading to indicate that something marked for omission is to remain.

ste-ve-dore, a dock laborer who loads and unloads vessels.

sti-pend, a settled salary.

stip-u-la-tion, a contract; an item in an agreement.

stock, *n.,* capital; cattle; store; supply; *v. t.,* to fill; supply.

stock-bro-ker, one who buys and sells shares and stocks for others.

stock com-pa-ny, a corporation whose capital is represented by shares held by various persons.

stock ex-change, a place where stocks are bought and sold.

stock-hold-er, one who holds shares in a corporation, etc.

stock-job-ber, one who deals in stocks.

stop-gap, a temporary expedient.

stop watch, a watch which can be stopped instantly, used in timing races, etc.

stor-age, the act of putting goods away for safekeeping; charge for storing goods.

stor-age bat-ter-y, a device for storing electrical energy.

store, *n.,* stock; shop; *pl.,* food, ammunition, etc.; *v. t.,* to put away.

store-house, a warehouse.

store-room, a room in which things are put away until needed.

stow, to put away; arrange compactly.

stow-age, the act of packing away; room in which things may be packed; charge for packing.

strike, *v. t.,* to hit; dash against; affect suddenly; *v. i.,* to hit; cease work in an effort to achieve wages, etc.; *n.,* a ceasing of work.

strike-break-er, one who takes the place of a man who has stopped work in an effort to gain higher wages or better working conditions.

strik-er, one who stops work in the hope of getting higher wages or better working conditions.

strin-gent, severe.

sub-com-mit-tee, an under committee.

sub-let, to let to another property that has been let to oneself.

sub-poe-na, *n.,* a writ summoning a witness into court under penalty; *v. t.,* to serve with a writ of subpoena. Also, SUBPENA.

sub-scribe, *v. t.,* to sign; assent to; promise; *v. i.,* to sign one's name to; approve or promise something by affixing one's name.

sub-scrip-tion, a signature; a formal attestation; amount pledged.

sub-sid-i-ar-y, *adj.,* aiding; auxiliary; tributary; *n.,* a helper; an assistant.

sub-si-dize, to aid with public money.

sub-si-dy, money granted by one government to another or to a private enterprise; a grant; bonus.

sub-stan-ti-ate, to prove; verify.

sub-sti-tute, *n.,* a person or thing in the place of another; *v. t.,* to put in the place of another person or thing.

sum-ma-ry, *n.,* an abridgment; *adj.,* concise; done quickly.

sump-tu-ar-y, pertaining to the regulation of expenditures.

sun-dries, *n. pl.,* various small articles.

sun-dry, several; various.

su-per, a prefix meaning over, above, beyond.

su-per-a-bun-dance, excess.

su-per-an-nu-ate, to impair by age; retire on a pension on account of old age.

su-per-car-go, an official who has charge of the cargo and business affairs of a merchant ship during a voyage.

su-per-in-tend-ent, an overseer; supervisor.

su-pe-ri-or, *adj.,* preferable; finer; *n.,* one of higher rank or position.

su-per-nu-mer-ar-y, *n.,* a person or thing beyond the regular number; *adj.,* beyond the required number; superfluous.

su-per-scrip-tion, that which is written on the outside, as of an envelope.

su-per-sede, to set aside; take the place of.

su-per-struc-ture, something built above something else.

su-per-vise, to oversee.

su-per-vi-sor, an overseer.

sup-ple-ment, *n.,* an addition to a book, paper, etc.; *v. t.,* to add to.

sup-ply, *v. t.,* to furnish; *n.,* the act of furnishing or providing; store; *pl.,* reserve stores.

sur-charge, an extra charge; an excessive charge or burden.

sure-ty, security bail; one who becomes responsible for another for debt, etc.

sur-plus, excess.

sur-tax, an extra tax.

sweat-ing sys-tem, the system of employing poor people to do piecework for very low wages.

sweat-shop, a place where people are employed for low wages under poor conditions.

swin-dle, *v. t.,* to defraud; *n.,* a cheat.

swin-dler, a cheat.

syn-di-cate (sĭn'-di-kăt), *n.,* an association or combination of persons; *v. t.* (sĭn-dĭ-kāt'), to form into an association or company; offer literary work for sale to a number of periodicals.

sys-tem, an orderly arrangement or assemblage; method.

sys-tem-at-ic, orderly.

sys-tem-a-tize, to reduce to a system or regular method.

T

ta-ble d'hôte, a plan by which meals are served at a fixed price: opposite to à la carte, *Fr.*

tab-u-lar, arranged systematically or in the form of a table.

tales-man, a person summoned to fill a deficiency in a jury.

tal-ly, a score kept by notches, etc.

task-mas-ter, one who imposes a piece of work upon another.

tax, *n.,* an assessment; money paid to a government; *v. t.,* to impose a duty upon.

tax-a-ble, liable to taxation.

tax-a-tion, the act of levying taxes on persons or property; taxes collectively.

tech-ni-cal, relating to the mechanical arts, any art or science, or to the mechanical side of any branch of learning.

tech-ni-cal-i-ty, something relating to the mechanical part of any art or science; formal or trifling nicety.

tell-er, a bank clerk who receives and pays money.

tem-po-ral, worldly; not eternal.

tem-po-rar-y, transitory; not permanent.

tem-po-rize, to delay.

ten-a-ble, capable of being defended or maintained.

ten-an-cy, a holding property as a tenant; in law, ownership by title.

ten-ant, one who rents or leases real property; an occupant.

ten-der, *n.,* an offer; money offered in payment; *v. t.,* to proffer.

ten-e-ment, a house or apartment for renting.

ten-e-ment house, a large building occupied by many families.

ten-ure, a holding; the conditions under which real estate is held.

ter-cen-te-nar-y, the 300th anniversary.

ter-mi-nal, *adj.,* pertaining to, or forming, the end; *n.,* a limit; an end; point of departure or arrival of a common carrier.

ter-mi-nate, *v. t.,* to end; *v. i.,* to come to an end.

ter-mi-nus, an end, as of a railroad.

ter-ri-to-ry, a region of land; district.

tes-ta-ment, see *Will.*

tes-ta-tor, one who has died leaving a will.

tes-ti-fy, *v. i.,* to bear witness; give evidence; *v. t.,* to bear witness to; declare upon oath.

tes-ti-mo-ni-al, a certificate of one's ability; a gift in token of appreciation.

tes-ti-mo-ny, evidence; witness; affirmation; proof.

thrift, frugality; economical management.

tick-er, a telegraphic instrument which receives news and prints it on a strip of paper or "tape"; a similar instrument in a broker's office to receive and record the reports from the stock market.

tide-wait-er, an officer who watches the landing of goods to secure the payment of duties.

till, a money drawer or tray in a counter or desk.

time bill, a bill payable at some future date.

time clock, a clock by means of which employees record their time of arrival, etc.

time draft, a draft payable at some future time.

time-ly, seasonable; opportune.

time note, a note payable at some future time.

time-serv-er, one who adapts himself to the occasion without regard to principle.

time-ta-ble, a list of dates and hours for events, as of the arrival and departure of trains.

time-work, work paid by the hour: opposite to *piecework.*

ti-tle, right to the possession of property; evidence of such right.

ti-tle deed, the written evidence of one's right to a piece of property.

toll, a tax on vehicles or persons using a road or bridge; charge for long-distance telephone calls.

to-pog-ra-pher, one versed in the scientific description of a place.

to-pog-ra-phy, the scientific description of a territory or region.

tort, in law, wrong or injury not growing out of breach of contract for which damages may be obtained.

to-tal, the whole sum or amount; *v. t.,* to add; *v. i.,* to amount to a certain number, etc.

town-ship, a governmental unit; part of a county.

trace, to copy exactly, as a drawing; follow the course of.

trac-er, one who tries to locate lost letters, packages, etc.

trade, *n.,* commerce; business; *v. i.,* to carry on business or commerce; *v. t.,* to exchange.

trade ac-cept-ance, a draft drawn by the seller on the buyer of goods, and accepted by the latter for payment at a definite time.

trade dis-count, an allowance made by dealers to others in the same business.

trade-mark, the distinguishing mark of a merchant or manufacturer.

trade name, the commercial name of a commodity; the business name of a firm.

trade price, the reduced price charged by wholesale to retail dealers.

trad-er, one carrying on commerce; a merchant.

trade school, a school where trades are taught.

trade-un-ion, an organization of workmen in a trade to secure favorable working conditions.

trade-un-ion-ism, the principles or practice of organization of workmen.

traf-fic, *n.,* commerce; the movement of vehicles or pedestrians along a street or highway; *v. i.,* to barter; bargain.

trans-act, *v. t.,* and *v. i.,* to perform; manage.

trans-ac-tion, *n.,* the carrying on of any

business; negotiation; *pl.*, the reports of the proceedings of a society, etc.

trans-at-lan-tic, beyond or crossing the Atlantic Ocean.

trans-fer, *v. t.*, to convey; copy; *n.*, conveyance of something from one person or place to another.

trans-fer-a-ble, capable of being carried over from one person or place to another.

tran-sient, temporary; short-lived; staying for a short time.

trans-it, a passage through or over. IN TRANSIT, on the way.

trans-mit, to send; allow to pass through.

trans-port (trăns-pōrt'), *v. t.*, to carry across from one place to another; *n.* (trăns'-pōrt), a vessel or other conveyance for carrying troops, supplies, etc., from one place to another.

trans-ship-ment, the removal of goods or merchandise from one means of transportation to another.

treas-ur-er, one who has charge of funds.

treas-ur-y, a place where money or treasure is kept; the department of a government which has charge of the funds.

treas-ur-y notes, notes issued by the government and received in payment for all dues except those on imported goods.

trea-ty, an agreement between nations.

tres-pass, to intrude, as on another's property.

tri-al bal-ance, in double-entry bookkeeping, a statement of the footings of the debit and credit accounts to show whether the two sides of the ledger balance.

tri-al ju-ry, a jury called to try a case: opposite to *grand jury*.

trib-u-tar-y, subordinate.

tri-week-ly, occurring three times a week.

tro-ver, legal action to regain goods found and not delivered.

truck, *n.*, a vehicle for carrying heavy goods; vegetables raised for the market; *v. i.*, to barter; exchange.

truck-age, freight.

trust, *n.*, confidence; responsibility; a combination of business organizations; property held for another; *v. t.*, to believe; entrust; *v. i.*, to have con-

fidence; *adj.*, held in charge for another.

trust com-pa-ny, a corporation empowered by its charter to receive money and other property in trust, and to lend money on real and personal property.

trust deed, a deed giving power to a body of creditors to foreclose mortgages in the event of nonfulfillment of obligation on the part of the debtor.

trus-tee, one appointed to hold or manage property for another.

turn-o-ver, that part of the capital of a business available for the purchase of merchandise or other commodities.

two-ply, having two thicknesses.

type face, see *Face*.

ty-pog-ra-pher, a printer.

ty-po-graph-i-cal, pertaining to the art of printing.

ty-pog-ra-phy, the art of printing.

ty-ro, a beginner.

U

ul-te-ri-or, beyond what is expressed; more distant.

ul-ti-ma, the last syllable of a word.

ul-ti-mate, the last; final; utmost.

ul-ti-ma-tum (*pl.*, **ultimata, ultimatums**), the final statement or proposition.

ul-tra, extreme.

un-a-bridged, complete; having nothing omitted.

un-al-loyed, pure; unmixed.

u-nan-i-mous, of one opinion; agreeing.

un-der seal, a term, commonly indicated by *seal* or *L. S.*, in addition to the signatures of a contract to show lawful consideration for the agreement made in the contract.

un-der-sell, to sell below the trade price.

un-der-sign, to subscribe; write one's name under.

un-der-val-ue, to underestimate.

un-der-write, to write beneath; insure; subscribe.

un-der-writ-er, one who insures, issues stock, etc.

un-earned in-cre-ment, the increase in the value of property without effort on the part of the owner.

u-ni, a prefix meaning *one*.

un-ion, a combination; association.

un-ion-ism, belief in, or the principles of, trade-unions.

u-nit, one; a single group in an organization; a standard of measure.

un-war-rant-ed, unjustifiable; not authoritative.

un-writ-ten, not recorded in writing; understood though not expressed.

up-keep, maintenance.

up-to-date, in the latest style; according to the most recent facts or information.

u-su-fruct, the temporary right of use.

u-su-rer, one who lends money at exorbitant or illegal interest.

u-su-ry, a high or unlawful rate of interest.

u-til-i-tar-i-an, *adj.,* pertaining to utility or usefulness; *n.,* one who believes that utility should be the sole standard of moral conduct.

u-til-i-ty, usefulness; something serviceable.

u-ti-lize, to make use of.

u-to-pi-an, impractical; ideal.

V

va-de me-cum, a Latin expression meaning, *Go with me;* a constant companion, as a manual or handbook.

val-id, sound; legal.

val-i-date, to make sound or legal; confirm.

va-lid-i-ty, soundness; legality.

val-u-a-tion, appraisement; estimation.

val-ue, *n.,* worth; *v. t.,* to estimate the worth of; appreciate.

val-ued, highly prized.

val-ued pol-i-cy, an insurance policy in which the value is agreed on and inserted as liquidated damages.

val-ue re-ceived, a phrase used to denote that a note has been made or a bill accepted for a consideration and not for accommodation.

van, the front; a heavy truck.

van-tage, a superior position; advantage.

van-tage ground, a superior position.

vault, a place for safekeeping, as jewels, securities, etc.

ve-nal, mercenary; open to bribery.

ve-nal-i-ty, a mercenary spirit; prostitution of talents, etc., for money.

vend, to sell; peddle.

vend-ee, a legal term designating the person to whom a thing is sold.

vend-er, one who sells or peddles goods.

vend-ing ma-chine, a device from which products are automatically dispensed upon insertion of the prescribed coin or coins.

ven-due, a public auction.

ve-neer, *v. t.,* to overlay with a thin surface of finer wood; to hide behind superficial show; *n.,* a thin layer of wood overlaid above a less valuable wood; a surface polish.

ve-ni-re, a legal writ summoning a jury.

ven-ti-late, to supply with fresh air; utter publicly.

ven-ue, the place of action in a crime, etc.; the place where the trial is held.

ver-ba-tim, word for word.

ver-dict, the decision of a jury; an opinion.

ver-nac-u-lar, one's native tongue; vocabulary peculiar to a locality, business, profession, etc.

ver-sion, a translation; account.

ver-sus, against; *abbr., v.* or *vs.*

vest-ed, clothed; fixed; established by law and subject to no contingencies, such as vested interests.

ve-to, *n.,* the power of prohibiting; a refusal from one in authority; *v. t.,* to prohibit by authority.

vi-ce ver-sa, in reverse order; conversely.

vi-cin-i-ty, nearness; neighborhood.

vi-cis-si-tude, a change in circumstances; an unforeseen event.

vi-de, a Latin term meaning *see.*

vi-de-li-cet, *adv.,* to wit; namely; *abbr., viz.*

vis-à-vis, face to face.

vi-sé (in the United States usually **vi-sa),** *v. t.,* to examine and endorse; *n.,* an official signature approving a passport or other document.

vi-va vo-ce, by word of mouth; orally.

viz., namely; *abbr.* for *videlicet.*

vo-li-tion, will; decision; intention.

volt, the standard unit for measuring electric force.

volt-age, the amount of electromotive force in terms of volts.

vol-ume, a book; mass; compass of space occupied.

vouch, to guarantee; bear witness; answer for.

vouch-er, one who or that which bears witness; a receipt; certificate.

W

wages, payment for services rendered.

waive, to give up; relinquish.

waiv-er, the voluntary surrender of a right.

walk-out, a labor strike.

Wall Street, a narrow street in the lower part of New York City where the most important financial transactions of the country take place.

ware-house, a storehouse.

ware-house re-ceipt, a receipt, sometimes negotiable, given for goods in storage in a warehouse. See *Bonded Warehouse.*

wares, goods; merchandise.

war-rant, *n.,* an official paper giving authority to arrest, etc.; a guaranty; *v. t.,* to guarantee; authorize; justify.

war-rant-a-ble, justifiable.

war-rant of-fi-cer, a noncommissioned army or navy officer.

war-ran-ty, a legal guaranty; authority.

war-ran-ty deed, a deed in which the grantor guarantees that his title to the property is as represented.

wast-age, loss due to handling, leakage, etc.

waste, to spend recklessly.

waste-ful, extravagant.

wa-tered stock, stock, the par value of which has been added to without a corresponding addition to the assets for which it stands.

wa-ter-mark, a record indicating the rise and fall of water; a faint trademark made in paper during its manufacture.

watt, a unit of electrical power.

way-bill, a list of goods or passengers carried by a train or other conveyance.

week-day, any day but Sunday.

week-ly, *adj.,* happening in or continuing for, seven days; occurring every seven days; *n.,* a periodical issued every seven days.

weigh, *v. t.,* to find the heaviness of an object by weight or balance; ponder; *v. i.,* to have weight.

weight, heaviness, load; importance; *v. t.,* to add to the weight of.

wel-fare, prosperity; well-being.

wharf, a pier.

wharf-age, the fee for the use of a wharf; wharf accommodation.

where-as, considering that.

where-with-al, *adv.,* with which or what; *n.,* means or money by which anything can be done or bought.

whole-sale, a sale of goods in a large quantity: opposite to *retail.*

wild-cat, risky or hazardous, as a scheme or business.

will, a written declaration by which a person disposes of his property, to take effect after his death.

wind-fall, a piece of unexpected good fortune.

wind-ward, the direction from which the wind blows.

win-now, *v. t.,* to sift; separate; *v. i.,* to separate the chaff from the wheat.

wire-pull-ing, the act of using unseen means to gain one's end, as in politics.

wire tap-ping, the making of connection with another's telephone wires so as to gain information.

with-out re-course, words added to the endorsement of a note, etc., to exempt the endorser from liability.

wit-ness, *n.,* testimony; evidence; one who testifies; *v. t.,* to look at; see; testify.

work-day, a day on which labor is performed. Also WORKING DAY.

work-ing-man, a laborer.

work-man, a common or skilled laborer.

work-man-like, worthy of a skilled laborer; careful.

work-man-ship, the manner in which a piece of work is done; style of performance.

work-shop, a room where manufacturing is carried on.

worth, *n.,* merit; price; *adj.,* equal in value to.

Y

year-book, a book issued once a year, usually a report or summary.

Z

ze-nith, the point directly overhead; the greatest height.

ze-ro, a cipher; nothing; the neutral point on a scale, as of temperature.

INDEX

Agriculture *(cont'd)*
tion, 325; on food-preservation at home, 84; Forest Service, 325; Information, Office of, 325; regulatory programs, 324; research activities, 323, 324; Rural Electrification Administration, 325; Soil Conservation Service, 325; Statistical Reporting Service, 325. *See also* Agriculture; Farming and agriculture in the U.S.

Air conditioning in home and office, 230; air conditioners, types of, 231; comfort chart, 232; health benefits, 230; installation, 233; maintenance, 233; and office planning, 228; performance efficiency, 230

Aircraft industry, career opportunity in, 201

Air express service, 183

Air Force, U.S., career in, 204; enlisted men's ratings, 140; officers' rank, 140. *See also* Defense, Department of, U.S.

Air mail. *See* Postal information

Air transportation, career opportunity in, 201. *See also* Air express service

Alcohol, boiling point, 292

Alien, 161; and contracts, 7. *See also* Naturalization

Alimony, 416

Alphabetization, 167

American Automobile Association, 199

American Federation of Labor and Congress of Industrial Organizations, 297

Ampere. *See* Unit

Annuity, 80; table, 82

Antitrust statutes, 184

Apothecaries' weights and measures. *See* Weights and measures

Apple, seedtime and harvest, 318

Application, letter of, 206

Aptitude testing, 207

Arch, construction of, 375

Architect, 332

Area, measures of, 281

Arithmetic, commercial, 235; addition, 235, column, 236; check of nines, 240; circle, 243; cube, 244; division, 237 (table, 239); fraction, 241; mensuration, 241; multiplication, 238 (table, 239); numbers, 235; slide rule, 245; square, 243; subtraction, 237

Armed forces, U.S., commander in chief, 113; jobs in, 204. *See also* Air

Force, U.S.; Army, U.S.; Navy, U.S.

Army, U.S., career in, 204; enlisted men's ratings, 140; officers' rank, 140; Secretary of the, 114. *See also* Defense, Department of, U.S.

Assignment, 15, 73

Associated Credit Bureaus of America, Inc., 275

Atomic energy, career opportunity in, 201

Attachment, 73

Attorney General, U.S. *See* Justice, Department of, U.S.

Audit Bureau of Circulations, 386

Automatic machines, 225

Automobile, and arrest of driver, 191; associations, 199; driver's safety information, 192; driving costs, 190; driving outside the U.S., 198; gasoline tax rates, 195; horsepower, 200; insurance (*see* Insurance); license tax, 94; point system, 192; speed limit, 191; tax deductions, 191; touring mileage (tables), east, 196, 197; south, 195; west, 196, 197; traffic laws, 191

Automobile Manufacturers Association, 199

Aviation insurance. *See* Insurance

Avoirdupois weight. *See* Weights and measures

Babson's Business Report Service, 275

Balance, of trade, 159, 160. *See also* Accounts, keeping

Bail, 74

Bailment, 74

Bankruptcy, 107; agency, ends, 10; assignment, 109; and banks, 107; candidate for, 107; Chandler Act, 107; Chandler Railroad Adjustment Act, 107; composition, 109; Corporate Reorganization Act, 107; court, 109; and death of debtor, 107; Debtors' Relief Act, 107; debts, not affected by discharge, 110, priority of, 110; discharge, and conduct of bankrupt, 110; dividend, 111; duties of a bankrupt, 108; Frazier-Lemke Farm Mortgage Act, 107; and insurance companies, 107; involuntary, 107; Municipal Debt Adjustment Act, 107; property exemptions, 108; provable claim, 108; Railroad Reorganization Act, 107; referee, 109; settlement, 109; statutes of limitation, 112;